Praise for *Rome*

'In pages of trenchant prose, Hughes chronicles the art and architecture of Rome from the Emperor Augustus to Federico Fellini. This is quite an undertaking but Hughes is an entertaining, if at times highly opinionated, critic' *Spectator*

'If visiting Rome, you should certainly take this passionate, erudite bruiser's Baedeker with you – a superbly rich blend of history, art and travelogue' *The Sunday Times*

'We enjoy reading Hughes precisely because he avoids any of that corseted coyness which characterises too much art history writing nowadays. Thankfully not having to worry about securing professional tenure at a university or gaining a coveted gallery curatorship, he can speak with the candour of a visceral enthusiasm, savaging mediocrity and rhapsodically defending excellence'
Literary Review

'His love and knowledge of the city stand forth' *Sunday Telegraph*

'A story that lasts almost 3,000 years and is pivotal to so much of Western civilisation requires a chronicler of well-nigh unattainable erudition, who can write with the skill needed to prevent readers from succumbing to a literary version of Stendhal syndrome. Mr Hughes, the Australian-born art critic of *Time* magazine, comes as near as anyone to fulfilling that job description and for much of this wide-ranging volume he succeeds magnificently' *Economist*

'A tour of the great city with a great guide: who could do this better?' *Evening Standard*

'Hughes proves an entertaining and erudite guide. He is an impeccable raconteur, commanding, self-confident, witty'
Daily Telegraph

'In this Herculean undertaki⸻ ⸻the true spirit of Rome: the asp⸻ ⸻ite obstacles, setbacks or failure⸻

Robert Hughes was born in Australia in 1938. Since 1970 he has lived and worked in the United States of America, where until 2001 he was chief art critic for *Time*, to which he still contributes. His books include *The Shock of the New*, *The Fatal Shore*, *Nothing If Not Critical*, *Barcelona* and *Goya*. He has received numerous awards and prizes for his work.

By Robert Hughes

The Art of Australia (1966)
Heaven and Hell in Western Art (1969)
The Shock of the New (1980)
The Fatal Shore (1987)
Lucian Freud (1988)
Frank Auerbach (1990)
Nothing If Not Critical (1990)
Barcelona (1992)
The Culture of Complaint (1993)
American Visions (1997)
Goya (2003)
Things I Didn't Know (2006)
Rome (2011)

ROME

ROBERT
HUGHES

PHOENIX

A PHOENIX PAPERBACK

First published in Great Britain in 2011
by Weidenfeld & Nicolson
This paperback edition published in 2012
by Phoenix,
an imprint of Orion Books Ltd,
Orion House, 5 Upper St Martin's Lane,
London WC2H 9EA

An Hachette UK company

1 3 5 7 9 10 8 6 4 2

A CIP catalogue record for this book
is available from the British Library.

ISBN 978-0-7538-2305-7

Typeset by Input Data Services Ltd, Bridgwater, Somerset

Printed and bound by CPI Group
(UK) Ltd, Croydon, CR0 4YY

The Orion Publishing Group's policy is to use papers
that are natural, renewable and recyclable products and
made from wood grown in sustainable forests. The logging
and manufacturing processes are expected to conform to
the environmental regulations of the country of origin.

www.orionbooks.co.uk

CONTENTS

ACKNOWLEDGEMENTS

The last, and I daresay only, book I've written about a major city was over twenty years ago. That book was *Barcelona*, a city I'd visited frequently due to my long-standing friendship with the sculptor Xavier Corbero, and it was through his eyes that I discovered the Catalan gem that was to steal my heart and lure me back with its siren song, so magical and alluring. Several years ago, my literary agent, Lynn Nesbit, called on a bright, early spring day and proposed a book on the subject of Rome. Her enthusiasm and vibrant energy about writing this book rhymed with the emerging greens of the early spring unfolding outside, making it impossible to decline. Lord Weidenfeld, the formidable publisher of Weidenfeld & Nicolson, had been conceptualizing this book for many years and decided it must be done and as a complete history, to be called *The Seven Pillars of Rome*. To be handed his vision of this project was a privilege and an honour of which I am eternally grateful.

Rome is a city where I have spent much time, but unlike Barcelona, I had not had the opportunity to live and breathe the air for months on end. My knowledge of the history came to me by my profession as a writer and critic of art. It was the visual language in my travels in and around the city that built the foundation for my historical reference, and in taking on this challenge my internal reservoirs could begin to flow into a cohesive stream of history – Rome in chronology and through my own eyes, the eyes that have seen the priceless art and architecture, the structure of a city that, historically, will never be complete. The master craftsmen, artists, rulers, warriors and social anthropologists, now long gone, bestowed the world with one of the greatest treasures known to man.

Early on, during one of my first research visits to Rome, I realized what a mammoth undertaking this book was to be, something that was not lost on my wife, Doris Downes. I am deeply grateful on many levels for her support as a partner, her loyalty, her friendship and her own knowledge of the city. Because of my compromised state of mobility, the effects of a car wreck in the Australian outback thirteen years ago, I relied heavily on her and my many friends in Rome to help negotiate the sites and research facilities as well as the politics. In these noble tasks, I would like to thank Peter Glidewell, adviser for the Foundation for Italian Art and Culture (FICA), who spent his lifetime in this city and seemed to know every coin in every fountain with his sophisticated views on what Rome had been and what it is today. He spent much time organizing my agenda in and around a city that is not and can never be 'disabled-friendly' without razing every street of its paving stones. His knowledge and patience in working with me, as well as his loyalty, I will never be able to repay fully. In addition, I would like to thank my friends Alain Elkann and Rosy Greco for their hospitality in our visits to the city by offering their grace and generosity in providing me with a spectacular space in which to hang my hat, and to Lucio Manisco, my dear old friend and journalist in Rome.

Anyone who is familiar with my past acknowledgements knows that they are never complete without thanking a major hospital and entire wing of specialists and interns. This time, the gong goes to Policlinico Umberto Primo, located within the city proper. Without their careful attention, I would not have been able to complete this book. I would also like to give my heartfelt appreciation to Doris, who, putting her own important work aside, flew back to Rome to navigate the medical labyrinth of this sprawling teaching hospital and for managing a safe return back to New York.

I am deeply indebted to my indefatigable editors at Weidenfeld & Nicolson. I thank them for their patience and professionalism throughout this long process, as well as the Editorial Assistants, Production Editors, and Graphic Designers. At Orion

Books, I would like to thank Alan Samson, Bea Hemming and Helen Richardson. Nor could it have gone to print without the continued generosity of the New York Public Library in giving me access to the Allen Room, with the rare treasures that helped to bring this book to life in so many ways.

In closing, I would like to thank my stepsons, Garrett and Fielder Jewett, for their love and encouragement during the years of writing intermixed with my many bouts of self-doubt that it would ever come to completion.

PROLOGUE

I have eaten, slept, looked until I was exhausted, and sometimes felt as though I had walked my toes to mere stubs in Rome, but I have never actually lived there. I only ever lived outside the city; not on the mediocre *periferia* that grew up to accommodate its population surge in the fifties and sixties, but in places along the coast to the north, like the Argentario peninsula. I quite often came into Rome itself, but rarely for more than a week or two and not often enough to qualify as a resident by paying rent to anyone but a hotel-owner or having a kitchen wall on which to permanently hang my wicker spaghetti-strainer, which remained in Porto Ercole.

For a time in my adolescence – not knowing Rome in any but the sketchiest way – I longed to be a Roman expatriate and even felt rather hypocritical, or at least pretentious, for having any kind of opinions about the city. Everyone, it seemed to me then – this being a time that began in the early fifties – knew more about Rome than I did. I was nuts about the idea of Rome, but to me it was hardly more than an idea, and a poorly formed, misshapen idea at that. I had never even been to the place. I was still in Australia, where, due to an education by Jesuits, I spoke a few sentences of Latin but no Italian whatever. The only semi-*Romano* I knew was actually Irish, a sweet, white-haired, elderly Jesuit who ran the observatory attached to the boarding-school I had attended in Sydney, and who from time to time would travel to Italy to take charge of its sister institution, belonging to the pope (Pius XII, aka Eugenio Pacelli) and situated at Castelgandolfo outside the Eternal City. From there, doubtless enriched with recent astronomical knowledge whose dimensions I had no idea of, he would bring back postcards, sedulously and with obvious pleasure gleaned from their racks in various museums and churches at ten to twenty lire each: Caravaggios, Bellinis, Michelangelos. He would pin these up on one of the school noticeboards. Naturally they were Old Masters of the chaster sort: no rosy Titianesque nudes need be expected. I have no idea what success these gestures might have had in the direction of civilizing the robust cricket-playing lads from Mudgee and Lane Cove who were my schoolfellows. But I know they had some on me, if only because having such things in a church, however distant, seemed (and was) so exotic and therefore, if only in miniature reproduction, so attractive.

The religious art one encountered at a Catholic Australian school like mine (and, indeed, throughout Australia) was of a very different kind from this. It was made of plaster and conceived in a spirit of nauseating piety by a religious-art manufacturer named Pellegrini's, and it was all of a sweetness and sickliness that I hated then and whose remote memory I still resent today: cupid-lipped Madonnas robed in a particularly sallow shade of light blue, simpering Christs on or off the cross who looked like some gay-hater's fantasy with curly chestnut hair. I don't know how this *bondieuserie* was sold. Maybe Pellegrini's had some kind of primitive mail-order catalogue. Or maybe there was a salesman with a Holden panel van, lugging the samples from church to church: plaster Teresas and Bernadettes, virgins holding stems of plaster lilies, priced at so much per inch height. How one could be expected to pray through, to, or in front of this rubbish was an abiding mystery to me. As far as I could discover there was not one work of religious art in Australia that anyone except a weak-minded nun, and a lay sister at that, could call authentic.

Where could one see the real thing? Clearly, only in Rome. How would one know what feeling in religious art actually was authentic? By going to Rome. Come down to it, how would one know that art of any kind was any good? Mainly – if not only – by going to Rome, and seeing the real thing in the real place. Rome would be my entry-door to Italy and then to the rest of Europe.

And with that would come sophistication and taste and possibly even spirituality. Not to mention all the other more earthly delights I was also looking forward to. From this distance I am embarrassed to admit that I can no longer remember their names, but to me they looked just like the girls I saw in Italian movies. If I was lucky I might even be able to latch on to some of those unbearably chic pants, jackets and thin-walled shoes from Via Condotti, though where the money would come from I didn't know.

When I finally got there, in May 1959, much of this turned out to be true. Nothing exceeds the delight of one's first immersion in Rome on a fine spring morning, even if it is not provoked by the sight of any particular work of art. The enveloping light can be of an incomparable clarity, throwing into gentle vividness every detail presented to the eye. First, the colour, which was not like the colour of other cities I had been in. Not concrete-colour, not cold glass-colour, not the colour of overburned brick or harshly pigmented paint. Rather, the worn organic colours of the ancient earth and stone of which the city is composed, the colours of limestone, the ruddy grey of tufa, the warm discoloration of once-white marble and the speckled, rich surface of the marble known as *pavonazzo*, dappled with white spots and inclusions like the fat in a slice of mortadella. For an eye used to the more commonplace, uniform surfaces of twentieth-century building, all this looks wonderfully, seductively rich without seeming overworked.

The very trees were springing, tender green, not the more pervasive drab grey of the Australian eucalypts I was used to. Some of them were in blossom – the pink-and-white bursting into bloom of the oleanders by the roadsides. Azaleas were everywhere, especially on the Spanish Steps: I had been lucky enough to get to Rome at the very time of the year when florists bank the Scalinata di Spagna with row after row, mass upon mass, of those shrubs whose flowers were all the sweeter for being short-lived. And it was not only the flowers that looked festive. The vegetables were burgeoning in the markets, especially the Campo dei Fiori. Their sellers did not want to constrain them. Bunches of thyme,

branches of rosemary, parsley, bundled-up masses of basil filling
the air with their perfume. Here, a mountain of sweet peppers:
scarlet, orange, yellow, even black. There, a crate filled with the
swollen purple truncheons of aubergines. Next to that, a parade
of tomatoes, fairly bursting with ripeness – the red egg-shaped
San Marzanos for sauce, the broad-girthed slicing tomatoes, the
ribbed ones for salads, the green baby ones. Even the potato, a
dull-looking growth as a rule, took on a sort of tuberous grandeur
in this Mediterranean light.

Then became apparent something of a kind I had never seen at
home in Australia. All this vegetable glory, this tide of many-
coloured life, this swelling and bursting and fullness, welled up
around a lugubrious totem of Death. The piazza in which this
market is held, the Campo dei Fiori, translates literally as 'the
field of flowers'. There are several versions of how it acquired this
name; it was not always a garden; possibly it had never been a
garden, in the sense of a place where plants were cultivated and
picked. One version has it deriving from Campus Florae, 'Flora's
square', and thus named after the (supposed) lover of the great
Roman general Pompey, who (supposedly) lived in a house there.

But the male presence that dominates this beautiful, unevenly
built square is not Pompey, but someone later than classical
Roman: a dark, brooding figure, cowled, standing on a tall plinth,
his hands crossed before him gripping a heavy book – a book, it
seems, of his own writing. The whole piazza seems to circulate
around him; he is its still point. He is a vertical totem of bronze
darkness and melancholic gravity in the middle of all that riot of
colour, and it may take a moment or two to find his name on a
plaque half hidden behind the sprays of flowers. It is Giordano
Bruno, and even a tyro from Australia had heard of him. He was
a philosopher, a theologian, an astronomer, a mathematician and,
not least, both a Dominican monk and a heretic – all told, one of
the most brilliant and unorthodox Italian minds of his time, the
last half of the sixteenth century. One of the thoughts Bruno
proposed and taught was that the universe, far from being the tight
and limited system of concentric spheres conceived by medieval

cosmogony, all tied into orbit around their Unmoved Mover, was in fact infinitely large – a vast continuum consisting of sun after sun, star upon star, eccentric to one another and all in independent movement. This was the startling germ of a modern vision, and the more conservative, theologically grounded thinkers of the sixteenth century viewed it with alarm as opening an attack on the very idea of a God-centred universe.

It is difficult for anyone in the twenty-first century to grasp how radical Bruno's proposal that the stars we see at night are other suns, identical in nature to our own, seemed over four hundred years ago. The idea of a plurality of worlds, which we have no difficulty in accepting, was not merely novel but threatening in the sixteenth century.

Moreover, there were other difficulties with Bruno. He was fascinated by hermetic thought and by ideas about magic. He was rumoured, and by the ignorant believed, to traffic with the Devil. This idea arose from his extraordinary, pioneering researches into mnemonics – the art of systematic memory, a widely shared obsession among Renaissance intellectuals in which Bruno was a leader. For the unorthodoxy of his views, Bruno aroused further suspicion, especially from an inquisitor appointed to refute them – the formidable Catholic thinker, a Jesuit and a cardinal of the Church, in himself a spearhead of the Counter-Reformation against Luther, Robert Bellarmine (1542–1621), who lies entombed in the Church of the Gesù in Rome. This was no mere bigot, but one of the great conservative intellectuals of the Church, its leading authority on the theology of St Thomas Aquinas, and he saw in Bruno a dangerous philosophical enemy. The arguments went on, back and forth, for seven years. On 17 February 1600 Bruno was brought out of the prison cell – the last of several in which he had languished while on trial for a dozen heresies – and led to the centre of the Campo dei Fiori, where a pyre had been prepared. *Maiori forsan cum timore sententium in me fertis quam ego accipium*, he said to his priestly accusers: 'Perhaps you pronounce this sentence against me with greater fear than I receive it.' The brand was applied to the dry wood. As the flames came roaring up to envelop him Bruno was heard to utter neither a prayer nor a curse.

Thus perished one of the true intellectual heroes of the Italian Renaissance. He was burned alive for holding erroneous opinions about the Trinity, the divinity and incarnation of Christ, for denying the virginity of Mary, and half a dozen other heretical positions including belief in 'a plurality of worlds and their eternity' and 'dealing in magic and divination'. His chief inquisitor, Cardinal Bellarmine, demanded a full recantation, which Bruno refused. When the fire died down to cinders, whatever remained of Giordano Bruno was scraped up and dumped in the Tiber, and all his many writings, both philosophical and scientific, dozens of books, were placed on the Index, the Vatican's list of forbidden texts. The statue was put up in 1889, on the advice of a committee partly Roman and partly foreign, which included such distinguished non-Catholics as the German historian Ferdinand Gregorovius, Victor Hugo and Henrik Ibsen. The fruit and vegetables of the Campo dei Fiori would renew themselves for ever, in freshness, as his best memorial.

Giordano Bruno was the most distinguished but by no means the last person to be executed for his sins in the Field of Flowers. All sorts of people, from ordinary murderers to practitioners of the black arts, paid there with their lives in the seventeenth century. A surprising proportion of them were renegade priests. This must have suited other visitors to the square very well, since public executions were always popular in Rome – as, indeed, they were throughout Europe. Partly because of this, the Campo also supported a vigorous and profitable hotel trade. One of the best-known inns of the city, named La Locanda della Vacca ('The Cow'), which occupied the corner of Vicolo del Gallo and Via dei Cappellari, was owned by Vannozza Cattanei, the former mistress of Cardinal Rodrigo Borgia, who held the Papacy from 1492 to 1503 under the name of Alessandro VI. With matchless impudence Vannozza arranged to have her coat of arms emblazoned in quarter with the Borgia pope's; they can still be seen over the entrance in Vicolo del Gallo. Rome's oldest inn, supposedly, was the Locanda del Sole, built from *spolia* salvaged from the nearby ruins of the Theatre of Pompey. It is still open for business at Via del Biscione 76 as the Sole al Biscione Hotel.

I do not visit St Peter's every time I go to Rome. The atmosphere of faith is too imposing and even becomes, as rhetorical sublimity sometimes can, somewhat monotonous. Nor do I always make a beeline to favourite places like the Church of S. Maria della Vittoria, which contains Bernini's wonderful Cornaro Chapel. Sometimes I don't even enter a museum, because in a sense all Rome is a museum inside out. But the Campo dei Fiori, with its statue of Giordano Bruno, has been holy ground to me ever since I first encountered it, in ignorance, and I seldom fail to visit it and reflect on what it represents.

For how could I not? That piazza is quintessential Rome to me: essential Rome five times over. Essential, first, because of the terrible and authoritarian memory it summons up, of the Roman Church which without qualms could burn to death one of the most brilliant men in Italy for the crimes of teaching (as Bruno apparently did) that Christ was not God but an inspired magus, and that even the Devil might be saved. (How I wish I could have known him!) A quatrain circulated:

Roma, se santa sei,
Perche crudel se tanta?
Se dici che se santa,
Certo bugiardo sei!

'Rome, if you're holy/ Why are you so cruel?/ If you say you're holy/ You're nothing but a liar!'

Essential, secondly, because some three hundred years after killing him the city could change its mind (against the opposition of the clergy), retract its judgement and, in recognition of Bruno's individual greatness, raise a statue in his honour. A bit late perhaps, but certainly better late than never.

Thirdly essential, because Rome could build such a monument

only when the Church's temporal power over the city ceased to exist, after Rome was captured in 1870 by the newly formed Kingdom of Italy and became politically a secular city. Fourthly so, because the presence of Bruno's great dark totem is such a brilliant urban gesture, and the life that goes on around it is the life of the Roman people, not just of tourism. Fifthly and last, because of the daily superfetation of fruit and flowers, and the appetites they inspire, reminding us that in the presence of Death we truly and absolutely are in Life.

For Rome is certainly a city driven by her appetites. Much of the food one ate, in and out of this piazza, was quite unfamiliar to me, for all its simplicity. In Australia I was never, as far as I remember, offered something as exotic as *baccalà*, salt cod: it was simply not a part of the Australian diet, which was hardly surprising since there were no cod in the Pacific. In Rome, of course, *baccalà fritta* was a staple of street food: soak the board-stiff slabs of cod for several days in changes of water, take off the skin, remove the bones, cut it into pieces as wide as two fingers, drop it in batter and then fry it in oil to a rich golden brown. Nothing could be simpler than this, and what could taste better with a cold glass of Frascati, consumed at a table in a foreign piazza in early-afternoon sunlight?

The fried foods of Rome, the salads, even the humble cornmeal mush known as polenta were, in every way, a revelation for a hungry young man whose experience of Italian food was as limited as mine. I had never eaten a zucchini flower before getting to Rome. Nor had I ever come across a dish like the anchovies with endive, layered in an earthenware pan and baked until a crust forms, to be eaten hot or cold. Some of these dishes were doubly exotic because of their Jewish origins. As an Australian Catholic I was all but unaware of the existence of Jewish food, and because of the tiny Jewish population of Australia its recipes had never entered the mainstream of popular cooking, as they had in America. But Rome had ancient Jewish traditions, food among them. What foreign goy could be expected to know about those? One example was the Roman dish known as *carciofi alla giudia*,

Jewish-style artichokes, which I soon learned to dote on, as any goy might. Take your artichokes, strip off their tough outer leaves, and holding them stem upright, squish and whack them down on the table until the inner leaves spread outwards. Immerse them, like early martyrs, in boiling oil. Gradually the artichokes will turn spikily golden, like the petals of a sunflower, and then a rich brown. They are almost ready. With a hand dipped in cold water, sprinkle them and they will begin to crackle invitingly. Then sprinkle again with oil, and serve.

But food wasn't all that had me enraptured on my first hungry visit to the city. In Rome, for the first time in my life, I felt surrounded by speaking water. What trees are to Paris, fountains are to Rome. They are the vertical or angled jets, wreathing, bubbling, full of life, which give measure to the city. I had never seen anything like that before. In other places fountains are special events, but in Rome they are simply part of the vernacular of civic life; you notice them, you see them as exceptions to the surfaces of stone or brick, but it seems that they are there to be breathed, not just seen. In the centre of the great city one is always aware, if only subliminally, of the presence of water. No city (or none that I know) so incarnates the poetic truth of the opening lines of Octavio Paz's poem *Piedra del Sol* ('The Sun-Stone'), evoking the continuous movement of a city fountain:

A willow of crystal, a poplar of water,
A tall fountain the wind arches over,
A tree deep-rooted yet dancing still,
A course of a river that turns, moves on,
Doubles back, and comes full circle,
Forever arriving:

The fountain is, in its very essence, an artificial thing, both liquid – formless – and shaped; but the jets of Bernini's Piazza Navona, glittering in the sun, mediate with an almost incredible beauty and generosity between Nature and Culture. Thanks to its fountains – but not only to them – the Roman cityscape constantly gives you more than you expect or feel entitled to as a visitor or, presumably, as a citizen. 'What did I do to deserve this?' And the answer seems ridiculously simple: 'I am human, and I came here.'

Some of the most wonderful first glimpses of Rome, for me, were quite unexpected and rather close to accidental. I had meant to approach St Peter's as it is shown on the city maps – by walking up the broad direct avenue of the Via della Conciliazione, which runs straight from the Castel S. Angelo to the vast colonnaded space of Piazza San Pietro. Luckily for me, I got this wrong. I went too far to the left and approached the piazza, which I could not see, from near the Borgo Santo Spirito. After some trekking, during which I had little idea where I was, I came across what I supposed was a massive curving wall. It was nothing of the kind. It was one of the mighty columns of the piazza itself, and when I crept around it the space burst into view. No straight approach up the Via della Conciliazione could have offered this surprise. As generations of previous tourists have been, I was thunderstruck by the sight: the fountains, the vertical of the obelisk, but above all the curve of Bernini's double Doric colonnade. The idea of architecture of such scale and effort had never entered my mind before. Of course I had never seen anything like it – for the rather obvious reason that nothing else like Bernini's piazza and colonnade can be seen, in Australia or out of it. For a twenty-year-old student to go from memories of Australian architecture (which had its moments and its virtues, most conspicuously the Sydney Harbour Bridge, but none really like this) to such near-incomprehensible grandeur was a shattering experience. It blew away, in an instant, whatever half-baked notions of historical 'progress' may have been rattling about, loosely attached to the inside of my skull.

It was being gradually borne in on me by Rome that one of the vital things that makes a great city great is not mere raw size, but the amount of care, detail, observation and love precipitated in its contents, including but not only its buildings. It is the sense of care – of voluminous attention to detail – that makes things matter, that detains the eye, arrests the foot and discourages the passer-by from passing too easily by. And it goes without saying, or ought to, that one cannot pay that kind of attention to detail until you understand quite a bit about substance, about different stones, different metals, the variety of woods and other materials – ceramic, glass, brick, plaster and the rest – that go to make up the innards and outer skin of a building, how they age, how they wear: in sum, how they live, if they do live. An architect's flawless inkwash rendering of a fluted pilaster surmounted by a capital of the Composite order is, necessarily, an abstraction. But being an architecture student in Australia, it was all I knew about the old stuff. It has not become architecture yet, and it will really not do so until it is built and the passage of light from dawn to dusk has settled in to cross it, until time, wind, rain, soot, pigeon shit and the myriad marks of use that a building slowly acquires have left their traces. Above all it will not become architecture until it is clearly made of the world's substance – of how one kind of stone cuts this way but not that, of bricks whose burned surface relates to the earth below it. Now Rome – not the society of people in the city, but their collective exoskeleton, the city itself – is a sublime and inordinately complicated object lesson in the substantiality of buildings and other made things, in their resistance to abstraction.

This is an awareness that a student cannot really get from listening, however attentively, to lectures, no matter how skilled and sympathetic the lecturer. Nor is he or she well placed to grasp it by looking at photos, though photos are certainly a help. It needs to be got, and can only be acquired, from the presence of the thing itself. And of course the sense of it cannot come into existence, as a general characteristic of a city, unless the city has the clarity and deliberation of something that has been made, preferably by hand, and bit by bit – unless you can see that the depth of a moulding or the sculptural profile of a capital is not there by accident or habit, but by intent, by design. That it is wrought, not just slapped on. It is too much to expect that everything in a city should partake of this quality of attention and intention. But without it, you have a suburb, a mall, whatever you want to call it – not a real city. This is why Chicago is truly a city but Flint, Michigan, can never be.

Rome abounds in such realizations. Sometimes you think that every yard of every crooked alley is full of them. But for the new and uninstructed arrival, such as I was in 1959, it is naturally the very big and rather obvious ones that strike first, and for me the most decisive and revelatory of these first encounters was not in Piazza S. Pietro, that mythic centre of faith, but on the other side of the Tiber, up on the Capitol above Piazza Venezia. Its messenger was not a religious work of art, but a pagan one: the ancient bronze statue of the emperor Marcus Aurelius (reg. 161–80 CE) riding his horse, in the most noble silence and stillness, on a pedestal which rose from the centre of a twelve-pointed star, in the trapezoidal piazza Michelangelo designed for the Campidoglio. I had seen photographs of it, of course; who hadn't? But nothing really prepared me for the impact of that sculpture, both in its mass and in its detail. It is by far the greatest and, indeed, a rare surviving example of a type of sculpture that was widely known and made in the ancient pagan world: the hero, the authority figure, the demigod on horseback; human intelligence and power controlling the animal kingdom, striding victoriously forward. There used to be twenty or so such bronze equestrian statues in Rome, and yet more throughout Italy, such as the *Regisole* or 'Sun-King' in Pavia, which was so thoroughly destroyed in 1796 that not a skerrick remains and the only surviving trace of it is a mere woodcut on paper. All were toppled, broken up and melted down by pious, ignorant Catholics in the early Middle Ages, who believed that their vandalism was an act of faith, an exorcism of the authority of the pagan world. Only Marcus Aurelius survived, and by mistake. The good Catholics mistook the statue for a horseback portrait of the first Christian emperor of Rome, Constantine the Great. But for that sublimely lucky error, Marcus Aurelius would have joined all the other bronze emperors in history's indifferent melting-pot.

I, of course, knew next to nothing of this history when, aged all of twenty on that summer evening of 1959, I saw the bronze horseman for the first time, dark against the looming golden background of Michelangelo's Palazzo del Senatore, with the bats beginning to flit around. I knew even less about horses, old or new, bronze or flesh. I was a city boy, despite sojourns in the bush, and to me these animals were 'dangerous at both ends and damn unsafe in the middle'. The very idea of scrambling up on a four-teen-hand horse touched me with reluctance, even dread. But as I circled the pedestal, looking up at the magnificently robust displacements of space and shape afforded by the limbs and bodies of horse and man, I realized that this horse and this rider were beyond and outside any sculpture, indeed any work of art, I had seen before.

It may be that Australia had some equestrian bronzes in it – war memorials, perhaps? – but if it did, I do not remember them. It probably didn't, because the fabrication of a life-size bronze man on a bronze horse consumes a great deal of metal and is prohibitively expensive in a country that had no tradition of public sculpture. It also requires a special foundry and special skills to work in it, neither of which could have been available in my homeland.

But what really made Marcus Aurelius and his mount unique in my very limited experience was their confluence of sculptural grandeur with intimacy of detail. You can make a big generalized horse and a full-scale, generalized man without exciting the feel-ings that more detailed sculpture can produce. But that does not offer what Marcus Aurelius delivers, the passionate apprehension of small things combining and flowing into large ones, the ordered accumulation of details locked together in a larger image of life.

This is no rocking-horse: the lips, constrained by its metal bit, fold and grimace under the tension on the reins; they look fierce but they testify to imperial control. Marcus Aurelius' hair stands energetically up, a nimbus of corkscrewing locks, not a bit like the conventional signs for hair that plaster so many Roman marble crania. The extended right hand, in its gesture of calming power, is majestic (as befits the hand of an emperor) but benign (as a Stoic's well might be; this was the hand that wrote Marcus'

Meditations). The different thrusts and directions of the statue's limbs are adjusted to play off one another, the raised left foreleg of the horse against the splayed legs of the man astride it, with an uncanny appreciation of movement. And then there is the colour. The bronze carries the patina of more than two thousand years. It is something that cannot be replicated by applied chemicals. It speaks of long exposure, running out beyond the scale of two dozen human generations, each contributing its small freight of patches, gold blotches, green streaks and pinhole discolorations to the venerable surface. When I first saw the Marcus Aurelius, this process had been going on uninterruptedly, like some extremely slow maturation of wine, for a very long time and was part of the simultaneous but differently scaled ageing of Michelangelo's architectural frame for the horse and rider – the crisper contours of the pedestal, the bloom and discoloration of the mellowed surface of Palazzo del Senatore.

One's interest in the past is, at age twenty, minimal – it seems so distant and irrelevant and, in so many ways, imbued with failure. The future is equally inconceivable; one is overwhelmed by the romance of possibility. But that was the magic of Rome for my younger self. The city was my guide backward as well as forward. It provided insight into beauty as well as destruction, triumph as well as tragedy. Most of all it gave physical form to the idea of art, not simply as something ethereal for the elite but as something inspiring, even utilitarian. For me, that first time, Rome turned art, and history, into reality.

FOUNDATION

Although nobody can say when Rome began, at least there is reasonable certainty of where it did. It was in Italy, on the bank of the river Tiber, about twenty-two kilometres inland from its mouth, a delta which was to become the seaport of Ostia.

The reason no one can pinpoint when the foundation took place is that it never ascertainably did. There was no primal moment when a loose scatter of Iron and Bronze Age villages perched on hills agreed to coalesce and call itself a city. The older a city is, the more doubt about its origins, and Rome is certainly old. This did not prevent the Romans from the second century BCE onwards coming up with implausibly exact-looking dates for its origins: Rome, it used to be asserted, began not just in the eighth century but precisely in 753 BCE, and its founder was Romulus, twin brother of Remus. Here a tangled story begins, with many variants, which tend to circle back to the same themes we will see again and again throughout Rome's long history: ambition, parricide, fratricide, betrayal and obsessive ambition. Especially the last. No more ambitious city than Rome had ever existed, or conceivably ever will, although New York offers it competition. No city has ever been more steeped in ferocity from its beginnings than Rome. These wind back to the story of the city's mythic infancy.

In essence, the story says that Romulus and Remus were orphans and foundlings, but they could claim a long and august ancestry. It stretched back to Troy. After Troy fell (the legendary date of this catastrophic event being 1184 BCE) its hero Aeneas, son of Anchises and the goddess Aphrodite or Venus, had escaped the burning city with his son Ascanius. After years of wandering on the Mediterranean, Aeneas fetched up in Italy, where Ascanius (now grown up) founded the city of Alba Longa, not far from the eventual site of Rome, traditionally in about 1152 BCE.

Here, Ascanius' progeny began a line of kings, his descendants. The last of the line was called Amulius, who wrested the throne of Alba Longa from its rightful occupant, his elder brother Numitor. Numitor had one child, a daughter, named Rhea Silvia. Amulius the usurper used his convenient, newly seized power to make her a Vestal Virgin, so that she could not produce a son, who might be not only Amulius' heir but also a deadly threat to him. But the war god Mars, no respecter of either virginity or vestality, impregnated Rhea Silvia. Amulius, realizing she was pregnant, had Rhea Silvia imprisoned; presently she died of ill-treatment – but not before delivering her twin sons, Romulus and Remus.

We have the great historian Livy's word for what happened next. Amulius ordered his men to fling little Remus and Romulus into the Tiber. But the river had been in flood and its waters had not yet receded. So rather than wade right out into the current and get uncomfortably wet, they merely dumped the babies into the shallower floodwater at the river's edge, and went away. The level of the Tiber dropped some more, stranding the twins in the mud. In this state, wet but still alive, they were found by a she-wolf, which benignly nourished them with its milk until they were old and strong enough to be brought to adulthood by the royal herdsman, Faustulus. (Most visitors, when they see the bronze sculpture in the Museo dei Conservatori of the Foundling Babies sucking on the pendulous conical teats of the *lupa*, naturally think it is one original piece. It is not; the wolf is thought by some people to have been cast by an Etruscan craftsman in the fifth century BCE, but Romulus and Remus were added in *c*.1484–96 by the Florentine artist Antonio Pollaiuolo.)

In any case, in the myth they eventually overthrew Amulius and restored their grandfather Numitor to his rightful place as king of Alba Longa. And then they decided to found a new settlement on the bank of the Tiber where chance had washed them ashore. This became the city of Rome.

Who would be its king? This was settled by an omen in the form of a flight of birds of prey. Six of them appeared to Remus but twelve to Romulus, thus marking him – by a majority vote from the gods above, as it were – as the indisputable ruler of the new city.

Where exactly was it? There has always been some dis-agreement over the original, 'primitive' site of Rome. There is no archaeological evidence for it. It must have been on one of the Tiber's banks – which one, nobody knows. But the district is famous for having had seven hills – the Palatine, the Capitoline, the Caelian, the Aventine, the Esquiline, the Viminal and the Quirinal. Nobody can guess which one it may have been, although it is likely that the chosen site, for strategic reasons, would have been a hill rather than flatland or a declivity. Nobody was keeping any records, so no one can guess which one of these swellings, lumps or pimples was a likely candidate. 'Tradition' locates the primitive settlement on the modest but defensible height of the Palatine Hill. The 'accepted' date of the foundation, 753 BCE, is of course wholly mythical. There was never any possibility of authenticating these early dates – again, nobody was keeping any records, and since later attempts at recording the annals of the city, all belonging to the second century BCE (the writings of Quintus Fabius Pictor, Polybius, Marcus Porcius Cato), only began to be made five hundred years after the events they claim to describe, they can hardly be deemed trustworthy. But they are all we have.

Supposedly, Romulus 'founded' the city that bears his name. If things had gone differently and Remus had done so we might now talk about visiting Reem, but it was Romulus who, in legend, marked out the strip of land that defined the city limits by hitching two oxen, a bull and a cow to a plough and making a furrow. It was called the *pomerium* and would be the sacred track of the city wall. This, according to Varro, was the 'Etruscan rite' for the founding of a city in Latium. Ritual demanded that the furrow, or *fossa*, the small trench of symbolic fortifications, should lie outside the ridge of earth raised by the ploughshare; this ridge was called the *agger* or earthwork. The walls of the city were raised behind this symbolic line, and the space between it and the walls was scrupulously kept free of building and planting, as a defensive measure. The area within the *pomerium* would come to be called *Roma quadrata*, 'Square Rome', for obscure reasons. Evidently Remus took exception to it, for reasons equally unknown. Perhaps he objected to Romulus assuming the right to determine the shape of the city. He showed his disagreement by jumping over the furrow – an innocent act, one might think, but not to Romulus, who took it for a blasphemous expression of hostile contempt and murdered his twin brother for committing it. History does not tell how Romulus may have felt about slaying his only brother over a perceived threat to his sovereignty, but it is perhaps significant that the sacred group that ran around the *pomerium* at intervals to assure the fertility of Roman flocks and women in later years was known as the *luperci*, or wolf brotherhood.

So the embryo city, rooted in an unexplained fratricide, had one founder, not two, and as yet no inhabitants. Romulus supposedly solved this problem by creating an asylum or place of refuge on what became the Capitol, and inviting in the trash of primitive Latium: runaway slaves, exiles, murderers, criminals of all sorts. Legend makes it out to have been (to employ a more recent simile) a kind of Dodge City. This can hardly be gospel-true, but it does contain a kernel of symbolic truth. Rome and its culture were not 'pure'. They were never produced by a single ethnically homogeneous people. Over the years and then the centuries much of Rome's population came from outside Italy – this even included some of the later emperors, such as Hadrian, who was Spanish, and writers like Columella, Seneca, and Martial, also Spanish-born. Celts, Arabs, Jews and Greeks, among others, were included under the wide umbrella of *Romanitas*. This was the inevitable result of an imperial system that constantly expanded and frequently accepted the peoples of conquered countries as Roman citizens. Not until the end of the first century BCE, with the reign of Augustus, do we begin to see signs of a distinctively 'Roman' art, an identifiably 'Roman' cultural ideal.

But how Roman is Roman? Is a statue dug up not far from the Capitol, carved by a Greek artist who was a prisoner-of-war in Rome, depicting Hercules in the style of Phidias and done for a wealthy Roman patron who thought Greek art the ultimate in chic, a 'Roman' sculpture? Or is it Greek art in exile? Or what? *Mestizaje es grandeza*, 'mixture is greatness', is a Spanish saying but it could well have been Roman. It was never possible for the Romans, who expanded to exercise their sway over all Italy, to pretend to the lunacies of racial purity that came to infect the way Germans thought about themselves.

Several tribes and groups already inhabited the coastal plain and hills around the Tiber. The most developed in the Iron Age were the Villanovans, whose name comes from the village near Bologna where a cemetery of their tombs was discovered in 1853. Their culture would mutate by trade and expansion into that of the Etruscans by about 700 BCE. Any new settlement had to contend, or at least reach an accommodation, with the Etruscans, who dominated the Tyrrhenian coast and most of central Italy – a region known as Etruria. Where they originally came from remains a mystery. In all likelihood, they had always been there, despite the belief held by some in the past that the Etruscans' remote ancestors had migrated to Italy from Lydia in Asia Minor. The most powerful Etruscan city close to Rome was Veii, a mere twelve miles to its north – though the cultural influence of the Etruscans spread so far and wide that they made themselves felt far in the south, in what later became Pompeii. Until they were eclipsed by the rising power of Rome, around 300 BCE, they laid down the terms of culture in central Italy.

Never a centralized empire, the Etruscans created city-states along the Tyrrhenian coast of Italy: Veii, Caere (Cerveteri), Tarquinia, Vulci and others, all of them ruled by high-priestly kings called *lucumones*. Some of these settlements were linked in a loose federation, with ritual similarities and defence and trade agreements. Because of their military superiority – the Etruscan 'tank' was a bronze-fitted chariot, and the basic unit of Etruscan warfare was a heavy-armoured, close-knit phalanx, the ancestor of the

Roman legion – they could dominate the less tightly knit forces of their tribal rivals – until the Romans moved in.

Other minor tribal groupings held territory in the neighbourhood of Rome as well, one of these being the Sabines. They seem to have been hill people and shepherds, and their settlement may have been on the Quirinal Hill. An expansionist from the beginning, Romulus seems to have decided to go after this territory first. In order to lure the Sabines and their women within reach, Romulus is said to have held some horse races during the Festival of Consus (in August). The whole Sabine population turned up, and at a signal the Romans abducted all the young women they could lay their hands on. This amounted to a declaration of war between the Romans and the infuriated Sabines. (All Romans were Latins but not all Latins were Romans. Roman power, including the power to confer Roman citizenship, was vested in Rome, and it became an esteemed honour.) The Sabine king, Titus Tatius, gathered an army and marched against the Romans. But in another scene made legendary by artists such as Jacques-Louis David, the kidnapped Sabine women flung themselves between the two sides of furious males – brothers, fathers, husbands – and persuaded them to make peace, not war.

Peace and alliance between Sabine and Latin now prevailed. Romulus supposedly ruled the united tribes for another thirty-three years, and then dramatically vanished from the earth, wrapped in the thick darkness of a thunderstorm. Six kings are traditionally said to have succeeded Romulus, some Latin, others (notably the semi-legendary, sixth-century BCE rulers Tarquinius Priscus and Tarquinius Superbus, 'Tarquin the Arrogant') supposedly Etruscan. In legend, their succession began with Numa Pompilius, who reigned for forty-three years and established in Rome 'an endless number of religious rites and temples'. He was followed by Tullius Hostilius, who conquered the Albans and the people of the Etruscan settlement of Veii; by Ancus Marcius, who added the Janiculan and Aventine hills to Rome; by Tarquinius Priscus, said to have established the Roman Games; by Servius Tullius, who added the Quirinal, Viminal and Esquiline hills and

finished off the Sabines; and by Tarquin the Arrogant, who murdered Servius. His son, Lucius Tarquinius Superbus, made peace
between Latins and Etruscans.

These kings established the *mons Capitolinus*, the Capitoline
Hill, as the citadel and sacred centre of Rome. Here the temples
to the goddesses Minerva and Juno were raised and, most sacred
and important of all, the temple to Iuppiter Optimus Maximus,
'Jupiter Best and Greatest'. It was (supposedly) dedicated by King
Tarquin in 509 BCE. Although little is known about Tarquin the
Arrogant as a historical figure, he contributed to most languages
an expression which lives and is used down to the present day.
According to Livy (who was writing about half a millennium
later), the king taught a lesson with it to his son, Sextus Tarquinius,
the future rapist of Lucretia. Having just conquered an enemy
city, Tarquin was strolling with his boy in their garden when he
began to chop off the heads of the tallest poppies in it. This, he
explained, was the thing to do with leading citizens of a fallen
town who might cause trouble in defeat. Hence the modern term,
especially loved and all too often used by sneering Australians to
level the society around them: 'tall poppy syndrome'.

The authority of kings in Rome lasted about two hundred
years. Succession was not hereditary. During this time, the kings
were in essence elected – not by all classes of the Roman people,
but by the city's richest and most powerful elders, who (with their
families) came to be known as the *patricii*, the 'patricians'. These
constituted a governing class, choosing and then advising the
rulers of Rome. After the disappearance of the last king, Tarquinius Superbus, whom the patricians expelled and refused ever
to replace, a system evolved that was designed never to put such
authority in one man's hands again. Supreme authority was
granted to not one, but two chosen figures, the *consules* (consuls).
Their powers were exactly equal and one could overrule the other:
thus the Roman state could take no action on any issue unless
both consuls agreed on it. This at least saved the Roman state
from some of the follies of autocracy. From now on the prospect
of 'kingship' would be a political bogey to Romans; the consul

Julius Caesar, to take the outstanding example, would be assassinated by a cabal of republicans who feared that he might make himself a king. Meanwhile, the religious powers of the kings were hived off and invested in a supreme priest, known as the *pontifex maximus*.

Every Roman citizen not a patrician was classified as a plebeian. Not everyone who lived in Rome enjoyed citizenship; it was not extended to slaves or resident aliens, of whom there were many. The official upper caste of power was next enlarged after 494 BCE, when the plebeian citizens – fretting at the arrogance with which patricians treated them – went on strike and refused army service. This could have been a disaster for an expansionist state like Rome, surrounded as it was by potential enemies. It was averted by choosing each year two people's representatives known as 'tribunes', whose duty was to see to and protect the interests of the plebeians. Before long the number of officials granted the tribune's power, the *tribunicia potestas*, grew from two to ten. To clarify their field of action, written laws began to emerge, known at first in their primitive form as the Twelve Tables.

The city on the hill, or by now hills, was unstoppable. It continued to live and grow, to expand and conquer. It was singularly dynamic and aggressive, but about its life and physical traces we know very little, because of the absence of credible historical records and the crumbling-away and demolition of buildings. Whatever there was is buried by subsequent Romes. In the words of the French historian Jules Michelet, 'The Rome we see, which tears from us ... a cry of admiration, is in no way comparable to the Rome we do not see. That is the Rome that lies twenty, thirty feet underground ... Goethe said of the sea, "The further you go, the deeper it is." So it is with Rome ... We only have the lesser part.'

Perhaps, perhaps not. The deeper you go, the more primitive Roman architecture is apt to be. There are no legible traces of constructed Etruscan-Roman temples left standing. Much guesswork is needed to reconstruct the primal, Etruscan-based temple of Jupiter on the Capitoline, with its deep porch, heavy gabled roof with wide wooden eaves, and profuse terracotta roof decoration in the form of antefixes. The columns are very widely spaced, wider than they could possibly have been in stone construction: these forms belonged to wooden architecture, because they rely on the tensile capability of timber – stone is strong in compression and therefore excellent for posts and columns, but in tension, as a beam spanning a gap, it is weak. The emphasis of the building is on its front façade – unlike Greek temples, which were 'peripteral' or designed to be seen with columns all round, on four sides. Vitruvius, the first great classifier of ancient Italian architecture, called this style 'Tuscan', and so it remains.

What caused the gradual refinement of this kind of 'primitive' Etruscan-Roman architecture was the influence of Greek building in the Hellenic colonies on the Italian mainland – Cumae, Neapolis (Naples), Zancle, Naxos, Catana, Leontini. Their temples tended to have all-round columning and established 'orders' or styles of column-capital. It may be that liturgical changes favoured abandoning the single-front temple. Or perhaps the all-round design of the Greek buildings that were rising in Hellenic colonies on the Italian mainland prompted imitation. The fluted column, whose vertical striations, in Greek hands, may have been a highly stylized memory of wood-grain, never appears, but certainly the Etruscan builders' use of terracotta antefixes along their wooden roofs was adapted from Greek models.

Many of the Etruscan tombs and holy precincts that are recognizable today needed no columns at all, because they were built below ground level. Some of these, particularly in the country inland from Tarquinia, a city which overlooks the coast fifty miles north of Rome, are still in existence, a tiny minority of them beautifully if somewhat crudely painted with scenes of hunting, fishing, feasting, sacrifice, dance, ritual and (in the Tomb of the Bulls, behind Tarquinia) of sodomy. But these are hardly architecture – just decorated holes in the ground, or recesses under conical heaps of earth and stones.

Of their religion and gods frustratingly little is known. Plenty of inscriptions in Etruscan survive, but they are, for the most part, historically quite useless – mere chicken-scratched names, not even memorializing dates and certainly not deeds. Because of the letters' kinship with the Greek alphabet we can tell what the words probably sounded like but rarely what they meant. It may be that the triad of principal Etruscan gods, Tinea-Uni-Menvra, corresponds exactly to the Roman triad Jupiter-Juno-Minerva, whose worship would be installed on the Capitol, but it may not – though 'Menvra' is probably Minerva.

We know that some Etruscans were capable of exquisite sculpture in terracotta, and that some were experts in metalwork: this is clear from such masterpieces in bronze as the Arezzo Chimera; the hauntingly Giacometti-like figure disinterred from a tomb in Volterra and nicknamed, because of its extreme elongation, the *ombra della sera* ('the evening shadow'); the life-size and elegantly detailed bronze figure of an Etruscan orator, which is one of the treasures of the Archaeological Museum in Florence; and the aforementioned emblematic *lupa* or she-wolf which, glaring fiercely up on the Capitol, suckles little Romulus and Remus. Perhaps the greatest of Etruscan terracotta sculptures is the late-sixth-century BCE *Sarcophagus of the Spouses* now in the Museo di Villa Giulia in Rome, a large chest in the form of a bed on which the young couple gracefully recline, the massing and delicate linear balance achieved with such a light touch that, for many visitors, it is the most moving and beautiful image in all Etruscan art. What did they die of? Did they go at the same time? Who could guess now? It was found in Cerveteri, but the most esteemed centre of statuary in Etruria was Veii – so much so that the name of one of its artists, Vulca, who was commissioned to make statues for the great temple of Jupiter on the Roman Capitol, has come down to us, the rarest of commemorations.

The Etruscans seem to have had few if any indigenous potters of the first rank, but their taste for fine ceramics brought remarkable pieces from Greece to Etruria as trade goods, which ended their travels in the tombs of the Etruscan great; the most famous of these, because of the sensation and controversy that surrounded its sale to the Metropolitan Museum of Art in New York and its eventual return to its true custodianship in Italy in 2008, was the big Greek wine bowl known as the Euphronios krater, dug up and then stolen from the Etruscan necropolis of Cerveteri north of Rome. The indigenous pottery material, not found in Greece, was a black clay known as *bucchero*, used unpainted, from which thousands and thousands of utilitarian pots and bowls were made, some of robust monochrome beauty.

Their architecture and most of their sacred artefacts may be gone, but the influence of the Etruscans is written everywhere on the early city-state of Rome. It affected the calendar – its division into twelve months, each with its 'Ides' (the middle of the month), and the name of the month Aprilis, were of Etruscan origin. So was the way Romans personally named themselves – with a first and a clan name. The original Latin alphabet, of twenty-one letters, was probably adapted from an Etruscan adaptation of the Greek alphabet. The first temple on the Capitol was Etruscan. It was dedicated to Jupiter (Iuppiter) Optimus Maximus, with his companion goddesses Juno and Minerva. No ruins of it survive, but it appears to have been very large – two hundred feet square is a common estimate – and, because of the necessary column spacing, its roof was made of timber: this meant, inevitably, that it often burned down. One can probably get a good idea of the cult image of Jupiter on its roof from the 500 BCE terracotta Etruscan *Apollo of Veii* in the Museo di Villa Giulia in Rome.

Rome's *ludi*, the games and gladiatorial contests that were to assume such colossal political importance under the Caesars, originated in Etruria. Some of the lifelike qualities of Roman portrait sculpture were already present in the vivid immediacy of Etruscan terracotta effigies.

Some Roman technical achievements began in Etruscan expertise. While the Etruscans never came up with an aqueduct, they were good at drainage, and hence they were the ancestors of Rome's monumental sewer systems. Their land was criss-crossed with irrigation channels up to five feet deep and three feet wide, known as *cuniculi*; but after Etruria was crushed by Rome its drainage was not kept up, so that much of the campagna north of

Rome degenerated into malarial heath and swamp and would remain uninhabitable in places until Mussolini's government drenched it with insecticides in the twentieth century. It is probable that the Etruscans invented the segmental arch, without which Roman architecture could not have developed – the Greeks never had this structural form, but it is the basis of the Etrusco-Roman sewer system that culminates in the enormous, and still visible, exit of the Cloaca Maxima into the Tiber.

Some Etruscan forms of political organization were kept up, in a broad way, by the early Romans, starting (legend says) with Romulus and continuing through the early Republic. They retained the institution of kingship, backed by patricians or aristocrats. But kingship was not hereditary: because his office as war chief was of absolutely central importance, the king was elected (though not by the common people). As high priest of the state, it was his task to find out the will of the gods by augury and haruspication. He was in charge of taxation and the military draft. He was the military leader. These things made up his executive power, or *imperium*. It was interwoven with the advice of his advisory body, the Senate, composed entirely of free citizens of standing – no paupers, workers or freedmen (ex-slaves) allowed. The custom was that each patrician would enjoy the services of his plebeian 'clients', persons of inferior rank (such as ex-slaves and foreigners) who would serve him in return for a place, however small, in public life. The patron–client relationship would prove to be as durable in the future history of Rome as that between masters and slaves.

And before long, the institution of Roman kingship would wither away. By the fifth and early fourth centuries BCE the aristocracy was victorious, and it proceeded to replace the king's functions and powers with those of two consuls, one balancing the other. Any major state decision had to be agreed on by both. Each consul was elected to office for one year and had complete authority over civil, military and religious matters. If necessary the kingly power could be renewed, for a strictly limited term of six months, by a dictator – but this was not often resorted to as a political device, and nobody was prepared to equate or confuse dictatorship with kingship.

The largest class of Romans was the intermediary one, attracted to settle and work in Rome by the steady expansion of the city and its territory. Rome kept pushing outwards: in 449 BCE, for instance, it annexed a great deal of Sabine territory, and it was in more or less continuous confrontation with the tribes of the Volsci, who wanted – but failed – to cut off Latium from the sea. The Romans correctly saw it as essential to control both banks of the Tiber, and its mouth. The biggest danger of all, in the fifth century BCE, came from the north – the hostile Gauls, who had begun a piecemeal takeover of Etruria. One of their raids, in approximately 390 BCE, carried them right into Rome, though not for long. (A Gallic scouting party, so the story goes, had seen the tracks of a man on a cliff by the shrine of Carmentis on the Capitol. They managed to follow up, ascending in such silence that not even a dog barked; but just as they were about to fall on the Roman garrison at the top, they disturbed some geese which, sacred to Juno, were kept on top of the Capitol. The cackling and flapping of these birds gave the alarm to the Roman defenders, who drove the Gauls off.)

The need for strong defensive forces against the Gauls and others increased the value of the plebeians to the Roman state, which could not defend itself with patricians alone – particularly since its territory kept growing through conquest and alliance. In 326 BCE Rome had about 10,000 square kilometres; by 200 BCE, 360,000; by 146 BCE, 800,000; and by 50 BCE, nearly two million. The city on the Tiber was well on its way to ruling the known world.

Naturally, given their growing military and economic import-ance in their inferior position, the plebeians had demands to make. This was when the tribunician system was set up. The hereditary aristocratic system of Roman power became less stably fixed because of them. The plebeians wanted champions, men who would defend their interests. Several such men, 'tribunes', were appointed. And the spread of Roman power kept inexorably growing. By the mid-fourth century BCE Rome had swallowed up all the Latin cities, and all Latins in Rome enjoyed the same social and economic rights as Roman citizens. Part of Rome's political genius was that, when she absorbed another political entity – *socii*, they were called, or allies – she moved its citizens to full Roman rights. The typical arrangement, with the Samnites for instance, was that the *socius* tribes and cities kept their own territory, magistrates, priests, religious usages and customs. But this did not amount to democracy. There was a general feeling that government required special skills, which a citizen or an ally needed to learn and acquire – they did not simply come with territory and landownership. And meetings of the plebeians were very seldom held without patrician observers.

The Senate of Rome was distinguished from the 'people', the mass of Romans. But the two were always envisaged as working in harmony together. This is commemorated in what, since time immemorial, has been the official device of the city of Rome, its *stemma* or shield. Preceded by a Greek cross, four letters run diagonally downwards across the shield: S P Q R. These have had many jocular interpretations, from *Stultus Populus Quaerit Romam* ('A Stupid People Wants Rome') to *Solo Preti Qui Regneno* ('Only Priests Are in Charge Here'), and even, in a gesture towards the household marketplace, *Scusi, il Prezzo di Questa Ricotta?* ('Excuse Me, the Price of this Ricotta?'). But they just mean *Senatus Populusque Romanus* ('The Senate and People of Rome').

Few Romans saw anything amiss with the class relations that developed out of a state run by a patriciate. An exception was a pair of brothers, Tiberius Gracchus and Gaius Gracchus. Tiberius Gracchus was elected tribune in 133 BCE and tried to legislate a redistribution of land from the rich to the poor. It is doubtful whether he was inspired by wholly pure and disinterested motives. More likely the measures Tiberius Gracchus proposed were meant to curry favour with a plebeian majority so as to advance his own power. In any case the conservatives stamped on him, hard, and when Tiberius took the unprecedented step of seeking a second year's election as tribune, he was killed in a riot which they fomented. Much the same fate befell his brother Gaius, who in 122 BCE, likewise elected tribune, tried to bring in laws that would have given more power to plebeian assemblies and cheap grain to the needy. Patrician landowners viewed such measures with horror and arranged the lynching of Gaius Gracchus, and of several thousand of his supporters. In matters of class interest, the Roman Republic did not hesitate.

Undoubtedly the chief Etruscan legacy to Rome was religious. Polybius, the Greek historian of the second century BCE, argued that Roman power came from Roman religion: 'The quality in which the Roman commonwealth is most distinctly superior is, I think, the nature of their religious convictions . . . it is the very thing which among other peoples is an object of reproach, I mean superstition, which maintains the cohesion of the Roman state.' 'Superstition' did not mean false fear of untrue fantasies. It related, rather, to the shared idea of *religio*, 're-ligion', a strong binding together. There can be no question that the unifying power of a common religion, linked at all points to the institutions of the state, reinforced Rome's political strength and increased her powers of conquest. Cicero was one of many who agreed with this. 'We have excelled neither Spain in population, nor Gaul in vigour . . . nor Greece in art,' he wrote in the first century BCE, 'but in piety, in devotion to religion . . . we have excelled every race and every nation.' The highest praise, the supreme adjective, that one Roman could apply to another was *pius*, as in the *Aeneid*, Virgil's epic celebrating the mythic birth of Rome and the deeds of its founder, *pius Aeneas*. This did not mean 'pious' in the English sense. It implied veneration of ancestors and their beliefs; respect for the authority of tradition; worship of the gods; above all, consciousness of and devotion to duty. It was a firmly masculine virtue whose implications went far beyond our milky notions of mere 'piety'. The only national sentiment that approached the full sense of Roman piety – and even then, perhaps not completely – was the English Victorians' belief that God was truly on their side, sharing the white man's burden in the immense task of founding, expanding and glorifying the natural needs of the people in the face of the 'fluttered folk and wild' whom it was their destiny to rule. There has probably never been a civilization in which religious imperatives were more entangled with political intentions than they were in early republican Rome. This characteristic of the city would last, of course; it underwrote the enormous political power of religion there from antiquity through Papal Rome.

Certain religious practices came directly to Rome from Etruria. The native Roman religion, before it was reformed by the adoption of Greek gods, was animistic, not anthropomorphic. Its gods were rather vague and ill-defined spirits known as *numina*, from which our term 'numinous' comes. Some of the *numina* survived in later Roman religion, long after the main Roman gods had been personalized and had taken on the character of their Greek predecessors – Zeus becoming Jupiter, for instance, and Aphrodite becoming Venus.

Through early republican times and even into those of the Principate, which brought the beginnings of one-man rule by Augustus and turned the Republic into the Empire, Roman religion was an absurd bureaucratic clutter of minor gods without defined character, who presided over innumerable social functions and needed constant propitiation by prayer and sacrifice. For most of them, only their names and some rather obscure functions have come down to us. In the case of a baby, for instance, his cradle was supervised by Cunina, his breast-feeding by Rumina, his ingestion of adult food and drink by Educa and Potina, his first lispings of words by Fabulinus. Agriculture attracted a horde of godlets, who saw to ploughing, harrowing, sowing, and even the spreading of dung. One *numen* looked after the thresholds of doors, another after their hinges. Among the more important surviving *numina* were the *lares* and the *penates*, who guarded agricultural land and houses; the 'Genius', identified as the procreative power of the father (whence its eventual application to the idea of creative talent); and Vesta, guardian-goddess of the hearth, centre of family life, in whose honour 'Vestal Virgins', six in number, starting as children aged six to ten, were appointed by the high priest. The Vestals were supposed to tend the sacred fire on the state hearth in the temple of Venus, never letting it go out. If it did, they would be ceremonially flogged. This was in practice a lifetime appointment; it was supposed to last thirty years, but after such a term of office a Vestal, having known no other way of life, was most unlikely to marry and raise a family, especially since women in their late thirties or early forties were not considered eligible for childbearing.

Each of the principal gods had priests known as 'flamens' devoted to him, to make sacrifices and perform rites. Ancient taboos and rituals surrounded these sacred offices. A flamen could not, for instance, ride a horse, touch a she-goat, wear a jewelled ring or tie a knot in any of the clothes he wore. The origin of these and other peculiar taboos is, by now, not merely obscure but unknowable.

The flamens were important figures for two main reasons. First, their deliberations were the primitive basis of law and had something of its coercive force: you could not defy them with impunity. Second, because it was so desirable to have an idea of what the gods approved, from this need arose the practice of augury.

The Etruscans seem never to have done anything important without a religious motive, and respect for what the Romans called the *disciplina Etrusca* was passed on and remained embedded in the codes of Roman public and religious life. Well into imperial times, Rome maintained a 'college' of Etruscan diviners, a privileged group known as the *haruspices*, whose task was to read the will of the gods from lightning flashes (*fulgura*) and other portents, especially the flight of birds (what part of the sky they came from, what their speed and heading were) and the markings on the livers, gall-bladders and guts of sacrificed animals. Some believe that the requirements of these vatic birdwatchers influenced, or perhaps even once determined, the siting of temples (on hilltops) and the orientation of their façades (so that the migratory passage of bird flocks could be compared to them). *Templum* did not originally mean a building; it signified a place set aside for the utterance of formulaic words in augury. The augurs' requirements may also have determined the form of the temples: that they were set on tall podiums and had to have one single façade (unlike Greek temples) may have been ritual necessities. But there is no way of proving such things now.

The aim of augury was not simply to foretell the future. It was to find out whether a proposed course of important action was likely to have the approval of the gods. A common way of doing this was by consulting the sacred chickens. These otherwise ordinary fowls (there seem to have been no criteria for telling a sacred chicken from a non-sacred one) were carried in a cage to the field by Roman armies. Before the battle, they would be given chicken-feed. If they pecked at it with gusto, letting bits of food fall from their beaks, it was greeted by the augurs as an excellent omen. If they ignored the offering, it was a very bad sign. If they ate half-heartedly or seemed choosy, that too had its meaning for the augurs. Many Romans of the highest rank took this charade perfectly seriously. One who did not was Publius Claudius Pulcher, an admiral of the Roman navy who, just before an engagement between the Roman and Carthaginian fleets off Drepanum during the First Punic War in 249 BCE, cast the grain before the fowl and was told, by the ship's augur, that the birds would not eat. 'Then let them drink,' Pulcher exclaimed rashly, as he grabbed the chickens and threw them overboard. Alas, he lost the ensuing battle.

If *pietas* was one of the two defining virtues for ancient Rome, then *lex*, Law in all its guises and forms, starting with the great and fundamental distinction between civil law and criminal law, was the other. The Romans were tremendously energetic codifiers, and the corpus of Roman law, a conceptual edifice so vast that it defies any possibility of summary here, remains the foundation of all Western legal systems since. Its earliest form, drawn up by a special commission of jurists in the republican period (*c*.450 BCE), was the Twelve Tables, and so much importance was attached to them that four hundred years later, during the lifetime of Cicero, schoolboys were still obliged to recite them by heart, even though the code of law by then had so hugely expanded as to render the original Twelve Tables, while still fundamental, obsolete. They would remain the cornerstone of Roman law for the best part of another thousand years, until they were at last superseded by the *Corpus Iuris Civilis* of the emperor Justinian.

What was law in the Roman view? Certainly not the false principle that 'might is right', although – particularly in their dealings with non-Romans – you might often suppose that is what they believed. The code of law was not simply a code of power, and this made all the difference between Roman law and its more primitive antecedents. 'Justice,' wrote the jurist Ulpian, 'is a constant, unfailing disposition to give everyone his legal due. The principles of law are these: to live uprightly, not to injure another man, to give every man his due. To be learned in the law is the knowledge of things divine and human, the science of the just and the unjust.' Law was the god in the codex.

Its principles, written down by such jurists as Julius Paulus (late second century CE) and notably Ulpian (Domitius Ulpianus, d. 228 CE), seem so elementary and self-evident now that it is hard to believe they had not existed for ever, but of course they had not. 'He who has knowledge of a crime but is unable to prevent it is free of blame' (Paulus). 'He inflicts an injury who orders it to be inflicted; but no guilt attaches to him who is obliged to obey' (Paulus). 'In the case of equal conflicting claims, the party in possession ought to be considered in the stronger position' (Paulus). 'No one is compelled to defend a cause against his will' (Ulpian). And *nemo dat quod non habet* (Ulpian): 'No one can give what he does not have.' Such were a few of the 211 entries in the 'General Rules of Law' inscribed in the *Digest* of the emperor Justinian.

The making of law was, as the name implies, 'legislation'. Who made law under the Republic? Popular assemblies, divided at first into military units and later, after the third century BCE, a council of common (i.e., not royal or patrician) citizens known as the *concilium plebis* or 'council of the people'. Its votes and resolutions were known as *plebiscita*, from which stems our concept of a 'plebiscite' or general popular vote. At first the men of money and property, the patricians, vehemently objected to the idea that they should be subject to the same laws as commoners. They thought they should make their own for themselves. But in 287 BCE a dictator, Quintus Hortensius, passed a law that all citizens, patricians included, should be bound by any law passed by the council of the *plebs*. This 'Hortensian law' was a milestone in Roman class relations. It deprived the patricians of their last means of arbitrarily dominating the plebeians.

Much of the physical legacy of Justinian's reign would disappear. Most of the hundreds of churches, aqueducts and other public buildings erected by this sixth-century Christian emperor – with certain great exceptions, such as the Church of Hagia Sophia in Constantinople – have fallen into ruin or disuse, but not the epitomes he made of earlier Roman law. Justinian's *Corpus Iuris*, despite the Greek and Christian elements that entered it, remained essentially Roman law, and because the imperial constitutions were issued in the names of both eastern and western emperors and were held to be binding throughout the Roman Empire, they would eventually radiate – through the universities of England, France, Spain, Italy and Germany – to encompass the entire legal basis of Europe during the Middle Ages and on into modern times.

We speak of early Rome as a republic, which she was. Nevertheless she was not a republic in the modern American sense. The root of the term, *res publica*, meant 'public affairs', no more than that. But the essential quality of her political life as a republic was, as we have seen, that she was not ruled by a succession of kings, especially not a hereditary one. She had hammered out a system whereby her polity was split into two broad classes – patricians and plebeians. In the early years of the Republic the patricians held and controlled all the political and social power of the state. Only patricians could be elected to any office, including the all-important senatorships. Only they could serve as priests. The plebeians, by contrast, were excluded from religious colleges, magistracies, and as a rule from the Senate; early on, they were also forbidden to marry patricians. With lawmaking and religion in patrician control, what was left for plebeians? Only agitation and pressure. The patricians needed the plebeians, could not do without them, because they had to build armies; all military offices up to *tribunus militum* were open to them. As Rome kept annexing more and more land within (and then outside) Italy, larger prospects of economic independence gradually rose before the plebeians.

Rome was still a young republic when it began to acquire the overseas provinces that would form the basis of its immense empire. Doing this required naval supremacy in the Mediterranean, but for the first five hundred years of its history Rome had no warships. The naval power in the Mediterranean belonged to the city of Carthage, founded (allegedly) a little earlier than Rome, in 814 BCE, on the Tunisian coast of north Africa, by its legendary queen Dido. Carthage enjoyed immense trading power in the Mediterranean, and considerable strategic power as well, since it controlled the routes along which tin – that essential ingredient of bronze when alloyed to copper in a proportion of approximately 1:9 – was shipped and sold. (The hardness, but the brittleness too, of bronze increased with its tin content. Alloyed with zinc, copper became brass.)

All the islands in the western Mediterranean had been annexed and colonized by Carthage, except Sicily. But the Carthaginians had established a strong presence there, and Rome was worried that if it got any stronger the whole island would be theirs. In 264 BCE Carthage occupied the Greek colony of Messana in north-east Sicily. Rome entered an alliance with the Greeks and drove the Carthaginians out of Messana, expelling them (in 262 BCE) from the colonies of Segesta and Agrigentum as well. This was the beginning of the First Punic War. (*Punicus*, in Latin, meant Carthaginian.) It has often been said that Rome's war on Carthage was a blunder without real justification, but it was not. Rome needed *Lebensraum* by sea as well as by land. It could not move armies freely around the Mediterranean if Carthage remained the dominant sea power. Hence Marcus Porcius Cato the Elder's (234–149 BCE) monotonous sign-off cry at the end of every speech he made in the Senate, 'Delenda est Carthago', 'Carthage must be wiped out.' The defeat of Carthage took more than a century, but eventually it ended all serious obstacles to Rome's hegemony over the Mediterranean and the lands that enclosed it; the Mediterranean now became, in the full sense, mare nostrum, 'our sea'.

What kind of forces were locked in this war? How strong were they? The Greek historian Polybius gives what is probably the most balanced sketch. At sea, the Carthaginians were superior – they had been trading across the Mediterranean for generations, they understood shipping, 'seamanship has long been their national craft'. They had no standing army, however, and had to employ mercenaries. The Romans were far better at fighting on land. Their army consisted of Romans and their generally loyal allies: most Roman soldiers were fighting for their own land, their own families and nation, and for one another – inducements to courage and obstinacy which no mercenary army could be expected to have.

But as good as their army was, the Romans knew they could not defeat the Carthaginians without naval power. They also knew they had neither a fleet nor any naval tradition. So they set out to create themselves a navy from scratch. According to Polybius they were very lucky in capturing an enemy prototype they could copy: as the Roman forces were heading for Messana in Greek-built, chartered triremes and quinqueremes (oar-powered warships), the skipper of a decked Carthaginian ship got over-excited in pursuit and ran aground. The Romans 'built their whole fleet on its pattern . . . if that had not occurred they would have been entirely prevented . . . by lack of practical knowledge'. They even had to train their rowing crews in mock-ups, built on land. But it worked; the Carthaginian fleet was destroyed at sea off Mylae, a septireme (a battleship with no fewer than seven rowers to each of its enormous oars) and thirty quinqueremes and triremes all captured or sunk.

The trireme, which by the end of the sixth century BCE had become the standard warship of the Mediterranean, had three banks of oarsmen, one above the other, the topmost ones working from an outrigger. Its source of power was one man to an oar. The oars were manageable if not light, between 4 and 4.5 metres long. One reads, in classical sources, of quinqueremes with five banks of oars (or five rowers to an oar), and even sixteen-bank vessels, but it is most unlikely that so many oars, placing the rowers so high above the waterline, could possibly have worked, since they would have had to be unmanageably long.

A trireme's normal crew was two hundred men, of whom about 170 were rowers and fifteen were deck-hands. None of these, as a rule, were slaves; and the cartoonists' image of a Roman galley with its whip-wielding bosun striding through the hull and flogging the rowers is unlikely – generally the triremes had drummers and flautists to provide the rhythm of work, and there would have been little point in weakening a rower by corporal punishment. With this motive power, under favourable con-ditions, a trireme could manage an average of nine kilometres per hour over long distances, with bursts of possibly twelve when the ship was picking up speed to ram an enemy vessel. For that purpose it was built with a sturdy, bronze-sheathed ram projecting forwards, under-water, from its bow. The other weapon that proved decisive for the Romans was a massive hinged and weighted wooden hook known as a *corvus*, from its similarity to a raven's beak; it was raised, the enemy ship was rammed, and then the 'beak' was dropped, smashing through the opponent's deck and grappling the two vessels together so that the Roman soldiers could swarm to the attack. The width of the plank was about 1.2 metres, enough to form a bridge. The disadvantage of the *corvus* was its destabilizing clumsiness when raised upright, wobbling heavily in a seaway. Its great advantage was that it enabled Roman marines, always better soldiers than their Punic opponents, to board enemy ships on the high seas.

The cost of the war at sea, and of funding its mercenary army on land, put Carthage badly in debt. It could raise money only by launching a conquest of Spain, which it pursued under the generalship of Hamilcar and his sons Hasdrubal and Hannibal. This meant attacking Saguntum, a Spanish city south of the river

Ebro and an ally of Rome. The Carthaginians hoped to defeat Rome's army in the field and thus cause at least some of her allies to desert. This, Hannibal expected, would not reduce Rome to a minor power, but it might curb her aggression by rendering her one power among several. Carthage had no hopes or plans for conquering Italy as a territorial whole. 'Italy' was not yet a unified state under the control of Rome – it was a patchwork of tribal principalities. But Carthage did hope to regain Sicily, Sardinia and other lost territories. Hannibal was convinced that the only place for a war against Rome was Italy itself, 'whereas if no movement was made in Italy, and the Roman people were allowed to use the manpower and resources of Italy for a war in foreign parts, then neither the king nor any nation would be a match for the Romans'.

The Romans did not believe this. They embarked on the Second Punic War confident of victory. Now they had a strong navy and they designated two uses for it. The first was to take a Roman army under the consul Publius Cornelius Scipio to engage Hannibal in Spain and so neutralize him. The second was to send the other consul, Titus Sempronius Longus, to invade north Africa and conquer Carthage. This might have worked, but the Romans moved too slowly. Seeking a base in the Po valley, the Carthaginian army under Hannibal marched through southern Gaul and across the Alps into northern Italy. Why did the Carthaginians not invade Italy by sea? Because, now that it had a navy, Rome could blockade any fleet that tried to carry an army along the Spanish coast and down into the Tyrrhenian. Moving elephants around was not easy, either – but the land route, including the perils of crossing the Alps, seemed (for all its difficulties) the only practicable choice. By the autumn of 218 BCE Hannibal and his army were among friendly Gauls in the Po. In December the Romans lost the Po valley entirely to Hannibal.

And so began the Second Punic War (218–202 BCE). When Hannibal began his legendary march with his twenty-one war elephants into north Italy, he had an army of fewer than 35,000 men with which to confront a total Roman force of 700,000 infantry and

70,000 cavalry (not all of which, of course, could be marshalled together at the same time).

It is still a matter of argument among scholars which route Hannibal might have taken; the most favoured view is that he led his army over the western Alps, via the Mont Cenis pass. Even if he did, the conditions they all encountered were appalling; the descending path was so narrow and steep as to be nearly impassable to horses at one point, let alone to elephants. Landslides had carried away much of the mountain face. But disheartened though many of his troops were, Hannibal was able to show them something of their destination from the top of the pass; on a clear day, you could see 'the actual view of Italy, which lies so close under these mountains that when both are viewed together the Alps stand to the whole of Italy in the relation of a citadel to a city'.

One might have supposed that the odds were so much in Rome's favour as to render Hannibal's invasion hopeless. There is still disagreement over the usefulness of those elephants to Hannibal's campaign, but there is little doubt that they terrified many a Roman soldier, and the effort of getting these great beasts sliding and stumbling over the rocks and through the ice and snow of the Alps must have struck most of those who saw or even heard about it as astonishing. The march from Carthago Nova (Cartagena) had taken five months, and fifteen days had been spent in crossing the Alps. Hannibal arrived in Italy with his force reduced to 12,000 African and 8,000 Iberian foot, backed up by only 6,000 horse – and the remaining elephants, of which about half had died on the way. He was, however, able to pick up some reinforcements in northern Italy from the formidable Cisalpine Gauls, who were no doubt attracted by the prospect of loot in Rome.

Rome had long known that Hannibal was coming. The first encounter between a Roman army, two legions led by Publius Cornelius Scipio, and Hannibal's forces took place near Ticino in north Italy – gateway to the plains through which an army could move south towards Rome – in 218 BCE. The engagement was won by Carthage, so convincingly that thousands of tribesmen of the Boii, hitherto allied to Rome, defected to Hannibal's side. Like a snowball gathering mass as it rolls downhill, Hannibal's army grew as it moved south. It crushed the Romans at the battle of Trebia, crossed the Arno swamps, kept going past Faesulae (Fiesole) and Arretium (Arezzo), and reached Lake Trasimene in the spring of 217 BCE. Here, it was confronted by an army led by the consul Gaius Flaminius. It was another rout. Apparently, the Romans failed to see the Carthaginians, hidden by early-morning mist on the high ground beside the lake. By the end of that morning 15,000 Romans were dead, including the luckless Flaminius.

The Roman response to this disaster was to appoint a dictator to lead its army. The tactics followed by this supremo, Quintus Fabius Maximus, earned him the nickname of 'Cunctator', 'The Delayer'. Instead of confronting Hannibal's army head-on, he chose to follow and harass it, in the hope of distracting and enfeebling it without a definitive engagement. But Hannibal's forces kept marching unstoppably south, down past Rome, towards the Adriatic coast. Before long the Romans had tired of delays and longed for a decisive head-on encounter with Hannibal's army. On 2 August 216 BCE, sixteen Roman legions advanced to battle against the Carthaginians near the town of Cannae, in Apulia, south of Rome. The result was the bloodiest and most costly defeat Rome had ever suffered, or ever would.

At Cannae, in one day, Hannibal's army slaughtered some 50,000 of the Romans and their allies, out of 75–80,000 men who took the field. For comparison, one should consider that on the first day of the Battle of the Somme in 1916 there were some 57,000 British casualties, most of whom survived; less than 20,000 were killed outright, and the weapons they faced were German machine-guns, not Punic spears and swords. The sheer efficiency of the slaughter Hannibal's army inflicted on the Romans is amazing. Roman losses at Cannae were almost as great as American combat losses (58,000) in the entire Vietnam War. And it all happened within about nine hours, on a late spring or early summer day, blindingly hot, fogged with the clouds of dust kicked up by thousands of men in their relentless, terminal struggle. Varro, the Roman commander, had put the mass of his infantry in the centre, leaving his wings with cavalry weak but mobile. This was the classical deployment. But Hannibal reversed it, concentrating his weight of infantry on the flanks. In this way the Romans were soon enveloped, and then cut off from retreat by a Carthaginian cavalry charge across their rear. When the Romans tried to retreat, they were massacred.

They had little experience of defeat; certainly none on this scale. Defeat did not make sense to the Roman army. Rome was first and foremost a military state. The prime qualification of citizenship was the ability to bear arms against her enemies. The Roman army was organized as a militia: service in it was an inflexible condition of citizenship, and by the time of the Punic Wars, it was a highly sophisticated and organized machine. Its higher officers were aristocrats but the centurions, who commanded the basic fighting units ('centuries' of a hundred men), were commoners, from the same social class as the line soldiers. This contributed greatly to *esprit de corps*, as did the frequent swearing of loyalty oaths. Rome had never previously lost a major battle against a foreign enemy; certainly not a battle on this near-apocalyptic scale. In terms of discipline, arms, disposition of forces and chain of command, the Roman army was meticulously organized against such an event.

The key figure in this organization was the centurion, the non-aristocratic soldier who had been chosen for his valour and efficiency in leadership from the ranks of the enlisted men. The centurions, as John Keegan has pointed out, were 'long-service unit leaders drawn from the best of the enlisted ranks, [who] formed the first body of professional fighting officers known to history'. They were the backbone of the army, the repository of its accumulated service skills, and it was due to them and the example they set that the Romans fought better and with more tenacity than any other tribe or nation in the known world. The centurions turned soldiering into a self-sufficient profession; they did not see their work as a way of entry to the governing class;

this was what they were born and trained to do, and there lay much of their strength.

Numerically, the building-block of the Roman army was the legion, normally made up of 4,200 men; in times of crisis its strength was raised to 5,000. They were divided by age and experience. The youngest and rawest recruits were called *velites*. The next-older ones were *hastati*, or spear-carriers. Above them in seniority, men in the prime of life, were the *principes*, and above them came the *triarii*. Typically, a legion had 600 *triarii*, 1,200 *principes*, 1,200 *hastati*, and the remainder *velites*. The *velites* were the least experienced and the lightest-armed, with a shield (laminated wood, with a metal rim, about three feet in diameter), two javelins, a sword and a helmet. Often the tyro would cover his helmet with a piece of wolf skin, to make him look fierce, but also to make it easier for his commanding officer to identify him in a fight.

The *hastati* were more heavily armed. Each man carried a full shield (*scutum*), two and a half feet wide and four deep, giving maximum coverage to the body. Its convex curvature deflected the enemy's spears and arrows better than a plane surface. It, too, was made of wood planks glued together, probably with splined joints; then it received a canvas cover – animal glue again – and an outer sheathing of calf skin. Its edges were iron and in its centre was an *umbo* or iron boss, which gave further protection against sling stones and pikes and was good for bashing in the face of an opponent. It was heavy; reconstructions, iron and all, have weighed in at around 9 to 10 kilos.

Each man carried his *gladius*, a double-edged sword designed for thrusting, though it was excellent for slashing too. It was called a 'Spanish sword' and may have been adapted from the weapon carried by Carthaginian mercenaries in the First Punic War, a tribute to its qualities as a killing tool. It was short-bladed (about 60 centimetres including the tang) and therefore suitable for closely pressed fighting; infantrymen did not fence like d'Artagnan, they stabbed like butchers. A soldier would probably have a *pugio* or dagger on his belt as well. He would also be equipped with a relatively long-range missile, the *pilum* or heavy throwing spear, weighing perhaps 3.5 kilos and with an ash shaft, an iron shank and a barbed point. The soldier was normally issued two of these javelins, although lighter ones were available. Their accuracy, when thrown, was variable, and their effective range was at the most thirty metres, but within their limits the *pila* were formidable weapons, with enough inertial energy to penetrate the opponent's shield and the opponent himself. On the attack the Roman soldier would hurl his *pilum* and then charge forward to close combat with the *gladius*. Descriptions of Cannae feature the frightful hissing noise made by volleys of *pila*, which must have been as scary as the shriek of incoming shells in twentieth-century battles.

The two other types of pointed weapon in the Roman army were the cavalry lance, longer than the *pilum* and not thrown as a missile, and the *hasta*, a long thrusting spear. There was also artillery, of a primitive and awkward kind – large arrow-shooters or stone-flingers, which relied on the stored energy of twisted animal sinew. But these clumsy devices seem never to have played a decisive role in warfare: they possibly had some psychological effect, but their range was limited and their accuracy slight.

So much for weaponry. What about defence? On the collective level of the army on the march, the Romans displayed unique fortitude and energy in self-protection. Knowing that 'barbarians' in occupied territory were likely to attack at night, when the Roman invaders were tired from the day's exertions and darkness was likely to favour confusion and panic, the Romans did not end the day at the finish of each day's march. They first put up a camp: not a mere array of tents, but a fully fortified square *castrum* or encampment, almost an overnight town, with a wall, a ditch (produced by digging out the earth to throw up the wall), and everything that was necessary to protect the mass of troops. The wall or 'circumvallation' was some 200 feet out from the tents, so that missiles, shot or thrown from outside the barrier, could not reach them or do much harm if they did. The space between the wall and the tents also allowed for quick mustering, or for holding booty such as cattle. The whole perimeter was closely guarded, and fearful punishments awaited any soldier delinquent in his sentry duty. The customary one was the bastinado or *fustuarium* described by Polybius. The accused man was tried by a court martial of legionary tribunes. If found guilty, he was touched by one of the tribune's cudgels, whereon the whole camp attacked him with sticks and rocks, usually killing him in the camp itself. 'But even those who manage to escape are not saved thereby: impossible! for they are not allowed to return to their homes, and none of his relatives would dare to receive such a man in his house. So that [he is] utterly ruined.'

For defence of individual soldiers, armour existed. Each man had a helmet, either a plain basin of metal or the so-called (by archaeologists) 'Montefortino' pattern, with a narrow neck guard and large protective cheek pieces. Shin-protecting greaves are mentioned in the literature, though none have been found. Bronze *pectorales* to protect the heart were not uncommon, though not every soldier got one. Those who could afford it – they were not cheap items – wore a *lorica* or chainmail cuirass, a shirt made from metal rings, worn over a padded undergarment. This probably weighed about 15 kilos and would have been exhausting on a hot day like the one on which the battle of Cannae was fought.

The Roman system was designed to produce identical fighting-men with the same basic training. Hannibal's troops were not like this. Being mercenaries, they came from Africa and all over the Mediterranean, and had their own traditions and techniques of fighting, though their higher-ranking officers seem to have all been Carthaginian. The army contained Numidians, Iberians, Libyans, Moors, Gaetulians and Celts. There were specialists in types of warfare who came from particular areas. Thus the Balearic islands (Majorca, Minorca, Formentera) got their name from the slingers they produced in antiquity – *ballein* being Greek for 'to throw', as in 'ballistics'.

The Punic forces did not have the fierce allegiance to the legionary standards that helped rally the Roman army in moments of crisis, and only two things mattered to them in the end – winning, and getting paid. And this time, win they did, fighting with the most furious determination until the trampled soil of Cannae was a marsh of blood, guts, excrement and hacked limbs, so thick and slippery that a man could scarcely move on it without falling.

Cannae caused a paroxysm of social superstition in Rome. The winter of 216–15 BCE became a time of witnessed prodigies. In the Forum Boarium (cattle market) an ox escaped from confinement, climbed to the third storey of a house and then leapt out, as though committing suicide out of despair. In the Forum Holitorium (vegetable market) the temple of Hope was struck by lightning. A shower of pebbles fell out of a clear sky in Picenum. Men in shining garments were glimpsed in the sky. A wild wolf ran up to a sentry somewhere in Gaul and grabbed his sword from its scabbard with its teeth, running off with it. Worst of all, two Vestal Virgins named Opimia and Floriona were convicted of unchastity; one killed herself, the other was buried alive, as ritual demanded.

The number of prisoners taken in Hannibal's victory was so great that the Roman Senate had to devise a plan to rebuild the army. Hannibal was known to be short of cash; was he perhaps open to bribery? Could the captives be ransomed? No, said the Senate; that could exhaust the Roman treasury. Then the consul Tiberius Gracchus proposed that slaves should be bought with public money and be trained to fight. About ten thousand were forcibly enlisted in this way. Great emergency efforts, urged on by Scipio the Carthage-Destroyer, were made to build up Rome's fleet. The keels of thirty ships – twenty quinqueremes and ten quadriremes – were laid, the timber and all the gear brought from all over Etruria; within forty-five days of the arrival of the first consignments of timber, the historian Livy recorded, the first ships were launched 'with their tackle and armament complete'.

The defeat at Cannae also spread panic among Rome's allies in southern Italy, although the central Italians remained steadfast in their loyalty. 'The Campanians,' observed Livy, 'could not only recover the territory taken from them unjustly by the Romans, but could also gain authority over Italy. For they would make a treaty with Hannibal on their own terms.' This hope was delusive;

after Hannibal's defeat the Romans recaptured Capua, the capital of Campania, and inflicted dreadful reprisals on its citizens.

Hannibal's presence in Italy did not and could not last, although the Romans, due to his military genius, were unable to beat him on their own land. They slowly drove him southward and his army weakened as it went. His brother Hasdrubal led an army to Italy to strengthen Hannibal, but it failed, and in 207 BCE a Roman army defeated him at the river Metaurus. In the end, Hannibal could only leave Italy because Rome launched an expedition, under Scipio, against Carthage itself. This compelled Hannibal to withdraw to Africa to fight in defence of his own country. In 202 BCE, Hannibal was defeated by an Italian army for the first time, at the battle of Zama in north Africa, on Punic territory. The Romans now had at least a partial revenge for Cannae, though not on the same scale of slaughter. But Carthage would never be a Mediterranean sea power again; her place had been wrested from her, finally, by Rome.

The Hannibalic wars had inflicted changes on Rome that were longer-lasting and in some ways deeper than military loss. It sometimes happens that an extreme and traumatic defeat in war will provoke a spasm of religious faith among the losers, and this appears to have happened in Rome in the years after Cannae. All sorts of cults and previously exotic or marginal beliefs began to make their appearance, especially among Roman women, who could always be counted on for religious experiment. People traumatized by colossal defeat will not be satisfied by a merely ceremonial state religion. They will want the gods to come closer, to care and protect, to be more responsive to prayer and sacrifice.

These needs would not be met either by the vague gods of traditional Roman religion, or by the sterner new ones. But Greek gods filled the bill. Their images, and the rituals addressed to them, were less rigid, more humanly sympathetic and participatory. Rome now saw an expansion of Greek-based mystery religions. And there was a growing constituency for them, because Rome had an immense desire to be regarded as a part of the Greek-civilized world. Rome wanted a national literature on

Greek models, starting with Homer. More and more its intellectuals and politicians regarded Greek as the true language of civilization, especially now that so much of Greece had been absorbed by conquest and treaty into the heart and soul of Rome.

Rome was full of émigré Greeks and its air was dense with their voluble, seductive arguments, as the floors of temple and villa were thick with Greek (or Greekish) sculpture. True, some Roman shellback traditionalists resented and resisted the growing influence of Hellenic culture and philosophy on Roman ways. One of them was Cato the Elder, who 'wholly despised philosophy, and out of a patriotic zeal mocked all Greek culture and Greek learning ... he declared, with a rasher voice than became one of his age, as it were with the voice of a prophet or a seer, that the Romans would lose their empire when they began to be infected with Greek literature. But indeed time has shown the vanity of this prophecy of doom, for while the city was at the zenith of her empire she made all Greek learning and culture her own.' Cato was such an extremist in his dislike of luxury as a Greek distraction that he even tried – fortunately without success – to have water mains laid into private Roman houses ripped out.

The most consequential Roman to be formed, in a fundamental way, by Greek ideas and rhetoric in the midst of republican Rome was Marcus Tullius Cicero (106–43 BCE), Rome's greatest orator and a fervent supporter of the Republic. His education as a public speaker had begun when he was sixteen (89 BCE), under the consulship of Lucius Cornelius Sulla and Gnaeus Pompeius Strabo (Pompey). His cultural influence went far beyond the spoken word and did not diminish after his death. His letters were collected and he wrote treatises on rhetoric, morals, politics and philosophy; he thought his most durable achievement was to be his poetry (though he was wrong about that: Tacitus acidly observed that as a poet Cicero was less fortunate than Caesar or Brutus because his verse became known and theirs did not). He could be deadly in attack, even against minor figures: an otherwise forgotten politician was skewered by a single remark. 'We have a vigilant consul, Caninius, who never slept once during his entire term of office.' Caninius' term had lasted only one day.

Much of what he said about Rome and its rulers remains true today. 'Nothing is more unreliable than the populace, nothing harder to read than human intentions, nothing more deceptive than the whole electoral system.' He was completely undeceived about the wellsprings of most social action: 'Men decide far more problems by hate, love, lust, rage, sorrow, joy, hope, fear, illusion or some other inward emotion, than by reality, authority, any legal standard, judicial precedent, or statute.' And he was very sharp about human weakness: 'The greatest pleasures,' he remarked, 'are only narrowly separated from disgust.' What a psychotherapist this Roman would have made! One can always read Cicero with profit, and English writers of the seventeenth and eighteenth centuries, including Shakespeare, incessantly did, quoting from him freely.

Of all the currents of Greek thought that flowed into Roman intellectual life, it was Stoicism that had the greatest effect on Cicero and on Roman ideas in general. Stoicism was a school of Hellenistic philosophy founded in Athens by one Zeno of Citium in the early third century BCE. (The name came from a gathering-place in Athens where Zeno taught, a colonnade overlooking the Agora – the central meeting-place of Athens – known as the *Stoa Poikile* or 'painted porch'.) The basic assumption of Stoicism was that extreme, possibly destructive emotion was to be shunned; the wise man will free himself from anger, jealousy and other distracting passions and live in a state of calm and contemplative peace of mind; only in this way could he see what was true and guide his actions appropriately. 'Permit nothing to cleave to you that is not your own; nothing to grow on you that may give you agony when it is torn away,' counselled the Stoic Epictetus (55–135 CE). The ideal was *askesis*, 'inner calm'; the Stoic did not preach indifference or anaesthesia, far from it, but rather a reasoned concentration on the truths of life. Only thus could human reason be brought into accord with the 'universal reason of nature'. In the words of one of the more famous Stoics, the emperor Marcus Aurelius (121–80 CE, reg. 161–80 CE), 'Say to yourself in the early morning: I shall meet today ungrateful, violent, treacherous, envious, uncharitable men. All these things have come upon them through ignorance of real good and evil ... I can neither be harmed by any of them, for no man will involve me in wrong, nor can I be angry ...'

Clearly Stoicism went well with the Roman sense of duty and *pietas*. The Romans with whom it was popular – and there were many – were perhaps less interested in the Stoic view that all men were necessarily imperfect than in Stoic injunctions to face misfortune, grin and bear it, which had a powerful resonance throughout the culture of Rome and with many of its intellectuals and public figures. Cicero was one of these, and he also had a strong philosophical and meditative bent, which displayed itself in his many orations and voluminous writings. The great project of his political life was holding and defending the ancestral system of republican government. He wanted to bring about a 'concord' of the conservative, senatorial aristocrats and the rapacity of the growing class of equestrians, or hereditary knights, but this was beyond his powers, as it would have been beyond anyone's. Neither Cicero nor anyone else could deflect the movement towards one-man rule in Rome which, in the first century BCE, was the chief direction of its politics.

The emblematic figure of this movement was Julius Caesar. Some family lines last for centuries, are of the utmost nobility, and yet for unknown reasons produce no individuals of special achievement or eminence. One of these was the Julian clan – one of the oldest and most distinguished in Rome, with a generally accepted claim to be descended from Aeneas himself, from his mother the goddess Venus and from his son Iulus. Most of its members did little and were mediocrities. But there were two blazing exceptions, men who utterly transformed Rome, its internal politics, its culture and its relations with the rest of the world and were, without competition, the outstanding figures of power in their times.

The first of these was Gaius Julius Caesar (100–44 BCE). The second was his grand-nephew, his legal and political heir and

Rome's first emperor, Gaius Julius Caesar Octavianus (63 BCE–14 CE) known at first as Octavian and later, to Rome and the world, after his thirty-sixth birthday, as Caesar Augustus.

Julius Caesar's career had a slow start. He had spent the years 75–74 BCE studying oratory and rhetoric in Rhodes, from which he emerged as a perfected and highly polished speaker, superbly equipped for public political life. He was not a florid speechifier – that, as anyone knows who reads the crisp, unadorned prose of his later war commentaries, was not his way – but he had an exemplary talent for singling out the heart of an issue and driving straight to it. On the voyage back from Rhodes he gave a foretaste of his future toughness when his ship was taken by pirates and Caesar briefly became their prisoner. He swore that he would crucify every last one, and in time he did.

Cicero, so great an orator himself, was a more astute critic of oratory than any man alive and called him the most elegant of all Roman speakers. But others could perhaps rival Julius Caesar on the podium. Where he excelled was in the manipulation of politics and, later, in the command of armies on the battlefield. In politics, he first briefly inclined towards the *optimates* or 'top people'. This was the name adopted by the Roman upper class, the party of wealth and power which defined itself and its interests against the *populares*, a 'people's party' of workers, farmers and small traders originally mobilized and led by the Gracchus brothers in c.133 BCE. Before going to Rhodes to study rhetoric, Caesar had confirmed his growing allegiance to the popular party by marrying Cornelia, the daughter of Cinna, who was a chief opponent of Sulla (138–78 BCE), leader of the *optimates*, who had given Pompeins Strabo's son, also called Pompey, his basic political education.

Sulla was a vengeful and merciless patrician, who by sheer drive and cunning had obtained a consulship and the command against Mithridates, the Persian king of Pontus, who had rashly invaded Rome's provinces in Asia. Political enemies at home, members of the *populares* faction, cancelled Sulla's command, whereupon he retreated to Capua and gathered six legions that were prepared to go with him against the government in Rome and, once they

had taken over the city, to go after Mithridates in Asia. In 86 BCE
Sulla and his legions invaded Greece and captured Athens. From
there he returned to Italy, his army laden with booty. Landing at
Brundisium in 83 BCE, he and his army were joined by Pompey,
Marcus Crassus and an ultraconservative senator, Metellus Pius,
with all their men. The Roman government was not able to
withstand them for long. Within a year, Sulla had taken Rome
and was proclaimed dictator of Italy. He now began a reign of
terror through 'proscription', publicly listing for death everyone
who was or might have been an enemy; any soldier could murder
them, their property went to the state (namely, to Sulla) and all
citizens were encouraged to betray and denounce whomsoever
they chose – it was proleptic Stalinist justice, pure and simple. In
this way, Sulla is thought to have eliminated forty senators and
1,600 *equites*, whose sons and grandsons were also excluded from
public life. Such was the exemplar and political patron of Pompey.

In 68 BCE Caesar had been dispatched as a quaestor or magistrate to Hispania Ulterior (Further Spain); in that year his wife
Cornelia died, and he made what was clearly a political marriage
to Pompeia, a girl in Pompey's family. Now he was elected an
aedile, a position of great importance to the plebeians of Rome,
since it gave him charge of temples, markets and (most telling of
all) the corn supply, a great collector of votes. During this time he
spent lavishly on the restoration of temples and the holding of
public entertainment, especially gladiatorial shows. He had to
borrow the money from the immensely wealthy consul Marcus
Crassus, destroyer of Spartacus' slave revolt, who distrusted
Pompey but was not above financing his strategies for ingratiating
himself with the commoners. Naturally, the cost of winning popularity in this way put Caesar heavily in debt to Crassus and the
optimates, who did not altogether trust him. To get further as a
politician, he needed to bypass their suspicions: to become a
consul and then obtain a major military command, whose victories would be as irrefutable as Pompey's. In Rome, Caesar had
in 59 BCE become a senator. He made an alliance with Pompey
and Crassus (the 'First Triumvirate') and joined with Pompey –

now consul – in repealing some of Sulla's more extreme and biased alterations to the constitution. There was no sign, as yet, of any discord between Pompey and Caesar. In fact Pompey, in 59 BCE, married Julia, Caesar's own daughter by his first wife Cornelia, thus completing a neat matrimonial symmetry.

In 58, as proconsul, Caesar took on the control of both Cis- and Transalpine Gaul (the Po valley in northern Italy, and southern France, which he called 'the province', a name commemorated ever since as Provence) as well as Illyricum (Dalmatia). From 58 to 50 BCE he concentrated on Rome's northern, Gallic frontiers, methodically wearing down all resistance from them. He did not hesitate when it came to deciding what Rome's overseas policies should be. Rome had to conquer and intimidate any state or people that might give it trouble. That had been the chief lesson of Cannae. Everyone concurred in this, including Cicero, who rather disliked Caesar personally but admired him politically:

> He believed not only that it was necessary to wage war against those who he saw were already in arms against the Roman people, but also that all Gaul must be subjected to our sway. And so he has fought with the fiercest peoples, in gigantic battles against the Germans and Helvetians, with the greatest success. He has terrified, confined and subdued the rest, and accustomed them to obey the empire of the Roman people . . .

Caesar's conquest and pacification of Gaul were approaching completion by 56 BCE. Most of the country had come to heel and was now a Roman province, except for sporadic outbreaks of fierce resistance. In his *Commentarii de bello Gallico* Caesar described how the ferocious Helvetii, having left their territory of what is now Switzerland, had migrated into Gaul, intending to get as far as the English Channel and resettle there. Caesar's armies attacked them in their migration, and in Annecy on the river Arroux he wiped them out by the tens, perhaps hundreds, of thousands, turning the survivors back towards Switzerland.

The same infiltration into Gaul, followed by the same costly expulsion, was attempted by German tribes. North of the Seine were the so-called Belgae, a warlike people consisting mainly of Germans intermarried with Celts. They were extremely suspicious of Caesar, and well they might be. When Caesar established his winter headquarters on Gallic territory, and gave every sign of meaning to stay, they mobilized a full 300,000 warriors. Caesar's reply was to raise two more legions in Cisalpine Gaul, bringing his total force to eight.

The coherence of the Belgic armies now began to disintegrate, largely due to supply shortages. Only the tribe known as the Nervii could keep an army in the field, and Caesar annihilated them in a battle on the river Sambre in 57 BCE. Thus, the resistance in Gaul lasted for only two military seasons. In the end, fully a third of all Gauls of military age were killed and another third were sold into slavery: a toll which all but destroyed the male population of the province, made it incapable of further resistance, and made Caesar even more colossally rich than before. The Gallic leader Vercingetorix, a brilliant, charismatic figure who had given Caesar the most difficult and stubborn resistance of his career, was besieged and finally captured at Alesia in 52 BCE. Brought back to Rome in chains, he was paraded in Caesar's triumph and then ignominiously strangled in a dungeon.

By 52 BCE, little opposition to Rome was left and by 50 there was none. The conquest of Gaul changed Rome from a Mediterranean power to a pan-European one, since (in the words of the historian Michael Grant) 'a vast conglomeration of territories in continental and northern Europe had now been opened up to Romanization'. It also radically changed Gaul, transforming it, in effect, into an embryonic form of France. It was opened, though at great cost in blood and suffering, to classical culture.

With long-term thoughts of enlarging Rome's *imperium* still further, Caesar in 55 BCE dispatched an expedition across the Rhine to Germany, with inconclusive results; this was less an invasion than a probe. Its purpose was to show Roman power to the Germans on German territory, which would deter them from crossing into Gaul. A friendly, or at least complaisant, German tribe called the Ubii offered him boats in which his troops could cross the Rhine, but Caesar refused – it would not look good to depend on the Germans to get him into Germany. Instead, by engineering means that are not clear from his own account, his men built a timber bridge across the mighty river. His army spent three weeks or so marauding and burning villages on the German side, and then withdrew, having made its point, and demolished its bridge behind it.

Next came an expedition to Britain. Why Caesar wanted to invade the island, which had never been attacked by Rome before, is unclear. Perhaps he suspected that the Britons would join with the Gauls in some later counterattack; perhaps he was lured by exaggerated stories of fabulous wealth (gold, silver, iron and pearls) to be looted there. Or perhaps he merely wanted intelligence about this unknown place, and nobody could supply it to him. Whatever the motive, in 55 BCE he led a fleet of transports and men-of-war directly to the south-east coast of Britain, where they met with vilely contrary weather and stiff resistance from the 'barbarian' infantry and cavalry. The Romans eventually succeeded in landing (at the present site of Deal) and making the Britons sue for peace, but they did not penetrate far inland; it was a shallow victory at best, and they brought back little information and less booty.

Caesar tried again the next year, 54. He assembled a new fleet of some 800 vessels, carrying five legions and 2,000 cavalry. This time the conditions were more favourable, and the Romans fought their way north, crossing the Thames with intent to attack the British commander Cassivellaunus. They besieged this king's stronghold in Hertfordshire, and captured him; terms were made. But then news arrived that an insurrection was brewing among the Gauls, so with reluctance Caesar withdrew his army across the Channel; the complete conquest of Britain, and its reduction to a province of Rome, would have to wait for nearly a century, until it was achieved by the armies of the emperor Claudius.

But precisely because so little was known about Britain in

Rome, the very fact of going there endowed Caesar with mystique and celebrity at home, on top of the glory he had earned with his conquest of Gaul and the readership his brilliant *Commentaries*, the best book on war a Roman had ever written, had acquired. He was, moreover, extremely wealthy now from the sale of Gallic prisoners-of-war as slaves. He raised the scale of his influence-buying. One of the consuls of the year 50 BCE, Lucius Aemilius Paullus, is said to have raked in 36,000,000 sesterces from Caesar: this, at a time when a line soldier in the Roman army was paid 1,000 sesterces a year. Surpassingly rich, overwhelmingly popular: nothing could have been more propitious for a major political career in Rome.

The big problem was that he could not return to Rome. He could not come back with his legions, because by law no commander could enter the city with his troops. But he could not come back without them, for that would have meant laying down his command and exposing himself to prosecution by his many enemies.

But he had been moving south. In January 49 BCE the Senate sent him orders to disband his army. Caesar received them on the northern side of a small river called the Rubicon, the boundary between Cisalpine Gaul and Italy proper. (The name, deriving from the Latin *ruber*, red, referred to the colour of its clay-filled water.) Caesar's reaction to this letter was prompt and decisive. 'As for myself,' he declared in his *Civil War* (I.ix), 'I have always reckoned the dignity of the Republic of first importance and preferable to life. I was indignant that a benefit conferred on me by the Roman people was being insolently wrested from me by my enemies.' And so, in that legendary phrase which has come to mean taking any fateful and irrevocable decision, he crossed the Rubicon and entered Italy with his troops.

This inevitably meant civil war. The commander of Rome's troops in the war was Pompey – Gnaeus Pompeius Magnus (106–48 BCE) – a resourceful and highly skilled commander, the only man in Rome capable of standing up against Julius Caesar. Pompey's career, up to this point, had been marked by brilliant

successes which also served dramatically to highlight the weak-
nesses of the ageing republican system. From now on, Roman
politics would have less and less to do with democracy, becoming
more and more determined by ambitious individuals backed by
their own armies.

Quite early in his career Pompey showed every sign of developing into just such a prototypical strongman, utterly ruthless and
bent on power. Sulla had recognized that Rome's growing empire
could not possibly be governed by popular acclamation, by democratic votes. That system was too unwieldy. His policy, therefore,
was to shift the authority and policy-making power of the state
away from Rome's tribunes, magistrates and popular assembly,
which he regarded as mere rabble, and return them to the Senate.
Under Sulla's new system the senators got all their judicial powers
back, while consuls and praetors, shorn of their military power,
had to content themselves with being the Senate's good servants.
But there was a question: what if some new Roman warlord
turned on the Senate with his forces and simply threw them out?
Sulla's solution was to pass a law whereby there would be no
Roman armed force in Rome. As soon as any returning soldiers,
or their officers, crossed the limits of the *urbs Romae* they would
automatically have to lay down their arms, surrender their
command and become private citizens once more. Of course, this
needed enforcement, which Sulla, the winner of the war against
Mithridates, king of Pontus in Asia Minor, was prompt to supply.
He had accumulated huge reserves of booty and cash, and these
financed his own invasion of Italy in 83 BCE. Naturally this did not
go without a hitch, for there were strong anti-Sullan feelings in
both Sicily and north Africa, and Sulla enlisted the brilliant and
ruthless young Pompey to suppress them – which he did with
unrestrained butchery and bloodshed. By 81 BCE the anti-Sulla
factions were crushed, and Pompey – who was only twenty-five
at the time – was in a position to demand a full triumph from
Sulla on his return to Rome, and the cognomen Magnus, 'the
Great', attached to his name. There was no denying that Pompey
had burst through the exclusive ranks of Rome's upper estab-

lishment, the *optimates*. No previous Roman had won such an honour so early in his military career.

In 70 BCE he was appointed consul. The other consul, his reluctant and watchful yokefellow, was Marcus Licinius Crassus, the man who had put down Spartacus' slave revolt (it particularly irked him that Pompey, who had mopped up a last remnant of Spartacus' defeated army, took credit for suppressing the whole rebellion) and made a huge fortune by corralling the confiscated property of Roman citizens stripped of their assets in the proscriptions. Friction and ill-submerged conflict between the two billionaires, Crassus and Pompey, were inevitable.

In January 49 BCE, seeing that the Rubicon had been crossed and Caesar was now on Italian soil, the Senate voted martial law against him and turned over the government of the Republic to Pompey. But Caesar did not delay for a moment after crossing the Rubicon. He led his ever-growing army in a whirlwind march down the east coast of Italy, and Pompey and the Senate had to skedaddle out of Rome so fast that they even left the national treasury behind. The continuous presence of senators turned out to be a great encumbrance to Pompey. They kept demanding reports, criticizing plans, and in general getting in the way. This did much to neutralize what would otherwise have been a clear advantage for the Pompeians. They had ships and Caesar had no navy. They were able to assemble and train a large army at Dyrrhachium in the west of Greece. Caesar's troops were so poorly supplied that many were reduced to eating the bark off trees. And yet, by a combination of superior generalship and good military luck, Caesar was able to beat Pompey, who offered him battle at Pharsalus in August 48 and was roundly defeated. Unnerved, Pompey fled to take refuge in Egypt, where the Ptolemaic government – fearing reprisals from the dreaded Caesar – cut off his head and dispatched that grisly trophy to him.

Julius Caesar now ruled Rome and its enormous, ever-growing empire without opposition. In 46 BCE he made himself dictator for ten years, and in February 44 the appointment was extended for the whole of his future life. The official calendar, which stood badly in need of revision, was indeed revised, with the month that had been known as Quintilis renamed 'July'. Caesar's head began to appear on coins, a homage which up to then had been reserved for kings and gods. Caesar was the first man to overcome, and in essence overthrow, the ancient Roman republican aversion to kingship. Plutarch believed that Caesar planned to have himself turned into a deified king, and he was probably right, though the issue is still debatable. Certainly the masses of Rome came very rapidly to view him as the next thing to a living god.

Now that the wars were over and won, Caesar, with the support of a thoroughly complaisant Senate, awarded himself no fewer than five complete triumphs, four after destroying Scipio at Thapsus in north Africa in 46 BCE and one more for smashing the sons of Pompey at Munda in Spain in 45 BCE. The grandest was the triumph awarded him for his conquest of Gaul, but it was in his Pontic triumph at Zela over Pharnaces, the son of Mithridates, whom he suspected of trying to restore his father's kingdom in the east that Caesar was inspired to produce the most famous phrase in military history; on the victorious march-past he displayed on a placard the three laconic words, *Veni, vidi, vici* – 'I came, I saw, I conquered.'

These Roman triumphs were ceremonies of great importance and they followed a set pattern, whose origins lay in the Etruscan past. To qualify as a *triumphator*, the conquering hero had first to be acclaimed by his soldiers. He must hold a magistracy with *imperium*, the autocratic power to command. (If he did not have such a magistracy, there could be no triumph for him, no matter how resounding his victory.) He must show that he had killed at least five thousand enemy soldiers, and brought home enough of his army to demonstrate their complete victory. Because Rome itself did not fall within his *imperium*, he must now wait outside the city limits until the Senate had agreed to grant him that absolute power for a single day. Once that was done, the triumphant leader could enter at the head of his troops, preceded by his lictors, each of whom carried a bundle of rods and an axe – the *fasces* re-adopted by Mussolini in the twentieth century – to symbolize his power to arrest, punish and execute. A dictator had twenty-four lictors, lesser officials fewer. The soldiers raised a chant of praise, *'Io triumphe!'*, and sang mildly obscene songs, the 'Fescennine verses', poking fun at their leader; a typical verse about Caesar (who was bald, and renowned for his sexual appetites) ran:

Home we bring the hairless Fucker,
Roman maidens, bar your doors –
For the Roman gold you sent him
Went to pay his Gallic whores.

Usually the appearance of the victor would be preceded by a long parade of his spoils. Thus the triumph of Aemilius Paullus was preceded, according to Plutarch, by an entire day's march-past of some 250 wagons bearing the statues, paintings and colossal images looted from Perseus, king of Macedon. Then came a second day, during which looted Greek silver, bronze and gold was displayed on a similar train of chariots, along with captured armour. Not until the third day did triumphant Aemilius Paullus make his appearance, followed by Perseus, 'looking like one altogether stunned and deprived of reason through the greatness of his misfortunes', as he must indeed have been.

The conquering hero would, of course, dress for the occasion. His face would be painted with red lead, to signify his godlike vitality. He would be arrayed in triumphal purple, with a laurel crown on his head and a laurel branch in his right hand, and wear amulets to avert the evil eye. Addressing a mass gathering of civilian citizens and his troops, he would praise the patriotism of the former and the noble courage of the latter. He would distribute money and decorations to them. These gifts were expected to be lavish. And coming from Caesar, they were: every footsoldier of his veteran legions got 24,000 sesterces as his booty, over and above what he had received as wages. If you pay a lot for gratitude, Caesar well knew, it is likely to stay bought. But his men did love him, and for other, and equally compelling, reasons: his tremendous daring and military skill, his powers of charismatic leadership.

Mounting in a *quadriga* or four-horse chariot with his children and relatives around him on horseback, the victorious general would now begin his progress towards the Capitol; riding with him in the chariot would also be a public slave, holding over the victor a gold crown studded with precious stones, and repeatedly intoning the mantra, 'Remember that you are a mortal man.' The processional route ran from the Campus Martius outside the city, through the Triumphal Gate, to the Circus Flaminius – an anomalous public square in which, despite its name, races seem never to have been held, and in which there were no banks of seating for spectators, but where the spoils of triumph were displayed – and thence to the Circus Maximus. Then the procession would wind round the Palatine Hill, along the Sacra Via – the oldest and most famous street in Rome – and thence to the Capitol. In the Forum, he would order some captives of high rank imprisoned and put to death, and then ride on to the Capitol, where further rituals including sacrifices would be performed at the temple of Jupiter Capitolinus. Julius Caesar's sense of display and drama was such that when he walked up the final steps to the Capitol, he had forty elephants deployed to his right and his left, each carrying a torch in its trunk.

Naturally, these long and impressive ceremonies required a grand architectural backdrop. All during his campaigns in northern Europe, Caesar had built nothing; there was no time. But in 54 BCE he decided to leave a permanent architectural mark on Rome: a magnificent colonnaded square, the Forum Julium or Forum Caesaris, with a temple dedicated to Venus Genetrix, mythical ancestress of the Julian line, at one end of it. It bordered on the more ancient Forum which had begun as a general meeting-place and market and had become known as the Forum Romanum, to distinguish it from other existing fora like the Forum Holitorium and the Forum Boarium. Over the years a clutter of functions had converged and taken root in it. Lawyers, money-changers and senators mingled in its ancillary buildings, which sometimes served as markets. State archives were held in its *tabularium*, an all-important archive. Shrines were built – a circular temple of Vesta, the Roman hearth-goddess, was attended by six Vestal Virgins whose duty was to tend the city's sacred fire. The Forum Romanum also contained the small but ritually important shrine of Janus, the Roman god of beginnings, whose gates were ritually closed whenever peace in the Roman world was announced.

Julius Caesar's forum was the first of a number of fora to be built next to and north of the Forum Romanum; its successors were the Forum Augustum, the Forum of Nerva and the Forum of Trajan. The huge costs of Julius' forum would be met by the sack of Gallic cities and shrines, and by the slave trade, which Caesar dominated by now with his prisoners-of-war. The final cost of the land – and only the land – for the Forum Julium is said to have been 100,000,000 sesterces, because every square foot of it had to be purchased from private owners at a time of fierce commercial speculation.

This did not matter to Caesar; he was determined to put his parcel together at any cost, and he did. Inside it he erected a marble temple in a colonnaded square. He filled it with expensive works of art, including paintings of Ajax and Medea by the famous painter Timomachus, a golden statue of Cleopatra, a corselet made of British pearls, and a plethora of portraits of himself. Outside its entrance he is said to have installed the *Equus Caesaris*, another sculptural portrait of himself mounted on his favourite horse. Ancient accounts – Pliny, Suetonius – concur that this was a peculiar animal, recognizable by its near-human forefeet. But it is not clear whether it had toes, or just malformed hooves.

He was entirely the master of the Roman Empire now. For twenty years he had been head priest of the state religion, the *pontifex maximus*. It seemed that Caesar could go no higher, except by becoming a deified king.

Even that was on the cards. In 44 BCE his portrait head began to appear on Roman coins. Mark Antony (Marcus Antonius, 83–30 BCE), a close adherent of Caesar's, tried (but failed) to establish a cult of the living Caesar with himself as its priest. Caesar also inflated the numbers of the Senate with hundreds of patricians and equestrians he personally chose. He appointed many new magistrates, equally obliged to him, and established scores of new Latin colonies outside Italy to reward loyal army men. Buoyed up by his successes, feeling invulnerable, he also made a fatal mistake. He dismissed his Praetorian Guard.

Conservatives were waiting in the wings, burning with anger at the sight of Caesar's growing autocracy, and determined to return Rome to its supposedly pristine virtues as a republic. The only way, they reasoned, to be rid of Caesarism was to kill Caesar. They rapidly formed a cabal. Its leaders were Gaius Cassius Longinus and Marcus Junius Brutus. Cassius had fought on Pompey's side against Caesar's army during the civil war, but Caesar, with his usual magnanimity towards defeated Roman foes, had pardoned him, raised him to praetor in 44 and then made him consul designate.

Brutus, who led the cabal, was a man of intense probity and patriotism – 'This was the noblest Roman of them all' – whom the other would-be assassins thought indispensable to the plan of killing a hero so worshipped by the *plebs*. The fact that he was a usurer – Cicero, whom Brutus had served as quaestor in Cilicia, discovered that Brutus was getting 48 per cent annual interest on a loan he had made to a city in Cyprus – did nothing to diminish his reputation. To kill a man who had too much power and abused it was not necessarily repugnant to Romans. They had before their eyes the example of such heroic figures as Harmodius and Aristogiton, the Greek lovers who in 514 BCE assassinated the tyrant Hipparchus and were honoured by a statue in the Agora, much copied by Roman sculptors (or Greek ones working for Roman clients). That was how the cabal saw Caesar and they resolved to kill him, which they did with their daggers on the floor of the Senate House in Rome on the Ides of March 44 BCE. Shakespeare has the unprotected Caesar exclaiming *'Et tu, Brute?'* ('Even you, Brutus?'), but his last words were apparently not in Latin; they were Greek – *'Kai su, teknon?'*, 'You too, my son?' – as befitted one highly educated Roman addressing another, even at the point of death.

Chaos followed. The assassins left Caesar's corpse where it had fallen on the floor of the Senate House, at the foot of a statue of Pompey. They rushed out into the street brandishing their daggers and shouting '*Libertas!*' and '*Sic semper tyrannis!*' ('Freedom!' 'Thus always to tyrants!'). The general populace was unconvinced; they milled around, some hysterical with grief and confusion; they drove the conspirators to take shelter on the Capitoline Hill. Meanwhile Mark Antony, Caesar's consul and main friend, seized the dead man's papers, last will and money, and prepared to speak at Caesar's public funeral. His speech incited the crowd to a frenzy and the conspirators, who had convinced themselves that they would be hailed as saviours, hurriedly left Rome for the eastern provinces of the Empire.

At this early stage of post-Caesarian sorting-out, nobody paid any attention to Caesar's only male relative, his grand-nephew, a weedy eighteen-year-old named Gaius Octavius. But it turned out that in his will Caesar had posthumously adopted him as his son and heir, and left him three-quarters of his enormous fortune. Antony, who had usurped the role of Caesar's executor, flatly refused to give the lad this inheritance and, just as foolishly, refused to pay out the 300 sesterces Caesar had willed to each and every citizen of Rome. This incredible act of parsimonious folly sealed Antony's fate, depriving him of the goodwill of most Romans.

Meanwhile, barred from access to Caesar's fortune, Gaius Octavius used his own lesser but still considerable funds to raise a private army from among Caesar's veterans who had been settled in Campania and Macedonia. The name of Caesar was still magical to these old campaigners, and Octavius had inherited its mana. And although he was no warrior with any weapon but his tongue, Cicero attacked Antony with fourteen 'Philippic Orations', a title he had borrowed from Demosthenes for the hysterically ferocious speeches he made against the dead Caesar's friend.

Octavius now marched his army of hardened professionals on Rome. At the age of nineteen he was elected consul – the youngest in the city's history – and thenceforth was styled Gaius Julius Caesar Octavianus: Octavian, for short. After a meeting near Bononia (modern Bologna) with Mark Antony and the governor of Transalpine Gaul, Marcus Aemilius Lepidus, Octavian announced that the Second Triumvirate had been formed; this was confirmed by the Roman Senate, which had no choice about the matter, shortly after. The triumvirs would hold office for an initial five years. They would have absolute power over taxation and the appointment of officials, high and low. They would be free to proscribe whomever they wished, and they did so mercilessly – three hundred senators and two thousand equestrians died in the purges, their money and property gobbled up by the triumvirs.

And Cicero paid dearly for his insults to Mark Antony. He had scarcely begun his flight from Rome when a party of Octavian's soldiers overtook him on the Via Appia, in early December of 43 BCE. They buried his body but brought his head back to Rome. There are two versions of its fate. 'It is said,' wrote the chronicler Appian, 'that even at his meals Antony placed Cicero's head before his table, before he became satiated with this horrible sight.' Another version related that the head was nailed up for all to recognize in the Forum. Fulvia, Mark Antony's wife, prised open its jaws, pulled out the tongue and transfixed it with her hatpin: a fitting insult, she and others felt, for the organ that had so often and so calamitously libelled her husband.

❧ 2 ❧
AUGUSTUS

Until the advent of photography and then of TV, which effectively replaced them, propaganda statues were indispensable when it came to perpetuating the iconography of leadership. They were produced in mass numbers all over the world to celebrate the virtues and achievements of military heroes, political figures, wielders of every sort of power over all kinds of people. Most of them are wretched kitsch, but not all, and one of history's more successful icons of power is a marble statue exhumed in a villa that once belonged to the empress Livia, wife of Octavius and mother of the future emperor Tiberius, near the site of the Prima Porta, one of the main entrances to ancient Rome. It is a portrait of her husband, Gaius Julius Caesar Octavius, known to the world and to history as the first of the Roman emperors, Augustus (63 BCE–14 CE).

The statue is perhaps not, in itself, a great work of art; but it is competent, effective and memorable, a marble copy of what was probably a Greek portrait in bronze, showing the hero in military dress, in the act of giving a speech either to the state as a whole or, more probably, to his army on the eve of battle. As an image of calm, self-sufficient power projecting itself upon the world, it has few equals in the domain of sculpture. It does not ask of the viewer any particular knowledge of Roman history. But little is wholly self-explanatory. Take the design on the cuirass he is wearing, which shows – as most literate Romans would have known, though we can hardly be expected to – the recovery by Augustus of one of the army's military standards, captured and taken away by the Parthians on the eastern frontier in 53 BCE: the cancellation, therefore, of an unbearable disgrace. It also helps to

know that the little figure of the love-god Eros next to Augustus'
right leg is there to remind us that his family, the Julians, claimed
to have descended from the goddess Venus; its presence thus
reinforces the belief that Augustus was a living god, while the
dolphin next to it refers to Augustus' destruction of Antony and
Cleopatra's fleet in the sea battle of Actium.

We may be inclined to suppose that the Prima Porta Augustus
is a unique piece, but it almost certainly is not. The Romans
revelled in the cloning, copying and dissemination of successful
images – successful, that is to say, especially from the viewpoint
of ideology. If we think of this Augustus as an 'original' we are
probably wrong. All over the Empire, sculptors were busy chur-
ning out standardized effigies of Augustus, mostly in marble but
some in bronze. The artists were more often Greek than Roman,
and their production was organized, as far as one can tell, in
efficiently factory-like ways. There was more in common between
classical Roman art and the techniques of Andy Warhol than one
might at first suppose. A huge empire had to be saturated with
images of its deified emperor. As a 2001 study put it, 'A recent
count of [Augustus'] surviving heads, busts and full-length statues
reached more than 200, and recent estimates of ancient production
guess at 25,000–50,000 portraits in stone all told.'

Augustus (the name is a title bestowed by the Senate, meaning
'worthy of veneration', and it carried the implication of num-
inousness, of semi-divinity) was the son of Julius Caesar's niece,
adopted as his own son by Caesar himself. It is unclear what kind
of relations young Octavius had with his great-uncle, but there is
no question that Caesar's influence on him was definitive. In
particular the young man admired Caesar's political and military
daring. He made short work of avenging Caesar's death. The
Triumvirate's armies destroyed those of the rebels at the battle of
Philippi in 42 BCE. Brutus and Cassius committed suicide.

The triumvirs, now in complete control of Rome, instituted a
violent purge against the senatorial and equestrian classes of the
state. In the course of this, deep rifts between Octavian and Mark
Antony appeared. Their upshot was the brief Perusine War (41–

40 BCE), in which Lucius Antonius, Antony's brother, mounted an open revolt against Octavian. Archaeologists have unearthed not a few of its relics – stone and lead slingshot balls with rude messages scratched on them. 'I'm after Octavian's ass.' 'Octavian has a limp dick.' It was a brutal little war, won by Octavian, who had some three hundred prisoners of senatorial or equestrian rank sacrificed on the Ides of March at the altar of the god Julius. Antony's and Octavian's rivalry was patched up, after a fashion. In the new order of things, Octavian took control of Rome's western provinces, while Antony kept power over the eastern, including, fatally and famously, Egypt.

Now came the diplomatic and military fiasco of Antony's love affair with the last of the Ptolemaic rulers of Egypt, Cleopatra (69–30 BCE). The queen of the Nile had already had a liaison with Caesar (48–44 BCE) and borne him a son. Now she and Antony launched into their famous affair, beginning in 41 BCE. It produced twins. The extant coins and other effigies of Cleopatra do not seem to do justice to what those who knew her (especially Antony) considered her irresistible beauty. It may be that Blaise Pascal, many centuries later, was right in observing that if her nose had been shorter, the entire history of the world would have been different. But there are some things we will never know.

What is quite certain, however, is that Antony's and Cleopatra's obsession with one another had huge political repercussions. It was a godsend to Octavian, who by now wanted to destroy Antony altogether, but held back from doing so because an attack on Antony was likely to be interpreted as an attack on the sacred memory of Julius Caesar. He saw an opportunity when Antony took up with the Egyptian queen, and began promoting the idea that Cleopatra had perverted Antony's Romanness. Cleopatra was the power-crazed Greek strumpet of Egypt, a woman who would stop at nothing in her drive to undermine Roman interests in the Middle East, with Antony as her sex-fuddled dupe. She meant to make it all the way to the Capitol: she intended to run Rome.

Actually, the image of Cleopatra we have inherited is

completely misleading, a creation of propaganda and nothing more. She was, if anything, a woman worthy of respect, not least for her intelligence, which went far beyond mere sexual cunning. She had only two recorded affairs with powerful and charismatic men, Caesar and Antony, and children by each, to whom she was devoted. The picture of her as a scheming nymphomaniac is false in every way. But it certainly served Octavian's purposes. He used it to whip up Roman plebeians and patricians alike to a war frenzy. In the first place, they feared that Cleopatra, through her influence on Antony, would subvert the proper course of Roman politics – and do even more damage if she moved to Rome with him. In the second, they loathed the idea of a woman, any woman, having such political influence.

Thus Octavian was sure of popular support for an attack on Antony which would destroy both him and Cleopatra. The eventual result was a sea battle between the Triumvirate's ships and Antony's. It was fought in 31 BCE, off Actium, south of Epirus in Greece. The sixty ships of Cleopatra and Antony were put to flight by the Roman navy; most surrendered. Cleopatra fled back to Alexandria; Antony, likewise. Both committed suicide, he by running on his sword, and she – unable to bear the loss of her lover and the prospect of public humiliation in Rome, where Octavian was going to drag her through the streets for punishment – by the bite of an asp, the most famous snake in history.

Octavian went on to Egypt. He entered Alexandria on the first day of August, 31 BCE. There, he beheld the embalmed body of Alexander, his hero and model. It must have resolved him even further.

His enemies dead or scattered, his army and navy victorious, Caesar avenged and the Roman people, weary of war, hoping only for order and an honourable, lasting peace, Octavian now had absolute power over Rome. 'He was the first and the greatest and the common benefactor,' wrote Philo of Alexandria, 'in that he displaced the rule of many and committed the ship of the commonwealth to be steered by a single pilot, himself ... The whole habitable world voted him no less than celestial honours. These are well attested by temples, gateways, vestibules, porticoes ... That he was never elated or puffed up by the vast honours given to him is clearly shown by the fact that he never wished anyone to address him as a god.' Instead the Romans came up with a new name for him: no longer Octavian, but Augustus.

No such *imperium* as his had ever existed before. Rome now ruled the entire Mediterranean world.

The image we have of ancient Rome comes down to us in a heavily edited form. Much of the editing has been done by art and artists of later years: think of Nicolas Poussin. This city of the imagination, masquerading as a city of collective memory, is mostly white – the colour of classical marble, the stuff we imagine the city made of. (So at the outset we are misled, since the marble most valued by Roman builders to sheathe the brick and concrete cores of their buildings was very often coloured.) White cylinders of stone gleaming in the sun, surmounted by capitals, Doric, Ionic, Corinthian, Tuscan, Composite, linked by cornices, architraves and arches. White ramps, white colonnades, flights of white steps, and white foam from the plashing fountains. White people inhabit this townscape, of course, and they are wearing white togas. There is lots of air around these dignified Romans. As befits the owners and rulers of the known world, which extended from England to Africa, from the Thames to the Nile, from the Seine to the Euphrates, they are not crowded or hurried. Their gestures are dignified; they have become the statues of themselves. They are full of that very Roman attribute, *gravitas*.

If we were to pluck a real Roman from the real Rome of this time, the second century CE, or from the earlier city of Augustus, and set him down in this handsome and meaningful place, this site of classical order, he might feel out of place.

The real Rome was Calcutta-on-the-Mediterranean – crowded, chaotic and filthy. A few of its inhabitants might dwell in the palaces we imagine but most lived in warrens – tall, jerry-built, tottering blocks of flats known as *insulae* or 'islands', which rose as high as six storeys and were given to sudden collapse or outbreaks of fire. Building codes did not exist. The poet Juvenal complained, without exaggeration, that 'Here we have a city propped up for the most part by slats; for that is how the landlord patches up the crack in the old wall, bidding the tenants to sleep at ease under the ruin that hangs above their heads.' Because the *insulae* were usually built without chimneys, the tenants had to rely on charcoal braziers for warmth in winter, exposing them to death by carbon monoxide poisoning or accidental fires. Rome had about 1,800 *domus* or single-family dwellings and 46,000 *insulae*, but there was no regulation of the size or human capacity of an 'island' – it would hold as many people as a landlord could cram into it. If one thinks of a total population of 1.4 million people in Trajan's Rome, one will probably not be far wrong.

This made Rome a vast and consequential city, but it also condemned most Romans to live under conditions worse than the overcrowding and lack of basic amenities – water, fresh air, sewage services – that typified the worst slums of New York at the height of immigration in the 1870s. *Terrarum dea gentiumque, Roma*, wrote the poet Martial, *Cui par est nihil et nihil secundum* – 'Rome, goddess of lands and peoples, whom nothing can equal and nothing even approach.'

But the goddess stank. These being long before the days of mechanical transport, Rome's streets were laden with the excrement of horses, pigs, cows, dogs, donkeys and people, ton on ton of it, not to mention the dead babies and the corpses from periodic murders and muggings, and all the kitchen waste. Few facilities existed for collecting and getting rid of this stuff, not even for dumping it in the Tiber. And the Tiber, one should remember, still served as a principal supply of drinking water for many Roman households. Not until the reign of the emperor Trajan, in June 109 CE, did the eight aqueducts which formed the distribution end of the Aqua Traiana, bringing more than 220 million gallons a day of good spring water to the right bank of the Tiber, open for use – and most of that was monopolized by the ground floors of the rich. Only very rarely did an *insula* have rising pipes to bring good water to its upper floors.

Nevertheless, ancient Rome did have one hygienic advantage

over modern New York. Like most Roman cities, and unlike modern ones, it was generously equipped with public toilets. These were not of the sort familiar to modern users. Because the ancient Romans did not have the same taboos about elimination as we do, they did not insist on separate cubicles. The typical arrangement was a long stone bench, pierced with suitable holes. Everyone sat companionably, side by side. Underneath ran a channel of flowing water; and a channel in the floor outside the seat enabled the users to wash their hands when they were finished.

Since municipal trash disposal was as far from Roman expectations as automobiles or video, householders simply threw their rubbish into the street, where it lay and festered and was sometimes partly washed away by rain. At least there were sewers and storm-water channels to carry it off into the Tiber. In fact the Roman sewer system, which had been under construction since the sixth century BCE, was (for all its imperfections) one of the marvels of the world's civic engineering.

Nobody wants shit around. *Cacator sic valeas ut tu hoc locum transeas*, reads one of the many graffiti preserved under the ash of Pompeii – 'Do yourself a favour by shitting somewhere else.' And a city of a million or so people is obviously going to have its problems of sewage disposal. Rome had its system, and it was famous. Its main collector, the Cloaca Maxima ('principal sewer'), began its underground journey through Rome below the temple of Minerva in the Forum of Augustus, passed between the Basilica Julia and the temple of Vesta, went under the Arch of Constantine and the Piazza della Bocca della Verità, and discharged its noisome freight into the Tiber just below the Ponte Rotto through an arched opening five metres in diameter. None of the *insulae* seem to have any direct connection through downpipes to the sewers. Now and then, *plostra stercoraria* or shit carts might make an appearance, but not reliably. The ejection of garbage and waste into the public street usually happened at dusk. It was one of the drawbacks of ancient Roman life, especially since (as coarse terracotta cost nothing) it was a common habit to throw out the pot with its contents. Juvenal warned the visitor that 'You are truly negligent and careless if, before leaving the house to go out to dinner, you don't first make a will', because passers-by were so often brained by falling night-urns. 'Very often you might die for all the windows open along the streets you travel. Therefore . . . cultivate within yourself the forlorn hope that the windows will be content to pour out only the contents of their chamber-pots on your head.' Roman law did provide some redress for those injured by chamber-pots falling from on high: the victim should be compensated for his medical fees and lost work time. But he could not sue the owners or tenants of the *insula* for disfigurement caused by his wounds, since 'the body of a free man is without price'.

The wise night-rambler should wear a padded leather cap to protect his head, not only against such hazards, but from the assaults of other and more delinquent Romans. One of these, according to Suetonius, was the young emperor Nero, whose sport was to prowl the *clivi* and alleys of his imperial capital with a gang of friends and bash strangers insensible – 'he was in the habit of clubbing people on their way home from banquets, and if anyone fought back he would beat him badly and throw him in a sewer'. To be mugged and then half-drowned in excrement by a prowling emperor was the kind of fate which not even Georgian London, for all its bad sanitation and royal absolutism, inflicted on its visitors. But it would have been hard to tell if your assailant was a Nero or a mere commoner, since the streets of Rome were unlit and unpoliced. Either you found a *lanternarius* or slave to precede you with a flambeau, or you groped your way in fear and darkness. And naturally, the streets had no numbers or posted names.

The traffic made city life harder still. In 45 BCE, Julius Caesar issued an edict which banned carts, wagons and chariots from driving in the city between sunrise and mid-afternoon. This was a masterpiece of bad urbanism, since although it did something to make daytime walking and riding in Rome possible it immediately diverted all Rome's commercial traffic into the night hours, depriving most Romans of their sleep. Roman carts had wooden wheels with iron tyres, and the grinding and clanking of their progress over the ruts and stone pavements raised a din that mingled with the braying and lowing of beasts, the shouts of the carters, the merchants' bellowing quarrels and the crash and scrape of goods being loaded and unloaded. This went on all night long, and a stone could hardly sleep through it. It would keep a sea-calf awake on the bottom of the sea, Juvenal thought. It would give the emperor Claudius insomnia. Rome, the enemy of repose! And in the day it was little better, since although the traffic noise was not as bad, the sound of voices and pedestrian confusion was still unbearable. The only solution, and a partial one at that, was to be rich and ride at ease in a 'spacious litter' that one's slaves could hoist above the heads of the madding crowd. In it, one could close the windows and perhaps doze. But on foot, wrote Juvenal,

> The tide of the crowd before me is an obstacle, while the one following behind me like a compact phalanx is pressing at my back; one man elbows you in the side, another strikes you roughly with a cudgel; the next one bashes your head with a board, the next with a barrel. Meanwhile your legs grow heavy with mud, your feet are stepped on from all sides by enormous shoes, a soldier punctures your big toe with his hobnailed boots . . .

Before it could flow out of Rome, of course, the water had to flow in. It did so mainly through aqueducts. Eleven of these supplied the city with its drinking and washing water, eight entering by the region of the Esquiline Hill. Four more were added after the popes replaced the emperors, two of them in the twentieth century. No other ancient city had such a copious supply of water, and it earned Rome the name of *regina aquarum*, 'the queen of waters'. Almost all of them brought in drinkable water, except for the Alsietina, which carried water from the small lake of Martignano; some 33 kilometres long, it supplied an arena for naval battles which the emperor Augustus created on the present site of Trastevere. Probably the best water was that of the Claudian aqueduct, begun by Caligula in 38 CE and finished by Claudius in 52 CE; certainly the aqueduct whose construction created the most difficulty was the Aqua Marcia, begun in 144 BCE under the praetorship of Quintus Marcius.

Aqueduct maintenance was a never-ending occupation, done in the main by slaves. The channel or *specus* of each aqueduct was continually being narrowed by the build-up of 'sinter', deposits of calcium carbonate ($CaCO_3$), carried in the water and deposited on the channel walls. How fast it built up depended on several variables: the 'hardness' or lime content of the water, the texture of the channel (rough surfaces encouraged build-up, which roughened the surface more, increased friction and so trapped more sinter) and the speed of water flow. Research done on the channel of the great aqueduct at Nîmes in southern France indicates that sinter deposits (on both sides) narrowed its channel by 46 centimetres, or a third of its original width, in two hundred years. This yields a rate of about six inches per century, which may not sound like much, but over the hundreds of linear miles of the eleven aqueducts that supplied Rome with its water the tasks of grinding and chipping the sinter away added up, as did the maintenance of the terracotta or lead conduits themselves. Besides, four miles out of every five lay underground.

The distribution of water to its end users was done mainly through lead pipes. Lead gave its Latin name, *plumbum*, to those who worked with it, the *plumbarii* – who bequeathed it to their modern successors in England, the plumbers, and to those in France, the *plombiers*. It had large advantages for such work. It was soft, very ductile, and had a low melting point – about 375 degrees centigrade. Best of all, it was common and cheap, being itself a waste product. It had one disadvantage: it was highly poisonous, as the grieving parents of many a Victorian child who chewed too often on his lead soldiers discovered.

Rome used a great deal of silver, which was present in tiny quantities in its principal ore, galena (lead sulphide). The galena, when melted, separated into about one portion of silver to 300 of waste lead. A simple process afforded slaves (who were likely to die of lead poisoning in the end) the means of making lead pipe. Molten lead was flowed over an inclined, heatproof surface. When it reached the desired thickness and cooled, the resulting sheet was trimmed and then rolled around a suitable wooden mandrel. Its edges would be soldered together, and the result was water pipe, which usually came in ten-foot or shorter sections. The fact that Rome's water was delivered through lead conduits gave rise to a persistent myth: that the water was contaminated, and so lead poisoning killed or weakened those who drank it. This cannot have been so, because the water passed through the pipes too quickly (at its fastest, probably at 1.5 metres per second) to acquire any significant toxicity on the way. However, it often happened that wine was kept for long periods in jars or amphorae whose interiors had been treated with lead-based glazes, so it may well be that bibulous Romans were affected by it. But probably it was gonorrhoea, rather than lead poisoning, that made Romans ill.

How did water move into the city and get distributed? No pressure pumps existed. The entire distribution system for Rome's water, throughout the total 500 kilometres of the eleven aqueducts, was gravity-fed, and the feed had to be maintained across great distances: the original source point of Rome's Aqua Marcia was 91 kilometres from the city, and that of the Anio Novus hardly any closer (87). Since water will not run uphill against gravity, each aqueduct had to have a very gradual downward slope, continuous throughout its length. That of the Aqua Marcia, for instance, was 2.7 metres in every kilometre. But the natural form of the earth is never a steady, almost imperceptible decline. Consequently the aqueducts, on meeting a rise, had to go through a tunnel; and when the ground level fell too suddenly away, the channel of water had to be carried above it on arches. Hence the magnificent sight of the tall aqueducts converging on Rome, across the flat wastes of the campagna – mile upon mile of arches not yet fallen into ruin, imposing their proud rhythm on an otherwise undistinguished landscape, silently beautiful in the golden morning or rosy evening light.

But how to give them the necessary shape, the exact fall needed to convey the precious water into the heart of the city? This was accomplished by surveyors. They did not have modern equipment – the laser-levels and theodolites of today's surveyors did not exist. Yet they managed well with what would seem, by modern standards, to be very primitive instruments. The first of these was the *chorobates* or water-level, a long narrow trough (a straight, hollowed-out section of tree trunk would do) which could be propped up on stones and filled with water. Since a still water surface is always horizontal, this gave an excellent reference for sighting along, and when an assistant placed himself some distance away with a vertical, graduated measuring rod which had a moveable target, a surveyor with good eyes – Rome had no lenses or optical glass – could readily establish the rise or fall of the land between the two points. It was a clumsy instrument, needing a twenty-foot table to carry the trough, but in skilled hands it could plot variations in height with astonishing accuracy. No ancient remains of such a device have ever been found, but descriptions leave no doubt about its use. Similar surveying principles governed the boring of underground tunnels.

Next in usefulness was the *dioptra*, a flat disc mounted on a tripod, which could be both turned horizontally and tilted in the vertical plane. Through a sighting-tube fixed diametrically across the disc, it could measure both height and bearing of a distant target and was thus the ancestor of the modern theodolite. And finally there was the basic tool that every surveyor had to have, more for field-surveying than for the layout of aqueducts: the *groma*, consisting of two horizontal cross-pieces fixed at right-angles on the tip of a pole, with a plumb-bob hanging from each end of the pieces. It was indispensable for the other kind of big Roman engineering project as well: the laying-out of roads.

Along the length of the aqueduct, and especially just before it entered Rome, settling-tanks were built: a simple filtration system whereby the flow was allowed to pause so that particles and debris could sink to the bottom, there to be cleaned out periodically by the slave maintenance crews.

The oldest of the aqueducts dated well back into republican days: the Aqua Appia, sixteen kilometres long, mostly underground, built in 312 BCE and successively restored by Quintus Marcius Rex (144 BCE), Agrippa (33 BCE) and Augustus (11–4 BCE). It delivered 75,000 cubic metres of water per day. The next-oldest was the Anio Vetus (272–69 BCE), another mostly subterranean aqueduct which took its water directly from the Tiber above Tivoli, bringing it 81 kilometres to Rome and supplying some 180,000 cubic metres a day.

Rome's need for water increased rapidly in the second century BCE, as a result of its colonial victories, which swelled the population of the city. This produced the longest of all its aqueducts, the Aqua Marcia, which ran for 91 kilometres (approximately 80 below ground) and delivered 190,000 cubic metres daily.

Agrippa, builder of the Pantheon, also constructed two aqueducts, the Aqua Julia (33 BCE) and the Aqua Virgo (so called because its source outside the city was pointed out to his surveyors by a young girl). Between them they brought some 150,000 cubic metres a day into Rome. Two aqueducts started by the emperor Caligula (the Aqua Claudia in 38 CE, the Aqua Anio Novus in the same year) had to be finished by the emperor Claudius; between them they gave Rome a further 380,000 cubic metres a day. All in all, the eleven aqueducts provided some 1,130,000 cubic metres of water to meet the daily requirements of about a million people, which averaged out at about 1.13 cubic metres of water per person per day.

Not all of this water was used for drinking, cooking and washing. Water also had a strong, indeed essential, decorative and metaphorical aspect in ancient Rome, as it does today. Not every house had a garden, but many did, and those fortunate enough to have one needed a good supply of water for plants, pools and, of course, fountains. The fountains of Rome, celebrated in numberless paintings and poems as well as in music – one thinks of the charming trills and tinklings of Respighi's *Le fontane di Roma* – have always been a feature of the city and the culture it embodied. Because of the low water pressure in the days before

mechanical pumps, the 'abounding glittering jet' that spells 'fountain' to us today and was so magnificently choreographed by the
likes of Gianlorenzo Bernini in the seventeenth century was not
available in ancient Rome, but a lot of refreshment and relaxation
could be had from trickling basins, ornamental pools, shallow
waterfalls and *chasses d'eau* – the most grandiose project of this
kind being the celebrated Canopus in the garden of Hadrian's
Villa at Tivoli.

All this civic splendour, and much more, depended on a colonial
empire that had grown from a small seed in Italy, at the mouth of
the Tiber – Ostia, that vital port where the wealth of the growing
Empire came in and the administrative manpower went out, taken
from its original inhabitants in Etruscan times. Now, at the turn
of the millennium, its spread was prodigious. In Africa, Rome
commanded the provinces of Numidia, Mauretania, Cyrenaica
and Africa Proconsularis. Its African possessions did not supply
mineral wealth (that came largely from Spain) but they gave
Rome huge supplies of grain and other foodstuffs and, as a bonus,
supplied the wild animals for the shows in the arenas. Rome had
all of Egypt. Its command of the Iberian peninsula, modern Spain
and Portugal, was divided between the provinces of Tar-
raconensis, Lusitania and Baetica. It ruled Gaul (Lugdunensis,
Narbonensis, Belgica) and Britain. It had – insecurely, at times –
the frontier provinces of Germany and the lands along the natural
frontier of the Danube, such as Dacia. It had annexed Greece
(Macedonia, Achaea and Thrace) and much of Asia Minor. Its
furthest eastern provinces included Judaea, Syria and Mesopotamia.

At its height, the Roman Empire included fifty to sixty million
people – all under the absolute rule of one single man, all members
of subject populations: citizens of Rome, but also other Italians;
Europeans and Middle Easterners of all sorts, Gauls, Dacians,
Armenians, Mesopotamians, Syrians, Africans, Egyptians;
Britons, Spaniards, Germans, and so on, seemingly ad infinitum.
These formed a vast and bewilderingly complex mosaic of lan-
guages, histories, creeds and customs, some willingly passive to

Roman authority, most of them manageable by dint of colonial firmness, and a few – such as the ever fractious Jews – continually at odds with the system that had taken them over. Some of these peoples had very little effect on the core culture of Rome. Others, notably Greece, not only influenced but transformed it. *Graecia capta ferum victorem cepit*, wrote Horace, *et artes intulit agresti Latio*: 'When Greece was taken she enslaved her rough conqueror, and introduced the arts to cloddish Latium.'

Almost as soon as he had emerged victoriously from the battle of Actium in 31 BCE, Augustus launched an ambitious programme to restore his city's damaged prosperity. He took advantage of the long-term security of funds and work which his Principate – the word given to his rule as *princeps* or 'first citizen', a title Augustus had chosen to avoid the taint of absolutism or kingship – allowed. 'Professing himself satisfied with the tribunician power for the protection of the plebs,' wrote Tacitus, 'Augustus enticed the soldiers with gifts, the people with grain, and all men with the allurements of peace, and gradually grew in power, concentrating in his own hands the functions of the senate, the magistrates and the laws. No one opposed him, for the most courageous had fallen in battle . . . As for the remaining nobles, the readier they were for slavery, the higher they were raised in wealth and offices.'

It was an essential part of Augustus' political genius that, now and over the coming decades of his reign, he successfully maintained the illusion that he was not a dictator, just a saviour, the man who had restored the Republic and its primal virtues by handing it back to the Senate, and thus to the people, of Rome.

But it was a fiction – a necessary one. Augustus created a charade of restoring the Republic, but few Romans now remembered what it had once been. He had no intention of allowing republican chaos to seize the state again. He made a point of consulting the Senate, but the Senate reciprocally made a habit of never defying his will. He kept total command of the Roman army, and of the imperial provinces. He was also *pontifex maximus*, the supreme religious authority of the state.

Augustus was not a consistently great general, but he had his successes. Chief was the annexation of Egypt as a Roman province in 30 BCE, which gave Rome an unfailing and inexhaustible supply of grain. His armies completed the conquest of Spain. He also had military failures, the worst of which was undoubtedly the destruction of three whole legions in an ambush in the Teutoburg forest on the north side of the Rhine. The leader of the German attack, Hermann or Arminius, was one of the geniuses of German military history, his name invoked by every German leader from Frederick the Great through Bismarck to (of course) Adolf Hitler. For a long time after, it is reported, Augustus would beat his head on the wall at night and beseech the gods to 'Give me back my legions!'

But win or lose, the loyalty of the Roman army was always sworn by oath, by each individual, to Augustus personally. He was their paymaster. Their commanding officers were chosen by him, and the head commanders of their campaigns were usually members of his family – Tiberius, Germanicus or Agrippa. If the soldier lived long enough to complete his term of service (sixteen years, and later twenty) he would expect to be settled on a patch of arable land to complete his life as a farmer, and the matter of what land he received, and where, was decided by Augustus. He was, in short, their patron, and they were his clients: an arrangement wholly familiar from civilian life, but transferred with even more stringent bonds of obligation and discipline to the military.

For a few years after Actium, Octavian/Augustus shrewdly passed up the most obvious possibility raised by his victory – to declare himself dictator of Rome and its empire. In 28/27 BCE he made a move that seemed to confirm that he was no dictator, but rather was acting as the saviour of the Republic and its primal virtue, when he formally restored the supreme power to the Senate and People.

In a document entitled *Res Gestae* ('Things Done'), whose most complete text is not in Rome but, strange to say, bilingually inscribed in stone on the wall of the temple of Augustus and Rome in Ancyra (modern Ankara) in Galatia – the original was placed outside his mausoleum in Rome, but being written on bronze pillars was 'recycled' by later thieves – Augustus set forth this as the first of what he considered the main achievements of his reign: 'In my sixth and seventh consulships, after I had stamped out the civil wars, and at a time when by universal consent I was in absolute control of everything, I transferred the management of politics [res publica] to the discretion of the Senate and People of Rome. For this service I was given the name "Augustus" by a decree of the Senate.'

This was merely a façade, though. There was no 'permanent revolution', no automatic retention of supreme power – but he was placed in charge of Gaul, Spain, Syria and Egypt, where most of the legions were stationed, and he remained one of Rome's two consuls, exercising consular imperium (either as consul or as proconsul) until his death. To make quite sure that he did not suffer Julius Caesar's fate, he recreated a special, elite unit, another Praetorian Guard, for his personal protection.

His actual power, through the army and the consulship, was therefore close to absolute, and the bonds of deference and clientship did the rest. Moreover, they did so for a very long time. Just as England in 1900 had many citizens who had turned sixty without ever knowing any ruler but Queen Victoria, crowned in 1838, so at the time of Augustus' death (14 CE) countless Roman citizens had never known any form of government other than the stable Principate. The management of an empire without Augustus must have seemed to many people hard to imagine, almost a contradiction in terms.

Yet there are some things that not even the most inspired and determined leader can do, and one of the things he failed at – a vital part of his intentions – was his effort to restore ancient Roman virtues by means of legislation. 'By new laws passed at my instigation, I brought back those practices of our ancestors that were passing away in our age.' He had the Senate pass sumptuary laws limiting extravagance and the gratuitous display of wealth, and he tried to restore what he saw as the diminished dignitas of the upper classes by cracking down on the frequency of divorce and adultery among them. He was no puritan, and his own family was certainly no model of virtue – for reasons lost to history, he felt obliged to banish his adopted son Agrippa Postumus (12 BCE–14 CE) to the dull Mediterranean island of Planasia, where he was shortly murdered; in 2 BCE he had banished his only daughter Julia, and in 8 CE his granddaughter, also named Julia, both for sexual immorality. Apparently what irked Augustus particularly in his granddaughter's conduct was that, in the course of a wild party, she placed a chaplet on the head of a statue of the satyr Marsyas,* a gesture with pronounced sexual overtones. But Augustus' attempt to legislate his subjects into virtue was, like most such efforts before or since, a failure.

It was also a small matter compared to his achievements. He recreated the Roman state and its power, refreshed it, and set a pattern of Roman rule that would last some five hundred years. No other statesman of antiquity could have made such a claim. And to the extent that he could set a compelling example through his own way of life, he did that too. Augustus had none of the obtrusive vices of his successors. He believed in dignity but not pomposity; in ceremony, where necessary and within the limits proper to a chief priest, but not in Oriental showiness, despite the fact that he was regarded as a divine being, *Divus Augustus*. Nor was he given to luxurious display, despite his overwhelming wealth. Few later emperors – Claudius and Hadrian being among the exceptions – would show such an understanding of the difference between *auctoritas* (authoritative influence) and *imperium* (command from above).

---

* Whose story is as follows. The goddess Athena had invented the flute, but threw it away because playing it distorted her face. Marsyas found it where it lay, and taught himself to play it. He became so good at it that he had to challenge Apollo to a contest: his flute versus the god's lyre. Inevitably, the impertinent and libidinous satyr lost. Apollo's dreadful revenge was to string Marsyas up and skin him alive. This was always taken as an allegory of the opposition, in art as in life, between sexy spontaneity (Marsyas) and disciplined invention (merciless Apollo).

Augustus was no glutton. He lived, and ate, with moderation. 'He ... preferred the food of the common people,' recalled Suetonius, 'especially the coarser sort of bread, whitebait, fresh hand-pressed cheese ... and would not wait for dinner, but ate anywhere.' In oratory, he loathed what he called 'the stink of far-fetched phrases'. But he 'gave all possible encouragement to intellectuals; he would politely and patiently attend readings not only of their poems and historical works, but of their speeches and dialogues; yet objected to being made the theme of any work unless the author were known as a serious and reputable writer'. He also possessed a dry sense of humour, if one is to believe some of the stories about him. He went to a courtier's house for dinner and was served a poor, unelaborated meal. As he was taking his leave he murmured, 'I'd no idea I was such a close friend of yours.' Learning of the death of a Roman *eques* who (without anyone's knowledge) had contracted debts of 20 million sesterces, Augustus sent an agent to the auction of the man's property. There, he bought the man's pillow for his personal use. Eyebrows were raised. But, the emperor explained, 'The pillow on which he could rest with all those debts must be especially conducive to sleep.' And he could take a joke, or so it was said. Back in Rome after his victory over Antony and Cleopatra, he was approached by a man who offered him, for 20,000 sesterces, a tame raven that had learned to croak 'Hail, Caesar, victor, commander!' Augustus gave him the money, but then a friend of the bird's owner told him that he had a second raven, which he had trained to say, just in case, 'Hail, Antony, commander, victor!' The bird was produced. It did indeed hail Antony. Instead of taking offence, the emperor merely told him to split the money with the friend. He was whimsical with his presents, which might be gold plate or, just as easily, 'lengths of goat-hair cloth, or sponges, or pokers, or tongs'.

At the top of the social tree in this newly stabilized Rome, below the emperor himself, were the senators and their families. It was not in Augustus' interest to lord it over them, since that would have diminished his pretence to be *primus inter pares*, 'first among equals', and increased the risk that disaffected citizens might see him as a king. The senators were traditionally very much an elite, and Augustus was careful to preserve that status for them – even though, under his rule, they had less and less to do. Particularly important for senatorial self-esteem were the magistracies which they (and they alone) could hold. They were expected to set standards of dignity, and at times compelled by law to do so – no senator could marry an ex-slave, appear on stage as an actor, or (unthinkable liberty!) enter the arena as a gladiator. Property qualifications also existed: in practice, by Augustus' time, there was no senatorship for men who owned less than a million sesterces.

Below the senators were the *equites* or knights and squires. In earlier days of the Republic they were a cavalry force, hence relatively wealthy. This no longer applied, since under the later Republic and the Principate cavalry was supplied by Rome's allied states. But one still needed to be quite rich – 400,000 sesterces or more – to qualify as an *eques*.

Then came the *plebs*, or ordinary people – the majority of Roman citizens. Some were born free but others were *liberti* or freedmen, former slaves who had been manumitted by their owners. No stigma attached to being a *libertus*, and none to the free children of slaves. On the contrary: it was a matter for congratulation. When the novelist Petronius depicted the freedman Trimalchio in the *Satyricon* vaunting himself on his status, it was not with contempt, still less with hate: Trimalchio might indeed be vulgar, gross and a bit of a thug, like half the citizens of the Upper East Side today, but he had made it into respectability, and who was going to rebuke a former slave for waving his cash around?

At the bottom of the Roman social order one comes to the slaves, without whom the society as a whole could not possibly have functioned. Their legal status was simple. They were chattels, things, owned absolutely by their master, who could buy and sell them as he pleased, and assign them to do any work he wanted. The fact that slave labour was less efficient than free was well known to the Romans, because it is the first big thing a slave-owner learns. Pliny, for instance, attributed the high food productivity of pre-imperial Rome to its reliance on free workers on farms, and its fall in his own time to the general use of slave labour. 'In those days,' he wrote, more as a moralist than an economist,

> the lands were tilled by the hands of the very generals, the soil exulting beneath the ploughshare crowned with wreaths of laurel and guided by a husbandman graced with triumphs ... But today these same lands are tilled by slaves whose legs are in chains, by the hands of malefactors and men with branded faces ... And we are surprised that the yields from the labour of workhouse slaves are not the same as from the honest toil of warriors!

Nevertheless, given the choice, what Roman was going to do without his or her slaves? While most slave-owners had few, perhaps no more than one or two – just like most landowners in the slave South of America before the Civil War – the slave populations of some upper Roman capitalist families were truly impressive. The freedman Gaius Cacilius Isidorus, towards the end of the first century CE, left 4,116 slaves when he died. More than a few Roman bigwigs owned 1,000 slaves, and the emperor might be served by as many as 20,000. But the statistics are unreliable, especially for the top end of slave-ownership. It is conventionally supposed that about one person in three in imperial Rome was a slave.

What did they do? Just about everything. They served, performing an incredible number and variety of tasks and services, which rose almost to a madness of detail in the division of labour. Slaves worked as water-carriers, valets, bricklayers and litter-bearers. Their rural equivalents pruned the vines, fed the pigs, sowed and harvested the wheat. They were secretaries, draftsmen, accountants, stone-carvers and teachers. The great man's toilette would be taken care of by the bathing-attendants (*balneatores*), the masseurs (*aliptae*), the hairdressers (*ornatores*) and the barbers (*tonsores*). His food would be prepared by pastry-cooks (*libarii*), bakers (*pistores*) and other kinds of *cocus* or cook, and served up by the *structores* (major-domos), the dining-room attendants (*triclinarii*), the waiters who carried the dishes in (*ministratores*) and those who took them out again (*analectae*). Before any food was eaten by the owner it would be tasted, just in case an enemy had reached the kitchen, by the *praegustatores*. At intervals in the parade of dishes the emperor or aristocrat would be entertained by dancing-girls (*saltatrices*), dwarves (*nani*) and buffoons (*moriones*). If a slave was the body servant or the secretary of a master, that implied a certain trust, even closeness. It also meant, however, that the slave would be treated as one who had privileged information, which could lead to torture under interrogation.

The living conditions of domestic slaves in prominent households tended to be better than those of farm-labourer slaves out in the country, though they were not always so. But they were also unstable and came without guarantees. The law did not recognize that a slave could be punished by loss of status, for he or she *had* no status to lose. The master owned the slave's body and could do as he pleased with it: flog it, fuck it, work it three-quarters to death. The law of deference and obedience (*obsequium*) was made of iron. On the other hand, a slave might sometimes receive a sum of money, known as the *peculium*, from his or her master; this might be saved, and eventually go towards buying manumission. But it was entirely gratuitous and no slave had a right under law to such *peculia*.

The *peculium* was understood by all involved, slave as well as master, to be a tool for strengthening the bonds of deference and obedience. Sometimes slaves would help one another out, in the face of (sometimes hideously) unjust punishments. The emperor Commodus, for instance, displeased with one of his slave bath-attendants who had drawn him too cool a bath, ordered another slave to burn him alive in the palace's furnace. The attendant burned a sheepskin instead, and its smell deceived the emperor.

Almost all slaves were worth something; a slave needed to be very old, incompetent or mentally dangerous to be entirely worthless. Some of them, of the right kind and properly handled,

1 *Sarcophagus of the Spouses,*
6th century BC

Terracotta, 114 × 190 cm;
National Etruscan Museum, Rome

2 *Apollo of Veii,* c. 550–520 BC

Terracotta, 174 cm; Museo Nazionale
di Villa Giulia, Rome

CLOCKWISE FROM TOP LEFT

3 Leochares
Apollo Belvedere, c. 350–325 BC
White marble, 224 cm; Vatican Museums,
Vatican City

4 Apollonius
Boxer, 225 BC
Bronze; Museo Nazionale, Rome

5 *Pasquin*, 3rd century BC
Marble, 192 cm; Piazza di Pasquino, Rome

6 *Temple of Fortuna Virilis*, 75 BC

7 *The Pyramid of Cestius*, 12 BC
White marble, 37 m

8 *Augustus of Prima Porta*,
C. 15 AD

White marble, 205 cm;
Vatican Museums, Vatican City

9, 10 & 11 *Villa dei Misteri
friezes*, 1st century

Frescoes; Pompeii

15 *Baths of Caracalla, c. 212–216*

16 *Santo Stefano Rotondo, c. 468–483*

could make their owner rich. An example was the instructive career of that singular politician, speculator and slave-owner Marcus Licinius Crassus (c.112–53 BCE), who had been, with Pompey and Julius Caesar, a member of the First Triumvirate. Crassus' fortune had largely been made by his pack of loyal and well-trained slaves. Crassus had many silver-mines and huge agricultural holdings but, wrote Plutarch, all that was nothing compared to the value of his slaves, 'such a great number and variety did he possess – readers, secretaries, silversmiths, stewards and table-servants. He himself directed their training and took part in teaching them himself, accounting it, in a word, the chief duty of a master to care for his slaves as the living tools of household management.' But the big profits Crassus' slaves earned him were in property. He purchased slaves who were builders and architects. Then, after one or another of the catastrophic fires that were always breaking out in Rome, Crassus would move in and purchase the devastated sites and burned-out buildings for a pittance, using his enslaved professionals to renovate and build them up again: 'Then when he had more than 500 of these, he would buy houses that were on fire and those adjoining the ones on fire. The owners would let them go for small sums, because of their fear and uncertainty, so that the greatest part of Rome came into his hands.'

Crassus was also the man who stamped out the great slave rising led by the Thracian gladiator Spartacus in 73 BCE, which burst out in Capua and spread like wildfire across Italy. Competent, supremely brave, strong and humane, Spartacus was a brilliant and charismatic leader who eventually attracted an army of ninety thousand rebel slaves, many of whom were being trained as gladiators by their Roman masters. He and his army had fought and marched their way to Roman Gaul; they conquered several full Roman armies but were eventually destroyed in Lucania, in southern Italy, after their hope of crossing to Sicily failed. Crassus savagely crucified six thousand of the rebels (the unclaimed ones, of course; the rest went back to their owners, for Crassus had great respect for the laws of property) along the Appian Way.

Somehow it is difficult to mourn the fact that this supremely brutal real-estate king was captured and killed by the Parthians when they defeated his legions at Carrhae in Mesopotamia, during a failed punitive expedition in 53 BCE.

It is conventionally assumed that the coming of Christianity made the lives of slaves easier, but this is untrue. Early Christian emperors did not press for manumission, and fourth-century sermons were not filled with exhortations to Christian slave-owners to set their human property free. Rather they tended to follow the advice of St Paul – slaves should stay put and obediently serve their masters as the good served Christ. Most Church leaders and ordinary pious Christians were slave-owners themselves – a fact that was not going to be ignored in centuries to come, in the American South.

Slavery's impact on Rome was too vast to be only economic. It also changed, by steady and irreversible degrees, the nature of Roman education of the young. In the early days of the Republic, this had tended to be amateurish and tradition-obsessed. A child's teacher was his father, the *paterfamilias*, with some input (of an entirely conservative kind) from the mother. The curriculum consisted largely of learning about the national heroes of the Roman past, and the corpus of law known as the Twelve Tables. The chief skill taught by this conventional education was rote memory, coupled with a strong emphasis on physical culture and basic military knowledge. Plutarch, in his *Life of Cato the Elder*, recounts how Cato's father, who owned a slave named Chilo, an accomplished teacher of other boys, would not allow his own son to be taught by anyone but himself. 'He thought it improper to have his son reprimanded by a slave, or to have his ears tweaked when he was slow in learning; nor would he have him under obligation to a slave for so priceless a thing as education . . . In his son's presence he refrained from obscene language no less than if he were in the presence of the Vestal Virgins. Nor would he ever bathe with him.' This was just the kind of cold-bath upbringing that the importation of large numbers of Greek slaves was sure to dispel. As education passed into the hands of Greek instructors, its nature changed. It was Hellenized and liberalized. Instead of rote learning of conservative tribal wisdom, it favoured debate and speculation, philosophical argument, sophistry, and the study of literature, both Greek and Latin.

Most of all, it made oratory the chief skill to acquire, the true test of intellectual capability. Cicero describes how his boyhood and early manhood were devoted to learning it in different places and under different masters. First, he 'gave myself up wholly' to the instruction of Philo, an expatriate Greek philosopher who, with his intellectual friends, had fled from Athens because of the Mithridatic wars, and settled in Rome. He studies pleading with Molo of Rhodes, another Greek; dialectic, with Diodotus the Stoic, who actually moved into Cicero's house. 'The foremost teachers, knowing only Greek, could not, unless I used Greek, correct my faults nor convey their instruction.' Now it is time to go to Athens, where he studies with the philosopher Antiochus and goes 'zealously' into rhetorical exercises under the direction of Demetrius the Syrian. Next he travels through Asia Minor, attaching himself to one teacher after another, starting with 'the most eloquent man of all Asia', Menippus of Stratonicea. Such a varied, intense curriculum was, of course, unusual. But under the old Roman dispensation it would have been unthinkable, because no one would have thought it necessary.

The words 'Augustan Age' evoke the name of the poet Virgil as inevitably as the word 'modernity' does that of the painter Pablo Picasso. Publius Virgilius Maro was not born in Rome, but few of the writers who created the canon of Latin verse and prose were – Livy came from Padua, Catullus from Verona, Martial from a backwater in Spain. Virgil was from Mantua; on his deathbed he supposedly dictated the epitaph for his tomb: *Mantua me genuit, Calabria rapuere, tenet nunc / Parthenope: cecini Pascua, rura, duces.* 'Mantua bore me, Calabria brought me death, now Naples holds me; I sang of flocks, farms and leaders.' Modest enough, for the greatest poet Rome ever produced.

This was the man whose lifetime (70–19 BCE) and whose work associate him indelibly with the reign of Rome's first emperor.

Sixteen years of his life as a Roman citizen were disfigured by civil war, by the murderous proscriptions that followed the killing of Julius Caesar and the defeat and suicide of Cassius and Brutus at Philippi. And by the time Italy settled down somewhat, there were still the massive expropriations and evictions to contend with: Roman soldiers were rewarded by their masters with land confiscated from those who had owned it in peacetime, and this dislocated the rural society of Italy. Something like a quarter of the good land of Italy is thought to have changed hands in this disastrous way, and this trauma is reflected in Virgil's first published work, the *Eclogues* or 'Bucolics':

> A godless soldier has my cherished fields,
> A savage has my land: such profit yields
> Our civil war. For them we worked our land!
> Aye, plant your pears – to fill another's hand.

The speaker is the farmer Meliboeus, in Virgil's first *Eclogue*: and he is lamenting his loss of home, forced on him by the great, distant world of politics. '*Tityre, tu patulae recubans sub tegmine fagi / siluestrem tenui Musam meditaris auena: /nos patriae finis et dulcia linquimus arua: nos patriam fugimus.*' ('Tityrus, here you loll, your slim reed-pipe serenading the Muse beneath a sheltering canopy of beech, while I must leave my home place and the fields I love: we must evacuate our homeland.')

His family was moderately well off; well enough, at least, to send him to Mediolanum (Milan) and Rome to be educated in philosophy and rhetoric. It is possible, though not certain, that Virgil's family estates were lost in the massive confiscations that followed the battle of Philippi in 42 BCE, when free land was issued to Octavian's veteran soldiers, but other property was given to him near Naples, thanks to the benevolent intervention of his well-placed friend, Maecenas. He is said to have been worth ten million sesterces when he died, a handsome fortune which can only have come to him in gifts from Augustus.

Virgil was tall, dark and shy; he seldom went to Rome, preferring rural life. He had weak lungs (coughing blood for much of his life, he died at fifty-one, though that was not an uncommon age for death) and a fine reading voice; he is known to have read the *Georgics* aloud to Augustus for four days straight, taking turns with Maecenas when his throat got hoarse. Everyone praised the expression and dramatic power of his reading. It irked him to be accosted by admirers and when this happened on the street – as it often did, when the word of his poetic powers and his friendship with the emperor got around – he would hide in the nearest house. In Naples his modesty of speech and behaviour got him the nickname Parthenias, 'the virgin'. Of course he was no virgin, and his preference was for boys.

How did a poet make a living in ancient Rome? The short answer was: not at all, or else through patronage. This was only the literary extension of one of the most durable commonplaces of Roman life, the relation between the client and the patron in everyday dealings. There was little question – if possible, even less then than now – of a poet living off his royalties, since no pub-lishing industry existed. Books were made in small numbers but few people bought them. When Pompeii and Herculaneum were overwhelmed with lava from Vesuvius in 79 CE, thousands of statues and scores of wall paintings were buried and have since been found, but all the digging on these sites over the last couple of centuries has exhumed only one private library.

Some poets, at least, already had a degree of financial inde-pendence: Horace had enough cash to pay for a kind of university education in Athens and both Ovid and Propertius were her-editary squires (*equites*), the latter with senatorial relations and friends who were, or had been, consuls. Catullus came from a senatorial family and was not short of money, especially since his family was friendly with Julius Caesar. But for those who were not so luckily placed (and even for those who were, since having well-off relatives does not make a poet rich even if it gets him dinner invitations) the benign interest of a patron was all.

Patronage was one of the most characteristic institutions, or social habits, of ancient Rome. In early republican times a free man would seek the protection of a rich and powerful one to whom he offered his services. In doing so, he became that person's 'client'. A freed slave was automatically the client of the former owner. The relationship was not exactly contractual, though early Roman law did treat it as legally binding under some circumstances. The client's task was to dance attendance on his patron, come to greet him each morning, be a 'gofer' and offer him political support. He would be formally rewarded with a *sportula*, a dole of food and sometimes cash. Sometimes, but by no means always, the relationship between patron and client would develop into real friendship, but that was hardly predictable, since friendship presupposes feelings of equality and differences of class were very strong in ancient Rome. Patronage was an arrangement in which power flowed only one way. It survived long into modern times, of course, and particularly in Sicily: a perfect example of its workings was given by one memoirist who in the 1950s observed, in the dining-room of a major Palermo hotel, a *pezzo di novanta* (literally, a ninety-pound cannon, or 'big shot') walk in, doff his overcoat, and without looking drop it behind him, certain that someone would catch it before it touched the floor. Rome's satirists – chiefly Juvenal and Martial – had some bitter things to say about patronage. 'A man should possess "patrons" and "masters" who does not possess himself, and who eagerly covets what patrons and masters eagerly covet. If you can endure not having a slave, Olus, you can also endure not having a patron.' And in fact they had good reasons to be bitter, because the relationship between patron and client had degenerated appreciably under the Empire. The client was now little better than a parasite, a hanger-on. Originally, in Greek, a *paraseitos* was merely a 'dinner-guest' but it went downhill from there, acquiring strong overtones of contempt.

The transaction between patron and poet was not a simple one – not a matter of any poet offering to sell mediocre panegyrics to any would-be celebrity. Poetasters do not confer everlasting fame; their work dies with them, or (more likely) before. But there was always the possibility that a major poet might confer on his patron *memoria sempiterna*, 'undying memory', by praising him in verse. Thus Rome's first major epic poet before Virgil, the Calabrian Ennius (239–169 BCE), wrote in praise of the military achievements of M. Fulvius Nobilior, and is (unreliably) said to have been awarded Roman citizenship for doing so. However, the negotiation over patronage was a delicate matter, and tended to be done through a tastemaker, a middleman, who had the ear of the potential patron and enjoyed his trust. One such person, the most influential one in the so-called Golden Age of Latin writing, was the *eques* Gaius Maecenas, a friend and confidant of Augustus who claimed descent from Etruscan royalty and was also the patron of Horace. It is not difficult to glimpse the fine hand of Maecenas behind Horace's endorsement and celebration of Octavian/Augustus' victory over Antony and Cleopatra at Actium, the famous 'Cleopatra epode', which begins *Nunc est bibendum, nunc pede libero / Pulsanda tellus*:

> It's drinking-time, comrades, time to stomp the ground with an unfettered foot, to honour with Salian feasts the couch of the gods. Before now it was forbidden to bring out the Caecuban wine from ancestral cellars, so long as a Queen, together with her band of men stained with vile perversion, was preparing insane destruction for the Capitol and ruin for our rule, being so abandoned as to hope for anything imaginable, drunk as she was upon sweet fortune. But when scarcely a single ship escaped from the flames it lessened her madness, and Caesar reduced her thoughts to the stern reality of fear . . .

This was a great poem, but it is also unrestrained propaganda, libel run wild without a syllable of truth in it.

Maecenas was associated with, and helped promote, the poetry of Propertius and Varius Rufus as well as Horace. But his chief linkage, the one which fixed him permanently in literary history, was to Virgil. He did well by some of his poets: Virgil died rich, Horace received the free gift of a Sabine farm. But Virgil certainly did the most to earn the gifts he received, and became essentially the emperor's mouthpiece. His *Eclogues* are the main source of the pastoral tradition in Latin, and thus in English and French. His *Georgics* set the mode and pattern for didactic poetry, a form abandoned in the twentieth century but of great importance before it. The *Aeneid* was Rome's archetype of the heroic narrative epic. Augustus was extraordinarily lucky to have Maecenas steering his patronage in Virgil's direction.

In the *Georgics* Virgil evokes and idealizes the life which, he believes, Augustus is giving back to Italy – simple, direct, close to the earth and to the workings of Nature: pastoral heaven, in short. ('Georgics' derives from the Greek word *georgos*, 'one who works the soil'.) It is a life without ceremony, flattery, formality – and, we see, without intrusive clients:

> O happy beyond measure the tillers of the soil . . . Even if no
> high mansion with tall portals pours forth from every room
> a mighty wave of men coming to pay their respects in the
> morning; even if men do not gape at pillars inlaid with lovely
> tortoise-shell . . . or at Corinthian bronzes; even if the pure
> olive oil they use is not spoiled with perfume, yet they enjoy
> sleep without worry, and a life that cannot bring dis-
> illusionment . . .

Nothing is going to disturb such men; they have found their centres, they enjoy 'sleep without worry . . . gentle slumber beneath a tree', unmoved by military honours, the threat of Dacians 'swooping down from the Danube', the death-throes of kingdoms, the haves and have-nots.

> His furrows are ever piled high with harvest and his granaries
> are filled to overflowing . . . the pigs return well fed on acorns,
> the woods produce wild strawberries . . . Meanwhile, sweet
> children hang about his lips, his chaste household preserves
> its purity, the cows' udders hang full of milk . . . This is the
> life the ancient Sabines once cherished; so, too, Remus and

his brother; thus, surely, Etruria waxed strong, and Rome became the fairest thing on earth . . .

All of this would be echoed by Horace: *Beatus ille qui, procul negotiis / Ut prisca gens mortalium, paterna rura bobus exercet suis / solutus omne faenore.* 'Blessed the man who, far from wheeling and dealing, like the first of mortal men, ploughs his ancestral acres with his own oxen, free from all usury.'

The *Aeneid* was the most important long poem to be written in any European language since Homer's *Iliad*. Through it, Virgil achieved an influence over human thought, and the conception of poetry as an artform, that no other writer could claim. Not until Dante, who made Virgil his fictional guide through the *Inferno*, would any poet rival the imaginative achievement of the *Aeneid*. And of course Dante paid grateful tribute to his guide for showing him what writing could be and do. 'Since you my author and my master are / And it was from you only that I took / That lovely style that I am honoured for.'

Essentially, Virgil wrote the founding myth of the Roman people, setting forth what was expected of their nature and destiny under the guidance of Augustus. Its importance, both as art and as political utterance, was recognized long before it approached completion. 'Stand aside, Roman writers; give way, Greeks!' wrote that entrancing love-poet Sextus Propertius, who had been broken financially by the proscriptions of Octavian and Antony. 'Something greater than the *Iliad* is being born!'

Virgil freely admits that other peoples, such as the Greeks, are better at certain things than his Romans. 'Let others make more lifelike, breathing images from bronze, which they will,' he writes. Others can excel as orators, as astronomers. 'But Romans, keep in mind that your artform is government. You must keep men practised in the habit of peace, be generous to the conquered, and stand firm against the arrogant.' For the real Roman, the art of power is what counts. To show what this means, Virgil will tell the story of Rome's foundation by that man of destiny, the Trojan hero Aeneas, who with his venerated father Anchises and little son Ascanius escapes from the burning ruins of Troy and, pursued by the hostility of the goddess Juno, after many perilous wanderings by sea, founds the city of Rome, the second Troy, a city destined for an equally mythic greatness. 'I sing of warfare and a man at war,' the epic begins, or in John Dryden's translation:

> Arms and the man I sing, who, forced by Fate
> And haughty Juno's unrelenting hate,
> Expelled and exiled, left the Trojan shore,
> Long labours, both on land and sea, he bore . . .

In part, the *Aeneid* is an imitation of Homer's *Odyssey*. Aeneas was already a character in the *Iliad*. In some respects the *Aeneid* is almost impenetrably complicated but its story may be summarized, in a very simplified form. Setting sail from burning Troy (book I), Aeneas reaches Carthage, which is not written about as an enemy to Rome, but as a luxurious refuge from the terrors of the sea; it is ruled by the beautiful Queen Dido to whom he relates, in the manner of Odysseus, the fall of Troy and his voyaging (books II–III). Dido and Aeneas fall in love (book IV) but the gods oblige him to take to the sea again, deserting her, breaking her heart, driving her to suicide and, not incidentally, providing the substance of later operas. His venerated father dies; Aeneas holds funeral games for him (book V), sails on, and makes landfall in Italy, where he finds the entrance to the Underworld near Cumae (book VI). There he meets the shade of Dido, who bitterly reproaches him with many curses. Aeneas can think of no justification for his conduct – there is none – and is forced to the lame excuse that he didn't mean it: he left her because Jupiter told him to. There he meets the shade of his father, who tells him about the destiny of the city he is about to found, Rome.

In book VII Aeneas reaches Latium and seeks marriage to the princess Lavinia, whose previous suitor, Turnus, grows furious and, incited by the ever vengeful goddess Juno, makes war on Aeneas and the Trojans. In book VIII Aeneas acquires celestial armour, including a stupendously elaborate shield made by Vulcan. It is a prophetic object, showing a number of future events involving Rome, including Augustus' victory over Antony at Actium.

After prolonged warfare (books IX–XII) Turnus is killed and Aeneas' hegemony over the new Rome is complete.

It is, on one level, a majestically patriotic poem, suffused with an epic sense of scale and destiny. It recounts as its basic theme the establishment of those moral obsessions of ancient Augustan Rome, peace (*pax*), civilization and law (*mos* and *ius*). *Tantae molis erat Romanam condere gentem*, Virgil wrote: 'So hard and massive a task it was to found the Roman race.' Much the same might be said about the composition of Virgil's poem. Like Shakespeare, Virgil created an extraordinary number of phrases and images that so embedded themselves in the uses of his language that they seem always to have been there: clichés that continually refresh themselves. *Equo ne credite, Teucri. Quidquid id est, timeo Danaos et dona ferentes.* A real shudder of mystery in the presence of the Trojan horse: 'Don't feel safe with the horse, Trojans. Whatever it is, I fear the Greeks, especially when they bring gifts.' Or the warning about Hell: the road down to that place of damnation is easy, *Facilis descensus Averno*, but

Night and day the gates of Death's dark kingdom lie open:
But to retrace your steps, to find your way back to daylight –
That is the task, the hard thing.

The *Aeneid* reverberates throughout with hints and prophecies of Rome's destiny. Aeneas comforts and encourages his exhausted men (I. 205–10): 'We hold our course for Latium, where the Fates / Hold out a settlement and rest for us. Troy's kingdom there shall rise again. Be patient: / Save yourselves for more auspicious days.' Aeneas will found the city, and presently

Happy in the tawny pelt
His nurse, the she-wolf, wears, young Romulus

Will take the leadership, build walls of Mars,
And call by his own name, his people Romans.
For these I set no limits, world or time,
But make the gift of empire without end.

In the kingdom of the dead in book VI, Anchises prophesies
that 'Illustrious Rome will bound her power with earth, / Her
spirit with Olympus. She'll enclose / Her seven hills with one great
city wall, / Fortunate in the men she breeds.' And he instructs his
son Aeneas to

Turn your two eyes
This way and see this people, your own Romans.
Here is Caesar, and all the line of Iulus,
All who shall one day pass under the dome
Of the great sky; this is the man, this one,
Of whom so often you have heard the promise,
Caesar Augustus, son of the deified,
Who shall bring once again an Age of Gold,
To Latium, to the land where Saturn reigned
In early times. He will extend his power
Beyond the Garamants and Indians,
Over far territories north and south . . .

Thus the growth of Empire is foreordained.

After Virgil, the best-known of all Augustan poets, then as now,
was Quintus Horatius Flaccus – Horace. (Lucretius was certainly
influential, both in Rome and, later, through his influence on
Milton; but he was not loved and enjoyed as Horace was.) Horace
was five years younger than Virgil, the son of a freedman, his
father an auctioneer who had been a slave. His career, up to the
time he was noticed by Maecenas and brought into the Augustan
circle, had been an uneven one. In fact he had served in the army,
fighting on the side of Brutus and Cassius and with the high rank
of military tribune, against the future Augustus at Philippi.

Horace was certainly indebted to Maecenas, but he did not feel a bit inferior to him – rather he addressed him as an equal, a friend – 'Maecenas, son of royal stock / My friend, my honour, my firm rock.' A relaxed intimacy seems to prevail between the two men. At one point, in *Epode* 14, Horace even refers to an erotic liaison between Augustus and an actor, Bathyllus – a liberty which he could not possibly have taken if a trusting confidentiality did not exist between him and Augustus' friend Maecenas.

He makes a few mistakes at first, over-flattering Augustus, attributing a politically unwelcome divinity to him. He follows the Augustan line on sexual immorality and public weakness a little too sedulously for some tastes: 'Teeming with sin, our times have sullied first the marriage bed, our offspring, and our homes; sprung from this source, disaster's stream has overflowed the people and the fatherland . . . The young maiden even now trains herself in coquetry and, impassioned to her finger tips, plans unholy amours.' But soon the right proportion of praise is found, and in the meantime Horace has developed into a wonderful singer of the light of pleasure and, sometimes, of the remorse which can be the shadow of that sun.

He was short and stout, grey-haired and a connoisseur of wine, gardens and conversation. He was urbane, humorous and without rancour in the face of human folly. If you can judge a man's qualities from his poetry, he was an ideal companion. He loved the country farm that Augustus, through Maecenas, had given him: its orchard, its bubbling spring of water 'shinier than glass'. He was presumably homosexual. He never married, and some of his most beautiful verses are addressed to a Roman youth called Ligurinus. But he certainly had no animus against the opposite sex, celebrating it in some of the finest lines ever addressed by a man to a woman, however imaginary:

Quis multa gracilis te puer in rosa
Perfusus liquidis urget odoribus,
Grato, Pyrrha, sub antro?
Cui flavam religas comam,
Simplex munditiis?

'What slim youngster drenched in liquid scents presses against you, Pyrrha, under some pleasing grotto? For whom are you binding back your blond hair in simple elegance?'

Other remarkable poets enjoyed the favour of Maecenas and, through him, the largesse of Augustus: Sextus Propertius, Tibullus. The characters of their poetry would recur in English verse up to the nineteenth century, thanks to the classical basis of upperclass English education: Propertius' Cynthia, and the girl whose slave Tibullus declares he is, Delia.

But the most irresistible of these poets, and the 'bad boy' of Augustan writing, was Ovid: Publius Ovidius Naso, born in a valley of the Apennines east of Rome, 43 BCE, died in exile on the western Black Sea coast in the village of Tomis (now Constanţa in Romania), c.18 CE, while his books were removed from Rome's public libraries on Augustus' orders. It might actually have been a lot worse, for he was allowed to keep his property in Rome. Exactly what Ovid had done to deserve this condign punishment – Augustus never banished another writer of quality – is not really certain, and Ovid himself never did more than hint at it in his writing beyond saying that it was caused by a *carmen* (a song) and an *error* (a mistake). The mistake was probably sexual and it may have involved Augustus' wild and sexy granddaughter Julia, who was some twenty-five years younger than the poet and would herself be banished to a Mediterranean island for immorality at about the same time that Ovid was sent to Tomis. As for the disapproved song, any number of Ovid's would have fitted the bill. 'Posterity, recognize who it is you're reading, / the poet of fun, kindness, love,' declares his *Tristia* ('Lamentations'), written in exile, to assert his innocence. Witty, fluent, thrice married, with a worldly charm that shines through every line of his *Ars amatoria* ('The Art of Love') and his magnum opus, the *Metamorphoses*, Ovid was the first of the great literary *boulevardiers*, and to kick him out to a provincial hole like Tomis, whatever the rustic charms of its landscape and its women, was a terrible waste of life-enhancing talent:

> As I can,
> I solace myself with song.
> There is no one to listen.
> In pretence I spend the day.
> The fact that I am alive, that I put a firm front on hardship,
> That I look sorrow in the face,
> I owe to poetry. It offers me comfort,
> Rest and remedy,
> It is my guide and companion . . .
> Our age has produced great poets,
> But my reputation stands,
> There are many I rank above myself,
> But others rank me with them,
> And I *am* the best-seller.

No wonder that he was; no Roman writer, and few later ones, wrote as stylishly about sexual intrigue as Ovid. Here he is giving his advice to a girlfriend:

> And once you get to the bedroom
> Fill it with every delight; let's have no modesty there.
> Once you are out of there, though, abandon abandonment, darling –
> Bed is the only place where you can act as you please.
> There it is no disgrace to fling your dress in a corner,
> There it is no disgrace lying with thigh under thigh,
> There it is proper for tongues, as well as for lips, to be kissing,
> There let passion employ all the inventions of love.
> There use all of the words, the helpful cries, and the whispers,
> There let the squeak of the bed appear to be keeping in time.

And husbands, particularly older ones, are there to be cuckolded
by their lovelorn, randy wives:

> Tacticians recommend the night attack,
>   Use of the spearhead, catching the foe asleep,
> Lovers use them too – to exploit a sleeping husband,
>   Thrusting hard while the enemy snores.

Such cheerful promiscuity did not conform to the standards of
'family values' that Augustus was determined to reinforce in
Rome. Augustus believed in restraint; Ovid, no. Anyone who has
ever had hot sex on a hot afternoon is his co-conspirator: in comes
his Corinna –

> Sheer though it was, I pulled the dress away;
> *Pro forma*, she resisted, more or less.
> It offered little cover, I must say,
> And why put up a fight to save a dress?
> So soon she stood there naked, and I saw,
> Not only saw, but felt, perfection there,
> Hands moving over beauty without flaw,
> The breasts, the thighs, the triangle of hair.

Ovid's free sexuality certainly contributed to his popularity,
and is one of the reasons he is still read today, but the main
reason for his influence in Roman times – which rivalled that
of Virgil – was that his verse became Rome's main source for
Greek mythology. The divinities of Roman religion tended to
be nature spirits – Fortuna, Mens Bona – without personalities.
It was Ovid who gave the Roman gods faces – and genitals to
go with them. He did most to invent the idea of mythology
as entertainment, a comedy of manners, full of dramatic or
scandalous stories about the gods' doings on Olympus: as
Richard Jenkyns observed, 'Ovid is nearer to Offenbach than to
Homer.' He became the favourite and most imitated Latin poet
of the Italian Renaissance and was often rendered into English,

especially by Chaucer and Spenser. Echoes of him appear in Shakespeare and one of the greatest lines in Christopher Marlowe's plays, uttered by Dr Faustus as he awaits damnation, is quoted directly from Ovid: *O lente, lente currite, noctis equi,* 'Run slowly, slowly, horses of the night.'

We know little about Augustus' own sexual predilections. But we do know about some of his tastes in other areas, and particularly that of architecture and city planning. Literature would ensure some part of his cultural survival, but marble would do so even more solidly.

Augustus had a great enthusiasm for building. He wanted to make Rome unsurpassably beautiful. For that reason, it had to become Greek; but bigger. His famous declaration that he had found a city of mud-brick and left it marble was, to a surprising extent, true. The marble was more often a thick facing veneer over common brick than solid masonry blocks. But not always so. Much of it was of an intimidating, or inspiring, solidity, of which the extreme example was the enormous Forum of Augustus itself. He fulfilled Julius Caesar's plans for a monumental rebuilding – a creation, really – of the architecturally diffuse heart of Rome, which had been left undone by his murder. To say Augustus mobilized the Roman building industry is to understate it. He declared he had built (or restored) eighty-two Roman temples alone in one year – many gods, many temples – apart from other structures, and this was no mere boast.

The show-material was marble, the best available, from the Luna quarries in Carrara in the north. Luna marble was the finest available if you wanted perfect whiteness, which Augustus and his builders did. Its whiteness rivalled that of the moon, from which it took its name. Luna marble tended to be very homogeneous and, to the extent that any sedimentary and metamorphic rock can be, free of internal veins and cracks. This reduced the risk of unexpected disfigurements appearing in the whiteness of an architrave or, worse, in the cheek of a Venus or a general. On buildings it was combined with other marbles whose variety of origins symbolized the vast spread of the Roman Empire, which could bring any kind of stone from anywhere in the conquered world, from Asia, the Near East, and all over the Mediterranean. Pink marble came from the Greek island of Chios; a greeny-blue marble known as *cipollino* from Euboeia, yellow from north Africa. There were many others, though not as many as would be exploited by late imperial designers or, at the extreme, by those of Baroque Rome. The discreet use of bands and veneers of these stones enlivened what might otherwise have been a certain monotony of surface in Augustan buildings.

The best thing about Luna marble, apart from consistency of colour, was its firm crystalline structure. This made for an even 'grain' in the stone, which in turn favoured crispness and depth of detail. And some details of Augustan buildings were very elaborate. The principal architect and theorist of the Augustan age was Vitruvius Pollio, who wrote the fundamental text on classical Roman building, the ten-volume *De Architectura* (25–23 BCE) – the only treatise on fine building to survive from ancient Rome. He discussed not only architecture but also town planning, water supply, engineering and war engines, but his views on architecture, set forth in great detail, lay at the core of European practice for the best part of a thousand years. No actual buildings by him have survived and practically nothing is known about his life, except that he served Augustus' army as an artillery engineer, designing *ballistae* and siege engines.

Vitruvius was intensely alert not only to the practical aspects of building, but also to its metaphorical content. Thus his disquisitions on the 'orders' of architecture and their meanings. Doric, Ionic, Corinthian, Tuscan – each one had its human and divine significance:

The temples of Minerva, Mars and Hercules will be Doric since the virile strength of these gods makes daintiness entirely unsuitable to their houses. In temples to Venus, Flora, Proserpine, Spring-Water and the Nymphs, the Corinthian order will be found to have special significance because these are delicate divinities and so its rather slender outlines, its flowers, leaves and ornamental volutes will lend propriety where it is due. The construction of temples of the Ionic order to Juno, Diana and Bacchus . . . will be in keeping with the middle position which they occupy: for such buildings will be an appropriate combination of the severity of the Doric and the delicacy of the Corinthian.

The most prominent of the Augustan 'orders' was a new type of capital, known as 'Composite', which combined the acanthus leaves of the Corinthian order with the volutes of the Ionic. This hybrid became one of the typical forms of Augustan architecture but it required rather more skill to carve successfully than most Roman stonemasons had. Greek marble-cutters had to be imported, because Greece trained better stonemasons than first-century BCE Rome.

These Greek workmen did more than carve architectural details. They did statues too; someone had to churn out all those effigies of the Princeps and his family. This helps account for the fact that the portraiture of the imperial period tends to lack the realistic, sometimes sharply frank likenesses of earlier Roman portraiture. The carvers had never set eyes on Augustus and so had no first-hand idea of what he 'really' looked like, and no conception of his personality other than the one diffused by imperial propaganda. But Augustus was a god, and Greek sculptors were well used to depicting gods. This also helps account for a certain sameness in the representations of Augustus throughout his reign and across the Empire.

But more than flooding the culture with numberless coins, busts and statues, the Greeks had a profound and lasting influence on the physical city. Two monuments in Rome itself which clearly showed the continuing Greek influence on Roman art and architecture were the Forum of Augustus, finished around 2 BCE, and the Ara Pacis Augustae, dedicated in 9 BCE.

In layout the Forum is entirely Roman, as it should be: a

rectangular open space lined with porticoes, in which people met and business was done. One end was closed by a large temple on a high podium, that inheritance from more ancient Etruscan conventions; and there were statues of heroes of the state, including, of course, Augustus himself. But Greek details understandably insinuate themselves. The capitals of its columns are Corinthian; the presence of a line of caryatids (load-bearing, columnar figures of women) in the upper storey of the colonnades is a direct reminiscence of those on the porch of the Erechtheum in Athens.* The scale of the whole complex was immense. The columns of the temple were some eighteen metres high, made of the gleaming white Luna marble from the quarries of Carrara that was Augustus' architectural signature. The flooring of the colonnades, by contrast, which survives only as fragments, was done with the most highly coloured marbles in the Empire: Phrygian purple (*pavonazzetto*) from Turkey, Numidian yellow (*giallo antico*) from Tunisia, red and black *africano*.

The Ara Pacis Augustae, or Altar of Augustan Peace, is an even more direct quotation from Greek norms and forms. Its purpose is to celebrate the end of conflict and dissension – the settling of the Roman state by its great uniter, Augustus, who is seen as presiding over a Rome that has been reborn from the dissent that finished off the Republic. The altar rises on steps, themselves contained within high screen walls of Luna marble with open entrances on the east and the west sides. On either side of each entrance are mythological panels of carved stone. They depict the spiritual and material benefits of Augustus' reign, and are clearly by Greek artists. One of them, for instance, promises the return of the Golden Age. Here, enthroned at the centre of the panel, is *Natura naturans*, Nature being Nature – Mother Earth in her

---

* The Caryatids, bearing the architrave on their heads, were emblems of slavery. The city of Caria, in Asia Minor, had resisted the Athenians, and thenceforth its women were depicted as defeated load-bearers.

sweetest and most fertile guise, with two infants sporting in her arms. Fruit and flowers surround her, a cow and a sheep lie contentedly at her feet, and she is flanked by two benign nature spirits representing Ocean and Water. The mood and content are those of Virgil's fourth *Eclogue*, in which the poet tells of the coming age of Apollo:

> Ours is the crowning era foretold in prophecy:
> Born of Time, a great new cycle of centuries
> Begins. Justice returns to earth, the Golden Age
> Returns, and its first-born comes down from heaven above.
> Look kindly, chaste Lucina, upon this infant's birth,
> For with him shall hearts of iron cease, and hearts of gold
> Inherit the whole earth – yes, Apollo reigns now.
> And it's while you are consul – you, Pollio – that this glorious
> Age shall dawn . . .

Who is this first-born child 'from heaven above'? It is still a mystery. Christian interpreters after Virgil's death had no doubt that it was the infant Jesus, but the wish was certainly father to the thought: Virgil was not writing Christian prophecy, although many people have wished he was.

Elsewhere on the carved walls of the Ara Pacis, we see Augustus as Aeneas making sacrifice, in his fundamental guise as the peace-bringer, establishing the city of Rome, having at last transcended the dreadful conflict and loss of Troy. The lesson is not to be avoided: there is a saviour before us, a saviour who repeats the primal act of foundation by establishing the Roman state for the future in accordance with its ancient laws and pieties. What is more, the saviour's family is and always will be the metaphor of the good state. Such is the 'Augustan Peace'.

The other Augustan building that survives, after a fashion, in Rome and is a parallel to the Ara Pacis is Augustus' own family mausoleum, whose original form has been so broken down over the ages that, apart from its circular shape, it is hardly legible. The Augusteum (in which there remains, of course, not a speck of the dead emperor's dust) is really more an earthwork than a building – a big shallow cone, eighty-nine metres in diameter and forty-four high, reminiscent of much earlier Etruscan monuments. The first member of Augustus' family to be interred in it was probably his favourite nephew Marcellus, poisoned in 23 BCE by Augustus' third wife Livia, who wanted her own son Tiberius to inherit the throne. In less ancient times, once the remains of Augustus himself were lost, it acquired many uses, none of them particularly glorious; it was fortified and used as a military base by the Colonnas in the twelfth century, then it was quarried for travertine, and in 1354 the corpse of Cola di Rienzo, mutilated by the daggers of the Roman mob, was cremated in it. Later it became a huge kitchen garden and later still, when the fashion for things Spanish reached Rome in the nineteenth century, it was turned into a bull-ring. Not until the 1930s, when Benito Mussolini is said to have contemplated being buried in it, did it regain some of its archaeological dignity – a dignity now hopelessly compromised by the clutter of waste paper, sweet-wrappers, empty cigarette packets and other rubbish left on it by passing Romans.

Augustus' commitment to building was felt with particular zeal at the edges of Empire, where such major architecture was less dense. Some of the greatest structures of the Augustan era are 'provincial' in location – far from Rome, but governed by it – and yet as sophisticated as anything in Rome itself. One of the most beautiful of these Augustan monuments is the Pont du Gard, an aqueduct near Nemausus (modern Nîmes) in Provence, with its rhythm of arches spanning a valley; for those who have seen it, and perhaps even for those who only know it from photographs, this huge and exquisitely proportioned three-level structure is *the* aqueduct, the archetype of its genre.

Being a major provincial centre, the capital of Gallia Narbonensis, Nîmes also has an amphitheatre, seating some twenty-five thousand spectators and built towards the end of the first century CE. The Augustan jewel of Nîmes, however, is the temple honouring Augustus' grandsons, Caius and Lucius Caesar, known as the Maison Carrée or 'Square House' (*c.*19 BCE). It is extremely well preserved, probably because it was converted into a Christian basilica in the early Middle Ages. Some of its details, in particular the design of the Corinthian capitals, resemble those of the great temple of Mars Ultor dedicated a few years earlier in Rome, and they reflect Augustus' partiality for the Corinthian order. Likewise, the frieze decoration – continuous acanthus scrolls – mimics that of the Ara Pacis. The Maison Carrée had been enormously admired for centuries when it was first seen by an American, Thomas Jefferson, in 1784. He seized on its design as the ideal prototype of dignified, official architecture for the new conception of democratic politics which he had the honour to represent in France: noble and Augustan, yet fine-boned and somehow intimate. Thus the influence of the Maison Carrée crossed the Atlantic, supplying the prototype of the new 'State House', the capitol of Virginia. It was not a passive copy: Jefferson had to make changes, substituting Ionic capitals for the Corinthian ones, since he feared (no doubt correctly) that local Virginian masons would not be able to carve all those complicated acanthus leaves. But the Virginian Capitol in Richmond showed, in Jefferson's own words, that 'We wish to exhibit a grandeur of conception, a Republican simplicity, and that true elegance of Proportion, which correspond to a tempered freedom excluding Frivolity, the food of little minds.' How Augustus himself would have approved!

The first century CE also saw the decorative arts flourish in the private sphere. Probably the best paintings were imported from Greece, or done in Rome by Greek artists. There was a strong tradition of easel painting throughout the Greek and Roman world, but we only know this from literary sources – the works themselves, victims of time, have not survived except as fleeting glimpses. There is no sign that Roman walls in Augustus' time had anything comparable in quality and in charged, intricate grandeur to the red-background mural paintings of initiatory scenes in the Villa of the Mysteries in Pompeii, built in c.60 BCE.

Little is known of Roman garden design, but it existed, though whatever Augustan gardens there may have been were obliterated long ago by later building. One can infer its character from what survived in Pompeii – the fishponds and shell grottoes, the paved walks, vine arbours, pergolas and painted shrubberies. Floor mosaics were popular, whether made of pebbles or of glass tesserae. Middle-class Romans seem to have been excessively fond of kitsch ornamental sculpture, too: the garden of the Pompeiian house of Marcus Lucretius Fronto, if one can judge from photographs, looks like the terrace of Luigi's Pasta Palace in coastal New Jersey, crammed with sculptures that are more like garden gnomes – a Silenus standing in a *nymphaeum* and pouring water from a wineskin, birds, satyrs, a generic bearded herm, a cupid riding a dolphin. Some of this stuff may have been inherited, but most of it was undoubtedly turned out in local factories to the householder's order.

In the midst of all this building, what was the single most important monument built by the Romans, still visible in some part today? We think of 'monuments' as vertical, rearing up in stately fashion and visible from a distance. *Exegi monumentum aere perennius*, wrote the poet Horace: 'I have earned a monument more durable than bronze', meaning the fame of his own poetry.

But the greatest of the physical monuments, which occupied the best energies of Roman surveyors, planners, engineers, labourers, masons and slaves for centuries and made possible the growth and administration of the largest empire the world had hitherto known, was neither a mighty building nor a statue but a thing both ponderously physical and entirely horizontal and thus, at least from a distance, rather hard to see: certainly invisible, and very hard to imagine, as a whole. This was the enormous road system without which the Roman Empire could not have existed. Estimates of its size vary a good deal, depending on how many secondary and tertiary roads are figured in. But it was certainly not less than 80,000 kilometres and possibly as much as 100,000 or even 120,000, including its many bridges thrown over foaming rivers, culverts above swamps and tunnels hewn through mountainous rock. It was a stupendous feat of surveying, planning and labour, and all done without earth-moving machines, graders or explosives – just hand-tools and muscle.

You can no more imagine Roman power without its sustaining road network than you can imagine that of America's empire without radio, TV, telephones, the Internet and every other sort of electronic communication. It enabled information to pass between distant points faster than ever before in history. It took only eight days to ride across Italy from Rome to Brindisi along the Via Appia. The road had its own support system, the ancestor of the garages and rest-stops along today's autostrada – workshops and inns, well-equipped stables, vets for the horses. If your vehicle, of which the most common type was known as a *carpentum* (whence, 'car'), threw a wheel or broke an axle along the way, you could call for a mechanic or *carpentarius* (whence, 'carpenter') to repair it. If carless, the ordinary pedestrian could walk perhaps twenty kilometres in a day. A marching soldier might do thirty to thirty-five.

In the past, other great imperial powers (the Egyptians, and in Persia the Achaemenids) had road systems, sometimes large and well-maintained ones. But either their use was restricted (in Egypt, all roads were royal and off-limits to commoners) or they were poorly integrated with existing ports, making the relations of land and sea transport decidedly iffy. The Roman system worked with a smoothness never achieved before in history, and every *civis romanus* (Roman citizen) who had anything to move – an army, a wagon-train, a roll of papyrus with an important or trivial message, a basket of melons – had access, either personally or through his representatives and clients, to it. From the point of view of trade and strategy, nothing like the roads of Rome had ever been imagined, let alone built, before. Without the roads the strategy could not have existed. The administration of so many subgroups within an empire was extremely time-consuming. Speed of communication and accurate placement of force were essential. Imperial cohesion, then as now, depended on communication.

The size of the road network, given the labour required to

create it, is astonishing now and was almost inconceivable two millennia ago. It encircled the entire Mediterranean basin. Given enough time, a traveller on horseback or in a wheeled vehicle who started out from Rome and headed east through Ariminum (modern Rimini), then through Thessalonika towards Byzantium (not yet named after the emperor Constantine), and crossed into Asia could follow the same road south through Antioch, Damascus and Gaza and then have before him, still fully paved and serviced, the long westwards coastal run through Alexandria, Cyrene and Leptis Magna that would eventually finish at Banasa in what is now Morocco. There, he might find himself staring across the narrow strait that divided Spain from north Africa at another traveller who had taken another Roman road west along the bottom of Europe, through Arelate (modern Arles) and Narbo (modern Narbonne), across the maritime foot of the Pyrenees to Tarraco (Tarragona), west from there to Caesaraugusta (Saragossa), and thence southward to Hispalis (Seville) and Gades (Cádiz), which gazed on the north African coast. The Roman geographer Strabo believed that more than 3,500 miles of roads had been completed by the Romans on the Iberian peninsula by 14 CE, and this total would presently rise to some 10,000.

To the north, the pattern was much the same. The conquered territories carried the mark of their subjugation in the form of Roman roads. One such road linked Mediolanum (modern Milan) to Augusta Vindelicorum (Augsburg) and so along the valley of the Rhine to Mogantiacum (Mainz) and Colonia Agrippina (Cologne). France was webbed with paved routes, from Lugdunum (Lyons) to Rotomagus (Rouen). And of course the network spread across the Channel to Britannia, thrusting north to link up with Hadrian's Wall, which was built to frustrate the hostile Scots in 122–5 CE. The roads' construction hardly varied, and depended entirely on exactingly supervised slave and military labour. First a large trench was dug, six or seven metres wide and perhaps 80 centimetres deep. Both sides of it were lined with *gomphi* or kerbstones, and then the roadbed was filled with layers of sand, gravel and small rocks, well pounded in. The final surface was given by flat slabs of stone, keyed together. The road-builders took care to give the surface a camber, so that water would run off to the sides.

Not all Roman roads were like this. Many were cambered, edged but unpaved. Some, like the great military road that linked Carthage to Theveste in north Africa, were paved and assiduously maintained. These included the Via Appia between Rome and Capua, and the Via Egnatia across the Balkan peninsula from the Adriatic to the Aegean – which would be extended to Constantinople. But many roads disintegrated over time, from the stress of wheeled traffic, and would hardly be traceable today but for their surviving milestones, squat cylindrical columns which indicated the traveller's distance from the nearest major city. (The 'Roman mile' was about 10 per cent shorter than the modern mile at 1,620 yards.) Nevertheless the Roman road system was by far the most elaborate and far-reaching that human ingenuity would produce until the nineteenth century in Europe. Naturally, it long outlasted Augustus' own lifetime and was one of the most valuable parts of the enormous legacy that he left to his successors.

Augustus ruled Rome for almost forty-five years, dying a month before his seventy-seventh birthday. He had what he had asked the gods to send him: a quick and painless death. Though there were rumours that he had died of eating some poison-smeared figs brought to him by his wife Livia, this was only gossip. The transition of power went smoothly: Livia's eldest son by him, Tiberius, was Augustus' main heir and received the *imperium*. No one expected that anyone could measure up to the immense achievements of the Princeps; and of course, neither Tiberius nor anyone else did so. Dying, according to Suetonius, '[f]inally he kissed his wife with "Goodbye, Livia; never forget whose wife you have been."' It cannot have been a much needed injunction.

❧ 3 ❧
THE LATER EMPIRE

We are used to thinking of most Roman emperors after Augustus, with the exception (thanks to Robert Graves' sympathetic novels) of Claudius, as beastly degenerates – the proof that absolute power corrupts absolutely. It is not true, but one can understand why so many have imagined it was.

The most prominent offenders were those two reliable crazies Gaius Julius Caesar Germanicus, known as 'Caligula' (12–41 CE), and Lucius Domitius Ahenobarbus (37–68 CE), or Nero. Caligula got his pet name from the legions – the word roughly translates to 'Bootikins' – by wearing tiny versions of the legionaries' combat boots, *caligae*, as a child, when he was the mascot of the Rhine armies, shortly after the death of his much adored father Germanicus in 19 CE. The one thing everyone knows about him is that he was quite mad and excessively fond of his horse Incitatus (a name which meant, roughly, 'Go-Go'). Not only did he give this animal a marble stable, an ivory stall, purple blankets, slaves and a jewelled collar, but he actually appointed it consul. Or so the story goes. There is, however, no evidence that he made any such promotion. Consul Go-Go may just have been palace gossip of a somewhat recherché sort. Suetonius, our only ancient source on this, merely writes that 'It is said that he even planned to award Incitatus a consulship' – and planning something is not the same as doing it. The consul-horse story is likely no more than a variation on one of the twisted jokes Caligula was fond of making, as appears from other examples. One can imagine him losing his temper with the unfortunate Senate and calling its members dumber than his horse.

Can anything be said for Caligula? Probably not much, although the Roman gladiators and their owner-managers were doubtless grateful for his obsessional interest in arena fighting. However, he did make distinct contributions to public works. Realizing that the water supplies of Rome's seven aqueducts were not enough for a growing city he ordained the construction of two more, the Aqua Claudia and the Anio Novus, though he did not live long enough to see either completed; they were finished by his successor, Claudius. He began a project which (until Claudius finished it) kept thirty thousand men busy for eleven years levelling and tunnelling a mountain to drain the Fucine Lake in central Italy – a Roman equivalent to the appalling labours to which Stalin's political slaves would be condemned in digging the White Sea canal.

Without question, however, Caligula's most popular contribution to the architecture of Rome was on the Ager Vaticanus, an enormous circus or race-course known as the Circus of Gaius and Nero. Almost all of it lies underneath the basilica and piazza of St Peter, and there is a simple and logical reason for this. This was the circus where Nero put Christians to death in the spectacular persecution that followed the fires of 64 CE, for which the members of that sect were blamed. Early Christian tradition also held that it was the site of St Peter's martyrdom. Both Caligula and Nero were obsessive enthusiasts for chariot-racing, and they competed with the professionals on this track.

The much later emperor Elagabalus, who reigned from 218 to 222 CE, drove *in Vaticano* too, except that his chariot was drawn not by horses but by a team of four elephants, which does not suggest lightning speed, especially since his ponderous *équipe* kept knocking over tombs on the way. Elagabalus lives in legend as the demented homosexual transvestite who once arranged for his guests to be smothered in rose petals, dropped through trapdoors in the ceiling of his palace. His sexuality made Caligula's seem almost routine, although the two were not dissimilar; Elagabalus surrounded himself with actors, dancers and charioteers, all seeking to outdo one another in perversity. He was at least bisexual enough to have three wives: Julia Paula (who lasted one year),

Aquilia Severa (a Vestal Virgin, whom he married, divorced and married again, each time for a year) and Annia Faustina, a relative of the late, great Marcus Aurelius whom he seems to have espoused for the sake of prestige. She, too, lasted a year.

To make quite sure that he had something for everyone, Elagabalus also caused annoyance to religious conservatives by bringing his own god with him from the east, the black stone of Emesa, itself an object of reverence, representing Baal. Having been proclaimed emperor in 218 by rebellious legions of eastern troops, he was persuaded by his grandmother – a fearsome old harpy who dominated him completely and, in effect, ran the palace with his mother – to adopt his cousin Severus Alexander as his son and Caesar in 221. Perhaps inevitably, this lad's presence sent Elagabalus into shrieking fits of jealousy: the western imperial troops liked Severus better than the emperor. Elagabalus planned to have him killed, but the soldiers killed him instead, with his mother. Thus perished the only emperor who gave Caligula some competition as the most dissolute in Roman history.

The personal behaviour of both Caligula and Nero fluctuated, according to the rather meagre reports it left – mainly in the writings of Suetonius – between the eccentrically aesthetic and the utterly mad, the indulgent and the insanely cruel. Caligula is said to have raped his sister Drusilla, and to have made a habit of public incest with her and two other sisters at banquets, while (one imagines) the less than enthusiastic guests stared in glum silence at their roast peacock. He could also be even more public in his entertainments. It was Caligula who habitually condemned criminals *ad bestias* (to be devoured by wild beasts in the arena), or had them forced into narrow cages where they were sawn in half – 'merely for criticizing his shows [or] failing to swear by his Genius'. What made life under Caligula especially difficult was that he expected to be applauded, not just by his courtiers but by the whole Roman public, as a great tragic-comic and sporting personality. Gladiator, singer, dancer, chariot-racer, actor: there was nothing he did not excel at. Perhaps there is a touch of Caligula in every showbiz star, but Caligula himself was *all* Caligula, and nobody who outdid him in performance was likely to live long. Besides, he was no fool in literary matters. He might rave and shout but he knew all his references. The emperor had a captive audience, and he knew it. To imagine a more modern, though hardly more threatening, equivalent one should perhaps think of Adolf Hitler singing at Bayreuth, with a member of the Gestapo posted behind each seat in the theatre.

But some of his efforts at self-dramatization (and they were many) defy any attempt at rational explanation. Suetonius relates how, while on campaign in Gaul facing the English Channel, Caligula had had his men drawn up in battle array, backed by various engines of war – *ballistae* and the like – pointing at the distant coast of England. He then boarded a trireme and put to sea, for a short distance. Then his warship turned round and brought him back to shore, where he clambered up on its high poop and shouted the order 'Gather sea shells!' Nonplussed but obedient to their commander-in-chief, his troops did so, filling their helmets and tunics with what Caligula termed 'plunder from the sea, owed to the Capitol and the Palace'. He then promised every man in his army a bonus of four *solidi* or gold pieces, though there is no record that this was actually given out. The sea-shells were dispatched back to Rome as 'booty'. As Caligula's most recent biographer has written with some understatement, 'This episode has provided much grist for the scholarly mill.'

It may be that this bizarre incident was nothing more than training manoeuvres; but this was winter, the weather and the seas were adverse, and even if Caligula (who was terrified of the sea, and could not swim) had not realized it, any of his captains could have enlightened him about the impossibility of launching an invasion of Britain at that time of the year. No matter: he planned an ovation for himself on having invaded Britain and he even chose some sturdy Gauls to grow their hair long, dye it red, and act like conquered soldiers, which in a general way they were. But it was not enough for Caligula to be fêted and admired as a hero, the conqueror of Germany and Britain. He was determined to be worshipped as a living god. Now it was true that previous emperors had been seen, and within limits revered, as divine. Virgil included Octavian/Augustus as one of the *presentes deos* ('gods amongst us') and it was common in the Greek east of the Empire to pay divine honours to members of the imperial family. But divine homage to living emperors was far less usual in Rome itself than in the external Empire, the definition of divinity itself could be rather fuzzy, and in any case some emperors found it excessive, even embarrassing: Tiberius, for instance, refused to allow a temple to be dedicated to himself and Livia in 25 CE. Dead emperors could be worshipped as gods and have temples dedicated to their cult, but Caligula was the first (though not the last) to take this a step or two further. According to Suetonius he decided to live with Jupiter Optimus Maximus on the Capitoline. It was said that he planned to have Phidias' renowned sculpture of Olympian Zeus transferred there as his cult image, presumably given a new head, but was somehow dissuaded; he then had a full-length statue of himself, life-size, made in gold. Every day the slaves dressed it in a different outfit from Caligula's extensive wardrobe.

All in all, perhaps the most surprising thing about Caligula's short and demented reign – he died in 41 CE at twenty-eight, assassinated by the officers of his own guard, having ruled Rome for not quite four years – was that he managed to last as long as he did. What happened to the sea-shells is unrecorded.

His successor was a man widely regarded as the family idiot, humiliated and condescended to by his nephew Caligula: Tiberius Claudius Drusus (10 BCE–54 CE), known to history simply as Claudius, the last male member of the Julio-Claudian line. But he was popular with the Roman public, and with the army as well; certainly he was much better respected and liked than the repulsive Caligula. Nothing, one might have supposed, prepared him for the *imperium*. He was lame; he drooled and twitched when excited; and some chroniclers, notably Suetonius and Tacitus, treated him as a ridiculous figure, inept and stammering. Some of his traits were consistent with Tourette's syndrome, but this is not easily judged. Moreover his sexual tastes, compared to those of most Roman emperors, seemed downright eccentric, almost perverse: according to Suetonius he had no interest in men, only in women. Unfortunately he had a way of marrying the wrong ones: first a lumpish horse of a creature named Urgulanilla, then a termagant called Aelia Paetina, then his first cousin Valeria Messalina, a money-crazed nymphomaniac who, according to the often unreliable testimony of Tacitus, once competed with a prostitute to see which of them could take on the most sexual partners in a night; and finally Agrippina, a descendant of Augustus and the mother of Nero. From childhood on, Claudius was mercilessly bullied and deprecated as a fool by his mother Antonia and his grandmother Livia, and this seems to have set a pattern of domination by scheming women which infected his entire married career.

Claudius was fifty years old when Caligula was murdered. In the general confusion that followed the assassination, he ran into hiding behind a door-curtain in the palace. One of the guardsmen, Gratus by name, spotted his feet beneath the curtain and pulled him out. Claudius, thinking his last moment had come, clasped the soldier's knees and started begging for mercy – but to his mingled terror and relief, the soldier bore him off to the palace guards' quarters, where he was acclaimed as the new emperor. He was the first emperor to be proclaimed by the Praetorian Guard rather than by the Senate; but obviously, the Senate had little choice in the matter.

This may not have been a very auspicious start to his reign, but Claudius proved to be a surprisingly good ruler – much better, certainly, than either his crazed predecessor Caligula or *his* predecessor, the mediocre Tiberius, who after a promising start, with wide military experience on the German frontier, ended his reign as an elderly, cruel debauchee on the island of Capri while leaving the effective control of Rome to his Praetorian captain Sejanus. Claudius, of whom less had been expected, did much more. He considerably enlarged and strengthened the Empire by planting *coloniae*, fortified settlements, in remote zones; such places as Colchester in Britain and Cologne in Germany were originally

Claudian settlements. To Claudius belongs the distinction of leading the successful conquest of Britain, which began in 43 CE. Having captured the British general Caractacus, he spared his life and treated him with unusual clemency. Caractacus was allowed to live out his natural life on land given to him by the Roman state, instead of being garrotted in prison, the usual fate of those who dared lead a resistance against Rome. This, one need not doubt, did wonders for the colonial relationship between the British and their conquerors.

Claudius was a gifted administrator with (as it must have seemed to citizens who had grown used to the arbitrary habits of Caligula) an intense regard for the minutiae of the law. He presided at public trials, viewing his presence there as both a duty and a pleasure, although some of his edicts make strange reading today; one of them, according to Suetonius, promoted unrestrained farting at table as a health measure. In particular he was committed to programmes of public works – the building of aqueducts, the draining of the Fucine lake. (The latter almost proved a disaster; due to miscalculation by the engineers, the lake waters came rushing out too soon and backed up in a too narrow sluice, nearly drowning Claudius and his party, for whom a great banquet had been prepared on the bank of the channel.) The Fucine drainage scheme, underwritten by a syndicate of businessmen in return for ownership of the reclaimed land, may have taken eleven years, but is said to have eventually returned a profit. Probably the most important of these works was Claudius' creation of a deep-water harbour at Ostia, complete with a tall lighthouse; this transformed Rome's access to Mediterranean trade, especially during the winter storm season.

His main contribution to popular entertainment was his unbridled enthusiasm for arena fights. Claudius – according to Suetonius, our only source on this – was unusually bloodthirsty, even by Roman standards. If an accused man was to be tortured to extract testimony, Claudius liked to watch. Sometimes, when he had spent the whole morning watching gladiator fights and wild-beast shows, 'he would dismiss the audience, keep his seat, and not only watch the regular combats but extemporize others between the stage carpenters . . . as a punishment for the failure of any mechanical device'. Nothing survives of Claudius' work as a historian – which is a considerable loss, since he wrote many books about Roman, Etruscan and even Carthaginian history from sources that were extant two thousand years ago but have now disappeared.

He was gluttonous, and this led to his death. His favourite dish was mushrooms, and at a family banquet his last wife, Agrippina, served him a dish of *funghi porcini* laced with poison. This killed him, conveniently preparing for the succession of Agrippina's son, Lucius Domitius Ahenobarbus, better known as Nero.

Nobody could say that Nero lacked the advantages of education as well as birth.

Coming from Spain, Lucius Annaeus Seneca (d. 65 CE) was Nero's tutor, and a stupendously voluble writer; his surviving prose works alone run to over a thousand closely printed pages. He took great pride in his Stoicism, but no Stoic was ever longer-winded or more self-infatuated. He could argue both sides of a case – when Claudius died it was Seneca who composed the eulogy delivered on him by Nero, his successor, but also Seneca who wrote a satire on the departed emperor, the 'Apocolocyntosis' or 'Pumpkinification' of Claudius, who was imagined as turning into a dim-witted, sententious vegetable-god. Seneca was a hypocrite almost without equal in the ancient world. He sang the praises of moderation: 'To be a slave to self is the most grievous kind of slavery; yet its fetters may easily be struck off . . . Man needs but little, and that not for long.' Fine words, which unhappily bear little relation to the real facts of Seneca's life: he was a mercilessly greedy usurer. Few can have mourned him when, on direct orders from Nero, he committed suicide by opening his veins in a hot bath.

Nero's most notorious act of vandalism was (supposedly) burning much of the city of Rome.

It is not sure that, as legend durably insists, he fiddled while doing so – though a keen amateur musician, his preference was for giving long vocal recitatives, generally of a tragic kind, some of whose titles – though, perhaps mercifully, not their libretti – have been preserved: among these were *Canace in Childbirth*, *Hercules Distraught* and *Orestes the Matricide*, in which he would wear the masks of heroes, gods or goddesses modelled either on his own face or on the features of a current mistress.

Nevertheless, the image of Nero fiddling away while the flames leapt upward has entered the English language (and most others) and is unlikely to vanish soon. Even without the accusations of arson, Nero's treatment of others – including his own family – was, to put it mildly, defective. The list of his victims was long, and it included his mother Agrippina, with whom he was alleged to commit frequent incest. He had no hesitation in ordering the murder of anyone who displeased him, however trivial or fictional the offence. Not even his wives were exempt: his empress Octavia, daughter of Claudius and Messalina, died in exile on the desert island of Pandateria in 62 CE, thus freeing Nero to marry, deify and then kick to death (in pregnancy) his second spouse, Poppaea, merely because she had dared to complain that he came home late from the races. He had his aunt Domitia Lepida murdered with an overdose of laxative. In all, as Suetonius remarked, 'there was no family relationship which Nero did not criminally abuse'. He made every effort to mock real family relations by parodying them: thus his obsessive relation with his catamite Sporus, whom he castrated and then married. 'The world,' remarked Suetonius acidly, 'would have been a happier place if Nero's father Domitius had married that sort of wife.'

It is said that for his own amusement Nero launched an attack on several granaries near the future site of his Golden House, knocked down their walls with siege engines and then had his troops set the contents ablaze. Naturally he found a public reason for this – slum clearance. The old buildings were decrepit, and he was only finishing off a fire hazard. However, there is no evidence that Nero was personally responsible for the fires that broke out and spread during demolition. They could have been, and probably were, entirely an accident. If Rome was anything like seventeenth-century London – and it was, being overcrowded and a firetrap, filled with tinderbox *insulae* which would go up at a breath and were unprotected by water pumps and safety ordinances – then living in it must have been a constant menace, especially since the reliance on open braziers in cold weather must have filled their rooms with carbon monoxide and further reduced the level of sleepers' consciousness.

Whatever their origin, these fires soon joined up in one continuous blaze, lasted for six days and seven nights, and destroyed not only the rickety *insulae* of Rome's public housing but also numerous mansions and temples dating back as far as the wars against Carthage and Gaul. It started on 18 June 64 CE, the exact anniversary of the burning of Rome by its Gallic invaders in 390 BCE. It did enormous damage not only to the residential quarters of the Aventine and Palatine hills but also to the Forum itself, most of whose monuments it destroyed. Nero is said to have revelled in watching the fires and it was rumoured that, to celebrate what he called 'the beauty of the flames', he donned the costume of a tragedian and proceeded to sing, from start to finish, a lengthy dramatic piece about the burning of Troy entitled *The Fall of Ilium*. This may perhaps have been heartless but it is hard to think what action of a practical sort Nero could have taken to extinguish the flames. What could he have done, flouncing around in his fancy dress, except get in the way of the hard-pressed firemen? And what person, emperor or commoner, would fail to get the best vantage-point from which to view the irresistible spectacle of a city fire?

This tale is of course the origin of the much-worn saying. According to Tacitus the fire broke out among the shops of the Circus Maximus and ran through the level portions of the city that contained no masonry walls to interrupt its spread. It outstripped the puny efforts to control the flames, 'so completely was the city at its mercy owing to the narrow winding lanes and irregular streets which characterized old Rome'. When the blaze took hold in earnest Nero was not in Rome, but in Antium (Anzio), south of the city. Nothing, it seemed, could contain the flames, but Nero, hurrying back to Rome, threw open the Campus Martius, the public structures of Agrippa, and even his own gardens, and had emergency shelters erected in them. But the effect of such well-meant measures was less than it might have been, because by now the *plebs* of Rome were convinced of the rumour that their emperor, the deified firebug, was to blame for the destruction of so much of the city.

After this veritable orgy of site clearance, Nero's own idea of a suitable new building was the Domus Aurea or 'Golden House', one of the legendary structures of antiquity of which so little remains that one can form only the haziest idea of its splendours. There had been a huge palace linking the Palatine and Esquiline hills, and when it burned down Nero had it rebuilt with a statue of himself 120 feet high in the entrance hall (for comparison's sake, Bartholdi's Statue of Liberty in New York harbour is roughly 150 feet from toes to crown). Behind it, a pillared arcade ran for a mile, flanked, said Suetonius, 'by buildings made to resemble cities' and artificial woodlands in which every kind of domestic and wild animal sauntered and grazed at its ease. Inside, the walls of the Golden House earned its name by being both gilded and inlaid with mother-of-pearl and precious stones. Nero's dining-rooms had ceilings of ivory fretwork which, on command, released gusts of perfume or rose petals on the reclining guests. The main dining-room, where Nero held his feasts, was circular and its entire roof, fretwork and all, revolved in a stately harmony with the sky, day and night. 'He believed,' wrote Suetonius of Nero, 'that fortunes were made to be squandered, and whoever could account for every penny he spent seemed to him a stingy miser.' Nero's own comment on the Golden House, once it was finished, was merely that now, at long last, he could begin to live like a human being.

Little enough is left of the Domus Aurea, and much of that remains to be excavated. The enormous Baths of Trajan were built on top of Nero's palace. Unfortunately most of its valuable décor – the coloured marble veneers, the gilded panels, and of course the carved ivory – was stripped and looted as soon as the palace was abandoned; all that remained was the painted plaster on the walls of secondary rooms. But this fascinated the artists who, in the sixteenth century, burrowed down through the baths into the remains of the palace to study them, and it became the basis of whole arrays of light and playful décor known as *grotteschi*, 'grotesques', because they had been found in 'grottoes'. These would influence European design and décor, especially through the work of Englishmen like the Adam brothers, for two centuries. The foremost exponent of decorations based on the remains of the Golden House was Raphael, who admired and copied them and was followed not only by other artists, but by a horde of intrepid sightseers who braved the subterranean dark with torches, and sometimes left their names scratched on the mouldering walls – among them, Casanova and the Marquis de Sade. Raphael would use *grotteschi* for his decoration of the Loggetta in the Vatican (c.1519), and they gave him a limitless fund of invention and caprice – even though, as the art historians Mary Beard and John Henderson mischievously noted, the subsequent popes were parading about in what were, in effect, copies of Nero's servants' quarters.

Under the original ceilings and beside the Domus Aurea's scented pools, Nero would give himself up (wrote Suetonius) to 'every kind of obscenity'. These included dressing in the skins of wild animals, and attacking the genitals of men and women who stood helplessly bound to stakes in the imperial gardens. Presumably it is not possible for one man to practise all the known or imaginable sexual perversions; but Nero clearly had as impressive a repertoire as any Roman. And he famously compounded them by fastening the blame for Rome's misfortunes on one particular group. These were the tiny sect known as the Christians, whom he persecuted with quite demented severity after the fire.

It had not taken long for the cause of the great fire that had consumed so much of the city to be assigned, by the plebeians, to the emperor himself. For that reason alone, Nero had to find someone else, another group, to divert the blame for it: and that was the Christians. The historian Tacitus explained why: these

Christians were already 'hated for their abominations', not only in Judaea but also in Rome, 'where all things horrible or shameful from all parts of the world collect and become popular'. Those who confessed, on interrogation, to being Christian were convicted 'in great numbers' – 'not so much of guilt for the conflagrations as of hatred of the human race', and then 'mockery was added to their deaths':

> They were covered with the skins of wild beasts and torn to death by dogs, or they were nailed to crosses and, when daylight failed, were set on fire and burned to provide light at night. Nero had offered his gardens for the spectacle, and was providing circus games, mingling with the populace in the dress of a charioteer ... Hence, though [the Christians] were deserving of the most extreme punishment, a feeling of pity arose as people felt they were being sacrificed not for the public good but because of the savagery of one man.

As indeed they were. The first representation in art of Christ crucified is a derisive graffito from somewhere on the Palatine Hill, near the Circus Maximus. It shows a crudely scratched figure with a donkey's head, hanging on a schematic crucifix, with a man raising his arms in homage and adoration. A scrawled caption says, 'Alexamenos worships his god'. The donkey, in popular Roman lore, was an utterly despised animal, lower than a pig. The graffito is no older than the second century CE – which suggests how very slowly the story of Christ's crucifixion seeped into popular awareness. 'It is now generally accepted,' writes an authoritative scholar of the subject, 'that there are no securely datable Christian archaeological remains before the second century or about AD 200.'

'The blood of martyrs,' a famous saying went, 'is the semen of the Church.' This was indisputably true. How did Christianity manage to detach itself from the peculiar tangle of competing creeds that jostled one another in the fourth-century Roman world? There were mystery cults of varying degrees of eccentricity, drama and peculiarity. There was Mithraism, a powerful import from the Middle East, which had a strong following among the Roman military. Rome harboured a large minority population of émigré Jews, who of course stood by the tenets of their faith and practised its rituals. Deified emperors received various forms of devotion. There were cults of Isis, Dionysus, Hermes, Serapis and of the patron of doctors, Asclepius, the human healer transmuted into a dog. Often, when the cult of a spring-goddess or a fertility-god had been established for years, it was merely renamed and began a new votive life. The Christian belief that gods were likely to punish disobedient humans was not, on the whole, a feature of pagan religion. The weight of guilt or sin did not bear heavily on the worshippers. The pagan moral world was, in this respect, as in others, a universe away from the spiritual environment of Judaism and Christianity, so largely animated by guilt and the desire for expiation and forgiveness.

But the greatest difference was in ideas of past and future. Roman religion presented its faithful with only the haziest conception of an afterlife. Its dreams of felicity were focused on a long-past Golden Age; perhaps it could be recaptured, but it was certain that the present was a descent from it. Christianity, however, had no powerful notions of lost happiness in an earlier life. What mattered most to the Christian was happiness or anguish after death, both eternal, both irrevocable. With the help of Jesus, the Christian soul had charge of its fate to a degree not imagined by classical religion. Hence the unimagined power of Christianity. Now the Christian and pagan paths were about to cross, with totally unforeseeable results.

A visit to the decaying remains of the Golden House of Nero can be disappointing, and there is unlikely to be much to see in another fifty or a hundred years. The most complete Roman building to survive from antiquity was constructed somewhat later, during the reign of the emperor Hadrian. This is the enormous concrete and stone masterpiece of engineering that is the Pantheon. It was built to replace the original Pantheon, constructed and dedicated in the aftermath of Octavian's victory at

Actium by Marcus Agrippa during his third consulship, in 27 BCE.
This building burned down, along with others next to it, in a huge
fire in 80 CE. It was rebuilt in its present form in about 125 CE by
the emperor Hadrian. Rather confusingly it bears on its pediment
the legend M.AGRIPPA.L.F.COS.TERTIUM FECIT, which
stands for *Marcus Agrippa, Lucii filius, consul tertium fecit*, meaning
'Marcus Agrippa, son of Lucius, consul for the third time, made
this'. But he did not make it – Hadrian did. Agrippa was long dead
(12 BCE) by the time the Pantheon was finished.

The Greek word *pantheion* means 'all the gods', which makes
the building polytheistic. Cassius Dio, a Graeco-Roman senator
writing some seventy-five years after the present Pantheon was
built, opined that 'It has this name ... because its vaulted roof
resembles the heavens.'

In the audacity and thoroughness of its engineering, in the
grand harmony of its proportions and in the eloquent weight of
history with which it is imbued, the Pantheon is certainly the
greatest of all the surviving structures of ancient Rome. The
Colosseum exceeds it in mass and size, but it is the form of the
Pantheon that elicits one's amazement: that huge dome, opened
at the top by an oculus which seems not merely to show but to
admit the sky, is a landmark in the history of construction and,
one might add, of architectural metaphor. Even today, two millennia after it was finished, the alert visitor is likely to be struck
less by its great age than by its inexhaustible newness. This is truly
Roman architecture, not Greek. Greek building was a matter of
straight posts and straight lintels. The Roman genius was to conceive and build three-dimensional curved structures, of which the
Pantheon's dome is the sublime archetype. This could not be
done, at least not on any scale, in hewn stone. A plastic, mouldable
substance was needed, and the Romans found it in concrete,
whose use was unknown to Greek architecture.

Roman concrete was a structural ceramic that set hard, not
from the action of heat (as pottery does in a kiln) but from the
chemical interaction of hydrated (slurried or water-saturated)
ingredients. It consists of an aggregate (small pieces of hard stone)

mixed with a semi-liquid mortar of hydraulic cement, made from a mixture of water, lime and a crushed volcanic ash deposit known to the Romans as *pozzolana*. This thick liquid is then tamped into a mould, known as a 'form'. It may be reinforced with metal rods to increase its tensile strength, although this was not the Roman practice. Chemical changes in the mass as it dries make it set into a hard impervious block, whose shape is that of the negative space inside the form. The mould is dismantled and removed; the concrete block remains.

Ancient Roman builders would mix their ingredients, wet lime and volcanic ash, in a barrow, spread it over the rock fragments of the aggregate, and then pound it well together with a hefty wooden compactor known in English as a 'beetle'. The less the water, the better the amalgamation of mortar and aggregate, the stronger the result: and it is amazing what Roman builders could do by hand, without mechanical compactors, rotary mixers or any of today's motorized tools. Vitruvius' *Ten Books on Architecture* (*c.*25 BCE) recommended a ratio of one part of lime to three of *pozzolana* for buildings, and one to two for underwater work. *Pozzolana* concrete behaved like Portland cement. It also had the extraordinarily useful merit of drying under seawater, which made it invaluable for maritime structures; the emperor Claudius had a harbour mole built at Ostia by the simple expedient of using a whole large ship as a form, filling it with *pozzolana*, lime and water and then sinking it, so that it set into a (literally shipshape) block.

With concrete, the Romans could build aqueducts, arches, domes and roads; it opened up means of rapid transport, storage and defence that had not existed in earlier masonry cultures. Concrete built hundreds of bridges that gave the Roman army swift access to the most remote parts of the Empire. It was the stuff of power and discipline. It was ugly and always would be – the brief mid-twentieth-century vogue for *béton brut* produced some of the most hideous, grime-attracting surfaces in all architecture, as a visit to London's Festival Hall will confirm. But it could be rendered with stucco or faced with thin sheets of stone, and it was very strong and cheap, enabling very large structures to be built with it. And size – raw, powerful size – had great appeal to the Romans in building their empire, as it would to the Americans in building theirs two thousand years later.

The Pantheon is circular, and it rests on a ring beam of concrete 4.5 metres deep and more than ten metres wide. The drum walls are six metres thick, and solid: the only light for the interior comes from the great oculus in the dome above. The dome of the Pantheon was constructed from concrete elements shaped by wooden formwork. It was not necessary to do this in one continuous pour. What was essential was a complete control of the dimensions of the formwork, which produced the stepped coffering within the dome; of the angling of the elements, which gave a perfect circular shape to the oculus (8.92 metres in diameter, the edge originally ringed with bronze); and of the varying density of the concrete mix. This last was essential, because the dome, in the interests of structural stability, had to be lighter at the top than at the bottom; its thickness increases from 1.2 metres around the oculus to 6.4 at the bottom, where the base of the dome meets the drum. Moreover, the integrity of the structure depended on using a lighter aggregate at the top – pumice stone and tufa – than the brick and travertine at the base. The builders took care to add the concrete in small batches and tamp it very thoroughly to expel air bubbles and water before adding the next batch. In sum, the construction of this five-thousand-ton dome was a marvel of architectural forethought – what we would call systems planning today – and an architectural historian might well long for a sight of the wooden formwork, scaffolding and shuttering that its construction must have entailed.

The statistics, bare as they are, remain. With a diameter of 43.3 metres, it is the world's largest unreinforced concrete dome, surpassing the diameter of St Peter's cupola by just 78 centimetres. There are larger domes on earth. But they are segmental and reinforced with steel, like the 100-metre dome of the 1960 Palazzetto dello Sport in Rome. No modern architect would dare to attempt another Pantheon using the same structural principles.

Nobody would insure it. But the Pantheon has stood for nearly two thousand years and shows no prospect of collapse.

It has, however, endured some damage. Originally the great dome was sheathed in gilded bronze, all of which was plundered by the Christian (Byzantine) emperor Constans II in 655 CE. Pope Gregory III replaced it, more prosaically, with lead sheets a century later. It had long been believed that the Barberini pope Urban VIII, patron of Bernini, had the bronze beams of its portico removed, melted down, and recycled as the *baldacchino* in St Peter's and as cannons for the Castel S. Angelo. Alas, some historians now doubt this story.

Imperial Rome also gave birth to what must be, bar none, the greatest piece of narrative sculpture from the ancient world. It stands in the remains of the Forum Traiani, rising up as one of the chief landmarks of the city. Much of the sculpture of Trajan's enormous forum was destroyed in Christian times, either burned for lime or taken away to embellish other buildings – thus several reliefs on the Arch of Constantine (315/316 CE), showing battles between Romans and Dacians, were taken from the Forum, altered by inserting portrait heads of Constantine and Licinius, and installed on the Arch.

Trajan's Column, on the other hand, is virtually intact. However, it is still impossible to 'read' as a continuous story, because of its form: a continuous stone frieze, 700 feet long, carved in low relief and wrapped in a spiral around a 100-foot-high vertical cylinder. It is a huge ancestor of the comic strip. Other monuments to this great emperor have disappeared; there was, for instance, in the middle of the Forum of Trajan, a magnificent equestrian statue of the emperor, offered to him by the Senate but later destroyed in one of the barbarian invasions of Rome (or perhaps by the Catholics). But the column still stands, well preserved. It is an astonishingly ambitious piece of propaganda but there is no vantage-point from which it has ever been possible to see more than segments of the whole design, and of course (for a spectator at ground level) the detail towards the top tends to vanish in the recession of its perspective, although the artist or artists who designed it made an effort to counteract this by gradually increasing the height of the figures from 0.60 metres at the base to 0.90 at the top. It represents that frustration with narrative sequence which would not be conquered until the invention of the movie camera.

The column is carved from seventeen drums of Luna marble. Each drum is about ten feet in diameter and hollow inside, to accommodate a cramped spiral staircase of 185 steps, so that (with difficulty) one can climb to the top; the stair is lit by forty-three small slit windows which are virtually invisible from the outside. The drums were cut separately, but the matching of the figures and the lack of damage at the joints are such that it looks like one seamless cylinder. The sculptors were Roman artisans, many of whom must have been Greek slaves: the scenes are full of figures that descend from Hellenistic prototypes, and Greek-trained sculptors were usually preferred to Roman craftsmen. How many carvers worked on this enormous project is of course unknown, but there must have been many.

Dedicated in 113 CE, it commemorates Trajan's campaigns in the Dacian wars on the Danube frontier in 101–2 and 105–6 CE. For anyone with good binoculars, a sustaining interest in Roman military history and a crick-proof neck, this is a mesmerizing document, if 'document' is the right word for something so big, stony and solid. Nothing tells us so much about the Roman army at work – not just killing and capturing barbarians, but marching, bridging, foraging for supplies, maintaining weapons, building camps, listening to the speeches of its commanders and bearing its standards. Every detail of uniform, armour and weaponry is correct. So is the depiction of barbarian arms, which are prominently shown as military trophies on the column's rectangular base as well as in the scenes of conflict along the band. Throughout the narrative helix of 2,600 figures there are some sixty Trajans, speaking to the troops, receiving envoys, conferring with his generals, offering sacrifices to the gods. One may also notice a large river-god, the personification of the Danube, blessing the Roman army as it crosses. The dexterity with which this story is unrolled is still as amazing as the clarity of detail with which it is set forth in the stone.

Unfortunately the bronze statue of Trajan himself which used to stand atop the column was removed and melted down in Christian times, to be replaced in 1588 by one of St Peter, who had nothing to do with the Dacian wars. If you look closely at the base you can make out another relic of Christianization over the door to the column's interior – the outline of the roof of what was once a tiny church, S. Nicola de Columna, recorded in the early eleventh century but demolished by the sixteenth. The main feature of the interior, a gold urn containing Trajan's ashes, was inevitably looted long ago.

Of the phrases that have survived into English from classical Latin, certainly one of the best-known stands for social irresponsibility, fatuous hedonism: the public's desire for 'bread and circuses'. It comes from a satire of Juvenal, launched against the 'mob' of his fellow Romans of the first century CE. Juvenal has seen mob violence directed against Tiberius' right-hand man Sejanus, through his many public effigies:

The ropes are heaved, down come the statues,
Axes demolish their chariot-wheels, the unoffending
Legs of their horses are broken. And now the fire
Roars up in the furnace, now flames hiss under the bellows:
The head of the people's darling glows red-hot, great
Sejanus
Crackles and melts. That face only yesterday ranked
Second in all the world. Now it's so much scrap-metal,
To be turned into jugs and basins, frying-pans, chamber-
pots.
Hang wreaths on your doors, lead a big white sacrificial
Bull to the Capitol! They're dragging Sejanus along
By a hook, in public. Everyone cheers . . .
They follow fortune as always, and detest
The victims, the failures. If a little Etruscan luck
Has rubbed off on Sejanus, if the doddering Emperor

Had been struck down out of the blue, this identical rabble
Would now be proclaiming that carcase an equal successor
To Augustus. But nowadays, with no vote to sell, their motto
Is 'Couldn't care less'. Time was when their plebiscite
elected
Generals, Heads of State, commanders of legions; but now
They've pulled in their horns; only two things concern
them:
Bread and the Games.

Duas tantum res anxius optat / panem et circenses – the public
which once cared passionately about serious matters of power
and public welfare, such as consulships and the army, now merely
longs for two things, bread and circuses. One might suppose this
was a poet's licence, but it was closer to fact. The Caesars had
discovered one of the better aids to governing a large, potentially
unruly state, once the capacity for power inherent in citizenship
of a republic had been collapsed into the single power of the
dictator: keep the citizens diverted, at state expense. The immense
political power of amusement, and the social anaesthesia it fosters,
was something that no one had fully acknowledged before. The
Romans would use it to spectacular effect.

To wit, the Caesars underwrote leisure, the blank tablet on
which amusement is written. First, it created more public leisure
than any state had ever imagined giving its citizens, or ever would.
This became addictive. The Roman year was divided into days on
which ordinary business could be done (*dies fasti*) and days on
which it could not, for fear of offending the gods (*dies nefasti*). As
the number of leisure days or *dies nefasti* grew, so the number of
dies fasti had to shrink. Earlier on, in the time of the Republic,
Rome had holidays on which *ludi*, or games, were held in honour
of various gods; the Ludi Romani, lasting two weeks, began in
366 BCE, and these were joined over the next couple of centuries
by the Ludi Plebei, the Ludi Floreales (in homage to the goddess
Flora), and various others. In all, there were fifty-nine such holidays. But then, on top of these, one must add the thirty-four days

of games instituted on various pretexts by Sulla and the forty-five *feriae publicae* or general feast-days, such as the Lupercalia in February (celebrating Romulus' and Remus' nurture by the *lupa* or she-wolf), the Volcanalia in August, and the riotously entertaining Saturnalia in December. Then there were the various days that Roman emperors designated to honour themselves, or which were awarded them by an obsequious Senate. All in all, by the reign of emperor Claudius Rome had 159 public holidays a year – three a week! – most of which were accompanied by games and shows paid for with public money. And reckoning in the irregular feast-days that emperors were apt to decree on the slenderest pretexts, one might not be far off the mark in saying that imperial Rome had one holiday for every day of work.

This may seem an absurd disproportion to modern eyes, and indeed it is, but it kept the *plebs* in line and had two major side-effects. It meant that Rome was perennially short of useful, productive free labour, and this shortfall had to be made up by slaves, the only ones who did not share in the unremitting fun of the festivals; its dependence on slave labour meant that Rome would always lag in certain areas of technology and invention. And secondly, it meant that the food, handed out by the emperor's minions, was an essential accompaniment to the pacifying distraction of the circus games, since a man and his household must eat whether they work or not. The mob is volatile. A populace that is both hungry and bored is a powder-keg, and the successors of Augustus would take no such risk. At any time there were probably 150,000 people in Rome living on 'public assistance', meaning free food and games. To give them a common cause of anger might be politically risky.

In the short run, the addiction to state-sponsored amusement was very effective. 'The height of political wisdom,' the second-century commentator Marcus Cornelius Fronto called it. 'The success of government depends on amusements as much as on serious things. Neglect of serious matters entails the greater detriment, of amusements the greater unpopularity. The handouts of money are less eagerly desired than the shows.'

What were these shows? Basically they were of three kinds: horse-races, theatre and, most popular of all, gladiatorial combat.

The horse-races were run in 'circuses', race-tracks specially designed for them. Rome had three principal circuses: the Circus Flaminius, the Circus Gaii ('of Gaius', named after the emperor nicknamed Caligula, who had it built on the site of what is now the Vatican); and, grandest of all, as its name implies, the Circus Maximus. All have since been buried beneath the structures of a later Rome. The form of the circuses never changed, though their sizes did. Two long strips formed a rectangle with a half-circle at one end. The strip between them was called the *spina* or backbone. The public sat on long tiers of raked seats, parallel to the *spina* and facing it across the track. The Circus Maximus could hold some 250,000 spectators, though estimates vary; it was a gigantic structure, 600 metres long by 200 wide, or over a kilometre and a half per lap, of which there were normally seven per race. With a gross area of about 45,000 square metres, it had twelve times the area of the Colosseum.

Each driven by a single charioteer, the chariots would thunder around this track. The chariots, the horses and their drivers were kept in their *carceres* or starting-pens until the signal was given; then the doors would spring open, and the race would be on. The starting-pens were made of tufa, and the posts marking the turning-points were of wood. The emperor Claudius improved on this by having the pens reconstructed from marble and the turning-posts from gilded bronze, which gave an even grander aspect to the races. Some chariots were *bigae*, or two-horse rigs; others, *trigae*, three horses, *quadrigae* (four), and so on up; the most common and popular type of racer was drawn by four horses, but eight-horse chariots were not unknown.

The charioteers commonly began as slaves, and won their freedom through skill and ruthless success on the track. Driving to win in the circus was the most effective way for a fearless, illiterate athlete to rise above the mob and become a hero: a charioteer who consistently won was a star, he had the mob on his side and, besieged by groupies, was enormously rewarded both in prestige and in cash. Nothing essential would change between the day of the Roman chariot-hero and that of the modern stock-car racing star, except of course that two thousand years ago the charioteer did not get to endorse products and had to live on his prize money alone. But this could be enormous. Undoubtedly the most successful charioteer in history was Gaius Appuleius Diocles, originally from Lusitanian Spain, who competed in more than 4,200 races over a twenty-four-year career and retired in 150 CE, having reached his early forties and having won or been placed 2,900 times, amassing 35 million sesterces. But unsurprisingly, no other drivers had the skill, the stamina or the blind luck to equal this barely credible record. Some did very well: the charioteer Scorpus, for instance, won or was placed 2,048 times. But by far the more common fate of the charioteer was to end up in his early twenties dead or a crippled pauper, crushed under the wheels of his opponents.

Theatrical shows were popular with the Roman mob but they could hardly compare with the drawing power of the circus; the three principal theatres of Rome (the Theatre of Pompey, the Theatre of Marcellus, the Theatre of Balbus) probably had a combined seating capacity of fifty thousand, huge by modern standards but nothing to equal the capacity of the Circus Maximus. The shows they put on tended to be gross, melodramatic and simple-minded – in the same vein, one might say, as most of the offerings on television today. There was no Roman equivalent to Sophocles or Aristophanes. As Barry Cunliffe points out, 'Creative theatre in the Greek sense was already dead. Plautus and Terence represent not the beginnings of a new Roman approach to drama and comedy, but the end of the Greek-inspired tradition.'

But they were only theatre, not reality. The headiest stuff of Roman spectacle, barbaric and frightful and (to us) incomprehensible as it was, were the *munera*, the spectacle of men slaughtering other men in gladiatorial combat in an arena built for that specific purpose. Virtuously, we recoil from the very thought of these dreadful entertainments. We cannot imagine (we say) queuing up to see them. They represent an idea of the value of human life so totally opposed to our own – or what we would like to claim as our own – as to extinguish all comparison between ourselves and the ancient Romans. We good and gentle people do not have such sadistic voyeurism simmering beneath our skins – so we would prefer to think.

But if the existence and popularity of the *munera* are an indication, civilized men (and women too) can and will do almost anything, however strange and terrible, if they see others doing it and are persuaded of its normality, necessity and entertainment value. Moreover, Romans took the *munera* as a lavish gift from the Caesars to themselves. A succession of autocrats, starting with Pompey and Julius Caesar, treated them as the greatest imperial show of all and hence a great public gift. In his list of *Res Gestae*, the things he had done for the state, Augustus recounted that 'I gave a gladiatorial show three times in my own name, and five times in the names of my sons or grandsons; at these shows about 10,000 fought ... Twenty-six times I provided for the people ... hunting spectacles of African wild beasts in the circus or in the Forum or in the amphitheatres; in these exhibitions about 3,500 animals were killed.' Not to have attended such bloody extravaganzas, not to immerse oneself in the entertainment, would be a sign of base ingratitude. Not that the emperor up in his *pulvinar* (royal box) would have noticed; but your fellow Romans well might, and treat you with derision and contempt for it.

The Romans attributed ancient origins to the *munera*. Many thought they had begun with the foundation of the city, when such duels had supposedly been fought in honour of the god Consus, one of the primitive forms of Neptune. Probably the first 'games' of this kind, albeit on a modest scale, were fought between gladiators in the Forum Boarium (cattle market) in Rome. They soon became extremely popular, and were rapidly enlarged: at the funeral games of *the pontifex maximus* Publius Licinius Crassus Dives in 183 BCE, sixty pairs of gladiators fought to the death. A variant on these man-to-man combats was the man-to-beast encounter in which criminals suffered the particular humiliation of *damnatio ad bestias*, condemned to destruction by wild animals. The first example of this practice is supposed to have happened the year after the consul Aemilius Paullus, following his military victory at Pydna in 168 BCE over the Macedonian king Perseus, had his deserters crushed to death by his war elephants.

Amphitheatres appeared wherever cities grew. By the second century CE, seventy-two were to be found in Gaul, twenty-eight along the towns of Rome's northern frontier, nineteen in Britannia – a total of some 186 sites throughout the Roman world. By far the largest, and the best-known, of these was the Colosseum in Rome. It was originally called the Flavian Amphitheatre, the largest example of a type of building peculiar to imperial Rome, used for spectacles and gladiatorial contests in which thousands of men and beasts struggled and died for the entertainment of a mass audience.

The earliest of these amphitheatres dated from 53 BCE and stood in the Forum Boarium, where early 'games' were held in honour of Decius Brutus Scaeva some two centuries before – a link to the gloomy and chthonic ceremonies of Etruscan death. Little is known about either its architecture or the gladiatorial shows it staged. Presently it was replaced by the Amphitheatrum Castrense, a three-storey oval structure built not far from the present site of Santa Croce in Gerusalemme, a broad oval in plan with a long axis of 88 metres. At first the Castrense was the only amphitheatre in Rome.

But this building, though impressive in size, was completely dwarfed by the arena which came to be known to all and sundry as the Colosseum. The word does not mean 'gigantic building' – it meant 'the place of the Colossus', a necessary distinction, because the 'Colossus' in question was an actual statue. It was a portrait of the emperor Nero, cast in bronze by the Greek sculptor Zenodorus, nude and some 120 Roman feet high (according to Suetonius), which stood at the entrance to Nero's prodigy of extravagance, the Domus Aurea or Golden House on the side of the Velian Hill. This monster of imperial narcissism hardly outlived its subject. After Nero died his successor, the emperor Vespasian, who understandably did not want to be overshadowed by the largest effigy of another monarch in the Roman world, had his artists and engineers convert it into an image of Sol, the sun-god, by equipping it with a radiant headdress, something like the Statue of Liberty's, with seven rays, each 23 Roman feet long. In 128 CE the emperor Hadrian had the whole thing moved to a site just north-west of the Colosseum – a square in the street surface, seven metres by seven, marks the spot. Hadrian was no stranger to huge engineering projects – this was, after all, the man who built the Pantheon and his own magnificent villa at Tivoli – but the transfer of Nero's statue was one of his largest. It was moved standing up vertically, hauled by twenty-four elephants. After Hadrian died, in 138 CE, a successor, the deranged, dissolute Commodus, had the head of the Colossus removed and replaced by a portrait of himself, glaring across the city. (There was a strong relation between the arena of the Colosseum and the fantasies of Commodus, who identified with Hercules and was obsessed with being a gladiator. He had been known, among other proofs of skill, to ride around the arena lopping off the heads of terrified ostriches, like some madman in a park decapitating tulips with swings of his walking-stick.)

In due course the attributes of Commodus were stripped from the Colossus and it became Sol once more. The frequent rituals held to venerate it gradually petered out and by the end of the eighth century CE it was no longer mentioned, so presumably it had been demolished and melted down for its bronze. It left behind it a famous cliché. The English monk and chronicler known as the Venerable Bede (673–735), who had never actually been to Italy, wrote that *quamdiu stabit colossus, stabit et Roma; quando cadet, cadet et Roma; quando cadet Roma, cadet et mundus*: 'So long as the Colossus stands, Rome will stand; when it falls, Rome will fall too; when Rome falls, so will the world.' This was echoed by many a later English writer, most memorably by Byron in *Childe Harold's Pilgrimage*, who transferred the supposedly eternal endurance of the statue to the arena itself:

'While stands the Coliseum, Rome shall stand,
'When falls the Coliseum, Rome shall fall;
'And when Rome falls – the world.' From our own land
Thus spake the pilgrims o'er this mighty wall
In Saxon times . . .

This enormous oval arena stood on a portion – though only a
small one – of Nero's Golden House. Its design, like that of the
Golden House itself, was accomplished after the Great Fire. It
may be that Vespasian's architects, of whom little is known beyond
their names, meant to produce a *cavea* or internal space with some
eighty regular arched openings, framed by engaged Tuscan, Ionic
and Corinthian columns. It had begun as an ornamental lake,
which had been turned into a series of fountains and grottoes,
ringed by the Velian, Oppian and Caelian hills. The idea was to
build the largest and most beautiful of all amphitheatres, but it
was too grand and time-consuming a project to be carried out by
any single emperor. The floor plan was an ellipse, the long axis 86
metres long, the short 54.

Vespasian (reg. 69–79 CE) pushed its construction to the top tier
of the second arcade of the outer wall before his death in 79. The
emperor Titus added the third and fourth storeys of seating.
Domitian (reg. 81–96 CE) is said to have completed the topmost
storey of the amphitheatre *ad clipea* – as far up as the emblematic
gilded bronze shields that ringed the top storey of its exterior. It
must have been a formidably impressive sight when finished,
although a series of lightning bolts and earthquake tremors
damaged it over the years. It was struck by lightning in 217, shaken
by the earthquakes of 442 and 470, and seriously attacked by
demolishers who were after the massive stonework and marble
facings of which the Colosseum was built, material that was later
recycled into other buildings of Rome. In the sixteenth century,
for instance, the steps of St Peter's were built of stone quarried
from the Colosseum.

By then, the wreck looked much as it does today, an enormous
array of ring-corridors. Through these radiated *vomitoria* or radial

corridors, along which the audience streamed in and out to take up or vacate their places on the raked seating of the show. Underneath them were the cells for the gladiators, the cages for the wild beasts whose deaths were such a popular part of the Colosseum 'games', and the elaborate, ponderous stage machinery. Although none of the seating survives, it is clear that the arena itself was an ellipse, floored with heavy planks of wood which were strewn with sand for traction and could be removed for 'special effects'. What these effects were remains, to some extent, obscure.

The auditorium could hold as many as fifty thousand and perhaps even seventy-five thousand people, and one has to imagine this mass audience stomping, hollering and baying for blood; these 'games' were the most barbarous form of orgiastic release ever devised, and their addictive power was immense.

All fighters were trained in the *ludus gladiatorius*, or gladiators' school, generally attached to an amphitheatre. Each school was organized and run by an entrepreneur known as a *lanista*, some-times an ex-gladiator himself, a tough and ruthless man who trained up his fighters from the bottom of the heap: from the endlessly replenished supply of prisoners-of-war and condemned thieves and murderers, from slaves and even from paid volunteers, down on their luck and desperate for cash. Perhaps one gladiator in five was a free man. Gladiatorial fighting in what was called the *hoplomachia* (a Greek term meaning 'heavily armed struggle') did at least create the possibility of freedom and reward for a really successful thug, if he won enough fights in the arena. Generally the gladiator, once downed, would be doomed to die; a dreadful figure symbolically costumed as Charon, ferryman of the dead, or Hermes Psychopompos, carrier of souls, would step forward with a heavy wooden mallet and smash in his forehead. But if the gladiator had killed enough, and the audience and emperor approved with the thumbs-up signal, he might be awarded the *rudis* or wooden sword, symbol of his favour and manumission. Then he would be allowed to live and be laden with treasure – silver salvers, gold baubles.

One of Cicero's letters (to Atticus, VII.14) mentions that in

Capua alone there lived five thousand gladiators, and it was from the gladiators' school in Capua in 73 BCE that the Thracian hero Spartacus arose to lead the most dangerous and nearly successful slave revolt in Roman history.

It was necessary, for the sake of dramatic variety, to keep the audience on its toes by having various types or classes of gladiator. One kind fought with sword and full-length shield; another, with a shorter dagger and a round leather buckler. The *retiarii*, their weapons chosen in homage to the god Neptune, carried nets in which they strove to entangle their opponents, and razor-pronged tridents with which to impale them. The custom was to make them fight *murmillones*, who were netless but wielded swords and were identified by fish on their helmets. It was considered especially piquant to send different kinds of opponents out on to the sands of the arena – one learns of 'a bold array of dwarves – they give and suffer wounds, and threaten death – with such tiny fists!'. Women, untrained in a gladiatorial school, would be sent out to hack and bash awkwardly at one another on the sands, or pitted against dwarves – a certain crowd-pleaser.

One also sometimes reads of naval battles being fought in arenas specially flooded for the occasion, but if this happened at all it must have been very uncommon. The only well-attested event of that kind in Rome took place in a *stagnum* or artificial pond somewhere to the south of what is now Trastevere, where (at the command of Augustus) there was a scaled-down restaging of the battle of Salamis, involving thirty full-sized biremes and triremes. But although it caused much loss of life, the wretched crews cannot have had much room to manoeuvre: the pond was only half a kilometre long.

Since the gangs of gladiators were privately owned and hired, they were quite often deployed outside the arena and the training-school in street violence fomented by the political ambitions and enmities of their rich masters – becoming, in effect, private armies.

Then there were the fights between man and beast, or beast and beast, known as *venationes*. The former were simulated hunts – except that the animals had no way out, no caves or forests to escape into. They were kept penned and caged below the floor of the amphitheatres and released to come charging up ramps to face the *bestiarii* or animal-killers. Outstanding gladiators might win themselves considerable prestige, though not nearly as much as heroic chariot-racers – but a *bestiarius* had none and was regarded as somewhere between a butcher and a common criminal, as indeed he usually was. These entertainments were first presented in the early to mid second century BCE. The Roman Empire in Africa furnished its arenas with what seemed, at first, to be an inexhaustible supply of wild animals, captured by intrepid hunters in its deserts and savannahs and then shipped back, caged and alive, to be tormented to a pitch of fury and then done to death in the various arenas. Among them were elephants, lions, panthers, tigers and – unlikely though it may sound – hippopotami, which somehow survived the sea voyage in their cages. (Despite its placid, portly and waddling appearance, the hippo if enraged is quite fast on its feet and can easily kill a man.) As a result of their use in the arenas, north African elephants became extinct in Roman times. During the opening slaughters of the Colosseum in 80 CE, at the behest of the emperor Titus, some five thousand beasts were killed in a single day, either by human butchers or by other animals.

But not every Roman approved of the *munera*. Some were disgusted by them and emphatically said so. One such person was Seneca, who described in his *Moral Epistles* how he went to a midday show and found that

> It is pure murder. The men have no protective covering. Their entire bodies are exposed to the blows, and no blow is ever struck in vain ... in the morning men are thrown to the lions and the bears, at noon they are thrown to their spectators. The spectators call for the slayer to be thrown to those who in turn will slay him, and they detain the victor for another butchering. The outcome for the combatants is death ... And when the show stops for intermission, 'Let's

have men killed meanwhile! Let's not have nothing going
on!'

Cicero attended a *venatio* and came away feeling distinctly let
down. 'I ... saw nothing new in it. The last day was that of the
elephants, and on that day the mob and the crowd was greatly
impressed, but manifested no pleasure. Indeed the result was a
certain compassion, and a kind of feeling that that huge beast has
a fellowship with the human race.'

The origins of the *munera* must lie in more formalized human
sacrifice, and are lost in antiquity; presumably they descend
from the gloomy funeral customs of the Etruscans – the
assumption being that bloodshed reconciles the dead with the
living.

There can be no doubt that the Roman public was debased by
the gladiatorial shows. How could it not have been? Was any
counter to this supplied by the state? None whatever; but at least
the Caesars gave their subjects another somewhat less murderous
source of pleasure: the public baths. These structures did little but
good. For most citizens of Rome, private bathrooms were all but
unknown: they were too costly to heat, and their water supply
was at best irregular. But public baths were the great amenity of
Roman city life. They began to make their full appearance in the
second century BCE, and in 33 BCE Agrippa had a census made of
the public baths with paid admission in Rome: there were already
170 and by Pliny's time the total was closer to a thousand, many
of which were presumably tacky if not outright filthy. But the great
imperial bath complexes, whose construction probably began in
the late first century BCE and continued into the third century CE,
were entirely another matter: huge, splendid and overwhelmingly
popular. Their role as a point of contact between imperial largesse
and the desires of the Roman public can hardly be overestimated.
The *thermae* were not a mere amenity, but a core element of
civilized life in Rome and throughout its empire. One finds, for
instance, an edict of the emperor Caracalla from 215 CE, banishing
as possible subversives all Egyptians living in Alexandria except

for 'pig dealers, river boatmen and the men who bring down reeds for heating the baths'.

The first of them was begun by Agrippa in about 25 BCE, close by the Pantheon. It had a *laconium* or dry sweat bath and was heavily adorned with works of art, including pictures (both encaustic and fresco) which were recessed into the walls of even the hottest rooms.

The second great bath complex was the *thermae* built in 62 CE by the emperor Nero, struck by lightning and burned, and at last finished in 64 – just in time for the catastrophic fire that swept through Rome in that year, which it survived. It occupied a site between the north-west corner of the Pantheon and the stadium of Domitian, now Piazza Navona, and although it has almost entirely disappeared, two grey granite columns from it were used, in the seventeenth century, to repair the porch of the Pantheon, and other *spolia* were cannibalized for later palaces, while another column and a piece of cornice were dug out from beneath the piazza outside S. Luigi dei Francesi and set up in Via di S. Eustachio as late as 1950. None of these fragments give any idea of the scale of the Baths of Nero, whose plan was about 190 metres by 120.

The third major Roman bath was that of Titus, dedicated in 80 CE, the same year as the Colosseum – another vast structure built on part of the site of the Golden House of Nero, of which little remains except the brick cores of some columns of its porch, facing the Colosseum.

The fourth, built after 104 CE on a huge rectangular section of the burned-out ruins of the Golden House, 250 metres wide by 210 deep, was the Baths of Trajan. The fifth was officially known as the Baths of Antoninus, although everyone calls them the Baths of Caracalla. They were completed early in the third century CE, and they are vast, covering eleven hectares. The sixth, the Baths of Diocletian (*c*.306), was even bigger, with an area of thirteen hectares. Today its site and vestiges contain a large church, an oratory and one of the greatest collections of antique art in Italy, the National Roman Museum. Due to the administrative and fiscal chaos into which so much of the management of Italian museums has fallen, whole tracts of this notionally sublime collection are closed to the public – for instance, none of the Ludovisi collection, except the Ludovisi Throne itself, is open to view. But it is still extraordinarily rich, not only in sculpture, but also in ancient Roman painting, in which it nearly rivals the unsurpassable collections of the Naples Museum.

The parts of the imperial baths that are still standing have afforded continuous inspiration to architects – including, especially, those of the past century. Roman *thermae* supplied the models for those mighty expressions of the mystique of nineteenth-century American travel, Grand Central Station and the former Pennsylvania Station (1902–11), by McKim, Mead & White, with its waiting-room modelled on the Baths of Caracalla but enlarged by a quarter – demolished in 1963 when, in one of the worst outrages ever inflicted on Manhattan, it was torn down to make room for the squalid warren that has replaced it. The Baths of Caracalla also furnished the prototype for another nineteenth-century masterpiece in New York – the cool, august spaces of the entrance hall of Richard Morris Hunt's Metropolitan Museum of Art. But the influence of these ancient *thermae* extended well into the twentieth century, and will continue to be felt in the future by any architect who values mass and volume above mere transparency.

A Beaux-Arts architect like Hunt tried to get back to the magisterially pristine form of the Roman baths. Sixty years later, another genius of American design, Louis I. Kahn, was inspired by their state as ruins. The various baths, including those of Caracalla and Diocletian, had been built of concrete and brick, then sumptuously clad in limestone and coloured marble. All this surface and carved detail was stripped away after the death of the Empire, and the brick set in to crumble, leaving only the rudiments of architecture behind it: mass, space, light. These were the rudiments Kahn set himself to capture in new structures, and his search for them began in his experience of Roman ruins, particularly the *thermae*, with their giant vaults made possible only by that Roman invention, the poured concrete arch that generated the vault (if extended) and the dome (if rotated) – so unGreek, so prototypically modern.

Whatever the architectural differences of individual buildings, the process of bathing – and the divisions of space and use that it implied – hardly varied. Naturally, all the functions of the bath palace had to be grouped under one roof, a huge quadrilateral, with shops, exercise and massage rooms along its outer sides and the bathing facilities within. The rituals of the Roman bath were, so to speak, processional. On entering, one shed one's clothes in the dressing-room or *apodyterium*, stowed them in a locker, and then headed for the *tepidarium* or warm hall, which had on one side the *frigidarium* or cold plunge-bath and on the other the steam-room, the *caledarium*. Next to that was the hot-air sweating room, the *sudatorium*. The necessary heat for this system, which was enormous, came from furnaces stoked with firewood or reeds. One could lose a lot of weight in such places, sweating out one's surplus fluids. Seneca described (vividly, though perhaps with some exaggeration) what it was like to live over a bath-house. The grunting and groaning were enough to make him queasy:

> When the stronger fellows are exercising and swinging heavy leaden weights in their hands ... I hear their groans, and whenever they release their pent-up breath, I hear their hissing and jarring breathing ... Add to this the arrest of a brawler or a thief, and the fellow who always likes to hear his own voice in the bath, and those who jump in the pool with a mighty splash as they strike the water ... Imagine the hair-plucker keeping up a constant chatter in his thin and strident voice [and] the varied cries of the sausage dealer and confectioner and all the peddlers of the cook shops ...

The *thermae* were not only for bathing. The larger ones, in Rome, were likely to contain libraries and galleries. Some were so richly endowed with sculpture, both copies and original pieces in marble and bronze, that they were almost museums in their own right: the Laocoön, considered by eighteenth-century connoisseurs to be the very quintessence of achievement in classical sculpture, was allegedly disinterred in the ruins of a bath-house. Probably the presence of such works of art did much to appease the objections of conservative Romans who felt that the athletic prowess celebrated by bath culture was anti-intellectual. The baths rightly inspired civic pride. 'With so many indispensable structures for so many aqueducts,' remarked Frontinus, 'compare, if you will, the idle pyramids or the useless, though famous, works of the Greeks.' This was not empty boasting, even though it is unclear why Frontinus should have regarded Greek architecture as useless. Certainly, to a Roman the pyramids of Egypt, those prodigies of stonework with no function beyond the burial of a single man, must have seemed 'idle' – the extravagances of religions other than one's own do tend to look that way. But a Roman took great pride in his city's baths. Their size and magnificence did not overpower him – rather the reverse, for they reminded him that he was the reason for the state. In form and meaning, they were the very quintessence of public architecture.

The emperor Gaius Aurelius Valerius Diocletianus (reg. 284–305 CE), or Diocletian, did much more than build the immense baths in Rome that bear his name. He was a straightforward soldier from Dalmatia, with little formal education, not even Roman by ancestry (his original name, Diocles, was Greek) and of the humblest birth. This was a prime factor in his control of the army, and in the army's loyalty to him. The social gap between army officers and enlisted men now yawned; it was not just an inconvenience, as the social distance between an officer earl and Tommy Atkins might have been in the British army, but an ever present danger to the coherence of the Roman forces. The more the army had to fill its ranks with 'barbarians' rather than true *Romani*, as it did, the less patriotic ardour it could expect from the men who fought for Rome. At least the line soldiers, knowing that their emperor began as a low-class outsider like themselves, were more likely to stick with him.

Diocletian was very pious, devoted to the Roman gods, and

this must have caused family stresses when both his wife Prisca and his daughter Valeria converted, as it was said, to Christianity. He was also imbued with an extreme arrogance, which he regarded as a necessity of power. Augustus had begun the tradition of the Principate by which the emperor was always *primus inter pares*, first among equals; he had loathed being addressed as *dominus*, 'Lord', although in practice his power was absolute. Later emperors observed this formula, with varying degrees of conviction.

The earlier emperor Vespasian (Titus Flavius Vespasianus, 9– 79 CE), for example, had viewed the fantasy of the Divine Emperor with a most commendable scepticism, but he was the only emperor to do so. He was a sound, fair, hard-boiled military man, who had won honours under Claudius for his role in the conquest of southern Britain in 43 CE, and in 66 CE had commanded three legions in the Jewish War. He loathed pretension and effeminacy, qualities which had not been in short supply under previous emperors. When a dandified young officer, smelling heavily of scent, came to thank Vespasian for his promotion, the emperor brusquely remarked that he would rather he smelt of garlic, and busted him back to the ranks. He also had an ironic sense of humour and no patience with the mumbo-jumbo of deification – a fact commemorated in his famous deathbed remark as he was expiring of a fever in 79 CE: *Vae, puto, deus fio*, 'Oh, no! I think I am becoming a god!'

Diocletian was not going to be anything but a god. He completed the evolution of the Principate to the Dominate – undisguised, ceremonious and absolute monarchy: Oriental monarchy, as many thought. The subject, approaching the presence of the emperor, had to prostrate himself and, when he spoke, address him as *dominus et magister* – 'Lord and Master'. As we have seen, there had been moves in this direction made by previous emperors. To be treated as a god on earth – that had been expected by Caligula, Domitian and Commodus. By the time Diocletian became emperor there was nothing unfamiliar or freakish about emperor worship, and it meshed perfectly with the great third-century jurist Ulpian's declaration that 'the Emperor is above the laws'. Possibly Diocletian regarded this as entirely benign, a corollary of his belief that, as emperor, he was the *pater patriae*, father of the Roman people. But once you have tasted godhood it is not so easy to de-deify yourself.

However, he was earthbound enough to recognize that the sheer size and complexity of the Roman Empire, and the slow communication this size meant, demanded changes in the administration of its government. He therefore introduced the 'Tetrarchy' or 'Rule by Four'. It actually began as a diarchy, rule by two. In 285 he designated his lieutenant Maximianus as 'Caesar' and put him in charge of the western half of the Empire, while he kept the eastern. (Diocletian was worshipped as the earthly incarnation of Jupiter, and now Maximianus became, for religious purposes, Hercules.) In 293 Diocletian appointed two more Caesars: Constantius, father of the future Constantine the Great, who was to rule Britain and Gaul in the west, and Galerius, who got the Balkans in the east. But he had to be sure that ambitious sub-Caesars did not become too powerful, so he split the provinces: divide and rule. There would henceforth be six dioceses in the east and six in the west, divided into about a hundred provinces, each with its own governor. The roster, in its essential features, would last for centuries – it was the basis of most subsequent national divisions.

Inflation was a huge, intractable problem, which Diocletian lacked the economic ingenuity to control. He tried, and failed, to fix prices by issuing edicts limiting both wages and the sale price of every sort of commodity and service. An army *modius* of ground millet, for instance, would cost 100 *denarii*; a pound of best pork leg, 20; oysters, a *denarius* each; and so on. An arithmetic teacher was to earn 75 *denarii* per month, a carpenter 50 per day, a scribe 'for second-quality writing' 20 *denarii* per hundred lines, a lawyer 1,000 for pleading a case, and a cloakroom attendant in a bathhouse 2 *denarii* per person. None of this worked; it merely produced a runaway black market. The Empire's coinage, meanwhile, became so debased as to be almost worthless. Nobody trusted it.

There was not enough gold and silver bullion in the Empire to reinstate the currency, and eventually Diocletian was forced to accept tax payments, and to pay his soldiers, in kind rather than in cash. Meanwhile there were imperial headquarters to be built for the tetrarchs: in the east at Nicomedia, Antioch and Thessalonika, in the Balkans at Sirmium and in the north at Milan, Trier and York.

One would have thought all this would have distracted the god Diocletian from such matters as a small, peripheral Jewish religion, but far from it. For the first two decades of his reign he paid no attention to the Christians, but towards 303 he began to worry about the infiltration of their faith into high places, mainly through the conversion of governors' wives and daughters. It worried him, understandably in view of his own immense egotism and his piety towards the old gods, that such families were moving away from the imperial cult, especially since some of the more intelligent members of the army high command were becoming Christians too. This canker had better be excised; even the oracle of Apollo at Didyma near Miletus urged the emperor to attack the Church. The result was a fierce renewal of persecution of Christians, designed to force them to accept the imperial cult and worship Diocletian as a god – which, of course, few of them would do. It is not known how many were killed in the 'Great Persecution' of 303–13; severe as it was, Christian writers like Lactantius were bound to exaggerate it and to demonize Diocletian, 'inventor of wicked deeds and the contriver of evils ... ruining everything'. (One should, perhaps, remember that Lactantius had a bit of an axe to grind. He had been summoned from Africa to teach Latin rhetoric in Nicomedia, an extremely important academic post, given that Nicomedia was scheduled to become one of the new Romes. Then, during the Great Persecution, Diocletian fired him. To lose such a job was a very severe blow that demanded literary revenge, which Lactantius certainly exacted with a blood-curdling text, *On the Deaths of the Persecutors*.)

There is a temptation – fostered, of course, by pious impulses – to suppose that Christianity somehow 'triumphed' over Roman paganism by the fourth century, completely changing the religious horizon of Rome. Nothing could be further from the truth.

With the establishment of the Tetrarchy, no emperor spent any length of time in Rome. Once the *caput mundi*, it was no longer an effective centre of power; its monopoly of that was gone. Perhaps because of this, its pagan institutions continued to flourish. The building of its huge defensive bulwark against barbarian invasion, the Aurelian walls (309–12 and 402–3), with their fifteen-metre height and their 380 towers, created what Richard Krautheimer called 'the greatest monument of late antique Rome'. Any list of the pagan enterprises of Rome in the thirty years before the arrival of its first Christian emperor, Constantine, would need to include the Baths of Diocletian, the Senate House on the Forum Romanum (rebuilt after a fire in 283), the Basilica Julia (rebuilt after the same fire), the colossal hall of the Basilica Nova, with its three huge barrel-vaulted niches, built by Maxentius in his six-year reign (306–12), the apsed hall of the temple of Venus and Cupid, and much more. Forums, temples, sanctuaries, shrines were constantly being repaired and rebuilt. Through the fourth century Rome seemed to visitors 'an essentially classical, secular and pagan city'. The fourth-century gazetteers listed, among its contents, 28 libraries, 11 forums, 10 basilicas, 11 public baths, 9 circuses and theatres, 36 triumphal arches and 46 brothels. Even after Constantine's death, the persistence of pagan memory was strong. There may have been a 'New Rome' and Constantine would of course change the city, but not so huge that it suddenly rendered Old Rome itself irrelevant. Cities do not die at the stroke of a pen. The persistence of pagan memory was too strong for that. Rome remained a stronghold of enlightened paganism, drawn from Gnostic and Neoplatonic philosophies, strengthened by some of the greatest art and literature the world had ever seen, and supported by powerful and conservative local aristocrats. In those decades, to be conservative was to be anti-Christian – indeed, to regard Christianity itself as an intrusive low-brow sect, not worth a civilized person's attention except as an example of the kind of folly that was coming out of north Africa. If anyone had suggested to such a Roman that, at some future date, this little sect would be larger, richer and more powerful than any number of Roman empires, he would have thought the proposal lunatic. And the struggle over that transfer of power would be fierce.

For what could have been more powerful than Rome, then? Or richer? The Tetrarchy may have disbanded the central power, but the more wars Rome won, the more its empire expanded, the richer it got: this was inevitable. And the richer it got, the more luxurious its life became. Not everyone's life, obviously; but for the top five per cent it took on a character of manic overindulgence and extravagance, unpleasantly reminiscent of the life of the super-rich today. *Frangitur ipsa suis Roma superba bonis*, wrote Sextus Propertius: 'Proud Rome is now brought low by her wealth.' Pliny the Elder, writing as early as the first century CE, estimated that at the 'lowest reckoning' the expensive imports from India, China and the Arabian peninsula 'drain our Empire of 100,000,000 sesterces every year – that is what our luxuries and womenfolk cost us'. Granted, Roman writers (just like those two thousand years later) were fond of invoking the good old days of the early Republic, when men were men, life simple and morality stricter. Why did frugality prevail in olden times? Because, Tacitus explained, we were once all citizens of one city. 'Even when we were masters of Italy alone, we did not have the temptations of today. Victories in foreign wars taught us to devour the substance of others, victories in civil wars, our own.' Inveighing against recent luxury and decadence, Seneca pulled out all the stops:

> We think ourselves poor and mean if our walls are not resplendent with large and costly mirrors; if our marbles from Alexandria are not set off by mosaics of Numidian stone, if they are not covered all over with an elaborate coating variegated to look like painting; if our vaulted ceilings are not concealed in glass; if our swimming-pools – into which we lower our bodies after they have been drained weak by copious sweating – are not lined with Thasian

marble, once a rare sight in a temple, or if the water does not flow from silver spigots . . . We have become so luxurious that we will tread upon nothing but precious stones.

In the view of the historian Livy, writing a few decades earlier, the appetite for debilitating luxury came to Rome from its conquests in the east, and was brought back by the military:

It was through the army serving in Asia that the beginnings of foreign luxury were introduced into the city. These men brought into Rome, for the first time, bronze couches, costly coverlets, bed curtains, and other fabrics, and what was considered at the time gorgeous furniture – one-legged tables and sideboards. Banquets were made more attractive by the presence of girls who played on the lute and the harp . . . The cook, whom the ancients regarded and treated as the lowest form of slave, was rising in value, and what had been a servile task began to be looked on as a fine art.

What did these Romans eat and drink? The answer is a little disappointing, if your expectations of Roman food are based on the legendary blowouts recorded in Petronius' *Satyricon* and other accounts of high living. We read of Trimalchio, a former slave grown immensely rich through speculation, entertaining guests in his house in Campania. They are shown a bronze donkey – Corinthian bronze, the most expensive kind – with panniers on its sides, one full of white and the other of black olives. There are silver dishes 'laden with dormice sprinkled with honey and poppyseed . . . [and] sausages smoking-hot on a silver gridiron, with damsons and pomegranates sliced up'. Each dish is engraved with Trimalchio's name and its own weight, so that all the guests know what it is worth. The *pièce de résistance* is a basket full of straw, with a carved wooden pea-hen sitting atop it, her wings spread. Two slaves set it down; trumpeters play a fanfare; the slaves rummage in the straw, finding egg after egg. Trimalchio exclaims: 'My friends, I ordered pea-hens' eggs to be set under a hen, and by Jove I fear they are half-hatched already; but let us try whether we can still suck them.' Each guest is given a silver spoon 'weighing at least half a pound' and they start on the eggs, which turn out to be made of 'rich pastry'. Within, hidden in the yolk, the narrator finds a fine, plump fig-pecker, a great delicacy, then as now.

This kind of gastropornography is what springs to mind when most people today think of Roman food, but it has little to do with what the vast majority of Romans actually ate. Their daily fodder was much more likely to be polenta (a corn porridge, either hot and gloppy or, when congealed, fried in slices), beans and bitter herbs, with meat (preferably pork) as a rarity, and eggs and an occasional chicken. Most working-class Romans subsisted largely on pulses and bread. Cheeses were much eaten, and there cannot have been much difference between the *pecorinos* or sheep's-milk cheeses consumed today and those of Roman times. Vegetables also made an appearance in such forms as a delicious preparation of young zucchini known as *scapece*, which is still served in some Roman restaurants. There would also be fish, though without refrigeration it cannot often have been fresh. The very rich were able to maintain fishponds – there are even horror stories about slaves being fed to their enormous eels. The universal stimulant of appetite was a decoction of rotting fish guts, which seems to have resembled a very smelly and salty ancestor of Worcester sauce and was called *garum*. Roman households consumed it rather as some today consume tomato ketchup, putting it on everything. We tend to assume that *garum* merely stank of rotten fish, but it must have had a more subtle taste than that.

The potato, the tomato and all other imports from the undiscovered New World were, of course, unknown. So was sugarcane. When a Roman cook wanted to sweeten a dish he did it with honey.

Another outlet for Roman wealth and decadence during this time was art. Just like today, the prices of fashionable 'fine' art were fantastically inflated: ancient Rome, it seems, had its equivalents to the hysterical, grotesque pricing of Pablo Picasso, Andy

Warhol and Jasper Johns. The orator Lucius Crassus paid an incredible 100,000 sesterces for two silver goblets engraved by Mentor, a famed Greek silversmith, 'but he confessed that for shame he had never dared use them'. Corinthian bronzes were so prized for their workmanship that they cost whole family fortunes. Pliny reported that one ivory table changed hands at 1,300,000 sesterces – 'the price of a large estate, supposing someone preferred to devote so large a sum to the purchase of landed property'.

Another was jewellery: the display of precious stones by some Roman matrons was grotesquely excessive, and the matrons themselves monsters of vulgarity, just like today's. Here was Lollia Paulina, third wife of the emperor Caligula, whose beauty equalled her vulgarity, 'at an ordinary betrothal banquet covered with emeralds and pearls interlaced with each other and shining all over her head, hair, ears, neck and fingers, their total value amounting to 40,000,000 sesterces, and she herself ready at a moment's notice to show the bills of sale in proof of ownership'. By the Tiber as under the lights of Broadway, diamonds really were a girl's best friend. The spread of Empire inevitably brought with it an increased supply of luxury goods and precious baubles: emeralds from Egypt and the Urals, sapphires from Sri Lanka, amethysts and diamonds from India. The finest Chinese silk traded for gigantic prices: a pound of silk for a pound of gold was not unknown. Perhaps the favourite Roman jewel was the pearl (*margarita*), yielded by all Rome's oceans. Naturally the abundance of precious and semi-precious materials helped create a large class of luxury craftworkers. More relics of their industry would, no doubt, have come down to us if Rome had not so frequently been sacked.

The most spectacularly ostentatious piece of art-stuffed real estate in Roman antiquity – surpassing even the Golden House of Nero – was a villa built for the emperor Hadrian at Tivoli, twenty miles north-east of Rome. To call it 'Hadrian's Villa' seems a complete understatement, since its site was about the same size as central Las Vegas, some 300 hectares, twice the area of Pompeii.

Like some abandoned Mayan city, Tikal perhaps, it has been only partially excavated, despite the enormous quantity of statues and other works of art removed (looted) from it over the last few centuries and dispersed to museums in London, Paris, Berlin, Los Angeles and St Petersburg, not to mention Rome itself and, of course, unlisted private collections. Some historians of antiquity think that only 10–20 per cent of the full built area of the 'Villa' has been dug up and disclosed, which would make it the biggest unstudied ancient site in Italy or the Roman world.

One particular kind of ancient statue is associated with the Villa – the naked, idealized likeness of Hadrian's lover Antinous, the Greek homosexual pin-up *par excellence*, whose fetching body and pouting Elvis mouth proliferated all over the Empire after he drowned in the Nile in 130 CE. But the contents of the Villa reflect a general culture of intense imitation in which one version after another of Greatest Sculptural Hits was turned out to imperial order by craftsmen whose sole task was to create a cultural dreamscape: a wondrous Greece recreated in (or just outside) Rome. The idea of 'heroic invention', which is the basis of modern worship of the new, did not exist in classical times, and would have been regarded as a zany aberration, not as a sign of excellence. One of the results has been that Roman copies, or (relatively) free variants, of Greek originals have become almost all we know of the original art of Greece; with the exception of a few indisputably Greek-made masterpieces, such as the Parthenon marbles, Greece is now largely Roman. And because so many 'Greek' masterpieces were either made by Greeks in Rome for Roman clients, or by Romans in Rome, or completed in Rome by local craftsmen after the original block had been roughed out in Greece, the problem of saying anything certain about the origins and nature of classic art objects is usually insoluble. But one thing seems fairly certain. In its quality of sculpture ancient Rome could never rival ancient Athens. Phidias had many Roman imitators, but there was no Roman Phidias. Most Roman sculpture is, at best, faithfully descriptive – one thinks of the realistic funerary portraits of slightly grim-looking citizens, tight with virtue. Great sculpture, like the panels celebrating Augustus on the Ara Pacis, is very much the exception and when it occurs one may fairly suppose the authorship of Greek or at least Greek-trained carvers. Virgil was right: the great art of Rome was not sculpting, but ruling.

❧ 4 ❧
PAGANS VERSUS CHRISTIANS

It makes little real sense to speak of 'the end of the Roman Empire' as though that enormous social structure suddenly came undone or ceased to exist. In forms both powerful and merely vestigial, it continued to provide the framework of international society throughout Europe for hundreds of years. That said, starting with the reign of Constantine, the battle between the old pagan rule and the new Christian might would slowly erode the Empire's potency.

The first persecutions launched against the Christians by Rome's emperors were relatively small affairs, but none the saner for that. It must seem strange that a city as abundant in sects and cult objects as imperial Rome should have persecuted anyone for holding unorthodox beliefs – there was, one might have thought, more than enough superstition for everyone – but in imperial times that was not how the ruling and priestly classes saw the matter, and for two reasons.

One was that the Christians refused to pay divine honours to the emperor. They would not pray or sacrifice to him as a god. Even a token participation in Roman religious rituals would probably have satisfied the authorities. But to refuse them altogether was an act of defiance. It was resented as a crass form of lese-majesty. Christians seemed bound together by ties of common belief and worship which had nothing to do with the ordinary relationships between Romans and their gods. Those relationships underwrote the stability of the Roman state. The Christians seemed more loyal to their secret society, which could only mean that they were disloyal to Rome.

The second, related reason was that, after a period of relative indifference, Christianity began to attract hostile and fantastically inflated rumours about the numbers, conduct and beliefs of its devotees, and the dangers they might pose to an orderly society. They were becoming a more visible sect, which – thanks to its slowly growing popularity among the common folk of the Roman Empire in the third century CE – was attracting the kind of hatred that success breeds. Christians had arrived only recently, boasted one of them, Tertullian, 'and we have filled everything of yours – cities, islands, forts, towns . . . Palace, senate, forum. We have left you only the temples.' This was an extreme exaggeration. But nearly everything that was said about Christianity in its earliest years was an exaggeration, and none more so than the popular notions among pagans of what Christians actually believed and hoped for.

Given the success of Christianity in the coming years, given that this embryonic cult would soon become an all-dominating and world-embracing religion that drove the pagan gods from their sanctuaries and niches, one might have expected a surge of opposition to it right from the start; actually there was little. If no threat was presumed, Romans tended to be quite tolerant of minority religions, even when the 'minority' was large. The emperor Augustus, for instance, knew that a large tract of Rome beyond the Tiber was owned and inhabited by Jews. Most of these Jews were Roman freedmen, who had been brought to the city as prisoners-of-war and then manumitted by their owners. They did not worship the Roman gods, or perform obeisances at Roman shrines. But because they caused no trouble either in doctrine or in action, Augustus saw that no pressure was put on their synagogues; no Jew was prevented from meeting with his or her brethren for the exposition of the Law – 'on the contrary, he showed such reverence for our traditions that he and almost all his family enriched our Temple with expensive dedications. He gave orders for regular sacrifices of holocausts to be made daily in perpetuity at his own expense, as an offering to the Most High God. These sacrifices continue to this day, and will continue always, as a proof of his truly imperial character.'*

Christians, few but growing in number, led little-noticed lives in the forest of sects and cults that the decay of 'official' Roman religion produced; as a religion it seemed hardly worth contesting. To most Romans who thought at all about the matter it would have seemed of little consequence and the idea that the civilized world would before long date its events from the lifetime of a carpenter's son from Galilee would have seemed merely ludicrous.

There is a passing reference in Suetonius' account of Claudius (page 25, paragraph 4) to disturbances caused by Jews in Rome 'at the instigation of Chrestus', but it is not at all clear if Chrestus was the same person as Christ. No pagan writer even bothered to attack the ideas of the Christians until 178 CE. (He was a Neoplatonist named Celsus and his writings are lost; we know only that he wrote them because a Christian apologist, the Church father Origen, attacked him for them.)

Unrestrained calumnies were let fly against the Christians, 'a rabble of unholy conspirators', given to sharing 'barbarous foods . . . for the sake of sacrilege', according to the converted Christian writer Minucius Felix. The result of the mere presence, let alone the growth, of Christianity (according to those Romans who disapproved of it) had been general moral decay in the Empire and, everywhere, 'a kind of religion of lust'. Christians were accused of every sort of perversion and impropriety, including ritually murdering children and eating their flesh – a fantasy which must have arisen from Christ's Eucharistic instructions to his disciples, to eat his body (the bread) and drink his blood (the wine), and to 'do this in memory of me'. This form of banqueting was 'notorious; everywhere, all talk of it'. The Christians wanted to bring about the end of the earth, moon and stars with fire, and be

* Here, the word 'holocaust' is given its earlier and correct meaning: a multiple sacrifice and incineration which is pleasing to the Lord, not the mass murder of an unwilling people.

'reborn after death from the cinders and the ashes'. In sum, the apocalyptic nonsense that anti-Semitism would soon be spouting against Jews was being marshalled by some Romans to incite and justify the persecution of Christians.

Whence such virulence? A rational person might have had his reservations about Christian behaviour and found reasons to disagree with, even dislike it. But the idea that Christianity wanted to bring about the destruction of the world must seem exotic, or at least a tad far-fetched, to those who, like nearly everyone today, think of it as a benign and gentle religion. Others destroy; Christians temper, comfort and forgive. But it could very well not have seemed so to a Roman in the first century CE, when confronted by the rhetoric not only of the sect's faithful, but of its founder, the aggressive Galilean, Jesus Christ.

Early Christians were not milky-mild or forgiving at all. We know this because we know what they believed, which was what Christ had told them to believe. At the back of all Christian minds lay his injunction to intolerant militancy: 'I come not to bring peace, but a sword.' The New Testament's record of early Christian belief is contained in the Acts and the Epistles. They are saturated with apocalyptic rhetoric: some of it, no doubt, garbled and touched up – the New Testament was put together a long time after Christ's death – but without reasonable doubt a fair epitome of what Christ, and the early Christians, believed and said. And (no less important) of what the Romans thought they were saying.

The principal content of these beliefs was that the world was coming to an end. St Peter had no doubt about this. 'The end of all things is at hand,' he announced. 'The time is come that judgement must begin at the house of God.' This would happen at any moment, because these are 'the last days' – a phrase that would be used and reused in Christian eschatology for the next two thousand years. St Paul was of a similar view, eagerly awaiting the day 'when the Lord Jesus shall be revealed from heaven with his mighty angels, in flaming fire taking vengeance upon them that know not God, and that obey not the gospel of our Lord Jesus Christ: who shall be punished with everlasting destruction'.

Jesus' own words on these terrible events to come are recorded in the Gospel of Matthew: 'For nation shall rise against nation, and kingdom against kingdom; and there shall be famines, and pestilences, and earthquakes, in divers places. All these are the beginning of sorrows ... ye shall be hated of all nations for my name's sake ... I say unto you, This generation shall not pass, till all these things be fulfilled.'

Christians did not believe that such prophecies, promises and threats were in any way metaphorical. They were truthful in essence and soon would be in fact, as well: not in the distant future, but imminently, within this generation. Rome was doomed to be destroyed in a few years, a few decades at the most. The New Testament had not been written yet, but such beliefs were preached, described, made part of the essential public lore of the new religion and its adherents. To them, it made perfect sense, because it was Revealed Truth. But to the Roman authorities it made sense too, of a different kind. It meant that the Galileans *wanted* this promised destruction – as no doubt many of them, being fanatics, did. The radical who dreams of bringing a whole society crashing down on the heads of its inhabitants, who fantasizes about the fiery end of the social order, would become a familiar figure – hero to some, nightmare to others – throughout the twentieth century: the anarchist with the bomb, the Falangist general crying *Viva la muerte!*, the Arab teenager blowing himself and a Jewish school bus to a bloody, smoking pulp for the sake of 'martyrdom'. There seems to be little room for doubt that a civilized, law-loving Roman might have believed what the Jesus freaks said about the future of history and their mission within it, and concluded that the best thing to do with this hostile though marginal sect was to wipe it out before it spread any further. Of course, the end of the world did not come – a relief to sensible people, though no doubt a disappointment to some loonies. But to threaten it, which was what Rome thought Christians were doing, was – how to put it? – a deeply antisocial act. It made the thought that Christians were motivated by 'hatred of the human race' seem quite plausible.

Undoubtedly the most crazed and sadistic attack on Christians by any Roman emperor was the one launched after the Great Fire in Rome in 64 CE, when Nero needed a scapegoat for said fire. According to the historian Tacitus, the Christians were already 'hated for their abominations' in Judaea. The Jews, particularly the very orthodox ones, would have liked nothing better than to see them disposed of – to gratify their apparent longing for holy martyrdom. Thus they welcomed their persecution by Nero, even though the need for it did not, according to Tacitus, convince the Romans themselves. They thought it freakish: 'Nero provided his Gardens for the spectacle, and exhibited displays in the Circus, at which he mingled with the crowd – or stood in a chariot, dressed as a charioteer. Despite their guilt as Christians, and the ruthless punishment it deserved, the victims were pitied. For it was felt that they were being sacrificed to one man's brutality rather than to the national interest.'

There was no sudden transition between Nero's obsessions and the victory of the Christians – how could there have been? – and yet, looking back on it, it is surely possible to see in the violence of Nero's attack on the little sect a foretaste of what was to come two and a half centuries later. The epochal event which divided the history of the Roman Empire was a battle won just outside Rome, and fought in 312: the battle of the Milvian Bridge, which spanned the Tiber. It marked – though of course no one realized it at the time – the end of the old Roman imperial system and the beginning of the Byzantine Empire. It was predicted by a line in Homer cited, with some relish, by the Roman gossipmonger and historian Suetonius when writing of the first-century emperor Domitian: 'Too many rulers are a dangerous thing.'

So indeed they proved to be.

Under Diocletian, the unified Roman Empire had split and assumed a new shape: at the dawn of the fourth century CE it consisted of an eastern and a western Empire, ruled by the tet-rarchs – not one but two senior emperors, each known by the honorific 'Augustus' and supported by his own 'Caesar' or junior emperor, making four rulers in all (*tetra* being Greek for 'four'). The best-known depiction of this odd system was created by an unknown artist in Constantinople, looted by Crusaders in 1204 and brought to Venice, where it was built into the façade of St Mark's Basilica. It depicts two pairs of tetrarchs, the Augustus and the Caesar of east and west respectively, embracing one another. They are solid, heavy, thick-necked, and shown grasping their swords with their free hands. It is an image of firm, one might say implacable, loyalty, though there is no indication of their names.

In the spring of 305 Diocletian, the Augustus of the eastern Empire, as Maximian was of the western, had formally abdicated. He now retired to his gigantic palace whose ruins still stand at Split, formerly Spalato, on the Dalmatian coast. He was succeeded as Augustus of the east by his fiercely anti-Christian colleague Galerius, who had moved up from his previous post as Caesar of the east (and was succeeded in that role by his nephew, Maximinus Daia). Similarly, Maximian abdicated as the Empire's western Augustus and was replaced by Constantius Chlorus, up to then the Caesar of the west.

What threw this ponderous imperial game of musical chairs into chaos was that in 306 the barbarian border tribe of the Picts, ancestors of the modern lowland Scots, tried to invade Roman Britain. Constantius Chlorus would not put up with such effrontery and sailed for Britain with an army and his warrior son Constantine, determined to put the Picts down. He managed to do so; but then Constantius himself died, of unknown causes, at York in the summer of 306. This left his heir, the ambitious young Constantine, as imperial ruler of Britain, Gaul and Spain, with the full rank and title of Augustus. Or rather, it was expected to: but Galerius, the reigning Augustus of the east, did not want the boy to succeed him immediately. Constantine wrote to him asking to be ratified as the Augustus. Galerius would give him only the second rank, that of Caesar. Constantine accepted this, no doubt reluctantly but with as much grace as he could muster.

But in Rome, neither the army nor the majority of the people would go along with that arrangement. For reasons too prolix to go into here, stemming from their resentment at the prospect of forced tax levies, they wanted Maxentius, the son of Maximian, as Caesar. And once Maxentius was installed, he asked his father to come back from retirement and become, once again, the Augustus. Galerius, who wanted the next Augustus to be a military strongman (but not as strong as himself) named Severus, objected to this proposal and ordered his army to attack Maxentius. They lost; Severus' troops mutinied and killed their leader; and this left Maxentius and his legions in command of Rome. In retrospect, though of course it would hardly have seemed so at the time, the most important thing about Maxentius' power over Rome and its empire was, like Diocletian before him, an implacable dislike of the small and still rather marginal sect of the Christians.

Constantine launched himself across the Alps from Gaul, at the head of an expeditionary force numbering some forty thousand troops, perhaps a quarter of his whole army, in the spring of 312. His target was a heavily fortified Rome, where Maxentius had dug in. The cities of northern Italy offered little resistance. Some of them, notably Milan, effusively welcomed Constantine, because Maxentius' occupation of Rome had deprived them of much of their importance and power. As Constantine advanced southwards it became ever clearer that Maxentius was preparing for a siege. But when Constantine's force had come almost within striking distance of Rome, the Romans themselves lost confidence in their ability to resist a long siege; rumour and oracles persuaded them that Constantine was invincible, and so Maxentius realized that he would have to come out and fight, on the north side of the Tiber. The bridges across the river to Rome had all been destroyed, but Maxentius had a new, temporary one created from boats and pontoons where the more solid Milvian Bridge had stood. Across this structure, anchored against the flow of the Tiber, Maxentius and his army marched forth to confront Constantine on 28 October 312.

The result was a disaster, a rout.

In years to come Constantine gave his version of the battle of the Milvian Bridge and swore, under oath, that God had granted him a miraculous victory preceded by signs and omens. As he was leading his army south towards Rome, he claimed, he and every man under his command had seen a cross of light shining in the sky, with the words *In hoc signo vinces*: 'In this sign, conquer.' That night, when Constantine was asleep in his tent, Christ appeared to him in a dream holding that unfamiliar emblem of the cross and directed him to have new standards made for his army in its form.

What could this really have meant to him? In the early fourth century most people, Constantine included, had no idea of the symbolism of a cross. He was not a Christian, not yet, but there were some Christians among his advisers, such as Ossius, Bishop of Córdoba, and they all concurred in pointing out that the cross was the emblem of the greatest of all gods, and that if Constantine adopted it he could not be defeated. Well, Constantine seems to have thought, try anything once. The pagan standards were flung away, on went the crosses, and soon Maxentius' troops were on the run, in chaos and confusion. The boat-bridge disintegrated and Maxentius himself is said to have drowned under the weight of his armour while trying to get back across the Tiber.

Just before battle was joined, Constantine declared for Christianity. After the Milvian victory in 312, state persecution of Christians in the Roman Empire – torture, murder, confiscation of goods and property – effectively ceased. It was removed from state policy. There would be no more libellous assertions about the new sect such as had infested the policies of Diocletian, who regarded the cult as treasonous and diabolical and was not above torturing any suspected Christians on unfounded charges of arson, burning them alive, demolishing their chapels.

Constantine ordered that property and wealth confiscated from Christians under Diocletian's mandate should be given back. But it is far too easy, in Constantine's case, to ascribe to pure religious faith what was more like a continuous exercise in realism, carried out by a hard-headed soldier with a polytheistic background.

Certainly, he must have ascribed his victory over Maxentius, at least in part, to the intervention of some powerful god. It is always wise, as well as easy, for a winner to declare that God was on his side. But pagan symbols continued to appear on his coinage for twenty years after the battle of the Milvian Bridge. Constantine was not even baptized a Christian until he was dying, a quarter-century later, in 337. To say that he unambiguously 'converted' to a new faith, a new spiritual discipline, is to invoke a myth – however useful this myth became to Christian propaganda, as it assuredly did. What did it mean, to say that Constantine was the first Christian emperor? Not, perhaps, as much as later Christians made out. At this distance, and across such vast cultural differences as those between his time and ours, it is hardly possible to know.

Nevertheless, it is clear that there was a marked change in the religious landscape. The recognition of a new tolerance was inscribed in the so-called Edict of Milan, 313, which emerged from a wish of the now dying Galerius that Christians might be allowed to 'again rebuild the houses in which they used to meet'. (Christian religious ceremonies were generally not held in churches, but in *tituli* or houses of the faithful – 'meeting-houses' exactly describes them. Since there were relatively few churches yet dedicated as such, those shrines and meeting-places were commonly part of *tituli*: so this law was also an affirmation of personal privacy of worship. *Tituli* were usually named after the owners of the private property, as in Titulus Ceciliae or Titulus Anastasiae, or the Titulus Byzantii, named after the Roman senator Byzantius, who gave his house to the Christians as a place of worship. By the end of the fourth century about twenty-five of these were known in Rome. There may have been more, but this was in any case a tiny presence of Christians among the forty-four thousand *insulae* or apartment blocks and more than a million inhabitants Rome had in Constantine's time.) So, after his victory at the Milvian Bridge, Constantine and his co-emperor Licinius met at Milan and issued a declaration that Christians from now on must have complete religious freedom, that they should no longer suffer confiscations and, as Galerius wished, that their houses of worship, if taken from them, must be restored. This had large cultural as well as religious consequences, because it opened a space in which specifically Christian iconography and symbolic detail could flourish and develop, moving away from, though in many ways building on, Roman prototypes. A vivid example of this process is the sarcophagus of Junius Bassus (d. 359), one of the first Roman patricians to embrace Christianity. In form, it is a pagan sarcophagus. But on its sides, carved in deep relief, are scenes of such biblical events as the sacrifice of Isaac, the trial of Christ before Pilate, and Adam and Eve's shame at their nakedness, replacing such familiar sarcophagus images as gods, goddesses and battle scenes.

At the very least, Constantine knew he owed Christianity a great deal, since the new god on the cross had clearly overseen his utter defeat of Maxentius and placed him on the imperial throne. He also knew that debts have to be paid, especially when owed to such powerful gods; henceforth, the Christian Church would receive massive underwriting from the Roman state.

First, Constantine wrote to Maximinus, the ruler of the eastern Empire, pointing out that since Maxentius was dead and as the Roman Senate had now recognized him as the senior member of the imperial college, he had the absolute authority to order Maximinus, his junior, to cease from any and all persecution of Christians within the east, whether by tax, violence, confiscation or (God forbid!) martyrdom. Whatever had been taken from them must be given back. They must not be molested in or out of their places of worship.

Constantine had all officials appointed by Maxentius purged, and replaced by Christian-friendly ones. And in a decision whose consequences would echo down the centuries – granting any cultist quack and televangelist in modern America, for instance, openings to huge immunities and profits – he exempted the churches from tax. Shrewdly, he imposed no penalties on those among his subjects (and there were many, at first) who wanted to continue worshipping the older gods. One does not change the religious practices and loyalties of a whole empire merely by issuing an edict. Instead, he gave Christianity the status of the most favoured religion, then let social pressures take their course.

The most spectacular sign of the new order was the opening to the young Church of Constantine's imperial coffers. This happened most evidently in Rome, where its results could be seen by the most people. What did most favoured status mean unless the emperor disbursed as much on the temples of the new religion as his predecessors had on the old? With Christians among Constantine's advisers as early as 313, the Church was turning into a major political force already, and by acquiring new landholdings it became an important economic one as well. Constantine turned much of the revenues from Roman colonies in north Africa, Greece, Syria and Egypt towards underwriting and embellishing the new Christian foundations, perhaps four thousand gold *solidi* a year, the approximate equivalent in today's currency of $25–30 million.

With such funds it was possible to build actual churches, not merely convert private houses to places of worship.

On the east side of the Caelian Hill, by the Aurelian wall, was a site formerly belonging to an *eques* or knight named Plautius Lateranus; Constantine had acquired it and was determined to build a magnificent church on it, one that would hold two thousand worshippers, as an ex-voto thanking Christ for his victory over Maxentius. (Plautius Lateranus had been unwise enough to befriend Constantine's defeated rival Maxentius, and it must have gratified the emperor to demolish the barracks of his Horse Guards, who had apparently supported him against Constantine.) It was on the edge of the city, though just inside its walls, and this position meant that Constantine did not have to embark on demolitions that would offend the still-pagan elite whose shrines to traditional gods were crowded in the centre of Rome.

This elite continued to matter a great deal in the fourth and on into the fifth century CE. Christian writers were given to boast that they and their co-religionists were taking over, but nothing is so simple. In the fourth century Christian buildings were certainly being constructed, but it took centuries for the Pantheon to be rededicated as a Christian church by Pope Boniface IV in 609, and a further three hundred years went by before the next Roman temple, that of Fortuna Virilis, was Christianized. Why? It is not certain, but pious Christians may have imagined these buildings were contaminated by a residue of evil spirits. Certainly that was what people believed about the Colosseum. Meanwhile, pagan monuments were being repaired or even newly built – fora, streets, aqueducts, shrines and even temples. Indeed, to its most sophisticated residents the culture paganism stood for – learned, aesthetically rich and well embedded – was the only one worth having.

The siting of the Basilica Constantiniana, or San Giovanni in Laterano (as it came to be known, in recognition of the site's original owner), was of both symbolic and political importance, not only because it was the first great Christian church in Rome but also because it declared that it was not the Christian ambition to obliterate the more ancient Roman order: coexistence was the watchword between Constantine and the old aristocratic families. San Giovanni in Laterano was and remains the cathedral of Rome (not, be it noted, St Peter's, despite what so many tourists think). It is the mother-church of all Christendom and its role is stated in the inscriptions cut not once but twice on its façade: *omnium urbis et orbis ecclesiarum mater et caput* – 'the mother and head of all churches of the city and of the world'.

It set the archetypal form of Christian churches in the west by adapting, with minimal alterations, a Roman architectural form: the 'basilican' plan, so called after the Greek term meaning 'royal house': a long rectangular nave, a public space with entrance and apse on the opposite short sides. Side aisles, framed out from the body of the nave, provided space for ambulatories and chapels. This had been adapted from pagan Roman models (the first basilica in Rome had been built by Marcus Porcius Cato back in republican times, in 184 BCE). It served the same type of ceremonies: queues of acolytes, stately processions towards a designated focus, such as are involved in the sacraments of Holy Communion and Confession. The basilican plan lends itself to a clear and strict separation of the celebrant (the priest) from his communicants, as the centralized plan of the Greek rite does not. But the basilican Christian plan was open to a wide variety of forms: it could have several naves (some had up to nine of these aisles, separated by rows of columns). Rectangular, axial basilicas of this kind were less costly to build than the centrally planned ones, roofed with masonry domes, favoured in the east, because they did not require the elaborate curved shuttering needed to construct arches and domes.

It was, by the standards of its time (or any time), an enormous building, with a four-aisled nave 98 metres long and some 56 wide. Its main columns were of red granite, and its secondary aisle columns were recycled from ancient buildings and were of green marble. Apart from the enormous cost of construction, Constantine donated enough sheet gold – all looted long since – to decorate the apse.

This was not Constantine's only ecclesiastical venture in Rome, of course. He endowed what became a private chapel for the devotions of his mother Helena (250–330), S. Croce in Gerusalemme, in the Sessorian Palace. In c.326 the future St Helena made a pilgrimage to the Holy Land, from which she brought back shiploads of relics, including some tubs of soil from Calvary, and (a considerable engineering feat, if true) the stairs which Christ was believed to have climbed in the palace of Pontius Pilate in Jerusalem.

Some early Christian churches in Rome are almost-bewildering palimpsests. A case in point is the Basilica of S. Clemente, less than half a mile from the Colosseum. It was begun in the first century CE, raised on the foundations of a building, perhaps a warehouse, perhaps an apartment complex, burned out in the Great Fire of 64 CE and owned by a consul named Titus Flavius Clemens, a great-nephew of the emperor Vespasian. According to the Roman chroniclers Dio Cassius and Suetonius, Clemens was executed in 95 CE on charges of impiety connected with 'godlessness' and Judaism, brought by the emperor Domitian. Whether this indicated some connection with Christianity is a matter of debate; the pious like to believe it was. What is fairly certain, however, is that by the late second or early third century the dark, dank, cave-like space within the former *insula* had become a Mithraic temple, which was abandoned when, in the fourth century, Mithraism – imported to Rome largely by legions returning from Asia Minor after the campaigns of Pompey* – was outlawed by the now victorious Christians.

Frustratingly little, and from documentary sources almost nothing, is known about this religion. It was one of those mystery cults that has managed to keep most of its secrets down to the present day. Mithras, or Mithra, was a god-hero who embodied light and truth. His acolytes knew him as, among other honorifics, 'lord of the wide pastures', and his central, mythic action was the capture and killing of a wild bull, which he dragged to a cave and then slaughtered. From its blood sprang life and grain. The sacrificing god was known as Mithras Tauroctonos, 'Mithras the bull-slayer'. The killing of the bull was therefore a highly gen- erative act, and it may be that its memory is preserved, in a much mutated form, down to the present day in the Spanish cult of the bullfight. This story may descend from the Greek myth of Perseus killing the Gorgon Medusa, and may have originated with King Mithridates VI of Persia, who was named after Mithras but claimed descent from Perseus.

Mithraism never claimed a mass collective audience such as Christianity acquired. It had no need of huge basilicas – its cave- like gathering-places were usually no more than sixty by twenty- five feet. Moreover, the congregation it did have was deliberately restricted. Mithraism was a masculine warrior cult from which

---

* Mithraism was practised by the pirates whom Pompey suppressed in 67. It took hold in ancient Rome in the first century BCE. Its spread was so rapid that the Emperor Commodus was initiated into the cult at the end of the second century CE, and it was an important factor in the religious initiation of Julian the Apostate, in the fourth century.

women were strictly excluded. *Mithraea* (the term for its meeting-places) have been found in Rome, about a dozen in all, the largest being the Mithraeum Thermarum Antonianum underneath the Baths of Caracalla. The remains of others exist in Ostia, a reminder of how common Mithraic worship was in ports, among sailors and travellers.

There were similarities between the cults of Mithras and of Jesus, but they generally turn out to be superficial and there is little support for the once common view that Christianity developed out of Mithraism. Certainly Mithraism was more like Christianity than any of the other eastern mystery cults that found adepts in Rome. But the two were also very dissimilar. Christianity wanted to spread; one of its main strengths was among women, and the idea of excluding half the human race from the faith would have been incomprehensible to the early Church, whatever its suspicions of the female sex.

Above the lowest, Mithraic floor of the *titulus* of Clemens (or Clemente, as his name is given in Italian) is another level, dating from the late fourth century and clearly associated with Christian worship. Over the centuries it was adorned with a series of frescoes and mosaics, of which the most beautiful is a depiction of the Tree of Life in its apse – Christ crucified, with white doves roosting on the arms of his cross, and writhing spirals issuing from the base of the tree to fill the gold semicircle of the background. Of all the early Christian monuments of Rome, this twelfth-century mosaic is one of the most decorative and satisfying.

Various legends cling to the church. One is that after S. Clemente, third successor to St Peter as Bishop of Rome, was flung into the Black Sea in 98 CE by the impious Romans with an anchor tied to his neck, his body was recovered by two Slavic saints, Cyril (826–69) and Methodius (815–85), brought to Rome and buried in the church that bears his name. Another is recorded in a fresco in the nave. It tells how a Roman husband, peeved by his wife's constant attendance at Mass, referred to the clergy of S. Clemente's as *fili dele pute*, 'sons of whores'. Not only is this a surprising inscription to be found anywhere in a church; it is said to be the earliest known writing in vernacular Italian.

Constantine had (why, it is uncertain) a particular devotion to an early Christian martyr named St Lawrence (San Lorenzo). This was the deacon who, in the third century, was supposedly roasted to death on a gridiron. (The pious story that he defied his pagan tormentors by exclaiming, after a few minutes had brought him to medium-rare, 'Turn me over, I am done on this side' is no doubt apocryphal.) Constantine had Lawrence's grave identified (at least at a guess), and then covered with a handsome silver grating, glorifying the original grill. Then he raised a *basilica major*, complete with inlaid cosmatesque decoration, to mark the spot.

In a move to expiate the fierce injustices of pagan persecution, he underwrote various martyrs' shrines, of which the most important in terms of its cult power was the Church of the Apostle Peter in the Vatican. There had been a longstanding cult concerning the remains of St Peter, martyred in Rome during the persecutions of Nero. There is no proof that the bones in whose honour Constantine had this basilica constructed actually belonged to that Apostle, to whom Jesus allegedly entrusted his newborn church (*'Tu es Petrus, et super hanc petram aedificabo ecclesiam meam'*). The fact that successive rebuildings of St Peter's, culminating in the stupendous pile marvelled at by today's faithful, are believed to stand above the saint's actual bones proves nothing; the issue, as one Christian historian tactfully put it, is 'clouded by confessional loyalties'.

Another main recipient of Constantine's civic largesse was Palestine – in particular, the city of Jerusalem. His mother Helena, like many another woman of humble origins who comes into great wealth and power, was unrestrained in her generosity; she founded and had built the Church of the Nativity in Bethlehem, dedicated to Mary Mother of Christ, and another church on the Mount of Olives to mark the point of her son's ascent into heaven. But the grandest construction was Constantine's own, designed to mark the special relationship between the emperor and God. On what was believed to be the site of the crucifixion, overlapping on to Christ's tomb, the emperor ordained the construction of a magnificent basilica. This entailed the destruction of a Roman shrine to Venus, and in the course of the work the excavators found a chamber, containing not a body (one would certainly not have wanted to find a body, given the dogma of the Resurrection – 'He is risen, He is not here,' said the angel) but a quantity of wood, which (of course) could only be the wood of the True Cross on which the Son of Man had expired. Splinters of this timber would fill the Christian world's reliquaries in centuries to come. Those inclined to believe in such things also identified a small stone room, hardly more than a hole, abutting what was rebuilt as an ambulatory, as being the prison in which Christ had been mewed up before his crucifixion.

These links between the New Testament account of Christ's passion and death and the discoverable fabric of the excavated building were tenuous, but they did not deter Constantine's representatives from saying with certainty that the site of the Holy Sepulchre had been found. The work of expanding and ennobling it began almost at once, on Constantine's orders. All who saw it agreed with Eusebius, the Bishop of Caesarea (c.260–340), Constantine's chief admirer and interpreter, in finding the Church of the Holy Sepulchre a building beyond compare, encased in marble and with a coffered ceiling gilded from end to end. Moreover it contained, in a small side-chapel, what was believed to be the place where Jesus himself had expired on the cross – the Rock of Calvary. In its original form, the Church of the Holy Sepulchre, when it was formally dedicated in 336 on the thirtieth anniversary of Constantine's coronation as Roman emperor, was the supreme architectural marvel of Christendom, the gold-sheathed and jewel-studded house that testified to the triumph of God.

Unfortunately little of it remains. In 614, after the Persian conquest of Jerusalem, the Holy Sepulchre was sacked. Some restorations took place over the next few hundred years but then, catastrophically, the caliph Al-Hakim, a religious fanatic who believed that no Christian institution should be allowed to stand on ground associated in any way with Islam, ordered the complete demolition of the Sepulchre. But by then there were many other

Christian churches in what had been the pagan east, built and supported by funds from the confiscation of temple treasures, and untouchable by any caliph.

Constantine did not, of course, confine himself to church-building. He was an indefatigable legislator who also rewrote many of the laws relating to behaviour and punishment. Noting that eminent Christians of the past, like St Paul, had complained of the obligation to sue one another in pagan lawcourts over civil matters, he made it legal for them to take their cases out of the hands of civil judges and into the arbitration of bishops, whose verdicts would be final. This greatly increased the Church's power over civil life, as Paul had hoped it would. In the criminal domain, he abolished crucifixion as a punishment, holding that Our Lord's manner of death should no longer be the atrocious and degrading thing that pagan Rome held it to be; it was wrong to subject common criminals to what Christianity held to be a fearful but now hallowed form of sacrifice.

This was not due to squeamishness. When it came to inflicting pain, Constantine could be as brutal as any other emperor. On the complicated matter of sexual behaviour his views were so extreme as to qualify as psychotic, and must certainly have seemed so to anyone accustomed to the more relaxed attitudes of pagan family law.

In an edict of 1 April 326, he totally forbade married men to keep mistresses. Only men (husbands, fathers, brothers or uncles) could bring denunciations of adultery within a family – women, never. Rapists and seducers must be burned alive, a punishment which could also be inflicted on any girl who eloped without parental approval, and on anyone who aided the elopement. If a nurse encouraged a girl to take off in this way, her mouth would be forced open while boiling lead was poured down her throat. But a girl who lost her virginity to a rapist also deserved punishment; clearly she had been asking for it – she could have stayed at home. Worse, Constantine ordained that, once raped, she must lose the right to inherit property from her parents. This condemned her to the marginal life of a reject, since it deprived her of the dowry without which no man would marry her.

It might seem difficult to reconcile the author of such repugnant statutes with the man often praised for bringing the message of Gentle Jesus to a pagan world. But within the soul of Constantine an innate sadism was looking for an outlet, and found it in the misogynistic lunacies of Christian asceticism. This can be seen from the wretched fate of Crispus, Constantine's eldest son by an early marriage. A young married man who enjoyed a brilliant reputation as a military prodigy, and had already served as Caesar to his father's Augustus, Crispus certainly would have succeeded to the imperial throne. But for reasons which are still obscure, Constantine's newer wife the empress Fausta accused him of violating her. It was her word against his, there was no proof. In an ungovernable rage, Constantine put Crispus on trial with himself as sole judge, declared him guilty, and had him executed. But then Constantine's aged mother Helena, who did not believe the story about Crispus and Fausta, seems to have received some persuasive evidence that Fausta had concocted it to cover her adultery with a palace slave. When it was revealed to Constantine, he had Fausta shut in the hot-room of the imperial palace baths, whose furnaces were then stoked so that she boiled to death.

Crispus had been put to death in Pola. This had caused some political embarrassment and it is probably why Helena, Constantine's mother, went on an ostentatious pilgrimage to the Holy Land in 326. It cannot have been an easy trip, since she was in her mid seventies when she set out. But the dowager empress played her role with impressive determination, her son encouraging her to spend whatever was needed to help people forget the Crispus–Fausta scandal and the delicious gossip it had ignited. It was during this trip that she endowed those two churches in Palestine, the one in Bethlehem to commemorate Mary and the nativity of Jesus, and the other dedicated to his ascension into heaven from the Mount of Olives. She gave generously to whoever approached her on her progress through the Holy Land – soldiers, priests, the poor – and released prisoners from jail and from the mines. She acquired enormous and bulky relics, such as the aforementioned stairs up which Jesus was supposed to have climbed in the house of Pilate, and shipped them to Rome. Then, worn out by her travels and benefactions, she died, probably in Nicomedia. Her body was placed in a massive porphyry sarcophagus and carried, under military guard, back to Rome.

As the religious as well as the political leader of the Roman Empire, Constantine inevitably had to deal with matters of heresy. Heresy had not been a problem for the older Roman religions, which left their devotees much freer in their selection of cults and rites than Christians would, or could, ever be. But Christianity was an intolerant religion which placed extreme emphasis on orthodoxy of belief. More and more, bristling phalanxes of bishops and theologians stood ready to do battle over the smallest inflection, the least quillet of doctrinal meaning. The result was a nightmare of religio-political correctness, in which the stakes were not simply the tolerance or disapproval of others but (it was believed) the soul's prospect of eternity in hell. This gave a terrible seriousness to theological argument. Ridiculous as many such debates may seem from a twenty-first-century viewpoint (there can be few believers left who care how many angels can dance on the point of a pin), in the fourth century they gave rise to the first Christian persecutions, in which one wing of the faithful tormented and killed members of another over what now look like absurdly minuscule differences of belief.

The first such split was over 'Donatism'. This heresy had caused a schism in the Church of Africa, which had only slight repercussions in Europe. It arose, quite simply, from the fact that during the persecutions of Diocletian some Christians had knuckled under, denying their faith to save their skins. Now that Diocletian was gone and Christianity had become the state religion, these quislings sought to rejoin the Church and be forgiven. But a strong group opposed this, tooth and nail. To them, there must be no future forgiveness for former collaborators. Their leader was a Carthaginian priest named Donatus. This, one might have thought, could have been resolved at the lower levels of the

Church, but it proved insoluble. The emperor himself had to rule on it – and he did, ordering the army to force the Donatists into submission. Thus began the first orthodox, official Christian persecution and martyrdom of 'heretic' Christians.

There would be others. The most spectacular, bitter and bloody of them was the fourth-century Arian persecution, which split the Church down the middle and caused seemingly illimitable suffering to many as Christians rejected, tormented and frequently slaughtered one another over a single vowel, an extra o, descriptive of Christ's relationship to God the Father and the Holy Spirit. Was Christ *homoousios* with God the Father (made of the same essence as God, and existing from the beginning of time) or merely *homousios* (similar in essence but not the same, and created after the Father, there having been 'a time when he was not')? This seemingly absurd dispute originated in Alexandria with a highly intellectual priest named Arius (d. 336), who fiercely objected to any prevalent reading of the Scriptures that claimed that Christ was the Son of God, 'begotten, not made', sharing the Father's divine essence and existing for all time. Orthodox Christianity disagreed. It regarded the dogma of the Trinity – God consisting of three persons, the Father, Son and Holy Ghost, who form one substance – as a basic and central tenet of faith, which it was heresy to deny. It was this 'one substance' clause, as it were, that generated the passion over whether Christ was *homoousios* or *homousios* with his Father. The dogma of the Trinity was a 'mystery', not comprehensible through human logic; there were later attempts to rationalize it, though, as when a Victorian cleric argued that one need only imagine a carriage with three persons riding in it – to which another Victorian cleric retorted that one should try instead to envision three carriages with one single person riding in them.

The dispute was settled, after a fashion, when Constantine himself felt obliged to intervene. In 325 he summoned a council of bishops in the city of Nicaea to pronounce on the ideas of Arius. Their verdict, not unexpectedly, was that Arianism was a heresy to be stamped out. This was enshrined in the Nicene Creed, a document repudiating Arius and agreed to, pro forma, by all the bishops of the Catholic Church. Jesus was now officially *homoousios* with his Father.

Despite Constantine's gestures towards relative tolerance, by 325 paganism was a lost cause within the Roman Empire. Many of the supporters of Constantine's erstwhile co-emperor Licinius, still a pagan, were killed off after his death. (Constantine was said to have had Licinius himself strangled, though the circumstances remain murky.) Most of the survivors were dismissed. Pagan rituals, such as sacrifice to the gods, divination or the consultation of oracles, were now banned absolutely. In effect – and luckily for the archaeology of the future – pagans could keep their shrines, temples and sacred groves, not demolish them but not worship in them. Constantine made sure that no more pagans, or even those who had recently abjured pagan beliefs, would be appointed as magistrates, prefects or provincial governors. All preference would go to Christians. But active persecution of pagan religions was not required, since it might provoke violent counter-reactions. Constantine wanted peace, albeit peace only on terms of submission to Christianity.

Apart from Christianity itself, the great beneficiary of Constantine's power was the city of Constantinople, which he founded in 330, not quite a quarter-century after he was proclaimed emperor. To say that Constantinople was in any real sense the 'new Rome', replacing the original by a single act of will, is of course a foolish simplification. But Constantine was determined to found a new and great Christian city where he and later Christian emperors could hold their court in an environment not contaminated by physical memories of paganism – no temples to the gods, no relics of pre-Christian institutions. This ruled out rebuilding the site of Troy, which he seems to have briefly considered for its mythological attractions but then rejected because he did not want his actions attributed to Homeric inspiration.

On Europe's most south-easterly peninsula, between the salt-water strait known as the Golden Horn and the inlet from the Sea of Marmara called the Bosphorus, was a neck of land on which

17 *Santi Cosma e Damiano Apse, 526–530*

18 *San Clemente basilica mosaic, 12th century*

19 *Cola da Caprarola,*
San Maria della
Consolazione,
Todi, 1508

20 Raphael
The School of Athens,
1509–1510

Fresco, 500 × 770 cm;
Apostolic Palace,
Vatican City

21 Michelangelo
Moses, c. 1513–1515 Marble, 235 cm; San Pietro in Vincoli, Rome

22 Raphael
The Liberation of St Peter from Prison, early 16th century.

Fresco; Stanze di Raffaello, Vatican Palace, Vatican

23 Raphael
The Triumph of Galatea, 1513

Fresco, 295 × 224 cm
Villa Farnesina, Rome

24 Raphael
Portrait of a Young Woman ('La Fornarina'), 1518–1520
Oil on wood, 85 × 60 cm; Galleria Nazionale d'Arte Antica, Rome

25 Michelangelo
Piazza del Campidoglio,
1536–1546

FACING PAGE
26 Michelangelo
The Last Judgement, 1537–1541
Fresco, 1370 × 1200 cm;
Sistine Chapel, Vatican City

OVERLEAF
27 Michelangelo
Sistine Chapel, 1537–1541
Fresco, 4050 × 1400 cm;
Sistine Chapel, Vatican City

stood the remains of a Greek settlement and the beginnings of a minor Roman city, its origins dating from the seventh century BCE. This city was known as Byzantion. It had obvious strategic and trade advantages. It stood at the intersection of the land route from Europe to Asia and the sea route from the Mediterranean to the Black Sea. It was well placed for self-defence. Most of it was girdled by the waters of the Golden Horn, to the north, and the Sea of Marmara, to the south. It needed only a wall across its base, between the bodies of water, to make it very difficult to invade. The Via Egnatia linked it to Rome, while from it two other roads led east towards Asia Minor. The land behind it was indulgent to crops and fruit, and rich in building stone. The sea around it fairly teemed with fish. Aqueducts gave it water, and as soon as serious building work began on the new city they would be supplanted by many large cisterns, some forty of which survive (and are full of fresh water) to the present day – water palaces, one of which is known to the Turks as 'the Cistern of a Thousand and One Columns', which must be close to a factual description.

Here, a new capital could be built – the capital of what would from now on be the eastern Empire. It would owe a triple allegiance to geography. It lay at the eastern end of the Mediterranean, between the worlds of Rome and the east, right on the borders of Europe and Asia. Yet it fully shared the character of neither. The Asia Minor to which it partly belongs was neither geographically nor ethnoculturally a part of Asia, though it belongs in a sense to the Asian continent. By the same token, the eastern Balkans on which Byzantion and its territories abut are in most senses remote and disconnected from what an Italian, a German or a Greek would be inclined to call 'Europe'. Byzantion, no matter how or how far it was developed, was almost certain to be an anomaly to both Europeans and Asians. This suited Constantine very well. He threw the resources of his domain into this project and the resulting metropolis was naturally named after him: Constantinople.

Less is known of the archaeology of Constantinople than of Rome. There are various reasons for this, but the chief one is that since it was conquered by the Muslims in the early Middle Ages the Turkish authorities have been at best reluctant, and at worst opposed, to having their city dug up in search of Christian remains, at the possible expense of later, Islamic ones. This deadlock is unlikely to be freed in the imaginable future; it would be too unpopular with today's radical or even moderate Islam.

The building of Constantinople, spurred by Constantine's desire for a new capital, went on very fast. In some respects it repeated the layout of Rome, with a central forum, a senate house, an imperial palace and a main street, the Mese. Its centre was the hippodrome, where some of the great dramas of the city – political as well as sporting – would be played out after Constantine's death. It did not, however, have a gladiatorial arena and its churches took the place of temples. Constantine's churches were almost always designed on the basilican plan, which produced a huge, long interior space without internal supports, similar to the basilica he had built in Trier when he was still Caesar there. Their ultimate model was the Roman Church of San Giovanni in Laterano, his vast thanks-offering for victory at the Milvian Bridge.

Constantine died in 337. It is likely, though not certain, that despite his colossal achievements he was afflicted by a sense of failure: having killed his eldest son and likely successor, the gifted Crispus, along with his wife Fausta, he could hardly have felt wholly fulfilled. He had three other sons, all formally recognized as Augusti: Constantine II, twenty-one years old at his father's death, Constantius II (twenty) and Constans I (seventeen). Deadly quarrels immediately broke out among them. In 340 Constantine II – who had inherited control of the western part of the Empire – attacked Constans I, ruler of Italy and Africa. The attack failed, and he was defeated and killed, which placed all the western Empire (including Britain and Germany) in Constans' hands, while Constantius II controlled the eastern part. But Constans' rule in the west was so harsh that his troops rebelled – an extraordinarily rare event in the Roman army – and in 350 he was deposed and killed. After much skirmishing, the officers who had led this revolt succumbed to internal bickering and were finally destroyed by the third brother, Constantius II, who emerged in 353 as the ruler of a united Roman Empire.

After all this murdering and much more manoeuvring, Constantius II found himself seeking a co-emperor: the task of running so vast an empire was more than one man could handle. He found a collaborator, as he thought, in Flavius Claudius Julianus (331–63), nephew of Constantine. As it happened, Constantius had already arranged in 337 for the murder of Julian's father and most of his close relatives, sparing Julian (and, for a while, his half-brother Gallus) only because of their youth. This proved to be a grievous error. Julian had grown up with Gallus, in semi-internment under the thumb of Constantius in the remote provincial village of Macellum in Cappadocia. Clearly, he was not happy about the massacre of his family (what anguish of survivor guilt did it raise in him?) and he never forgave Constantius for it.

Julian had been raised strictly as a Christian and had even taken lower orders as a *lector* in the Church. His eventual 'apostasy', his turning-away from the Christianity espoused by his egomaniac bully of an uncle Constantius II, seems to have been a classic example of what can go wrong when beliefs are shoved down the neck of an intelligent, sensitive youth temperamentally unfitted to receive or practise them. Constantius II, from the historian Ammianus Marcellinus' account, took orthodoxy to new heights, and was rigidly obsessed with making his godlike stature felt: 'He both stooped when passing through lofty gates (although he was very short), and as if his neck were in a vice, he kept the gaze of his eyes straight ahead and turned his face neither to left nor to right ... neither did he nod when the wheels jolted nor was he ever seen to spit, or to wipe or rub his face or nose, or move his hands about.'

This narcissistic and crazed formalist was hardly the kind of person to raise a young intellectual. He demanded from the lad a hostility for all Hellenic culture; and Julian's predictable response was to embrace classical Greece, its art, its philosophy and Platonic ideals, with enthusiasm. He took up studies in Athens in 355, in his early twenties. He also showed a real and unexpected talent for military command. Also in 355 Constantius II dispatched him to Gaul, to quell dissent among the Franks and Alemanni. Though completely untested in battle, Julian proved highly successful as a victorious general – this still in his early twenties. So successful was he, in fact, that his troops were more loyal to him than to their remote commander Constantius. When Constantius wanted to move Julian's legions to fight in a coming Persian campaign, they mutinied and proclaimed him Augustus. Civil war loomed; it was averted only because Constantius unexpectedly died, leaving Julian as emperor – he would be the last pagan emperor of Rome.

To the young Julian, Constantius II's mindset seemed bigoted and barbaric – as indeed it was. Julian had a deeply religious temperament but not a Christian one. His natural bent was towards what was called 'theurgy', the pantheistic mysticism favoured by the Neoplatonist philosophers of his time. Undoubtedly there were quacks and charlatans among the theurgists, but at least it can be said that they did not have the fanatical character common among the early Christians, and no one was persecuted by them. Julian believed in the idea of 'metempsychosis', proposed by followers of Pythagoras: the direct transmigration of souls, from one body to another. (Julian apparently believed that his body was occupied and, as it were, animated by the spirit of Alexander the Great.)

'Theurgy' meant, in Greek, 'divine work'; it was a kind of mystery religion, part Neoplatonist and part esoteric ritual based on (now lost) Greek texts known as the Chaldean Oracles. The theurgist hoped to learn how the universe worked and then apply its workings to his own advantage. Thus the soul would be purified. It clearly had a powerful appeal to Julian and other intellectuals who wished to preserve some of the character of the old worships. But since the rites of theurgy were understood to compel divine powers and not merely invoke them, it was not always easy to distinguish theurgy from magic. To a polytheist the magic was white; it depended on a belief in hidden sympathies and affinities between different parts of the cosmos. To Christians the magic was black, and had to be opposed because it was thought to summon demons. Julian's beliefs, to the extent that they could be revealed to anyone outside his circle of fellow theurgists, struck Christians as being little short of witchcraft.

Just as Constantine had restricted his powerful favours to Christian petitioners, so Julian reserved his for pagans. He would not persecute 'Galileans', as he scornfully called the followers of Jesus, but he scarcely tolerated them; he withheld both his respect and his help from them. 'When the inhabitants of Nisibis sent to beg his aid against the Persians who were about to invade the Roman territories, he refused to assist them because they were wholly Christianized. He would neither reopen their temples nor resort to the sacred places, and he threatened that he would not help them, nor receive their embassy, nor come to enter their city until he had heard that they had returned to paganism.'

In his political views, Julian looked back to an earlier Rome. What he admired was Augustus' conception of the emperor as *primus inter pares*, 'the first among equals', a citizen not ostentatiously raised above his fellows, not a despot, and scorning the apparatus of imperial power. 'The luxury of the palace excited the contempt and indignation of Julian,' wrote Edward Gibbon, 'who usually slept on the ground ... and who placed his vanity not in emulating, but in despising the pomp of royalty.' He deeply disliked such signs of servility as being addressed by inferiors as *dominus* or 'Lord'. He dressed simply and let his beard grow, which exposed him to ill-tempered satire. After the death of his wife he is said never to have looked at another woman.

He felt a duty to assert the rights of his adoptive tradition against the arrogant presumptions of the state-sponsored Christians. In fact, because of his commitment to *apostasis* or 'standing up' against Christian doctrine, he was known in his time and ever since as Julian the Apostate. Having won the status of official religion to the Roman Empire, the once marginal sect of Christians went on the attack – and this began even before Julian's ascendancy to Augustus. In the Theodosian Code, 357 CE, the emperor Constantius issued bans on soothsayers and astrologers, whose 'evil teachings' must henceforth 'become silent' and 'for

ever cease'. They must all be deported from the city of Rome.
Christian punishment for haruspication, the 'heinous' ancient
Etruscan practice adopted by Rome, seemed to know no limits.
But the punishment of those who worshipped traditional gods at
their traditional shrines was deliberately and cleverly left to those
new fanatics, the Christian masses themselves, who could be
relied on to do more damage in their effusions of zeal than need
ever be planned by Christian bishops. Posses of hymn-chanting
monks, the 'black-robed tribe' of whom the traditionalist Libanius, a justly renowned orator and writer (314–93), complained
to the emperor Theodosius, pious drunkards 'who eat more than
elephants', assailed the unprotected temples with stones and
crowbars. 'Then utter desolation follows, with the stripping of
roofs, demolition of walls, tearing-down of statues and overthrow
of altars. The priests must either keep quiet or die. After demolishing one they scurry to another, and to a third . . . Such outrages
occur even in the cities.'

But they were worst in the countryside, where by ravaging the
ill-protected temples the Christians condemned countless sites to
religious and therefore social and economic barrenness. 'Temples,
sire,' Libanius tried to point out to Theodosius,

> are the soul of the countryside; they mark the beginning of
> its settlement, and have been passed down through many
> generations to the men of today. In them farming com-
> munities rest their hopes for husbands, wives, children, for
> the oxen and the soil they sow and plant. An estate that has
> suffered in this way has lost the inspiration of the peasantry
> along with their hoes; for they believe that their labour will
> be in vain once they are robbed of the gods who direct their
> labours to their due end . . . One god supports the might of
> Rome, another protects for her a city under her sway, another
> protects an estate and grants it prosperity. Let temples every-
> where continue to exist, then, or else let these people agree
> that you emperors are ill-disposed to Rome since you allow
> her to act in a manner that will cause her harm.

Constantius II, in his last will, had recognized Julian as his lawful successor and now, with this authority confirmed, Julian set about restoring the damaged prestige of polytheism.

His first tactic was to reduce the Christian churches' income, so lavishly bestowed on them by Constantine. Large sums had been confiscated, or in plain terms looted, from the pagan temples and given to the churches. Julian saw to it that they were given back, along with the income-earning lands taken by the churches. This could not, of itself, restore the loss and damage that the pagan religious foundations had undergone since the conversion of Constantine. But it went some way to rectify things – if only briefly. Sometimes one detects a heavy-handed, chortling irony in Julian's abjurations. Thus he took obvious pleasure in imposing heavy fines on the Christians of Edessa for 'the insolence bred by their wealth', by invoking Jesus' praise of the poor and lowly: 'Since by their most admirable law they are bidden to sell all they have and give it to the poor so that they may attain more easily to the kingdom of the skies ... I have ordered that all their funds that belong to the church of Edessa ... be confiscated; this in order that poverty may teach them to behave properly and that they may not be deprived of the heavenly kingdom for which they still hope.' And to cancel the Christian laws against pagan practices, which Julian did, was a great step in the liberal direction. He had little time or respect for Christians, but he was too shrewd a strategist to persecute them. Instead he offered toleration to every faith and cult – especially to 'heretics' and to Jews. 'I affirm by the gods,' he declared, 'that I do not wish the Galileans to be either put to death or unjustly beaten, or to suffer any other injury; but nevertheless I do assert absolutely that the god-fearing must be preferred to them. For through the folly of the Galileans almost everything has been overturned, whereas through the grace of the gods we are all preserved.'

His one wholly anti-Christian enactment, which infuriated the 'Galileans', was to forbid them to teach the classics in schools, for classical literature was still the basis of all higher education: let them stick to their own beliefs, Julian in effect said, and preach to their own kind about the glories of monotheism, but leave others to teach earlier Roman literature in the polytheistic spirit which originally lay behind it. 'I think it is absurd that men who expound the works of [the classic writers] should dishonour the gods whom these men honoured ... since the gods have granted us liberty, it seems to me absurd that men should teach what they do not believe to be sound.' No Christian, therefore, who presumed to teach grammar, rhetoric or especially philosophy could be considered a good person, since he was preaching what he did not practise or believe in. He would be a hypocrite and so was bound to corrupt the young, even when he did not want to. If this policy could be carried out, Julian believed, the whole educated elite of the Roman Empire would, within a couple of generations, be pagan once again. Meanwhile, the pedants and monotheists must leave him and his likeminded people alone. 'I worship the gods openly, and the whole mass of the troops who are returning with me worship the gods ... The gods command me to restore their worship in its utmost purity, and I obey them, yes, and with a good will.'

As well as seeking restitution of confiscated pagan land and buildings, Julian worked hard to reassert the independent power of the *curiales* or city councils (as against the influence of the bishops). This alone, quite apart from his religious beliefs, was bitterly resented by the Christians. He tolerated Christians not because he liked them or respected their beliefs, but because he recognized the truth of the saying that the blood of martyrs is the seed of the Church. He did not want to give the 'Galileans' victim status, or do anything that might have aroused sympathy for them. Noting the doctrinal squabbling among Christian clergy and theologians, and the fierce rivalries it caused, he thought it wise to play a waiting game and let the 'Galileans' weaken one another. Could this have worked? It is unlikely but in any case we cannot know, because in 363 Julian was killed during a campaign against the Persians. A spear-thrust pierced his liver. This fatal wound may have been inflicted by a Persian or (possibly) a disloyal Christian in his own army. He was the last pagan emperor and all his immediate successors did their best to eliminate whatever he might have achieved. Julian's hostility to Christianity was deeply felt, but it was slight and measured compared to the fury with which Christian emperors after him would persecute intellectual pagans, staging ferocious witch trials on various concocted pretexts, usually the possession of 'wrong' or heretical books.

Julian was succeeded as emperor by the relatively moderate Christian Jovian (331–64). He reigned for only a year and died of carbon monoxide poisoning, from a defective brazier. His ill-educated successor, Flavius Valentinianus (321–75), known as Valentinian, showed tolerance towards pagans but was fatally short-tempered; he lost his temper so completely during a peace negotiation in 375 that he suffered a stroke and died. The throne now passed to his pious and sadistic younger brother Valens, who instituted a series of purges of real or suspected pagans, carried out with a 'monstrous savagery', wrote the fourth-century chronicler Ammianus Marcellinus, that 'spread everywhere like a fiercely blazing torch'. The record of denunciation amassed by Valens' inquisitors was such that no literate or philosophic-minded person felt safe under his rule, so that 'throughout the eastern provinces owners of books . . . burned their entire libraries, so great was the terror that had seized upon all'. Merely to be accused of sorcery or unChristian beliefs led to summary execution; men were maimed, hideously torn with hooks, and dragged off to the scaffold and the chopping-block. And, as in Germany a millennium and a half later, 'the scene was like a slaughtering of cattle': and

> Innumerable writings and many heaps of volumes were brought together from various houses and under the eyes of the judges were burned – being pronounced unlawful, to allay the indignation at the executions, although the greater number were treatises on the liberal arts and on jurisprudence.

But history would soon have its revenge on Valens, and, as many would come to see it, on Rome itself. It erupted from the

Germanic people known as the Visigoths, who had settled in the early fourth century CE in a former Roman province known as Dacia – approximately, modern Romania. These people were invaded soon after by other Germanic tribes, who in their turn had been displaced by invaders from central Asia known as the Huns. Driven by starvation and deprivation, the Visigoths in 376 petitioned the imperial government in Constantinople to be allowed to cross the Danube and seek refuge in Thrace. Instead of refusing them, the eastern emperor Valens made the error of allowing the Visigoths free entry to his territory. His motive was simple and wrong: he thought he could co-opt the loyalty of the new immigrants, and get their warriors into his armies, which already contained numerous Visigoths. He also expected that his own soldiers could get their hands, by cunning fraud if not by violence, on the wealth the Visigoths would bring with them.

So as soon as they were across the Danube, the Visigoths found themselves in conflict with Roman officials. They were battle-hardened, badly deprived people who realized that the Romans were ready to cheat them blind. So they fought back. In 377 their revolt spread to include other groups, especially slaves. Much to the amazement of imperial officialdom, the rebels forced a Roman retreat.

Valens could hardly believe this, but he resolved to crush the Visigothic rising. And so, on the eastern frontier, near the modern city of Edirne in Turkey, then known as Adrianople, battle was joined. By now the Roman army, once so unified, homogeneous and dreaded, consisted largely of mercenaries who were not fighting for their homelands. It did not have the *esprit de corps* of former days, and presently an incredulous Roman citizenry would learn that the barbarians had overwhelmed it at Adrianople – the Visigothic victory was so complete that the corpse of Valens could not even be found beneath the heaps of Roman dead, containing two-thirds of the Roman army and some thirty-five of its senior officers. Fritigern, the Visigothic leader, could not have dared to expect so total a triumph.

The catastrophe at Adrianople shook Roman self-confidence

so badly that it has been regarded, ever since, as comparable to Rome's stupefying loss to Hannibal at Cannae, six centuries before.

This did nothing to ease the transition from paganism to Christianity. At this point most worshippers of the old gods saw no reason whatsoever to give up their faith, and many regarded the new Christians as a pack of arrogant, moralizing primitives. In response, the Christians, emboldened and presumptuously certain that they alone possessed the Truth, could and did behave with an equal high-handedness and violence towards 'obstinate' pagans – it was their turn to do some persecuting. There were many cases of this, and some of the flare-ups were deadly. One was the destruction of the Serapeion in Alexandria at the end of the fourth century. This temple, dedicated to the Egyptian god Serapis, was one of the most famed and revered sites of pagan cultism in the Mediterranean, and attracted numberless worshippers. It had remained intact and unmolested through the reign of Constantine the Great. But in 391 it was seized, sacked and desecrated by a mob of Christians, at the behest of Theophilos, Bishop of Alexandria: 'The statues were removed, the *adyta* [secret places where objects used in worship were kept] were exposed; and, in order to cast disrepute on the pagan mysteries, [Theophilos] made a procession for the display of these objects, the *phalli*, and he made a public exhibition of what ever other objects ... were, or seemed to be, ridiculous.'

Offended by this grossly provocative insult, the pagans at the Serapeion attacked the Christians, killed a number of them, and seized the temple. Reprisals were violent and prolonged, culminating in the crucifixion of several Christians and a declaration by the emperor Theodosius I that the dead Christians were blessed martyrs and candidates for sainthood. Realizing that the next step was likely to be a full-scale attack by imperial forces, the pagans of the Serapeion panicked and fled.

The Serapeion was the best-known but certainly not the only pagan foundation in which this sort of takeover occurred. Strangely enough, at first sight, such conversions were late in coming to Rome itself. The first Roman temple to be converted to Christian use was the Pantheon, which in 609 was finally rededicated as S. Maria ad Martyres by Pope Boniface IV. What did this suggest? Only that people tend to be slow in giving up the religions they are used to, and that when a city has a large population of believers – and Rome had the largest – they will be correspondingly slower. For centuries after the death of Christ, Rome would remain a city in which all manner of cults continued to flourish. But now Christianity had taken its majority-holder's place in the general repertoire of belief, and nothing was going to dislodge it. From that point on it could only grow, and, in growing, push out weaker cults whose survival no longer had the mandate of a growing popularity.

5

MEDIEVAL ROME AND AVIGNON

Roman Christianity began (largely) as an imperial project. That is to say, it came up from below but was consolidated on high. The first Christian churches in Rome, such as the first St Peter's, were paid for by the emperors, notably by Constantine. This was bound to change as the Church accumulated power, prestige and money – as the political concept we think of as the Papal States replaced the older forms of the Roman Empire, as the Papacy took over from the Imperium. The building that most vividly marks this transition is S. Maria Maggiore, one of the city's earliest pilgrimage churches, atop the Esquiline Hill. In this undertaking, for the first time, the onus of church-building shifted from the emperor to the pope.

S. Maria Maggiore has been so much restored and rebuilt that almost nothing visible in it today, except for its mosaics, dates from before the Renaissance. The original foundation of the church, however, was made by Pope Liberius in 352–6. It was financed by a rich Roman patrician couple, who were childless and so wished to make a spectacular offering to Mary, the mother of Jesus. Near the site of this church had been a Roman temple dedicated to a goddess of childbirth, Juno Lucina, much frequented by women in late pregnancy; the raising of a basilica to the Christian birth-goddess Mary in such a spot is one of the direct transferences of pagan into Christian cult in which the early history of Christian Rome abounds. It is also called the Church of Our Lady of the Snow, because of a miraculous snowfall that supposedly took place outside it in August, at the height of the Roman summer, perhaps in 358. In memory of this supposed event, every year a bagful of white petals is shaken free high up inside the nave and allowed to drift to the floor.

The outstanding works of art in S. Maria Maggiore are the apse mosaics, depicting the *Coronation of the Virgin*, by the thirteenth-century painter Jacopo Torriti, who had worked on frescoes for the Upper Church of S. Francesco in Assisi and came to Rome to work for the Franciscan pope Nicholas IV in the 1280s. In them, the figure of the Virgin has equal importance and size with that of her son Jesus – an iconographic invention which would soon become commonplace, but was not at the time. The chronicler Gregorovius described how the apse mosaic 'fills the building with a solemn golden splendour, which is more than earthly when illumined by the sunlight falling through the purple curtains; it reminds us of that glowing heaven, basked in whose glories Dante saw St Bernard, Francis, Dominic and Bonaventure. Then the spell of the work seizes us with its radiance, like the music of some majestic anthem.'

This is one of the few mosaic works in Rome that compares, in grandeur and intensity, with the Byzantine mosaics in Ravenna. Another is to be found in one of the ancient Roman churches, that of SS. Cosmas and Damian. Its history is actually much older than Christianity, since it was built, in the early sixth century CE, into and on top of two Roman structures whose remains stood in the Forum of Vespasian. One of these was the Temple of Romulus – not Romulus the legendary co-founder of the city, but one Valerius Romulus, son of the emperor Maxentius, who died in 309 and was designated a Roman god, with a Roman basilica raised in his honour. The other, adjacent to it, was the Biblioteca Pacis or Library of the Forum of Vespasian. Both these sites were given by Theodoric the Great, the Christian king of the Ostrogoths, and his daughter Amalasuntha, to Pope Felix IV (reg. 526–30) in the early sixth century.

The pope had the idea of uniting the two buildings with a new structure over them, which was dedicated to a pair of Christian Arab doctors, Cosmas and Damian, brothers martyred during the persecutions of Diocletian. He seems to have meant it to be a

Christian version of, or answer to, the cult of the pagan twins Castor and Pollux, to whom a nearby temple had been dedicated. Fortunately this radical change did not end in the destruction of the old temple fabric; in fact, the Temple of Romulus, which now serves as a vestibule to the church, compares with the Pantheon as the best-preserved ancient temple in Rome.

The finest thing about the church, however, is the sixth-century mosaic in its apse, depicting the *parousia* or Second Coming of Christ. In its centre, his right arm extended in a gesture of recognition and blessing of the faithful, is Jesus Christ, robed in gold and descending a heavenly stair of many-coloured clouds, in whose strata pink and crimson predominate, fading out to silvery grey as the eye moves higher.

It is, almost literally, a stairway to Paradise.

On the right of Jesus is St Peter, and on the left St Paul, both in white Roman togas; they are ushering the martyrs Cosmas and Damian into his divine presence. The new saints carry martyrs' crowns. On the far left is Pope Felix, holding a model of his new church; a figure of St Theodore, or more likely Theodoric the Great, the donor of the site, appears on the far right. Below this zone, which fills the curving wall of the apse, is a band of mosaic sheep, those ancient symbols of obedience – the flock of the faithful. There are twelve of them, symbolizing the twelve apostles.

Rome has seven chief pilgrimage churches, the greatest of which is the Basilica of St Peter, where the apostle and first pope was allegedly buried after his martyrdom. The others are the Basilica of St Paul Outside the Walls, S. Giovanni in Laterano (the actual cathedral of Rome), St Sebastian Outside the Walls, S. Maria Maggiore (the greatest church dedicated specifically to the cult of Jesus' mother Mary), S. Croce in Gerusalemme, St Lawrence Outside the Walls. The 'walls' in each case are the Aurelian wall, erected c.271–5 CE to girdle the city. Only one of them, St Sebastian Outside the Walls, has no works of art of special interest; its attraction – now much diminished, because of the general loss of interest in the cult of relics as distinct from the drawing power of famous works of art – lay in its relics, among which is a stone carrying the footprints of Jesus, an arrow which once pierced the body of that popular third-century martyr St Sebastian, and a fragment of the column to which he was tied while his fellow soldiers, having learned of his Christian conversion, used him for target practice. Of course, other pilgrimage churches do contain artworks, some of them fine; but the emphasis had always been more on their saintly associations than on their quality, sometimes very slight, as aesthetic objects.

Another of these pilgrimage churches was dedicated to St Lawrence (San Lorenzo), the deacon martyred by the emperor Valerian in the year 258.

Pious legend (no more than that) has it that the Holy Grail, the cup, dish or chalice from which Christ and his apostles drank at the Last Supper, which had contained the wine converted into his holy blood, passed into St Peter's hands and thence to St Lawrence's safekeeping, and that he hid it: in Huesca in Spain during the third century, according to one version, or in the sanctuary of Montserrat in Catalunya, by another. Yet another version of Grail fantasy has the precious chalice entrusted to the protection of the Knights Templar. A third places it in the hands of a noble Irish family, the Dwyers; a fourth holds (insecurely) that it was brought to Lake Memphremagog in Canada a century before Columbus sailed the Atlantic. There are many versions of the post-crucifixion wanderings of the Grail, some pseudohistorical, others openly fictional, all of them absurd.* Several Roman churches are dedicated to St Lawrence. The place of his burning is marked by the minor Church of S. Lorenzo in Panisperna. His supposed burial spot is commemorated by the pilgrimage Church of S. Lorenzo fuori le Mura. The two chief relics of his martyrdom are the gridiron on which he was supposedly roasted (in another Roman

---

* Of these the most popular was *The Da Vinci Code* by Dan Brown, a wretchedly ill-written but hugely successful tale in which the holy relic is secreted in a Scottish chapel and under the floor of the Louvre.

church, S. Lorenzo in Lucina) and his burned head, kept in a reliquary in the Vatican but not, it seems, regularly shown to the faithful. Considering what this gruesome souvenir might look like after the ravages of fire and time, this may be just as well.

The Roman Church has always had a *tendresse* for early Christian virgin martyrs, the prettier the better. One of the earliest of them, the most honoured, and the only one to have a pilgrimage church dedicated to her, was the fourth-century St Agnes, whose faith remained steadfast through trials (inflicted, according to one version, during the persecution of Diocletian, while others claim it was that of Decius) that would have sunk any ordinary virgin.

She was twelve or thirteen. No sooner had the imperial edict for Christianity been published than she publicly declared that she was a Christian. First, the enraged pagans tried to burn her to death, and as a prelude stripped her naked; but she was able to cover her body and hide it from the onlookers with her flowing hair, which miraculously grew to an immense length before the very eyes of witnesses. Then a pagan judge threatened to consign her to a brothel – but when a young man cast lascivious looks on her, God struck him blind. Finally she was dispatched with a sword. A shrine was built on the place of her martyrdom, on the edge of what is now Piazza Navona. Gradually S. Agnese in Agone (as it came to be known) was added to by the faithful, and then by architects working for those papal sponsors the Pamphili family, the greatest of whom was Francesco Borromini.

Of Rome's seven pilgrimage churches, the 'old' Basilica of St Peter was by far the most important. First, and most obviously, it was believed to be the shrine of the Apostle Peter, whom Christ had entrusted with the task of maintaining his Church. Here, from Charlemagne in 800 onwards, emperors were crowned; they were not recognized as emperors throughout Europe unless they had undergone the papal rituals of St Peter's. Here, important treaties were signed, sealed and deposited on the apostle's tomb. Here, Romans and all foreigners went to pray for intercession.

This first St Peter's – destined, in the sixteenth century, to be torn down and then gradually replaced by the enormous basilica which occupies its site today – was largely built of pieces of demolished ancient Roman buildings. These recycled fragments were known as *spolia*, 'spoils' or 'leftovers', and from the fourth century until the thirteenth this process of gradually building a new Rome from the recovered, refurbished and recycled fragments of antique buildings was the biggest single industry the city had. Medieval Rome did not merely rise on the site of ancient Rome; it was, quite literally, made from its remains. The first St Peter's was the most important example of this process, but medieval Rome had more than twenty major churches – S. Maria in Trastevere and SS. Cosmas and Damian being only two of these – built around salvaged Roman colonnades. The two most important of them were Constantine's: the cathedral, S. Giovanni in Laterano, and the first St Peter's. The Lateran had two sets of recycled columns: some forty big granite ones, each thirty feet tall, in the nave, and forty-two much shorter ones of *verde antico* marble from Thessaly dividing the aisles. Though all vestiges of the first St Peter's were lost in the demolition of the church, the architects' records show that its forty-four main columns were recycled shafts of grey and red granite, *cipollino* and other marbles.

Ancient Roman builders had been fond of using highly coloured marbles for their shafts, terminating in white Composite capitals. Colour was a sign of preciousness, particularly since coloured stone had to be brought a long way; there was none in the environs of Rome. The stone came from all over the Empire: red porphyry from Egypt, green serpentine from Sparta, *giallo antico* from Tunisia, *pavonazzetto* from Turkey. These imports were ostentatiously expensive in ancient Roman times, and hardly any cheaper in medieval Christian ones – but the skilled labour force required to shape them, which no longer existed, was not needed for these ready-mades. In any case, with the weakening of the Empire and its navy, blocks of exotic stone could no longer be brought to Rome from the outer parts of the Empire, and medieval builders could not have used them. So 'found' column shafts had to be employed. Some were exported from Rome to distant parts of Europe. When the emperor Charlemagne was creating his Palatine chapel at Aachen in the late 780s, his builders brought luxurious ancient marbles, and in particular whole columns, from Rome and Ravenna. And sometimes, in an effort to assert a more metaphorical connection between the ancient Romans and Charlemagne, they faked it: some of the 'Roman' capitals in the chapel at Aachen are actually Carolingian imitations of *spolia*, made on the spot.

There is no doubt that, for the early medieval faithful, the presence of ancient Roman columns supporting God's 'modern' Roman house signified continuity – the passage of Rome's lost authority to Christianity. It must have powerfully contributed to the sense that the first St Peter's was the true centre of the true faith.

As a result, a kind of 'third Rome' – which to the pious soon became the First Rome – grew up around the pilgrimage church of St Peter's. It centred on the Castel S. Angelo, that huge, drum-like fortification built around the original tomb of Hadrian. It was defined by the 'Leonine walls', a line of enclosure dating from the time of Pope Leo IV (reg. 847–55), which ran from the Castel S. Angelo up to a point behind St Peter's, turned, and descended to the bank of the Tiber. These defined and sheltered the *città Leonina*, or Borgo, consisting of the basilica, the smaller churches, papal apartments, monasteries, living-quarters for the clergy and hostels for pilgrims: a clutter of buildings which, because of their papal associations, enjoyed an ill-defined juridical independence from the rest of Rome which continued until the late seventeenth century. This independence was an origin of what became, by law, the separation of the Vatican City (which corresponded, more or less, to the Borgo) as the last vestige of the Papal States.

As early as the ninth century the Borgo had five hostels for pilgrims, six monasteries to serve these hostels and the basilica, and temporary cells, a warren of them, attached to the basilica for hermits and the poor. But by the thirteenth century the Borgo had swollen to become the undisputed tourist centre of the city – 'the Via Veneto of ancient Rome', in Richard Krautheimer's words. It had so many rival inns and *locande* that their owners competed to steal one another's guests by force, which must have led to some picturesque and noisy squabbles on the piazzas.

Beyond the Borgo were the sectors of Rome known as the *abitato* and the *disabitato*. The *abitato* was where people lived, worked and worshipped. The *disabitato* was a kind of suburban desert, where nobody wanted to be and invaders came to grief. A chronicler in 1155 recorded how, on the edges of the *disabitato*, half the army of Barbarossa had been killed by 'green snakes, black toads and winged dragons ... whose breath poisoned the air as did the stench of rotting dead bodies'. But the *abitato* was busy, mostly with Christian expansion. By the fourth century Church revenues from its holdings in north Africa, Greece, Egypt and Syria amounted to 3,700 gold *solidi*, roughly $25 million in modern money, every year, and much of this was funnelled directly to Rome for its building plans. Thirty-three churches are mentioned in the *abitato* before 1050, of which twelve still exist today. Many more would come later.

One of the chief parts of the *abitato*, in the abutment between the Vatican, the Borgo, the Tiber and the Janiculan Hill, came to be known as Trastevere – the name a compression of *trans Tiberim*, 'across the Tiber'. By the end of the thirteenth century it had become the only *rione* (*regione* or district, number XIII) on the far side of the river, and it was united to the Borgo in 1585 – an administrative gesture which was supposed to reduce, but in fact did not, the Trasteverini's persistent habit of seeing and speaking of themselves as the only true and authentic Romans, and of all other Romans as foreigners. This is embedded in the name of Trastevere's main annual festival, the *festa di Noantri*, the 'festival of us others'. Local pride has always been a big matter in Trastevere, whose inhabitants traditionally resent any effort to horn in on it. A famous example, undocumented but almost certainly true, is said to have been an attempt by Mussolini to intrude upon the procession that accompanied this *festa*. Part of its festivity was a row of pasteboard arches spanning the Via di Lungara, which led to the area's main church, S. Maria in Trastevere. Advised by his sometimes maladroit propaganda chief Starace, the Duce was gratified to see that these arches bore patriotic mottoes – 'Trastevere, Trastevere, now you shine with a new light / You have the Madonna *and* Il Duce, watching over you!' But alas for the dignity of the occasion and its propaganda, some Trasteverino got to the arches the night before with a ladder and a paintpot and scrawled on the back of them another message. *Stanchi di tanta luce*, it ran: 'Sick and tired of all this light, we want to stay in darkness: tell them all to take it up the ass, the Duce, the Madonna, and the King.'

The emblematic figure for Trasteveran dissent and bloody-mindedness was, without rival, the Roman dialect poet Giuseppe Gioacchino Belli (1791–1863). A life-size stone portrait of him in frock-coat and top-hat presides over a square in the popular quarter. It was paid for by public subscription – a rare, perhaps unique, indication of a Roman poet's popularity. His following in Trastevere can perhaps be gauged by the fact that the public kept filching the wooden walking-stick with which the sculptor had endowed his effigy. Nobody could question Belli's supremacy as *the* dialect bard of the Roman people. Partly because he wrote only in *romanesco*, the Roman language – a parallel tongue to Italian, but difficult for non-Romans to grasp – he has always been the favourite literary son of the city. (Dante may belong to all Italians, but nobody but a Roman owns Belli.) 'Infected with clap? Me?' begins one sonnet of 1832, 'The Honest Whore',

But you amaze me –
I am as clean as an ermine,
Look here, how this linen blouse,
Would put a lily to shame with its whiteness!

He wrote with an undeceived pessimism, interlaid with raucous humour, that rose from the lower levels of Roman life. 'Faith and hope are beautiful,' says a sonnet on the Carnival of 1834, 'but in this wide world there are only two sure things: death and taxes.' But there is another reason, too, for his popularity. Belli's black humour, his spasms of obscenity, his blithely cutting

disregard for the proprieties of Papal and clerical Rome, all rever-
berate with the spirit of popular Roman dissent   a spirit in which
he alone seemed able to publish. He wrote entirely in terms of
the Petrarchan fourteen-line sonnet, and produced more than
2,200 of them, which add up collectively to an anti-image of Papal
Rome – its excesses of wealth and poverty, the decadence of its
ecclesiastical rule, its pantomimes of sanctity, the gross super-
stitions of its faithful. And he came up with burning denunciations
of hypocrisy:

> Truth is like the shits –
> When it gets out of control and it runs
> You waste your time, my daughter, clenching your ass,
> Twisting and trembling, to hold it in.
>
> In the same way, if the mouth isn't stopped,
> Holy Truth sputters out,
> It comes out of your guts,
> Even if you vowed silence, like a Trappist monk.

As sometimes happens with those who were radical in their
youth, Belli turned conservative later. This master of insult to
authority joined the papal government and served it as a political
and artistic censor, repressing work by such supposed enemies of
religious order as Shakespeare, Verdi and Rossini. (The official
prejudice against Verdi stemmed from the fact that the very initials
of his name offended some Italian conservatives: VERDI could
be read, and was, as a disguised form of propaganda for Italian
unity under the king rather than the pope – *Vittorio Emanuele Re
d'Italia*.)

In the middle of the river, linked to its Trastevere bank by the
Ponte Cestio and to the other side by an ancient footbridge (62
BCE), the Ponte Fabricio, is the Tiber Island. Legend (for which
there is no historical basis) claims it began to grow up on the
Tarquin kings' grain stores which, around 510 BCE, an indignant
Roman citizenry dumped in the river; mud and silt accumulated

on these and presently an island formed. A temple to Aesculapius, god of healing, was built on it at the end of the third century BCE. But soon Rome was stricken by a plague against which its medical resources were powerless. The Sibylline Books were consulted. They directed that the fourth-century effigy of Aesculapius should be removed from its cult centre at Epidaurus and brought by ship to the Tiber. The boat grounded on the island and a giant snake, the incarnation of the god himself, was seen to slither overboard and take up a position on dry land. The plague receded. From then on, the Tiber Island was associated with healing, and hospitals for the sick were built there.

However, if there was any single factor in changing the map and layout of ancient Rome, producing a new medieval shape for the city, it was the combination of St Peter's supposed grave and the Borgo. And added to that were the relics, prime target of faith tourism, which connected to the institution of periodic jubilees.

The word 'jubilee' derives from the Hebrew *yobhel*, meaning a year of special significance in which the *shofar* or ram's horn trumpet was blown to announce a period of peace and social equality. The Old Testament laid down that jubilees were to be commemorated every fifty years, but this was not insisted on by the New Testament. Originally there was a connection between jubilees (also known as 'Holy Years') and pilgrimages to the Holy Land, but after the seventh century the Muslim conquest of Palestine made this all but impossible for Christians. So the idea of the Jubilee became focused on Rome, and the first was announced in 1300 by Pope Boniface VIII (reg. 1294–1303). Originally Boniface had meant there to be a Jubilee every hundred years. But in 1350 Pope Clement VI (reg. 1342–52), exiled in Avignon, shortened the gap to fifty years, and in 1390 Boniface IX (reg. 1389–1404) shortened it once more, to thirty-three years, the length of Christ's life on earth. The humanist pope Nicholas V brought the interval down again, to twenty-five years. The last Jubilee year celebrated by the Catholic Church was 2000. Then there were 'extraordinary' jubilees, outside the normal liturgical calendar. Relics played an important part in all of these, stimulating devotion and strengthening religious fervour.

It is difficult to believe, but hardly possible to exaggerate, what the cult of relics meant for medieval Rome. In Krautheimer's words, it was the relics 'that made Rome the glowing centre of the thirteenth-century world, that with the [papal] court made Rome rich by drawing pilgrims to it'. Today, millions of people flock to Rome to see — or at least, be exposed to – famous works of art. Their fourteenth-century forebears did not care so much about the art, which in itself was not considered a reason to travel. But as Gregorovius pointed out, in that Jubilee year of 1300 'immense profits accrued to the Romans, who have always lived solely on the money of foreigners'. In that holy and hysterical year, at the great pilgrimage Church of S. Paolo fuori le Mura, two clerks could be seen standing all day and all night with great rakes, raking in the coins left by pilgrims. The Florentine chronicler Giovanni Villani thought that two hundred thousand pilgrims were in Rome at any given moment in 1300, not even counting people who were there on other business or just passing through, without religious motives – 'and all was well ordered, without tumult or strife, and I can bear witness to this for I was present and saw it'.

If true, and it probably was, this was an enormous figure. No tourism industry, except in the crudest and least organized form, existed then. There was no system of mass travel. No jumbo jets or hotel chains existed and there were, of course, no American or Japanese tourists. The population of Europe was far smaller than it is today. Tourism, to borrow the unpleasant term of today's jargon, was solely 'faith-based' and undertaken in the hope of benefits in the afterlife. This was the attraction of the Holy Year of 1300. Villani's account makes it clear that large, indeed extravagant, spiritual rewards were promised by the pope. 'Within the whole course of this said year [1300] to whatever Roman should visit continuously for thirty days the churches of the blessed apostles St Peter and St Paul and to all other [non-Romans] who should do likewise for fifteen days, there should be granted full and entire remission of all their sins, both the guilt and the punishment thereof' – after full confession, of course.

These were definitely major benefits, affecting the whole after-life of the soul.

The relics these pilgrims hoped to see and venerate differed in importance. The main stem of the cult of relics was the remains of early Christian martyrs, whose burial places could be found – or at least, were alleged to exist – beyond the walls of ancient Roman cities, and Rome itself in particular. Many of them were exhumed from the catacombs, those underground tunnels full of burial niches in which early Christians interred their dead. (The word comes from the Latin *catacumbae*, meaning 'recesses' or simply 'holes'.) There is a persistent myth that these were hiding-places for the faithful in times of persecution. It is picturesque but completely untrue, especially since the pagan authorities would have known where all the tunnels were: nobody could have hidden down there. Even if a person had been executed for treason, it was quite licit for his relatives and friends to bury him – but that burial, like all others, had to be done outside the city walls. Hence, for instance, the burial under Roman law of the dead Christ after his crucifixion in a sepulchre 'where none had ever been laid'.

Naples, Malta and parts of north Africa all had Christian cata-combs, but the greatest concentration of them was naturally outside the city walls around Rome. Their exploration began with an antiquarian named Antonio Bosio (1576–1629), who nearly got lost for ever in the Catacomb of Domitilla, but found his way out and lived to write *Roma Sotterranea* ('Underground Rome', 1634). There may be sixty to ninety miles of these passages originally containing up to three-quarters of a million bodies, all housed in *cubicula* or chambers containing *loculi* or niches, whose entrances would then be closed by a *tegula* or stone slab sealed with cement to prevent the stink of putrefaction getting out.

Occasionally a Mass or some family ritual would be celebrated in such chambers. A few are sparsely decorated with painted images of a patron saint or a biblical scene. There are, however,

no masterpieces in catacombs. It is thought that many of these
passages have not been discovered or excavated, but in fact there
would not be much point in doing so, since their contents tend to
be insignificant: Christians did not believe in burying goods for
the afterlife with their dead. Once a passage was filled with tombs
the *fossores* or gravediggers might dig down and open another and
lower level; some Roman catacombs have four, five or even seven
such levels, like inertly stacked cities of the dead.

But they were never inhabited, except briefly and for ceremonial purposes, by the living. Strong taboos existed against
the pollution of the enclosed area of cities by corpses, but as
Christianity took hold there was a stronger and growing demand
for martyrs to be shifted into the city, where their remains could
be reburied beneath the altars or in the crypts of new (or newly
consecrated) churches devoted to their cult. When the Pantheon
was rededicated as a Christian church, at the behest of Pope
Boniface IV in 609, under the name of S. Maria ad Martyres,
fully twenty-eight wagonloads of supposed martyrs' bones were
reverently dumped beneath its main altar.

Reliquaries became cult centres, and quite rapidly assumed
importance in the new configuration of cities as pagan religion
was displaced by Christian cult. The old monumental centres –
in Rome, for instance, the Capitol – which were heavy with
pagan association were displaced by new basilicas, which turned
into episcopal churches, whose special claim to religious importance varied with the relics they contained. And so the significance of the churches was bound to narratives of sacred
history which, in turn, could be read from the importance of
the martyrs' relics they housed. The holy martyr had become,
as it were, portable, and a part of the body could signify the
entire saint. Reliquaria replaced actual burial spots, which meant
that a saint could be efficaciously prayed to wherever his remains
could be put.

The first man to become the subject of an extensive relic cult
was the first Christian deacon and the first Christian martyr: St
Stephen. Having incurred the wrath of established Judaism, he

had been brought before the court of the high priest and elders in Jerusalem, sentenced, and stoned to death. One of the witnesses to his lapidation was Saul, the future Apostle Paul, whose acute feelings of guilt at assenting to it are said to have helped in his later adherence to Christ.

Bits and pieces of Stephen would be revered in churches all over the Mediterranean, but the major ones were concentrated in Constantinople and later migrated to Rome, where they share a tomb with the remains of St Lawrence in the pilgrimage Church of S. Lorenzo fuori le Mura.

The church in Rome which actually bears his name, S. Stefano Rotondo, may or may not contain a major relic of him. It was built during the pontificate of Pope Simplicius (reg. 468–83), and is one of the few commemorative buildings in Rome (others being the Pantheon and the tombs of the emperors Augustus and Hadrian, the latter now the core of the Castel S. Angelo) with a circular plan. Some antiquarians have argued that this plan was copied from that of the Holy Sepulchre in Jerusalem, but it seems uncertain. What is quite certain, however, is that S. Stefano carries on its walls the most complete frescoed anthology of scenes of Christian martyrdom ever painted in Italy. The work was done at the behest of Pope Gregory XIII (reg. 1572–85) and it survives as an almost hysterically extreme statement of the values of the Counter-Reformation: by commissioning these encyclopaedic scenes of torment and sacrifice the pope wished, by implication, to draw a parallel between the hostility of Protestantism to the true faith and the heroic resistance of Catholic believers. No work of art in Rome more vividly embodies the didactic style recommended by the Council of Trent, which had been summoned by the Church to define what was, and what was not, tolerable to Catholic orthodoxy.

In its posturing figures, all contortion and clumsy *maniera*, it is a kind of Sistine Chapel for sentimental sadists. Its creator, a Mannerist artist from Volterra named Niccolò Circignani (*c.*1530–92), better known as Pomarancio, produced it in the early 1580s – a Herculean labour, twenty-four large panels complete with explanatory inscriptions, including the names of the emperors who ordered the martyrs' torments. It starts, at the entrance, with the crucifixion of Christ and the stoning of Stephen. One then proceeds to every sort of piercing, burning, flogging, skinning, bashing, strangling, drowning and even cooking in boiling oil, like a Trastevere artichoke. Here is St Thecla torn apart by a pair of bulls. Here is St Ignatius (an earlier one, not the founder of the Jesuit Order) thrown, most satisfyingly, to the lions in the Colosseum. Sts Gervase and Protase are nailed to trees in parody of the crucified Jesus. St Eustachius is roasted alive inside a bronze bull. One martyr is crushed under a slab of stone, another is chopped up by heartless axemen. It may be that these dreadful scenes of suffering had some real didactic value, for the church was placed under the charge of the Hungarian Jesuits at the end of the sixteenth century and many a Jesuit was subjected to frightful torments when on missionary duty; perhaps Pomarancio's frescoes prepared them for what was coming. Certainly they are much more vivid than any dry-as-dust relic of the holy Stephen could ever be. However, time and fading have deprived them of much of their original vividness, which must have been quite lurid; and given the number of more important works of art in Rome which stand in equal or worse need of restoration, and the very limited money available for this endless task, they are not likely to be restored in the imaginable future.

In a culture that drew no very distinct line between the natural and the supernatural, relics were a powerful instrument of social control, striking awe into the sceptical and the impious. The holiest and rarest relics of all were, of course, those of Jesus Christ himself. The most significant was in Rome: the imprint of Jesus' own face, miraculously preserved on the veil with which St Veronica had wiped away his sweat on the way to Calvary. Before this wonderful image preserved by the woman Dante called *la Veronica nostra*, faithful pilgrims would throng in obeisance; during the Holy Year of 1300, it was shown to the public every Friday and on all solemn feast-days in St Peter's, and on one occasion the crush of the faithful crowd was so great that an

English Benedictine monk, William of Derby, was trampled to death.

That such a thing could happen today is, to put it mildly, unlikely. Veronica's Veil is still preserved in a reliquary above Bernini's statue of Veronica herself in one of the mighty piers that carry the dome of St Peter's, but it is seldom shown and kept so far from the congregation that no one could tell if the faint marks on it constitute the image of a face. It is said to be even less legible than the now generally discredited 'Holy Shroud' of Turin, which bears the supposed imprint of Jesus' body but is probably a fourteenth-century fake. There are a multitude of fabric remnants as, at the height of the relic mania, the custom arose of lowering long strips of cloth into a saintly grave; if it touched the remains, it became a relic in itself by holy contagion.

Relics associated with Jesus Christ were, naturally, valued above those of his saints, even if – like the Veil – they were not parts of his body but merely things associated with his suffering and death. The most unwieldy relic may be the one in the Roman Church of S. Croce in Gerusalemme. It is one of many brought back from the Holy Land by Constantine's mother, St Helena, who built a basilica to house them. Its floor was packed with earth that the empress had carted back from the hill of Golgotha, site of Christ's crucifixion. How much earth was involved is not known. A steady trickle of visitors still arrives to view, or at least stand in the presence of, St Helena's earth relic.

Her other large souvenir of the Holy Land was brought back in pieces and reconstructed in Rome – the flight of twenty-eight marble steps from the residence of Pontius Pilate in Jerusalem. Jesus Christ was believed to have walked up these steps on the way to trial and judgement by the Roman procurator, and the Scala Santa or Holy Staircase, as it is known, was reconstructed in Rome in its former papal residence, the Lateran Palace.

How Helena got this enormous cult object from the Middle East to Rome is not recorded, but of course the task, though daunting, would not compare with the logistics of transporting whole granite obelisks from Egypt to Rome in pagan times. The marble steps are now encased in wood, since it would not be right for ordinary human feet to tread on the stones which Jesus' own footprints have sanctified. Glazed peepholes have been cut so that pilgrims can venerate the stains in the marble, left by the blood of Jesus (who had just been scourged at the pillar, and so was leaving spots and smears everywhere).

Large indulgences go to those pilgrims who climb the whole flight of the Holy Staircase on their knees. The future heresiarch Martin Luther is said to have tried, but failed, to do this when he was a young monk, getting only halfway to the top. But in the nineteenth century, when Italy's king Vittorio Emanuele was about to invade Rome (and thereby begin the process which led to the confiscation of the Papal States), the vehemently conservative seventy-eight-year-old Pope Pius IX managed the climb on his knees – not that it did him or his political future any good. Interestingly, the stairs are still crowded with modern pilgrims, although handrails have been installed on either side for their convenience.

Since Christ ascended into heaven body and soul, he left behind on earth only one bodily relic, which was surgically removed from him by the high priest of the Temple in Jerusalem when he was an infant. Theoretically the Holy Foreskin, enshrined in a provincial church not far from Bomarzo in Latium, ought to be the least contested of all relics, but its unique claim to that title has unfortunately been challenged by another foreskin, housed in a rival church in the Abruzzi.*

---

* However, the Chapelle du Saint-Sang (Chapel of the Holy Blood) in Bruges claims to possess a phial containing drops of Jesus's blood, collected by Joseph of Arimathea, which had been given to Thierry, count of Flanders, by the patriarch of Jerusalem in 1149. Other claimants to possession of specimens of this precious fluid are Weingarten Abbey in Germany and the cathedral of Menton in France. One of the rival Crowns of Thorns, acquired by Saint Louis, king of France, and kept in the Sainte-Chapelle, disappeared during the French Revolution and is unlikely to resurface except, perhaps, as a fake of a fake.

But there were, and are, innumerable smaller relics of saints, so many thousands throughout the churches of Rome (and Italy, and the rest of the world) that no effort has ever been made to count them. The most esteemed were bone relics, such as the head (or heads) of St Paul. Of course they are all beyond veri-fication. How does one 'authenticate' the holy phial of the blood of San Gennaro, patron of Naples, which is kept in the church named after him and is expected to liquefy each year on the saint's festal day, to the edification of crowds of prayerful worshippers?

S. Croce in Gerusalemme itself has a whole chapel devoted to relics of Christ's passion. It possesses not one but two thorns from the Crown of Thorns. It has splinters from the True Cross, a piece of the Good Thief's cross, and one of the three iron spikes with which Christ was nailed to his cross. (It is said to be fairly intact, despite the medieval habit of scraping filings from the Holy Nails and incorporating them in minor relics in order, so to speak, to soup them up, like adding pepper to a cutlet.) S. Croce in Gerusalemme also has the column at which Christ was scourged, although it might be safer to say *one* of the columns: a thirteenth-century Crusader, Robert de Clari, who took part in the sack of Constantinople, mentions being shown Christ's whipping-post there in 1204, so either it was in two places at once or there were two columns; perhaps he had a hundred lashes at one and the rest at the other. It also has the crib in which his mother laid him in the stable at Bethlehem, and (in some ways most wondrous of all) the mummified index finger which Doubting Thomas sceptically poked into the wound left by Longinus' spear in Christ's side.

Among the oddest of these relics is a part of the *titulus Crucis*, the label that was affixed to the cross bearing the legend, in Latin, 'Jesus of Nazareth, King of the Jews', in red paint on a worm-eaten wooden plaque. Supposedly it was purchased by Helena and, after vicissitudes – brought to Rome, hidden from the invading Visigoths, forgotten until the fifteenth century, found in a sealed lead box – became part of the Passion reliquarium. In the cloisters of San Giovanni in Laterano, that ancient pilgrimage church which is the first cathedral of Rome, is even kept the stone on which the Roman soldiers attending the crucifixion cast dice for his garment.

Ever since Luther, the matter of relics has been a thorny one for the Catholic Church. The cult seems so blatantly superstitious, so comical. Yet within living memory, you could hardly enter an Italian church of any age without encountering scores of reliquaries that contained a profusion of bones, snippets of cloth, vials of dried blood and other curiosities. Relics were in immense demand in early Christian times, but in a more sceptical age their cult has been greatly reduced. It would probably be fair to say that most people who visit these collections are more interested in their reliquaries, those rhetorically magnificent examples of the metalsmith's art, than in their contents.

There are numerous competing heads, hands and legs of the same saint – an apostle, a virgin martyr – but these are the merest fraction of the number of holy relics that used to be displayed in Catholic churches a century or two ago.

We laugh, of course. How superstitious, how easily fooled through an excess of naive faith, our medieval ancestors and some of their more pious descendants were! But we – or at least, some of us – are no better. At the end of the twentieth century bidders were competing to buy, on eBay, a miraculous (though by then, rather stale) piece of bread that some American householder had popped in the toaster and seen come out with the Virgin Mary's face burned on it. On 22 November 2004, an Internet casino called GoldenPalace.com paid $28,000 for this relic – the most expensive slice of toast in history. Miraculous statues of Jesus or Mary, which weep tears or exude blood (but turn out to have cunningly concealed tubes, sacs of red dye and other handy miracle aids), periodically turn up in faith-sodden America. No moment in history is free from superstition; and as for the hysteria of relic-hunting, what but a sordid and comical piety could have driven wealthy Americans at a Sotheby's auction of Jackie Kennedy's effects to bid for one of her late husband's golf-clubs and for a worn tray on which the drinks of America's Holy Family might have been served at Hyannisport?

The cult of relics gave rise to much swindling and fakery, but holy mementoes were not the only things being faked. Forgeries of documents have played important parts in history, and none more so than an imaginative one of uncertain date (probably somewhere between 750 and 850) known as the Donation of Constantine.

What this document, which has been recognized as a forgery since the sixteenth century, attempted to prove and for ever ensure was the pre-eminence of religious over secular power. It was claimed to have been written by the first Christian emperor, Constantine, in the fourth century. It was 'discovered' – that is, written – in the ninth century, but it supposedly describes relations between Constantine and Pope Sylvester I (reg. 314–35). Its subject is the extent of papal power over the secular world, which it makes out to be all but limitless. The will of the pope supersedes that of any emperor, writes 'Constantine'. He can create emperors, and depose them. He has this right because the chief concern of human life is eternal salvation, beside which such matters as the accumulation of wealth and the exercise of worldly power are (relatively) trivial.

Constantine's address, then, is divided into two parts. In the first, the *Confessio*, he recounts how his pagan life ended when he was instructed and baptized in the Christian faith by Pope Sylvester, and how this miraculously cured him of 'a horrible and filthy leprosy'. Doctors had been summoned but could do nothing. After them came the pagan priests of the Capitol who recommended a grotesque replay of the Massacre of the Innocents: Constantine must set up a font on the Capitol 'and fill it with the blood of innocent children and by bathing in it while it was warm I could be healed'. Numerous children were duly rounded up, but when 'our serenity perceived the tears of their mothers', Constantine was filled with abhorrence and cancelled the project. Now Christ sent Sts Peter and Paul to speak to the still leprous emperor. They instructed him to seek out Pope Sylvester, who with his clergy was hiding from Constantine's persecutors in the caverns of Mount Serapte: 'When thou hast called him to thee, he will show thee the pool of piety.' Three times immersed in it, Constantine would be cured. And so he was. Constantine was so grateful for this miraculous baptism that he called together all his governors, senators and officials and ordered that 'The sacred see of Peter shall be gloriously exalted above our empire and earthly throne.'

How would that be done? As boldly as possible, by the means set forth in the second part of the forgery, the *Donatio*. Constantine, instructed by God, confers on the pope as successor to St Peter the primacy over the world's four patriarchs, those of Antioch, Jerusalem, Alexandria and Constantinople. The chief Roman ecclesiastics must have the same honours and rights as the senators and the pope must have all the same rights as the emperor, including the right to wear a golden imperial crown. But, the forger goes on to recount, Pope Sylvester refused to wear such a crown. The emperor instead bestowed on him a *phrygium*, a tall white cap of authority – ancestor of the papal mitre. He also gave the pope all his western lands, cities and possessions, including Rome and its Lateran Palace, as a present (*donatio*), making them 'a permanent possession to the holy Roman Church'. As a last formality he officially removed the seat of imperial government to the east, to the capital of Constantinople, since 'it was not right that an earthly emperor should have authority [in Rome], where the rule of the priests and the head of the Christian religion have been established by the Emperor of Heaven'. Such are the main clauses of the fictitious 'Donation', the most outrageously self-serving secular deception ever foisted on its believers by a Western religion.

It would, however, become the basis of an aggressively expansionist Papacy in the twelfth and thirteenth centuries. Whoever the forger was, he wrote a free ticket to the popes to embark on world dictatorship. The meaning of the Donation is spelled out in a remarkable cycle of frescoes in the small chapel of St Sylvester, part of the larger fortified basilica of the SS. Quattro Coronati, on the heights of the Caelian Hill not far from the Lateran Palace, former residence of the popes. Much ancient, medieval and

Renaissance art is political on some level, intent on the promotion and praise of some powerful men and ideologies, while attacking and downgrading others. But few early frescoes are as bluntly, explicitly political as these.

SS. Quattro Coronati, the Church of the Four Crowned Saints, originally celebrated the acts of faith of four Roman soldiers named Severus, Severinus, Carpophorus and Victorinus, martyred in one of the persecutions of Diocletian for refusing to sacrifice to the god Aesculapius, the Roman form of the Greek god of healing, Asclepius. (If it seems a little excessive, even self-contradictory, to kill men for displaying insufficient reverence for the founder of the art of medicine, then welcome to the oddities of pagan cult.) These Christian soldiers are not the only ones honoured in the basilica, which was built between the ninth and twelfth centuries. It also contains, in a ninth-century crypt under the altar floor, the remains of five Christian-convert sculptors from Pannonia (modern Hungary) named Castor, Claudius, Nicostratus, Sempronianus and Simplicius, who were put to death for refusing to make a statue of the same god. For many years the commercial stone-carvers of Rome, especially the ones dealing in recycled ancient marble from demolished buildings, preferred to have their shops near the church of these sculptor-martyrs.

But the art content of SS. Quattro Coronati is chiefly remarkable for its thirteenth-century frescoes by an unnamed hand, illustrating the Donation of Constantine. We see Constantine recovering from leprosy; Constantine baptized by Pope Sylvester; and most significant of all, Constantine offering the pope his white *phrygium* of authority and leading the papal horse by its bridle, thus assuming the subordinate posture of a *strator*, a groom. There could be no clearer statement of the Church's belief in the Donation forgery. The emperor must bow the knee – both knees, in fact – to the pope. Religious authority is, and always must be, above the claims of temporal power, which it need not ask for legitimacy.

The pope whose policies and actions were most opportunistically and flagrantly based on this belief was Innocent III (b.

Anagni 1160 – d. Perugia 1216). He did more than any other pontiff to shape the politics of Italy, internal but especially external, in the early Middle Ages. He came to the Papacy young; with few exceptions, popes tended to be older men, but Lotario de' Conti, son of Count Trasimund of Segni, was voted into the Papacy at the age of only thirty-seven, a man brimful of energy, highly intelligent and completely dedicated to his own conception of the Church Militant.

Such a man was not likely to be content until he had put his own stamp on the mania that seized pious Europeans in the twelfth century, and he became the chief voice of that expression of mingled religious zeal and territorial frenzy: the Crusades.

It seems extraordinary, looking back on the Crusades from nearly a thousand years later, that they could ever have been conceived as anything but a mirage, a long bout of collective religious delusion. What good could it do to 'free' a portion of the Middle East from its inhabitation by Muslims, for no better reason than that a Jewish prophet had once lived, preached and died there? But territoriality, especially when conceived in religious terms, heightened by the hope of eternal life and sharpened by xenophobia, is a murderous and intractable passion, and many Christians in the Middle Ages felt it intensely. Crusades were the ultimate form of that fear and hatred of the Other which underlies the sense of racial and religious selfhood, and a man conscious of his honour would have needed an almost superhuman detachment to resist their impulse, once it was roused by preacher and pope.

All over Europe, and not least in Italy, men were seized by a common delusion: that, as Christians, they collectively owned a tract of territory on which none of them had ever lived – that they had an unquestionable right to it because their Saviour had once walked and prayed and died on it; and that the most meritorious of acts imaginable would be to wrest control of it from non-believers, the sons of the Prophet, the Arabs whose mere presence in the Holy City of Jerusalem defiled that Saviour's memory – despite the fact that the 'Holy City' had been in Muslim hands since the seventh century. The Holy Land was defined by certain emblematic sites, closely associated with Jesus. They included, apart from Jerusalem as a whole, the Church of the Nativity in Bethlehem, the Garden of Gethsemane and the Mount of Olives, Calvary and the Holy Sepulchre. Pilgrims had been visiting these since the third century.

So the Crusaders engaged in what their enemies would call a *jihad*, a holy war, having trudged, ridden and sailed thousands of miles under the most adverse conditions to do so. They were fighting not forest dwellers, but highly trained, well-armed and, often, strategically brilliant armies. Crusaders were both warriors and pilgrims. That double determination was the peculiar strength of their enterprise. Fortified by a sense of their own holiness, bound to one another by the red crosses reverently sewn to their tunics, the Christian soldiers or *crocesignati* talked obsessively about the 'recovery' of the Holy Land – in total disregard of the fact that it was never lost, because they had never possessed it, except in collective fantasy. Such was the impetus for the start of the First Crusade (1096–9).

A spontaneous and disorganized parallel campaign, known as the Peasants' Crusade, miserably failed. But the 'professionals' were victorious, taking Jerusalem in 1099. Encouraged, the Papacy gave permission for the Second Crusade (1145–9). It was only a partial success, directed against the Muslims who commanded the Iberian peninsula. These Crusaders, led by Alfonso I of Portugal, managed to dislodge them from Lisbon, but the Muslims remained firmly in command of Spain and in 1187, led by the great general Salah-el-Din (Saladin), they recaptured Jerusalem from the Knights Templar.

The Third Crusade (1189–92) was famous mainly for the participation of England's mighty Moor-killer, King Richard I 'The Lionheart', who strove but failed to recapture Jerusalem. Then came the great betrayal of the Fourth Crusade (1202–4), one of the two worst fiascos of Innocent III's papacy and perhaps of the Catholic Church's entire history. Innocent never played down his desire to 'recover' the Holy Land. Muslim 'occupation' of the

Holy Places was an unceasing annoyance to him. It provoked him to make the mistake of authorizing a full Crusade, the Fourth. Unfortunately Italy was neither well placed nor properly equipped to ship the necessary troops and their supplies across the Mediterranean for such a campaign.

Italy had one Christian naval power, Venice, 'Queen of the Adriatic'. Approached by the pope, the Venetians agreed to transport the entire army of invasion to the Holy Land, with supplies for nine months, for 85,000 marks. The Crusaders – a ragtag assembly of knights and peasants, mainly French, and led by Baldwin of Flanders, Boniface of Montferrat and Geoffroy de Villehardouin – could not raise this, so another deal was struck. Its essence was that Venice would use the assembled crusading forces to besiege and take Rome's only great rival in the Mediterranean, Constantinople, on their way to the Holy Land. In this way they would finance the whole Crusade. Venice would pay for the entire expedition, if the Crusaders would briefly divert the attack on its way to Jerusalem and conquer the city of Zara in Dalmatia on Venice's behalf. They would then go on to take Constantinople and restore the Byzantine emperor Isaac Angelus to the throne from which he had been deposed. The man who delivered this proposal, Isaac's son Alexius, undertook to add more men and supplies to the crusading army, bringing its strength to some eleven thousand men, heading for Constantinople in a huge fleet (by medieval standards) of two hundred ships. They were accompanied and directed by the formidable old Doge Enrico Dandolo.

Zara fell easily, and by July 1203, this force was besieging the land walls of Constantinople. Its citizens, all Greeks and Christians, were taken utterly by surprise: it had never been imagined that a huge Christian force, sworn to eject the Muslims from Palestine, would stop off on the way to attack a Christian city – let alone the greatest of all Christian cities after Rome itself.

The outcome was inevitable: by April 1204 the defences of Constantinople were breached in a climactic attack and the

Crusaders surged in, despoiling the churches and palaces, killing the priests and raping the women. It was the most merciless sack ever inflicted on a Christian city. Baldwin of Flanders was proclaimed emperor and the Greek Orthodox Church, which had no say in the matter, was finally united with the Roman, under the authority of the pope.

It may be said to Innocent III's (rather limited) credit that he did not authorize, still less organize, this atrocity. He protested against it and even excommunicated those Venetians who had facilitated it. On the other hand, he was not reluctant to see his Church benefit from it. He did nothing to force the Venetians to restore their loot to the prostrate city. The matchless Greek bronze horses from Constantinople were installed on the façade of St Mark's, never to return. Hundredweights of precious stones were lost to the Venetians; many of them may still, a thousand years later, be seen set in the Pala d'Oro, behind the high altar of St Mark's. Gold, silver and bejewelled reliquaries, monstrances, ciboriums, pyxes, patens and chalices by the ton were distributed to church treasuries all over Europe but especially in Italy. The very icons were torn from the churches and broken up in thousands, burned to extract the precious metal from their gold-leaf backgrounds, which ran down into glittering puddles amid the ash. And nobody knows (though it is not hard to guess) what happened to such things as the high altar of Hagia Sophia, which beggared the descriptive powers of such Crusaders as Robert de Clari, the aforementioned unlettered knight, dictating a memoir of the sack years after his return to France:

> The master altar of the church was so rich that it was beyond price ... made of gold and precious stones broken up and crushed all together, which a rich emperor had made. This table was fully fourteen feet long. Around the altar were columns of silver supporting a canopy over the altar which was made just like a church spire and it was all of solid silver and was so rich that no one could tell the money it was worth.

'Now about the size of the city,' recalled de Clari,

> about the palaces and the other marvels that are there, we
> shall leave off telling you. For no man on earth, however
> long he might have lived in the city, could number them or
> recount them to you. And if anyone should recount to you
> the hundredth part of the richness and the beauty and the
> nobility that was found in the abbeys and the churches and
> in the palaces and in the city, it would seem like a lie and you
> would not believe it.

Neither richness, nor beauty, nor nobility could do anything
to deflect the horde of ravening Frankish thugs who stripped
Constantinople in the name of Jesus. The city was replete with
other wonders, not of an artistic kind. It had a magical tube the
size of a shepherd's pipe hanging by the silver portal of Hagia
Sophia, 'of what material no man knew'; if a sick man put one
end in his mouth 'it sucked out all the sickness and it made the
poison run out of his mouth and it held him so fast that it made
his eyes roll and turn in his head, and he could not get away until
the tube had sucked all the sickness out of him'. And of course
there were relics in profusion: wonder-working icons, pieces of
the True Cross, the iron of the lance that pierced Jesus' side on
Calvary, the robe of Our Lady, the head of John the Baptist, 'and
so many other rich relics that I could not recount them to you or
tell you the whole truth'.

So much has been said about the importance of the Crusades
as the collision of two utterly incompatible world-views that their
significance is habitually overblown. In the end they did not make
much difference to either Islam or Christianity, except as largely
symbolic events.

The eleventh- to thirteenth-century assaults of Christian forces
were a peripheral affair in the Muslim world, while the Muslim
counter-attacks hardly menaced the stability of the Christian
empire. (The later Ottoman surge against Europe in the sixteenth
century, so memorably beaten back from the walls of Vienna and

repulsed by the galleys of Don John of Austria at the battle of Lepanto, was of course quite a different matter.) Nevertheless their memory retained enormous rhetorical power, casting the Arabs in European eyes as cruel, barbarous infidels and the Christians in Muslim eyes as culturally bestial thugs. It is why the Islamic media, to this day, continue to refer to the Western armies in Iraq as 'crusaders' – not by any means the compliment that the stupider voices of American faith fancy it to be. What gets ignored in this clang and rattle of poisoned stereotypes is the immense cultural heritage shared between Islam and Christianity – though not the Christianity of the ranting American fundamentalist bigots, nor the Islam of the murderous low-brow ayatollahs. As Christians once built Chartres and St Peter's, Muslims once built the Blue Mosque of Istanbul and the Great Mosque of Córdoba, the courts and gardens of the Alhambra. Their librarians preserved all that we have of classical drama and philosophy. They created in 'al-Andalus', the Arab name for Moorish Spain, one of the supreme cultures in world history – supreme, not least, in its tolerance for other faiths and creeds, a tolerance not shared by the anti-Semitic Catholic brutes who did the dirty work of the *reconquista* for Ferdinand and Isabella.

Today, Islam's fundamentalist descendants can invent nothing, preserve nothing, create nothing. Comparing them with the remarkable figures of their own history is like comparing some illiterate IRA knee-capper to Seamus Heaney or William Butler Yeats. And it is the same on our side, where the Christian fundamentalists have no sacred art to show, no writing of aesthetic significance, and little architecture beyond drive-in megachurches.

Next only to the Fourth Crusade, the worst of all exercises in medieval crusading took place inside Europe and was also launched by Pope Innocent III. It was directed, not against the Byzantine Church, not against Saracens and other 'infidels', but against Europeans: a heretical religious movement of the French, the Cathars, whom Innocent III and his hierarchy were determined to wipe out by all possible means, by proscription, fire and the sword.

'Catharism' comes from the Greek root *katharos*, meaning a cleansing, a purification — which the Cathars saw as their appointed mission in a spiritually fallen world. It was strongest in France, where the tragic and bloody denouement of its growth and repression took place in the early thirteenth century; but at its height, Catharist 'cells' grew up all over Europe, including Italy, where they survived until the early 1300s and were experienced, by Rome, as a powerful threat to Christianity itself – as cancerous, potentially, as Stalinist cells in Western democracies were seen to be by the Catholic Church and the Western governments in the postwar years of Pius XII's papacy.

The first reports of Catharist belief communities actually came from Cologne in 1143. But France was the stronghold of the cult, and in particular the Languedoc in the Midi region of France, with its strong sense of exception, its remoteness from the great power centre of Paris, its separate language (Provençal, close to Catalan), and its traditions of vehement pietism.

Where did the Catharist faith come from? Because nearly all its 'scriptures' and holy books were destroyed, burned along with the Cathars themselves,* it is difficult to be certain about this, but most scholars seem to agree that it was an eastern import whose roots lay in the Balkans and the Byzantine Empire. It was related to the beliefs of the Bogomils or 'friends of God' who, being particularly strong in Bulgaria, were also known as the Bougres – whence our durable term of extreme disparagement, 'buggers'.

What did the Cathars believe? This can no more be summed up in a few sentences, or even a single book, than the theology of medieval Catholicism can. Besides, the Catholic effort to extirpate it was all too successful. After the texts were burned, only the merest traces and outlines of their content remain.

---

* Among the survivors, which give at least a partial and fragmentary idea of Catharist belief and were preserved by the Catholics as examples of heresy, were *The Book of Two Principles* (an exposition of the Catharist doctrine that the world had two gods, one evil and one good), the *Rituel cathare de Lyon*, and the *Nouveau Testament en provençal*.

Fundamentally, they thought in terms of a dualist universe ruled by two creative principles, one good, the other evil. The good was entirely spiritual. The evil was material, created by a demiurge whom the Cathars identified with Satan and referred to as the 'King of the World', *Rex Mundi*. The world we inhabit, including our own bodies, was his product. Sexual procreation, in the Cathar view, was an act of unsurpassed cruelty, since it brought down a helpless and undeveloped soul into a world of utter imperfection. The great object of mankind's spiritual quest, therefore, was to escape from a hopelessly debased world of substance and material desires ruled by the Devil and his minions, and to enter a world of pure articulate Spirit, beyond desire.

This difficult evolution could hardly be achieved in a flash of insight, or even in a lifetime, although some exceptionally illuminated souls were believed to manage the latter. Generally it required reincarnation: a second life, and perhaps a third and even a fourth, to achieve the journey towards Perfection. Those who did so were known as *perfecti*, and were a revered minority within the Cathar cult; they corresponded to the hierarchy of Catholicism (though the Cathars absolutely rejected the idea of priesthood), and were marked by their extreme asceticism. The majority, the rest of the Cathars, the *credentes* or simply 'believers', led relatively normal lives in a normal world, farming and trading, but abstaining from meat, milk, cheese and other animal products, not swearing oaths or engaging in acts of violence.

One might have thought that such mild people presented about as much threat to society as a gaggle of vegans – whose spiritual ancestors, in a sense, they were. But that was not how Rome saw the matter.

The pope and clergy perceived the Catharist doctrine of resurrection as the rankest heresy.

Because the Cathars saw the material world as intrinsically evil, they regarded Jesus' coming to earth as the incarnate Son of God as a fraud. If he was made flesh, he became evil; he became, or was allied with, the creator of material existence, *Rex Mundi*, and could not be worshipped as the God of love and peace. To the

Catholic argument that he had died to redeem material creation, their response was that by dying to redeem an evil thing, he was himself evil. (As with many structures of religious 'reasoning', once you granted the initial premises the rest made logical sense. That is why Catholic theologians came up with that very useful phrase, 'a mystery of faith'.)

The Catharist doctrine was the polar opposite of what Catholicism taught about Jesus' nature and the supreme value of his sacrifice on the cross. When a Catholic learned that a Cathar despised Christ and held the crucifixion to be of no spiritual value, or that Catharism rejected all belief in Hell and Purgatory, the sacrament of the Eucharist or the doctrine of the Trinity, he would be horrified. He would think of such ideas as literally diabolic, emanating from the Devil. And Catharism's other doctrines aroused an equal hostility. 'Resurrection', for instance, meant different things to Cathars and Catholics. To a Cathar it was the means whereby a soul passed from one incarnation to another, in its progress towards perfection. It was essentially the same as the Pythagorean belief in 'metempsychosis', the transmigration of souls. Whereas to a Catholic it had the narrower meaning of the physical resumption of life after death, emergence from the grave, like Jesus or like Lazarus.

There were other features of Cathar belief that Roman Catholicism found equally repugnant. In the Middle Ages, before general literacy and hence before a widespread reliance on written contracts, the swearing of oaths was of paramount importance. But the Cathars regarded oath-taking as wrong – the practice came from *Rex Mundi*. They were pacifists and did not believe in war, capital punishment (a most radical departure from medieval norms) or marriage vows. Nor were they at all keen on propagating children; the enormous value placed on sacred copulation and childbirth by the Catholics was not shared by them. And they loathed Roman Catholicism, believing it to be the creation of *Rex Mundi*, the Devil, utterly unworthy of veneration. The cult of relics – old bits of bone, splinters of wood and scraps of cloth with deluded pilgrims bowing before them – they rightly held to be a sham, merely another form of matter-worship. The Cathars must renounce all aspects of Rome: utterly renounce them, not merely criticize them. Rome was Babylon – hugely rich, corrupt beyond redemption. In fact the Cathars were so different from Roman Catholics that they positively begged to be stamped out, as in Hilaire Belloc's disillusioned little distich:

> Pale Ebenezer thought it wrong to fight,
> But Roaring Bill (who killed him) thought it right.

Roaring Bill, in this context, was none other than Pope Innocent III. With the Fourth Crusade over, and the treasure-houses and reliquaries of Venice crammed with the loot of Constantinople, Christ's Vicar on Earth now turned his attention to the hapless and heretical Cathars. So determined was the Cathar resistance, spiritual rather than military, that it took the pope's formal crusade, misnamed the Albigensian Crusade though it was not born in and did not attack Albi, twenty years to extinguish it. Yet in the end the job was done; Innocent III's Final Solution to this particular heresy was at last achieved.

But how to raise the necessary papal armies? The Cathars may not have had the riches of Venice. Indeed, most of them had no riches at all, in terms of jewels, gold or other palpable treasures. But they and their sympathizers in the Languedoc, including many rich nobles, did have land. Innocent III therefore let it be known, and had his preachers declare, that whoever successfully brought a Cathar to trial and thence to death would receive his lands in reward. It was a most effective strategy, because it attracted predatory, land-hungry nobles from the north. Besides, one did not need a huge army to launch an internal crusade. Medieval armies were tiny by modern standards. The pitched battles that determined the fate of whole regimes involved forces that would hardly have made dents in either side today. Ten thousand soldiers, twenty at the most, would more than do.

But the Cathars also had their share of loyal supporters. Weary of the money-grubbing and sexually debauched behaviour that they saw everywhere in the upper hierarchy of the twelfth- to thirteenth-century Church, many Catholics stood with the Cathars in a bond of moral superiority. The reputation of the medieval Church in Provence was very low, and getting lower all the time.

The Church in the Midi was not, though, entirely discredited by the behaviour of its clergy, their love of luxury, their usurious money-grubbing and sexual debauchery. There were always some humble priests, honest bishops, and congregations who valued them. But the moral superiority of the Cathars to the general run of Catholic prelates was no empty claim, and knowledge of it won many converts and tolerant allies for Catharism, doing limitless damage to the Church. Innocent III heard about these doings in Languedoc, of course.

At first, the Church in Rome tried to deal with the Cathars by peaceful persuasion. In the last half of the twelfth century various missions were dispatched to the Languedoc; all failed. The resolutions of Catholic Church councils – Tours in 1163, the Third Lateran Council in 1179 – had negligible effect. The nobly born Domingo de Guzmán, the future St Dominic and founder of the religious order that bears his name, began a conversion drive in the Midi, declaring that 'Zeal must be met by zeal, humility by humility, false sanctity by real sanctity, preaching falsehood by preaching truth.' It had little success, although it was attended by at least one spectacular miracle, sometimes represented in art: locked in a debate between Cathars and orthodox Catholics, the two sides flung their books on a fire: the book of the Albigensians was burned, but Dominic's collection of his writings was spared and floated up above the flames. The mendicant Dominicans whose passion against heresy earned them the name of *Domini canes*, 'the hounds of the Lord' (their emblem, a black-and-white dog, duplicating the black-and-white habit of the order and holding a flaming torch in its jaws), were frustrated by the Cathars' stubborn adherence to their own faith. 'In my country,' Dominic declared, 'we have a saying, "Where words fail, blows will avail."'

The blows soon came raining down. In 1208, Innocent III's legate Pierre de Castelnau was sent to meet, and threaten, the most powerful ruler in the Midi, Count Raymond VI of Toulouse. Believing (probably correctly) that the count was soft on Cathars and had been known to shelter them, Castelnau excommunicated him. Vengeance immediately followed: Castelnau was murdered on his way back to Rome, by one of Count Raymond's knights. This left Innocent III no choice, or none that he could see. Exasperated, he called for a full Crusade against the Cathars, and land-greedy northern French noblemen donned their chain-mail, saddled their horses and, brandishing the red insignia of the cross so hated by Arabs and Cathars alike, flocked to the papal banner.

Thus began the (misnamed) Albigensian Crusade, French against French, instigated by an Italian pontiff. Of course, it was not Innocent III's only piece of international meddling: he had received the feudal allegiances of Aragon, Bohemia, Leon and Portugal, tampered with the politics of succession in Sardinia, and had intervened relentlessly in English affairs, even declaring Magna Carta invalid. Nevertheless, the Crusade against the Cathars joined the Fourth Crusade as the apogee of Innocent's political adventurism, not because he organized it – he did not – but because he gave permission for it.

The pope placed the vanquished territory under the command of a Cistercian abbot, his papal legate, Arnaud-Amaury. He began his Crusade in the summer of 1209 by besieging what was supposed to be a Cathar stronghold, the town of Béziers. Béziers also had a Catholic population, who were given the option of leaving the town unharmed: significantly, few of them did, many preferring to stay and fight alongside the Cathars. One of Arnaud's fellow Cistercians asked his commander how he would tell a Cathar from a Catholic, and the reply became legendary: *Caedite eos, novit enim Dominus qui sunt eius*, 'Kill them all, the Lord will recognize his own.' When the Crusaders entered Béziers, where many had taken refuge, they killed some seven thousand people right away, and thousands more later. They were blinded, maimed, impaled, strung up as targets for archers and dragged behind horses. The town was then gutted by fire. 'Today, your Holiness,' the abbot Arnaud reported with obsequious satisfaction to Innocent III, 'twenty thousand heretics were put to the sword, regardless of rank, age or sex.'

This initial slaughter was followed in 1229 by the establishment of the Inquisition throughout southern France. Over-zealous thugs interrogated thousands of suspected Cathars, and those who seemed guilty were hanged or publicly burned at the stake. For almost a year the last redoubt of the Cathars, the almost inaccessible fortress of Montségur (the name means 'safe mountain'), was besieged by troops of the Archbishop of Narbonne. It fell in March 1244 and a large massacre followed, in which more than two hundred *perfecti* were incinerated on a killing-field below the castle, the Prat des Crémats or 'Field of the Burned'. Though this did not eliminate all the Cathar faithful, it scattered them and broke the back of the resistance. The last Cathar leaders, Pierre and Jacques Autier, were executed in 1310.

So the Papacy was well able to repress the challenges of heresy, but for a long period it was obliged to move out of Rome altogether. The 'Avignon Papacy', which lasted from 1305 to 1376, began as a temporary exile of papal authority to France, but for a time looked like its complete removal to what some people called a 'Babylonian captivity' of the Church. Its origins lay in an irreconcilable conflict between the French monarchy and Rome's papal authority, whose ultimate source was that hobgoblin of medieval power politics, the spurious 'Donation of Constantine'.

The papal authority involved, at the beginning of the fourteenth century, was the implacably arrogant Benedetto Caetani, who belonged to one of the more powerful clans of medieval Rome and was elected pope as Boniface VIII in 1294. Boniface believed absolutely in the Donation's dictum that the Papacy ruled over all Christendom, taking precedence over any secular authority, including the king of France. He soon locked horns with that king, Philippe IV, over the issue of tax. The French state derived no small income from the taxes French feudal lords levied on their clergy. Boniface vehemently opposed this and in his bull

Clericis laicos (1296)* he decreed that no taxation on the Church, its clergy or its by now immense properties could be levied by any secular authority. (The next year he wavered a little, granting Philippe IV the right to impose taxes on the clergy in certain emergencies. But this was soon rescinded in the wake of the triumphant Jubilee year of 1300.) Obviously, an expanding Church needed every penny of its own money.

Boniface's confidence in defying King Philippe was inflated by the mighty success of the Holy Year he had proclaimed for 1300, in which a total of two million pilgrims inundated Rome; after such a display of faith, it made no sense to ask 'How many battalions has the pope?' Boniface issued two further bulls: *Salvator mundi*, cancelling all privileges issued to French kings by earlier popes, and *Ausculta fili*, ordering Philippe IV to present himself forthwith before a papal council. Philippe would have none of that: 'Your venerable stupidity,' he wrote back, 'must know that we are nobody's vassal in temporal matters.' He then issued accusations of simony, sorcery, heresy and even sodomy against the pope.

This was hardball, and not to be outdone Boniface in 1302 issued the bull *Unam sanctam*, which laid it down as 'necessary to salvation that every human creature be subject to the Roman pontiff'. Impossible to be more categorical than that, and Philippe's response was in deeds, not words: he dispatched a delegation, which was really a military squad, with orders to bring the pope from Rome to Paris, to answer the king's charges before a French council. He even arranged for the cardinals of that exceedingly powerful Roman clan the Colonnas, who hated the Caetani, to humiliate Boniface. Philippe's men seized Boniface in his residence at Anagni outside Rome. He died of illness brought on by his apoplectic outrage some weeks later, aged sixty-seven.

---

* A papal bull, meaning an official declaration of policy from the pope, was so called because of the *bulla* or seal affixed to such documents, affirming their papal origin.

His successor was another Italian pope, Benedict XI. He was not as tough as Boniface and could not so readily defy the French king. His timidity made him impotent in the face of big Roman clans like the Colonnas. Unsurprisingly, he was poisoned and in 1305 a new pope had to be chosen. This time it was an Italian cardinal who took the name of Clement V (reg. 1305–14). This was a political triumph for Philippe and the other French cardinals in the Curia, and Clement found the very idea of moving to Rome repugnant.

For, quite apart from the clan hostilities within the Roman elite, Italy itself was close to civil war. It was being shredded by the deadly struggles between Guelf and Ghibelline. Its greatest writer, Dante Alighieri, called it 'the abode of sorrow' and 'a place of prostitution'.

A country so riven by vicious political factionalism was clearly no safe place for a foreign pope, and no Frenchman could forget the attack on Boniface VIII at Anagni – an act of lese-majesty that could only have happened with the connivance of the Roman nobles. So it was quite understandable that the French popes of the fourteenth century refused to hold their court in Rome, and set up their own papacy at Avignon. Avignon was not Italian. But neither was it French. It was an enclave within France, independently papal, like the Vatican today, only much larger. It ruled the territory known as the Comtat Venaissin. A French cardinal could feel much safer there than in Rome, but still be on papal ground.

It is often imagined that to have a pope living outside Rome was an unusual violation of Church custom. This was not true at all. There were lots of precedents for it. In the century between 1099 and 1198, the pontiffs spent a total of fifty-five years away from Rome, eight of them in France. In the two centuries from 1100 to 1304, they spent an aggregate of 122 years out of Rome, some remaining in Italy, others not.

Gregory IX (reg. 1227–41) passed more than eight of his fourteen years' papacy away from Rome. Celestine V never saw Rome at all – elected in 1294, he lasted only five months before he resigned, defeated by the intrigues that swirled around him, thus delivering *il gran rifiuto*, 'the great refusal', the abandonment of the Papacy for which Dante placed him in the Inferno. Innocent IV (reg. 1243–54) was elected and consecrated in Anagni but spent no more than a single year in Rome; Boniface VIII spent far more time in Velletri, Orvieto or Anagni than in the Lateran Palace.

In sum, the only precedent-breaking aspect of the Avignon Papacy was its length – about seven decades. This filled some observers with alarm and foreboding. Papal withdrawal, said one, could be more economically and spiritually disastrous for Rome than even the barbarian invasions. The German historian Ferdinand Gregorovius called the Avignon popes 'slaves' of the king of France, and this was not an uncommon view among writers and intellectuals at the time. And yet it would be difficult to maintain realistically that the removal of the Papacy from Rome to Avignon was inherently bad for the Church. In some ways, it even meant its improvement: the Church turned out to be more readily centralized, with a more efficient administration, from Avignon. But the ostentation of papal life there certainly grated on those who did not benefit by it. The poet Petrarch, who lived in Avignon, was horrified. 'Here reign the successors of the poor fishermen of Galilee,' he wrote to a friend in 1353:

They have strangely forgotten their origin. I am astounded ... to see these men loaded with gold and clad in purple, boasting of the spoils of princes and nations ... Instead of holy solitude we find a criminal host and crowds of the most infamous hangers-on; instead of sobriety, licentious banquets; instead of pious pilgrimages, preternatural and foul sloth ... In short we seem to be among the kings of the Persians and Parthians, before whom we must fall down and worship.

Though one might take this for the rhetoric of a disgruntled poet, it was close to literal truth. The papal court at Avignon eclipsed most others in Europe by its sheer extravagance. In the

Palace of the Popes, a far more imposing building than the old Lateran Palace in Rome, the floors were covered with splendid Flemish and Spanish carpets, and the walls with silk hangings. The popes and their swarms of courtiers ate from gold plate and gold trays, lidded goblets, ewers, sauce-boats and flagons, using gold cutlery with handles of jasper or ivory. Pope Clement V's stock of plate weighed 700 marks or 159 kilos; that of Clement VI, in 1348, weighed almost 200 kilos. Their clothes were tailored from the richest materials: silk from Tuscany, gold Venetian brocade, white woollen cloth from Carcassonne, linen from Rheims and Paris trimmed with ermine or sable. Fur was used with abandon: Pope Clement VI had 7,080 ermine pelts in a new wardrobe that included several capes and no less than nine birettas (fur-trimmed hats).

Nor did the Avignon popes keep frugal tables. Their feasts were catered on a royal scale which, if anything, surpassed the extravagance of the Burgundian courts. In November 1324, Pope John XXII gave a wedding feast for the marriage of his great-niece, Jeanne de Trian, to the young nobleman Guichard de Poitiers. It is uncertain how many guests were invited, but they were served 4,012 loaves, nine oxen, 55 sheep, eight pigs, four wild boar, 200 capons, 690 chickens, 580 partridges, 270 rabbits, 40 plovers, 37 ducks, 50 pigeons, 292 'small birds', four cranes and, rather anti-climactically, only two pheasant. They also dealt with 3,000 eggs, 2,000 apples and pears and 340 pounds of cheese, washed down with eleven barrels of wine.

When the guest of honour was a pope, however, these relative austerities were abandoned. The Italian cardinal Annibale di Ceccano threw a reception in Avignon for Pope Clement VI in 1343. 'The meal,' he reported,

> consisted of nine courses, each having three dishes. We saw brought in . . . a sort of castle containing a huge stag, a boar, kids, hares and rabbits. At the end of the fourth course the cardinal presented the Pope with a white charger worth 400 florins, and two rings, one set with an enormous sapphire

and the other with an equally enormous topaz. Each of the sixteen cardinals received a ring set with fine stones, as did the prelates and the noble laymen.

After the seventh course a jousting tournament, with lances and horses, was held in the dining-hall, and dessert followed: 'Two trees were brought in; one seemed made of silver, and bore apples, pears, peaches and grapes of gold. The other was as green as laurel, and was decorated with crystallized fruits of many colours.'

The climax of all this jollity took place outside, where the guests were shown a wooden bridge over the nearby river Sorgues. It was a dummy structure which seemed to lead to the scene of further festivities. But once it was thickly crowded with monks, nobles and other guests, it collapsed and 'the artless sightseers all tumbled into the water' – one of those coarse practical jokes of which medieval humour was so fond, like the *giochi d'acqua* (water games) which were among the hazards of Renaissance gardens.

While such things were going on in Avignon, the very opposite was happening in Rome. There, the continued absence of the popes, the Curia and the general life of the Catholic Church had impoverished the city to wretchedness. Suddenly its main business was withdrawn; or if not withdrawn, then brought to a near-standstill. The contrast between the misery of the Eternal City and the luxuries of Avignon only got worse as time went by. The withdrawal of the Papacy effectively deprived Rome of its chief occupation – the effect was comparable to what might happen to modern Los Angeles if the whole entertainment industry, the production and promotion of movies, TV, pop music, was suddenly wiped out. The economy stagnated and the population plunged. Grass grew in the streets. No pilgrim was safe. Licence and disorder reigned. The rivalries fought out between the powerful clans of the city, the lawless aristocrats named Colonna, Savelli, Orsini, Caetani, multiplied in number and violence. Bandits who enjoyed the cynical protection of these big-shots could not be controlled; no lawful traveller or trader was safe on a Roman street. It seemed that Rome was going bankrupt and careening into anarchy. Then, as sometimes happens, the fermentation of chaos and greed threw up what appeared to be its own antidote – from below.

His name was Nicola Gabrini, and his origins could scarcely have been humbler. His parents were both Romans: mother a washerwoman, father a small-time tavern keeper, Lorenzo Gabrini. In the usual Italian way his first name was shortened and attached to his father's, so that he became known as Nicola di Lorenzo – 'Lorenzo's boy Nicola' – or, with vernacular elisions, Cola di Rienzo. There was nothing in his background to suggest the powerful and idealizing effect he was destined to have on Rome, and on Italy in general. But Cola di Rienzo had a vision of Rome, of what it had once been and might become again. He yearned for Rome to rise from the squalor to which the disappearance of the popes to Avignon had condemned it, and become once more the *caput mundi*, the capital city of the world.

Cola was born in Rome around 1313 and spent his early years in Asnani. He advanced rapidly, becoming a promising notary. He had not travelled, but he had read widely in the classics, particularly Livy, Seneca and Cicero; he studied the inspiring monuments, those traces of Rome's vanished greatness. Enthusiasm is the best teacher, and Cola was filled with it. He had found his life's mission early.

He also had a religious vision, not merely an antiquarian one. He was inspired by religious men he came to know, the *fraticelli* or spiritual brothers who were given to proclaim that the age of the official Church had come to its necessary end, and that a new age, presided over by the Holy Ghost, was dawning. No doubt this belief was reinforced, for Cola, by a mission on which he had been sent in 1343 to Pope Clement VI in Avignon. There he was able to witness very clearly and with his own eyes the corrupt extravagance of the Avignon Papacy, and contrast it with the brutal and impoverished state of Rome, so weak and so exploited by its own aristocracy.

He came back to Rome in about 1344 and soon gathered around him a group of young, like-minded men, all determined to work for public honesty and social justice. He hated the Roman aristocracy (on principle, but also because one of its members had murdered his brother) and was resolved to lead a revolt against them. The stage was now set for the emergence of the first popular leader the city had had since antiquity.

In May 1347, on Whit Sunday, the coup was detonated. Promising a general assembly of citizens on the Capitol, Cola di Rienzo appeared before the crowd, magnificent in full armour, and led a huge procession to the ancient focus of Roman power and Roman rights. He harangued the people – *his* people, it was at once clear – 'with fascinating eloquence' on the glorious past, present servitude and future deliverance of their Rome. He unrolled a series of new and more just laws for the governance of the city. The crowd of Romans acclaimed him as its tribune – *Nicholaus, severus et clemens, libertatis, pacis, iustitiaeque tribunus, et sacrae Romanae reipublicae liberator*: 'Nicola, strict and merciful, tribune of freedom, peace and justice, and liberator of the sacred Roman Republic.' The corrupt nobles simply melted away in fear, leaving the young hero in command of the city and its people.

A honeymoon period followed, but it did not last very long. In July Cola proclaimed the sovereignty of the Roman people over the rest of Italy and sent letters to all its chief cities, demanding that they send legates to what was meant to be a general congress in Rome, ratifying what he conceived as his dictatorship over the whole peninsula. This was a fantasy. Cola's assumption of national power was taken seriously in some places, such as the Kingdom of Naples. In others it was not: what kingdom, with its own traditions, was going to bow the neck to Rome on the say-so of one Roman tribune? Nevertheless, later in 1347 the delegates of twenty-five cities did converge on Rome, and stood in homage before Cola. A magnificent procession to the cathedral, S. Giovanni in Laterano, was formed, and Cola bathed in the enormous font in which Constantine had been baptized a Christian – a ceremony gravid with the deepest meaning, signifying, in effect, that Cola had assumed the powers not only of a tribune but of an emperor. This, he announced, symbolized the 'rebirth of Italy', and he audaciously told the papal representative that in future he, Cola di Rienzo, could govern Rome without help (or, as he saw it, interference) from the pope.

No such announcement had ever been made before, and its hubris marked the turning-point in Cola's fortunes. The noble families of Rome, which hated him, now had papal approval to stir up trouble afresh. In November, having gathered an army, Cola went to battle with the nobles' forces outside the Porta Tiburtina, and succeeded in killing their ringleader, Stefano Colonna. But he had underestimated Pope Clement, who issued a bull of deposition calling him a heretic and a criminal, even a pagan. On 15 December 1347, the bells on the Campidoglio began discordantly to chime and a crowd assembled, shouting 'Popolo! Popolo! Down with the tribune!'

Cola lost his nerve. Fearing a revolt, he fled to Castel S. Angelo, shed his insignia and, in plain clothes, ran for refuge to Civitavecchia, the port on the Tyrrhenian forty miles north. From there, after some delays and confusion, he abdicated his tribuneship and retreated into deeper exile – first to Naples, then among the fraticelli of the Apennines. With these monastic followers of the pious, radical mystic Joachim di Fiore, he waited out a manhunt by papal troops for two years.

By then he was even more strongly convinced that he had been chosen, not only by the Romans but by the Holy Ghost, to lead Italy back to virtue and towards the unity it had never had. He wrote a plan full of apocalyptic visions for the reform of the Church and the regeneration of the world, and in 1350 presented it to the emperor Charles IV in Prague, urging him to invade Italy and make him, Cola, the imperial Vicar of Rome. Unimpressed, the emperor clapped him in jail, kept him there for a year, and then handed him over to the tender mercies of Pope Clement, who was delighted to have this unstable populist rebel in his clutches at last.

Cola was surrendered to the papal authorities in Avignon in August 1352, tried before a trio of cardinals and sentenced to death. But he was not executed; he was kept in prison (despite eloquent but vain pleas from Petrarch for his release) and, in another of the dizzying turns of fortune's wheel, he was saved by the sudden death of Pope Clement at the end of 1352. The succeeding pontiff, Innocent VI, who detested the Roman nobles, pardoned Cola, released him and appointed him senator.

Cola went money-raising in Perugia, one of the cities that had supported his quest for Rome's *imperium* over Italy. He raised enough cash to hire a force of five hundred mercenaries, and in 1354 he led them in a march on Rome.

At first the populace greeted him as a liberator, but this illusion soon dissolved. Cola's apocalyptic fantasies, nourished in hiding among the monks of the Apennines, had taken him over. His tribune's rule showed signs of increasing tyranny, with arbitrary arrests, executions and bombastic pronouncements. At last the people who had once adored him had had enough. A mob besieged Cola's palace on the Campidoglio and set it on fire. In disguise, Cola escaped – but he was recognized almost at once, near the top of the great flight of 124 steps that he himself had built up the flank of the Capitoline Hill, leading to the Church of S. Maria in Aracoeli. The mob butchered him with its daggers. It must have been a scene worthy of Sergei Eisenstein. In fact, in his short life and violent death Cola di Rienzo provided more material for fiction, verse and drama than any Roman since Julius Caesar. Petrarch addressed one of his most beautiful odes, '*Spirito gentil*', to his memory. In the nineteenth century Cola fuelled the dreams of republicans and became a Romantic hero, the quintessence of the leader raised from humble origins by a grand fate. To Byron he was heroism incarnate, and he was the hero as well of a novel, no longer read but popular in its day, *Rienzi: Last of the Tribunes* by Edward Bulwer Lytton. Richard Wagner wrote an opera about him, *Rienzi* (1840). Indeed, one might almost say that he was commemorated not only in art, but in real life. For the twentieth century would produce in Rome the man who seemed, in so many ways, the only successor to Cola di Rienzo: Benito Mussolini, another 'vertical invader' from the lower classes, who would convulse all Italy with his apocalyptic dreams of a historical revival centred on Rome.

6

THE RENAISSANCE

The overwhelming fact about architecture – the built, man-made environment – is that it tends to be the first thing you see in cities. It gives them their character. It is a thing in the world, irrefutably present, not an illusion like painting. So when we mention the word 'Renaissance' it is the architecture that comes to mind as the most potent symbol of that spirit of rebirth that swept European culture starting in the fourteenth century. Architecture refers, first and foremost, to large man-made things, which afford shelter and gathering-places to social groups and have a clear-cut political intent behind them. At the same time, the origin of these things, their roots, is often deep-buried and obscure. No single person 'invented' Gothic architecture, and we will never know who was the primal inventor who laid a horizontal tree trunk across the tops of two vertical ones. But there has never been much dispute about who the 'father' of Renaissance architecture was. He was Filippo Brunelleschi (1377–1446), the son of a Florentine notary, who was (in the words of the art historian Vasari) 'sent by Heaven to invest architecture with new forms, after it had wandered astray for many centuries'.

The new forms, of course, were old forms: those of ancient Rome. This picture of Brunelleschi as a saviour sent from on high to redeem the art of building and rescue it from the barbarous, pointy-arched Gothic squalor into which it had fallen may seem, to put it mildly, a little simplified today – but as far as the sixteenth and seventeenth centuries were concerned, it was the plain and only truth. Everything Brunelleschi designed and built, from the Ospedale degli Innocenti and the Pazzi Chapel to the immense octagonal dome of S. Maria del Fiore, the cathedral that dominates

the city, was done in his native Florence. But many of their prototypes, the structures and remnants by which his architectural
thought was stimulated, were in Rome. Brunelleschi was no
copyist, but he was wide open to inspiration from the remote
past. The great dome of ancient Rome, the Pantheon, is not like
Brunelleschi's dome on S. Maria del Fiore. It is a structure that
relies entirely on mass, whereas Brunelleschi's dome is a highly
sophisticated framework covered with a membrane. Nevertheless, Brunelleschi derived his language of building *all'antica*
from Rome, and part of the excitement his buildings still transmit
comes from the rapturous sense of making the old new which
accompanied his discovery of ancient architecture in Rome.

Curiously, although early humanists had talked quite a lot about
the physical antiquities of Rome, none of them seem to have made
a concentrated effort to examine and record the ruins before
Brunelleschi. Ancient Roman texts, inscriptions and manuscripts,
eagerly sought and examined by literary humanists, were of
course a different matter.

Little is known about Brunelleschi's early life, but certainly he
did not begin as an apprentice architect. Though his father
expected him to be a civil servant like himself, the son showed
early artistic ambitions, enrolling in the Arte della Seta, the silk-
workers' guild, among whose members were goldsmiths and
bronze-workers. He had a vocation for work in gold and semi-
precious metals, diligently turning himself (wrote his first biographer Antonio Manetti, 1423–97) into 'a perfect master of niello,
enamel and coloured or gilded ornaments in relief, as well as the
cutting, splitting and setting of precious stones. Thus in any work
to which he applied himself . . . he always had wonderful success.'
In 1398 he was recognized as a master goldsmith. His first important building, the Ospedale degli Innocenti or Foundlings' Hospital
in Florence, was paid for and commissioned by the goldsmiths'
guild in 1419 and finished around 1445. With its long portico of
round arcades carried on eight-metre-high Corinthian columns it
was the first clear echo of classical Roman architecture in Florence.
It had resulted from a study trip Brunelleschi had made with his

friend the sculptor Donatello to Rome, after they had both been narrowly defeated by Lorenzo Ghiberti in the competition for the design of the east doors of the baptistery of Florence Cathedral. Manetti has the disappointed Brunelleschi reflecting that 'It would be a good thing to go and study where sculpture is really good', and so, around 1402–4:

> He went to Rome, for at that time there were plenty of good things that could be seen in public places. Some of the things are still there, though few. Many have since been stolen ... by various pontiffs and cardinals, Romans and men of other nations. While looking at the sculpture, as he had a good eye and an alert mind, he saw the way the ancients built and their proportions ... [H]e seemed to recognize quite clearly a certain order in their members and structural parts ... it looked very different from what was usual in those times. He proposed, while he was looking at the statues of the ancients, to devote no less attention to the order and method of building.

It must have been one of the great dramas of discovery in art's history, a Quattrocento buddy-movie: Brunelleschi and Donatello, one at each end of the measuring-string, flushed with effort and determination, clambering over the ruins, chopping aside the entangling bushes and creepers, measuring heights, widths and spacings, tirelessly noting inscriptions, discovering a lost Rome. It requires a real effort of imagination to envisage what Rome looked like in those far-off days. The Forum was a kind of wilderness with ruins, commonly referred to as the *campo vaccino* – the 'cow-pasture' – which it actually was, with animals grazing about. Shops, restaurants, workplaces – forget them. One traversed the place by stumbling hither and thither. Nothing was self-evident, as Roman ruins are today. The city was a jumble of old fallen columns and ruinous early walls, collapsed vaults, broken arches. The Roman natives who saw them at work on their quest for 'the excellent and highly ingenious building methods of the ancients and their harmonious proportions' thought they were nothing more than crazy treasure-hunters – which in a sense they were. 'Neither was bothered with family cares because neither had a wife nor children ... Neither was much concerned with how he ate, drank, lived or dressed himself, provided he could satisfy himself with these things to see and measure,' according to Manetti.

In this way the bones of the Eternal City surrendered their secrets to Brunelleschi and Donatello, even though the latter, wrote Manetti, was not much interested in architecture as such. 'Together they made rough drawings of almost all the buildings in Rome ... they had excavations done in order to see the joinings of the parts of the buildings, and whether those parts were square, polygonal or perfectly round, circular or oval ... From these observations, with his keen vision, [Brunelleschi] began to distinguish the characteristics of each style, such as Ionic, Doric, Tuscan, Corinthian and Attic, and he used these styles ... as one may still see in his buildings.'

A powerful aid to doing this was the new system Brunelleschi was working out for representing solid objects in depth, known as linear perspective, which relies upon the fact that objects seem to get smaller the further they are from the viewer's eye. If a reliable way could be found to create this illusion by constructing it on a flat plane, such as the surface of a panel or a sheet of paper, then it would be possible to represent the world and its contents, such as buildings, in a coherent and perceptually accurate manner. Brunelleschi's systematic researches were taken up by another architect – though he was much more than that – Leon Battista Alberti (1404–72). Showing the world in this way enabled the artist to give his scenes a new credibility, with what seemed to be real people moving in real space and even, startlingly enough, showing real emotions to one another. Wrote Alberti in a treatise on painting (1435): 'I like to see someone who tells the spectators what is happening there; or beckons with his hand; or menaces with an angry face and with flashing eyes so that no one should come near; or points to some danger or marvellous thing there and invites us to weep or laugh together with them.'

In Alberti's eyes, perspective was not merely a means towards illusion – it was a tool of empathy. It helped give painting, and its representation of architecture, the dignity of a 'liberal art' and raised both above the domain of mere craft.

Truth of representation, allied with a scientific and pragmatic fascination with the forms of antiquity. Such was the beginning of Renaissance architecture. Its canonical early buildings were not raised in Rome, but in Florence; yet they would not have existed without the examples of Roman antiquity, as interpreted by Brunelleschi and Alberti.

Alberti's likeness was cast in a bronze medal in 1454–6 by the sculptor Matteo de' Pasti. On one side is a profile portrait of Alberti, a strikingly handsome man of fifty. The reverse shows his *impresa* or heraldic device, a flying eye with flames bursting from its corners, carried on wings, like Jove's thunderbolt – speed and acuity of perception. Around it is a laurel wreath, declaring his certainty of success. And below, the motto: QVID TUM, 'What next?' It is a declaration of man's faith in the future, in the power of human invention. Nobody could have deserved it more than Leon Battista Alberti, for if anyone gave meaning to the term 'Renaissance man', it was he. He was architect, theorist, sculptor, painter, archaeologist and writer; his subjects included such matters as cryptography and family ethics, as befitted someone used to the close-knit and often secretive world of Renaissance courts. He contributed much to the use of vernacular Italian, as distinct from Latin, in prose writing. He composed the first Italian grammar. He wrote treatises on architecture, painting and sculpture. Moreover he is said to have been an outstanding athlete, and he even wrote a treatise on horses, *De equo animante*. He designed some of the most beautiful and visionary buildings of the fifteenth century: in Florence, Palazzo Rucellai (*c.*1453) and S. Maria Novella (1470); the Tempio Malatestiano (1450) in Rimini; for Lodovico Gonzaga, the churches of S. Sebastiano (1460) and S. Andrea (1470) in Mantua – but in Rome itself, he did nothing except restoration. His literary masterpiece was the ten books of *De re aedificatoria*, the first comprehensive treatment of Renaissance architecture ever published and the first treatise written on classical architecture since Vitruvius in antiquity. Its effect on architects – at least, on those who had Latin, since Alberti did not write it in vernacular Italian – was as wide and fundamental as Vitruvius' had been. Indeed it has a serious claim to be the most influential text on architecture ever written.

Although he did not build in Rome, Alberti had great influence there and his medium for it was the pope, Nicholas V (1397–1455). Born Tommaso Parentucelli, this new pope, who ascended the papal throne in 1447, four short years after Alberti had settled in Rome as a member of the court of Pope Eugenius, was a humanist like Alberti and had been his friend since their university days in Bologna. Both men in earlier years had served the Florentine grandee Palla Strozzi as a tutor. Vasari affirmed that Nicholas had 'a great, resolute spirit, and knew so much that he was able to guide and direct his artists as much as they did him'.

Just how this translated into practice is not certain. Without doubt, Nicholas V and Alberti talked often and long about architecture and town planning – so long and so often that the pope became the natural person to whom Alberti would dedicate and present his *De re aedificatoria*. 'By God!' Alberti wrote at one point, 'I cannot but rebel sometimes when I see monuments, which even the wild barbarians spared for their beauty and splendour, or even time itself, that tenacious destroyer, would willingly let stand for ever, falling into ruin because of the neglect (I might have said the avarice) of certain men.' And to mitigate this constant erosion of Rome's historical fabric he began to collect all the knowable facts about the city's monuments and to present them in a way that made preservation possible, if not easy. His friend the pope was all in favour of that work of memory.

Unlike many of his predecessors – all of whom were of course literate, but some not much more than that – Nicholas V was a ravenous bibliophile. 'He searched for Latin and Greek books in all places where they might be found, never regarding the price,' wrote Vespasiano da Bisticci (1421–98), who would have known, being the principal bookseller of Florence: 'He collected many of the best scribes and employed them. He brought together a number of learned men and set them to produce new books, and also to translate others not in the libraries, rewarding them liberally ... since the time of Ptolemy there had never been collected such a store of books.'

Nicholas' book-collecting enthusiasm formed the basis of the Vatican Library, and cost a fortune. Thus he became 'the ornament and the light of literature and of learned men, and if after him there had appeared another Pope following in his footsteps, letters would have achieved a position worthy of them'. This did not happen, because later popes did not entirely share Nicholas' bibliomania. But even his library-building was quite modest compared to his architectural enterprises. Vespasiano da Bisticci remembered how Nicholas 'used to say that he would like to do two things, if ever he had the money: form a library and build, and he did both during his pontificate'.

The formation of the library was quite gradual. In the mid-fifteenth century it consisted of only 340 volumes, two in Greek. Modern scholars point out that Nicholas V was the first pope to give the formation of the papal library a high priority, but by 1455 its collection amounted to no more than 1,160 books; there were others in Italy the same size or bigger. The honour of being the true founder of the Vatican Library as an institution, therefore, goes to a later pope, Sixtus IV, who was lucky enough to have the scholar Bartolomeo Platina as his librarian (1475–81). Later expansions, particularly that of Leo X in the sixteenth century, would far surpass that. Yet Nicholas certainly had the vision of a library for the Vatican, 'for the common convenience of the learned', and nobody could accuse him of stinginess. He even carried a bag with hundreds of florins in it, which he would give away by the handful to people he thought deserving.

Leon Battista Alberti he thought particularly deserving. Alberti stood out for two reasons. First, because in addition to his other writings he composed a *Descriptio urbis Romae*, a 'description of the city of Rome', which covered the main buildings of antiquity and the principal churches built during the Christian era, along with the city walls and gateways, the course of the Tiber and other matters – a huge step up from the one that had been the only guidebook to the antiquities of Rome, the legend-infested *Mirabilia*, or 'Marvels' of the Eternal City, a text riddled with hearsay and extreme inaccuracies, which became a much needed prelude to the Jubilee year of 1450 which Nicholas had just announced. 'There was not the least remain of any ancient structure,' Alberti would write with pardonable pride, 'that had any merit in it, but that I went and examined, to see if anything was to be learned from it. Thus I was continually searching, considering, measuring and making drafts of everything I could hear of, until such time as I had made myself perfect master of every contrivance or invention that had been used in those ancient remains.' It is probably no exaggeration to say that Alberti ended up knowing more about ancient Roman building than most ancient Romans had.

The second reason lay in the pope's own archaeological interests.

In addition to all his other talents, Alberti had the novel distinction of being the world's first underwater archaeologist. The object of his search was an ancient Roman galley from the time of Trajan, which thirteen hundred years before had sunk, presumably during a *naumachia* or mock naval battle, to the muddy floor of Lake Nemi. Its location was known, because it kept fouling fishermen's nets. But nobody had figured out a way to raise it, and without underwater goggles divers could see no more than a vague bulk looming in dark water. Commissioned to do so by Cardinal Prospero Colonna, Alberti brought it up with grappling-hooks, cables, floating barrels and winches. Only the prow came clear of the water before the hull broke in half and sank again, and Alberti was able to observe – the first account of ancient Roman naval construction – that it was built of pine and cypress 'in an excellent state of preservation' and covered with tar-soaked linen which was then sheathed in lead secured by bronze nails.

Although this feat must have caused a good deal of buzz and

flutter in court circles, what most cemented Alberti's position as Nicholas V's adviser on building was his large and ever-growing knowledge of architecture, its theory, practice and history. In addition, he had no illusions about whom he was designing and, if possible, building for. 'Do everything possible,' he exhorts the reader, 'to obtain commissions only from the most important people, who are generous and true lovers of the arts. For your work loses its value when done for persons of low social rank. Can't you see the advantages to be had in the furthering of your reputation if you have the support of the most influential people?' Moreover, 'the safety, authority and decorum of the state depend to a great extent on the work of the architect'.

With the patronage and encouragement of Nicholas V, Alberti became the successor to Brunelleschi, with the difference that he was also the first architect of the Renaissance Papacy. (Brunelleschi, despite his great influence on other architects, did not design for popes.) Certainly, though Alberti believed in the supremacy of Roman norms and forms, he also believed strongly in individual taste and would never have considered imposing a strict, formulaic canon of beauty. A building might well have the proportions of a human being, but what kind of human?

> Some admire a woman for being extremely slender and fine shaped; the young gentlemen in *Terence* preferred a girl that was plump and fleshy; you perhaps are for a medium between these two extremes, and would neither have her so thin as to seem wasted with sickness, nor so strong and robust as if she were a Ploughman in disguise, and were fit for boxing: in short, you wou'd like her such a beauty as might be formed by taking for the first what the second might spare. But then, because one pleases you more than the other, would you therefore affirm the other to be not at all handsome or graceful? By no means ...

It seems fairly certain that Alberti had the strong hand in crucial restorations of a dilapidated Rome, although we do not know

how many. Nicholas had ambitious plans for the city's renovation.
One of the keys to it was the aqueduct of the Acqua Vergine,
which had been so important to the water supply of the ancient
city. Now tracts of it had fallen in, and much of the rest was
blocked by sinter or accumulated lime deposits. Those who lived
in districts once served by the Acqua Vergine were obliged to drink
the filthy water of the Tiber, teeming with bacteria. Prompted by
Alberti, Nicholas V ordered a complete rerouting of the aqueduct,
entering Rome near the Porta Pinciana and finishing at the Campo
Marzio in three outlets called the Fontana di Trevi, designed by
Alberti but later to be demolished and replaced by Nicola Salvi's
enormous stone festivity into which Anita Ekberg waded for
Fellini's camera and generations of tourists threw their coins.

Alberti oversaw the restoration of the Ponte S. Angelo, which
brought traffic across the Tiber to the Castello S. Angelo, formerly
Hadrian's Tomb. He was also busy restoring ancient and infirm
churches for Nicholas, such as S. Stefano Rotondo, the circular
church with its majestic ring of internal columns erected in early
Christian times.

Nicholas V had no doubts about the importance of architecture – a new architecture, one which would centre and stabilize
the faith of Christians. In 1455 he declared that

> To create solid and stable convictions in the minds of the
> uncultured masses there must be something that appeals to
> the eye ... a popular faith sustained only on doctrines will
> never be anything but feeble and vacillating. But if the auth-
> ority of the Holy See were visibly displayed in majestic build-
> ings, imperishable memorials ... belief would grow and
> strengthen like a tradition from one generation to another,
> and all the world would accept and revere it.

But the great work on which Nicholas and Alberti hoped to
embark was the replanning and construction of St Peter's, the
navel of Christianity. Constantine's original basilica, by the fifteenth century, was in poor repair and Alberti saw that whole

sections of it had to be rebuilt. 'A very long, big wall,' he noted, 'has, very unadvisedly, been built over a number of large voids', with the result that the buffeting of north winds over the centuries had pushed it six feet out of plumb – so that any extra pressure or subsidence could bring it crashing down. Alberti recommended that the whole wall be bound in with new masonry, and Nicholas ordered more than two thousand cartloads of building stone to be quarried from the Colosseum and brought to the site of St Peter's. But the gigantic task of rebuilding the old Constantinian basilica was not achieved; the pope died, and the responsibility for the great church passed into other and even more ambitious papal and architectural hands.

The architectural ones were those of Donato d'Angelo (1444?–1514), commonly called Bramante – a nickname that meant 'ardent' or 'intensely desiring'. (His maternal grandfather had been nicknamed Bramante too: perhaps intensity was a family trait.) He was a farmer's son, born in a village of the Papal States near Urbino. Undoubtedly he witnessed the construction of the Ducal Palace and he would have had some contact with artists who attended its highly cultivated court at the invitation of its ruler and patron Federigo da Montefeltro, including Alberti and such figures as Piero della Francesca. He was one of a constellation of early Renaissance figures who were born around the 1440s – Perugino, Botticelli, Signorelli and, in 1452, Leonardo da Vinci. Later, when he moved to Milan, he came to know Leonardo, but how well it is not possible to say. Probably a small book on ancient Roman architecture that appeared anonymously around 1500 and was dedicated to Leonardo was by Bramante. Certainly both men worked for the Sforza court in Milan in the 1490s. Presumably Bramante got his introduction to Duke Ludovico Sforza through his aunt, Battista Sforza (d. 1472), who had married Federigo da Montefeltro. Bramante was to spend two decades in Milan doing some building for Duke Ludovico. He did not become a star there; as an outsider to the city he did not secure the big commissions. However, he did design the Church of S. Maria presso Satiro, and was involved with the design of the Milanese Monastery and

Church of S. Maria delle Grazie, where Leonardo painted his disastrously ill-preserved *Last Supper* – that now almost vanished icon of the High Renaissance. Bramante designed a tribune at the end of the nave which was originally meant to be a mausoleum for the Sforzas.

Bramante's move to Rome we owe to political history. When the French armies marched into Milan in 1499, they expelled the duke and dislocated the city's cultural life entirely. They also perpetrated what is doubtless one of the greatest crimes against art ever committed: Leonardo's clay model for the giant bronze horse, which was to be the monument to Gian Galeazzo Sforza, Ludovico's father, ignominiously fell to pieces after the French crossbowmen used it for target practice – a great loss indeed. Like the bitterly frustrated Leonardo, Bramante was one of the figures who left for Rome, and Milan's loss was very much Rome's gain. Like any other architect of talent, he was soon absorbed in the grandeur and purity of its ancient structures.

Quite soon Bramante's obvious talents would be snapped up by one of the great 'building popes' of the Renaissance, Pope Julius II. But he designed several non-papal buildings first, and the most significant of them was hardly bigger than a summerhouse – a diminutive domed circular temple in the courtyard of the Spanish Franciscan Convent and Church of S. Pietro in Montorio, up on the Janiculan Hill. This 'tempietto', as it is known, may have been inspired by the ancient Temple of Vesta in Rome. The sixteen columns of its outer ring are all Doric, the order considered most suitable for commemorating robust and virile heroes, which Peter, no plaster saint, certainly was. Bramante worked to a modular scheme originally set out as a recipe for internal harmony by Vitruvius – all the chief dimensions, such as the diameter of the interior, are multiples of the column diameters. The Tempietto is the first completely Doric building of the Italian Renaissance, as another pioneer architect, Sebastiano Serlio, pointed out: 'We should give credit to Bramante, seeing that it was he who was the inventor and light of all good architecture which had been buried until his time, the time of Julius II.'

Julius II was the name taken, at his election to the Papacy by the College of Cardinals, by Giuliano della Rovere (1443–1513). This impatient, bellicose and thunderously energetic man was the greatest patron of art the Roman Church had ever produced, and he would remain so until the partnership of Urban VIII Barberini and Gianlorenzo Bernini more than a century later. His architect was Bramante, his sculptor Michelangelo, his painter Raphael.

This trio formed, without much question, the most remarkable body of artistic talent ever assembled by a single European.

Raphael frescoed his suite of private papal apartments on the second floor of the Vatican, the chief one of which was known as the Stanza della Segnatura because in it Julius signed his name to essential documents. Some think that Julius himself, rather than Raphael, chose the narrative of images for these rooms.

As for Michelangelo, Julius was by far the most important, if difficult, client he ever had – just as Michelangelo was the most difficult and important artist Julius had ever employed. The sculptor embarked upon a colossal and never-to-be-finished project for Julius' tomb in the Church of S. Pietro delle Vincole. He very reluctantly frescoed the ceiling and end wall of the chapel in the Vatican which, having been built by Julius' uncle Pope Sixtus IV (reg. 1471–84), was known as the Sistine, and later decorated the Pauline Chapel, also in the Vatican, with scenes of the conversion of St Paul and the crucifixion of St Peter.

And Bramante – an ageing man when he came into Julius' employ, more than sixty years old – took on the Herculean task of finishing the work Alberti had started, creating a new symbolic centre for Christianity by demolishing Constantine's basilica of St Peter and building an entirely new one. It would be the biggest church in the world.

That Julius II was a monster of will and appetite has never been in doubt. You could not defy him with much hope of survival, let alone success. He was known to his court and the rest of Rome as *il papa terribile*, 'the terrifying pope' – or, if you wanted to shift the meaning an inch or two, the Dreadful Father. He did not call himself Julius for nothing. His model was antiquity's Julius the First – the all-conquering, all-seeing, all-remembering and godlike Julius Caesar, conqueror of Europe and re-maker of Rome, *Roma triumphans*, the city around which the rest of the world turned. He was determined to restore, not just superficially refurbish, the scope of the Catholic Church's political power, which had suffered all too apparent losses through the translation of the Papacy to Avignon.

For this, it was necessary to expand the Papal States, an effort that could be tried by diplomacy but underwritten only by military force. Thus Julius II became the first and last pope to lead an army from horseback, wearing plate armour. (His papacy also brought the foundation, on 21 January 1506, of the Swiss Guard, who today are merely pushy Vatican cops with flapping yellow uniforms but, in the sixteenth century, were a serious force of halberdiers dedicated to protecting the person of the pope – an ecclesiastical Praetorian Guard.)

Much of the money for his military enterprises came from Italy's textile industry. The dyeing of cloth requires a fixative, which in the sixteenth century was a mineral, alum. Most alum had come from Turkey, but large deposits of it were to be found north of Rome in an otherwise unremarkable spot named Tolfa. The fortunes of the mines of Tolfa, with their virtual monopoly on the mineral, rose with the textile trade and so were a large source of income for the Papacy.

In 1503, when Julius was elected pope, the city of Rome was in difficult straits. In some respects it hardly functioned as a city – it lacked a strong central government and was divided up into quarrelsome and isolated districts, run in an improvised way by the entrenched heirs of medieval clans. It was plagued by crime, particularly in the dock areas of the Tiber, the Ripa and the Ripetta, where trade was dominated by Mafioso-like thugs. Some banks had closed, unable to hold up against the creeping devaluation of the currency. The price of corn had doubled. The ancient water-supply system was near collapse, despite Nicholas V's earlier efforts to fix it. There were frequent outbreaks of plague. Some riverside parts of Rome had turned malarial – even Julius II had a bout of malaria, though not a grave one.

Against this background Julius' actions, though resented by many Romans, made considerable sense. He stabilized the price of bread by setting up public bakeries. He brought in cheap grain from Sicily and France, and prohibited immigration. He tightened the screws of tax collection and confiscated the estates of several immoderately rich cardinals who had conveniently died. They were replaced by newly appointed cardinals, all friends of Julius, who were also rich but could be relied on to obey him. And of course the Church was directed to wring every penny it could from the sale of indulgences, that abusive and superstitious practice by which the faithful could supposedly buy remission from Purgatory in the next life by giving hard cash to Rome's agents in this one. 'When you open your purse-strings and the cash-bell rings, the soul flies out of Purgatory and sings.' Disgust at the indulgence trade would be one of the forces that drove the Protestant Reformation, but at first the Catholic hierarchy did not realize how furious an industry it was growing to be. Thanks to these emergency measures the papal treasury, which had about 300,000 ducats in 1505, swelled to 500,000 in 1506.

Julius was lucky to have a close friend and astute money-manager in the Sienese papal banker Agostino Chigi (1466–1520), recognized as the wealthiest merchant banker in Europe, who had more than one hundred offices spread from Cairo to London and at one point held the papal tiara in pawn as security on his loans.

Thus Julius was able to indulge his appetite for Caesarian glory. This became especially clear after the papal armies annexed Bologna and expelled its Bentivoglio rulers in 1507, when an imperial procession exactly reminiscent of the original Caesar's triumphs was arranged for him in Rome; along streets flanked by cheering crowds he rode under triumphal arches to the Capitol. In 1504 a new and revalued silver coin, bearing his portrait and known as the *giulio*, was minted in his honour. The following year, Julius II commissioned from Michelangelo an enormous figure of himself which was mounted on the façade of the Bolognese Church of S. Petronio; but three years later, when his forces lost control of the city, this bronze giant was torn down, broken up, and recast as cannon. But by then Julius' attention was pre-empted and occupied with other projects by Michelangelo, as well as by Raphael and Bramante.

Architecture took first place. Through new building on a grand scale Julius intended to renovate the 'decorum' of Rome, returning the city to the grandeur and authority its ancient buildings had once conferred on it. Julius Caesar had given Rome a renewed spiritual centre through his constructions. Julius II would do the same, by rebuilding St Peter's on a hitherto unimagined scale.

In 1505 Bramante began a series of additions to the Vatican Palace: the terraces of the Belvedere courtyard. These were private, of course; indeed, so much so that they were designed to be seen from one main vantage-point, the window of the pope's study, that part of the papal apartments overlooking the downhill slope towards the Tiber known as the Stanza della Segnatura. They were modelled on the huge imperial palaces of antiquity – Nero's Domus Aurea, Hadrian's Villa; they would tell the visitor that a new Catholic and Papal Rome comparable in every way to the old imperial and pagan Rome was on its way. Naturally, Julius wanted this gigantic affair, a hundred metres wide and three hundred long, with its stairs, ramps, formal gardens, arcades, fountains, *nymphaeum* and open-air theatre, to be finished tomorrow, if not yesterday. It would have the most impressive and precious collection of antique sculpture that existed; the Apollo Belvedere, the Laocoön, the Belvedere Torso, all were there. The words of Virgil's Cumaean Sibyl, warning off the ignorant, *procul este, profani* ('Begone, you uninitiated'), were cut into the stone of the spiral staircase ramp near the sculpture court. You could ride a horse up this ramp. Its architrave bears on a series of columns, which get slenderer and more refined as one ascends: the Tuscan order at the lowest level, giving way to the Doric, and then to the Ionic and finally the Composite.

The fresco of Parnassus was painted on the north wall of the

Stanza della Segnatura, above its window. The view from the window was of a part of the Vatican hill traditionally considered sacred to Apollo. Another part of its mythic history was that Etruscan priests used to watch for auguries and make prophecies (*vaticinia*) from this spot. Hence the name 'Vatican' for the general area. The Apollo was installed on the Belvedere as an act of naming not so much the sculpture as its site. Having Raphael's fresco of Apollo and the Muses right at the spot from which one observed the distant sculpture of Apollo confirmed the mantic tradition of the place, and this was enriched by the further myth that St Peter had been crucified there.

The Belvedere, with its size and levels, could almost be a town in itself, and certainly Bramante's town-planning ambitions, though never fulfilled, were part of his reputation in Rome. Two years after his death a writer named Andrea Guarna put Bramante in a comedy titled *Scimmia* ('The Monkey'). He dies and arrives at the gates of Paradise, telling St Peter – the original pope, one should remember, the prototype of Julius II – that he will not come in unless he is employed to rebuild the whole place:

> I want to get rid of this hard and difficult road that leads from earth to heaven; I shall build another, in a spiral, so wide that the souls of the old and the weak can ride up it on horseback. Then I think I will demolish this paradise and make a new one that will provide more elegant and comfortable dwellings for the blessed. If you agree, then I shall stay; otherwise I shall go straight to Pluto's house, where I shall have a better chance of carrying out my ideas . . . I shall make an entirely new hell and overturn the old one.

Neither Bramante nor Julius hesitated to get rid of old buildings, however venerable, if they got in the way of their plans. It is no surprise that one of the architect's nicknames was 'Bramante *ruinante*', Bramante the Wrecker. It was used a lot as he prepared to undertake the biggest project of his life, perhaps the biggest project of any architect's life (unless you count later mile-high skyscrapers in Arab sheikhdoms or mega-airports in China): the design and building of the new St Peter's Basilica.

Both the pope and the architect believed, with reason, that the old building erected in the fourth century by Constantine would no longer do. In the reign of Nicholas V (1447–55) a survey had shown its walls were tottering out of plumb, and there was a real danger that an earthquake tremor (to which Rome, in the fifteenth to sixteenth centuries, was more prone than it is today) would bring the whole thousand-year-old fabric down. Both men were conscious of their own mortality, and in fact would die within a year of one another, Julius in 1513 and Bramante in 1514. If history were to remember them as the authors of this colossal enterprise, they would have to hurry. Moreover, they needed to move the project as far along as possible, so that the next architect and the next pope would be stuck with their conception, unable to make radical changes.

Unfortunately, since Bramante did not run an architects' office in the modern sense, there are practically no written or drafted records of how ideas might have passed to and fro between him and Julius, and the only first-hand record of Bramante's intentions is a drawing known as the 'parchment plan', in the Uffizi. It shows a central dome and two domed chapels, forming a Greek cross, though with no indications of size. But there were strong motives for making it enormous, and one can imagine Julius and his architect discussing how, now that Constantinople had fallen (in 1453) to the Turkish infidel and Hagia Sophia had become a mosque, the largest dome should be the centre of Christendom. The questions raised by the demolition of a building as venerated as old St Peter's would be silenced by the phrase inscribed on a medal depicting its intended elevation: TEMPLI PETRI INSTAURACIO. *Instaurare* meant to restore, to make new; the pope and the architect could say that they were only 'restoring' the ancient fabric, though of course they were replacing it altogether.

Bramante's inspiration for the new church was essentially Roman, not Florentine. That is to say, it was modelled on the gigantic bath complexes of ancient Rome and, like them, made

of concrete and brick, with various facings of marble and limestone. As built, the basilica is 218.7 metres long, its main nave 26
metres wide and 46 high from floor to roof. The transept is 154.8
metres long. The whole fabric contains forty-six altars. It covers
an area of 5.7 acres. None of these raw figures gives more than a
faint impression of the vastness of a building that can, if the
congregation is packed in, hold up to sixty thousand people
(though not comfortably). For comparison, the Duomo in Milan
can hold about thirty-seven thousand. St Peter's dome is the tallest
in the world – 448 feet from the floor to the top of the external
cross on the lantern. In diameter, it is fractionally smaller than the
ancient dome of the Pantheon and Brunelleschi's 'modern' dome
of Florence cathedral. The tradition that it is built over the actual
site of St Peter's tomb is only that – a tradition, for which there is
no compelling historical or archaeological evidence.

Not the least impressive aspect of the cupola was its lighting,
splendid and theatrical. Today it is done with electric floods and
spots, but from the Seicento to the end of the nineteenth century
it was achieved (on special occasions, such as the *festa* of St Peter)
with a superabundance of several thousand lamps, lanterns and
torches, all of which, on the orders of a theatrical maestro, would
be lit simultaneously. Everyone who saw this, before the age of
electricity, was astounded by its grandeur. Goethe, who witnessed
it, recorded that 'If one reflects that, in that moment, the great
edifice serves only as the frame of a fantastic orgy of light, one
can well understand that nothing else like it can be found in the
world.'

The design of the basilica was heavy with liturgical symbolism:
thus (to take only one instance) the early drawings for the church
specify twelve doors, alluding to the twelve tribes of Israel and to
the twelve Apostles. The most essential thing about it, from both
Bramante's and Julius' viewpoint, was that it should be based
on 'perfect' geometrical forms, the square (symbolizing, among
other things, earth) and the circle (the heavens), one inscribed
within the other. It was not built that way, but in another building
by Bramante – not in Rome – one can get some idea, on a smaller

scale, of the general effect. This is the far smaller pilgrimage
Church of S. Maria della Consolazione, built on a hillside below
the town of Todi, in Umbria. Its dome rises from a drum which
in turn rises from a square block, from which grow four polygonal
apses each roofed with a half-dome. There is no town around it;
it simply emerges from the earth, flooded with light inside. No
mosaics, no statuary, no gilt, no marble: only strong, ideal, geometrical form. To have such an interior to oneself, in the light of
a spring morning, is to grasp a fleeting sense of what Dante
meant – *luce intellettual, piena d'amore*: 'the light of the mind,
suffused with love'.

The construction of St Peter's took 120 years and lasted for the
lifetime of twenty popes. When Bramante died in 1514, he was
replaced by Giuliano da Sangallo, Fra Giocondo and Raphael.
Sangallo and Fra Giocondo both died the next year, which left
Raphael as the master architect until he, too, died in 1520.

Antonio da Sangallo now took over the revision of the design
and stayed with it until his own death in 1546, by which time
Michelangelo, old, reluctant and increasingly infirm, was handed
the enormous task. By then Sangallo had built the crossing piers
that would support the dome, and vaulted some of the arms of
its immense Greek cross.

But the dome itself did not exist yet.

Michelangelo's first step was to cancel Sangallo's plans
altogether and tear down whatever structures by Sangallo he did
not like. He wanted to revert to a Bramantian purity and in a
famous letter he sent to the Fabbrica or office of works of St
Peter's he wrote that 'any who have deviated from Bramante's
arrangement, as Sangallo did, have deviated from the truth'.

Sangallo had cut off all the light from Bramante's plan, or so
Michelangelo thought, creating dark corners where nuns could
be molested and false coiners could do their nefarious work. In
the evenings, when the basilica had to be locked up, it would
take twenty-five men to clear out anyone hiding inside. And so,
'Winning [the commission for St Peter's] would be the greatest
loss to me, and if you can get the Pope to understand this you will

give me pleasure, because I don't feel well.' It was no use. Having no choice, Michelangelo accepted, full of misgivings, in 1547. He sent off to Florence for clay and wooden models of its Duomo. These became the first inspiration for the double-shelled cupola of St Peter's raised on its sixteen-sided drum. It had come nowhere near completion before Michelangelo died in 1564. It was eventually finished by Giacomo della Porta in 1590; his design had a somewhat more pointed, upward-reaching quality than Michelangelo's hemispheric outer dome.

Meanwhile, Raphael had been at work inside the Vatican.

Raphael was born in 1483 in Urbino, which, though small, was no cultural backwater. His father Giovanni Santi was a painter, attached to the court of the city's duke. The first duke, the *condottiere* Federigo da Montefeltro, had been ennobled by the pope – Urbino was part of the Papal States – and largely thanks to him the town had become what W.B. Yeats would later call 'the mirror-school of courtesies / Where wit and beauty learned their trade / Upon Urbino's windy hill'. As the gifted son of a court artist, Raphael was raised in an environment where polished manners, tact and all-round *gentilezza* counted immensely; this place, this tiny social world, was to be the model for Baldassare Castiglione's classic manual of behaviour, *The Book of the Courtier* (1528). So although Raphael did not get a top-flight education as a humanist scholar – his Latin always seems to have been a little shaky – he had one in the manners and skills of a court artist. Moving gracefully in high circles was never to be a problem for him, as it often was for other Renaissance painters. Other artists, as Vasari pointed out, might be hampered by 'a certain element of savagery and madness, which, besides making them strange and eccentric, had ... revealed in them rather the obscure darkness of vice than the brightness and splendour of those virtues that make men immortal'. Not Raphael.

Of his precocity there was never any doubt. Right from the start, as his earliest surviving drawings (done when he was sixteen or seventeen) amply show, Raphael's hand was both brilliant and disciplined. He was apprenticed to the studio of one of the best-known and most successful painters in Italy, Pietro Perugino (1450–1523). According to Vasari, young Raphael imitated Perugino's style, in all its elegance and sweetness, so closely that their paintings could hardly be told apart; 'his copies could not be distinguished from the master's originals'. What made him more than an epigone of this fine but provincial artist was a sojourn in Florence, where 'he changed and improved his manner so much from having seen so many works by the hands of excellent masters, that it had nothing to do with his earlier manner; indeed, the two might have belonged to different masters'.

Clearly, the road pointed towards Rome, where thanks to Julius' patronage a new interest in painting, as in architecture, was simmering. It is not known how word of Raphael's existence reached Julius II's ears. Perhaps Bramante, who came from the same part of Italy, recommended him. In any case, by 1508 the young painter, now in his mid-twenties, had been summoned to Rome and given the difficult and prestigious job of decorating the papal apartments in the Vatican Palace. From then until his death, he would be occupied with this commission, which required him to hire more and more assistants, including Giulio Romano – who would presently transfer what he had learned from Raphael about architectural design to Raphael's Villa Madama in Rome and about fresco to his own gloriously eccentric masterpiece for the Gonzagas, the Palazzo del Te in Mantua. Giulio Romano was often accused of vulgarity, but in his hands in Mantua this became a virtue; since he could not incorporate his life-affirming coarseness into Raphael's rooms for the pope, it went instead into the Mantuan frescoes, some of which fairly burst with stylish libido, and the enjoyably pornographic prints he made as illustrations to the work of the bawdy writer Aretino. It hardly surfaced in his Roman work.

The first room Raphael addressed in the Vatican Palace was the pope's library and office, the Stanza della Segnatura. The themes he chose, or was given, were those appropriate to Theology, Poetry, Jurisprudence and Philosophy.

'Poetry' called, of course, for a scene of the gathering of ancient and near-contemporary genius on Parnassus, grouped around an Apollo who is making music below his emblematic laurel tree. At the top are his agents the nine Muses, the Greek deities of astronomy, philosophy and the arts. The daughters of Zeus and Mnemosyne, they are Calliope (Muse of the heroic epic), Clio (history), Euterpe (flute music), Terpsichore (dance), Erato (lyric poetry and hymns), Melpomene (tragic drama), Thalia (comedy), Polyhymnia (mime, sacred poetry and agriculture) and Urania (astronomy). Ancient poets in the fresco include Homer, Virgil, Sappho, Propertius, Horace, Tibullus. Among the more modern writers, some of whom were Raphael's contemporaries, are Petrarch, Ariosto, Sannazaro, Boccaccio and of course Dante. It is an anthology of what a person would need to have read before he could call himself civilized.

Traditionally, and rightly, *The School of Athens*, representing 'philosophy', is the grandest of the four compositions in the Stanza della Segnatura. The arch of the wall opens out into a perspective series of further arches: we seem to be in a majestically vaulted but unfinished architectural space. Blue sky can be seen through its gaps, suggesting that the building is the new St Peter's, of which Raphael was now the supervising architect. To a sixteenth-century visitor seeing this image for the first time, it would have suggested a pristine Rome, being rebuilt and restored – just what Julius II wanted his papacy to suggest.

It is filled with figures, explaining, arguing, reading or writing. At their centre, the vanishing-point of the perspective, two men are advancing towards us. The one on the left, in the red garment, pointing upwards, is Plato, indicating to his listeners, and to us, that the source of all ideal form is to be found in the heavens. He is holding a copy of his late work, the *Timaeus*, which was devoted to natural science and sought to describe the relationship between gods and man in the world. The world, the *Timaeus* asserts, is eternal, because it is subject to eternal laws. Next to him, Aristotle in the blue cloak contradicts this; he points downwards to the earth, indicating that true knowledge is to be found empirically, in the world as it is and its contents as they are. He carries a book inscribed 'ETH[IC]A' – the *Nicomachean Ethics*, regarded by Christianizing humanists of the day as the summit of Aristotle's thought. Each man has his eager group of listeners and disciples. The heroes of thought are sometimes given the faces of Raphael's contemporaries. Plato, for instance, has the archetypal-sage features of Leonardo da Vinci.

Raphael wants his fresco to represent not the physical production of books, but the processes of thinking that go into them and undergird their arguments – along with the buzz of discussion that thought produces. If one man is writing something down, another is reading it over his shoulder. *The School of Athens* is often taken for an image of 'classical' composure, but in fact it is almost as animated as a battlepiece, criss-crossed with vectors of agreement, exposition and surprise. There in the right foreground is a knot of figures watching a savant with protractors, drawing a geometrical figure on a tablet. He represents Euclid, demonstrating one of his theorems. But his face is that of Bramante, in whose buildings geometry played so large a creative role. In a corresponding position on the steps to the left is Pythagoras, busily writing in a book. Solitary, sitting apart, wrapped in a keep-away melancholy (the saturnine artist in contemplation) is Michelangelo, his pencil poised over a page. What is he thinking about? We don't and can't know – but we know what Raphael has been thinking about, and that is the permeability, the exchange value, of thought itself. And surely he could think about that, and find such a fluid, continuous embodiment for it, because he could draw on the help and interpretative support of the humanists in and around Julius II's court. Perhaps such a painting as *The School of Athens* could be called, in that sense, a collaborative work of art. Other painters worked under Raphael as painting assistants on the Stanza della Segnatura, but who worked with him in deciding its cast of characters and implied themes?

The theme of Raphael's frescoes in the Stanza d'Eliodoro is broadly political. They represent God's way of protecting His Church from various possible threats. Is its wealth threatened? Then the would-be thief has to consider a once obscure incident related in the Apocrypha (II Maccabees 3), where the larcenous general Heliodorus has been planning to loot treasure from the Temple of Jerusalem. We see him sprawling, blinded, and furiously attacked by two spectacularly beautiful youths while a horseman sent by heaven tramples him down. From the left, this scene is watched by Julius II seated in a litter, which is borne by an entourage that includes likenesses of Raphael himself and his assistant Marcantonio Raimondi.

Is there concern or scepticism about the truth of dogma? Then the visitor must consult Raphael's fresco of *The Mass at Bolsena*, where we see a priest celebrating Mass; it is the climactic moment of the ceremony, the consecration of the Host, when at the words *Hoc est enim corpus meum* ('This is indeed my Body'), first uttered by Christ at the Last Supper, the bread – so Catholics are required to believe – is transformed into the veritable flesh of Jesus. This Mass in the lakeside town of Bolsena, north of Rome, had a sceptic in its congregation who was unsure about the Transubstantiation, and to convince him God caused the Host in the priest's hands to bleed Jesus' own sacred blood. Raphael has this event watched by the kneeling figure of Julius II, who never saw it but wished to emphasize his devotion to the Eucharist.

Thirdly, is the seat of the Church, Rome itself, in danger of invasion? Raphael symbolizes this in *The Meeting of Leo the Great with Attila*, the least inspired and satisfactory of the four scenes, in which we see Attila the Hun and his barbarian hordes reeling back from the walls of Rome at a mere gesture from Pope Leo I. Raphael's figure of this pope is a portrait of the tenth Leo, Giovanni de' Medici.

Finally, is the person of the pontiff in danger? Then the viewer must consider the fourth wall of the Stanza d'Eliodoro with its fresco of *The Liberation of St Peter*, Raphael's superb night-piece of the saint incarcerated in the darkness of the Mamertine prison in Rome, glowing like a firebrand beside the shiny black armour of his guards. The sense of life restored, the contrast between the vitality of the saint and the moribund, beetle-like quality of the guards' bodies, shows how carefully Raphael must have taken note of similar contrasts between the risen God and his slumbering captors in earlier paintings of the resurrection of Christ. This must have been the last fresco of Raphael's that Julius could have seen; he was painting it in 1513, the year the pope died.

The work of frescoing the Stanze continued well past Julius' death and was still absorbing Raphael while he worked as papal architect on St Peter's. The clearest reference to the new pope, Leo X, is quite indirect: it shows a miracle performed by his namesake, an earlier Pope Leo, the fourth (reg. 847–55), who miraculously extinguished a fire that threatened to destroy St Peter's along with all the buildings of the Borgo. In the so-called Stanza dell'Incendio, in the fresco *Fire in the Borgo*, he appears as a small distant figure making the sign of the cross on a balcony, near the vanishing-point of the composition. Unless you look for him you hardly know he is there, but the clue is given by the distant, agitated women beseeching him from below his balcony. The emphasis of the fresco is on the frantic Romans in the foreground, scurrying to and fro, disoriented by the threat of the blaze. The fire rages on the extreme left. On the right one sees a crowd of women carrying pots of water to put out the flames. There, in the foreground, is a strong young man carrying an older one piggy-back, accompanied by a boy: a direct reference back to images of Aeneas accompanied by his son Ascanius and carrying his old father, Anchises, away from the flames of Troy, on their way to found Rome. A mother hands her swaddled child over a wall, into the receptive arms of a helper; a naked man hangs by his fingertips from the wall, about to drop to safety. (This is a fairly operatic moment, since it would clearly have been just as easy for the naked man to scoot around the end of the wall. But that would have deprived Raphael of the pretext to paint that magnificent body, muscles tensed at full stretch.)

In the years he worked on the Stanze, Raphael did not limit himself to fresco. He also had a large output of portraits and devotional paintings. His portrait of Baldassare Castiglione is to be ranked with Leonardo's *Mona Lisa* as one of the suavely inventive masterpieces of that genre. His most popular religious paintings were of the Madonna and Child, usually with the infant John the Baptist. The common complaint about Raphael concerns these images, which remained steadfastly popular from the sixteenth to the nineteenth century and influenced generations of artists, down to Ingres, who wrote that 'We do not admire Rembrandt and the others at random; we cannot compare them and their art to the divine Raphael.' The group of German artists in Rome who called themselves the Nazarenes (Overbeck, Pforr and others) venerated the early more than the later Raphael. Others thought him sentimental, stereotyped and oppressively masterly; nine-teenth-century English artists like Millais and Holman Hunt called themselves 'Pre-Raphaelites' because they wanted to paint as though he had never existed.

But today, it is difficult to have more than a glancing acquaint-ance with Raphael's devotional easel paintings without suc-cumbing to their charm, and then realizing what unsurpassed mastery lies behind them. No matter how often one sees baby Jesus and the infant Baptist playing together, however strongly one may react against the repeated theme – the prophetic Baptist showing the little saviour a stick, or wand, with a cross-piece which Jesus eagerly reaches out for, since it is a prefiguration of the cross on which he will die – the sheer beauty and fluency of the painting gets you every time. 'Immortal', 'divine', 'per-fection' – such words, which Raphael's work evoked from earlier admirers, may die on our modern (or postmodern) lips, but their memory cannot be entirely effaced.

And certainly no need to be rid of it was felt in the early sixteenth century. Raphael was the ideal secular as well as religious painter, faultless in his production, his meanings always clear as spring-water, his saints holy, his men noble and thoughtful, his women desirable, his technique impeccable. What other artist could have painted two little angels like Raphael's into an assump-tion of the Virgin, giving them an enchanting air of childish detachment while not distracting at all from the majesty of the event? The answer is: none. Nobody had a word to say against him, except the notoriously prickly Michelangelo, who learned that Bramante had let Raphael into the Sistine Chapel for an early, unauthorized look at its first completed ceiling section when its scaffolding was dismantled in 1511. 'Everything he knew about art he got from me,' the titan grumbled, though serious enmity did not persist between them.

Raphael never let a client down, and among those clients were some of the most powerful men in Italy. Apart from the pope, his chief patron was the papal banker Agostino Chigi, for whom he painted two chapels in the churches of S. Maria del Popolo (Chigi's own burial chapel) and S. Maria della Pace. For Chigi he also painted his only major mythological subject, a *Triumph of Galatea* (*c*.1511–12), frescoing it on a wall of Chigi's Villa Farnesina in Rome. Where did this delectable sea-nymph come from? Possibly, indeed quite probably, she is a portrait of Chigi's mistress. In the myth, Galatea was uncouthly loved by the monstrous Cyclops, Poly-phemus, in the *Odyssey*. (Polyphemus himself is depicted in a nearby fresco in the villa by Sebastiano del Piombo.) She escaped from him over the sea, in a boat drawn by two dolphins, and in Raphael's version of the event one sees that one of these charm-ingly stylized marine mammals is chewing up an octopus, a 'polyp', in its sharp jaws – a sight Raphael no doubt remembered from a visit to a fish-market, but which equally alludes to the defeat of Polyphemus. Nereids and other sea-deities sport around her, putti flutter in the sky above. Galatea herself is enchantingly pretty, surfing along in graceful *contrapposto*, but she may not have been directly painted from a living model. 'To paint a beauty, I should have to see a number of beauties, provided Your Lordship were with me to choose the best. But in the absence of good judges and beautiful forms, I make use of an idea which comes to my mind.'

By then Raphael was famous throughout Europe and so esteemed in the papal court that the pope's treasurer, Leo X's chief minister Cardinal Bernardo Bibbiena, actually offered his niece to the painter in marriage. Even more remarkably, the painter politely refused. There seem to have been two reasons for this: the first being that Raphael's life was full of other women, notably La Fornarina, who was his adoring mistress for years. If his portrait of her (*c*.1518) in Rome's Galleria Nazionale is truthful, which presumably it was, and correctly identified, which it may not be, one can well understand why he might not have wished to switch. The second reason is said to have been more practical: there was a possibility that Leo X might make him a cardinal, an office to which married men could not be raised. If that had happened, Raphael would have been the first and only artist in history to receive the red hat for his services. But neither that nor the marriage took place: six years later, at the excessively young age of thirty-seven, Raphael died – as a result, some said, of a fever caused by a particularly energetic night of love with La Fornarina, 'the baker's daughter', his delicious black-eyed woman of the people from Trastevere. He was buried in a niche in the Pantheon, with the epitaph cut on his tomb slab, an elegant distich by his friend the poet Pietro Bembo: ILLE HIC EST RAPHAEL, TIMUIT QVO SOSPITE VINCI / RERUM MAGNA PARENS, ET MORIENTE MORI: 'The man here is Raphael; while he was alive the Great Mother of all things [Nature] feared to be outdone; and when he died, she too feared to die.'

The frescoing of the Stanze was one of the two chief achievements of Julius' patronage. The other, it goes almost without saying, was the employment of Michelangelo Buonarroti. It was for Julius that Michelangelo, sometimes with the deepest misgivings and resentments, frescoed the ceiling of the Sistine Chapel, producing what remains the most powerful – if not in all ways the most likeable or even comprehensible – series of images of the human figure in the whole history of European art. It would be followed, more than twenty years after Julius' death, by *The Last Judgement* on the altar wall of the chapel, conceived by Pope Clement VII late in 1533, commissioned by Pope Paul III Farnese in 1534, started as cartoons in 1535 and as fresco in 1536, and finally unveiled to very mixed reactions in 1541.

In between these fell the tragic debacle of Julius' tomb, Michelangelo's obsessive project. It was to have been a sculptural block, about 24 by 36 feet, and thus with a 'footprint' of over 70 square metres. It was designed to be on three levels, containing some forty-seven marble figures. It would have been in St Peter's, where, since Bernini had not yet appeared, it would have been the greatest sculptural project of the Christian world. And Michelangelo being what he was, maker of the colossal David in Florence, it would have been entirely the work of one man. Ascanio Condivi, who knew Michelangelo and wrote his life, relates that

> All around about the outside were niches for statues, and between niche and niche, terminal figures; to these were bound other statues, like prisoners ... rising from the ground and projecting from the monument. They represented the liberal arts, and likewise Painting, Sculpture, and Architecture ... denoting by this that, like Pope Julius, all the virtues were the prisoners of Death, because they could never find such favour and nourishment as he gave them.

This was never achieved. Julius II died in 1513 but none of his successors was able, or willing, to support the project. Before long it was relocated, in a much diminished form, to Julius' former titular church in Rome, S. Pietro in Vincoli. Though it contains one tremendous finished sculpture for the tomb, the *Moses*, Julius II's final resting place does not even remotely resemble in scale, size, site or imagery what Buonarroti had in mind. Julius himself had undermined Michelangelo's chances to complete it by ordering him to paint the Sistine instead. Paul III had ruined them by insisting that he lay down hammer and chisel to paint *The Last Judgement*. Then there were the architectural projects for the Medici, such as the Laurentian Library and the façade of S. Lorenzo, the Medici church in Florence. A man, even if that man is Michelangelo, can only do so much.

The Sistine Chapel was so called, as noted earlier, because it had been built thirty years before Julius' papacy by his uncle, Pope Sixtus IV della Rovere (reg. 1471–84). Its architect was the otherwise unremarkable Giovannino de' Dolci. Its walls were

frescoed by some of the greatest Quattrocento artists, including
Luca Signorelli, Sandro Botticelli, Domenico Ghirlandaio and Bernardino di Betto, better known as Pinturicchio; but nine out of
every ten people who visit the Sistine go there only for the ceiling.

The layout of the Sistine reflects a particular medieval conception of world history. It was believed, in the Middle Ages, that
humanity's past divided into three sections or epochs. The first
was the story of the world before God gave the Law to Moses.
The second was the Law as laid down to Moses. The third, life
since the Law, centred on the birth and life of Christ: the period
of the New Testament. Sixtus IV's artists had illustrated the third
part and some of the second. However, this left the first
untouched, and so it was to Michelangelo that Julius II entrusted
the task of illustrating, on the ceiling, the epic narrative of the Old
Testament.

The ceiling was blank, or almost. The only decoration on it
was a uniform coat of ultramarine blue, dotted with golden stars.
It was enormous, 40.5 metres long and 14 wide, and every inch of
it had to be painted by Michelangelo. The contract to paint the
vault was drawn up and signed in May 1508 and the work was
finished in October 1512 – a little more than four years, which
included an interruption of close to a year between 1510 and 1511.
Considering that all, or nearly all, of the painting was done by
Michelangelo and not delegated to assistants, as Raphael might
have done, this was an astounding speed of execution. Of course,
he did have assistants – carpenters to erect the high scaffolding
and the ladders, studio men to grind the colours and mix the
plaster, labourers to carry the paints and buckets of water up the
ladders to the top of the scaffold, *stuccatori* to apply the wet plaster
to the ceiling, and assistants to help hold the cartoons or design
drawings in place while their lines were transferred to the plaster,
whether by scratched-in marks from a stylus or by 'pouncing'
lines of powdered charcoal dots through holes pricked in the
paper. No one man could have done all that donkey work. The
conception of the grand design must have been formed by conferring with others, chiefly Julius II and whatever clergy and

theologians he might have brought in – not many, one suspects.

But all the rest – which is to say, about 95 per cent of the actual work, all the painting of more than ten thousand square feet of ceiling – was done by Michelangelo alone, and the more one knows about the technique of *buon fresco*, as this kind of painting was called in his native Florence, the more astounding the achievement of the Sistine becomes.

An artist could not just paint his design on a hard, dried plaster surface. That invited disaster, and when even an artist as skilled as Leonardo da Vinci tried it with *The Last Supper* in Milan, disaster obligingly came. The reason is that no wall made of bricks, mortar and plaster is ever completely dry and impermeable. Waterborne salts work their way in from outside and will destroy an oily paint film lying on top of plaster inside. This does not happen, or not as gravely, when the coloured pigment is integrated with the plaster, and such is the essence of *buon fresco*. For the paint to be integrated with the plaster, it must be applied while the plaster is damp – ideally, two or three hours after the laying of the *intonaco*, as the fresh lime plaster is known. Then the two form an indissoluble chemical bond when they dry.

But fresco has its peculiarities, and the chief one is that it has to be done piecemeal. The artist must complete painting a section of the *intonaco*, before it dries. (If the pigment is put on dry plaster, as it sometimes has to be for retouching and correction, it is said to be done *a secco* and lacks the durability of true fresco. However, not all pigments are suitable for fresco, because some – particularly the blues and greens, such as ultramarine and malachite – are vulnerable to the alkaline action of the lime. These were used *a secco*. The preferred fresco pigments included the ochres, brown and yellow earths, haematite reds, umber, burnt sienna, ivory black and vine black. The borders of each section must therefore be planned, like a large jigsaw. Each is limited to the work that can be done in a single day. The patch of each day's surface was known as a *giornata*, and it is easy for a trained eye, close up, to follow the outlines of each *giornata* and thus reconstruct the order in which the fresco was done. If repair work is needed, as it sometimes was, it was done by brushing water-based paint on to the now dried *intonaco*. A further complication is that in fresco, colours do not dry the way they look when wet – a problem that does not arise with oil paint or watercolour. Pigments with a green or black hue dry lighter, while iron-oxide pigments dry darker; matching up wet and dry demands from the artist the most acute powers of visual memory.

It is not known exactly how the narrative of the ceiling was composed. Michelangelo undoubtedly had input from others (especially the pope) in doing it. (He claimed he invented it all, but he was given to claims like that.) The basis of the vault we see now is nine scenes from the Book of Genesis, framed in fictive (painted) stonework, running crosswise between the long walls. They begin at the altar end of the chapel with three scenes of cosmic creation, *The Separation of Light from Darkness*, *The Creation of the Sun and the Moon* and *The Separation of Land from Water*. Then follow three more: *The Creation of Adam*, *The Creation of Eve* and *The Temptation of Adam* combined in one panel with *The Expulsion from the Garden of Eden*. Finally one sees *The Sacrifice of Abel* (or perhaps that of Noah), *The Flood* and *The Drunkenness of Noah*, complete with the ancient patriarch's eldest son committing what had become known as the Sin of Ham – not overindulgence in *prosciutto crudo*, but gazing upon his inebriated father's nakedness.

Gazing on masculine nakedness was, of course, Michelangelo's unwavering obsession. On the painted stone frame surrounding these scenes sit the *ignudi*, the beautiful naked youths who have no part in the biblical narrative but are purely the invention of the artist, and make up the grandest anatomical repertoire in Western art. They serve to hold up garlands and painted bronze medallions. The spandrels of the chapel hold mighty figures depicting those who foretold the coming of Christ to the ancient Gentiles (the Sibyls) and to the ancient Jews (the Prophets). They alternate down the walls: the Libyan Sibyl, then Daniel, then the Cumaean Sibyl, then Isaiah, and so on. It seems, the more one looks at this huge vocabulary of human form, that Michelangelo did more than any artist before him to give posture and gesture their utmost eloquence. Here is the Libyan Sibyl, arms spread wide to hold open her enormous book, showing her back but looking over her shoulder. Here is the figure of Jonah, just released from the mouth of the whale – which is actually more the size of a large tarpon – leaning back and gazing upwards in astonishment at a sky that he never thought to see again. Goethe, after visiting the Sistine, wrote that no one could have any idea of what a single individual could accomplish on his own unless he had stepped inside this huge hall. It is still true, and no other work of art can deliver that.

The effort of painting the ceiling, lying on his back, was brutal and interminable, even for a man in his mid-thirties in peak physical condition. Michelangelo wrote a sardonic sonnet about it, addressed to his friend Giovanni da Pistoia. 'I've grown a goiter at this drudgery,' it begins,

> The kind wet cats get in the Lombard swamps
> Or in whatever country the things live –
> My belly's rucked up underneath my chin,
>
> My beard points up, my memory hangs down
> Under my balls, I've grown a harpy's breast,
> And all the while my brush above me drips,
> Spattering my face till it's an inlaid floor.

He feels crippled, permanently deformed; 'I am recurved like a Syrian bow', and his thinking is distorted:

> A man shoots badly with a crooked gun.
> And so, Giovanni, come to rescue me,
> Come rescue my dead painting, and my honour –
> This place is wrong for me, and I'm no painter.

The Sistine ceiling is almost all body, or bodies; the only sign of a nature that is not flesh is an occasional patch of bare earth and, in the Garden of Eden, a tree. Michelangelo was not even remotely interested in landscape; in this respect, as in many others, he was completely the opposite of Leonardo da Vinci. The human body, preferably male, its structure, musculature and infinitely diverse postures, framed all the expressive powers he wanted to use; but a dumb *tree*? A patch of unconscious *grass*? A wandering, arbitrarily shape-shifting *cloud*? Forget it. None of these, in Michelangelo's eyes, had the grand complexity, the sublimely purposeful integration, of the human body, created in God's own likeness. Leonardo might suspect that universal laws lay hidden in the behaviour of water pouring from a sluice-gate into a still pond, but such speculations were of no interest to Michelangelo.

Twenty-one years after the ceiling was complete, in 1533, Michelangelo began work on his fresco for the altar wall of the Sistine, and this time the work contained nothing but bodies (though there is a small patch of water, representing the river Styx, at the bottom). The subject of this monumental musclescape was the Last Judgement. It is a huge creation, and he took eight years over it, finishing it in 1541 at the age of sixty-six – twice the age he was when he began the Sistine ceiling.

Politically, a great deal had happened in Italy in those thirty years, and the most traumatic event of all had come in 1527 with the Sack of Rome. Barbarians and other enemies had got as far as the walls of Rome in previous years, but none had actually succeeded in breaching them on a large scale. The sack of 1527, however, was almost another Cannae in its traumatic effects on Roman self-possession and self-confidence.

Europe had now become an immense cockpit in which national factions were battling it out for international dominance. Long and inconclusive wars (1526–9) were fought in Italy between the troops of the self-styled Holy Roman Emperor, Charles V, and the hodgepodge alliance of France, Milan, Florence and the Papacy. There was considerable truth in the saying that the Holy Roman Emperor was neither holy, nor Roman, nor in any real sense an emperor. Nonetheless Pope Clement VII had thrown his lot in with him so as to avert France's defeat at the hands of Charles's army. But the imperial forces did defeat the Franco-Florentine-

Papal alliance – only to find there was no money to pay the troops their promised fee. Frustrated, the imperial forces mutinied and forced their commander Charles III, Duke of Bourbon, to lead them in an attack on Rome. Rome was a fat, rich city, full of treasure – so it was assumed. The army of the Holy Roman Emperor contained a substantial number of Lutheran sympathizers grimly delighted at the thought of attacking the throne of the Great Whore of Babylon, the Catholic Church; and whatever their religious views, all the thirty-four thousand soldiers wanted their promised back-pay. So they marched south, spreading rapine and chaos as they went, and arrived beneath the Aurelian walls of Rome in early May 1527.

The city was not strongly defended. It had better artillery than its attackers, but only 5,000 militia and the small papal force known as the Swiss Guard. Duke Charles III died in the attack – the great goldsmith-sculptor Benvenuto Cellini, never averse to self-promotion, claimed to be (and possibly was) the marksman who shot him. With him died the last possibility of restraint from the imperial invaders, among whom were 14,000 fearsome German *Landsknechte*, thirsting for blood, sex and gold. The Swiss Guard was cut down almost to the last man on the steps of St Peter's – out of its five hundred members only forty-two escaped and, with commendable bravery and guile, managed to smuggle Pope Clement VII by a secret corridor out of the Borgo and to precarious safety as a prisoner in all but name in the Castel S. Angelo. About a thousand defenders of the city and its churches were summarily killed. Then the sack began.

Before long, it was for the living in Rome to envy the dead. Priests were dragged from their sacristies, savagely humiliated and put to death, sometimes on their own altars. Hundreds of nuns were gang-raped and then killed, starting with the younger and more attractive ones. Monasteries, palaces and churches were gutted and torched, and the higher clergy – including many cardinals – had to pay heavy ransoms to the implacable soldiers. Some of the minor scars of these days can still be seen today: in one of Raphael's Stanze a mutineer left his scratches on the fresco of Heliodorus. The chaos went on for weeks. The emperor Charles V was unable, and not altogether willing, to stop his troops. Not until 6 June, after a month of unremitting plunder and rape, did Clement VII formally surrender and agree to pay a ransom of 400,000 ducats for his life.

It was spared, but there was no way to restore the prestige of his papacy, or the sense of inviolability that went with Rome's position as *caput mundi*. If God had allowed this to happen, what reliance could be put on Rome's supposedly divine mission? In minds all over Europe, the Sack of Rome was an omen, joining in terrible synergy with the Reformation, which was by now a ten-year-old movement with undeniable staying power. God was abandoning the city; had already abandoned it, perhaps. A judgement had fallen. This was the end of the Renaissance Papacy in Rome, that short and glorious thing. And although Michelangelo, who witnessed these things, was not given to writing about current events, it is surely not wrong to see in the titanic pessimism of the Sistine *Last Judgement* some character of response to the sacking of the helpless city six years earlier. Possibly, indeed probably, the image of Charon, the diabolic ferryman, whacking the terrified souls out of his boat with his oar harks back to some moment Michelangelo had witnessed when a gleefully ruthless *Landsknecht* was driving a gaggle of helpless citizens out of their shelter with stabs and swipes of his halberd.

The wall of figures is huge; it is also almost unbearably claustrophobic, because there is no 'space' in the ordinary sense of the word; no landscape or skyscape in which you can imagine your own body moving. It is packed almost to immobility with enormous bodies. Its actors are vehemently corporeal, and yet not of this world. We see, as we have seen in other *Last Judgements*, the division of the damned from the saved, the former going down to Hell, the latter rising to glory under the aegis of Judge Jesus. And yet there is something disquietingly irrational about the scene, if something as huge and dispersed as this can rightly even be called a 'scene'. Why does Jesus look more like a relentless, Apollonian Greek god than the 'normal' judge and saviour of other *Last*

Judgements? Why does Jesus' mother crouch so submissively by his side, as though terrified by the revelation of her son's capacity for wrath against sin? Perhaps both are related to the line of Dante's which had probably inspired Michelangelo before, when he carved the adult and supremely beautiful dead Christ lying in his mother's lap, *Figlia del tuo figlio*, 'Daughter of your son'. But why does St Bartholomew, customarily depicted holding up his own skin (which was flayed from him in his martyrdom), hold up a human skin whose collapsed face is unmistakably that of Michelangelo himself? And why on earth did Michelangelo give the blessed Bartholomew himself the face of that most unsaintly writer, the satirist and pornographer Pietro Aretino, whose collection of sexual 'postures', illustrated by Giulio Romano, was one of the repressed classics of High Renaissance titillation? These and a dozen other questions rise unbidden whenever one enters the chapel and gazes at its altar wall, and they bring with them the thin thread of possibility that they could be answered, at least partly, if only one could see Michelangelo's work as it had been when his brush left it.

In the meantime both the ceiling and *The Last Judgement* had been condemned to woeful indignities. Some popes later than Paul III quite vehemently disliked it. Paul IV Carafa (reg. 1555–9) called the *Judgement* 'a stew of nudes', meaning stew in the Renaissance sense of a public bath, a *stufato*, a whorehouse. Another Medici pope, Pius IV (reg. 1559–65), ordered some of the figures to be made decent with painted loincloths; this task was assigned to a good painter, Daniele da Volterra, who ever after was known as *il braghettone*, the trouser-maker. Clement VIII Aldobrandini (reg. 1592–1605) wanted the whole thing white-washed over, but fortunately was dissuaded by his clerics.

No art-interested person who was in Rome in the late 1970s and early 1980s is likely to forget the passions roused by the project of cleaning the Sistine. Lifelong friendships were broken; the field of discussion, usually a relatively tranquil one, was swept by hails and cross-fires of moral disagreement.

The argument tended to revolve around one central question.

Was the greyness, the almost monochrome character of so much of Michelangelo's colouring, deliberate or accidental?

There is always a certain resistance to cleaning any beloved work of art. The thought of damage, the natural fear of radical change, combine in what sometimes amounts to an anguished conservatism. And sometimes it is not a bit unreasonable: those who remember certain paintings in London's National Gallery, before the director Sir Philip Hendy's restorers were unleashed to use their swabs and solvents upon them, bitterly recall that they were not merely spruced up but skinned alive. The puritanical belief that cleanliness is next to godliness, that the more you take off the closer to the original truth you come, was still very strong in some quarters of the picture-cleaning trade in the late 1970s, and in the early 1960s it was virtually a dogma. The reduced colour of the Sistine ceiling seemed to accord very well with the belief that Michelangelo was primarily a sculptor, a man who naturally thought in terms of monochrome substance. People didn't want to think that the greyness which lent the figures a marmoreal grandeur even as it deprived them of detail was just dirt, soot and centuries of grime.

Elaborate explanations were devised by the anti-cleaning faction which, it is only fair to say, included some of the most distinguished art historians in Italy and elsewhere. The most popular of these was that Michelangelo, disliking the relative brightness of the Sistine frescoes, had applied an *última mano*, a 'final touch' in the form of a darkening and unifying wash of pigment and animal glue size. Obscure and ambiguous ancient texts about the use of *atramentum*, a dark tonal wash, in antique painting were resurrected to suggest that Michelangelo had used it too.

Glue there certainly was, and dark-wash pigment too. But Michelangelo did not put them there. They were later accretions. The pigment was mostly airborne soot, from hundreds of years of burning candles. (Before the age of electricity, the Sistine was lit by large, stout candles, smoking away on an internal ledge below the level of the frescoes. They were not beeswax, which burns relatively cleanly, but the kind of black gunk you get on a barbecue from grilling chops.) And the glue was animal size, much of it also applied long after Michelangelo's death by intrusive conservators who sought to bring up the higher tones in the frescoes by darkening the lower ones. The net result was a messy obscurity. Various attempts were made over the years to clean some of the film of dirt away, but none succeeded.

If you wanted to know what colours Michelangelo really pre-ferred in a painting, it made sense to look at his one surviving complete easel picture, the *Doni Tondo* or *Holy Family*, c.1504. Bright, singing colours, *colori cangianti* as they were called, the hues of shot silk, the crinkled sky-blue of Mary's skirt, the opulent yellow of Joseph's garment, the general clarity of light – none of this looked remotely like the colours of the Sistine ceiling. Inevitably, when the ceiling was cleaned and colours similar to those of the *Doni Tondo* began to appear, there were cries of protest from art historians who felt that Michelangelo had been traduced: the 'new' colours were those of later, Mannerist art, characteristic of an artist such as Pontormo or Rosso Fiorentino. The obvious deduction from this should have been that the bright *colori can-gianti* of Mannerism had been copied from the Michelangelo of the Sistine, by artists who regarded Michelangelo as the ultimate guide and wished only to follow him in homage, when they flocked to the Sistine to see his new work. But critics of the restoration were determined to put the cart before the horse.

Seeing the Sistine frescoes in their renewed state a decade later, one can only guess what the hysteria of opposition had been about. They can now be seen in their full plenitude of colour, and it is one of the world's supreme sights. At this point I should perhaps confess a bias. Working for what was then a major Ameri-can magazine, *Time*, I was lucky enough to get extended access to the *ponte* or moving bridge between the Sistine walls on which the cleaners worked, and spent the better part of three days up there, with my nose a couple of feet from the fresco surface, seeing the way Michelangelo's colour was coming alive once more after so long a burial under waxy residue, and how the forms were being reborn. This was a privilege, probably the most vivid one I had in a fifty-year career as an art critic. It left me in no doubt that the Vatican team's meticulous high-tech efforts, inch by inch, were as great a feat of skill and patience as John Brearley's magnificently discreet cleaning of Velázquez's *Las Meninas* in Madrid, and that an enormous cultural truth, once obscured, was now coming to light.

Michelangelo's frescoes are, of course, a magnetic point of concentrated attraction for visitors to Rome – so much so that it is no longer possible to appreciate them in peace, because of the intolerable, jam-packed, year-round crowds. Michelangelo's Roman architecture is, however, a different matter. Its chief undertakings were three: the reform of the Capitol (complete with its bronze of Marcus Aurelius on horseback), the design of the grandest palace in Rome, Palazzo Farnese, and the development of the Basilica of St Peter's.

Sometimes, while he was working on *The Last Judgement*, Michelangelo was approached in the hope that he would turn to public architecture projects. With the *Judgement* finished and the Pauline Chapel behind him, he was relieved to give himself over to architecture, and the first of the schemes in which he immersed himself was the redesign of Rome's mythic and historic nucleus, the Capitol (in Italian, *Campidoglio*). The need for a renewed Capitol had become clear in 1536, nine years after the sack, when the victorious Charles V made a state visit to the still horribly scarred Rome and Pope Paul III realized that, although temporary processional arches were run up to greet the emperor along the old Roman route of triumph, there was no great central piazza for a reception ceremony.

The Capitoline Hill, with all its historical associations, seemed suitable, and in 1538 Paul III ordered the bronze statue of Marcus Aurelius on horseback to be moved from its site outside the Lateran to a new spot on the Capitol. The pope thought, wrongly, that it was a statue of the emperor Constantine, hence Christian. It was a fortunate mistake, since only the fact that all Romans in the Middle Ages had assumed it to be Constantine (or, later, the Christian Antoninus Pius) had protected it from being demolished and melted down as a pagan monument. Michelangelo, interestingly enough, opposed placing the Marcus Aurelius there – it is uncertain why, but fortunately for Rome the pope overrode him. He was made an honorary citizen of Rome in 1537 and, flattered by this compliment, he pressed ahead with ideas for the Capitol. He designed an oval base for the statue, which he surrounded with an oval pavement, replacing the amorphous piazza in front of the Palazzo del Senatore. He put in two symmetrical staircases on the face of that palace, and designed a fine wide stepped ramp, the Cordonata, linking the piazza to what is now the level of Piazza Venezia below. So the visual axis of the Cordonata runs through the Marcus Aurelius and up to the junction of the twin stairs on Palazzo del Senatore. Now the statue needed a new architectural environment. To one side of it, built on the ruins of what was once the temple of Jupiter, was the fifteenth-century Palazzo dei Conservatori. Michelangelo gave it a new façade, with powerful full-height Corinthian pilasters, and on the other side, facing it, he drew up plans for the matching Palazzo Nuovo, now the Capitoline Museum, which holds its prodigiously rich collection of Roman antiquities.

In this way Michelangelo instigated the creation of one of the greatest urban centres in the history of architecture; only a few others in Italy, such as Piazza S. Marco in Venice and the Campo or shell-shaped piazza in Siena, compare with it in spatial beauty, and none can approach its phenomenal richness of art content. Nothing could rival it, or ever will. Its effect on visiting aesthetes was summed up in a much later drawing by the neo-classical artist Henry Fuseli, who had moved to Rome for an eight-year sojourn in 1770. It showed a figure, head buried in his hands in despair, seated before the enormous marble foot and hand of Constantine, which are still on the Capitol. Its title is *The Artist in Despair over the Magnitude of Antique Fragments*. It was an emotion often felt, and by many; but not by Michelangelo. Raphael was the more enthusiastic preserver of the two.

Through his short life, Raphael actively promoted the pre-servation of Rome's innumerable ancient ruins and monuments. There was a report on their decay submitted to Julius II's successor, Leo X, who in 1515 appointed Raphael to be Prefect of the Antiquities of Rome. This did not give Raphael the power to block the plunder of ancient marble. Rather the reverse – it put him in charge of gathering ancient material to be used in building the new St Peter's. So there is something hypocritical about the lamentations of the report. It is not clear who compiled and wrote it. Unsigned, it has been ascribed to Bramante, Raphael, the writer Baldassare Castiglione and others. Since a draft copy of the report written in Baldassare's hand was found in the Castiglione family library, and since Raphael (1483–1520) was not only the architect-designate of St Peter's and the chief adviser on aesthetic matters to Leo X but also an intimate friend of Castiglione, it is very likely that the two men wrote the report together.

The author(s), says the report, have been all over Rome, looking, drawing, measuring, and it has been a decidedly mixed pleasure: this knowledge of 'so many excellent things has given me the greatest pleasure; on the other hand, the greatest grief. For I beheld this noble city, which was the queen of the world, so wretchedly wounded as to be almost a corpse.' In Rome, antiquity had been mercilessly despoiled by the Romans themselves, the fine stone of the ruins looted, the columns felled and carted away, the marble statues and friezes burned for lime, the bronzes melted down. This had been going on for hundreds of years, without hindrance from pope or Senate. The Romans had done more damage to Rome than the worst barbarian invasions. Compared to them, 'Hannibal would appear to have been a pious man.' 'Why should we bewail the Goths, the Vandals, and other perfidious enemies of the Latin name, when those who above all others should be fathers and guardians in defence of the poor relics of Rome have even given themselves over to the study – long study – of how these might be destroyed and disappear?' This Ubuesque project of demolishing the ruins, this relentless urbicide, was Rome's biggest, almost its only, industry.

How many Pontiffs, Holy Father, who have held the same office as yourself, though without the same knowledge ... have permitted the ruin and defacement of the ancient temples, of statues and arches and other edifices that were the glory of their builders? How many allowed the very foundations to be undermined so that pozzolana might be dug from them, so that, in but a little time, the buildings fell to the ground? How much lime has been burned from the statues and ornaments of ancient times?

This piecemeal destruction of the city by its ignorant developers was 'the infamy of our times', an atrocious historical castration. Raphael and Castiglione – whom one may assume to have been the authors – knew very well whom they were pleading to. He was Giovanni de' Medici, successor to the mighty Julius II, the last layman to be elected pope, the second son of Lorenzo the Magnificent of Florence, then only in his early forties. He had received a good humanistic education at Lorenzo's court in Florence, from such luminaries as Pico della Mirandola, Marsilio Ficino and the poet Angelo Poliziano. Both in Florence and in Rome, he had been immersed in art and literature; his reverence for the classical past was thoroughly instilled, not just an affectation or a pseudo-intellectual quirk. Moreover he did not have automatic respect for the opinions of earlier popes, especially on such matters as architectural history.

'Since God has given us the Papacy,' Giovanni de' Medici famously remarked after his election as Leo X, 'let us enjoy it.' He set out to do so, and he did. He was, wrote Venice's ambassador to Rome, Marino Giorgi, 'a good-natured and extremely free-hearted man, who avoids every difficult situation and above all wants peace ... he loves learning; of canon law and literature he possesses remarkable knowledge'. He had a menagerie of pets, including a tame white elephant. He was, according to the 1525 testimony of Francesco Guicciardini, an active and unembarrassed homosexual, 'exceedingly devoted – and every day with less shame – to that kind of pleasure which for honour's sake may not be named'. And he was culturally serious. Leo X restored the University of Rome, which had fallen on hard times during the pontificate of Julius II. He increased the salaries of its professors, expanded its faculties, and underwrote a Greek printing-press which created the first Greek book to be published in Rome (1515), an important step in the implantation of humanistic ideas in the city. He gave papal secretaryships to scholars and poets, such as Pietro Bembo and Gian Giorgio Trissino.

All this cost money – a great deal of it. Leo X badly depleted the papal treasury in two or three years. Naturally it embarrassed him, as Christ's Vicar on Earth, to find himself presiding over a city as miserably shorn of its ancient glory as Rome had become. The Church needed defences, of which new buildings were the manifest and concrete proof. Julius II and his architect Bramante had begun to replace the old St Peter's with a vast new basilica and now Leo X set out to double its size, a thing unheard of in the previous history of Christianity. Much of the time these expansions were chaotic, since new popes tended quite often to allow the projects of those before them to lapse. The military, political, architectural and artistic ambitions of successive pontiffs drove the Papacy into long spasms of bottomless debt, causing inextricable woes to its bankers. Leo X was certainly not exempt from these financial horrors, and his short-term palliatives for them were a disaster for the Church. He was one of the most feckless spenders in the history of the Papacy. One cannot help liking him for his attachment to the fine arts, especially for his encouragement of literature and scholarship. But the Church needed a more restrained man, and restraint was not a virtue Leo X understood. He needed immense sums, not only to support his luxurious tastes, but to finance large projects, of which the largest was building the new Basilica of St Peter's. He therefore opened the door to one of the worst rackets in ecclesiastical history: the large-scale sale of indulgences.

When not enough cash was flowing in from this, Leo sold (to selected buyers, of course) the prestige of association with the Papacy. He invented all manner of new papal offices, and sold them to the highest bidders. It was reliably estimated that, when Leo died, more than two thousand people were paying for offices he had created, generating a capital value of three million ducats, which yielded the pope 328,000 ducats a year. Cardinals' hats were commonly sold, and this caused the higher levels of the hierarchy to silt up with avaricious crooks. Leo was even reported to be pawning and selling some of the artistic contents of the Vatican – furniture, plate, jewels and works of art.

It is not certain that Leo X fully understood the determined anger that propelled the epic change in the history of ideas and of worship that was about to rock Europe; there could hardly have been two more dissimilar men than the Medici pope and the German monk named Martin Luther who, in the fourth year of Leo's papacy, on 31 October 1517, nailed his ninety-five theses to the church door in Wittenberg. Luther was a deeply educated man, but he had none of the hedonistic delight in culture that animated Leo. In no way could he have been called a sensualist, which Leo in all respects was.

The indignation and disgust that Leo's money-raising activities caused among the faithful was to be one of the prime causes of the Reformation, in which for doctrinal reasons the epochal split between Catholicism and Protestantism took root. But at the same time that Leo was disposing so recklessly of such magnificent works of art, he was acquiring others, notably books and manuscripts for the ever-growing Vatican Library. In the process, the pope who gave rise to the Reformation was also fostering a new intellectual elite: the Roman humanists.

7

ROME IN THE SEVENTEENTH CENTURY

You cannot imagine modern Rome without the changes that a single pope, Sixtus V, imposed on it in the sixteenth and seventeenth centuries. Because of his patronage of titans like Michelangelo, we are naturally inclined to think of Julius II as the supreme 'building pope' of the sixteenth century. And so he was, in a sense – but if the scale of Sixtus V Peretti's changes to the urban structure of Rome is not appreciated one is fated to misunderstand the city. It was Sixtus V who laid the groundwork of Baroque Rome, the city whose exoskeleton the visitor sees today but is apt to take for granted.

He was elected pope in 1585, inheriting a chaotic city, riddled with crime, close to bankruptcy and dotted with half-abandoned ruins. In the apogee of its imperial years, Rome held over a million people. Now it had possibly twenty-five thousand, and probably fewer. The economic depression of the fourteenth century, forced on Rome by the Great Schism that drove the city into a plunge, had turned Rome into a veritable ghost town with monuments.

The seven main churches of Rome were foci for a steadily increasing flow of religious tourism which, unlike later and more exploitative forms of mass tourism, did little for the city's general economy. True, every year the number of pilgrimages by the faithful increased. But the connective tissue between them – the living body of the supposedly Eternal City – seemed to be shrivelling at an alarming rate. One project of renewal stood out: Michelangelo's masterpiece of urban design, the remaking of the Capitol, which was begun in the 1540s – long before Sixtus V's papacy. But too little had been built anew, and the order on which Rome depended for its continued civic life had disappeared, replaced by a chaos reminiscent of New York City in the 1970s or Washington DC in the 1990s. Some people believed the bandits had taken over. One estimate said there were twenty thousand of them, about one for every law-abiding citizen. This hardly seems plausible, but certainly the crime rate had increased beyond computation.

Such a crisis cannot be averted by one person. Yet it cannot be defeated without strong leadership, either – without a ruthless intensity of will that committees cannot usually summon. But as sometimes happened, the crisis called forth the man – a cleric who, in the closing years of the sixteenth century, became pope and thus took over Rome and its administration. He was Felice Peretti, Cardinal Montalto, a Franciscan who had been elected pope by the conclave that followed the death of Gregory XIII, and had assumed the Papacy under the name of Sixtus V.

He was a farmer's son, born in Grottammare, an obscure *paese* near Montalto in the Papal States. It was said that as a boy he was a swineherd, which may easily be true. He rose rapidly within the Church as a Minorite friar, becoming the rector of successive convents in Siena (1550), Naples (1553) and Venice (1556). He was appointed counsellor to the Inquisition there a year afterwards. Fierce and fanatical Inquisitors were no novelty in Venice, but even there Peretti seems to have been abnormal in his zeal, and by 1560 the Venetian government demanded and got his withdrawal.

In 1566 Pope Pius V made him a bishop and in 1570 he took the cardinal's red hat. Fifteen years later he was elected pope. He was said to have entered the chamber of the electoral conclave on crutches, feigning extreme infirmity. No doubt he hoped this would improve his chances of being elected as an interim, short-term pope. The instant his election was confirmed by the white smoke rising from the chimney, he flung the crutches away, standing before the assembled cardinals erect and fairly bristling with vitality. The story is untrue, but *se non e vero*, as the Romans habitually say, *e ben trovato* – if it's not true, it ought to be.

In some respects Sixtus V was a terrifying figure, in others an ignorant one, and in all ways formidable. But he could never be reproached for either indecision or lack of creativity. The atmosphere of reform that seized the Church had brought forth a man whose belief in authority, especially his own as pontiff, was absolute. However, being a man of iron will, he was not inclined to listen to those he considered his inferiors – which meant anyone else in the One Holy Roman Catholic and Apostolic Church.

This showed in all his actions, from city planning to biblical scholarship.

In the late 1580s, Sixtus took charge of publishing the 'Sixtine Vulgate', or official Latin text of the Bible. This was a religious necessity, because it would give Italians the definitive printed form of the fundamental text of Christendom, protecting it from heretical incursions like Lutheranism. But Sixtus did not take kindly to editors. He saw them as quibbling nuisances, and brusquely ignored their suggestions. This edition, published in 1590, became a bibliographic rarity because it was so full of mistakes that it had to be suppressed – after his death, naturally.

Nothing like that happened with his plans for Rome itself. Thinking holistically, on a citywide scale and not just building by building, Sixtus transformed the shape of Rome.

But first, he had the crime problem to deal with.

Non veni pacem mittere, he told a fellow cardinal who congratulated him on his election, *sed gladium*: the words of Christ, 'I come not to bring peace, but a sword.'

The papal blade first swung, with deadly effect, at Rome's population of thugs and thieves, who found themselves arrested, beheaded, garrotted, or hanging from gibbets and the Tiber's bridges. Sixtus V emphatically did not believe that citizens had the right to bear arms. What he did believe in was judicial terror. When four innocuous youths with sheathed swords were seen following one of his papal processions, he had them summarily executed. This policy was so effective that before long the Papal States were considered the safest domain in Europe. Sixtus celebrated this achievement by having a medal struck with his face on one side and on the other a pilgrim sleeping beneath a tree, with the motto *Perfecta securitas*.

In case villains tried to get away, Sixtus was the first to arrange for extradition treaties with neighbouring states. No ruler was going to risk papal displeasure by ignoring them. If the death penalty could improve civic order, it could also do wonders for moral order. Among the actions Sixtus declared punishable by death, apart from theft and assault, were abortion, incest and paedophilia. Theoretically these had carried the death penalty before, but Sixtus made it absolutely mandatory and without exceptions. Lesser crimes, such as failing to keep holy the Sabbath day, were punished by condemnation to the galleys. (The Papal States still had a modest-sized fleet, though its ships were probably less used for warfare than for the punishment of sinners at the labouring oar.) Rome was swarming with prostitutes, who had scarcely been disturbed by previous papacies; Sixtus had them banned from major thoroughfares during daylight hours, and from all Roman streets after nightfall. He meant it, too: if a girl was caught plying her trade in the wrong place or out of hours, she would be branded on the face or breasts.

With crime and vice under some kind of control, Sixtus next turned his attention to the planned but unfinished urban work of his predecessor, Pope Gregory XIII. This pontiff had already made his own changes to the city. A Holy Year was scheduled for 1575. It would bring many pilgrims to Rome, multiplying its circulation problems. By way of preparation for this, Gregory had cleared a wide street called the Via Merulana, running from S. Maria Maggiore to the Lateran. He also revised the building codes, to encourage larger and more impressive civil structures.

But this was small stuff compared to the projects Sixtus V now embarked on, through his architect-in-chief Domenico Fontana (1543–1607).

Much earlier, in 1576, Fontana had designed a huge (and ever expanding) villa on the Quirinal Hill for Sixtus, the Villa Montalto. He advised the pope on the restoration of one of the most beautiful early churches in Rome, the fifth-century S. Sabina, with its twenty-four matching Corinthian columns recycled from some ancient pagan temple. He designed a large but undistinguished building to house what is now a great collection, that of the Vatican Library (1587–90), and chose the painters who frescoed it with such scenes as the Cumaean Sibyl presiding over the burning of the Sibylline Books.* Sixtus was not in favour of keeping the Palace of S. John Lateran, parts of which dated from the sixth century and which until the fifteenth had been the chief papal residence. Pope Nicholas V had moved out of it and into new quarters in the Vatican. Since then the old building had decayed through neglect and much of it was uninhabitable, certainly not popeworthy. Sixtus decreed that it should be razed to the ground, and in its place Fontana built a new Lateran Palace, which was finished in 1588.

The particular concern of Sixtus V, though, one which amounted almost to an obsession, was the shape and circulation of the city of Rome itself. It was not enough for the pope to ban all overhanging wooden structures on its streets, though he did. The streets themselves needed radical surgery. In the end Sixtus either paved or resurfaced about 120 streets in Rome, and laid out some ten kilometres of new roads within the city.

The city maps of the earlier sixteenth century show its seven pilgrimage churches: S. Giovanni in Laterano, S. Pietro, S. Paolo fuori le Mura, S. Maria Maggiore, S. Lorenzo, S. Agnese and S. Sebastiano. Meandering between them were roads, most of which were mere cattle paths. This messy informality offended the pope's sense of order. In future, straight streets would join up at

---

* The Cumaean Sibyl was the most famous of that sisterhood. Her prophecies and oracles, filling nine volumes, were offered to the last king of Rome, Tarquinius Superbus, at a high price. He refused; the Sibyl burned three of the books and offered the remaining six to Tarquin at the same price. He refused again; she burned three more of them and offered the remaining three to Tarquin, who finally bought them. These *Libri Sibyllini*, filled with prophecies and advice on how to avert divine anger, were entrusted to the care of patricians. The Sibyls came to be thought of as equal to the Old Testament prophets and figure as such in Michelangelo's Sistine Chapel.

focal points, in orderly progressions. For instance, he directed the layout and construction of avenues that linked S. Maria Maggiore directly to the Lateran Palace, and the Lateran with the Colosseum. A wide, handsome street named the Strada Felice (after the pope's own name), and later renamed the Via Sistina, was driven three kilometres from S. Croce in Gerusalemme, on to S. Maria Maggiore, and so to S. Trinità dei Monti. No existing building impeded the clearance of these avenues. If anything was in the way, down it came. The pope had an unquestioned right of eminent domain on secular as well as ecclesiastical buildings, and he exercised it without restraint.

Nor did he have the slightest regard for the classical monuments. Sixtus V was a man of superficial culture, never inhibited by humanistic reverence for the Roman past, or even the memories of the Renaissance. His predecessor Gregory XIII had set up ancient statues on the Capitol; Sixtus objected to this, saying that they were no more tolerable than any other pagan idols, and had them carted off. He told one of his courtiers that this gave him particular enjoyment because he had dreamed of Gregory XIII, whom he hated, suffering in Purgatory. He took pleasure in spending the recorded sum of 5,339 *scudi* on destroying the ruins of the Baths of Diocletian. Without a qualm he demolished the remains of the magnificent façade of the Septizodium of the emperor Septimius Severus (dedicated in 201 CE), so admired by fifteenth- and sixteenth-century artists, and had its *spolia* of precious marble dispersed through the city as part of his own building projects. He wanted to see the four-sided arch of Janus Quadrifrons in the Forum Boarium demolished, so that his court architect Fontana could use its marble to make a base for the obelisk in front of St John Lateran, and gave orders for the destruction of the tomb of Caecilia Metella, even though it was well outside the city limits. He also thought the Colosseum should be turned into a wool factory to increase employment in the city. This latter plan was going forward, but on Sixtus' death in 1590 it was dropped. So (luckily) was another and far worse idea of his, which was to tear down a whole section of the Colosseum to make way for a new, straight avenue connecting the Campidoglio to St John Lateran.

When the question arose of what to do with the two great antique columns of Rome, those of Trajan and Marcus Aurelius, Sixtus went right ahead without regard for the original meanings of these monuments, installing a statue of St Peter (cast from the bronze of ancient statues melted down) on top of Trajan's Column and another of St Paul on that of Marcus Aurelius. In dedicating the statue of Peter, His Holiness explained that such a monument as Trajan's could become worthy to bear the effigy of Christ's Vicar on Earth only if it was rededicated in the cause of the Catholic Church – an astonishing piece of casuistry.

The truth was that Sixtus V, like many another man of unbridled power, believed more in the future than in the past, because the future could be shaped but the past could not. At his core he simply did not see why the remains of a defeated paganism should be allowed to impede the progress of a living, triumphant faith. He was in that respect an ideal pope for the Counter-Reformation. Everything that was built, restored, carved or painted under his papacy had to exemplify the power of the Church Triumphant. If a fountain was to be designed, its subject could no longer be the pagan Neptune surrounded by sea-nymphs and tritons. It would have to be Moses striking the rock, releasing the gushing water of Faith.

Water was a prime metaphor of devotional art by now. Much of Fontana's work depended on his construction of a new aqueduct which, in homage to the pope's birthname of Felice Peretti, was known as the Acqua Felice. 'Happy water', indeed; until then, new building in Rome had mostly been confined to the low-lying areas along the Tiber. The Acqua Felice entered Rome higher up its hills, finishing at Piazza S. Susanna, by the Baths of Diocletian, the present site of the Museo delle Terme. This wider distribution of precious water opened up much more of the *disabitato*, the 'abandoned' or 'empty' tracts of the city, for development and occupation. Naturally, it was much easier to build on empty land than to 'do a Haussmann' and have to demolish and clear every site first.

So there was always work, but the one project by which Fontana is remembered, and which gave him a deserved immortality as an engineer, was moving and re-erecting the obelisk of St Peter's, that huge spike rising from what would become the heart of Christianity.

Sixtus V had a vast liking for obelisks, and Rome had more of them than any other European city – thirteen, to be exact, all except one either broken or lying prone, or mostly both.* His enthusiasm was satirized by one of the acrid couplets that made the rounds during his papacy:

Noi abbiamo basta di guglie e fontane:
Pane vollemo, pane, pane, pane!

We've had it up to here with obelisks and fountains:
It's bread we want, bread, bread, bread!

These angry rhymes were known as *pasquinades* because they were traditionally affixed to a worn antique statue named, since time immemorial, Pasquino. Rome had a number of such 'talking statues', which served as vents for civic annoyance at a time when Romans had no access to any press. Another was a female bust, now rather battered, known to Romans as Madama Lucrezia, attached to the wall of the Palazzetto Venezia, next to the corner of the Basilica di San Marco, the church of Rome's Venetian colony. But the most famous pair of talkers were Pasquino and his old friend Marforio. Marforio, an ancient river-god, used to be at the entrance of the Mamertine prison, but then he was moved up to the Capitol and is to be found reclining at the entrance to the Capitoline Museum. Pasquino is in the little piazza named after him, the Piazza di Pasquino, behind Piazza Navona. Marforio would speak (through a placard) and Pasquino would reply (or

---

* It is thought that there had once been more than forty; the fate of the rest remains unknown.

vice versa) and their dialogue, usually in a dialect incomprehensible to the non-Roman, was one of the great comic acts of Rome.

Pasquino, like Marforio, is ancient: a worn and beaten classical torso of Menelaus from the third century BCE dug up during the repair of a nearby street. It was installed in its present place by a cardinal in 1501. The name is supposed to have come from a tailor in a nearby shop who was dangerously free with his impertinent criticism of the papal government. But there are so many legends about Pasquino's origins that it is probably impossible to disentangle the true one.

In any event, one day during the reign of Sixtus V Pasquino was seen wearing a horribly filthy shirt. Why, Marforio wanted to know, did he wear such a stinking rag? Because Donna Camilla has become a princess, came the answer. Donna Camilla was the pope's sister, who in her humbler days had been a washerwoman but had just been ennobled by His Holiness.

There was a limit to what great figures would endure from Pasquino, and this crossed the line. It got to the ears of Sixtus, who let it be known that, if the anonymous satirist owned up to writing it, his life would be spared and he would receive a present of one thousand *pistoles*, cash. But if anyone else found him out and denounced him, he would be hanged. Naturally, the nameless graffitist – for who was going to turn down such a reward? – confessed. Sixtus V gave him the money and spared his life, but unsportingly added that 'We have reserved for Ourselves the power of cutting off your hands and boring your tongue through, to prevent your being so witty in the future.' But nothing would shut Pasquino up; he had a hundred tongues and two hundred hands. The very next Sunday he was seen draped in a freshly laundered, still-wet shirt, to dry it in the sun. Marforio wondered why he couldn't wait until Monday. 'There's no time to lose,' said Pasquino, thinking of His Holiness's taxation habits. 'If I stay until tomorrow perhaps I'll have to pay for the sunshine.'

The obelisks of Rome were souvenirs of the Empire's conquest of Egypt, and most of them had been brought to the city in imperial times. Ancient Egypt had three basic commemorative forms: the pyramid, the sphinx and the obelisk. But the task of moving an obelisk (never mind a sphinx or a pyramid) across the Mediterranean was hardly less daunting than making the thing from scratch – which was difficult enough, indeed insanely so, and could only have been undertaken by a theocratic anti-state like ancient Egypt.

All known Egyptian obelisks came from the same quarry – a deposit of extremely hard and fine-grained syenite, or reddish granite, at Aswan below the first cataract of the Nile. It lay 700 miles from Alexandria and 500 from Heliopolis, where the biggest concentration of finished obelisks stood. The tools of ancient Egypt were very simple. No stone-cutting saws or explosives, of course; no steel; and for moving the heavy blocks of granite, once they were free of the quarry, only the timber lever, the roller, the inclined plane, the wedge, palm-fibre ropes, grease and limitless manpower. Human muscle, at least, was not in short supply, and it was preferred to animal traction, since the fellahin could obey orders a team of oxen would not understand. Egypt had about 11,500 square miles of inhabitable terrain and a population, in Pharaonic times, of perhaps eight million people, a density of some seven hundred per square mile – six times more than China's or India's then.

The task of cutting out the granite block for an obelisk was simplicity itself – tedious, infinitely laborious simplicity.

You and other slaves marked the intended line of cleavage in the granite by gouging a channel for its full length, about two inches deep and two wide. Into the bottom of this channel you drilled a line of holes, each about three inches in diameter and six inches deep, spaced some eighteen inches apart.

You and your fellow slaves now had two choices.

The first was to hammer a wooden plug into each of these holes and then fill the channel with water, which other slaves would have brought in skins from the nearby Nile. If, despite the evaporative power of the Egyptian sun, the wood was kept soaked long enough, the plugs would swell and, with luck, cause the whole mass to crack away from its matrix.

The second choice was to build a fire the whole length of the channel and keep it burning until the rock was piping hot; then sweep away the ash and embers and quickly douse it all with cold water, which (with luck) would also crack the granite.

No tools for work on the obelisks have ever been found, except for a single bronze chisel at Thebes. Iron tools, if they existed at all, have entirely disappeared, rusted away (some think) by the highly nitrous Egyptian soil. Possibly the chisels had diamond teeth. For the long and arduous task of smoothing the granite faces of the obelisks, there must have been abrasives of some kind – emery, corundum, or even diamond dust. The main ingredient, of which ancient Egypt was never short, was limitless amounts of human labour.

How the obelisk got its final sculptural shape, with the 'pyra-midion' or point on top of the shaft, is not known. It cannot have been done with abrasives – there was too much rock to remove – but trying to split the waste rock off accurately at 60 degrees on all four faces must have been, to say the least, chancy.

Nevertheless it was done, and now came the problem of getting the thing to its intended site. But this was not a matter to deter a really serious pharaoh. In the nineteenth dynasty, about 1300 BCE, Rameses II had a 900-ton effigy of himself dragged 138 miles from its granite bed to the Memnorium in Thebes, on some kind of enormous sledge with obedient Egyptians pouring oil on the sand in front of its runners to reduce friction and thousands of other Egyptians hauling on ropes. The obelisk's granite bed was not so far – at least, not unthinkably far – from the Nile. The best guess is that the Egyptians built a dry-dock on the bank of the river, at low water. Inside this, a transport barge was constructed. Now the obelisk would be dragged from the quarry to the dry-dock on another massive timber sledge, an operation requiring perhaps fifty thousand men in double or quadruple lines and miles of palm-fibre rope.

Thus the obelisk would be loaded slowly, slowly into the barge;

there to wait for the great event, the annual inundation of the Nile. This would raise the laden barge, which then, with great luck and skill, would be floated down the river to a place as close as possible to the obelisk's appointed site. There, the patient Egyptians would run through the whole process again, this time backwards, building another dry-dock, securing the barge in it, waiting for the Nile water to recede, dragging the obelisk from the barge and the embankment to its eventual pedestal, and raising it vertical.

How this might have been done was entirely conjectural, and so it had to be reinvented again and again. First, the ancient Romans of the time of Cleopatra and Ptolemy had to reinvent it, no doubt with a great deal of subservient Egyptian help. Then, more than a thousand years later, the Italians had to invent it once more, since there were no records of the original moves.

Of the ships that brought the obelisks to Rome, not a trace remains. It is presumed that they were enormous galleys, each custom-built, quinqueremes with at least three hundred oarsmen, and that the prone obelisk was ballasted with many tons of wheat or dried beans in sacks packed around it to prevent it shifting, since any instability in so immense a load would have rolled the ship and sent it to the bottom at once. (Underwater archaeology has found an amazing variety of objects in ancient wrecks, including what is presumed to have been a primitive ancestor of the computer off the island of Antikythera – the 'Antikythera Mechanism' – but no obelisk so far.)

Once the ship and its cargo had reached Ostia, the entire process had to be repeated in reverse: the dry-dock, the sledge, the hauling, and the inch-by-inch journey to Rome. Some obelisks, at least, were raised vertically on their bases in the Circus Maximus and elsewhere, but it is not known how. Most of them were broken into several pieces, either by toppling over in unrecorded antiquity or by damage from earthquakes or ground subsidence as they lay prone. There was, however, one perfect unbroken obelisk still standing in Rome in the sixteenth century. It was the largest intact one outside Egypt. It dated from the nineteenth dynasty, and had been brought to the Eternal City on the orders of none other than Caligula, having been raised first at Heliopolis. Caligula decreed its transport to a site on Nero's Circus which, more than a thousand years later, turned out to be the back of the old St Peter's Basilica. It was a tapering granite shaft, eighty-three feet and one inch to the tip of its pyramidion, weighing 361 tons. On top of the pyramidion was a bronze ball, which nobody had ever opened; it was reputed to contain the ashes of Julius Caesar.

Pope Sixtus V had often looked at the obelisk from afar, and was not satisfied. It should not be behind the new Basilica of St Peter's, which was then nearing completion. It must be moved to the front. A simple matter of civic punctuation – shifting the exclamation mark in the sentence. A great piazza would be made in front of the new St Peter's (and so it was, years later, to the designs of the as yet unborn Gianlorenzo Bernini). Let the obelisk be brought round and planted *there*, plumb in the centre, to the wonder of pilgrims now, the edification of the faithful in centuries to come and the eternal memory of Pope Sixtus V.

But, how to move it?

The pope appointed a commission to look into the problem. Throughout 1585, some five hundred experts from all over Italy and as far afield as Rhodes, who had had previous experience with colossi, were consulted. Some were for transporting the obelisk prone, others for doing it standing upright, and at least one proposed, for inscrutable reasons, moving it at an angle of 45 degrees. Some wanted to move it horizontally and then turn it upright by means of a gigantic half-wheel to which it would be fixed. Others proposed raising it off its pedestal with wedges. Scores of solutions were proposed, most of which looked ineffective and some downright lethal.

Before too long Sixtus V wearied of looking at these notions, and appointed the man he had had in mind all along: his own architect, Domenico Fontana. The hitch was that Fontana was only forty-two, and therefore seen by some papal officials as too young and inexperienced. So the commission appointed a watchdog: the distinguished Florentine architect Bartolomeo

Ammannati, who was seventy-four and had to his credit a number
of architectural masterpieces, such as the courtyard of Palazzo
Pitti in Florence, the Ponte Santa Trinità spanning the Arno, and
the Villa Giulia in Rome.

Ammannati was an outstanding architect but he was hardly
needed, since Fontana was the greater engineer. What Fontana
proposed was to set one pair of massive timber pylons on each
side of the obelisk. Each of the four pylons would consist of four
vertical members, each 92 feet long, made of 20-by-20-foot timbers
lap-jointed securely together with 1.5-inch-thick iron lag-bolts and
iron bands. The timber baulks were brought from twenty miles
away. Ropes would run over pulleys at the top of the pylons and
be secured to the obelisk, which was to be padded with straw and
then encased in 2-foot-thick planks for its whole length, to give it
some degree of protection – though if it dropped, nothing could
save it from shattering. These cables would connect to eye-bolts
fixed to iron bands clasping the sheathed body of the obelisk. The
cables would run to windlasses on the ground, turned by horse-
powered capstans, like the capstans used to raise the anchors
of ships. Fontana calculated the gross weight of the obelisk, its
armature and metal lifting bolts at 681,222 pounds. A capstan
powered by four horses, he figured, could lift 14,000 pounds. So
he would need forty capstans to vertically lift 80 per cent of the
obelisk's weight – the remainder being done by five massive timber
levers. If the obelisk began to tilt it would initiate a catastrophe,
slipping sideways to the ground, so the most exquisite care was
going to be required to keep the tension equal on all those forty
cables, fanning outwards to the capstans around the obelisk. Win-
ching in the cables required pulleys based on ship's tackle, but of
a huge size never used on a ship – scores of double-sheaved pulley
blocks, iron-bound, the largest of them 5 feet 2 inches long. The
cables themselves, spun in an especially large ropewalk at Foligno,
were each 750 feet long, three inches in diameter, and with a
breaking strain (Fontana figured) of 50,000 pounds. This was the
largest order of equipment the Italian maritime industry had ever
known. But then, nothing like this had ever been tried in the

history of Italian civil engineering. It was going to need almost unheard-of care and coordination, which Fontana proposed to achieve with a system of sound signals – a trumpet to start each capstan pull, a bell to end it.

First the obelisk must be raised from its base, and then swayed down prone on the enormous carriage and rollers on which it would be dragged from the rear of St Peter's to the site in front. Then the pylons and capstans must be brought round, re-rigged, and used to stand the prodigious block of stone vertical again, gingerly lowered on to a base which had been prepared for it in front of the basilica.

Sixtus issued lengthy and detailed orders that no one 'shall dare impede, or in any way molest the work'. This meant invoking eminent domain over everything that lay along the route of the obelisk: if there was a house in the way, down it went. The whole operation, which took days and consumed the labour of nine hundred men and some 140 horses, was watched by most of the population of Rome – who were kept back by a security fence and had been warned, in no uncertain terms, that anyone who made a noise or spoke a word would be instantly put to death. Nobody uttered a peep.

However, it became part of the folklore of this tremendous operation that, at a certain point, the ropes carrying the obelisk began either to fray from the load or smoulder from the friction. Disaster stared Fontana in the face. Legend has it that the day was saved by an iron-lunged Genoese sailor named Brescia di Bordighera, who broke silence by bellowing 'Acqua alle funi!' – 'Water on the ropes!' Far from punishing the man for breaking silence, the pope, when he realized how the sailor had saved the project, rewarded him with blessings and annuities.

Unfortunately the story seems not to be true. Neither Fontana, who kept a log of the lowering, moving and raising of the obelisk, nor anyone else who was there, mentions the sailor and his saving cry, and it would hardly have been possible for anyone to find or bring the necessary water to Piazza S. Pietro in time.

When the obelisk was vertical Sixtus V could not contain his joy, crying in triumph, 'Cio che era pagano ora é l'emblema della cristianità' – 'The thing that was pagan is now the emblem of Christianity.' And that was the point: to Sixtus, the moving or 'translation' of this and other obelisks, achieved with such immense concerted effort and determination, symbolized the work of the Counter-Reformation, the reunification of the Church, the defeat and pushing-back of heresy.

The pope showered Fontana with honours. The bronze ball was opened and it contained no trace of Caesar; it was quite empty. So much for superstition.

The Vatican obelisk and the Acqua Felice were the most spectacular projects that Sixtus' papacy contributed to the fabric of Rome, but not by any means the only ones. An even bigger obelisk had been lying in three pieces near the cathedral, San Giovanni in Laterano. Originally commissioned by the pharaoh Thutmose III, it was removed to Alexandria by Constantine in 330 CE and then transported to Rome by Constantius II in 337 and set up in the Circus Maximus. It was 105 feet high – fully twenty feet taller than the enormous Vatican one – and weighed 510 tons. At Sixtus' behest Fontana managed to raise it, and repaired it so well that today its seams can be seen only if you look closely. He took charge of a third obelisk, which had also served as a marker in the Circus Maximus, and moved it to Piazza del Popolo, where it still stands. Compared to the Vatican and Lateran obelisks, this was almost child's play – a mere seventy-eight-footer, 263 tons. Finally he had the obelisk that lay in four pieces in Via di Ripetta, on the west side of the Mausoleum of Augustus, excavated and set up anew behind the apse of S. Maria Maggiore, in Piazza Esquilina. This was completed by the end of 1587.

This example was followed by several later popes, so that within a century a dozen obelisks were standing in Rome. The chief obelisk pope, after Sixtus, was Pius VI Braschi, who had three erected during his twenty-four-year pontificate (1775–99). The first was put up on the Quirinal Hill between its huge white marble statues of the horse-taming Dioscuri, Castor and Pollux. It, too, came from the Mausoleum of Augustus, where it had been found in the sixteenth century, reburied (it was a massive obstacle to riverside traffic on the Via di Ripetta), exhumed again in three pieces and, under the direction of the architect Giovanni Antinori, set up in 1786 in front of the Quirinal Palace. The second was installed at the top of the Spanish Steps, outside S. Trinità dei Monti, in 1789. The third, extracted from Augustus' mausoleum and known (on account of its ancient use as a gnomon on the enormous sundial) as the Obelisco Solare, went in five pieces to Piazza Montecitorio and was reassembled by Antinori where it still stands today, in front of the Palazzo dei Tribunali. Augustus had brought it back from Heliopolis in Egypt, where it had been made for the pharaoh Psammetichus I.

So Sixtus V's obelisk-raising was by no means unique. How, after inheriting a bankrupt Papacy, could this manic-impressive pontiff keep up the rhythm of building the public works that he insisted on? By the sale of offices, by the establishment of new *monti* or public loans (a money-raising device first employed by Clement VII in the sixteenth century) and above all by ferocious taxation. All this created a glut in the papal *fiscus* which, like some omnipotent Scrooge McDuck, he preferred to keep in bullion and specie in giant iron-ribbed coffers (still to be seen, but gaping empty) in the Castel S. Angelo. In these money-boxes he hid three million *scudi* in gold and 1.6 million in silver, the biggest mass of cash in Italy, one of the biggest in Europe. In fact his accumulation took so much cash out of circulation that it created severe economic problems for the Roman economy; money could not circulate as before, and so business stagnated. Either Sixtus was unaware of this, or he did not care about it. The public display, the rhetorical obelisk, was the thing.

In most respects his politics, particularly in the field of foreign policy, were a mess. He was given to grandiose fantasy. Wasn't he God's Vicar on Earth? He would conquer Egypt, he would bring the Holy Sepulchre to Italy, he would annihilate the Turks. He renewed the excommunication of Queen Elizabeth I of England, and agreed to give the Spaniards a large subsidy for the Armada which would conquer England – not, however, to be paid until the Spanish forces had actually landed, which of course they never did, so that their providential wreckage and dispersal by a storm in the Channel saved him a million crowns.

But the rethinking and rebuilding of Rome around those exclamation marks of the obelisks, the recreation of the expanse of the city as a pattern of rhetorical circulation – that was something new, worthy of another Caesar: and all done in five years of an incredibly short, obsessively active papacy. A fair epitaph was pronounced on Sixtus V by the nineteenth-century vernacular poet Giuseppe Belli (1834):

> *Fra tutti quelli c'hanno avuto er posto*
> *De vicarj de Dio, non z'è mai visto*
> *Un papa rugantino, un papa tosto,*
> *Un papa matto, uguale a Ppapa Sisto.*

> Among all those who have held the place
> Of God's vicar, there had never been seen before
> Such a quarrelsome, tough, crazy
> Pope as Pope Sixtus.

Nor would there ever be again. A visitor from Mantua, Angelo Grillo, reported that '[s]uch is the newness of the edifices, the streets, piazzas, fountains, aqueducts, obelisks and other stupendous marvels [with] which Sixtus V of glorious memory embellished this old city' that he could hardly recognize the place he had left ten years before. Later popes would build, but not with such a commitment to reorganize the basic pattern, the manifest sense of space, that was Rome. In a sense, the 'building popes' of the Baroque era stood in the shadow of Sixtus' obsession with the city as a pattern of movement and coordinated public declamation, not just a collection of separate monuments. So the visitor to Rome feels gratitude to this man, so inventive, so tyrannous and so dreadful in different ways. Yet few could be surprised to learn that a statue of him, erected in his honour on the Capitol when he was alive, was torn down by the common people of Rome – the 'rabble' – as soon as the breath was out of his body. They must have felt a right to smash it, since it had been put up with the tax money Sixtus extorted from them.

And what of his early-seventeenth-century successors? How did they change the appearance and layout of Rome? Very considerably, though perhaps not as radically as terrible Sixtus. The greatest scheme was the one accomplished during the pontificate of Alexander VII Chigi (reg. 1655–67) – the rebuilding of Piazza del Popolo, which lay just inside the Porta del Popolo, one of the chief entrances to Rome. 'Popolo' does not carry some protosocialist implication; in the Middle Ages, *populus* was a politically neutral term, meaning simply 'parish'.

Alexander VII cleared the way for his urban desires by reviving the Congregazione delle Strade, the planning commission for Rome which had fallen into disuse. He gave it the authority to demolish whatever it wished, whenever it saw fit. This was a powerful licence. It enabled him, for instance, to get rid of the Arco di Portogallo, which by constricting the Via del Corso caused endless traffic jams.

What Alexander favoured was generous squares approached by wide streets (no more medieval crimps and doglegs) marked out by distinctive buildings, fountains and groups of statuary: these he called *teatri*, 'theatres', and certainly Piazza del Popolo showed what he meant. It was the first part of Rome that most arriving foreigners saw, and it deserved special treatment. Gianlorenzo Bernini had designed its gate with the Chigi star carried proudly above it, and at the other end of the piazza now rose twin churches. Designed by the architect Carlo Rainaldi in 1661–2 and finished by Bernini and Carlo Fontana in 1679–81, these frame the entrances to the trident of streets (Via del Corso, Via del Babuino, Via di Ripetta) that plunge away into the core of Rome, and heighten the sense of anticipation that has already been raised by the Porta del Popolo. Everyone who sees them from the piazza, unless forewarned, admires them for their symmetry. In fact they are not symmetrical, being built on different-shaped sites. S. Maria in Montesanto (on the left, looking from the piazza) stands on a

longer triangular slice of ground than its companion. It therefore
has an oval dome, whereas S. Maria dei Miracoli has a circular
one. But nobody notices this (at first) from the outside, and the
illusion of symmetry is perfect until you look closer.

Rome of the Counter-Reformation – the late sixteenth and
early seventeenth centuries – did not offer much work to great
Italian-born painters, though it incubated some extraordinary
expatriates. There were, however, several outstanding exceptions,
some of whom (chiefly Bolognese painters in Rome) affirmed the
classical tradition, while others seemed completely to subvert it.
The first of the classicizers was Annibale Carracci (baptized 1560–
1609), along with his brother Agostino Carracci (1557–1602). They
were native Bolognese, and a third painter member of the Carracci
clan, their cousin Ludovico (1555–1619), chose to spend his life in
Bologna and never painted in Rome. Both Agostino and Ludovico
were fine painters, but the genius of the family was undoubtedly
Annibale.

How powerfully inventive he was can best be gauged by a
visit, if it can possibly be arranged, to the state rooms of Palazzo
Farnese. Generally this used not to be possible, since the palace,
originally built by that arch-nepotist Alessandro Farnese, the
future Pope Paul III (reg. 1534–49), and without much doubt the
most sumptuous *palazzo* in Italy, became the French Embassy and
access to it used to be so unbelievably restricted that even its
courtyard, the combined work of Antonio Sangallo and Michelangelo, was open to the public for exactly one hour a week,
between 11 a.m. and noon on Sundays. As for the state rooms,
forget it. This meant that one of the supreme works of seventeenth-century Italian painting could be known by the visitor to
Rome, and imperfectly at that, only from reproduction. Happily,
these conditions have now relaxed somewhat and guided tours
are offered. They should not be missed.

Odoardo Farnese decreed that its subject should be the Power
of Love, and earthly rather than divine love at that. Thus Annibale
Carracci set out, with tremendous zeal and brio, to cover the
twenty-metre barrel vault with frescoes representing the Triumph

of Love as symbolized by the cavortings of Bacchus and Ariadne – a surging, tumbling apparition of scenes from Ovid's *Metamorphoses*, a veritable firmament of classical flesh, anchored in references to Raphael's Loggia Farnesina and the *ignudi* of Michelangelo's Sistine ceiling, but as pagan as the art of painting could imaginably be. Annibale, a superb draughtsman, was one of the greatest re-inventors of the nude body that has ever existed, and the Farnese ceiling is virtually the last full-strength appearance of the classical impulse, at its outer boundaries of ambition, in Italian art.

If one wants to see the other extreme of Annibale Carracci's work, it too is in Rome, in the Galleria Colonna: the much earlier and more social-realist portrait of a worker tucking into his lunch of beans and onions, while clutching a bread roll and returning your gaze with a glare of feral possessiveness, mouth open, frayed straw hat on: *The Bean-Eater, c.*1583. It too is a masterpiece, though of a very different sort. Presumably it would be difficult, for today's dinner-guests in their *fracs* glancing up from their plates of *foie gras en gelée Lucullus* at the tumultuous joys of gods on the embassy ceiling above, to connect the two. It is sad to know that Farnese paid Annibale Carracci so stingily for his four years' inspired labour on the Farnese ceiling that the artist slid into depression, took to the bottle and died at the early age of forty-nine, reduced at last (one supposes) to eating beans.

The other major Bolognese artist working in Rome in the first part of the seventeenth century was Guido Reni (1575–1642). There can be few painters in history whose careers show such a spectacular rise to the heights of reputation, followed by such a plunge to the depths. For more than a century after his death, connoisseurs, tourists and other artists held him to have been angelically inspired; as famous, in his way, as Michelangelo, Leonardo or (for that matter) Picasso. Percy Bysshe Shelley, who died in Italy, thought that if some cataclysm overwhelmed Rome, the loss of Raphael and Guido Reni would 'be alone regretted'. Unquestioned geniuses, such as Gianlorenzo Bernini, thought he painted 'pictures of paradise' and took his work for a model, and other artists were unstinting in their praise. As well they might have been: as his allegorical frescoes in the Palazzo Rospigliosi-Pallavicini in Rome, such as the Raphaelesque *Aurora* (1614), amply demonstrate, Reni at his infrequent best had an exquisite sense of style. In the eighteenth and early nineteenth centuries his big altarpiece of the Trinity in S. Trinità dei Pellegrini was considered one of the sights of Rome, a mandatory spectacle for the serious young artist. But by 1846, in *Modern Painters*, John Ruskin was attributing to Reni 'a taint and a stain, and jarring discord ... marked sensuality and impurity'. Fifty years later, Bernard Berenson declared that 'We turn away from Guido Reni with disgust unspeakable' – not that it took so very much to disgust that severe and fussy aesthete. The nadir was reached fifty years after that, when you could easily get a ten-foot Reni (if you wanted it, which few did) for under $300 at auction.

What happened? A tectonic shift in taste. The Victorians did not mind sentimental high-mindedness, just as long as it was not hypocritical, and hypocrisy was the charge made, more and more often, against Guido after his death. He was proud, he said, of being able to 'paint heads with their eyes uplifted a hundred different ways', but this did not seem a virtue to later generations – not, at least, one that outweighed Reni's manifest vices, the saccharine of his expressions, the self-repetition, the overproduction.

Moreover his personal life was disastrous, a swamp of neuroses. Reni had the misfortune to be a gambling addict, always badly in debt, and turning out masses of hackwork to stay afloat. It has been surmised, no doubt rightly, that his gambling was inspired by masochism – losing was a form of self-flagellation for the sin of being alive. Since debts had to be paid, he kept an enormous studio – at one point, his biographer Malvasia noted with some amazement, Reni employed some two hundred assistants. At the same time he was socially inept, agonizingly aware of his poor education (which hampered him as a history painter and made him hopelessly awkward with sophisticates and scholars) and an extreme closet case. It was commonly assumed that he lived and died a virgin. He was not only a daily church-goer but morbidly superstitious. Women terrified him – he suspected them all of being witches, a suspicion they could allay only if they showed themselves to be the Virgin Mary, a hard thing to prove – and he could not bear it if anyone except his own mother touched his laundry.

Yet for all that, he was capable of extraordinary things. Perhaps his greatest painting was done in 1618–19, not long after leaving Rome for his native Bologna, and now in the Prado. This is *Atalanta and Hippomenes*. In the myth, Atalanta was a swift-running huntress who was determined to keep her virginity and refused to mate with any man who could not outrun her in a foot race. Nobody could, until she was challenged by Hippomenes, who had been provided with three golden apples by the interfering goddess Aphrodite. At intervals in their race, Hippomenes would drop an apple, which Atalanta could not resist; picking them up delayed her so much that she lost both the race and her virginity. Reni's vision is of two superb nudes that fill the picture space to the exclusion of everything except empty earth, bare sky and a plain horizon line. But there is little doubt about its subliminal meaning. Hippomenes is well ahead of Atalanta, who is greedily stooping for her second apple. But his gesture towards her is one of repulsion and banishment; he is fending off all possibility of contact with her, even though his victory in the race will, according to the myth, entitle him to claim her. He is racing for a prize that he does not desire. It would be hard to think of a more direct statement of homosexual repulsion (within the bounds of decorum) than this.

The word 'radical' became so comically overused in the late twentieth century that it has become worn to near complete vacuity. But there were times (now long gone) when it could (with due caution) be applied to things that happened in the arts. One such time was the early seventeenth century in Rome, and such an event was the appearance there of a young painter named Michelangelo Merisi, known by the name of his birthplace, the north Italian town of Caravaggio, where he had been born in 1571. There was no reason to suppose that anything of promise, let alone of transforming importance, would come out of a backwater like Caravaggio. It had produced almost no artists, had no intellectual life and could boast no aristocratic collections for a young painter to admire or copy. Yet Michelangelo Merisi was a genius and he possessed what all who knew him agreed was *uno cervello stravagantissimo*, a really weird turn of mind. What form did the weirdness take? In a word, realism. Caravaggio was not even faintly interested in the tricks and tropes of Mannerist painting – the elongated bodies, the balletic twisting and posturing, the arty metaphors and elaborate *concetti*. Roman painting in 1592, the year Caravaggio got there, had a great past but a mincing present. Much of it was as fatuous as the stuff that would come to be praised as 'postmodernism' there (and in New York and London) four centuries later. Pedantic, clever-clever, garrulous and full of weightless quotation. He wanted to see reality head-on, and paint it that way, direct from life, with the maximum impact and sincerity, down to the last callused foot and dirty fingernail.

This ambition, which seems admirably natural today, earned him much finger-wagging: he was called an 'anti-Michelangelo', as though that meant anti-Christ; an evil genius, a concocter of over-peppered stews and so forth. But Caravaggio's work really did turn the history of European painting around. For a time one had practically no choice but to be a Caravaggista. France, Holland, Spain, Germany and of course Italy itself were all subject to his influence. When he was born, almost all painters in Europe worked under the classicizing idealism of Michelangelo. Forty years later, after his early death, their descendants with equal unanimity were painting Caravaggios, neither classical nor idealistic. Scratch almost any seventeenth-century artist and you will find traces of Caravaggio: Rembrandt, Seghers and Honthorst in the Netherlands, Velázquez and Ribera in Spain, Georges de la Tour and Valentin de Boulogne in France, and a dozen more, omitting the scores of mere imitators.

There are two reasons why the hunger in Caravaggio's eye, the desire for complete and unidealized human truth, had such a powerful effect in its time, the early seventeenth century. The first was a general one: all over Europe, people were getting tired of the euphemism that tends to accompany abstraction. One sees this, for instance, in theatre: how the powerful and wrenching scenes of the Jacobean 'revenge' dramatists entranced their audiences:

Tear up his lids,
And let his eyes like comets shine through blood:
When the bad bleed, then is the tragedy good.

Or think of the fearful scenes in *Lear* – cold Goneril insisting that her father be blinded, not just put out of his misery by hanging – or in *Titus Andronicus*. Obviously the language of horror and dramatic extremity was not invented by seventeenth-century artists and writers, but it moved to the forefront of their imaginations, whether for titillation or for religious revelation, and thus became one of the main ingredients of Baroque art. Then one must add the fact that, horror or not, seventeenth-century Europeans were getting a lot more interested in the pragmatic and the factual. Fewer angels with gauzy wings; not so much disembodied spirituality. Instead, direct appeals to the senses of smell, touch, hearing, and to the actual look and feel of a world which, after all, God had created. If a painter set before a viewer an image of high, transcendent artificiality, it might not affect his beliefs. But an image which came out of the real world and referred dramatically back to it, one which inhabited the same kind of space as the viewer, which was subject to the same kind of feelings – that was more convincing. Such was the opinion of the Council of Trent, which resolved to find ways of making the doctrines of Roman Catholicism more vivid and direct to an unsophisticated public. The object of art would be not to out-argue Luther, not to win theological debates, but to assure the faithful of the Truth by means of a superior intensity, a more

palpable truth of events and emotions. And that, his patrons soon
realized, was where Caravaggio came in.

He certainly did not please everyone, but nobody could say
he went unrecognized. 'In our times, during the pontificate of
Pope Clement VIII,' begins a diatribe by the painter and theorist
Vicente Carducho (1570–1638), an Italian who had moved to
Madrid,

> Michelangelo Caravaggio rose in Rome. His new dish is
> cooked with such condiments, with so much flavour, appe-
> tite and relish, that he has surpassed everybody ... Did
> anyone ever paint, and with as much success, as this monster
> of genius and talent, almost without rules, without theory,
> without learning and meditation, solely by the power of his
> genius and the model in front of him? I heard a zealot of our
> profession say that the appearance of this man meant a
> foreboding of ruin and an end to painting ...

Though he finished as a sublime religious dramatist, Caravaggio began as a painter of benign nature. Granted, the worm is
in the bud sometimes – Caravaggio's early still-lifes often show
overripe, embrowned fruit – but the Caravaggian cave of darkness
was not invented overnight. His early Roman works, such as the
exquisite *Rest on the Flight into Egypt* (1594–5), are evenly and crisply
lit, in a way recalling the High Renaissance painters Lorenzo
Lotto and (more distantly) Giorgione. Mary, bent sleepily over
her infant, is a beautiful redhead (presumably Caravaggio's girlfriend at the time), and the elderly St Joseph holds up a score,
from which the angel is playing soothing music on his fiddle as
the mother and child doze.

Such works made him popular with the upper ranks of Roman
collectors. They included Cardinal Francesco Maria del Monte,
who owned eight of his paintings, and that discerning and deep-
pocketed *marchese* Vincenzo Giustiniani, who had fifteen.

Because of their even lighting and elegant variety of colour, we
are apt to think of this early work as 'untypical'. By his early

thirties, though, Caravaggio's essential character as an artist was formed. Its prime element was his mastery of gesture. Caravaggio saw things and set them down with uncanny accuracy: how people move, slump, sit up, point and shrug; how they writhe in pain; how the dead sprawl. Hence the vividness of Abraham's gesture in *The Sacrifice of Isaac*, as he pins his wailing son down on a rock like a man about to gut a fish. In *The Supper at Emmaus*, the characters seem ready to come off the canvas as Christ makes his sacramental gesture over the food (an ordinary Roman loaf); and the basket of fruit, perched on the very edge of the painted table, is ready to spill its contents at one's feet. And the cramped little Cerasi Chapel of S. Maria del Popolo, for which Caravaggio painted a *Conversion of St Paul* and a *Crucifixion of St Peter* (1600–1), is so small that it is impossible to get a distance from the paintings: they are almost pressed against you, like bodies in a crowded room, and one cannot believe this effect is not deliberate. Particularly this is true with the figures of Peter and his three executioners; they form a powerful X of flesh and dun-coloured cloth, the faces of two executioners hidden from us completely and the third turned away in shadow. Only Peter (who was crucified upside-down, according to pious legend, because he did not think himself worthy to die in the same way as the Messiah) is fully visible – that strong old man's body reflecting the light, those eyes staring in anguish at the iron nail driven through his hand and into the wood.

These are not invented or imagined figures, they have a tremendous physical presence, and one is left in no doubt that the stories about Caravaggio's way of working – that he found his models among the people on the streets, and painted them just as they were – are basically true. He clearly went to great lengths to arrange the directional lighting in his dark studio. But not much else is known about his way of working, because not a single attributable drawing by Caravaggio has survived. Perhaps he destroyed them all, or they were lost in one of his many moves between one improvised studio and the next, one city and another. But there is also the possibility, which one cannot reject out of hand, that he did not make any: that he drew directly on the canvas, without planning things first.

Naturally, this risky and exalted spontaneity – unlikely as it seems, and out of kilter with 'normal' studio practice – seems to fit the picture of Caravaggio that his way of life offers, from what we know of it. He died of a fever in 1610, at the age of thirty-nine, in Porto Ercole, then a malarial Spanish enclave on the coast of the Maremma north of Rome. The last four years of his life were one long flight from police and assassins; on the run, working under extreme pressure, he left altarpieces – some very great, and none mediocre – in Mediterranean seaports from Naples to Valletta to Palermo. He killed one man with a dagger in the groin during a game of tennis in Rome in 1606, and wounded several others, including a guard at Castel S. Angelo and a waiter whose face he cut open in a squabble about artichokes. He was sued for libel in Rome and mutilated in a tavern brawl in Naples. Saturnine, coarse and queer, he thrashed about in the etiquette of early Seicento Rome like a shark in a net. But the vivid piety of his work after 1600 was fundamental to Baroque painting, and he will always be remembered as one of the essential figures of Roman art on the verge of the Counter-Reformation.

The other artists were largely foreigners, drawn into the irresistible orbit of the world's art capital. While he was being fêted during an unproductive visit to Paris, the great Baroque sculptor and architect Gianlorenzo Bernini was shown the work of a number of French painters. They did not impress him. To the old maestro's implacable eye, they seemed small fry – hacks and bores, capable of an uninteresting decorum at best. There was, however, one artist whose works had been collected by Paul Fréart (1609–94), the sieur de Chantelou and steward to Louis XIV. This was Nicolas Poussin. To him Bernini responded strongly, looking long and carefully at his paintings and exclaiming, at last, 'O, il grande favoleggiatore!' – 'O, the great storyteller!' (except that favola suggests a kind of moral weight that goes beyond mere anecdote into serious allegory). Later, again to Chantelou, Bernini would point to his head and say admiringly that Poussin was an artist 'who works from up here'.*

It was true; and one reason for its truth was Rome. Poussin was the father and first great practitioner of French classicism. He lived most of his working life in Rome and only left it with the greatest reluctance. In cultural terms, everything north of Rome was merely a colony – especially France, the second-rate power he came from. 'We are indeed the laughing-stock of everybody, and none will take pity on us,' Poussin morosely wrote of the French, in a letter from Rome in 1649. 'We are compared to the Neapolitans and shall be treated as they were.'

For him, Rome and the countryside around it were, above all, the terrain of thought and of memory. The thought was not abstract; it was grounded in observation. The memory combined deep feeling about the observed, natural world with a kind of poetic erudition which was rare enough in the seventeenth century and is even less common in the culture today. William Hazlitt put his finger on it when he compared Poussin to John Milton. Poussin, he wrote, 'was among painters (more than anyone else) what Milton was among poets. There is in both something of the same pedantry, the same stiffness, the same elevation, the same grandeur, the same richness of borrowed material, the same unity of character.' Looking at certain Poussins, where a sturdy figure in a plain-coloured garment is walking through a leafy landscape, you cannot help remembering the last words of *Lycidas*, as the shepherd takes the rural path, having sung his song '[w]ith eager thought warbling his Doric lay': 'At length he rose, and twitched his mantle blue / Tomorrow to fresh woods, and pastures new.' Everything about Poussin's landscapes is ordered and coherent, but nothing in them is abstract; they are the 'Fair Champaign' of *Paradise Regained*:

---

* Paul Fréart was chiefly remarkable for accompanying Bernini on his visit to France, and reporting copiously on the sculptor's reactions to French art and his views on sculpture.

Fertil of corn the glebe, of oyl and wine,
With herds the pasture throng'd, with flocks the hills,
Huge cities and high tow'r'd, that well might seem
The seats of mightiest monarchs, and so large
The Prospect was, that here and there was room
For barren desert . . .

What Poussin offers above all is the earthiness of the world he
creates, and of the men, women and children who work, embrace,
play and doze in it. This is not an abstract world of lifeless marble.
You can imagine yourself desiring its inhabitants as flesh, not as
idealized stone: the long-thighed shepherdess who leans forward
with her shepherd companions (who clearly cannot read either)
to peer at the inscription 'Et in Arcadia Ego' on a forgotten sarcophagus in the woods, with a skull on top of it to remind you
that the ego in Arcadia, the self, is the inexorable presence of death;
or the ravishingly beautiful figure of the goddess Diana to whom
the infatuated Endymion, kneeling, declares his love. 'This young
man has the inner fire of the devil,' wrote one of Poussin's Roman
acquaintances, and in fact it was his vitality, breathing life into his
reimagining of the Antique, that distinguished his work from all
other archaizing painting that the seventeenth century produced
in Rome.

Even the play of children, watched by nymphs while charging
at one another on goat-back, has a certain chivalric intensity,
though it is at the same time a parody of knightliness as well. This
landscape lives and breathes, and looks as though nothing trivial
can happen in it. Poussin's goddesses and nymphs have not
dropped from Olympus; they grow up out of the earth. They
carry their archaism like a bloom, so that there is more sexual
tension between the white goddess and the kneeling shepherd in
Diana and Endymion (1628) than in a hundred Renoirs. This tension,
for Poussin, is part of classicism. 'The beautiful girls you will have
seen at Nîmes,' he wrote to a friend in 1642, 'will not, I am certain,
delight your spirits less than the sight of the beautiful columns of
the Maison Carrée, since the latter are only ancient copies of the

former.' It is an enchanting conceit, yet more than a conceit: the idea that the ancient orders of architecture were 'copies' of the ideal proportions of the beautiful human body was deeply embedded in Poussin's thinking, as it was in the ideas of many connoisseurs. This was what humanized ancient architecture and emphasized its relation to the present. And it emphasizes one's feeling that the women drawing water from a well in a Poussin have a relationship to the architecture behind them which is not simply formal, but in some historical way, spiritual.

In *Landscape with St Matthew* (*c.*1640) we see the evangelist surrounded by ruins – fallen columns, broken entablature – writing down on a sheet of paper the words of a visiting angelic being: its subject is the same as the Caravaggio in S. Luigi dei Francesi, the dictation to St Matthew of his Gospel. But in its companion-piece, St John writing the Apocalypse on the island of Patmos, Poussin produced what could almost amount to a self-portrait, sitting among the mighty ruins of antiquity, sketching their geometrical fragments (prism, cylinder, with an obelisk and an intact-looking temple in the background) – quite like himself encountering, in real life, the Roman ruins of the campagna. Wherever else he may be, he is not where he was born. He is where Fate and the necessity of his own art obliged him to go. He was the model expatriate. This was the story of Poussin's life.

He was born in Les Andelys, a provincial market town on the Seine in Normandy, in the vicinity of Rouen. Not much is known about his childhood, except that it clearly included some instruction in the classics, without which he could never have developed his enthusiasm for ancient Rome and its culture. Around 1612 he left home for Paris, and from there he is known to have made one unsuccessful attempt to reach Rome, defeated by illness and poverty (he got as far as Florence, but had to turn back). But then, in Paris, he had the good luck to meet the Italian poet Giambattista Marino (1569–1625), who was impressed by some drawings young Poussin had made for him on themes from Ovid's *Metamorphoses* and invited the budding artist to come to Rome with him. No urging was needed. In 1624 Nicolas Poussin arrived in Rome and began to make acquaintances whose regard for his work would stand him in excellent stead. One was Francesco Barberini, nephew of Urban VIII. The other was Cassiano del Pozzo, the Barberinis' secretary, a man of singular connoisseurship and some scientific knowledge.*

Poussin's main job in Rome, before his pictures started selling, was to draw records of classical sculpture for del Pozzo. This gave him excellent access to private collections, and the time to develop a repertoire of figures that would fill his work in years to come. The two men arranged for Poussin his first big commission, though a very uncharacteristic one – an altarpiece for St Peter's done in 1628, *The Martyrdom of St Erasmus*, an early saint who suffered disembowelment, his guts wound out on a windlass. In the painting, which is mercifully short of blood, Erasmus' intestines look like a long string of thin *luganiga* sausage. This would almost be Poussin's sole image of a human being in extreme pain. Its only competitor is the anguished face of a woman in *The Massacre of the Innocents*, which Francis Bacon thought was the most awful depiction of grief in all Western painting. Poussin was certainly able to paint extremes of human feeling, but he wisely kept them under control and used them only where they counted most.

Poussin devoted his early years in Rome to studying ancient architecture, drawing the live model (in the studios first of Domenichino and then of Andrea Sacchi) and making measured drawings of Roman statues and reliefs. But his work as a history painter came into full focus in the 1630s with two magnificent compositions, each depicting a heroic or tragic moment from the Roman past. The first was *The Destruction of the Temple at Jerusalem*, commemorating the emperor Titus' sack of the Holy of Holies. (There goes the seven-branched candlestick with the soldiers, presently to be carved on the Arch of Titus in Rome.) The second was *The Death of Germanicus*.

---

* As a result of Cassiano's instruction, Poussin became the illustrator of a later edition of Leonardo's work on optics.

Germanicus Julius Caesar, conqueror of Germany, was sent to command Rome's eastern Empire and died in Antioch in 19 CE, poisoned on the orders of his adoptive father the emperor Tiberius – so it was believed – by a jealous Roman governor. He soon became an archetype of the Betrayed Hero. In Poussin's picture the hero lies ashen and dying beneath the frame of a blue curtain, which suggests both a military tent and a temple pediment. On the right are his wife, women servants and little sons; on the left, his soldiers and officers. The common soldier on the far left weeps inarticulately, his grandly modelled back turned towards us. Next to him, a centurion in a billowing red cloak starts forward: grief galvanized into action in the present. Then a gold-armoured pillar of a general in a blue cloak (adapted from an antique bas-relief) projects grief forward into the future by swearing an oath of revenge. We do not see the man's face or its expression, which is Poussin's way to suggest that this death is not a private issue but one of History itself. The target of this socially ascending wave of resolution is not only Germanicus' exhausted head on the pillow but his little son, whose blue cloak matches the general's; the women suffer and can do nothing, but the boy learns, remembers and will act.

In 1629 Poussin moved in with the family of a French cook in Rome, Jacques Dughet, who cared for him during an infection of syphilis that would last the rest of his life. In the end, Poussin was so afflicted by the tremors brought on by the advanced stage of this disease that he could no longer paint with any confidence; in 1658, aged sixty-four, he apologized in a letter to Chantelou for not writing a separate letter to his wife 'because my trembling hand makes it difficult for me. I ask her pardon.' But there remained to him another twenty years of uninterrupted creativity. Poussin was lucky in being one of those men who did not care much about the social world. Selected friendships, such as his relationship with Chantelou in Paris, mattered greatly to him, but not the world of courts, whether royal, noble or papal. A story went the rounds of how his friend and patron the cardinal Camillo Massimi visited him in his modest house in Via del Babuino and wondered how Poussin managed without servants. 'And I pity your Eminence,' retorted the painter, 'because you have so many.' 'He avoided social gatherings as much as he could,' recalled one of his friends, the connoisseur André Félibien, 'so that he could retire alone to the vineyards and most remote places in Rome . . . It was during these retreats and solitary walks that he made light sketches of things he came across.'

Poussin was quite often accompanied on these walks by another French expatriate in Rome, Claude Lorrain (1604–82). The two men shared a passion for ideal and classical landscape, but were otherwise unlike one another; Poussin, compared to Claude, was a positively scholarly painter, well acquainted with classical poetry and philosophy, whereas Claude's knowledge of ancient Roman and Greek culture was relatively thin. He was less educated than Poussin partly because he came from a lower social level – his parents were of peasant stock, smallholders from the village of Champagny in Lorraine. He was not interested in alle-gory or the illustration of myth: Poussin was the *favoleggiatore*, not Claude. And this was just as well, since he did not have a jot of Poussin's aptitude for painting the human body, and hence not much gift for narrative.

His observation of trees, earth, water and especially of light was exquisite, rapturous; the figures in his landscapes (and convention demanded that they should be there) were con-ventional at their infrequent best and, at their more usual worst, looked like spindles or slugs – a fault shared, not incidentally, by Claude's great follower, J.M.W. Turner. No matter: Claude's mastery of, and inspiration within, the conventions of ideal pastoral landscape (some of which he invented) were so great that he became a model for several generations of painters, and the visitor to Rome is still likely to catch brief glimpses of Italy through Claudian eyes.

He came to Rome as a teenager, possibly as early as 1617. He seems to have had no artistic training in his native France, though it was often said that he had been a pastry-cook – indeed, he is sometimes credited with learning the technique of puff-pastry, *pâte feuilletée*, in Rome, and introducing it to France; this is possible, but undocumented. His first known training with a painter was in the studio of a German artist in Naples, Goffredo Wals. He did not stay there long, and soon was back in Rome as a studio assistant to the Italian landscapist Agostino Tassi. In 1625 he returned briefly to France, working for a minor court painter named Claude Deruet. But by 1627, or even a little earlier, Claude was back in Rome. He would remain there for the rest of his life, never revisiting France or travelling elsewhere in Europe, always at the same address in Via Margutta off Piazza di Spagna, the haunt of foreign artists in Rome. Everything about his life was low-key and modest. He scrimped and saved. He never married; and of his love-life, if he had one, nothing is known. Modest, hardworking and probably rather a bore when he was away from the easel, Claude's career was steadily successful; he sold nearly everything he painted, and at his death there were only four unsold paintings left in his studio. He was not interested in social climbing in the 'great world'; the world could find its way to him, and it did, reliably and regularly.

In fact by the mid-1630s he was so popular that he was plagued by fakers, Roman artists who saw in the manufacture of 'Claudes' a useful supplement to their modest (or nonexistent) incomes. The trademarks of a Claude were, at a certain level, easy to mimic: the parallel planes of the landscape, the luminous ultramarine skies (no cheap pigments for the maestro, only the very best), the feathery *repoussoir* trees framing a distant view of water or a Roman ruin – the Colosseum and the cylindrical tomb of Caecilia Metella, displaced, were particular favourites with collectors. To safeguard his own rights in his work, Claude came up with the practice of making records of his paintings – drawings of them in their finished state, which he annotated and bound in an album called the *Liber Veritatis* or 'Book of Truth'. Whatever was not in the Book of Truth was, by definition, false. In fact Claude did not copy all his work in this way, and this led to some acrimonious disputes about the authenticity of perfectly genuine paintings – but the *Liber Veritatis* was the first effort an artist ever made to keep a catalogue of his own work.

Claude's career exemplified the fact that no foreign artist could really consider himself a finished man unless he had studied and worked in Rome, though of course the lengths of apprenticeship to the great city varied. So many flocked there, from practically every country in Europe, that it would be pointless to try to list them all. The chief ones will have to do. From Spain, there were Jusepe de Ribera (baptized 1591–1652) and Diego Rodriguez de Silva y Velázquez (baptized 1599–1660).

Ribera, a brilliantly gifted realist painter of humble origins (he was the second son of a Valencian cobbler), was inspired by Caravaggio, whom he may have met in Naples. His most Caravaggian traits were his precise draughtsmanship, unideal street-life models and intense lighting, with faces and limbs plucked from surrounding darkness by brilliant shafts of light, in the manner of Caravaggio's *Calling of St Matthew* in S. Luigi dei Francesi. Though he passed almost all his working life as an expatriate in Naples, where he was affectionately known as *lo Spagnoletto* ('the little Spanish guy'), Ribera spent several early years in Rome, 1611–15, living with a bohemian group of Spanish and Dutch expats around the Via Margutta.

His main surviving early work there was an extraordinary series symbolizing *The Five Senses*. *Sight*, for instance, is a portrait of an introverted-looking thinker, no doubt one of Ribera's friends, holding a Galilean telescope and with a pair of spectacles and a mirror on the table before him. Earlier and more genteel painters might have symbolized *Smell* with flowers and flasks of perfume, in the hands of a nymph; Ribera painted a ragged and none-too-clean old man, who certainly stank, holding a split onion near his face. His opposite, however, is *Touch*, which one identifies at once with the cultural life of Rome – a well-kempt and decently barbered dealer in a brown jacket, his eyes closed in thought, running his discerning fingers over an antique head.

There is a certain family resemblance, caused by a common Caravaggian realism, between early Ribera and early Velázquez.

That, and Spanish blood, was all the two men had in common, and it is doubtful that they met more than briefly in Italy, if at all. Ribera by nature was a democrat and a populist, whereas Velázquez was a gifted courtier and a crushing snob. (In person, that is. Both painted low-life figures, common workers, bravos and tavern inhabitants, since the rich enjoyed seeing pictures of the poor on their walls in the seventeenth century, just as they would in the twentieth century with Blue Period Picassos.)

Velázquez was undoubtedly one of the greatest geniuses who ever held a brush, but he might have given up painting altogether for the sake of the right title. He was stiff, reserved, extremely conscious of lineage and protocol, religiously observant to a fault (you needed to be, for the right cardinals to give you the right commissions) and obsessed with winning membership in the noble Order of Santiago – a distinction he finally obtained, after years of lobbying, in 1658, only two years before his death, having tried throughout his life, without success, to prove that his family was of noble origin. In his self-portrait at the easel in his climactic masterpiece, *Las Meninas*, he is wearing the red cross of Santiago on his tunic. Membership of this exalted order entailed proving his *limpieza de sangre*, purity of blood – no Arabs or Jews allowed. He cannot have been an easy man to know. His contemporaries admired and respected more than liked him. But of his qualities there was little doubt: one of Italy's leading artists, Luca Giordano, called his work 'the theology of painting', the highest imaginable praise.

Velázquez was born in Seville and spent most of his career in Madrid, in the service of Philip IV, the king. He was apprenticed to a mainly religious painter, Francisco Pacheco (1564–1644), for six years. As an artist, Pacheco was a distinctly minor figure, but he knew a great deal about art theory and Christian iconography, which he imparted to the young Velázquez. As for his painting, its qualities were perhaps best summed up in a *boutade* which ran:

Who painted you thus, O Lord,
So dry and so insipid?

Some may say it was True Love –
But I can tell you Pacheco did it.

Pacheco had a wide acquaintance as a portraitist among the
upper crust of Seville, and this gave his student his first involve-
ment with Society. His apprenticeship ended in 1617 and Velázquez, now licensed to work as an independent painter,
celebrated by marrying Pacheco's daughter Juana and setting up
his own studio. What earned him the most kudos in these early
years, however, was less his portraits than his *bodegones* or genre
paintings – the word *bodegon* originally meaning a rough eating-
house with the simplest of meals and wine. *Bodegones* were not
considered a very serious form, but it was young Velázquez, above
all, who made them so by turning them into a vehicle for the
most detailed and exquisitely recorded perceptions of substance
and human character. There is no more beautifully painted glass
of water in European art than the one the old man is passing to
the boy in *The Waterseller of Seville* (*c.*1617–19), nor has a terracotta
water-urn ever been painted with more enraptured and sober
attention. It may be that these early Velázquezes bear a debt to
the early works of Jusepe de Ribera, but the debt is more like a
compliment. When a new Habsburg king, Philip IV, ascended
the throne of Spain in 1621, it was almost inevitable that young
Velázquez, who had already found favour with his grand adviser
Gaspar de Guzmán, the Conde (later Duque) de Olivares, should
have been on track to become the Pintor del Rey, to which office
he was raised in 1623.

To be the King's Painter in seventeenth-century Madrid was
not only a singular honour, but an extraordinary advantage. It
gave Velázquez unlimited access to one of the greatest collections
of painting in Europe. Since Spain had no public collections and
would not until the formation of the Prado in 1819, and since
common painters had no access to the Palace or the Escorial, this
gave Velázquez the edge over practically every other painter in his
country, and he made the fullest use of it – quite apart from the
social advantages that went with being Pintor del Rey. Then,

when Peter Paul Rubens arrived at the Madrid court from the Netherlands and Rome in 1628, an even wider world opened before the enraptured eyes of the thirty-year-old Spaniard. Rubens (who seems to have painted a number of his Madrid commissions in Velázquez's studio) urged him to go to Rome, the centre of the world, and of course Velázquez needed little persuading. Letters of release and introduction were arranged, and in 1629 he set off for Italy: Venice, Ferrara, Bologna. But the key destination was Rome, where he stayed for a year with the Spanish ambassador, the Conde de Monterrey. On this first visit he came as a young painter, albeit a brilliant one. On his second visit to Rome, twenty years later (1649–51), he arrived as an established, and as it were absolute, master.

What did Velázquez get from Rome that Spain could not have given him? A sense of pictorial possibility and sheer skill: no painting in Spain could rival in confidence, range and pictorial imagination what Italian art from the Renaissance on – Michelangelo, Raphael, Veronese, Titian, Caravaggio, the Carraccis – magnificently embodied. Then there was the Antique as well, the ancient statues which Velázquez was not there to copy, but which fortified his sense of possible continuity with the long past. There were no Roman paintings that look like Velázquez's *Surrender of Breda* ('The Lances', 1635), and yet he could hardly have managed that theatre of expression, that complex composition in deep space and that inspired frieze of twenty-four vertical lances (their rhythmic beat broken by just three oblique ones) without knowing and internalizing the achievements of Roman art.

For an ambitious artist with the skill and determination to work out its lessons, seventeenth-century Rome was indisputably the school of the world. It gave great liberties and opportunities to artists. For instance, in Velázquez's case, it encouraged a figure-painter to paint naked women. This practice, if not unknown in Spain, was very rare, because of the ignorant moral hostility of the clergy; as for the clientele, they could not display nudes on their walls, for fear of obloquy. But there was no risk attached to painting the female nude in Italy, and somewhere among the

horde of potential models who hung out for hire around Piazza
di Spagna Velázquez found the girl whose slender, lovely body
was destined to become one of the most celebrated in art history
and the first recorded nude by a Spanish painter: the pensive
mirror-gazing subject of *The Toilet of Venus*, or *The Rokeby Venus*
(*c*.1651).

Rome also presented him with the opportunity to create one
of the most mesmerizing and inquisitorial images of human power
ever put on canvas. This, of course, is the 1650–1 portrait of Pope
Innocent X Pamphili, which now hangs in the Palazzo Doria
Pamphilj in the via del Corso. Such is the nature of late modernist
fame that, by now, probably most people who are aware of this
painting know about it through the 'screaming pope' versions of
it done by Francis Bacon. These are among Bacon's best work but
they do not come near the original (which is not screaming: of all
men, the one least likely to scream, even privately, is this
Pamphili). Indeed, one is sometimes tempted to say that very few
portraits, if any at all, approach Velázquez's pope – even Innocent
X himself, on seeing it finished, is said to have called it 'too
truthful', and when one confronts its steely, interrogatory glare it
is all too easy to know what he meant.

The fourth great seventeenth-century expatriate to work in
Rome was not a Spaniard but a Fleming, originally from Antwerp:
Peter Paul Rubens (1577–1640). In terms of versatility, influence
and sheer historical and mythical power, there has never been
another artist to touch Rubens and it is likely that there never will
be. In his energy and his ability to fulfil great public roles, he puts
every twentieth-century painter in the shade. We are apt to regard
Picasso's *Guernica* as a very important piece of public art, and so
it is – for its time; but it is alone in Picasso's work, whereas Rubens,
the greatest northern painter associated with the Counter-
Reformation, could and did turn out such utterances, usually of
a religious sort although sometimes descriptive of politics, on the
grandest scale and with an eloquence and formal beauty that leave
Picasso far behind him. This kind of painting, with such ambitions
for the languages of paint, is simply no longer possible; its use has

been subverted by the decay of religion, the distrust of politics and politicians, the evaporation of belief in authority that characterize our own age. There can never be another Rubens because the intellectual and ethical backgrounds to his work, not to mention the educational systems and reverence for historical prototypes that supported and infused it, no longer exist. Nor can they be willed into being. The enormous fish has no water to swim in, and the estuary is dry.

There is no doubt that Rubens got his sense of the public role of an artist from a long visit to Italy and, in particular, to Rome. He made his first visit there at the end of 1601, when he was serving at the court of Vincenzo Gonzaga, Duke of Mantua. On his first trip and during a later sojourn there in 1606–8, Rubens was able to study the chief works of the Grand Manner, all of which were there: Michelangelo's Sistine frescoes, Raphael's Vatican Stanze. Their impact on him was immeasurable, and it was increased by the fact that the ancient Roman marbles, which had served these earlier artists as authoritative sources, were also there for Rubens to study and copy side by side: the Belvedere Torso, the Laocoön, and lesser but still instructive works like the *African Fisherman* (then thought to be a carved marble figure of the dying Seneca).

Given the wholly privileged position of the Church, the greatest collections of such antiquities were in the hands of wealthy clerics: the huge room in Palazzo Farnese, for instance, whose ceiling Annibale Carracci had frescoed, was crammed with ancient statues, and Cardinal Alessandro Farnese had already opened this collection of antiquities to scholars and selected artists (not yet to the general public) in 1589. In an age before public museums, this situation was tailor-made for Rubens, who used all his powers of charm, talent and ingratiation to get access to such aesthetic treasures and draw them, accurately, fast and from every angle. He made hundreds of such drawings, which served him as memory aids – these being the days before photographic reproduction – and furnished the basis of many of his own figures and compositions to come. Rubens would never cease to be a student of the art of the past, and drawing was his medium of study. To copy a work was to absorb it; to internalize it; to assimilate its DNA. This process is almost lost to us today, in an age of mass mechanical reproduction.

On this early visit, Rubens did not leave many works in Rome. He was not yet well enough known to get big commissions there, although he did an altarpiece for the Church of S. Croce in Gerusalemme, commemorating the empress Helena's acquisition in Jerusalem of the relics of the True Cross and the Holy Staircase contained in the church itself. But the experience of Rome, and in particular the sense of an immense sacred and aesthetic history transmitted through the ancient fabric of the city to the present day, would never leave him: it remained one of the basic messages of his art, the old vigorously underpinning the new. There was no artist who gave one a stronger sense of continuity in art than Rubens in Rome.

8

HIGH BAROQUE

The Catholic Church, faced with the stresses of the seventeenth century, responded with brilliant skill and energy. It marshalled its forces in defence of its own dogmas and powers, and the visual arts were one of the theatres in which this marshalling took place. This was part of the ideological and imaginative thrust known as the Counter-Reformation. Never, not even in the Middle Ages, had so much been expected of architects, sculptors and painters in defence of Catholic belief. If one had to choose a single sculptor-architect who completely embodied, in his person and his work, the spirit of the Counter-Reformation, there could be only one candidate. He was Gianlorenzo Bernini (1598–1680). Across a long and prodigiously fecund working life, Bernini epitomized what it could mean to be a Catholic artist in the fullest sense. 'Inspired' is a word that should be used with caution, but there is no more fitting adjective for him. Not only was there no angle between his beliefs and those of the royal personages and Catholic hierarchy for whom he worked: he drew an extreme stimulus from them, taking an unfeigned joy in satisfying their doctrinal requirements.

Bernini was the marble megaphone of papal orthodoxy in the seventeenth century. If you cut and worked stone at that time in Italy (and elsewhere in Europe, too), you worked in the shadow of this Roman prodigy. It was really as simple (but as complex) as that, and there have been few artists in European history who defined their age and their spiritual environment as completely as Bernini did. Looking back on him from a century whose defining cultural characteristic is doubt, it seems hardly credible that a man of such skill and *certezza* could have existed. But he did, and he found the right patrons to match his genius.

The presence of Baroque art is so massive now, so powerful in our reading of European culture, that it might always have been there. But it was not. 'Baroque' was a term of abuse, and the work it denoted was considered vulgar, hateful and (despite its technical skill) inept, right through the eighteenth and nineteenth centuries. Colen Campbell (1676–1729), the Scots protégé of Lord Burlington, whose *Vitruvius Britannicus* was such a strong influence on British architectural taste, saw the period as a descent from the heights of Palladian genius into 'capricious ornaments, which must at last end in the Gothick':

> I appeal to the Productions of the last Century: How affected and licentious are the works of Bernini and Fontana? How wildly extravagant are the designs of Borromini, who has endeavoured to debauch Mankind with his odd and chimerical Beauties, where the parts are without Proportion, Solids without their true Bearing, heaps of Materials without Strength, excessive Ornaments without Grace, and the Whole without Symmetry?

Nor did the succeeding two centuries bring much change of heart or opinion. For indignant Ruskin, to whom Gothic was the sublime mode for religious architecture, Baroque was merely 'the flourishes of vile paganism'. Charles Dickens, visiting Rome in *Pictures from Italy*, found Bernini's Baroque monuments 'intolerable abortions', 'the most detestable class of productions in the whole wide world'. The 1911 edition of that style bible of English architectural history, Banister Fletcher's *History of Architecture on the Comparative Method*, gave the whole seventeenth century thirty lines of text: writers on the Baroque were apt to content themselves with the mere exercise of stamping on its grave. It represented, wrote Fletcher, '[a]n anarchical reaction [to Palladio]. Sinuous frontages and a strained originality in detail are characteristic ... Ornamentation is carried out to an extraordinary degree without regard to fitness or suitability, and consists of exaggerated and badly designed detail ... Maderno, Bernini and

Borromini are among the more famous who practised this debased form of art.'

Such a picture of Baroque achievement, particularly in Rome, is unrecognizable today. Tastes change, as a matter of course; but in the case of seventeenth-century building and the reactions to it we might be looking at a different world – and in a real sense, we are. Where the Ruskins and Campbells saw disordered heaps of ostentation, a gratification of the lust for pomp without reference to true religious feeling, we are more likely to see the last great universal language of spirituality. The reasons for this begin and end with Bernini.

Bernini had his training in the studio of his sculptor father, Pietro Bernini, a Florentine Mannerist artist of some achievement who worked in Naples and settled in Rome, the art world's centre, around 1606 to work for Pope Paul V. His earliest known independent works belong to childhood: a small group of statues of the goat Amalthea suckling the infant Jupiter, done with the complex realism he must have learned from the Hellenistic marble carvings he saw in Rome and from his father's imitation of them – all those tangles of matted goat-hair, done with such relish! – dates to about 1609, when he was eleven. He was hardly more than a boy when his work first came to the attention of Cardinal Maffeo Barberini, who saw his carving of the martyrdom of St Lawrence, being grilled to death over hot coals and rising marble flames but looking fairly composed about it. It is said (*se non e vero, e ben trovato* . . .) that the twenty-year-old sculptor arranged a mirror and then put his leg into a fire, the better to see the anguish on his own face – although the expression of this Lawrence does not look unduly agonized. Or was it just that Bernini was unusually stoic? Probably not.

It was through Barberini that one of Rome's foremost art collectors became aware of young Bernini's work. This was Cardinal Scipione Borghese (1576–1633), nephew of Pope Paul V, connoisseur of antiquities, *bon vivant* and man of enormous wealth. He was the pope's secretary and, to all intents, he ran the Vatican government. He held a host of official positions, most of which returned him serious money; by 1612 his annual income was said to be a huge 140,000 *scudi*.

Pederasty in seventeenth-century Rome was a crime which, at least in theory, carried the death penalty. There is no doubt about Scipione Borghese's homosexual proclivities, but he was protected – indeed, armour-plated – by birth and wealth. He surrounded himself with *fanciulli* or pretty boys, and there is little doubt that their homoerotic content was a prime reason why early Caravaggios like *The Sick Bacchus*, *The Boy Bitten by a Lizard* and other works entered Borghese's collection. These pouting pieces of rough trade, with their lumberous dark eyes and hair like black ice-cream, were clearly much to the cardinal's taste.

His collection of ancient sculpture included some of the most admired pieces in Europe, such as the *Borghese Gladiator* (*c*.100 BCE), which Bernini strove to emulate. It was clear to Borghese that Bernini, hardly out of his teens, was a maestro in the making. And Borghese was not the kind of collector who would wait for, or be denied, anything that took his imperious fancy (one of his more odious actions was to confiscate more than a hundred pictures from the Cavaliere d'Arpino, a feeble Mannerist painter whose claim to distinction was to have taught Caravaggio for a while, for not paying his taxes). Borghese started amassing Berninis, and secured some of his best early works: among them, a life-sized figure group of Aeneas and his little son Ascanius fleeing the burning city of Troy, carrying his aged father Anchises, who himself carries the *penates* (household gods) of their lost home. This is a transcription in stone of Virgil's lines from the *Aeneid*:

> 'Then come, dear father. Arms around my neck:
> I'll take you on my shoulders, no great weight.
> Whatever happens, both will face one danger,
> Find one safety . . .
> Father, carry our hearth-gods, our Penates.
> It would be wrong for me to handle them –
> Just come from such hard fighting, bloody work –

Until I wash myself in running water.'

This sculpture, the spiralling movement of its bodies so strongly indebted to the great Mannerist sculptor Giambologna, was designed for Scipione Borghese's new villa at the Porta Pinciana in Rome, where it still stands. So was the extraordinary *Pluto and Persephone* (1621–2), in which the imposingly muscular figure of the king of Hades is seen carrying off the helpless daughter of Zeus and Demeter to be his prisoner and bride in the Underworld: a girl snatched, in Milton's lines, from

> That fair field
> Of Enna,* where Proserpin gathering flours
> Herself a fairer Floure by gloomie Dis
> Was gatherd, which cost Ceres all that pain
> To seek her through the World.

Persephone shrieks in vain; she struggles and wriggles helplessly, enticingly; we even see the marble tear on her cheek, and the yielding flesh of her thigh as Pluto's fingers sink implacably into it. It is an extremely sexy sculpture, and should be, since its subject is a rape; Scipione Borghese possessed an unsurpassed collection of antique Roman erotica, with which the young sculptor must have been happily familiar. The extraordinary character of this sculpture lies in a mastery over carving which transcends the puritanical mantra of modernism about 'truth to material', as though there were only some things that could legitimately be done with wood or stone, and that to go beyond them were a sin. Bernini leaves you in no doubt that stone can represent anything if the shaping hand is skilled enough. Is it wrong for it to look as though it were modelled rather than carved? Assuredly not, the marvellous surfaces and textures of Pluto's and Persephone's

* In Sicily.

bodies tell us. Is the effect a lie? Of course, but art itself is a lie – a lie told in the service of truth.

The showpiece of Bernini's early virtuosity is, however, the *Apollo and Daphne*, commissioned by Scipione Borghese after he gave the *Pluto and Persephone* to the pope's nephew to curry favour with the pontiff. It is a sculptural illustration of one of the more beautiful and poignant moments in classical poetry, which occurs in Book One of Ovid's *Metamorphoses*. Apollo has encountered the nymph Daphne, daughter of the river-god Peneus. The love-god Cupid, witnessing this, fires two arrows from his bow; one sharp and tipped with gold, which pierces Apollo's vitals, and the other blunt and lead-tipped at Daphne, who at once becomes unreachable by love. Apollo is now compelled always to pursue Daphne, who is likewise doomed always to flee. 'The marriage torches / Were something hateful, criminal, to Daphne', who entreats her father to 'Let me be a virgin always'. Apollo, of course, has other ideas. She runs,

> But Apollo,
> Too young a god to waste his time in coaxing,
> Came following fast. When a hound starts a rabbit
> In an open field, one runs for game, one safety,
> He has her, or thinks he has, and she is doubtful
> Whether she's caught or not, so close the margin,
> So ran the god and girl, one swift in hope,
> The other in terror, but he ran more swiftly,
> Borne on the wings of love, gave her no rest,
> Shadowed her shoulder, breathed on her streaming hair,
> Her strength was gone, worn out by the long effort
> Of the long flight; she was deathly pale, and seeing
> The river of her father, cried 'O help me,
> If there is any power in the rivers,
> Change and destroy the body which has given
> Too much delight!' And hardly had she finished
> When her limbs grew numb and heavy, her soft breasts
> Were closed with delicate bark, her hair was leaves,

Her arms were branches, and her speedy feet
Rooted and held, and her head became a tree-top,
Everything gone except her grace, her shining.
Apollo loved her still. He placed his hand
Where he had hoped, and felt the heart still beating
Under the bark; and he embraced the branches
As if they still were limbs, and kissed the wood,
And the wood shrank from his kisses, and the god
Exclaimed: 'Since you can never be my bride,
My tree at least you shall be! Let the laurel
Adorn, henceforth, my hair, my lyre, my quiver,
Let Roman victors, in the long procession,
Wear laurel wreaths for triumph and ovation . . .'
He said no more. The laurel,
Stirring, seemed to consent, to be saying *Yes*.

This, one might think, would have been an impossible thing to
illustrate with sculpture. Sculpture – at least until Bernini – always
depicted achieved actions and complete states. Nobody had tried
to illustrate in sculpture things in transition, to convey what was
incomplete or in the very process of change. Yet in *Apollo and
Daphne* we do see the change from girl to tree happening before
our eyes; the bark enveloping and encasing her lithe body; softness
giving way to ligneous toughness; movement turning into root-
edness. Moreover the sculpture seems to defy what we know is a
chief property of stone: its brittleness. How on earth (one
wonders), through what preternatural skill, did Bernini manage
to render those brittle stalks and thin, free-standing blades of
laurel leaf in marble, without snapping them off? It must have
been done with rasps, drills and abrasive; a hammer blow, the
touch of a chisel, would have ruined any of them. And once a
leaf was broken, there were no adhesives like epoxy capable of
mending it in the early seventeenth century. No sculpture, one
feels, could be riskier. Of course, one's admiration of Bernini's
technique is not confined to enjoying its Last-Supper-carved-on-
a-peachstone virtuosity, which has always been felt to go beyond

mere skill. There is no feeling that he has achieved such effects by some sort of trickery or legerdemain. They are there, factual, and it was not magic that put them there. And then there is the rendering of emotion and expression, which rivals the intensity of the work of the painter Guido Reni, the Italian artist whom, we know, Bernini greatly admired. In years to come, Bernini's work would deepen and acquire a wider emotional resonance. It, and he, would mature. But already, in his twenties, he showed himself capable of producing one of those works of art that seem to enlarge the scope of human possibility. Anyone who thinks of the young Picasso as a prodigy should reflect on the young Bernini, and be admonished. There was no twentieth-century artist, and is certainly none, so far, of the twenty-first century, who does not look rather small beside him.

He was a man of the utmost concentration and energy. Even in old age (and he lived to eighty-two) Bernini was quite capable of working on a marble block for seven or eight hours at a stretch. This vitality, which he never lost, combined with astonishing executive powers. He ran a very large studio, and had to, because of the number of commissions in sculpture and architecture, for the highest levels of government and religion, that he confidently undertook and completed. He was by far the most influential sculptor in Rome, or in the seventeenth-century world. Bernini was to become the supreme artist of the Counter-Reformation in sculpture and architecture, as Rubens was in painting.

And like Rubens, he was a man of strong and deep religious conviction. It is not, of course, true that to create important works of religious art one must be pious. Still less is it true that an artist's personal piety underwrites the quality of his art as art – much of the world's vilest, most sugary religious kitsch has been deeply felt and produced by honest and morally impeccable people. But there have been cases, uncommon but real, when deep religious impulses lend an authentic intensity of spiritual feeling to Crucifixions and Resurrections, one that detachment or agnosticism cannot provide. Bernini's was such a case.

The event that set the seal on Bernini's growing success came on 6 August 1623, with the election of Maffeo Barberini as Pope Urban VIII. Barberini (reg. 1623–44) was a Florentine and a man of the most unbridled political ambition. Indeed his papacy marked the high-water mark of the extent and power of the Papal States within Italy. It would hardly have been possible for him to remain aloof from politics anyway, not only because the Papacy ruled Rome but also because his reign coincided with twenty-one years of the Thirty Years' War.

But the patronage of art was also, for him, as important as the prosecution of war. He built extensively in Rome, and some of the results were glorious in their extravagance – notably his own residence, Palazzo Barberini on the Quirinale (Via delle Quattro Fontane 13). Its initial design – a villa with wings extending into the garden around it – was done by Carlo Maderno; later the work, interrupted by Maderno's death in 1629, was taken over by Bernini and Francesco Borromini. Its façade derives, in its essentials, from that mighty prototype of Roman Baroque palaces, the Palazzo Farnese. If he had built nothing else, Maffeo Barberini would deserve a place in architectural history for this private home, but he did much more. He was determined to leave a great indelible mark on Rome; like many before him, he chose to do so through its principal church, St Peter's. The man who would do this for him was young Bernini. On the very day of his election, Urban is said to have summoned the sculptor and declared: 'You have great luck to see Cardinal Maffeo Barberini Pope, Cavaliere; but ours is much greater to have Cavaliere Bernini alive in our pontificate.' Or words, at least, to that effect. Later Urban would write of his artist, 'Rare man, sublime artificer, born by divine disposition and for the glory of Rome to illuminate the century.'

Bernini was only twenty-three when he was made a *cavaliere*, a papal knight. This honour was merely a formal recognition of what everyone who had seen his early sculptures already knew: that of all the stone-cutters and bronze-casters working in Europe, Bernini was the most skilled, the most inventive: not only in his technical mastery of materials, but in his astonishing ability to create a *concetto* or 'concept' of sculpture. This gift went far beyond the ability to carve a strong Hercules or a desirable Venus, which was (relatively) easy. It had to do with inventing an entirely new kind of drama from posture, gesture and expression. It ensured Bernini his first papal commissions, of which the principal ones had to do with St Peter's. In fact for the next half-century, after 1623, hardly a year would pass in which Bernini would *not* be involved in the decoration of this prodigious basilica, and it was Urban who brought him into it as the master of papal works, starting with an enormous monument right below the dome, over the (supposed) burial spot of the Apostle Peter.

This was the *baldacchino*, or canopy of honour. It can never be too much emphasized that the shared project of Bernini and Urban VIII was to display to the world the triumph of Catholicism over Protestant heresy, and give unforgettable visual form to the tenets of the Counter-Reformation. The canopy was the first icon of this: a huge, exuberant declaration of the belief that St Peter, Christ's Vicar on Earth and first in an unbroken line of popes, lay buried *here* and nowhere else, that the only true version of Christianity was *his* faith and that of his successors, not (perish the thought!) Martin Luther's. It marks the foundation stone of the Church: *Tu es Petrus, et super hanc petram aedificabo ecclesiam meam*, Christ is recorded as saying, punningly, to Peter: 'You are Peter, and on this rock I will build my church.' These words are inscribed around the drum of the crossing, above the *baldacchino*, in letters five feet high.

The baldachin would have to be huge. In the vast space of that nave, under such a dome, seen from the distance of the entrance (the nave is 218 metres long), anything less than huge would look as trivial and incongruous as a beach umbrella. Obviously one could not use a real canopy, figured silk supported on poles. The size of the thing would have been too great for any kind of cloth, which would have perished anyway. So the canopy must be rigid, made of metal. The correct metal would be bronze. But a structure so large, with its superstructure of volutes and its twenty-metre-high twisted columns (of the type known as 'solomonicas', from the belief that spirally twisted columns were used in Solo-

mon's Temple in Jerusalem), would require enormous quantities
of this metal. Where would it come from? Where, but another
church? Urban VIII gave Bernini leave to strip the ancient bronze
cladding from the portico of S. Maria Rotonda, the new name of
the Pantheon, which had been adopted and reconsecrated for
Catholic rites and was the property of the Holy See. From this
and other sources of recyclable bronze, Bernini got the metal to
make the *baldacchino*, with enough left over to cast some cannon
for the Castel S. Angelo. This made some Romans indignant,
though in truth, while obviously it would have been better to have
both, it would be difficult to claim that the exchange of the
Pantheon's bronze for Bernini's baldachin was anything but a net
gain.

The *baldacchino* is the world's first incontestably great Baroque
monument. No wonder that Bernini's enemies derided it (behind
his back, of course) as a 'chimera' – it fell into no agreed category
of décor, sculpture or architecture. It still strikes the viewer with
awe, through the richness and complexity of its detail no less than
its astonishing size – the largest bronze sculpture in the world.
But is it sculpture? Or metallic architecture? Manifestly, both. As
a work of propaganda it has few rivals elsewhere in the fine arts.
Not only is it propaganda for Catholic doctrine and Catholic
archaeology, but for Maffeo Barberini himself. The bronze bees
that are crawling everywhere on it, giant insects the size of star-
lings, are the heraldic *api* of the Barberini family. The recurrent
suns and the laurels that twine around the massive corkscrew
columns are, likewise, Barberini emblems. *L'église, c'est moi.*

Maffeo Barberini's papacy was a fairly long one – twenty-one
years, from 1623 to 1644. It cannot be called a financial success; he
practised nepotism on too gigantic a scale. When he came to the
throne, the Papacy was 16 million *scudi* in debt, and Urban took
only two years to run that up to 28 million. By 1640 the debt stood
at 35 million, so that the interest payments on it alone consumed
more than four-fifths of the annual papal income. His political
adventures tended to be quite disastrous. Urban was the last pope
to go to war in the hope of expanding papal territory, and he

always lost his battles. Nor was his scientific sense much better. He vigorously opposed Galileo's heliocentric theory of the universe, the belief that the earth went round the sun and not vice versa, and summoned him to Rome in 1633 to make him recant. He also – to descend from the serious to the absurd – issued a Papal Bull, in 1624, that made smoking tobacco punishable by excommunication. The reason was that when smokers sneezed, their convulsion resembled orgasm, and this struck Urban as a mortal sin of the flesh.

Bernini far outlasted his patron in life, and glorified him after death in a tomb which occupies one of the most honoured spots in the basilica, enthroned and wearing the papal tiara (bareheaded was more normal in tomb sculpture). Nobody can miss the encompassing gesture of benediction with which he faces the viewer, but people do not always notice Bernini's attribution to him of eternal life: three bronze Barberini bees which have flown out of the sarcophagus and are heading upward, in illustration of Virgil's lines from the *Georgics* describing the immortality of those cooperative insects: 'There is no room for death: alive they fly / to join the stars and mount aloft to heaven.'

Nowhere could Bernini's diplomatic skills have been more evident than in his handling of the transition of power after Urban VIII's death to the new pontiff, Giovanni Battista Pamphili, who succeeded to the Fisherman's Throne in 1644 and reigned for eleven years under the name of Innocent X. Though he would spend a few years out in the cold, he bided his time; his sheer talent and unrivalled ingenuity would ensure his return to favour. Innocent had a visceral loathing for his predecessor, who had left the Papacy heavily depleted – patronage of one's own family, as Urban practised it, was a most expensive hobby.*

---

* This went both ways, for the Barberinis disliked the Pamphilis as much as the Pamphilis the Barberinis. In about 1635, the pope's brother, Cardinal Antonio Barberini, had commissioned a painting for the Church of Santa Maria della Concezione, the home church of the Capuchin monks, with whom his career had begun. It was by one of Rome's most esteemed

Innocent's acute dislike extended to the recipients of Urban's largesse, of whom the most conspicuous was Bernini. The great sculptor was detested by most artists and architects in Rome, since nothing breeds envy more than extreme success. It was therefore with an overwhelming sense of relief and *Schadenfreude* (that useful German word that has no exact English equivalent, but means roughly 'pleasure in the misfortunes of others') that the Roman cultural world not only saw him fail, but saw the pope do nothing to rescue him.

The stumbling-block was a design he made in 1637 for bell-towers on the façade of St Peter's. Apparently Bernini did not design a strong enough footing for them; the ground was more weakened by subterranean streams than the architect realized. Soon after it was built, cracks appeared in the left tower. To the unrestrained delight of his enemies, including his arch-rival Borromini, Bernini's towers had to be demolished. Because of Innocent X, it was politically safe for anyone to be as nasty about Urban VIII's once omnipotent protégé as he liked. For the first time in his life, Bernini was out in the cold. From the point of view of his prosperity this demotion from the exalted status of papal architect hardly mattered – there would be enough commissions from rich but lesser patrons to keep him busy till Doomsday. Still, losing the pope's favour was a severe blow, one that the great man could not accept.

And Innocent meant business. Once his mind was made up, he

---

painters, Guido Reni – a fact which guaranteed that every sophisticate in the city would come to see it. Its subject was the warrior archangel Michael with his sword, trampling underfoot a rebel demon whom he is casting down from Heaven. The prostrate and humiliated demon had the unmistakable face of Giovanni Battista Pamphili, the future Pope Innocent X. Despite the future pontiff's rage at this insult, the Capuchins hung on to their altarpiece, and it is still there – though nowhere near as well known as the other portrait, of an older Innocent X, by Velázquez, the 'screaming pope' frequently copied by Francis Bacon, which remains in its cubicle in Palazzo Doria on the Pamphilis' family square, Piazza Navona.

did not easily relent. Urban was hardly cold in the magnificent tomb Bernini had made for him in St Peter's before Innocent X brought suit against his relatives, the cardinals Antonio and Francesco Barberini, for misappropriation of public funds. They fled to France and took refuge under the powerful wing of Cardinal Mazarin, leaving financial chaos behind them; Innocent promptly confiscated their property.

He was also as given to meddling in the affairs of other countries as his medieval namesake, Innocent III: but this was still normal for a powerful sacrosecular state like the Papacy. One should not forget that the Papacy still ran the civil and political government of Rome. Its affairs were not only those of the Church, but of the state. The Church *was* the state. An extreme case of this meddling was Ireland. During the Civil War (1642–9) in England and Ireland, the pope dispatched a nuncio – an ecclesiastic diplomat – the archbishop Giovanni Rinuccini, to Kilkenny with a huge sum of money and ten tons of the best gunpowder. Though he declared, and with sincerity, that he meant to sustain the king, his purpose was to help the Irish Catholics throw off the Protestant yoke of England, restoring confiscated property to the Irish Church and the rights of Catholic worship to the Irish people. It went badly awry; instead of gaining its lost rights back, Ireland got the 'accursed butcher' Oliver Cromwell, who invaded with his New Model Army and in what could euphemistically be called a 'police action' mercilessly crushed the rebellion and ensured more than three further centuries of bloodshed between Catholics and Protestants within long-memoried Ireland – 'much hatred, little room', in W.B. Yeats's pregnant words. Archbishop Rinuccini was recalled by Innocent in 1649, his gunpowder wasted.

Preoccupied with his political adventures, Innocent X had little or no time for Bernini, who bided his time and worked on more private commissions. The greatest of these was the Cornaro Chapel in the Church of S. Maria della Vittoria, the work which signalled a new and audacious development in the sculptor's thinking. This is the project that brought together sculpture, scenography, narrative and architecture in a way which had never been done or even attempted before – a hinge-point, not only in Bernini's career, but in the history of seventeenth-century art.

It was a memorial, commissioned by the Venetian cardinal Federigo Cornaro (1579–1653), Patriarch of Venice, to commemorate both himself and his family. The saint it glorifies is Teresa of Avila (1515–82), the holy Spanish woman, founder of the Carmelite Order (to whom the church belongs) and teacher of St John of the Cross, whose copious writings include a vision of Divine Love, manifesting itself in the form of an angel with a spear. Her description of this vision has often been quoted, but it is worth repeating not only for its classical importance in the canon of mysticism but also because Bernini followed it to the very letter – and clearly, as a most devout Catholic, believed every word of it and strove to make it as concrete as sculpture could do:

> He was not tall but short, and very beautiful; and his face was so aflame that he appeared to be one of the highest rank of angels, who seem to be all on fire. They must be of the kind called cherubim ... In his hands I saw a great golden spear, and at the iron tip there appeared to be a point of fire. This he plunged into my heart several times so that it penetrated to my entrails. When he pulled it out, I felt that he took them with it, and left me utterly consumed with the great love of God. The pain was so severe that it made me utter several moans. The sweetness caused by this intense pain is so extreme that one cannot possibly wish it to cease, nor is one's soul then content with anything but God. This is not a physical but a spiritual pain, though the body has some share in it – even a considerable share ... if anyone thinks I am lying, I pray God in his goodness to grant him some experience of it.

In Bernini's sculpture, St Teresa is levitating, borne up on a marble cloud. Only three parts of her body are visible; her face, one bare foot, and a single nerveless hand. The rest of her is a mass of drapery, a near-chaos of folds and pleats, beneath which no sign of the body's form is discernible. All is agitation, the swirls and crumples of marble cloth standing as signs of the intense emotion caused by the vision's arrival. Her mouth is open, moaning; her heavy eyelids are lowered, stressing the internal power of her vision. Discreetly but without ambiguity, Bernini shows us a woman in orgasm – 'If that is divine love, *eh bien*,' said a worldly French diplomat on catching sight of *The Ecstasy of St Teresa* for the first time in the 1780s, 'I know it well.' (So, it should be added, did Bernini; he had an earthy-looking mistress named Costanza Bonarelli, whose bust he carved, voluptuously parted lips and all.) Compared to St Teresa, the angel is all unitary force, rising vertically beside her, his face a study in benign masculine sweetness, his eyes fixed on hers as he draws back the spear to plunge it, once more, into her welcoming flesh. (His left hand, touching the saint's disordered garment, is a superbly ambiguous touch: it could be seen as gently lifting the cloth to expose flesh which he can see but we cannot, or else as raising the whole body of the saint, weightlessly, upwards – a reminder of the levitation St Teresa said she had undergone.)

The space of the chapel, which is in the left transept of S. Maria della Vittoria, is quite shallow. Its focus is, of course, the marble group of Teresa and the angel. This is framed inside a niche, a sort of proscenium with a pediment that breaks forward on a curve and is framed on each side by a pair of darkish-green *breccia Africana* columns. The dark surround makes the white figures of angel and saint even more apparitional, especially since they are lit from above by a source we cannot see. In a chimney or light-well that is hidden from view, light cascades from a yellow glass window. (At least, it used to; the glass is now so dimmed by dust and pigeon-droppings that the Carmelites had to install an electric bulb to replace the sun.) The 'real' light falls on fictitious light – a burst of gilded sun-rays, fanning down behind the figures.

On the side walls of the chapel are two symmetrical niches, designed in false perspective to give the illusion of deep space running back. In them are seated white marble effigies of eight members of the Cornaro family: Cardinal Federigo, the donor, with his father the doge Giovanni Cornaro, and six earlier Cornaros, all cardinals too – a conclave of pious family power, spanning several generations. They lean forward in fascination at the miracle before their eyes; they turn to one another, talking and arguing (or since this is a church, whispering in awe) about it and its meaning; their astonishment parallels our own and increases it. This was the largest and most complicated essay in group sculptural portraiture (individual, lifelike portraiture, not merely figure groups) ever done. And it reminds the viewer, as so much of Bernini's work does, that he had a background in theatre: he relished designing stage set-ups, theatre sets and special effects like floods and sunrises, though we have little idea of how realistically they might have worked. We do know that they impressed and likely fooled the audience.* No wonder that the Cornaro Chapel keeps its magic of illusion even in an age of photography and film, and retains its talismanic power as a mixed-media masterpiece, melding sculpture, theatre, architecture and coloured marble surfaces in an inspired unity, a 'total work of art' that Wagner might have dreamed of.

Nobody of Bernini's genius can remain out in the cold in an age of public patronage for very long, and certainly Bernini did not. His restoration to papal favour came through the very pontiff who had revoked it: Innocent X Pamphili. No great Roman family was more bound up with an architectural feature of Rome than the Pamphili clan with Piazza Navona. It was 'their' square – actually, an elongated horseshoe which almost exactly followed

---

* Paul Fréart, sieur de Chantelou, who was *maître d'hôtel* for Louis XIV and closely accompanied Bernini on his visit to that monarch in France in 1665, recalled that Bernini had written several comedies for the stage, which 'caused a great stir in Rome because of the decorations and the astonishing contraptions he introduced, which deceived even those who had been forewarned'. See Elizabeth Gilmore Holt, *A Documentary History of Art*, vol. 2, p.125.

the track of the ancient Stadium of Domitian, which lay beneath it. Because foot races had been held in this stadium in ancient times (it was not a venue for either chariot-races or the murderous rites of the gladiators), it was relatively short and lacked a central divider or *spina*. Being a place of intense physical striving, it had become known as the *circus agonalis* or *platea in agone*, which became changed by Roman dialect into 'Piazza Navona'. A grand open space, ringed with palaces, closed at one end by the unwieldy bulk of Palazzo Doria, it had been distinguished by the pilgrimage Church of S. Agnese in Agone, built on the presumed site of the holy child-virgin's martyrdom, a Roman brothel. It was a modest church in its first form, but that would presently change by the orders of various members of the Pamphili family. Innocent X, in 1652, decreed a total rebuilding of Agnes's little shrine. This work was entrusted to Innocent's architect Girolamo Rainaldi. He had designed the Pamphili Palace next door, and he would work on S. Agnese until 1653, shortly before his death, when the project was taken over by his son Carlo. But in 1653 the work on the commission was also joined by Francesco Borromini, the depressive genius who was Bernini's chief rival. He redesigned the façade of S. Agnese as a concave, oval curve between bell-towers on either side. The church façade one sees from the piazza, therefore, is a palimpsest of three architects' work: Borromini up to the cornice, then a classical pediment by Bernini (1666), and finally the dome and the upper parts of the campanili by Rainaldi. It is a horse made by committee.

Nevertheless the piazza had evolved into one of the greatest festive precincts in Rome, frequented alike by the grandees taking their evening *passeggiata* and every kind of jongleur, contortionist, pickpocket, pimp, tart, hawker and gawker, whose descendants still throng the square as the day's light is fading. In a superb demonstration of civic theatre, there was until the end of the eighteenth century a custom of flooding the piazza with water, through which processions of horse-drawn carriages would festively parade round and round – a spectacle painted more than once by such artists as Hubert Robert. It must have been quite a sight, though prolonged immersion in water cannot have done much good to the wooden chassis and spoked wheels of the *carrozze*. But sometimes a Roman has no choice but to cut a *bella figura*, even when his carriage warps. Piazza Navona in the Baroque era was a centre for street theatre, replete with processions and ceremonies such as the Giostra del Saraceno, a jousting contest in which the target of the riders' lances was an effigy of a Saracen mounted on a pole. But none of these delights of the *effimero barocco* (temporary Baroque) could compare with what Innocent X, through the ministrations of Bernini, made of the piazza.

At the beginning, the pope did not mean to use Bernini at all. Piazza Navona was the Pamphilis' backyard, their family precinct, and Innocent X was determined to convert it into a permanent memorial to his reign – the greatest public square in Rome. He saw to it that every sculptor-architect of proven quality in Italy was invited to submit designs for the remodelling of Piazza Navona – with the single exception of Gianlorenzo Bernini, who, being so conspicuously the favourite of the detested Barberini, was disqualified.

At first it looked as though Borromini was going to win the commission: it was he who conceived the idea of a sculptural centrepiece for the square, a great fountain outside S. Agnese, with figures representing four rivers and, perhaps, symbolizing the four quarters of the known world. He also devised a scheme for a new aqueduct which would bring enough water for the fountain. Project models would be displayed to Innocent and he would choose.

But unknown to Borromini and everyone else, including the pope, Bernini's friend Prince Niccolò Ludovisi had briefed the great sculptor on the situation and recommended that he make his own model, some say of silver; it would be secreted in a room where the pope would see it. Bernini chose the theme of the Four Rivers too – no doubt Borromini never forgave him for this plagiarism – and proposed to add an Egyptian obelisk, which Innocent X had previously seen lying in five pieces on the *spina* of the Circus of Maxentius, out on the Via Appia. If Sixtus V could have his obelisks, so could Innocent X.

But it was necessary to give it a more grandiose and memorable setting than other obelisks, and Bernini proposed that it should be moved and reassembled to stand on the fictive mountain of travertine where the statues of the Four Rivers were ensconced. These rivers were the Nile, the Plate, the Ganges and the Danube. Each of the rivers would represent one of the world's four then-known continents, Africa, America, India and Europe, respectively, identified by allegorical figures and implications: a lion for Africa, a pile of riches for the Plate (representing the promise of the New World), a man holding an oar for the Ganges, and a papal coat of arms for the Danube. The whole thing would be an astounding *coup de théâtre*: that giant spike borne up on a rough arch of rock, standing on a void above water – an image of the world, *imago mundi*, without parallel in earlier sculpture.

On top of the pyramidion would be a bronze dove, the *stemma* of the Pamphili as the bee was of the Barberini, proclaiming to the world the triumph of Christianity (the Holy Ghost, which a dove also symbolized) over Egyptian and all other paganism, and the happy identification of that same Holy Spirit with the Pamphilis in general and this pope in particular.

Then came a further level of meaning: the traditional form of Paradise contained, at its centre, a fountain, and from it sprang the four rivers that irrigated the four quarters of the world, the Gihon, the Pison, the Tigris and the Euphrates. Bernini's design alluded to this too, thus implying that the Pamphili pope was in charge of Paradise, and in a theological sense its actual gatekeeper.

The model was finished; Prince Ludovisi arranged for it to be set in a room in Palazzo Pamphili, through which Innocent always passed on his way from dinner. He was on his way with his brother cardinal and his sister-in-law, Donna Olimpia, when it caught his eye:

> On seeing such a noble creation and the sketch for so vast a monument, [he] stopped almost in ecstasy . . . after admiring

and praising it for more than half an hour, he burst forth, in the presence of the entire privy council, with the following words: 'This is a trick of Prince Ludovisi. It will be necessary to employ Bernini in spite of those who do not wish it, for he who desires not to use Bernini's designs must take care not to see them.' He sent for Bernini immediately.

And so Bernini's design for the Fountain of the Four Rivers went ahead.* Begun in 1648, it was finished in 1651, thanks to a cast of skilled assistants working to his designs – on a project like this, Bernini was more the master of works than the carver, although he reputedly did the horse, the palm tree, the lion, some of the rock, and possibly the bizarre hybrid creature next to Francesco Baratta's figure of the river Plate, which looks like nothing that ever lived but was meant to be an armadillo, an animal so exotic that neither Bernini nor anyone else in Rome had ever seen one or even an engraving of one. Bizarreries and jokes were designed into the stone: Antonio Raggi's figure of the Danube is holding up its hand, allegedly to shield its gaze from the unwelcome sight of Borromini's façade of S. Agnese. Because the source of the Nile was unknown, the figure of it carved by Giacomo Fancelli has a head swathed in cloth – but this blindfold was also said (falsely) to protect the Nile against a glimpse of Borromini's work.

The reassembly and erection of the obelisk was a major enterprise: not, perhaps, as monstrous as Fontana's task in shifting the obelisk of St Peter's for Sixtus V, but attended by great engineering

---

* It is not known what happened to the silver model. It may have ended up in the possession of the formidably avaricious Olimpia Maidalchini, who had been married to Innocent's late brother and now, in her widowhood, was believed to have become Innocent's mistress, wielding great influence over him. She was respected and disliked in Rome, both for her ruthlessness and for her sexual power, which led to her nickname, 'Olim Pia', roughly meaning 'Formerly Virtuous'. Certainly she would have been a useful and receptive person to bribe with a silver *bozzetto*.

problems. It is a gigantic spike balanced above a void. Bernini constructed the base from travertine, apparently solid rock but carved to simulate 'natural' stone, in the form of an arch. One can see right under and through it, from one side of the piazza to the other. This was the new base of the obelisk. One cannot but guess a connection between the emotional effect that the collapse of the bell-tower at St Peter's must have had on Bernini and the daring with which he set up the obelisk over the void at the centre of the Four Rivers Fountain. Let the public and the Papacy see, he in effect declared, what I can do! Let them know that the bell-tower fiasco was not of my own making! And then one realizes something else. This spike over a void within the 'legs' of an arch – what is it but a prefiguring of the feat Gustave Eiffel would bring off two and a half centuries later, in steel and in Paris, with his celebratory tower? Was this where Eiffel got his first idea for the structure which, at the end of the nineteenth century, would be identified more than any other with modernity? Tantalizing, and impossible to know.

The Four Rivers was by far the most elaborate, ambitious and delightful fountain Bernini contributed to Rome, but of course it was not the only one. His earliest was possibly the 'ship' or barcaccia in Piazza di Spagna. It may have been designed by his father Pietro, who was the official architect of the Acqua Vergine, the aqueduct through which its water came; but the son seems to be the more likely author. Created in 1627–9, it takes the low water pressure in that area and turns it to advantage: the motif is a marble ship half-sunk in a pool, dribbling rather than exuberantly spouting water from its gun ports. It may be that it has a political reference, since the patron who commissioned it was Urban VIII, who at the time was conspiring with France and Spain to launch a seaborne invasion of Protestant Britain. With consummate hypocrisy, Urban penned a distich which was engraved on the fountain and in translation reads: 'The ship of the Church does not pour forth fire, but sweet water, by which the flames of war are extinguished.'

Bernini had a hand in the original design of the Trevi Fountain, but it was not started by him and it fell to Nicola Salvi (1697–1751) to build and finish it in the mid-eighteenth century. The commissioning pope was Clement XII Corsini (reg. 1730–40). The fountain occupies one whole flank of Palazzo Poli. It is huge – 20 metres wide and 26 high. Its central figure, by Pietro Bracci, represents the sea-god Neptune, riding on an enormous shell drawn by sea-horses and guided by two Tritons. These in turn are flanked by allegorical figures of Abundance and Healthfulness, in praise of the benefits of papal government. It owes at least some of its popularity not so much to its grandiose and congested design as to that hardy perennial of 1950s sentiment, the movie *Three Coins in the Fountain* – that, plus the iconic sight of the young blonde bombshell Anita Ekberg wading stalwartly in it in Fellini's *La Dolce Vita*. There is an urban myth which says that if you stand with your back to the fountain and toss a coin over your shoulder into the pool, your return to Rome will be guaranteed. The other, and perhaps more attractive, legend of the fountain holds that if a lover drinks a cup of its water in the presence of his beloved, he will never be able to get her out of his heart. Presumably this story is connected to the source of the fountain's water, which used to be known as the Acqua Vergine because its upwelling, some miles away, was pointed out to ancient Roman water-seekers by a young girl.

The Bernini fountain that remains an outstanding favourite of the Romans themselves is the Triton Fountain in Piazza Barberini (1642–3), outside the Barberini Palace, itself partially the work of Bernini. If the Trevi Fountain is the most grandiose in Rome, the Triton Fountain is surely the most graceful and, if one may use the term, the most epigrammatic. In the middle of a geometric pool, four head-down dolphins bear up, on their tails, a gigantic scallop shell which has opened its ribbed halves, like a book, to reveal a Triton blowing his conch. The 'music' one expects to come from a conch is a vertical blast of water, glittering in the Roman sunlight. It is a fabulous *concetto*, scarcely diminished even by the parked cars that cluster around it, the *avvocato* Agnelli's hogs at a trough.

Italy was the only country in which Bernini's genius was able to spread its wings. The French monarch, Louis XIV, had him invited to Paris, and (cautioning His Majesty not to speak to him about small projects) the sixty-six-year-old culture hero actually made the long and arduous trip to discuss a possible rebuilding of the royal palace of the Louvre. Nothing came of this except some drawings and a magnificent, complex marble portrait bust of Le Roi Soleil, which survives and remains in France. Otherwise, it was an unproductive trip – though Bernini took a sardonic pleasure in seeing people flock to view him as though he was a travelling elephant.

The visit also gave rise to a tremendous display of the old maestro's bad temper, when he heard the architect Claude Perrault, Bernini's eventual successor as *architecte du roi*, commenting to Chantelou on a possible flaw in Bernini's design for pavilions. The two men were speaking French, of which Bernini hardly spoke a word. Nevertheless he thought he understood, and flew into a towering rage.

He wanted Perrault to know, Bernini said, that in the matter of design Perrault was not worthy to clean the soles of his shoes. That his work had pleased the king, who would be hearing about the insult personally. 'That a man of my sort,' he fumed on, 'I, whom the Pope treats with consideration and for whom he has respect, that I should be treated thus! I will complain of it to the King. I shall leave tomorrow. I do not know why I should not take a hammer to the bust after such an insult. I am going to see the Nuncio.' Eventually the great man consented to be soothed with apologies, and he never listened to a French official again. The point was taken. He retired, victorious, to Rome.

The size of Bernini's huge output in Rome defies short summary, and so does its 'mood', if that is the word. Bernini could be very funny in his unofficial work, as in his pen-and-ink caricatures of Vatican notables, which were not made for public display. The much-loved elephant of Piazza Minerva, bearing an obelisk on its back, shows his humorous fantasy at full stretch. In the seventeenth century an elephant, in Italy, was a veritable apparition, a rarity seldom seen. The very name of the animal was a synonym for the bizarre, the unexpected and (sometimes) the menacing – hadn't Hannibal used the great beasts to crush the Roman armies at Cannae?

But apart from three other churches,* the stairways, fountains, portrait busts, chapels, palaces and tombs, Gianlorenzo Bernini's enormous reshaping of Rome centres on the greatest basilica in Christianity, St Peter's. You cannot imagine this complex without Bernini and his powers, not only of architecture, but of stagecraft – not that the two are readily distinguished. Bernini was responsible not only for much of the church and its contents but for its link to the Vatican palaces, in the form of the so-called Scala Regia (1663–6). Before he installed this staircase, the passage between church and palace had to be negotiated by a flight of cramped steps up and down which the pope was carried, at some risk, on a litter. Bernini had this steep and undignified incline demolished and replaced it with a new stair, which had a break near the bottom. This point, at which one turned through ninety degrees left to ascend the last and longest run of stairs, he marked with a huge sculpture of the emperor Constantine on his rearing war-horse, stricken with his vision of the Cross – 'Conquer, in this sign', promising victory over Maxentius at the Milvian Bridge.

But now he had to resort to a perspective trick. The walls of the basilica and the palace were not parallel. They converged towards the top of the stairs. Bernini therefore introduced, on either side of the stairs, a run of columns which create a diminishing tunnel-vault, getting smaller as your gaze travels up, giving the impression that the walls do not converge.

Of all the Berninian features of St Peter's – the altar that carries the *cathedra Petri* or apostolic throne, the *baldacchino*, the numerous papal tombs and figures of saints, the nave decorations, the

* All belonging to the period of Alexander VII's pontificate: Sant'Andrea al Quirinale (1658–70), San Tommaso Villanova at Castel Gandolfo (1658–61) and the Chigi Church of the Assumption at Ariccia (1662–64).

twin fountains on either side of the central obelisk* – the one that absolutely typifies Baroque grandeur, that 'stands for' the size and inclusiveness of the seventeenth-century Church, is of course its piazza. St Peter's Square, which is not a square but a colossal oval colonnade, 'pulled apart' in the middle, has been known to hold tens of thousands of people who flock there to receive the papal blessing and is justly regarded, even by some Protestants, as the very epicentre of Christianity – a pair of immense arms, Bernini himself said, reaching out from the façade in a gesture of embrace to the world.

It is the greatest anthropomorphic gesture in the history of architecture.

It is also the stripped-down essence of Baroque, for it carries little of the elaborate detail and décor usually associated with Baroque design. Its columns – 284 of them, in four rows – are austerely Tuscan, not the more florid Corinthian one might expect from Baroque. Its frieze is unbroken Ionic, without sculptural ornament, though there are some three hundred sculptures – more than a lifetime's work, one might have thought, even for Bernini's corps of assistants – along the edge of the roof. But in the vast spaces and distances of the piazza, these cause no visual congestion. Some critics have said, truthfully enough, that the piazza pays no compliment to the enormous façade of the basilica, by Carlo Maderno, that closes it off. The front of St Peter's is too wide – some 115 metres – for its height. The loss of Bernini's bell-towers caused this disproportion. It is a flaw, admittedly, but a small one in the context of a scheme so gigantic both spatially and conceptually.

Bernini's rival architect in the formation of the Baroque style in Rome, his prodigious contemporary Borromini, did not build as much as Bernini, and he was not a sculptor; but his relatively small output of buildings is so concentrated, so inventive, as to set him alongside Bernini as one of the heroic figures in architectural

---

* One designed by Carlo Maderno; the other, its twin, by Bernini.

history. Moreover, it should be recalled that Bernini was not an architect to begin with, and much of what he learned about the design of buildings was acquired, usually without acknowledgement, from Borromini. It would be hard to find two architects of comparable talent who were, psychologically and temperamentally, less like one another. Borromini's life ended in a way utterly unlike the sense of fulfilment conveyed by Bernini's death; at the age of sixty-eight, harried by jealousy and an irascible sense of failure, he wrote out his will by candlelight and then gave himself what he hoped to be a truly Roman exit, falling on his sword. Botched and painful, it was neither a quick nor an easy death, just a tragic one.

That he was a misfit genius of the first order cannot be doubted. Melancholic by nature, he went to extremes in admiring Michelangelo's penchant for solitude and for *terribilità*. In a Rome where sexual morality among men was notoriously lax, he had a reputation for strict and extreme chastity, focusing only on his work and never indulging in stray affairs. He made a point of always dressing in funereal black, Hamlet-like, in the Spanish way. In another architect, this might have been a sign of dandyism; one may be fairly sure that with Borromini it was not. It was more like penance, or perhaps indifference to fashion in an intensely fashion-conscious cultural capital. Borromini was never popular with everyone in his own lifetime. His contemporary, Giovanni Baglione, a priggish but influential figure, denounced him as 'a most ignorant Goth and corrupter of architecture, and the infamy of our century'.

The innovations of detail and planning he wrought into his buildings were paralleled in the way he presented their designs to clients. Thus Borromini was the first architect to use the graphite pencil rather than ink-and-wash in his presentation drawings. Moreover he seems to have regarded these drawings as ends in themselves, finished works of art, rather than merely indications of what the structures and finishes would be. He liked to call his drawings his 'children' and often refused to be parted from them by sending them to competitions – 'sent begging into the world' was his phrase for this.

Borromini's origins were humble. He was the son of a builder, born in Bissone on Lake Lugano. The apprenticeship of a manual worker started early, and when he was only nine years old his father dispatched him to Milan to learn the basics of stone-cutting on the decorative details of the city's cathedral, then under construction. He was a thoroughly skilled *scarpellino* or stoneworker when, in 1619, he moved to Rome and found work on the construction site of St Peter's, to whose official architect, Carlo Maderno, he was (very distantly) related. At first he carved decorative details; then Maderno and others saw that he had talent and facility as a draughtsman.

He was developing a very wide knowledge, probably wider than any of his generation including Bernini's, of the history of architecture, both ancient and modern. He absorbed and venerated old Roman building, but also studied sixteenth-century masters from Bramante and Raphael through to Palladio and Vignola – and, especially, Michelangelo, whom he called 'Prince of Architects' and revered almost as a god.

This made him extremely valuable to the better-connected but perhaps somewhat less studious Bernini who, only a year older than Borromini, was engaged in the first big project of his fast-track career, the *baldacchino* for St Peter's. At that early stage, Bernini had no architectural experience, and he had to rely on Borromini, whom he hired to do all the working drawings for the baldachin, along with the designs for some of its details, such as the bronze vine leaves and the four marble column bases with their complex Barberini shields and heraldic bees. It is likely, too, but undocumented, that Borromini also designed the baldachin's dynamic top, the four bronze volutes that so successfully replaced Bernini's original idea of semicircular ribs. If so, this could have been the seed of the painfully frustrating rivalry that Borromini felt towards Bernini for the rest of his life: the volutes are a much admired stroke of architectural genius for which he got no credit.

Borromini's relations with Carlo Maderno, however, remained good, and they led to his work on Palazzo Barberini (1628–32), one of the archetypes of the grand Roman Baroque palace. Maderno also hired Pietro da Cortona and Bernini as co-designers, and the questions of who designed what and when are too complicated and uncertain to easily or briefly resolve. Maderno died in 1629, leaving the job to the three younger architects – a troika which seems to have been plagued by disagreements, hardly a surprise given how strong-willed each member was. Before long, Borromini left.

His first solo, independent commission came in his mid-thirties, in 1634, through the good offices of Cardinal Francesco Barberini. This was a monastery and church for the Discalced (or Barefoot) Trinitarians, an offshoot of the well-established Trinitarian Order, which had originally been formed in 1198 with the object of rescuing Christian captives from the Muslim 'infidels'. The Barefoot Trinitarians tried to set an example of reform through austerity – one might almost say that they stood in the same quasi-fanatical relation to the original order as Borromini did to Bernini. They had little money and few means of raising it. But their superior, Padre Giovanni della Annunziazione, became confessor to Barberini, who happened to be very rich. This was just as well, since the austere Discalced Trinitarians badly needed funds and a strong contact with the papal court. The friars had been horrified when Borromini presented them with his first drawings for the church and monastery that became S. Carlo alle Quattro Fontane, and they complained that they had wanted something that cost about a fifth as much. Eventually a compromise was reached, brokered by Cardinal Barberini, who presumably gave money to its construction – though it is not known how much.

What they got in return was one of the most radical and daring small buildings of the Roman Baroque. Despite the shortage of funds Borromini was able to develop and keep the three key elements of his project: the plan, the dome, the façade.

The plan became almost immediately famous, and

architectural visitors to Rome kept begging for copies of it (which they did not get, because Borromini did not trust them). It had begun as a central-dome church with four crossing piers. Because the site was long and narrow, this configuration was squeezed and the circular dome became an oval. This produced the further sensation that the walls were going in and out, 'breathing', almost like a live creature with lungs.

The dome is coffered. Its interior is very deeply shaped, the pattern produced by a series of interlocking hexagons and crosses that seem to recede from your eye as your gaze travels towards the centre of the dome, which is marked by an emblematic triangle representing the Trinity after whom the order is named – Father, Son and Holy Spirit. This is an optical illusion: the geometrical figures are getting smaller but the dome is not getting deeper. Nevertheless the spatial effect is very powerful. Borromini delighted in such tricks of false perspective: there is another, smaller one in Palazzo Spada, the palace in Piazza Capodiferro near Palazzo Farnese which he redesigned for Cardinal Bernardino Spada in 1652, consisting of an illusory Doric colonnade which, because of the sharply decreasing size of its framing pillars and the slant of its floor, seems to be twenty metres long though its actual length is only 8.6. This 'Prospettiva', as it was known, was (and is) one of the most charming minor sights of Rome. But when you catch sight of it and see how it works it is immediately readable as a trick, and it may have had a deliberate allegorical meaning: just as its size is an illusion, so too is worldly grandeur. No such ironic meaning attaches to the dome of S. Carlo alle Quattro Fontane.

Then there is the façade. Borromini is said to have talked wistfully about creating a façade from a single moulded sheet of terracotta, and the front of S. Carlo suggests this unachieved idea. It ripples and bulges, in – out, in – out. Actually not all of it is by Borromini. The lower half was done before he died, in 1667; the upper, posthumously, by followers of Bernini, whose ideas are somewhat passively applied in the oval medallion supported by angels above the entablature. What Borromini himself might have done with this upper façade, had he lived, is anyone's guess.

Fortunately for the modern visitor, though, he was able to complete the cupola of the church which is generally regarded as his masterpiece, Sant'Ivo alla Sapienza (1642–60), the chapel of the University of Rome. This quite small building, whose walls appear when one first sees them to be almost fluid, in continuous motion, is one of the most inventive in Italy – or in the world. It is a marvel of space-shaping, based on a hexagonal plan with sharp cut-outs and lobes, that form a steep tent from which light pours into the nave below. In the words of the architectural historian Rudolf Wittkower, 'Geometrical succinctness, and inexhaustible imagination, technical skill and religious symbolism, have rarely found such a reconciliation.' The geometry, imagination and skill are self-evident; the religious symbolism of Borromini's *concetto* is perhaps less so. It may be that the geometry of the plan refers to the Star of Solomon, the king whose proverbial wisdom chimes with the idea of the building as the church of *sapienza* (wisdom). The most striking feature of the church is its lantern, whose top Borromini designed as a spiral that corkscrews into three full turns anticlockwise – a wonderfully dramatic climax to the building, flame-like and aerial. Various interpretations of its symbolism have been made, none of them entirely convincing; but as an expression of sheer architectural brio, there is nothing else quite like it in Rome.

An age of great and mobilized spiritual awakening stands a good chance of producing strong and effective religious art, impelled by remarkable personalities – remarkable not so much for their piety, but for their intelligence and militancy. So it was with Baroque Rome; the energy of its art and architecture was equalled by that of its outward thrust in conversion and theology. The Protestant Reformation awoke the Roman Church and gave it a new, fiery *raison d'être*.

The most powerful force in the Roman Catholic recovery, the essential militant group produced by the Church in its fight against the Lutheran heresy, was the Society of Jesus – otherwise known as the Jesuits. This order of secular priests grew from a tiny nucleus – at first, two Basques, later to be canonized as St Francis Xavier and St Ignatius Loyola. Both were missionaries, one inside Europe, the other in the Far East. The one who took Europe as his field was the founder of the Society, Ignatius Loyola. The nature of the Jesuits cannot be grasped without their shared conception of discipline, and that discipline depended on the military background of their founder, Ignatius, the thirteenth and last child of the lord of Onaz and Loyola, in the Basque province of Guipúzcoa.

Loyola's family was military, both in origins and in practice. They were border chieftains, tough, violent, merciless to their enemies, endowed with an iron loyalty to their friends and allies. Two of Ignatius' brothers were killed fighting for Spain against Italy, one in the *conquista* of America. The young Loyolas of Ignatius' generation were obsessed with the projects of conquering the New World for Christ and, in the Old World, of driving the *Moros*, the occupying Arabs, from Spain and restoring the primacy of the Christian faith to the peninsula. They were enthusiasts or, not to mince words, fanatics who completely shared the belief that religious and national feeling were, and ought to be, the same. In their eyes there was little difference between the messages of early chivalric novels like *Amadis of Gaul* (the first book of knight-errantry printed in Spain) and the worship of the Virgin Mary. The corollary of this assurance, the certainty that Spain's supreme projects were the expulsion of the Jews followed by the eradication of the Moors, was a fanatical belief in the sword of the conquistador. This belief lent a nobility to the profession of arms that is difficult to appreciate and impossible to share in another culture four centuries later.

Ignatius of Loyola felt it to the extreme. Almost from childhood he saw himself as a soldier. He was never to write a memoir of his life but his 'Confessions', dictated after 1553, ignored his youthful years, merely saying that 'Up to twenty-six years of age, he was a man given to the vanities of the world and his chief delight was in martial exercises with a great and vain desire to gain honour.'

What he gained was not just honour, but disaster and an atrocious degree of suffering that changed his life. In 1521 the Duke of Nájera, viceroy of Navarre, was embroiled in a war of secession against the French, who had territorial claims on that part of Basque Spain. Ignatius went to fight for him but a French cannonball smashed both his legs – the right femur almost irreparably. Taking chivalrous pity on him, the French shipped him on a litter back to his native ground in Azpeitia, fifty miles away, where a long and grindingly difficult convalescence began. At first there seemed to be only two prospects for Ignatius: to die in agony from infection, or to survive as a helpless cripple. But he was a singularly tough and determined man, not to say a lucky one. When it became apparent that his injuries, if allowed to heal 'naturally', would leave him crippled for life, Ignatius submitted to having his leg broken and reset again. This butchery took place at the family home in Azpeitia, and was followed by equally horrendous sessions in which the newly fractured leg was stretched – at Ignatius' own insistence – in an improvised rack, so that both limbs would set to more or less equal lengths. How could he have endured it? One would need to be another Ignatius to know.

Without anaesthetics, antibiotics or any of the drugs modern medicine takes for granted, the sixteenth century was an age of almost insuperable pain. Not only that, but Ignatius had to endure the knowledge that the active life of a knight-errant was now closed to him. A lesser man's resolution might well have buckled under the stress of such disappointment, but nothing could dissuade the crippled cavalier from his ambition to make a pilgrimage to Jerusalem. Before that could be done, Ignatius' soul must be cleansed, and he set out to achieve this by going first to the ancient pilgrimage centre of Montserrat in Catalunya, home of the cult effigy of the Black Virgin, at whose altar he left his arms and armour, and thence to Manresa, the backwater village where he spent a year in fasting, prayer and deprivation.

Ignatius' self-mortification was not as extreme as the punishments inflicted on themselves by certain medieval mystics, such as Henry Suso, who recounted (in the third person, as was customary) how '[he] secretly caused an undergarment to be made for him; and in the undergarment he had strips of leather fixed, into which a hundred and fifty brass nails, pointed and filed sharp, were driven and pointed always inward to his flesh. He had this garment made very tight and so arranged as to go round him and fasten in the front, so that it might fit the closer to his body . . .'

Ignatius did not need to go to such masochistic extremes because his doctors, such as they were, did that for him. Nevertheless he cut a very strange figure in Montserrat and Manresa. He threw away his clothes and donned prickly sackcloth. He grew his hair into a long, matted thatch; his fingernails turned into an animal's claws; he begged, stank, starved himself and kept strange hours at night. He spoke of his desire 'to escape all public notice', but he was becoming one of the grotesques of the street. Gradually these hippie-like eccentricities abated, leaving behind a residue of strict self-denial in which there was no room for frailties and eccentric behaviour. Ignatius had little in common with such saints as Francis of Assisi, who shrank from cleaning his sheepskin out of tender pity for Brother Louse, or the obese theologian St Thomas Aquinas, who endearingly had a piece sawn from his dining-table to make room for his Falstaffian belly. His mind was fixed on missionary work, and this entailed different disciplines from those of the contemplative orders – especially, learning about the languages and customs of the very foreign cultures in which he and his fellow priests would be working.

The product of the soldier-saint's hard time in the outer desert was a small but immensely influential book, the *Spiritual Exercises* (published in 1548). This was the manual for all those who wished to take the road of submission to Ignatian rule, a discipline that few at first could contemplate adopting but that later became the essence of Catholic revival and recruitment. Of all the Spanish Catholic texts that sought to open a passage away from the world and to prepare the soul for its encounter with God, this was by far the best-known and most influential. Its strength lay in its relentless single-mindedness. 'Carefully excite in yourself an habitual affectionate will in all things to imitate Jesus Christ,' Ignatius wrote:

> If anything agreeable offers itself to your senses, yet does not at the same time tend purely to the honour and glory of God, renounce it and separate yourself from it for the love of Christ ... The radical remedy lies in the mortification of the four great natural passions, joy, hope, fear and grief. You must seek to deprive these of every satisfaction and leave them, as it were, in darkness and the void.

Ignatius' *Exercises* were a long and precisely divided feat of the imagination. First, the soul must be driven into repentance by the fear of Hell. This must go on for a week, at whose end the now terrified and malleable soul will be ready to receive enlightenment. Progressive stages follow, and their sequence amounted to an intense form of self-therapy, which would remain central to Jesuit practice for centuries to come. To see its effect on the humbled, sensitive and impressionable young mind, one need only read the description of the 'retreat' suffered and finally embraced by the Jesuit student Stephen Daedalus in Joyce's *Portrait of the Artist*. Once an initiate had undergone this, there would be no turning back. Here is Ignatius' description of the meditation on Hell, the fifth exercise of the first week:

> The first point will be to see with the eye of the imagination those great fires, and the souls as it were in bodies of fire.
>
> The second to hear with the ears lamentations, howlings, cries, blasphemies against Christ our Lord and against the Saints.
>
> The third, with the sense of smell, to smell smoke, brimstone, refuse and rottenness.
>
> The fourth, to taste with the taste bitter things, such as tears, sadness and the worm of conscience.

The fifth, to feel with the sense of touch how these fires
do touch and burn souls.

Each sense is mobilized, one by one. In this way, Ignatius
insisted, the utmost concreteness of feeling would be given to
spiritual experience. There would be nothing abstract or hypo-
thetical about it. Part of the discipline was learning to defy the
evidence of one's own senses, should obedience make that necessary. Then gradually, step by step, the novice is moved through
repentance to hope, and from hope to desire of the joys of heaven
and of union there with God: but each of these stages must be
fully visualized, imagined in completeness. The *Exercises*, as one
priest-psychologist put it, created a 'regressive crisis, with its con-
comitant dissolution of psychic structures and the weakening of
repressive barriers', whose product was 'a new identity'.

The whole process, from entry to the final emergence as a
future Jesuit priest, took some twelve years – and in addition to
the usual priestly vows of poverty, chastity and obedience, the
Jesuit had to take further vows of obedience to his superiors in
the Papacy, making it incumbent on him to go and work at the
task of evangelical conversion anywhere in the world, if the pope
so wished. It was a somewhat frightening responsibility, because
in the sixteenth and seventeenth centuries the world was a huge,
hostile and little-known place and the small corps of Jesuits was
spread thinly in it. But it grew slowly and steadily. At Ignatius'
death in 1556 there were 958 members of the order; seventy years
later, some 15,000; by 1749, 22,500. It was an order highly conscious
of its elitism, both intellectual and in terms of class. Other orders
of priests could, and did, focus on recruiting the poor. But there
is little doubt that, just as the intellectual elitism of the Jesuit
missionaries underwrote their enormous success in the highly
class-conscious society of eighteenth-century China, so their stoicism and military toughness enabled them to withstand and
survive the terrible sufferings visited on them by the savage tribes
of North America. They were the commandos of the Church
Militant.

The order won official recognition from Pope Paul III in 1540. Once papal approval was secured, the Society of Jesus had to have a home church in Rome, and it had to be splendid, which meant money. Fortunately for the Jesuits the man who volunteered the cash was Cardinal Alessandro Farnese, who became Pope Paul III and during the fifteen years of his pontificate (1534–49) showered money on his own family and its projects. He also did great things for the city itself: he spent huge sums on repairing the damage inflicted on Rome by the disastrous 1527 sack of the city, directed the creation of Piazza del Campidoglio, and instructed Michelangelo to move the ancient bronze rider statue of Marcus Aurelius there, thus instigating the most spectacular and influential urban scheme of the sixteenth century. But there is little doubt that the long-term effect on the Church of his recognition of the Jesuit Order at least equalled his urbanistic projects in importance. The Jesuits already favoured their own architect, the otherwise unremarkable Giovanni Tristano (d. 1575), who had designed their college in Rome in 1560. But for the mother church something much grander in spirit was called for, and the chosen designer was a favourite of Cardinal Farnese's, Giacomo Barozzi da Vignola (1507–73), who had entered papal service in the 1550s, designing a stream of projects for Rome and the Papal States. The greatest of these was the Villa Farnese at Caprarola (1559–73), which began as a five-sided stronghold but morphed into a grandiose country house, a hill town in its own right with magnificent approach ramps. There were smaller secular buildings, some of them masterpieces, such as the twin-pavilioned Villa Lante at Bagnaia.

But his most important church, paid for by Alessandro Farnese, was done for the Jesuits: Il Gesù ('The Church of Jesus', 1568–75), which (as the evangelical order of the Ignatians spread) provided a model for numerous – though usually more modest – Jesuit structures throughout the world. It was also the first church to take the name of Jesus himself.

The main requirement of Jesuit churches, faithfully carried out by Vignola and every designer after him, was that the ceremony of the Mass should be plainly seen and that the priest's sermon,

carrying the evangelical word of the Church into battle against
the claims of Reformation heresy, should be distinctly heard,
everywhere in each building. This had not been easy, or even
possible, in older church layouts. The work of the Jesuits centred
on preaching. So the Gesù had to have a large nave to fit in as
many celebrants as possible, with unimpeded views of the main
altar, and clear lines of sight and hearing to the main and side
pulpits. It would not need crossing spaces – shallow side-chapels
would be better than transepts. The Gesù's nave is some 75 metres
long and it has three main chapels: on the right, that of St Francis
Xavier, a memorial to Ignatius' missionary partner, who carried
the Catholic message to the Far East and was the means by which
Catholic doctrine and theology entered China, where he died in
1552; at the apse end, that of S. Robert Bellarmine, the great
Counter-Reformation theologian who died in 1621; and on the
left, indispensably, the chapel of St Ignatius himself, built to the
designs of the Jesuit artist Andrea Pozzo and containing a bronze
urn which holds Ignatius' remains. If one thinks of the soldier-
saint as a puritanical opponent of lavishness, which he certainly
was when alive, it is a good idea to see what became of him in
death: this is one of the most costly and extravagant tombs in all
Rome. Its columns are entirely sheathed in blue lapis lazuli, and
a globe of this rare and semi-precious stone, the largest in the
world, 'blue as a vein on the Madonna's breast' in Robert Brown-
ing's words, surmounts the whole confection. It was for this
reason that the Grand Duke of Tuscany suggested that the Jesuits'
motto, whose initials are IHS, ought to be rendered *Iesuiti Habent
Satis*, 'The Jesuits have got enough'.* One vividly realizes what
Goethe meant when he wrote (in Regensburg in 1786, on his way
to Rome) that

> I keep thinking about the character and the activities of the
> Jesuits. The grandeur and perfect design of their churches

---

* It is actually an abbreviation of the Greek form of the name of Jesus.

... command universal awe and admiration. For ornament, they used gold, silver and jewels in profusion to dazzle beggars of all ranks, with, now and then, a touch of vulgarity to attract the masses. Roman Catholicism has always shown this genius, but I have never seen it done with such intelligence, skill and consistency as by the Jesuits. Unlike the other religious orders, they broke away from the old conventions of worship and, in compliance with the spirit of the times, refreshed it with pomp and splendour.

Across the ceiling vault of the Gesù spreads the overwhelming rhetorical utterance of Giovanni Battista Gaulli's *Triumph of the Name of Jesus* (1678-9). Gaulli was born in Genoa but he came to Rome early, before 1658, and worked there for the rest of his life, very much under the spell of Bernini, who connected him to influential patrons like the Pamphili. His *Triumph* reminds one how fatuous the Victorian and modernist objections to Baroque art as 'too theatrical' are. One might as well decry theatre itself as 'too theatrical'. Theatre, on this roof, is of the very essence: emotion and seduction on the grandest scale, achieved through a billowing range of bodily contortion, facial expression and gesture.

The ceiling falls into three zones, distinguishable but not sharply divided. At the centre, the glowing apex, divine light streams from Christ's monogram, the IHS. Around it is a mass of clouds upholding the heavenly blessed, the Communion of Saints, drawn in towards it like filings to a magnet. Some of them are allowed to spill over, across the painted architectural frame, into 'our' space. Then, at the bottom of this enormous cartouche, we see the damned and disgraced falling in a torrent out of the sanctifying presence of Christ's name. As befits their earthly status, these are the most solid bodies of all, not transfigured by light like the saints, but writhing, toppling and (in some cases) clutching the emblems of their sins – Vanity has a peacock, the head of Heresy teems, like Medusa's, with snakes.

The Baroque ceiling painting that rivals Gaulli's masterpiece is also in Rome, and it too was dedicated to the founder of the Jesuits. It is by Andrea Pozzo, in the Church of S. Ignazio. Its theme is *The Glory of St Ignatius Loyola and the Missionary Work of the Jesuit Order* (1688–94). It represents Ignatius entering Paradise. This enormous fresco in the nave vault, spilling over tracts of fictional architecture which in turn can hardly be told from the real architecture of the church, joins with Gaulli's work to sum up the rhetorical grandeur of painted Baroque illusion. Once standing on the right 'viewing spot' (considerately marked by a metal disc in the floor) and looking up at the perspective convergence of the ceiling, it is only with difficulty that one can tell where the walls of the nave end and the ceiling begins. The barriers between illusion and reality are down and it takes a strenuous effort of the will and imagination to raise them again. It was important to have no visible break between what was happening in the sky and on earth: a seamless transition between the two meant a continuity which was both a promise of transcendence and a threat of failure. The walls seem to stretch up so far that they become misty in the open sky; the space between them is filled with a whirling gyre of figures, enacting a sort of spiritually drunken ecstasy. In these ceilings, Bernini's sculptural achievements in the Cornaro Chapel are equalled in the art of painting. Pozzo would go on to do other schemes for Jesuit churches, in Trento and Montepulciano and even as far afield as Vienna, but Rome remained his base and none of his later works surpass his frescoes there. Between them, Pozzo and Gaulli represent the furthest stretch of the art of Baroque mural painting in Rome. But when the great age of foreign cultural tourism opened in Rome after 1700, this was not what the *milordi inglesi*, the French connoisseurs or the Russian princes were going there to study and appreciate. They were in full pursuit of the Antique, and of the seemingly lost authority of ancient Rome.

9

THE EIGHTEENTH CENTURY: NEO-CLASSICISM AND THE GRAND TOUR

The modern traveller, gazing through his little porthole at the procession of the Alps below, glancing irritably at his wristwatch to see whether his flight is going to be thirty or forty minutes late into Fiumicino, can have no idea of what the trip from London to Rome in the late eighteenth century – that heyday of the Grand Tour – once meant.

It was trying, dangerous at times, protracted and above all unpredictable. All travel was for the rich. There was no such thing as 'mass tourism', for the simple reason that the masses had not yet learned to move, to go abroad for holidays or education, or even to imagine visiting Europe. The idea of 'going abroad' for relaxation was not yet invented. Abroad was bloody and foreigners were bastards. In 1780 most English people lived within a social radius of fifteen or twenty miles from their birthplaces, and the English Channel was a barrier to further exploration. The English-man in the English street did not think of going to France; the French, most of the time, were despicable enemies and would remain so for decades yet. Spain was simply not to be imagined – a country of misery, with a language none could speak, bravos who would slit your belly as soon as look at you, and oily, filthy food that none could digest. A pretty fair summation of English attitudes to the European foreigner was given by Thomas Nashe in *The Unfortunate Traveller* (1593), that masterpiece of abusive, inventive xenophobia:

> Italy, the paradise of the earth, and the epicure's heaven, how doth it form our young master? It makes him to kiss his hand like an ape, cringe his neck like a starveling, and play at hey-

pass, re-pass, come aloft, when he salutes a man. From thence
he brings the art of Atheism, the art of epicurising, the art of
whoring, the art of poisoning, the art of Sodomitry ... The
better sort of men, when they would set a singular mask or
brand on a notorious villain, do say that *he hath been in
Italy*.

Still, Italian tourism by England's rich and notable was not, strictly
speaking, an invention of the period in which it first flourished,
the eighteenth century. Sir Thomas Hoby (1530–66), for instance,
intrepidly made an Italian tour in his late twenties, when he was
young, rich and vigorous enough to defy the swarm of Italian
crooks, footpads, delators and Church spies that beset him.

But in those early years, English travellers in Italy tended not to
be welcome, especially outside the great centres of sophistication,
because they were assumed (correctly, as a rule) to be heretical
Protestants. The Italians they were likely to deal with abhorred
the Reformation; they themselves, with every parallel reason,
feared the Inquisition and its arbitrary power to throw strangers
into dungeons without *habeas corpus*. To go there at all in Elizabethan or early Jacobean times, one needed a travel pass from
the English Privy Council, and these were not lightly given out.
Generally English travel was confined to north Italy: Venice,
Padua (whose university accepted foreign Protestant students, as
no other academic institution in Italy would) and Vicenza. Rome,
being the capital of the Papal States, was much more difficult;
a prolonged stay there was always expensive and fraught with
administrative obstacles. And forget about Naples, that enormous
den of thieves and religious fanatics. All in all, one needed to be
rich or very determined, preferably both, to confront the difficulties of Italian tourism, and the awareness of this took centuries
to fade, even though it lost its primal Elizabethan virulence.

Someone who signed himself 'Leonardo', one of a group of
English poetasters called the 'Della Cruscans', issued a warning
against Italy in the late eighteenth century, when the Grand Tour
had become an institution. For the peninsula offered an even

worse threat to moral rectitude than it did to physical safety, no matter what its cultural benefits might be:

> But most avoid Italia's coast,
> Where ev'ry sentiment is lost,
> And Treach'ry reigns, and base Disguise,
> And Murder – looking to the skies,
> While sordid Selfishness appears
> In low redundancy of fears.
> O what can Music's voice bestow,
> Or sculptur'd grace, or Titian glow,
> To recompense the feeling mind
> For BRITISH virtues left behind?

Such people feared that not all the art on the Continent, no matter how good it was, could make up for Italy's contagious lack of moral fibre and common decency. Fortunately, most of those who could afford the trip ignored these late Puritan misgivings, and went anyway. You didn't have to be all that interested in art, either. So it was with the biographer of Samuel Johnson, James Boswell, for whom Italy was mainly a field for sexual tourism, like Thailand today. Boswell was quite undeterred by the pox, although, as one travel book remarked, 'A great many of our gentlemen travellers have reason enough to be cross on account of some modish distemper the Italian ladies may have bestowed upon them with the rest of their favours.' 'My desire to know the world,' Boswell confided to his journal, 'made me resolve to intrigue a little while in Italy, where the women are so debauched that they are hardly to be considered as moral agents, but as inferior beings.'

But to know that world – that was the problem. It is hard today even to imagine the difficulty of access that Italy presented in the eighteenth century. There were two ways of getting to it: by sea, and across the Alps. Both took weeks which (depending on the weather) could lengthen into months, especially with stops to examine works of art. The sea route entailed an overland crossing

through France to the Mediterranean, then a coast-hugging progress to the Franco-Italian border, and then a slow descent south
through Genoa, Lerici, and thus to the campagna and to Rome.
John Mitford (1748–1830), later Baron Redesdale, described part of
the sea passage he made in 1776:

> From Genoa the Lerici travellers usually pass in a felucca to
> avoid the fatigue of a mountain journey along roads where
> only mules can keep their feet. These Mediterranean vessels
> are not formed for bad weather and they are manned by no
> very skilful mariners. Scarcely ever an oar's length from the
> shore they creep under the rocks, and trembling at every
> wind are always afraid to hoist a sail. If the wind is very fair,
> eight hours will carry the felucca from Genoa to Lerici. But
> if the wind is the least contrary, or if it is so slight that these
> timorous seamen do not trust a sail, twenty hours' rowing
> will hardly suffice.

If the sea tourist suffered boredom, discomfort and seasickness,
the land traveller might have worse problems, for he had as a rule
to negotiate the Alpine pass of Mont Cenis. This was so steep and
tortuous, and the road surface so blocked with ice and snow, that
no horses could drag the coach over the pass. The vehicle then
had to be dismantled at the foot of the incline, and the horses sent
on, unencumbered. The wheels, axles and all components of the
coach, along with the tourists' luggage, would then be loaded on
to mules and sent ahead. At the Italian side of the pass, on the flat,
where it was safe to do so, the coach was reassembled and the
portmanteaux, crates and everything else reloaded. And what of
the passengers, who had been carried up the steep slope in chairs
on poles? Thomas Pelham, in 1777, reported (a little surprisingly)
that 'As to our own person there is neither danger nor inconvenience: it was so hard a frost that when we came to the top of
the mountains we left our chairs and descended in sledges, which
though very trying to the nerves was not unpleasant. It was the
clearest day imaginable and the view beyond description.'

The delays must have been irksome, and there were occasional sorrows: Tory, Horace Walpole's pet spaniel, was eaten alive by a wolf on his Alpine crossing. Surely not all tourists who attempted the Mont Cenis pass can have had the phlegm or adventurousness of a Pelham; but it was too late to retreat, Italy beckoned, and this was the only way to the land where lemon trees bloomed.

'I have not read the Roman classics with so little feeling,' declared the 8th Duke of Hamilton, 'as not to wish to view the country which they describe and where they were written.' This was at least part of the essential motive with which the Grand Tourist, recipient of a classical education, set out. Would the trip make it all worthwhile – the rigours of life at an English public school, the flogging, the fagging, the bullying, the hours spent construing Cicero and Virgil? Probably it would; but not always in the expected way.

Few visitors failed to be thunderstruck by the density of Rome's Settecento cultural milieu. 'As high as my expectation was raised,' ran one typical reaction, that of the English tourist Thomas Gray writing to his mother in 1740, 'I confess that the magnificence of this city infinitely surpasses it. You cannot pass along a street but you have views of some palace, or church, or square, or fountain, the most picturesque and noble one can imagine.'

Of course, it mattered very much whom you knew, or had introductions to. Though some exalted Englishmen complained of the dearth of social life to which they had access – compared to the heady whirl of cities like Venice or Milan – there were certainly hosts aplenty. Many of the continental aristocrats who came to Rome in the eighteenth century were taken in hand by the city's French ambassador, Cardinal François-Joaquin de Bernis, who entertained them most lavishly. In the papal Jubilee year of 1775 the visitors to Rome included Charles Theodore, the Elector Palatine; the princes of Brunswick; the Earl of Gloucester, brother of George III of England; the archduke Maximilian of Austria, and innumerable lesser nobility. Up to 1775 there was a steady stream of exalted foreign visitors to Rome, but in the last quarter of the century it became a flood. It was Bernis' firm conviction that the way he entertained his guests ought to be a direct reflection of the *gloire* of the king he represented, Louis XVI. His embassy near Piazza di Spagna was the centre of feasts so extravagant they confounded their guests, even though they were quite accustomed to shows of abundance; and when the cardinal's staff handed out the epicurean leftovers at the back door even the commoners of Rome were left in no doubt about which was the premier Catholic power of Europe. This variation on the spectacle of Roman charity was repeated by other noble houses, on a lesser scale, throughout the city. Unsurprisingly, Bernis later complained that the cost of being Louis XVI's ambassador had nearly bankrupted him.

This mania for high-price private and official entertainment meshed with Rome's insatiable desire for public extravagance. No Italian city, except possibly Venice, loved a parade or a ceremony as much as the papal capital, or staged as many. Just like in Caesar's day, Rome and everyone in it, from its cardinals down to the raggedest urchin, was addicted to its Carnival, its *feste*, its holidays, cavalcades, illuminations and processions, not forgetting its huge firework displays and distributions of free food and wine to the poor. These were the points at which entertainment crossed with official life, including the still extremely vigorous life of religion and the all-reaching power of the Papacy. When a newly elected pope took office, he would enact the ritual of the 'Possesso', the 'taking possession' of Rome, with a long cavalcade from the Church of St John Lateran to the Capitoline Hill – re-enacting, in effect, the route of ancient Roman military triumphs. In the basilica, he would affirm his spiritual leadership of the Church; on the Campidoglio, where the leading magistrate gave him the keys of Rome, his political power over the city.

A more regular event, the 'Chinea' ceremony, staged every year but abandoned in 1787,* was eagerly awaited. This was the day when the feudal dues of the Kingdom of Naples, a fief of the

---

* The year in which Naples refused to continue to accept its status as a papal fief.

Papacy through most of the eighteenth century, were paid to the pope. They came as a bag of gold carried by a white donkey, the *chinea*. The money would be accepted by papal representatives and handed over in Piazza SS. Apostoli, in front of a stupendous piece of pasteboard architecture, vulgarly known as the *macchina* or 'contraption', designed by a leading architect and paid for, traditionally, by the Colonna family.

At first it was difficult for a visiting *Inglese* to grasp how very essential an aspect of Roman (and more generally, Italian) life the profusion of servants in the houses of the rich was. Private property in England was more private than here. The English lord had his dependants, and some hangers-on, but as a rule nothing like the number of accepted parasites that swarmed around the noble Roman household and were taken with equanimity as part of the cost of blue blood. It was common for a wealthy aristocrat – a Corsini or a Borghese, an Odescalchi, a Chigi or a Colonna – not even to know how many domestics he employed, or even what they did. Rome was Europe's capital of the bow, the scrape and the extended palm. The visitor was expected to distribute *mancie* (small tips) to everyone for everything – and often, it seemed, for nothing. This was profoundly unfamiliar and, for the foreign visitor, annoying. The Romans themselves saw it differently: giving to importunate beggars, after all, fulfilled Christ's injunction to care for the poor.

The foreignness of Rome was vividly felt in the position and conduct of its clergy. Both politically and socially, the Rome encountered by the well-off visitor was ruled by that clergy: rich, respected, feared, constantly lobbied and supplicated, and active in all its grades from priest to monsignor to bishop to cardinal. No other society in Europe, not even France's, could show such an influential religious power group, or one so obsessed with matters of age and rank. Or, for that matter, so given to partying. Today, the presence of a cardinal in full rig would put a damper on most parties. Not in eighteenth-century Rome, where the hierarchy of the Catholic Church loved to gossip, drink and gamble, though not (one presumes) dance; in 1729 Cardinal Alessandro Albani caused a delicious scandal by losing the huge sum of 2,000 *scudi* at cards one evening in the palace of the Princess of S. Bono. It was assumed, however, that to become a cardinal was to be raised to the summits of wealth. Hence the bizarre custom by which, when news of a new cardinalcy got around, the favoured cleric would hurry to empty his house of all his furniture and valuables. Otherwise there was a good chance that the Roman mob would sack it.

Some of the hierarchy were sceptical about themselves and their position, and Goethe relayed a story about the same Cardinal Albani, who had been present at a seminarists' meeting where poems had been declaimed in their various national languages. It was, he wrote, 'another little story to show how lightly the sacred is taken in holy Rome: One of the seminarists turned towards the Cardinal and began in his foreign tongue with the words *"gnaja! gnaja!"*, which sounded more or less like the Italian *"canaglia! canaglia!"* [scum, or dirty mob]. The Cardinal turned to his colleagues and said, "That fellow certainly knows us!"'

Even if one did not have access to a great household, so much of Rome's life went on in public places – the piazzas with their cafés, *trattorie*, markets and ever refreshing fountains – that it hardly mattered. Bed, undoubtedly, was the poor man's opera, but just walking and sitting outside was his theatre, and a Roman or a *straniero* could slake his curiosity about life and art merely by poking his nose out of the door. You didn't soon forget what you saw in Rome. Thirty years on, a friend of Goethe's named Hofrath Meyer was still talking with delight about a shoemaker he had seen there, beating out strips of leather on the antique marble head of an emperor that stood before his door.

There would have been memories, new knowledge, and perhaps, for the more assiduous traveller, a journal to keep. That feeling about the ancient past – 'Heroes have trod this earth; 'tis on their dust ye tread', in Byron's words, from *Childe Harold's Pilgrimage* – might still be running strong in the minds of aristocrats who started off as ignorant as colts. Of poets too, and everyone in between, not to mention some who were both, such as Lord Byron. Probably the most beautiful poetic image of the Colosseum written by any foreigner came from his pen, when he described how, at night, the stars seen through the arches of the Colosseum glittered 'through the loops of Time'. His friend Percy Bysshe Shelley, when he arrived there in 1818, found that it was chief among 'the miracles of ancient and modern art' that exceeded all comparison, all expectation:

> The Coliseum is unlike any work of human hands I ever saw before. It is of enormous height and circuit, and the arches built of massy stones are piled on one another, and jut into the blue air, shattered into the forms of overhanging rocks . . . the copse-wood overshadows you as you wander through its labyrinths, and the wild weeds of this carpet of flowers bloom under your feet. The arena is covered with grass, and pierces, like the skirts of a natural plain, the chasms of the arches around. But a small part of the exterior circumference remains – it is exquisitely light and beautiful; and the effect of the perfection of its architecture, adorned with ranges of Corinthian pilasters, supporting a bold cornice, is such as to diminish the effect of its greatness. The interior is all ruin.

As a good anticlerical Shelley was distressed to see the Arch of Constantine nearby, built to commemorate 'the Christian reptile, who had crept among the blood of his murdered family to the supreme power', even though it was 'exquisitely beautiful and perfect'. To him, the identification of Roman ruins blotted out everything else. 'Behold the wrecks of what a great nation once dedicated to the abstractions of the mind! Rome is a city, as it were, of the dead, or rather of those who cannot die, and who survive the puny generations who inhabit and pass over the spot which they have made sacred to eternity. In Rome, at least in the first enthusiasm of your recognition of ancient time, you see nothing of the Italians.' Modern Italians did not, would not, live up to the image of their ancestors that was part of the traveller's baggage. 'There are two Italies,' wrote Shelley, one composed of green earth & transparent sea and the mighty ruins of ancient times, and aerial mountains, & the warm and radiant atmosphere which is interfused through all things. The other consists of the Italians of the present day, their works and ways. The one is the most sublime and lovely contemplation that can be conceived by the imagination of man; the other, the most degraded, disgusting and odious.

Nothing was entirely predictable. Little about Rome could be discovered without being there: 'Only in Rome can one educate oneself for Rome,' declared Johann Wolfgang von Goethe. 'What the barbarians left, the builders of modern Rome have destroyed.' This was a prophetic utterance, even truer today, more than two centuries after his arrival in 1786, than it was then. 'Nothing here is mediocre, and if here and there something is in poor taste, it too shares in the general grandeur.'

How one remembered it afterwards was another question. One's memories of Rome were necessarily a kind of artefact. Probably no visitor could have seen what he or she expected. For some, the city was a guaranteed disappointment. Some Protestants were automatically sceptical. To Sarah Bentham (Jeremy Bentham's widowed stepmother, who died in 1809) the city did not arouse hope as one approached it; seen from the campagna it 'appeared to be situated in a desert'. And once you entered the Eternal City, '[t]he streets are narrow, dirty and filthy. Even the palaces are a mixture of dirt and finery and intermixed with wretched mean houses. The largest open spaces in Rome are used for the sale of vegetables. The fountains are the only singular beauties ... Rome has nothing within, nor without its walls, to make it desirable for an English person to be an inhabitant.'

On top of this, one had to count the distaste that some English visitors felt for the prying, denunciation and bigotry of Roman Catholic rule, and the contrast it made with the relative frankness and freedom of England. The oppression was real enough, though some *stranieri* laid it on a little thick. The English expatriate Sacheverell Stevens, who lived in Rome for five years (1739–44), wrote in his introduction to *Miscellaneous Remarks Made on the Spot on a Late Seven Years' Tour* (1756) that he hoped to 'plainly shew under what a dreadful yoke the wretched people of other nations groan, their more than Egyptian task masters having impiously robbed them of that glorious faculty of their reason, deprived them of their properties, and all this under the sacred name of Religion'. One surpassingly zealous Scots Presbyterian actually tried to convert Pius VI during a ceremony at St Peter's, at which Dr John Moore, physician and cultural adviser to the Duke of Hamilton, was also present. 'O thou beast of Nature,' cried this fanatic, on being presented to the pope, 'with seven heads and ten horns! Thou mother of harlots, arrayed in purple and scarlet, and decked with precious stones and pearls! Throw away the golden cup of abominations, and the filthiness of thy fornication!'

The pope's reply (if indeed he made one) was not recorded. This unruly Protestant fundamentalist was seized by the Swiss Guards and briefly jailed. But then the pope not only had him released, but thanked him for his good intentions and paid for his return passage to Scotland.

From the confusing wealth of images and experience that the gentleman tourist would encounter on his way to Rome and in the Eternal City itself, there were basically three kinds of souvenir that he could bring back to his London house or his country seat, proof that he had made the instructive pilgrimage and passed through history's great Finishing School.

He could purchase examples of the Antique – a cinerary urn or a kylix, cameos and pieces of ancient sculpture (among which there were almost bound to be fakes, though they could well include a modern piece in the best classical taste, by Antonio Canova or one of his many imitators). The greatest collections of antiquities in Rome were usually in the hands of royalty or the Church, but adroit middlemen could sometimes prise them free. The Giustiniani collection of ancient art was sold to the Earl of Pembroke in 1720, the statues and vases amassed by the Odescalchi family went to the King of Spain in 1724, and the antiquities purchased by Cardinal Polignac in Rome were bought en masse by Frederick of Prussia in 1742.

The two leading English purveyors of fakes (or 'optimistic restorations', as they might be called) to the British were Thomas Jenkins and James Byres.

Jenkins (1722–98) was an intriguing, almost protean figure: salesman, tomb-raker, cicerone, banker, dealer. With a past as a painter, he had more than enough connoisseurship to realize he had little future as one. He had come to Rome in 1752, and wasted no time making friends in high places. Through his friendships in Vatican circles (which included two popes, Clement XIV and Pius VI, and were cemented by his role as an unofficial British representative to the Holy See) he was able to move into the higher reaches of both Roman and tourist society. By the 1760s and 1770s he had formed a considerable clientele from the visiting English gentry, who loved Jenkins to show them the sights of Rome (about which, to be fair, he knew a lot more than most Italian 'bear-leaders') and trusted him to find them fine antiquities – which were not always so very fine.

It was impossible to enjoy any standing as a connoisseur in Georgian England without a collection of old marbles. So Jenkins employed several Roman sculptors to carve them, and to give them an antique patina with the help of tobacco juice. In 1774 he even helped form a consortium to dredge the bed of the Tiber for antiquities. But he also dispersed whole ready-made collections of impeccable genuineness, such as (in 1785) the entire Villa Montalto-Negroni collection. Very large shifts in Roman ownership took place in the Settecento. In 1734 Clement XII bought some four hundred Roman sculptures, mostly busts, from that indefatigable collector Cardinal Alessandro Albani; these became part of the nucleus of the Museo Capitolino, the only museum in Rome at the time that was open to the general public, and for that reason a unique educational resource for the scores and then hundreds of young artists who were flocking to Rome to study the Antique. It was difficult, and usually impossible, for a young unknown sculptor to get access to the treasures of nobly owned palazzi –

thus the advantage for painters such as Velázquez and Rubens in gaining access to the great royal collections – and this lent even greater importance to the Capitoline Museum. And the number of foreign artists struggling to get to Rome was constantly growing. For them, the Grand Tours of others were an important career filter. If a British sculptor met another Briton in Rome, it was more likely that this traveller would be there to look at art, and thus receptive to the work of the newcomer.

Jenkins' speciality, other than marble, was ancient gems and cameos, both real and fake. The fake cameos were made in a *bottega* set up in a nook within the Colosseum, at the time a favoured location for rough-and-ready workshops and boutiques. Unfortunately his flourishing career was cut short by Napoleon's invasion of Rome in 1796. Because Jenkins had quasi-diplomatic status without diplomatic immunity, and greatly feared what the French might do to him, he had to run from Rome, leaving all his property behind.

What Jenkins was to sculpture, James Byres (1734–1817) was to painting. To him belongs the honour of having spent several weeks in 1764 guiding the historian Edward Gibbon, future author of *The Decline and Fall of the Roman Empire*, around the Eternal City. He offered the best-known course in the appreciation of antiquities; it lasted six weeks and was thought by all who took it to be rewarding if very hard work.

As dealers, Byres and Jenkins were not in competition. Byres was mainly concerned with paintings, although he did manage to acquire and re-sell one of the most famous objects now in England, the antique Roman cameo-glass vessel from Palazzo Barberini known as the Portland Vase, which passed through Sir William Hamilton's hands and from him to Margaret Bentinck, Duchess of Portland, in 1784. His most outrageous coup was to fraudulently extract one of Poussin's greatest masterpieces, the group of seven canvases comprising *The Seven Sacraments*, from the Bonapaduli collection in Rome, export them to England classified as copies, and sell them as the originals they were to the Duke of Rutland for £2,000.

There were paintings, drawings and prints to be bought, and many a great English collection began with things brought back from milord's Grand Tour: Raphael, Michelangelo and Titian if possible – which it seldom was – but plenty of other Masters appealed to the taste of the eighteenth century as hardly less estimable: Veronese, Guido Reni, the Carraccis and Domenichino. Grand Tourists did not buy 'primitive' art; the products of the early Renaissance did not appeal to them, and Gothic painting seemed positively barbarous, wooden, inexpressive. They responded to the grand and suave eloquence of the sixteenth and seventeenth centuries, and to the beautiful, fleshy girls masquerading as madonnas and saints that it so often described. But it would be quite wrong to suppose that English tourists were the only ones buying. Rome attracted connoisseurs and collectors from everywhere, and it was a competitive business. Joseph II, the Holy Roman Emperor, vied with Catherine II, Empress of Russia, and Augustus III, King of Poland, who were in competition with Prince Nicholas Yussupov and the Grand Duchess Maria Feodorovna of Russia. Rome had a booming, open market for paintings, more than for antiquities, and it was served by (among others) expatriate artists doubling as dealers. It was the Scottish painter Gavin Hamilton, for instance, who purchased in Rome what became two of the greatest treasures of the National Gallery in London: Raphael's *Ansidei Madonna* in 1764, and Leonardo's *Virgin of the Rocks*, in 1785.

However, the Roman painters most admired in Italy in the eighteenth century were not necessarily the ones most eagerly snapped up by English and other Grand Tourists. The arch-example was probably Carlo Maratti (1625–1713), whose grand classical style of decoration, intimately linked to the doctrinal and emotional requirements of the Catholic Church, did not travel well in more Protestant latitudes. But Maratti's success in Italy was huge. His mythological and religious work energized young painters all over Europe, and he served seven popes. The death of Bernini in 1680 left Maratti as the unchallenged leader of the Roman school of art. The major Roman churches for which he

painted altarpieces include S. Croce in Gerusalemme, S. Maria
Sopra Minerva, S. Maria della Pace, S. Maria del Popolo, and a
dozen others including St Peter's Basilica itself. His fame and
influence were so great that he was widely known as the 'Roman
Apelles', after the Greek painter of the fourth century BCE, widely
regarded as the greatest of antiquity. And yet a century after his
death this vastly influential virtuoso had sunk with hardly a trace;
there has never been a retrospective of Maratti in a modern
museum, an extraordinary omission.

A Grand Tourist's second choice of memento was somewhat
more modest. Rome was already making tourist souvenirs. They
were, of course, more palatable than the trash stamped out in
Asian sweatshops (the Vatican naturally prefers to call these 'workshops' or 'studios') for today's tourists: phosphorescent plastic
rosaries, gummily smiling aluminium pope medals, three-inch-
high replicas of the Capitoline she-wolf. Nevertheless the eighteenth-century versions had a slightly industrial character, though
this would have been noticed only if you lined them up next to
each other. Various studios made small bronze replicas of famous
statues, the Apollo Belvedere or the Laocoön; the best-known of
these was run by the sculptor Giacomo Zoffoli. Giovanni Volpato,
a ceramicist of high reputation (and a friend of Canova's), did
porcelain objects, to a high standard of finish. Cork models of
ancient buildings, precise in scale, were made by the firm of
Giovanni Altieri – the British architect John Soane bought several
of these.

The part of this memory trade that verged on real art was the
making of micro-mosaics. The Vatican had employed a small
army of mosaicists for the decoration of St Peter's. But when their
employment waned the mosaic-workers, expert in their trade,
turned to producing tiny, portable mosaic images for the visiting
milords. The virtuoso of these *mosaicisti in piccolo* was Giacomo
Raffaelli, who composed his diminutive architectural views, landscapes and even copies of famous paintings in near-microscopic
tesserae made from *smalti filati*, glass threads coloured with
various metal oxides and rendered opaque with oxide of tin, then

cut into pinheads. There might be more than twelve hundred of these tesserae to the square inch. You could have a brooch with the whole Colosseum on it (microscopic gladiators might cost extra), or a snuffbox with a view of the Forum on its lid, all in imperishable glass.

The third choice – open only to, and all but obligatory for, the rich – was to commission paintings, possibly of Italian landscape scenes but certainly of oneself, with or without one's family. These were true acts of patronage, not just of souvenir-buying, and the chief recipient of these commissions among British landscape artists was a Welshman named Richard Wilson (c.1713–82). Wilson's father, a clergyman, had given him a most thorough education in the classics, particularly in Latin poetry; he knew, and could quote, long tracts of Horace and Virgil by heart. This meant that most of the places he was likely to paint, and that his clients were likely to have visited – Lake Nemi, for instance, haunt of the Sibyl, or the waterfalls near Tivoli, where later he would enjoy a contemplative and jolly picnic with the Earls of Thanet, Pembroke and Essex, travel companions in Rome – were in a literary sense familiar to him before he set eyes on them. The fact that he shared such a background with them made his mellow paintings all the more agreeable to his educated English patrons, who regarded him as the Claude Lorrain of England.

But whether or not he brought back a classical landscape of the 'holy ground' that he had trod, by the real French Claude or the 'English Claude', the Grand Tourist was almost bound to have his portrait made there. It would be set in a vista of the Eternal City, with the Colosseum or the Castel S. Angelo (always favourites, because easily identified) in the background, pointing with a pink and didactic hand at some exemplary work from the glorious Roman past – the *Borghese Gladiator*, perhaps, or the *Dying Gaul*, the Belvedere Torso, or the Laocoön. See! This is what I have seen, and in some sense appropriated! And just as I have returned with this painting, so I have come back with the knowledge of the cultural setting that it implies!

The maestro of such transactions, the first choice for the foreigner seeking to have his Roman portrait done, was the son of a goldsmith, Pompeo Batoni (1708–87). Born in Lucca, trained in part by his meticulous father, he had moved to Rome in 1727 to study painting, and almost from the beginning of his Roman life he showed a large and ever-growing talent for copying antique statuary. This in itself might have been enough to earn him a steady income from selling his beautiful and highly finished drawings to rich English visitors, who wanted to take home reminders of the classical masterpieces they had seen in the Vatican and elsewhere in Rome. But Batoni also had strong ambitions to be a painter of religious and historical subjects, and such appetites could only be satisfied by working for the Church. At first, his ecclesiastical work brought him unremitting success. His subject-paintings were popular with the *Inglesi* and, more importantly, Pope Benedict XIV appreciated him and saw to it that he received commissions for some of the greatest churches in Rome, among them S. Maria Maggiore (1743). What should have been the early apotheosis of his career came in 1746, when he was commissioned to paint a *Fall of Simon Magus* for the altar of St Peter's itself.

Batoni had laboured on this enormous project, the most important that a painter in Rome – or, indeed, anywhere in Italy – could have been offered, for almost ten years. And it defeated him. The Vatican meant to have his oil-painting executed in mosaic, because canvas, given the unexpected dampness of the air inside the basilica, succumbed to mould; but a temporary crimp in the papal income prevented that, and to Batoni's intense disappointment and chagrin the giant canvas was moved to the Church of S. Maria degli Angeli, where it still remains.

For any ordinary artist this would have been a prestigious spot, but Batoni was not an ordinary artist, and he felt the loss of a place of such honour as St Peter's very keenly – so bitterly, in fact, that he gave up his ecclesiastical work altogether and resolved, from then on, to concentrate on the more profitable field of portraits of the visiting nobility and gentry. He worked with such speed and virtuosity that by the time of his death he had done some two hundred of these affluent tourists, most of whom were already peers or would presently inherit a title. He was to Italy what the great portraitist Sir Joshua Reynolds was to England. Reynolds, it seems, detested his Italian rival. Batoni was doomed in advance, Reynolds declared in his fourteenth *Discourse*, written after Batoni's death: 'However great their names may at present sound in our ears, [they] will very soon fall into what is little short of total oblivion.' Reynolds did not believe that *De mortuis nil nisi bonum*.

He was right about most of the painters he mentioned here – who today remembers Imperiale or Massuccio? – but wrong about Batoni, although he was nearly right about him too, since Batoni's name was on the verge of disappearance by 1800. Most of the men who had bought his work were dead, and those who remained were old. Their heirs thought the ancestral portraits old-fashioned and banished them from positions of honour in the sitting-room to dark landings on the stairs. Few other people saw them, because the portraits had never been exhibited: they had gone straight from the maestro's studio in Rome to their owner's wall, and there had been no intervening exhibitions in which a public might have had the chance to see them. Hence, although he had many clients in Britain, his public was never large enough to make him popular. So even today (or perhaps especially today) Batoni's work has the charm of the unfamiliar. Admittedly, some of it looks routine, although one ought to be alert to its very real charms – the delightful palette which seems to preserve the complete freshness of encounter with a living creature, the fluent and ever accurate drawing, and the wholly delectable polish. Because the human subjects are so long dead, we can no longer appreciate the lifelike qualities that earned them such praise. Yet there are Batonis that compel not only by their immense skill but by a certain oddity – their theatrical faithfulness, it seems, to the self-confidence of the upper-class Briton abroad among the foreigners.

The outstanding one among these is his portrait of a Scots aristocrat, Colonel William Gordon. It is almost a definition of what used to be called the 'swagger portrait'. There is the noble laird, leaning on his ostentatiously drawn sword. (And why would a tourist be pulling out his sword in Rome?) He is swathed in yards of his family tartan, which becomes a bizarre sort of Caledonian toga. He looks as though he owns the place and is getting set to defend it against the Italians.

The subject of the best of all the foreigner-in-Italy portraits, however, was neither rich nor titled, nor English, nor was he painted by an Italian. The symbolic, over-life-size portrait of Goethe in the Roman campagna (1786–7) was by Wilhelm Tischbein (1751–1829). Tischbein and Goethe were longstanding friends and their meeting in Rome was deeply stimulating for both men. Born in 1749, Johann Wolfgang von Goethe was a German literary celebrity at twenty-four, the prodigy of Frankfurt on the Main. Within a year or two his reputation had spread throughout Europe. As Nicholas Boyle points out in the first volume of his magisterial biography, Goethe wrote in *Faust* 'the greatest long poem of recent European literature ... Goethe was not just *a* poet – for the whole Romantic generation in Germany, England and even France, he was *the* poet ... he affected all subsequent notions of what poets are and poetry does.' But his previous works had already cemented his reputation and, since he had at last fulfilled a lifelong desire by making the journey to Rome, this was seen by Tischbein (and other German cultural expatriates who were already installed there) as a very consequential act even before all its literary results were apparent. This has to be remembered when one looks at Tischbein's portrait. At the time of his arrival in Rome, Goethe was a little older than most members of the vigorous colony of German artists there: he was thirty-seven, Tischbein thirty-five, and none of the others past forty. Apart from Tischbein, his closest artist friend in Rome was the abundantly gifted and celebrated Swiss painter Angelica Kauffmann (1741–1807), who lived with her husband Antonio Zucchi in a studio at the top of the Spanish Steps, on the Via Sistina. With her, Goethe had many illuminating talks about art.

Tischbein painted him at full length. Goethe's energy was boundless, his thirst for historical understanding through art and architecture unquenchable, and the resulting image conveys both. Shaded by a wide-brimmed artist's hat and wrapped in a voluminous white cape – which looks appropriately like a toga but subliminally conveys the thought of the inspired prophet, although it was only a practical garment – Goethe reclines amid the overgrown relics of the campagna. His gaze, at something out to the right which we do not see, is strong and reflective. His right hand, his writing hand, is emphatically in view. He is not pointing at a famous work of art, as Batoni's clients were apt to do in their pseudo-proprietary way. The circular tomb of Caecilia Metella on the Appian Way rises in the distance. It was a favourite of both Tischbein and Goethe, and of Byron too, who wrote of it in *Childe Harold's Pilgrimage*; his hero, approaching Rome, sees it thus:

> There is a stern round tower of other days,
> Firm as a fortress, with its fence of stone,
> Such as an army's baffled strength delays,
> Standing with half its battlements alone,
> And with two thousand years of ivy grown,
> The garland of Eternity, where wave
> The green leaves over all by Time o'erthrown; –
> What was this tower of strength? within its cave
> What treasure lay so locked, so hid? – A woman's grave.

In the foreground is a fragment of ancient bas-relief, a fallen Composite capital, and the clutter of stone blocks, which may be the pieces of a toppled obelisk, on which Goethe is taking his ease. Rather, the ancient vestiges that surround the poet are painted as part of his natural environment of thought and reflection. They are not potential 'souvenirs'. And the bas-relief (as Nicholas Boyle pointed out) has a quite specific meaning in relation to Goethe's own work. It depicts the 'recognition scene' from *Iphigenia*, whose dramatic adaptation Goethe was then writing; and its marble block is overgrown, or crowned, with ivy, symbol of immortality.

'I shall never rest,' Goethe declared in a magnificent passage, written in Rome in June 1787, 'until I know that all my ideas are derived, not from hearsay or tradition, but from my real living contact with the things themselves. From my earliest youth, this has been my ambition and my torment.' In this spirit, he approached the enormous bulk of the city and its antiquities.

And so, Rome took time. Not only for Goethe, but for any serious visitor. 'It is as impossible for a man to dash through it,' noted Charles Cadogan in 1784, 'as it is for him to fly.' To set his impressions in order, get smooth access to collections, and have the whole confusing panorama of ancient Rome explained to him, the Grand Tourist would need help. It could be at hand in the form of a 'bear-leader' – a travelling tutor, preferably English, experienced in antiquity, who might be found living as an expatriate in Rome but was more likely to have been brought over in the tourist's party. Some of them were harmless clergymen of no high distinction, but Pelham retained no less a figure than Anton Mengs to show him around Rome, and men as eminent as Thomas Hobbes and Adam Smith were also well known as bear-leaders – in fact, guiding the bear-cubs, as the young and the rich were known to the Italians, was practically the only way an impecunious intellectual could afford to get to Italy himself.

One of the most popular guides to the city was the great German art historian Johann Winckelmann, 'than whom no one has greater skill in antique statues' (said Edward Wortley Montagu). He was besieged with requests for such services from bigwigs on the Grand Tour. Goethe observed his happy relations with ordinary (and less ordinary) Romans, but '[h]e experienced considerable pain at the hands of visitors from abroad. To be sure, nothing is worse than the ordinary tourist in Rome. In any other place, the traveller can go his own way; however, those who fail to do as the Romans do are a horror to the true Roman.' Such provincial sightseers – narrow-minded, unobservant, always in a hurry, arrogant – Winckelmann cursed more than once and repeatedly swore never again to act as their guide, only to relent on the next occasion ... Yet he also benefited considerably from serving as a guide to persons of position and reputation.

Some of the bigwigs, particularly the English, disgusted him:

Frederick Calvert, Lord Baltimore, appeared in Rome with a harem of eight women, some of whom were stout and others thin; the fat ones were fed sour food, and the thin a meat-and-dairy diet. Winckelmann, a fastidious homosexual, found both them and their master repellent. The Duke of York, George III's brother, seemed to be 'the greatest ass I know, no credit to his rank or country'. Naturally, the scholar kept these opinions to himself. He did a little bear-leading, but others did a lot, and without these guides, the novice – as a friend wrote to the painter George Romney – would not be ready for the shearing; he would walk through whole palaces of pictures

> [like] an upholsterer through the Vatican. They have been told of the *gusto* of the antique, but where to find it, or how to distinguish it, they know no more than their mothers. *Virtù* however is to be purchased, like other superfluities, and in the end their *Cicerone* lays them in for a bargain, perhaps a patchwork head of *Trajan* set upon a modern pair of shoulders, and made up with *Caracalla's* nose and *Nero's* ears ... home they come privileged *Virtuosi*, qualified to condemn every thing that their own countrymen can produce.

Some Grand Tourists collected on a huge scale. Richard Boyle, 3rd Earl of Burlington, who presided over the Palladian 'Revival' in England, was a shining example of what intelligent patronage – allied, in his case, with equally intelligent collecting – could do. The 'Apollo of the Arts', as Horace Walpole called him, collected on a lavish scale during two Grand Tours of Italy, the first in 1714–15, the second in 1719. Burlington came back from his second tour in 1719 with no fewer than 878 pieces of luggage, crammed with works of art. He bought with the utmost discrimination, finding, for instance, more than sixty original drawings by Palladio, together with prints and rare books of the master's work, during his sojourns in Verona and Vicenza. Lord Burlington was one of those exceptionally rare talents who could have altered the history of architecture as a patron, but who did so instead as a genius of creative design in his own right. By involving himself directly in architecture as a designer rather than simply as a patron, he shifted the social relation in England between patron and artist. And certain of his buildings, such as his own Palladian villa Chiswick House, or the grandly pure Assembly Rooms in York, are of a near-minimalist intensity that exceeds most of their Palladian prototypes.

Among the materials Boyle brought back from Italy would certainly have been various editions of the Roman etchings of Giovanni Battista Piranesi, printmaker extraordinary and architect manqué. No artist has ever done more to record the posthumous image of a great city than this Venetian brooding on the ruins of Rome. In effect, he created and recreated the Eternal City and its obsessively present antiquities for a mid-eighteenth-century public, ruin by ruin, almost stone by stone. In the course of a working life of forty or so years, Piranesi made etchings of every kind of structure in Rome: amphitheatres, baths, churches, monasteries, bridges and arches, forums, piazzas and free-standing columns, perspectives of streets, gardens and grottoes, obelisks, mausoleums, aqueducts, fountains, ruined temples, tombs, theatres, villas and palaces both abandoned and lived-in, sewers and crematoria.

The writer and connoisseur Horace Walpole urged artists to 'study the sublime dreams of Piranesi, who seems to have conceived visions of Rome beyond what it boasted even at the meridian of its splendour ... Fierce as Michelangelo, and exuberant as Rubens, he has imagined scenes that would startle geometry ... He piles palaces on bridges, and temples on palaces, and scales heaven with mountains of edifices. Yet what taste in his boldness! What grandeur in his wildness!'

He reproduced inscriptions that had been chipped and worn to near-illegibility by the gnawing of time, *tempus edax*. He designed tripods, urns, trophies, shields, imaginary armour, lamps, marble maps, Egyptian-style beds, Etruscan-style candlesticks and yawning, cavernous Roman fireplaces. He did huge decorative initials: a letter V made of sections of lead piping leaning one against the other, a D featuring the Roman *lupa* glaring toothily at the reader from inside its curve. He created a set of clocks and another of designs for sedan-chairs and coach doors, as well as some Egyptian Revival decorations (which featured sphinxes, vultures and a Nile crocodile but, alas, were destroyed long ago) for the inside of the Caffè degli Inglesi, and a set of haunting *capricci* showing the gloomily enfolding spaces of imaginary prisons, which for many people remain his supreme imaginative achievement and had more effect on writers than any etchings of the eighteenth century. He also designed elaborate furniture, nearly all of which has since disappeared – the sole apparent survivor being a carved and gilt side-table from the Quirinal Palace in Rome, designed for one of his principal patrons, the cardinal and future pope Clement XIII, Carlo Rezzonico, which ended its travels in the Minneapolis Institute of Arts.

Piranesi died in 1778, at the relatively advanced age of fifty-eight. He left some 1,024 engraved images, an output unrivalled by any other graphic artist of his age. More than seven hundred of his preparatory drawings also survive. But there is only one building standing in Rome that he designed and built: the church and headquarters of the Knights of Malta on the Aventine. For a man who styled himself a 'Venetian architect', it must have been something of a disappointment to have built only one building. Yet in the end, his colossal output of prints and drawings had more effect on the experience of architecture, on what many people expected of that art, than anything he could have achieved with real buildings. Their effect was powerfully felt all over the Western world, in structures as far apart from one another as John Soane's Bank of England (1798) and Benjamin Latrobe's Baltimore Cathedral (1805–18). His prints could and did travel everywhere, with an ease that no actual building could possibly rival. These 'buildings I never saw', as the great English designer Robert Adam wrote in 1755, 'are the greatest fund for inspiring and instilling invention in any lover of architecture that can be imagined'. In them, memory, fantasy and scholarship all combined to produce a parallel Rome, in many ways as actual as the city itself: a Rome that was both permanent and for ever lost. This must have consoled Piranesi for his lack of built buildings. This hugely ambitious artist recreated not only a city, but several ages of it.

Which is not to say that his instincts about its past were necessarily right. Piranesi managed to convince himself that the root of all classical architecture, Greek as well as Roman, was actually Etruscan. He even compared Etruscan buildings to the architecture of the Egyptians. (Of course, Piranesi had never been to Egypt.) He never wavered from this belief, which had no shred of evidence to support it. He had studied the Roman systems for water distribution and sewage removal, starting with the Cloaca Maxima. Knowing that the Etruscans had been experts in drainage, he wrongly supposed that they were masters of the same kind of massive tunnelling and vaulting that the Romans had developed. He imagined Etruscan architecture as massive, stonily articulated, vast in its spaces and recessions – all qualities which, he believed, lay at the root of Roman building. Actually, though some Etruscan temples and sacred spaces were artificial caves hollowed out of bedrock (the soft and easily cut tufa), those that were built, such as the sixth-century BCE Portonaccio temple in Veii, were made of timber and mud-brick and bore no resemblance at all to Piranesi's massive fantasies.

Born in Venice in 1720, Piranesi was the son of a mason, and he grew up fascinated by the question of where the roots of classical architecture in Italy lay. One should remember that Venice was the only major Italian city that, due to its watery site among the lagoons, had no Roman-era building and therefore no Roman ruins; this must have immensely increased the impact of the Rome that young Piranesi saw, when he went there for the first time. This happened when he was aged twenty, and a draughtsman on the staff of Marco Foscarini, the Venetian ambassador to the court of the new pope, Benedict XIV. Piranesi already had an enthusiasm for antiquity. It had been nurtured by his older brother

Angelo, a Carthusian monk who had encouraged him to read Livy, Tacitus and other historians of Rome.

There were large and magnificent buildings in Venice, but none of them were Roman at all, let alone Roman on the scale of the Baths of Caracalla or the Flavian Amphitheatre. Moreover, because Venice (like its cradling sea) was flat, Piranesi grew up without seeing anything like the tumbled, precipitous palimpsest of seven-hilled Rome, with its gigantic overlay of columns, fallen cornices, collapsed vaults and ancient excavations. Its impact on him would be immense, and it would liberate his imagination. It would encourage him to turn big things into titanic ones. 'These speaking ruins,' he would write, 'have filled my spirit with Images that accurate drawings, even such as those of the immortal Palladio, could never have succeeded in conveying.'

These images were often intensely theatrical. There is no evidence that Piranesi, as has sometimes been said, ever actually worked with the chief stage designer of Italy, the Venetian Ferdinando Galli da Bibiena (1657–1743), but he certainly knew Bibiena's work – as who in Venice did not? – and he did an apprenticeship with two somewhat less celebrated Venetian stage designers who worked in a similar mode, Giuseppe and Domenico Valeriano. He also became an expert in the dramatic use of angular perspective, under the tutelage of an engraver, Carlo Zucchi.

Venice was the natural home of such exercises, which went by the name of *capricci*, and were the stock-in-trade of earlier painters who clearly had an impact on the young Piranesi, such as Canaletto and the Tiepolos. So one will find his views of ancient Rome populated by the figures of people scattered among the ruins – ragged, gesticulating, tiny people, very different from the more elegant and composed travellers to be seen in other 'views' of Rome, sometimes troglodytic, as if they had just crawled out of holes between the rocks. These contributed to the impression given by Piranesi's later collections of architectural and topographic prints, such as the four-volume *Le antichità Romane* (1756) – that the Rome whose remains he was etching had indeed been the creation and home of earthly giants, a now vanished race whose like would not come again, sublime in ambition and unlimited in scope of grandeur.

Piranesi was lucky to reach Rome when he did. Any talented artist would have been. It was a clearing-house of ideas, a place where one went to learn, irrigated by the talent of scores of foreign artists (John Flaxman, Henry Fuseli, Angelica Kauffmann, Anton Mengs, Pierre Subleyras, Claude-Joseph Vernet), Italian ones (Marco Benefial, Pietro Bianchi, Giuseppe Cades, Pier Leone Ghezzi, Corrado Giaquinto, Benedetto Luti, Giovanni Panini, Piranesi, Francesco Trevisani), British architects (William Chambers, Robert Adam, George Dance and John Soane) and cultural theorists (notably Johann Winckelmann), and hundreds of intelligent tourists from all over Europe, some highly cultivated and others eager neophytes.

Among the former, Piranesi found a professional context. In the ranks of tourists, he found an abundant market. Chipped marble heads and Ionic capitals were not easy to carry back from Italy but sheets of paper were, and large numbers of Piranesi prints from his major series (the *Antichità Romane*, the *Della Magnificenza ed Architettura de' Romani*, and all the other series he made, not forgetting his fanciful studies of chimney ornament and of designs for vases, candelabras and gravestones) found their way back to England, where they were pored over and used as inspirational models by dozens of architects. True, it was sometimes difficult to mimic Piranesi's effects in the materials of the real world. The layers of massive, rusticated stones in his view of the understructure of the Castel S. Angelo seem to be bulging, extruding their very substance under the weight of the primeval masonry above. However, the care which Piranesi brought to depicting his Roman-ruin architecture is so dedicated as to challenge belief. In some of the plates, which purported merely to depict the technical aspects of ancient building, he was able to invest tools and techniques – like the lifting-tackle for large masonry blocks – with the drama of the technological sublime, a project dear to the heart of other eighteenth-century figures. At the same time, fantasy ruled the world given in other prints. Thus when he rendered the Pyramid of Cestius, in reality quite a small and almost delicate affair (as pyramids go), erected near the Porta Ostiensis in memory of a man about whom almost nothing is known, he gave it an Egyptian scale and mass.

In making his Roman ruins look like chasms and cliffs of stone, Piranesi was protecting the Roman genius for mass from dilution, as he saw it, by Greek artificiality. Much of this was fiction, of course. There could be little in the world – not even the Roman part of it – quite like those disturbingly congested views of the Via Appia in its heyday, stretching away in a surreal perspective, crammed cheek by jowl with statues, tombs, sarcophagi, urns and obelisks. No wonder that such things would become a rich source of plunder for later and lesser artists – Eugene Berman and Salvador Dalí – seeking to project a disquieting dream world of never-never architecture.

Making large etchings is an expensive business, and to do it on a Piranesian scale required large financial support. The patron from whom Piranesi expected most was a young Irishman: James Caulfeild, 1st Earl of Charlemont, to whom he wrote in 1757 that 'I believe I have completed a work which will pass on to posterity and which will endure so long as there are men curious to know the ruins which remain of the most famous city in the universe.' Charlemont seemed to Piranesi like a good potential patron; he was rich (though not, as it turned out, as rich as the artist supposed), and in 1749 he had set up an academy, though a short-lived one, for British artists in Rome to study antiquities, about which he was passionately enthusiastic. It looked a splendid idea, both to him and to Piranesi, to have his noble name attached to such a turning-point in archaeology as the *Antichità Romane*.

But unhappily, Charlemont had no idea – and since he was an amateur without earlier experience of publishing, how could he? – of the overwhelming mass of work and expense in publishing the four volumes and more than 250 plates of the *Antichità*. He had supposed he would be paying for a single volume about tomb chambers and now he was faced with the cost of this mammoth work, all of it, the fruit of more than ten years of study and meditation. Not only did Piranesi plan to show all of ancient Rome above ground: his engravings would also show what was hidden – the foundations and footings, the drainage conduits and water-supply systems. Poor Charlemont had something much simpler in mind, and much more saleable: picturesque *vedute* of the Eternal City. Not surprisingly, his resolution buckled and he dropped the project altogether, fleeing back to the British Isles.

This was the greatest disappointment of Piranesi's life and he never really got over it, even though he was able to find other supporters for the *Antichità*. Perhaps he would have killed the traitorous, chicken-hearted Charlemont (as he now thought of his ex-patron) if he could have got away with it, but he did not have the chance, and so he had to be content with a kind of *damnatio memoriae*. His title-page had originally carried a rather fulsome dedication to James Caulfeild, inscribed on an ample plaque surrounded by attributes of antique ruin. Piranesi now removed Caulfeild's name from the plate. This was in imitation of the Roman Senate, which after 212 CE had erased the once honoured but now disgraced name of Geta from a dedicatory inscription on the Arch of Septimius Severus in the Forum Romanum.* Presumably Caulfeild would have recognized this insult, even if few others did.

One area of Piranesi's output departed into pure fantasy, and has always seemed separate from his archaeological and view-making work. This is the series of fourteen plates known as the *Carceri d'Invenzione* or 'Imaginary Prisons', which first appeared in 1745 and were reissued in 1760. Unlike all his other work, as their title implies these are not based on any known buildings.

---

* Publius Lucius Septimius Geta (b. 189 CE) was the younger brother of the Emperor Caracalla. The two hated each other to the point where their palace in Rome had to be physically divided. In 211 CE, Caracalla had Geta stabbed to death – in his mother's arms! – and tried to have his memory obliterated by having his portraits defaced and removing his name from all public inscriptions – the *damnatio memoriae*, Rome's last and worst insult to the dead.

They are emanations of the artist's mind and, right from the start, it was recognized that they had little relation to real architecture. What they depict, essentially, are limitless underground chambers with no exit, the space knitted together, but never resolved, by ramps, stairs, bridges, galleries, catwalks, vestibules and arches that all assert a powerful presence but actually lead nowhere. They seem self-replicating and this was what spoke, with peculiar directness and vividness, both to Samuel Taylor Coleridge, sunk deep in his own laudanum addiction, and to his friend Thomas De Quincey, an addict as well. When Coleridge eloquently described the *Carceri* to De Quincey, they did not have copies of the prisons to hand. But Coleridge thought that these strange and paranoid imaginings recorded 'the scenery of his own visions during the delirium of a fever'. De Quincey seemed to recognize them too, from Coleridge's vivid account of the 'Gothic halls', the wheels, cables, pulleys, levers and racks. And he recognized some of the features of his own opium hallucinations: 'With the same power of endless growth and self-reproduction did my architecture proceed in dreams.'

In one sense these images hark back to Piranesi's earlier years as a student of stage design. Prison scenes were common and popular in the eighteenth century and through into the nineteenth, as an acquaintance with Beethoven (*Fidelio*) or Verdi (*Tosca*) reminds us. Many artists designed prison sets, whose towering arches and claustrophobic, vast-space, no-exit character all suggest affinities with Piranesi's dream prisons. What had been palatial now turns penal. Huge spaces had been taken to magnify their inhabitants' importance, in a world of wealth, power and privilege. But in the very different world of the *Carceri*, magnitude reduces man to a crawling, suffering insect.

In all their oppressive power, the *Carceri* had a strong appeal for writers, particularly for English Romantics. One of the first to set out his response to them was William Beckford (1760–1844), the dilettante who, fabulously wealthy from inheritance in the slave trade and the sugar business, had taken his Grand Tour in 1780. He was in Venice and his gondola floated him under the Bridge of Sighs. 'I shuddered while passing below,' he would recall later. 'Horrors and dismal prospects haunted my fancy on my return. I could not dine in peace, so strongly was my imagination affected; but snatching my pencil, I drew chasms and subterraneous hollows, the domain of fear and torture, with chains, racks, wheels and dreadful engines in the style of Piranesi.'

Memories of Piranesi's *Carceri* would infest Beckford's imagination for years to come, pervading the landscapes of his novel *Vathek* (1786). They were filled with a fear of vastness and indeterminacy – the *Carceri* could not be reconstituted in the mind's eye as real, architectural space, betokening security. This, of course, was what gave them their grip on the dreaming mind. In the 1960s, when the 'drug culture' was looking for antecedents to its often obsessive interest in hallucination, efforts were made to find a parallel between Piranesi's carceral visions and the visions caused by pot or LSD. It was argued, or at any rate suggested, that the connecting thread may have been attacks of malaria, caught by Piranesi while sketching aqueducts and ruins in the mosquito-infested campagna outside Rome: a common treatment for malaria was large doses of the opiate laudanum. But this is unprovable and probably has more to do with the atmosphere of the 1960s than that of the 1740s.

There were several reasons why such images might have caught the attention of a liberal-minded public. The whole issue of imprisonment – of crime and punishment, of what could deter the errant soul from sin – was much to the fore in English literary thinking around the turn of the nineteenth century. What was an appropriate architecture, a 'speaking' architecture, that would make a building truly carceral and would distinguish itself from other structures not designed to punish, intimidate, reform? George Dance the Younger (1741–1825) seems to have extracted part of his answer from the ideas of Piranesi, whom he met in Rome in 1763 and whose *Carceri* he undoubtedly saw. In 1768, after he got back from Rome, Dance was given the job of rebuilding London's main prison, Newgate. This task occupied him for the best part of seventeen years. It was hardly a coincidence that Dance's design for Newgate, dreadful though it may seem today, emerged just as the movement for penal reform in England began to stumble into life, urged along by its pioneer, John Howard, with his monumental report on punishment, *The State of the Prisons in England and Wales* (1777). We do not know if Dance read this tome, but its message was certainly in the air among the enlightened and reasonably Whiggish Englishmen whose values George Dance esteemed. Dance did not wish to create a jail along the traditional English lines – a sump of misery and social chaos, without decent ventilation, lighting, heating, sanitary provisions or even segregation of the sexes. In the 'new' Newgate he paid some attention, within a tight budget, to all of these matters, supplying such necessities of overcrowded life in a cold climate as stoves and privies. The walls of Newgate had to be blind, with no openings through which prisoners might conceivably escape to, or even glimpse, the world outside. In this, the design showed some debt to the claustrophobic spaces of Piranesi's prisons.* Further touches were directly taken from the *Carceri*, such as the festoons of carved stone chains over the prison's entrance.

It was the custom among successful architects to hire assistants and apprentices, as lawyers took articled clerks. For four years, 1768 to 1772, Dance employed a young assistant who was to change the language of English architecture, largely as a result of his visit to Rome and the influence of Piranesi. He was John Soane, to whom Dance was a 'revered master'.

Some architects come from a background of wealth and relative ease, though in the eighteenth century few did. Certainly Soane did not. He was the son of a bricklayer, always short of money, proud of his craft background, which gave him confidence in his

---

* However, the main influence on Dance here was Italian but not Piranesian. Its source was the massive rusticated stonework of Palladio's Palazzo Thiene in the centre of Vicenza, which Dance had seen on his tour and now adopted for his imagery of impenetrability and retribution: the heavy stones deliberately used as emblems of the weight of sin and crime on the crushed human conscience.

own building, but socially insecure when dealing with his 'betters'. The degree of that insecurity can be sampled, if not judged, from his change of name. His father's name was Soan; the son added a terminal e, because it seemed classier. Thenceforth he would always be referred to as 'Soane', and he would not be drawn into any conversations about his background, becoming irritable and touchy whenever social position came up in conversation. He even went back over his own early drawings when he could get at them, and 'corrected' the signatures.

Soane, with the backing of the architect William Chambers, who was the Royal Academy's influential treasurer, was awarded a travelling studentship which would finance a three-year tour of Italy. It was a well-timed stroke of fortune. His tour was not 'grand', but his sojourn in Rome put him in touch with other Englishmen who were Grand Tourists and would become his clients and colleagues in years to come. Among them was Thomas Pitt, cousin of England's future prime minister, William Pitt. Soane loved Italy so much that every year he celebrated 18 March as the day on which, aged a hopeful twenty-four, he had set out in 1777 for the wondrous south. It was not his birthday. But it was the day of his professional birth, which counted for rather more. It was just around the time that Thomas Pelham was writing home to complain about the surfeit of English tourists he encountered in Rome. The Eternal City had, he wrote, 'too great a resemblance to [Brighton], being crowded with about seventy English visitors'. (Crowded! Just as well, perhaps, that Pelham was not granted a prophetic vision of English package-tourists harried along in their thousands from bus to museum to Michelangelo to pizza-bar two centuries later.)

Soane quickly found lodgings in Rome and made the Caffè degli Inglesi in Via Due Macelli on the south side of Piazza di Spagna, rendezvous of foreign artists and intellectuals, his postal address. With his friend Thomas Hardwick, another postulant architect, he started measuring Roman buildings, both ancient and more recent: the Pantheon, the Temple of Vesta, S. Maria Maggiore, S. Agnese fuori le Mura. And, as Chambers urged, he looked up Piranesi, with whom he began a steady friendship.

But it was Soane's misfortune – which at first he mistook for good luck – to spend part of his tour with Frederick Augustus Hervey, later Bishop of Derry and presently to become the 4th Earl of Bristol. This culturally literate but deeply unpleasant cleric regarded Soane as part servant, part pet, and as a reputable creative figure only from time to time. When the two men were exploring the ruins of the Villa of Lucullus south of Rome, Derry turned to Soane and announced that he wanted to see designs made for a 'classical dog-kennel, as I intend to build one for the hounds of my eldest son'. Instead of treating this dotty idea with the repudiation it deserved, for no English architect with a sense of his own future was likely to want to spend his time housing dogs, even for a noble bishop, poor Soane – whose embarrassment at his own humble origins had not equipped him for dealing properly with the rich and titled – took the bishop seriously, went off and drew up designs for a kennel in the ancient Roman taste, decorated with every sort of doggy detail that his febrile imagination could muster. To Soane's mortification it was never built. Neither was anything else he proposed for Derry. The bishop had capriciously half-promised that Soane would get more serious work at his seat, Downhill, building for people rather than animals, when they got back to Ireland. Soane impulsively cut short his Italian trip by almost a year, went to Ireland at his own expense and spent a month there measuring and sketching. But nothing came of it; Derry dismissively dropped the idea, and the bitter disappointment this caused Soane was to skew his relations with clients for the rest of his life.

Soane was not the only person made miserable by Hervey's egocentric and brutal behaviour. The earl-bishop's wife, Elizabeth Hervey, was reduced to what her husband unkindly called a 'majestic ruin' by his vile moods. She described herself, in a sad letter to her daughter in 1778, as 'almost such a skeleton as Voltaire . . . wizened like a winter apple'.

But happily, Hervey was by no means the only person with whom Soane was significantly involved in Rome, and others were more seriously helpful. To a great extent Soane's tastes, and his way of displaying them as a collector, were formed by his acquaintance with the Roman cleric Cardinal Alessandro Albani (1692–1779). Albani was very much the child of privilege. He had been born in Urbino in 1692 and his uncle, Giovanni Francesco Albani, became pope (as Clement XI) in 1700. To the young man's mortification, this uncle had so sharply attacked the nepotism widespread in the papal court that he was unable to do much for his own relatives, including Alessandro. The young man showed promise as a linguist, a student of the classics, and a horseman; the last talent recommended him (since nepotism was not yet quite dead, this being Italy) to be made a colonel of the Papal Dragoons. His uncle Clement XI died, nepotism was given full revival, and Innocent XIII bestowed the cardinal's red hat and *fiocchi* on Alessandro at the age of twenty-nine. (It was possible to be made cardinal without being a priest first.)

Albani's nominal task in Rome was to look after the interests of its German community as 'Protector of the Holy Roman Empire'. But his main interest was a peculiarly rapacious form of archaeology; it was even said that when the catacombs were being opened and the pious nuns were sieving the dirt inside them for anything that could be called, however optimistically, a relic of an early Christian saint, Albani was right at their backs, snatching any cameos, intaglios, coins, rings or other antique titbits that might turn up. His position in the Vatican meant that he could indulge his acquisitive passions to the full, and deal without restraint. When Soane and Albani met, the cardinal had only a year to live, could barely walk, and was blind as a mole – but there was Albani's enormous, eclectic and ruthlessly acquired collection, begging to be imitated. Rivalling it became one of the central passions of Soane's later life, when he became an avid collector himself.

In addition to sponsoring neo-classicist theory and practice – Anton Raphael Mengs painted an enormous and frigid *Parnassus* for His Eminence's library, considered then and ever since, though not always with undiluted admiration, to be among the key works of neo-classicism – Albani was a formidable collector of antiquities. His palatial villa on the Via Salaria was a museum stocked with bronzes, marbles, coins and other *tesori dell'arte antica* raked in from the excavations that were going on around Rome and, in particular, from Hadrian's Villa at Tivoli. Soane visited Albani whenever he could wangle an invitation, and since Albani's hospitality to young foreigners was cast wide there were many of them.

Having Albani for a model might not seem realistic for a bricklayer's boy whose career was only just opening, but in 1784 Soane married, and richly. The bride was the niece of a wealthy English builder and property speculator. From then on Soane would never be less than comfortable. Not only could he pick and choose between projects, but he could make his own private museum, like a (less generously endowed) Cardinal Albani.

This is the wondrously diverse accumulation of architectural fragments, plaster-casts, Greek and Etruscan vases, cinerary urns and other antiquities, prints, paintings by Hogarth, Turner, Fuseli and a host of others, architectural drawings, cork models and other delights, such as the ponderous alabaster sarcophagus of the Egyptian king Seti I – all acquired by Soane over the years – that makes a visit to his house in Lincoln's Inn Fields such an adventure. No other museum in the world conveys such a powerful feeling of passing through the convolutions of another person's brain. It is the polar opposite of those boring epics of standardized taste that so many museums, especially in America, have become.

In terms of Soane's career prospects the most generous new friend he made in Rome was Thomas Pitt, the future Lord Camelford. With Thomas's cousin William Pitt's backing and encouragement, Soane was appointed Surveyor (or chief architect) to the Bank of England in 1788. This put him, at the age of thirty-five, in charge of the much needed redesign of the building, one of the most important in the city.

There are certain forms beloved by Soane that you can recognize, instantly, as coming from Piranesi's version of the ruins of Rome. One of these is the segmental arch that seems to rise from ground level, rather than being borne up on columns – a form that is all curve, no springing. It is low and gives an impression of primeval weight. It derives from the actual Roman arches that Soane had observed and drawn, half-buried in the earth. It is an extremely powerful shape, and Soane used it as the main motif in the new Bank rotunda – a ring of windows, providing the top-lighting he so prized. Soane was so enamoured of this effect that he actually commissioned the painter Joseph Gandy (1771–1843), a visionary illustrator of architectural themes who often did renderings for Soane, to create a painting of the rotunda of the Bank (1830) as a ruin.

Robert Adam (1728–92) was, with William Chambers and John Soane, the most influential British architect of the late eighteenth century. Born in Fifeshire, the son of a leading Scots architect, he was not rich but he managed to embark on a medium-Grand Tour to Europe, sharing expenses with his friend Charles Hope, younger brother of one of his father's main clients, the Earl of Hopetoun. Embarking in 1754, they travelled together through Paris, the south of France and central Italy. It was there, in Florence, that Robert Adam met the slightly older man who would prove so decisive to his career, a Frenchman who, he wrote, 'has all these Knacks, so necessary to us Architects'. This was Charles-Louis Clérisseau (1721–1820). In the course of his immensely long life, Clérisseau did not put up many buildings, though he did collaborate with Thomas Jefferson on the State House in Virginia, based on the Maison Carrée in Nîmes. His fame came from his drawings: he produced an enormous corpus of gouaches and watercolours of ancient, Renaissance and Baroque Roman monuments, both real and imaginary. He had, Adam wrote, 'the utmost knowledge of Architecture, of perspective & of Designing & Colouring I ever saw, or had any conception of; he raised my ideas. He created emulation and fire in my Breast. I wished above all things to learn his manner, to have him with me at Rome.'

The wish was granted. In Rome, Clérisseau became Adam's teacher and cicerone. His other guide was Piranesi, whom Adam met, came to know and believed was the only Italian 'to breathe

the Antient Air'. Adam did not emulate the dramatic massiveness of Piranesi's visions of ancient Rome, but his work even at its most delicately articulate was never spindly or effeminate, and he sometimes borrowed decorative details such as those in Piranesi's engravings of chimney-pieces.

He did not confine himself only to houses, either. A grandmaster of design, he filled them with furniture (chairs, chimneyboards, tables, escutcheons, doorknobs, chandeliers, carpets) and ornamented their walls and niches with painted 'Etruscan' designs and quasi-Pompeian grotesques whose twining imitated the *grotteschi* he had seen in Rome. All this was done with a consummate precision and light-handedness, not to say light-heartedness. Though he was so successful in business that he had to employ a small army of assistants and draughtsmen to satisfy the demand, there is hardly such a thing as a dull or self-repeating Adam design for anything. 'We flatter ourselves,' he remarked in the introduction to his *Works* (1773–8), '[that] we have been able to seize, with some degree of success, the beautiful spirit of antiquity and to transfuse it, with novelty and variety, through all our numerous works.' This is of course true of the greatest Adam buildings, such as Syon House, Osterley Park, Kenwood House and Kedleston; but its spirit informs all of Adam's work, and makes it perhaps the most refined and complex architectural response to Rome built anywhere in England, perhaps in Europe, in the eighteenth century.

At the time when the influence of Rome on foreign architecture was reaching its eighteenth-century meridian, the impetus of building in Rome itself had slowed considerably. There were no popes cast in the Baroque mould of architectural ambition. In fact the whole eighteenth century saw the creation of only one scheme that compared with the vast projects of an earlier Rome under Sixtus V, Julius II or Alexander VII. This was the three-flight stairway connecting the flood plain of the Tiber below to the system of streets laid out by Sixtus V above, rising from Piazza di Spagna with its Bernini ship-fountain to the triumphant, climactic surge of the Church of S. Trinità dei Monti and its attendant obelisk. Rome, being a city of hills, is also a city of steps and ramps, but the 'Spanish Steps' are the grandest and most spectacular of all its staircases – its only rival being the flight of steps down the side of the Campidoglio that connects S. Maria in Aracoeli to Piazza Venezia. The Spanish Steps were constructed between 1723 and 1726 to the designs of Francesco de Sanctis (c.1693–1731), the very young architect of the French Minims who owned the whole hillside down from the church, and it was his only major work in Rome. The commissioning pope was Innocent XIII. It grew out of an unrealized project of Gianlorenzo Bernini's, who in the 1660s was thinking of a monumental ramp connecting the Piazza di Spagna below to the church above. It would include an equestrian monument to Louis XIV as its centrepiece. For various political reasons this was not carried out. The division of the stairway into three major flights and three landings refers to the Trinity (Father, Son, Holy Spirit) after which the church at its summit is named.

The Spanish Steps are the only great rococo monument in Rome, and in fairness, they should not be called Spanish at all, but French. (They got the name from the building at number 50 Piazza di Spagna, which was and is the Spanish Embassy to the Holy See.) The French Minims controlled and supplied the funds to build them, and de Sanctis had worked for them since 1715. This masterpiece, however, finished the architect's career. In 1728 defective engineering combined with freakishly heavy rains caused the upper part of the stairs, linked to the Viale del Pincio, to collapse; and although repairs were made, and the disaster was not de Sanctis's fault, he got no more projects in the city he had so unforgettably embellished.

Today, most visitors to this part of Rome have little or no interest in the Spanishness of the Spanish Steps. They, or rather their flanking buildings, have other claims on one's attention. Two of the greatest English poets of the nineteenth century are associated with them. In a tiny museum room with a view in the Casina Rossa, as the building at 26 Piazza di Spagna is called (for its colour), the poet John Keats lived for a time, and died at the age of twenty-five on the evening of 23 February 1821; his gently smiling death-mask is preserved there, along with a lock of his hair and a carnival mask worn in Venice by his fellow poet Lord Byron. English doctors had sent Keats to Rome, hoping it would cure his tuberculosis, but it did not. He was buried in the Protestant cemetery not far from the Pyramid of Caius Cestius, in a tomb which bears the famous inscription, 'Here lies one whose name was writ in water.' His friend Percy Bysshe Shelley lies nearby, in the 'New Cemetery' of non-Catholics, along with August, the only son of Goethe (1789–1830), and the Marxist political theorist Antonio Gramsci.

The flood of information about ancient art, of archaeological discovery, of new specimens, fragments and entire masterpieces that was appearing every month from the plum-pudding of Italy was bound to produce its interpreters. The leading one – the man who revolutionized archaeology by creating a framework in which antiquities could be classified by style and time of origin – was Johann Joachim Winckelmann (1717–68).

To the extent that Winckelmann is read at all today, it is by scholars of the discipline of art history, not by art scholars. The almost papal influence and prestige his writings acquired in the eighteenth and early nineteenth centuries have evaporated, but his position as one of the 'fathers of art history' is secure and presumably always will be. 'Winckelmann must be regarded as one of those who developed a new organ,' wrote Georg Hegel, 'and opened up fresh perspectives in the world of art.' Goethe regarded him as hardly less than a moral hero. 'While the characters of many men, and especially of scholars, tend to disappear from view as we look at their achievements, the opposite is true of Winckelmann: everything that he produces is great and remarkable because it reveals his character.' To see that character in action, in all its fervent enthusiasm for the Greek ideal, one should consult his famous dithyramb on the marble statue known as the Apollo Belvedere, 'the most sublime of all the statues of antiquity':

An eternal spring, such as reigned in the blessed Elysian fields, clothes the attractive manliness of full maturity with delectable youth, and plays about the majestic frame of his limbs with soft tenderness. Pass with your spirit into the kingdom of incorporeal beauties and try to become a creator of a heavenly nature, to fill your spirit with beauty that rises above nature: for there is nothing mortal here, nothing that human appetite demands. No veins, no sinews, heat and stir his body . . . His delicate hair plays about the divine head, like the slender and waving tendrils of a noble vine, stirred, as it were, by a soft breeze; it seems to be anointed with the oil of the gods . . . my breast seems to dilate and swell with reverence . . . How is it possible to describe it?

It sounds faintly ridiculous now. One doubts the truth of such ecstasies. It might not have been entirely possible, but many a visitor to the Vatican Belvedere, where the Apollo stood (enclosed in a kind of wooden sentry-box to protect it from unauthorized eyes), tried very hard. To see the Apollo was considered both a privilege and a high point of one's Roman visit, and Winckelmann, in his position as librarian to Cardinal Albani (whose near-total blindness had not impeded his appointment as head of the Vatican Library), was the gatekeeper of such occasions. When the painter Benjamin West came to Rome, its cognoscenti were agog with curiosity about what the American's reaction to the Apollo would be. Not a few supposed that, being American, he was some kind of Noble Savage complete with feathers, and were politely surprised to see before them a young Philadelphia Quaker. Thirty carriages had followed him and Winckelmann to the Vatican. The marble deity stood revealed; West exclaimed, 'My God, a young Mohawk warrior!' Winckelmann was thrilled; this could only confirm his argument that the Greek masters had created archetypes of mankind, true across all cultures.

Winckelmann was a cobbler's son from the provincial town of Stendal who, by dint of fierce application, studied Greek, Latin and theology at the universities of Halle and Jena. He taught classics and became a librarian. By 1754 he was involved as a librarian with the court of Augustus III, Elector of Saxony, and began – while having seen, as yet, very little of classical art beyond some engravings – to develop his theories about the relative merits of Greek art, which he regarded as the supreme aesthetic achievement of mankind, and Roman art, which to all intents he dismissed as a corrupt imitation, unworthy of its Greek prototypes. His library work in Dresden brought him into contact with the man who changed his life, the papal nuncio to the court of Saxony, Count Alberigo Archinto. It happened that Archinto, mortally bored with what he regarded as his 'Babylonian exile', had a friend at court – the papal court, far away in Rome. This was Cardinal Passionei, scholar and *secretarius brevium*, in charge of the promulgation of all papal briefs, who (by a nice coincidence) was looking for a librarian who could set in order his collection of three hundred thousand volumes. Archinto recommended Winckelmann to him. Passionei responded favourably, and offered the young German aesthete a room in his own palace in the Vatican. Winckelmann realized that this kind of offer would not be made twice. Everything was drawing and pushing him to Rome, the centre of the world's art.

For convenience and to show his sincerity, Winckelmann underwent conversion to the Roman Catholic faith, a move which horrified his Lutheran associates but opened to him a far wider field – of clerical contacts, of collections, of access of every sort – than he could ever have had as a mere Protestant neophyte, a naive heretic in the Eternal City. Lutheranism would do nothing for a man whose obsession was with antiquity. Rome and its clergy could do everything. Winckelmann had no family ties that could impede a conversion to Catholicism. His beloved mother was long dead; his father, in 1750, had succumbed to epilepsy. Winckelmann also knew very well that without first-hand contact with Rome, that immersion in antiquity far deeper than anything he could scratch together by looking at engravings in books, he would never win recognition as an *Aufklärer*, a wise and enlightening connoisseur. Expatriation or obscurity, go or die: there was no other choice, he would go to Rome. But before he went, he would write.

His first attempt at art criticism rested on wobbly foundations. Published in 1755, the year he left for Rome, *Gedanken über die Nachahmung der griechischen Werke in der Malerei und Bildhauerkunst* ('Reflections on the Imitation of Greek Works in Painting and Sculpture') was his effort to enshrine ancient Greek art at the topmost and purest pinnacle of taste. It suffers, in retrospect, from the fact that Winckelmann at the time literally did not know what he was talking about. He had scarcely seen any Greek art; he had only read about it, and seen a few engravings. But this was also true of his own readers and it made very little difference; the essay was an immediate success. One phrase from it in particular became a standard utterance in the presence of the Ideal, a motto of neo-classicism: the characteristic of high Greek sculpture was *eine edle Einfalt, eine stille Grösse* – 'a noble simplicity, a calm grandeur'. This essay later became the basis of his most influential and elaborate work, his *Geschichte der Kunst des Alterthums* ('History of Ancient Art', 1767).

Winckelmann was chiefly responsible for implanting the modern belief that later classic art, Greek and Roman, was a degenerate form of the 'pure', early Hellenic tradition. There were no limits to his admiration for Hellas. 'Our race is not likely to produce as perfect a body as the "Antinous Admirandus", nor can our ideas conceive anything beyond the superhuman and harmonious proportions of a god as they have taken shape in the "Apollo Belvedere". Here is the consummation of the best that nature, art and the human mind can produce. I believe that imitating the Greeks can teach us to become wise more quickly . . . They have marked for us the utmost limits of human and divine beauty.' This, Winckelmann believed, was partly because the Greeks had achieved a sort of genetic transcendence, expressed in the 'great care' they took to 'have beautiful offspring'. They sought to avoid any distortion of their own bodies; Alcibiades 'refused to play the flute in his youth because it might distort his face, and the Athenian youths followed his example'.

In the true and exemplary art of Greek antiquity, Winckelmann saw the refutation of much of his own age and its cultural expressions. Modern artists had gone off the rails, and the Baroque filled Winckelmann with disgust. Among his contemporaries, 'especially the famous ones' (meaning the school of Bernini), admiration was reserved for 'exaggerated poses and actions, accompanied by an insolent "dash" that they regard as spiritedness ... Their favourite concept is "contrapposto", which for them is the essence of everything that makes for artistic perfection. They want their figures to have souls as eccentric as comets.' Since *contrapposto* – the depiction of a standing figure with its main weight reposing on one leg – was an absolutely fundamental device of classical Greek art later than the archaic, one may well wonder what Winckelmann thought he was getting at.

Nevertheless, it was really Winckelmann who invented the idea of stylistic development within antiquity, a master-story of rise and decline. He was also the first writer to create a sexual narrative within his subject. As noted earlier, Winckelmann was homosexual – when his friend Casanova interrupted him in mid-grapple with a servant one Roman afternoon, he unconvincingly explained that he had undertaken this sexual adventure in the interests of research, since he wanted to know what it was that the ancient Greeks had liked so much. But his yearning, lip-smacking descriptions of the ideal Greek body obviously come from deeper sources: and his descriptions of the canon, in which (for instance) the left testicle is always larger than the right, are permeated with desire.

Unhappily, his sexual passions not only supplied fuel for his art interpretation, they led to his death. In the spring of 1768, after a meeting with the empress Maria Teresa in Vienna, he was passing through Trieste on his way back to Rome when his eye was caught by a young, pockmarked hustler on the waterfront, by the name of Francesco Arcangeli. Winckelmann made the classic mistake of boasting to Arcangeli about his exalted friends in Rome, and showing him some valuable medals the Empress had given him. They were both in Winckelmann's room, no. 10 in the comfortable Locanda Grande, when Arcangeli turned on Winckelmann, tried to choke him with a cord and then repeatedly stabbed him.

Few sexual encounters between foreigners and natives in Rome had such drastic outcomes, but it need hardly be emphasized that prostitution was one of the most commonplace and visibly eternal aspects of the Eternal City. For the visitor its very air was saturated with sex, offered, bought, paid for and consummated. If you were male and could manage a trip to Rome without getting laid, this could only be because you did not want sex. The frequency with which tourists indulged their tender passions is certainly hard to gauge, since letters home do not always describe it – sex with Italian strangers, socially high or low, was not the first thing you would tell the family about – and diaries were often censored and tampered with by the traveller's descendants. But the availability of Italian women – not only professionals, but more or less respectable married ones as well – was a well-known fact among English travellers. 'If Italy don't spoil his Chastity and Germany his Sobriety, I flatter myself he will preserve the character he sets out with, as an honest worthy young man,' wrote Sir George Oxenden of his son Henry (1721–1803). Few Grand Tourists could have been unaware of the major punishment of vice, death by venereal disease, or of the painful and usually ineffective treatments eighteenth-century medicine reserved for the pox. Among others Charles Howard, Viscount Morpeth, succumbed to it in Rome in 1741 in his early twenties, necessitating a by-election in Yorkshire.

The perils of vice had been a well-known feature of Rome since antiquity, when prostitutes were called *lupe* or she-wolves, perhaps in homage to the original *lupa* who suckled Romulus and Remus, and brothels – particularly dense in the area of the city known as Suburra – were known as 'lupanars'. We owe one of our commonest sex terms to the humble environment in which so many of the street girls traded; they offered sex out of doors, in the arches or *fornices* of the city; hence, 'fornication'.

There were myriad steps between this commonplace rutting and the much more costly engagements offered by quality ladies – between the ordinary work of the whores (*puttane*, from which comes the name of the delicious *pasta alla puttanesca*, a simple dish using olives, anchovies and onions, easily prepared while in between clients) and that of the *meretrici* or, at the top, of the *cortegiane*, the courtesans, who could expect to be escorted out on ceremonial occasions and receive a place at table – and even enjoyed real social and political power. Such women counted nobles, prelates and even cardinals among their clientele. The scale of their income was recognized by realistic and heavy taxation, which at times became necessary to the income balance of the Roman state. Some even endowed their own churches. Areas of the city were set aside for them, not only in life, but in death as well; a favoured spot for the burial of ordinary whores, in unconsecrated ground, was by the wall known as the Muro Torto at the ancient entrance to the Villa Borghese. This practice fell into disuse, perhaps because the hookers' cemetery ran out of space.

An effort was made in September 1870 to systematize the sex trade in Rome by the introduction of *casini* or 'closed houses' – so called because their blinds and shutters were kept closed, by law – in a very limited number of locations. By 1930 there were nineteen of these highly ordered and state-supervised brothels, with strict rules: the client had to be able to show his age (the prescribed minimum being eighteen years, three months and a day), and could enjoy the services of the sex-workers only between 10 a.m. and midnight, never staying the night. Naturally, the actual business done in these places was only a fraction of the whole prostitution industry of Rome, but one had to start somewhere.

Any great society like Rome's, at almost any time, is bound to have its sex-goddesses who are not, in fact, prostitutes: women famed for their beauty and desirability who are known to everyone but are not in the trade. Rome, of course, had several, and the most famous of them is commemorated in a statue. Her marble effigy reclines in its own chamber in the Villa Borghese, queening it over all the rest of the women (except Bernini's) in the building. This is Antonio Canova's full-length, semi-nude, reclining marble portrait of Maria Paolina Bonaparte (1780–1825), the sister of

Napoleon who, renowned for her beauty, had married Prince Camillo Borghese. It is one of the absolutely iconic images of woman in Western art, as justly celebrated in its way as the *Mona Lisa*, and not without a parallel mystery of expression, which is hinted at in its title, *La Venere Vincitrice*, 'Victorious Venus'. This is a masterpiece at the end of a tradition which runs from the earlier reclining nudes of Titian and Giorgione to Jacques-Louis David's slightly later portrait of Madame Récamier.

That Antonio Canova (1757–1822) was the last of the line of great and generally admired Italian sculptors, the eighteenth-century successor in fame and reputation to Gianlorenzo Bernini in the seventeenth century, without rivals in his lifetime or successors after his death, can hardly be doubted today. His very presence in Rome, and his art's relation to Roman prototypes, seemed to confirm that the city had kept an undiminished vitality as a centre of the world's culture. His success as a professional artist was on an almost Berninian scale, even though, unlike Bernini, his architectural ambitions were modest and he built nothing in Rome and only one major building outside it – but the work kept pouring from the studio and the commissions kept pouring in. No Italian artist since Bernini had the relations Canova enjoyed with the great and the good of his day: with the popes he served, depicted and memorialized (Clement XIII, Clement XIV, Pius VII); with bankers and politicians; with princesses and other powerful women; with every sort of foreigner.

Canova never married and had no children. He may have been homosexual but there is no real evidence for that: only the famous but rather ambiguous story about Paolina Bonaparte, who, on being asked if she had never felt some frisson of anxiety being naked in the studio with the maestro for so many hours and days, retorted that 'With Canova there was never any danger.' More likely he was one of those artists whose entire libido is subsumed in his creativity, leaving no room for the distraction of sexual expression. This could not have meant that he was an introvert, or in any way a selfish man. Rather the contrary: he had a large and thoroughly deserved reputation for generosity. A tireless worker in the studio, he also spent large sums from his own earnings giving support to other and less successful Italian artists, including students, and on the commendable project of keeping Italian art in Italy, defending it against the merciless suction of foreign capital.

He constantly visited archaeological sites (Naples, Paestum, Pompeii, Pozzuoli), acquired Roman antiquities for the Vatican museums, and did his best to stem the export of works of art. He was helped in this difficult and distracting task by Pius VII's appointment of him as *ispettore generale* of antiquities and fine arts for the Papal States, which gave him the power to block foreign sales of significant artwork. In 1815, after the fall of Napoleon, it was Canova who went to Paris to earmark for return the major works of art the French had abducted from Italy and the Papal States during the Napoleonic wars, an essential part of Italy's cultural patrimony that included the Apollo Belvedere and the Laocoön.

Canova had never been to Greece, but that did not imply that he was ignorant of classical Greek sculpture. Some was to be seen in Italy, and though little of that was in Venice when he was a young artist, he eagerly drew and imitated the plaster-casts of ancient Greek sculptures assembled there in Palazzo Farsetti by Filippo Farsetti, a Venetian collector who wanted to provide his city's young artists with a sense of quality. His reputation as *the* authority on ancient sculpture was such that the English government brought him to London to certify the Phidian origins of the Elgin Marbles from the Parthenon. Critics who were against their purchase (often out of venomous dislike of Lord Elgin, masquerading as a desire for economy) wanted to dismiss them as vulgar Roman copies from the age of Hadrian, not even Greek, let alone by Phidias. Canova's opinion as the greatest living sculptor was rightly considered to be decisive: he thought the marbles genuine, 'stupendous and unforgettable', and said that any attempt at restoring them, even to touch them with a chisel or a rasp, would be 'sacrilege'.

Among the English *milordi* in particular, Canova had an immense vogue. Although nobody could mistake one of his carvings for an ancient marble of the kind he sometimes indirectly quoted, English connoisseurs and collectors credited him with the authority of the best Graeco-Roman antiquity. The Hanoverian king George IV bought his work, and as prince regent presented him with a diamond-studded snuffbox bearing his royal portrait in miniature. Canova did not take snuff. He was urged to try a pinch, and on opening the box the sculptor found a five-hundred-pound banknote in it. And in the early nineteenth century, a pound was very much a pound.

Canova designed a cenotaph for the royal Stuarts in St Peter's which Stendhal, no less, thought was the touchstone of one's appreciation of sculpture – if it left you cold, you had no feeling for the art. Practically every English or European writer of note was deeply affected, sometimes even shocked, by encountering his work. 'The devils!' William Wordsworth exclaimed on catching his first sight of Canova's entwined lovers, *Cupid and Psyche*. But the overwhelming feeling it induced was nostalgia – a kind of longing for an imagined Golden Age of antiquity, when emotions, whether of patriotic valour, of piety or of young love, were pure and unsullied. A partial list of the well-known British writers who found themselves stirred to the marrow by Canova would include Keats, Coleridge, Thomas Moore, the Brownings and, of course, Byron. 'Italy has great names still,' Byron wrote in the preface to Canto IV of *Childe Harold's Pilgrimage* (1818); 'Canova, Monti, Ugo Foscolo ... will secure to the present generation an honourable place ... and in some the very highest: Europe – the World – has but one Canova.' If one added the French, German, Russian and of course the Italian ones, the list would be even more eminent. Small wonder that collectors all over Europe, from the Devonshires at Chatsworth in England to Russian royalty in St Petersburg, competed to possess his work and vied to pay the highest prices for it.

Canova was tirelessly and exuberantly inventive, creating entire new conventions for such constantly worked-over problems as the design of tombs. As a funerary sculptor and an interpreter of myth in stone, nobody in his time could approach him. He was, for instance, the first artist in modern times to find something fresh in one of the most ancient of all commemorative forms, the Egyptian pyramid, that symbol of grief, permanence and transcendence. The finest of Canova's pyramidal tombs (1798–1805) is in the Augustinian church in Vienna, and contains the ashes of Maria Christina of Austria. In the tombs of the past, figures had been included or integrated with the structure. Canova had the simple but brilliant idea of detaching them so that they move, as it were, from our space into the domain of death; they form a procession of young and old mourners towards the dark doorway which contains the corpse invisibly and swallows up the visible living. Canova was thinking of the pyramids of Egypt, but even more of the Pyramid of Cestius, which he had seen so often in Rome.

No artist who came later, with the single spectacular (though very different) exception of Auguste Rodin in France, achieved Canova's measure of fame and influence in his own lifetime. He was, and still is, the only sculptor in all history to have a monument erected to him while he was still alive.

After his death in 1822, all this fell apart. The reaction against him began in England, with John Ruskin, who fulminated that the demand for Canova's work only went to prove the decadence of the upper classes – cold, over-idealized, boring. By the twentieth century good taste had come to neglect or even to utterly despise him, and the praises heaped on him in earlier times looked like so much fustian, the products of some kind of collective delusion against which modernism, happily, had inoculated most of us, leaving only reactionaries to admire his like. Nobody seemed to be speaking up for him, even in his native country, whose unrivalled culture hero he once had been. Its most powerful art critic, Roberto Longhi, let fly at 'the funereal blunders of Antonio Canova, the still-born sculptor whose heart is buried in the church of the Frari, whose hand is in the Accademia and the rest of him buried I know not where'.* We critics all make mistakes, but this was an extreme one; one may or may not share Canova's idealism about the body – he was perhaps the last great sculptor to implicitly share Spenser's belief that 'Soule is Forme, and doth the Bodie make' – but there is hardly a 'funereal blunder' anywhere in his large and immensely refined output.

If ever an artist appeared at the exact moment when his society most needed him, it was Antonio Canova. He was the last of a line of geniuses who redefined the art from the late fourteenth century, through Andrea Pisano in the late Middle Ages to Donatello in the Quattrocento, to Michelangelo in the High Renaissance and Bernini after them. But after Canova there would be no more such figures.

Inevitably, one's feelings about the singularity of Canova are increased by his isolation within his moment in Italian cultural history; aside from him, that history, at the start of the nineteenth century, was at a low ebb – the lowest it had ever reached, though not as debased as it would be by the start of the twenty-first. Its long-lasting cultural primacy, especially in the plastic arts (painting, sculpture, architecture), was a thing of the past. There were no Italian writers who could be even fleetingly compared to Dante; Alessandro Manzoni, the future author of *I Promessi Sposi*, had not yet appeared, and neither had the romantic genius of Giuseppe Verdi emerged to vitalize Italian music. The situation of the arts in Italy echoed, broadly speaking, the miseries of politics: almost all authority gone, almost all power in the hands of foreigners, most conspicuously Napoleon.

The heyday of the Grand Tour was well and truly over by 1800. The French Revolutionary war broke out in 1792 and it had immediate repercussions on continental travel, especially for the

---

* This refers to the reverent dismemberment of Canova's body for burial. Most of his body was interred in his own museum–mausoleum in Possagno, his birthplace in northern Italy. However, his heart was placed in the monument to Canova in the Church of the Frari, Venice; and his amputated right hand is in an urn in the Accademia di Belle Arti, Venice.

English. The threat of French naval action against Rome and Naples was taken very seriously. Britain entered the conflict in 1793; no Englishman now could contemplate a journey across France, and although it would perhaps have been possible to plan a trip to Italy by the sea route through the Bay of Biscay and the straits of Gibraltar, the fear that the French might get complete control of the Mediterranean and thus be able to interdict British shipping going either way was a powerful discouragement to civilian travel to Italy by sea.

The spectacle of the Terror made matters worse. Who, for the sake of culture, was going to risk leaving his head in a basket at the foot of the guillotine? The Grand Tourist's noble and illustrious contacts on the Continent were being killed or forced to flee. British diplomats were being withdrawn. Banking was in chaos. Access to Italian monasteries, nunneries and academies closed down. The art market collapsed in the face of massive confiscations; Lord Derry's large collection of antiquities, for instance, which had imprudently been left in storage in Rome, was simply seized by the French as loot; portable ones, such as the Laocoön and the Apollo Belvedere, were taken to Paris (whence Canova would retrieve them in due course); immovable ones, like murals, rendered harder to get to. The French occupied Rome in 1798 and founded the Roman Republic; Pope Pius VI went into exile (in France) in 1799. The entire cultural world of Europe, in short, was in upheaval and shock.

৵ 10 ৵

THE NINETEENTH CENTURY:
ORTHODOXY VERSUS
MODERNISM

Deep change in Italy was set off by Napoleon, when he invaded the north in 1796. Napoleonic ideas never found a following among the illiterate peasantry who made up most of the Italian population, which certainly had no say in how it was governed. But Buonaparte could challenge the authority of royalty and the Papacy and not look like a foreign intruder, because, on the simplest level, he was of Italian blood – or could plausibly claim to be, since his native Corsica had been Italian territory right up to the moment Genoa sold it to France less than three decades before, in 1768.

At this time, there was no sense in which Rome could have been called the political 'capital' of Italy, except that the Papacy was based there. Italian politics had no capital. The whole country was crippled by what it called *campanilismo*, the bewildering profusion of municipalities, local centres of power. A traveller descending the river Po had to traverse no fewer than twenty-two customs barriers, submitting to search and the payment of imposts at each stop. No common currency existed: in Piedmont one paid in lire, in Naples with *ducati*, in the Papal States with *scudi*, in Sicily with *oncie*. Exchange rates fluctuated, often at the whim of whoever was manning the customs and excise barriers. Merely to say 'Sono Italiano' was to invite mirth or, more likely, incomprehension. One was Roman, Neapolitan, Sicilian – not Italian. But Florentines despised Venetians, who loathed Neapolitans, who felt nothing in common with Abruzzesi, who looked down their noses at Sicilians, who resented any imputation that they might be from the mainland across the Strait of Messina.

The result was that, although the tiny minority of Italian

highbrows and literati were able to feel various cultural bonds in common – such as sharing the homeland of Dante or Michelangelo – this was much less of an option for the illiterate or the culturally indifferent who comprised most of the population. Moreover, it placed great importance on local dialects, which were immensely varied and whose differences all but guaranteed cultural disunity. So understandably the Code Napoléon, the uniform legal system the conqueror sought to impose on Italy, though attractive to a few educated Italians longing for good, responsible government, was met with disdain by the masses, who did not believe that such a government could exist. And besides, they had become used to and even protective of the patchwork of ill-framed laws that defined their civic lives.

Nevertheless, Napoleon went right ahead with his plans. On taking charge of a conquered Italy he proceeded to depose all its kings except those of Sardinia and Sicily, whose kingdoms, protected by the British Navy, were able to keep their independence. He was determined to cancel the powers of the great landowners and of the Catholic Church, which, working together, provided the utmost resistance to his rule. To the impotent horror of Italian conservatives, he evicted the pope from Rome and took over the temporal power of the Church, dissolving the Papal States as a political entity. At a stroke of his pen he reduced the number of Italian states to three – Piedmont, Naples and his own conquered territory, including the former Papal States, which he renamed the Cisalpine Republic. Little by little, French Revolutionary ideas began to take hold in Italy.

But they hardly had the time to fix themselves there. Napoleon was defeated at Waterloo in 1815, and with his fall the Congress of Vienna immediately set about reassigning the states of Italy to their former rulers. The Bourbon monarchs reclaimed Naples and Sicily (the so-called Kingdom of the Two Sicilies). Austria recovered her former possession Lombardy, and was given Venetia as well. The Grand Duke Ferdinand III, brother to the Austrian emperor, was restored to his dominion over Tuscany. And most important of all, the central states of Italy reverted to the Papacy.

28 Annibale Carracci
The Bean-Eater, 1580–1590
Oil on Canvas, 57 × 68 cm;
Galleria Colonna, Rome

29 Annibale Carracci
*The Triumph of Bacchus
and Ariadne, 1597*
Fresco; Palazzo Farnese, Rome

35 Diego Velázquez
Portrait of Innocent X, 1650
Oil on canvas, 114 × 119 cm;
Galleria Doria Pamphili, Rome

41 Borromini
Sant'Agnese in Agone,
1653–1657

42 Borromini
Sant'Ivo alla
Sapienza, 1660

Meanwhile, that formidable exponent of counter-revolutionary tactics Prince Metternich of Austria, who had some seventy thousand men within the 'quadrilateral' of central Lombardy, made a military alliance with Naples, whose object was to indefinitely maintain Austria's 'right' to interfere in Italy. For him the very term 'Italy' had no meaning; it was, he memorably said, merely a 'geographic expression'.

Thus Italy was, if anything, even more disunited than she had been before Napoleon's invasion. It was a situation bitterly lamented by her writers and intellectuals, including the poet Leopardi (1798–1837):

> I see the walls and arches, O my Italy,
> The columns and the images, the solitary
> Towers of our ancestors,
> But this I do not see:
> The glorious laurels and the swords they bore
> In ancient times . . .
> Who brought her down to this? – and what is worse,
> Both her arms are bound about with chains . . .
> Weep, for you have good cause, my Italy.

By the early nineteenth century Rome was swarming with foreign artists; despite Napoleon's invasion, the city had come to be regarded, once again, as the world's school. Several of these expatriates rivalled the native Italians not only in reputation, but in the demand for their work: if you could not secure a piece by Canova, for instance, a very good neo-classical sculpture by the Danish sculptor Bertel Thorvaldsen (1770–1844) was an acceptable replacement and could well be available.

Thorvaldsen, who spent most of his working life in Rome, first went there on a scholarship in 1797 after entering the Royal Danish Academy of Fine Arts at the precocious age of eleven.

It was not always easy, at first sight, to distinguish Thorvaldsen's mature work from Canova's. The subjects were much the same, drawn from Homeric poetry and Grecian antiquity in general:

Thorvaldsen's over-life-size *Jason with the Golden Fleece* (1803–28) produced many similar commissions – *Ganymede*, *Hebe*, *Apollo* and so on. He was also a prolific and fluent portrait sculptor – Byron's letters reveal how eagerly he was waiting for Thorvaldsen to complete his bust and that of his adored Venetian mistress. Canova's sculptures had more surface polish and Thorvaldsen's tended to be matt, but this difference was sometimes reduced or even abolished by over-energetic cleaning. Most of his major sculptures found their way to his native Copenhagen, where, emulating the example of Canova's museum at Possagno, he endowed his city with a large and comprehensive collection of his own work. Nobody could have accused this Dane of a hampering modesty: one of his larger self-portrait sculptures represented him as Thor, the thunder-god.

Not the least aspect of Thorvaldsen's sojourn in Rome was his support of other expatriate artists, mainly from the north, whose work he thought significant. He was particularly attracted to the work of the so-called Nazarenes, a group of young Germans who had set themselves up in Rome – they were given the nickname by more sceptical Germans in Rome for their demonstrative piety. He bought their work in some quantity, forming the city's most important collection of modern works of art in Rome. The Nazarenes' chief figures were Joseph Anton Koch, Peter Cornelius, Wilhelm Schadow and their leader, Friedrich Overbeck (1789–1869). The chief literary influence on Thorvaldsen's and his friends' work was an essay by the German cultural ecstatic Wilhelm Wackenroder, *Outpourings from the Heart of an Art-Loving Monk*. In it, as the title suggests, art was discussed as a holy activity akin to prayer, leading to an unshakeable belief in divine nature. Other artists and writers might feel they were part of the great movement towards the secularization of culture which was under way throughout Europe at the end of the eighteenth century, but Overbeck and his friends in Rome did not, and wished only to oppose and reverse it. They felt their duty was to create a revival of religious art in Germany and, spreading outwards from there, throughout Europe. Religion, Overbeck came to believe, was the true foundation of art. Merely secular painting was culturally impotent. This was the basis of the revulsion he felt at the wholly secular, classicizing teaching methods of the Academy he attended in Vienna (1806–9). But the starting place for its assimilation into visual culture, he concluded, would have to be Rome, that mighty capital of past religious imagery. Other young artists he came to know at the Academy felt the same, and just as warmly; among them were Ludwig Vogel, Franz Hottinger and Franz Pforr.

Together they formed a small confraternity they called the Lukasbruder, or 'Brothers in St Luke' – the Apostle Luke, said to have painted the Virgin Mary from life, being the patron saint of artists. The past artists they most admired and sought to imitate were early Italians of the Renaissance, particularly Masaccio and Fra Angelico. These, the 'Lukes' believed, were more sincere and naively truthful in their responses to Nature and to religious faith than any painters of the Baroque or neo-classical persuasion. Baroque artists were coarsened by the rhetoric of their style; neo-classical ones, by an excessive refinement and the traces of paganism. It was hardly surprising that the ideas of the Lukes would presently cross to England and find strong echoes in the work of the Pre-Raphaelite Brotherhood.

'Art is to me,' declared Overbeck, 'what the harp was to David. I use it on every occasion to utter psalms in praise of the Lord.' But what had become of this sacred impulse, once so general among painters? It had irreversibly declined, wrote Franz Pforr in Vienna. The fact was that not all the art that was being made in Rome was 'sacred' or even Christian-religious in its general themes. Neo-classicism itself worked against so narrow a definition of the artist's role in Rome and it tended to contradict exclusively religious, or even primarily moral, readings of art and its functions – simply by holding up pre-Christian themes as desirable ones. In times gone by, 'few men can have had so strong an influence upon morality and virtue' as artists. But now, in these fallen times, it had declined and could only be brought back with difficulty. 'When we consider the ends for which [art] is now used, one can only deplore that its decay is so very general. Formerly

the artist tried to charm the spectator into devotion by representing pious objects, and to induce him to emulate the noble actions
he depicted; and now? A nude Venus with her Adonis, a Diana in
her bath – towards what good end can such representations point?'

Both Pforr and Overbeck found the classical past, as promoted
at the academies, not only irrelevant to the present but even
slightly disgusting to a good Christian soul. 'Why do we seek
subjects so distant from our interests?' Pforr demanded. 'Why not
instead those that concern us? In the old Israelite stories we find
more material than anywhere else.' Overbeck was saying the
same, in more high-flown accents of faith.

It seemed to them that there was only one place where such
desires could be satisfied, where a young German could complete
his religious and artistic education; Rome, just by virtue of being
a religious capital, would provide the balance the young Germans
sought between stylistic tradition and living faith. Overbeck and
Pforr longed to immerse themselves in it, not for the ancient
marbles (they had seen quite enough of the Academy's plaster-
casts of those) but for the accumulated deposit of Christian belief
the city represented. The very name of Rome spoke to pious
young Germans like these with an intensity and promise that no
other place could offer. They were determined to move there.
And so, in May 1810, Overbeck, Pforr and the two other art
students, Hottinger and Vogel, left Vienna for the Holy City. They
entered Rome a month later, scarcely stopping to look at anything
on the way.

The city at the time was still occupied by the French, who had
closed and secularized a number of its religious institutions. One
of these was the Irish-Franciscan monastery of S. Isidoro up on
the Pincio above Piazza del Popolo. The Napoleonic occupation
had driven its monks out and the four youngsters, with minimal
bargaining, got a lease on rooms there. Wackenroder had written
about the monastic ideal of an artist's life, and where better to live
it than in a real, if admittedly disused and rented, monastery? The
pattern of activity was to work all day in one's cell and then meet
up in the refectory at evening, to argue, confess and carouse.

Many bottles of Frascati were consumed and then smashed. Soon, the group became known as the Fratelli di Sant'Isidoro, a nickname given special point by their way of dressing in cowl-like hats and monkish habits; the street where the monastery stood became the Via degli Artisti.

Their group was quite short-lived. They saw themselves as missionaries, bent on converting the 'heathens' of art. They sought to establish the primacy of religious art as it once had been, before art lost its purity to secularism and academic thinking. Fra Angelico, early Raphael, and such northern masters as Dürer and Jan van Eyck: these were their heroes and touchstones. Later Overbeck would produce a large painting for a German client, *The Triumph of Religion in the Arts*, accompanied by a lengthy written explanation of how 'true art' had petered out with the Renaissance and featuring some sixty portrait-heads of approved artists. Other young Germans would presently join this Roman nucleus of the Nazarenes. One was Julius Schnorr von Carolsfeld (1794–1872), son of a German history painter, who applied to Overbeck for admittance to the group, was accepted, and wrote his delighted thanks: 'You have judged me worthy to join your glorious ranks as a brother. Thus take me into your arms! My being is now tied to yours!'

Some of these artists, including Carolsfeld, were deeply influenced by the German practice, strong among the expatriates in Rome, of painting what they called 'friendship pictures', portraits of themselves and their German friends far from their native homes but locked in the fealty of common interest, a mutual loyalty sanctified by its enactment in the Holy City. One eloquent example among many was Wilhelm Schadow's *Self Portrait with Brother Ridolfo Schadow and Bertel Thorvaldsen* (1815).

Wilhelm and Ridolfo were the two sons of the eminent Berlin sculptor Johann Gottfried Schadow (1764–1850), who, as a friend of Canova's, had made the decisive pilgrimage to Rome and converted to Catholicism in 1785. Going to Rome themselves, they swore to one another that 'they would rather stay dead in Rome than return unknown to their home city'. Wilhelm's painting shows the taking of this oath. On the right, Wilhelm with his palette and brushes solemnly shaking hands with Ridolfo, who is holding his stonecarver's hammer; between them, the Danish sculptor Thorvaldsen, his left hand resting in comradely style on Wilhelm's shoulder, his firm gaze fixed on Ridolfo. Linking the figures in the group is the marble carving that won Ridolfo his early reputation in Rome, the *Sandalbinderin* or 'Girl Fastening Her Sandal'. It had been much admired for its truth and sincerity by Overbeck and other Nazarenes.

Overbeck refused to paint or even look at the female nude. To do so, he thought, was immoral. This shifted the terms of allegory; an earlier artist might have painted 'Italy' as a splendid naked nymph, but Overbeck would not. The painting that most expressed the Nazarenes' feelings about Italy was probably the pair of fully clothed figures by Overbeck, depicting the cultural union of Italy and Germany. Blonde Maria and dark Shulamit: the left-hand figure, crowned with a wreath of olive and bending attentively towards her companion, is 'Italia' and the landscape behind her is that of Italy – rolling hills, a rural *casa colonica*; the one on the right, who bends eagerly forward, holds Italia's hand and whispers lessons about painting and morals to her, is 'Germania' with her rosebud chaplet, her plaited braids, and the German city-on-the-hill with its medieval spire in the background.

Overbeck firmly maintained what he held to be his duties as an artistic and moral teacher. Basically he believed that nothing good had happened since the Renaissance – he must have viewed the monuments of Baroque Rome with horror – and so he missed out on the powerful spirituality of the newer art made by such Italians as Bernini in the seventeenth century. But he did not have much opportunity to do public art in Rome. His biggest commission came from Pius IX: it was a scene of *Christ Evading His Pursuers on the Mountain near Nazareth*, an allegory of the imprisonment of Pius VII by Napoleon, painted on one of the ceilings of Palazzo del Quirinale – a devout but insipid work at which few visitors, if any, look today. The Nazarenes certainly left an impression on Roman art, but it did not prove to be deep or lasting; and meanwhile the cultural energies of Italy had shifted almost entirely to the sphere of politics and its contentions. Pius IX, in particular, was so preoccupied with trying to hold on to his domains in the Papal States that he had little time for art patronage. But in Germany Overbeck's influence, and that of the Nazarenes in general, was widespread.

Interestingly, it also spilled into one area of French painting. The French had rarely been influenced by stylistic events in Germany, but in a city bustling with so many foreign artists, it was bound to happen and did, because of one major French artist who was resident there. The oldest of the various foreign academies in Rome was that of France; it had been instituted in 1666 under Louis XIV, impelled by Colbert and Charles Le Brun. In a very short time it had acquired great prestige, and its *pensionnaires* (as the painters, sculptors and musicians whose talent, officially recognized by the Prix de Rome, had been rewarded with a stipend from the French government and a spell on its premises) were considered to have made an important start to their public careers. In 1806 the brilliantly talented young painter Jean-Auguste-Dominique Ingres was awarded a *pension* from the Academy and settled in Rome. The Academy had been located in Palazzo Mancini in Via del Corso, but in 1803 one of the great sites of Rome became available to the French government, which bought it: the Villa Medici, at the head of the Spanish Steps. This became Ingres's studio and home for much of the rest of his life.

The nineteenth century was an exceptionally rich period in the history of the French Academy in Rome. Among its *pensionnaires*, apart from Ingres, were the architects Baltard and Garnier, the sculptor Carpeaux, the composers Berlioz, Bizet and Debussy. Ingres worked there as a *pensionnaire*, staunchly defending the classical tradition that surrounded him in Rome, from 1806 to 1820, and after a return to Paris he came back to Rome in 1835, now as the director of the Villa Medici. In this position, as the Grand Cham of French art teaching, the paladin of the classical style, he exerted an incalculable influence on thought and practice in French art. He was not a man prone to self-doubt, and one of the pictures he was proudest of was his first official commission in Rome since the fall of Napoleon in 1815 – *Christ Giving the Keys to St Peter* (1820). It depicts the moment at which Christ entrusted the future of his newly formed Church to the first of the line of future popes, St Peter, who kneels at his feet and looks up at him; Christ, too, is looking up, but to his father in Heaven, while with his left hand he points to the keys in Peter's hands, the power to open or close the doors of salvation which he has just passed on to his successor. Everything about this image, but especially its almost stonily firm construction and its powerful sense of hierarchy, points to the origins of at least some of Ingres's ideas in Nazarene painting – hardly a surprise, since the monastery where Overbeck and Peter Cornelius had been working was next door to the Villa Medici.

All this artistic flourishing took place against a turbulent political landscape. Especially post Napoleon, Italy was considered so hopelessly divided that it could barely have been called a single country at all. 'We have no flag, no political name, no rank among European nations,' lamented one of the patriots whose efforts would eventually bring about its unification, Giuseppe Mazzini (1805–72), who had been born and raised in Genoa, then under the rule of the French empire, being part of the Ligurian republic.

We have no common centre, no common market. We are dismembered into eight states – Lombardy, Parma, Tuscany, Modena, Lucca, the Popedom, Piedmont, the kingdom of Naples – all independent of one another, without alliance, without unity of aim, without organized connections between them ... eight different systems, of currency, weights and measures, civil, commercial and penal legislation, of administrative organization, and of police restriction, divide us and render us as much as possible strangers to one another.

As Mazzini was coming of age, there was a slowly growing current in the direction of change. What increasing numbers of

Italians – liberals, intellectuals, dissenting patriots, anti-imperialists who resented the rule of Austria – looked towards and longed for was a *risorgimento*, or 'resurgence', that would unify Italy as an independent country, free of Austrian influence. Of course, Italy never had been unified; it was always a patchwork of post-medieval entities, its dominant unit being the Papal States, whose size, wealth and centrality gave enormous political power to the pope as a temporal ruler.

At first, the main revolutionary action came from a secret society called the Carbonari or 'charcoal-burners'. They were originally centred in Naples from about 1806 onwards, and they were hailed as brethren by all Italians of a radical disposition, as well as by such foreigners as Lord Byron, who called them his 'cronies' and generously gave them rooms in his residence in Ravenna in 1821. 'My lower apartments are full of their bayonets, fusils, cartridges and what not. I suppose they consider me as a depot to be sacrificed in case of accidents! It is no great matter, supposing that Italy could be liberated, who or what is sacrificed. It is a grand object – the very *poetry* of politics. Only think! A free Italy! Why, there has been nothing like it since the days of Augustus!'

The Carbonari were fiercely persecuted: to be caught meant jail or death, and often they were the same, since the usual jail was the dreaded Spielberg fortress in Moravia, by all accounts the most miserable sort of place imaginable. (One unfortunate Italian writer named Silvio Pellico, arrested in 1820 for a trivial offence, wrote a book about his treatment there, *Le Mie Prigioni* ('My Prisons', 1832), which was said to have damaged Austria more than a lost battle.) But sometimes they were executed right away in Italy, with hardly more than the semblance of a proper trial.

This was the fate of two such dissidents in November 1825, Angelo Targhini and Leonida Montanari. They had long been cooking up plots against the papal government of Leo XII Sermattei della Genga (reg. 1823–9), being fiercely opposed to the continuation of that pope's absolute power in the Papal States. One can hardly blame them. Leo XII was one of the vilest reactionaries ever to occupy the Fisherman's Chair. Not only did he insist on all court proceedings of the Papal States being conducted in Latin by ordained priests; he forbade Jews, especially those in Rome, to own property, and ordered that they sell their possessions without delay and attend Christian catechism. Their only recourse was to emigrate outside the political control of the Church – to non-papal states such as Lombardy or Tuscany. All charitable institutions in the Papal States were put under direct Church supervision, as were all libraries and, of course, schools. The pope's neurotically suspicious dread of enemies only made the enmities, and his reaction against them, worse. If a dressmaker designed low-cut or in any way revealing dresses, she would be excommunicated. If her clients wore them, the same applied. Papal fear of unorthodoxy led to a system of denunciation, torture and arbitrary arrest for imagined doctrinal crime beside which the excesses of the Inquisition paled. And it often ended in death for the suspects.

So it was with the unfortunate Targhini and Montanari, whose paths in Rome had crossed with that of a papal double-agent named Spontini. On finding out Spontini's real mission, which was to entrap Carbonari, Targhini enticed him on to a dark Roman street and stabbed him in the chest. The blow was not fatal, but in the denunciations that followed it both Targhini and Montanari were condemned to death. Papal law decreed their beheading. They declared their innocence and impenitence right up to the last moment.

The pope, as monarch of the Papal States, had his very own *boia* or executioner – a functionary named Mastro Titta, who later (without the least trace of remorse) wrote his memoirs. Targhini and Montanari were beheaded on Piazza del Popolo in November 1825.

The Carbonari had unofficial enemies too. The Sanfedisti, a secret society supported by nobles and peasants alike, took an oath 'not to spare anyone belonging to the notorious gang of liberals, regardless of his birth, lineage or fortune ... and to spill the blood of the infamous liberals to the last drop, regardless of sex or rank'. The Sanfedisti were an Italian equivalent of such hysterically rightist Spanish terror organizations as the Exterminating Angels. But their membership came nowhere near that of the Carbonari, of whom there were claimed to be between three hundred thousand and a million. The loathed *sbirri*, or political police, could not field a fraction of that. Nevertheless Mazzini, who had joined the Carbonari in 1830, estimated that his home district of Lombardy contained three hundred police agents, 872 gendarmes, 1,233 police guards and a swarm of semi-official delators, all of whom reported back to Vienna. In 1830, while in his mid-twenties, he was arrested and locked up without trial for conspiring against the Piedmontese state. When his father protested to the governor of Genoa, he was told: 'Your son is a man of some talent, and he is too fond of walking by himself at night deep in thought. What on earth has he to think about at his age? We do not like young people to think unless we know the subject of their thoughts.' Mazzini was then clapped behind bars in the Savona fortress.

He was freed in 1831 but offered the unappetizing prospect of what amounted to permanent house arrest in a provincial town. Instead he chose exile, moving to Marseilles, where he started a society called La Giovane Italia ('Young Italy'), whose political programme was based on the creation of a free Italian republic by the merger of several states. It had some success in the next few years, claiming sixty thousand adherents by 1833 – not enough to convert all Italy, but certainly enough to perturb the government of Savoy, which ruthlessly clamped down on the young movement, sending twelve of its members to the gallows. Mazzini's best friend, Jacopo Ruffini, killed himself. Mazzini, tried and convicted *in absentia*, was forced into exile in London; from there he sent out a stream of letters and pamphlets to other countries – Germany, Poland, Switzerland – urging the creation of independence movements by national youth. He even tried to foment one among army cadets in Turkey, known, prophetically, as the 'Young Turks'. From their ranks, Kemal Atatürk, the future westernizer of Turkey, would eventually arise.

Mazzini theorized and argued incessantly, but he never led a militant revolt. His hopes for a continuous ignition of riots proved delusive. Every insurrection failed. Austrian police power was too strong. The movement's centralization on Austria was so extreme that, at one point in the 1840s, worn-out police boots had to be sent to Vienna to be repaired. Nevertheless through the 1830s and 1840s brushfires of dissent kept flaring up across Europe, demanding local constitutional rather than Austrian colonial rule. Their emblematic focus was Italy. In 1846 a Roman pamphleteer complained about unrestrained police power. 'The police can imprison a man, banish him, confine him to a district, rob him of office, forbid him to carry arms or to leave his house at night. They open his letters in the post and make no effort to conceal it. They can invade his house, close shops, cafés and inns, and fine us at their pleasure.' In Rome, political suspects (and it took very little to qualify as one) were confined to their houses from sundown to morning. They were also obliged to take the sacrament of Confession once a month, and what they told the priest under the seal of the confessional was routinely disclosed to the authorities as part of the 'special surveillance of the class called thinkers'. Most foreign books were proscribed or placed on the Index, the banned reading list; even private reading-groups focusing on economic theory were banned, and old or dying suspects were refused absolution by their priests unless they betrayed their friends and relatives.

The Italian liberals and nationalists struck back as best they could, sometimes with ingenuity; thus in January 1848 the protesters staged a civil disobedience strike in Lombardy, which consisted of citizens collectively refusing to smoke or play the state lottery; this caused grievous embarrassment to Austria through loss of income, both the lottery and the tobacco industry being state monopolies. Pro-constitutional revolts and demonstrations broke out in Tuscany, Naples, Sicily and Milan. But serious, open conflict did not come until the appearance of Giuseppe Garibaldi.

Garibaldi had been born and raised in Nice (Nizza), then a part of the Kingdom of Savoy with a large Italian-speaking population.

He took naturally to the sea and was working as a merchant marine captain when, laid over for a few days in 1833 in the Russian port city of Taganrog, he made the acquaintance of a political exile from Italy, Giovanni Battista Cuneo. Cuneo, a follower of Mazzini, was a member of the illicit Giovane Italia, and he soon converted the young Garibaldi. From now on the sea captain would be dedicated to the vision of an Italy free from Austrian control. It made him feel, he said, 'as Columbus must have done when he first caught sight of land'.

He met Mazzini in Italy, joined the Carbonari and rather prematurely agitated for insurrection in Piedmont. This merely made him a marked man – one more malcontent on the police lists. A Genoese court tried him *in absentia*. He fled from Italy to Marseilles. From there, Garibaldi wandered.

His peregrinations took him to Brazil, where he fell in with a republican uprising over meat taxation. The Brazilian gauchos, who regarded themselves as the backbone of the country, had come to bitterly resent the high taxes imposed on the sale of *charque*, Brazilian dried and salted beef, a staple food. Feelings ran so high that a minor civil war known as the Guerra dos Farrapos, the 'War of Tatters', broke out; the *farrapos* were the rebels and Garibaldi, scenting an invigorating conflict in the making, joined them in 1839. During the war he met and fell in love with a very brave and spirited woman, Ana Ribeiro da Silva, known as 'Anita', who fought right next to him in a series of engagements. It is said, though it is not certain, that Anita invented what became the Garibaldian uniform of red shirt, poncho and wide beret – the red cloth coming from a factory in Montevideo in Uruguay, which had originally been contracted to sell it to the cattle slaughterhouses of Argentina. Some believe that this gaucho outfit was the origin of the use of red as a sign of revolution, which would later pass to Russia and the Bolsheviks.

In 1842 the pair moved on his ship to Montevideo, where they raised an 'Italian legion' to support the Uruguayan liberals in a civil war against the conservative *caudillo* Juan Manuel de Rosas. But the situation in Italy moved steadily to the forefront of

Garibaldi's concerns; revolution was in the air all over Europe, he was Italian and not South American, and his duties as an insurgent were owed to Italy, not Uruguay. Garibaldi's mind was made up by the mistaken news that the recently elected pope, Pius IX, was apparently a liberal and sympathetic to reform. This was given credibility by the fact that, in 1846, the pope had granted amnesty to all political prisoners in the Papal States.

In 1847 he wrote a letter to the papal offices offering 'to shed our blood in defence of Pius IX's work of redemption'. The next year he sailed back to Italy with sixty men, a fraction of his legion. He offered their support to the king of Sardinia-Piedmont, Charles Albert, who had just granted a constitution to Piedmont, but soon he was to transfer his allegiance to the more promising Milanese, who in March, after five days of struggle against the Austrian occupation, had expelled the Austrians from their city. Venice, too, rose against its Austrian overlords and proclaimed a republic. Likewise, the Papal States – to the horror of Pius IX – declared for republicanism.

Now Garibaldi, encouraged by the ever premature Mazzini, moved down to Rome with the hope of taking military charge of it. In November, Pius IX fled south from Rome to Gaeta. But this was not a victory for Garibaldi. Louis Napoleon, the future Napoleon III, was determined to restore the pope and his temporal power, thus safeguarding the Papal States. He dispatched an army to throw Garibaldi out of Rome. At first this force, though larger than Garibaldi's, failed at the very gates of the city, in April 1849. But then French reinforcements arrived and, after a four-week siege, they forced Garibaldi and the republican army into retreat. Under a hastily negotiated truce, he led his men – by now around four thousand in number – out of Rome, on 2 July 1849. His idea was to keep up the pressure on Rome, guerrilla-style, from strongholds in the Apennines. 'Wherever we are,' he announced with impressive defiance, 'there Rome will be.' When this did not work the refugee army began heading for Venice, but most of its strength was eroded on the way; by the time its remnants reached San Marino only 250 men were left, and the ever courageous Anita had died near Comacchio on the retreat. Her death could only make her widowed husband more determined for victory than ever, although some years passed before he had another chance.

Meanwhile the French army entered Rome and re-established the military and political power of the pope. After brief sojourns in New York (1850), Peru (1851) and even Australia (1852), Garibaldi bought land on the Italian island of Caprera, north of Sardinia, and settled down to farm. This was merely an interlude. In 1859, he was made general in a war of independence launched by Sardinia against the Austrian government, leading a force of 'Alpine Hunters' to harass the Austrians in the mountains.

He won Sardinia's independence in 1860, the year Piedmont was able to assimilate several northern duchies – those of Tuscany, Modena, Parma and the Romagna. The next in line, in the sights of Italian nationalists, was to be the Kingdom of the Two Sicilies, comprising southern mainland Italy (its centre, Naples) and the island of Sicily itself, ruled by the Neapolitans. Garibaldi by now was quite resolved that the only hope for unification would be monarchy under Vittorio Emanuele.*

From Genoa, he planned an attack on Sicily and Naples, with the backing of Prime Minister Cavour, and carried it out with the covert support of the British. In May 1860 an expedition on two steamships set sail from near Genoa, carrying a thousand volunteers under Garibaldi's command.

The expeditionary force, under the name of Mille (Italian for 'the Thousand', volunteers drawn mainly from Lombardy and Venetia, and otherwise known as the 'Redshirts'), landed at Marsala in western Sicily, where Garibaldi announced that he was setting up a dictatorship over all Sicily in Vittorio Emanuele's name. The Mille won their first battle, against a two-thousand-

---

* Victor Emmanuel II (1820–78), eldest son of Charles Albert of Sardinia and Maria Theresa of Austria, had assumed the throne of Piedmont–Sardinia in 1849, following the abdication of his defeated father.

man detachment of the Neapolitan army, at Calatafimi, in mid-May. Now Sicilians, previously uncommitted, began to join them – there were even desertions en masse from the Neapolitan army. Soon the Mille had increased to about four thousand men. Garibaldi laid siege to Palermo, Sicily's capital, and at the end of May his forces took the city. Other victories followed – Milazzo, Messina. By the end of September resistance to Garibaldi in the *mezzogiorno*, the south, had all but collapsed; Garibaldi's troops had crossed the narrow strait to the Italian mainland and occupied Calabria, against the advice of Cavour but to the delight of Vittorio Emanuele II. Louis Napoleon's forces, which had been propping up the papal territories, now let the Piedmontese army come through from the north to lend decisive support to Garibaldi. Francis II, king of the Two Sicilies, was forced to leave his throne in Naples, transfer to the fortress of Gaeta, and eventually to seek exile in friendly Austria. In October 1860 a plebiscite formally confirmed the annexation of the Kingdom of the Two Sicilies to that of Sardinia, at which point it collapsed. The new Kingdom of Italy – an entity which at that point excluded Rome – was established in March 1861, with Vittorio Emanuele as its king, proclaimed in Turin by the first Italian parliament; Garibaldi handed over authority for southern Italy to the new king. He retired to his farm on the island of Caprera, a national hero, and declared himself ready to leave the rest of the work of unification to Vittorio Emanuele.

This did not happen because many, in some places most, southern Italians refused to acquiesce to rule by Piedmont. More than half the national army of 120,000 men had to be sent, an army of occupation in all but name, to the Two Sicilies to repress the discontents of former Bourbon subjects. The strong Catholicism of southern peasants supported every kind of opposition to the new regime. At first the southern clergy supported the papal officials against Vittorio Emanuele – they were particularly incensed by new laws nationalizing Church property. They angrily resented all efforts to strip the Papacy of its temporal possessions. When their efforts to frustrate the new policies failed, they resorted to encouraging 'brigandage', which southerners saw merely as an expression of their territorial rights. Priests in their sermons openly referred to the brigands of the *mezzogiorno* as their brothers. They preached that the Virgin would be bound to perform the miracle of driving the Piedmontese and their 'usurping king' back where they belonged, to the north.

Many of the discontented southerners managed to take ship for America. The brigands who stayed mutated, in large part, into the Mafia, which could never have become such a strongly self-protective society without the repressions of Vittorio Emanuele II and the Piedmontese. The defiance of such repression was summed up in the practice of *omertà*, 'manliness', or the code of silence – keeping a shut mouth, never blabbing to strangers or, especially, to the *sbirri*, and above all never testifying to higher authority in court against anyone who was accused of anything at all. Cala Ulloa, the Bourbon who acted as 'prime minister' of the Neapolitan government in exile, spoke in 1863 of the 'rigorous and pitiless enforcement of martial law'. The Piedmontese, however, 'have kept Naples under martial law for six months; and Neapolitans are treated by them not as people fighting for their independence, but as slaves who have revolted against their masters'.

Moreover, the pope in Rome would not get out of the way of unification. He was determined to hold on to the Papal States and viewed any effort to absorb them into a united single country of Italy as an atrocious trespass on his God-given rights. Garibaldi, however, living on his island, was determined to take Rome. So was Cavour, who in a speech in 1861 declared that 'Rome is the only city in Italy with more than merely local memories . . . Rome, Rome alone must be the capital of Italy . . . We must go to Rome, but on two conditions: we must go there in agreement with France, and the true independence of the Pontiff must not be lessened. We must go to Rome, but civil authority must not extend its power over the spiritual order.'

By now there seemed to be only three possible solutions to what had come to be known as the 'Roman Question'. Either the whole territory of what had been the Holy See would be reconquered by foreign troops and held for the pope as it had been before 1849; or the pope's total loss of these dominions would be agreed upon; or a small amount of the former papal territory surrounding Rome would be assigned to the pope and protected by foreign troops. This last, with France as occupying guarantor, was now the case. The first was clearly impossible and the second would never have met with Pio Nono's agreement.

In 1862 Garibaldi and his Redshirts tried to assail Rome, but were beaten back before their march really got under way, although Garibaldi himself was shot in the foot. In 1864 the 'September Convention' extracted an agreement from Napoleon III to withdraw his troops from Rome within two years. However, the people of Rome did not, as the republicans expected, rise against the pope. Instead, they fortified the French and papal armies. As a result, Garibaldi and the Redshirts were beaten back at the battle of Mentana, in 1867, in which six hundred Italian volunteers died. Once again, a march on Rome had been defeated. But the cause of Italian unification was not – in 1870 war broke out between France and Prussia and the French armies were defeated at Sedan. This meant that the French forces had to be withdrawn from Rome, and in September 1870 the troops of Italy marched in and took their place. At long last Rome became the capital of an Italy united under its new king, Vittorio Emanuele II.

Few Italians and no one outside of Italy seem to have regarded the new king as any kind of political genius. 'Lazy, uncouth, jealous, petty and boisterous' was a commonly echoed judgement, and the British Foreign Minister George Villiers opined that 'Vittorio Emanuele is an imbecile; he is a dishonest man who tells lies to everyone, he will end up losing his crown and ruining both Italy and his dynasty.' He was certainly philoprogenitive. In addition to the eight children he had by his cousin Maria Adelaide of Habsburg (1822–55), he had several by various mistresses, two by his *maîtresse en titre*, or chief mistress, Rosa Teresa Guerrieri, two by Laura Bon, two by Virginia Rho, and various daughters by others less remarked. He was a decent patriotic man who seems to have deserved his popular nickname of *il re galantuomo*, 'the gentleman king', but he left little trace of wit or thought behind him.

He did, however, strongly believe that Italy ought to be one country, with himself as its king, wily architect of unification Cavour as its prime minister, and the Papal States – along with the temporal, if not the spiritual power of their ruler Pius IX – reduced to a cipher.

It would be idle to suppose that such political events were directly reflected in Italian culture, particularly in painting in Rome. Mainly, writers got stirred by them. It is true, however, that there was a rhyme, though not a causal connection, between what happened in nineteenth-century Italian painting (some areas of it, at least) and what was brewing in politics. But what was happening in art, for a change, did not start in Rome.

In the mid-nineteenth century a group of ten or so artists formed in Tuscany. Their meeting-place was the Caffè Michel-angiolo in Florence and their shared interest was in landscape. They were all opposed to the formal teachings of the Florentine Accademia delle Belle Arti and, in a general way, they supported Italian unification, as most young artists naturally did – Italian unification symbolized Italian freedom, a freedom they wanted every part of. After 1799, when Napoleon invaded Tuscany and expelled the Austrian grand duke Ferdinand III, the official style of art in Florence was neo-classical in the French manner: David and later Ingres (who worked and taught in Florence from 1820 to 1824) were its models, and its seat was the Fine Art Academy. The chief ornament of this institution, who specialized in imperial commemoration, was the laborious history painter Pietro Benvenuti (1769–1844), whose biggest work for Napoleon was a painting of his victory at Jena in 1806, *The Oath of the Saxons* (1812). But younger artists were not so interested in replicating these neo-classical 'machines'. Gradually the conviction grew among them that what counted more was direct truth to tone, expressed in chiaroscuro – the relations of light and darkness, described in tonal relationships of increasing clarity and simplicity, as seen in quite ordinary things. Because the painters – whose major figure was Telemaco Signorini (1835–1901) – expressed these relationships in terms of broad strokes and patches, they became christened (by a hostile critic, of course) Macchiaioli, splotchers.

It would be wrong to think of these young artists as provincials. They were not displaced Impressionists, but different kinds of painters entirely. Some of them visited Paris and were well aware of Impressionist developments; they also drew some of their impetus from photography, which in the 1860s was coming strongly into its own as a source for both urban and landscape painting. (The Florentine photographic firm of Alinari Brothers, which supplied mementos and records to the once again increasing flow of tourists, saw its first developments in the 1860s.) Signorini went to Paris in 1868, '74, '78, '81, '83 and '84, partly to visit other painters (he counted Degas among his particular friends), and displayed a quite precocious modernity after a trip to Ireland with his painting *Leith* (1881), which is dominated by a huge theatrical poster glued to the wall of a general store – Pop Art long before its time. Nevertheless there is nothing to suggest that he or any of the other Macchiaioli were impelled by political feelings to paint what was local or modern into their views of Italy. Some of them did enlist to fight for their belief in Italian unification; and Silvestro Lega (1826–95) painted squads of unification sharpshooters leading captives to imprisonment in Garibaldi's war against the Austrians in 1859. For the most part, though, politics came second to art.

The longest-lived and most prolific of the Macchiaioli was Giovanni Fattori (1825–1908). More than eight hundred oil paintings by him are known, most painted after 1861, and they all show a consistent, stubborn attachment to Nature. But they have very little to say on Rome itself: Fattori's chief subject was rural, the landscape of the Maremma to the north of the city. This was yet another instance of how far-reaching and vivid changes, even convulsions, in a society's political opinions may produce very little direct reaction in what its painters do.

But it is sometimes otherwise in architecture. Vittorio Emanuele, the Gentleman King, died in 1878 and was succeeded by his
son, Umberto I. Spurred by Umberto's filial piety – an emotion
not always so easy to tell apart, especially in Italy, from costly and
displaced narcissism – the Italians now proceeded to plan and
build the largest and most stupefyingly pompous memorial ever
dedicated to a national leader in Western Europe. It is all the more
remarkable because the late nineteenth century was a period of
almost complete barrenness for Roman architecture. Apart from
the monument to Vittorio Emanuele II, practically nothing that
was built in Rome in the latter half of the nineteenth century
repays more than cursory inspection. It is by far the largest act of
architectural commemoration ever accorded to an Italian ruler,
or indeed to an Italian of any kind, since the days of Julius Caesar.
Nothing raised in memory of Dante, Michelangelo, Christopher
Columbus or any other world-changing Italian comes even close
to competing with it in size or visibility. There are not many parts
of Rome from which it cannot be seen, and few over which its white
mass does not appear to loom – a singular disproportion, given the
personal mediocrity of the man it so crushingly celebrates.

It is 443 feet wide and 230 feet high, chopped and gouged with
utter ruthlessness and a complete disregard for context into the
flank of what had so long been regarded as one of Rome's most
sacred ancient spots, heavy with history – the hill on which the
Capitol stood and which is surmounted by Michelangelo's piazza
with its statue of Marcus Aurelius, gazing down upon Piazza
Venezia. Visually, it completely obliterates everything else on that
hill. It is safe to say that, a hundred years later, it would have been
quite impossible to clear the space for even a chicken-coop there
against the protests of conservationists, but that hardly mattered
then. The late nineteenth century was not the late twentieth and,
in any case, Italians then had a more exalted idea of the importance
of their own recent history than they do now.

Dozens of medieval buildings and even some ancient churches
were accordingly flattened to make room for this cyclopean
monster. Work on it began in 1884 and continued long past the

death of its architect, Giuseppe Sacconi, in 1905; it was inaugurated in 1911 but not deemed completed until 1935. By then, Benito Mussolini – a man of pronounced architectural enthusiasms – was the absolute ruler of Italy, but Il Duce seems not to have interfered with Sacconi's almost insanely florid designs. They perfectly illustrate Alexander Pope's line on the new-rich lord's estate: 'Lo, what great heaps of littleness abound!' The building contains the Tomb of the Unknown Soldier, complete with eternal flame, a body selected from a dozen equally anonymous and unrecognizable ones at the war's end by a bereaved Italian mother from Gradisca d'Isonzo. It also houses the Museum of Italian Unification, full of the clutter of busts, documents, maps and weapons that one would expect to see there. School parties visit it from time to time, and some of the more energetic tourists manage the climb to the curved colonnade that crowns the enormous edifice, but it is not one of the more crowded institutions of the city – or one of the more beautiful, as some of its nicknames remind you. It has been variously known as the *macchina scrivere*, 'the typewriter', for its resemblance to a vintage writing-machine; as the *zuppa Inglese*, 'English soup', the common name for the dessert known as trifle, and the *torta nuziale*, or wedding-cake; as the 'false teeth', an allusion to its ever-dazzling whiteness; and, most popular of all, as the *pisciatoio nazionale* or National Urinal.

Not only is the National Urinal the largest structure in Rome, its materials are absurdly conspicuous. Nothing can make it fit in. The general colour of Roman buildings is ivory to buff to terracotta: the warm hues of tufa, brick, travertine and other local materials. The stone of which the Vittoriano was made is not local at all. It is *botticino*, a corpse-white marble imported by rail and wagon, at great expense, from geologically distant Brescia. Neither in design nor in material does the typewriter look Roman, and in point of fact it is not. It is Graeco-Teutonic. Its architect was certainly Italian, but his inspiration was the German architect Leopold von Klenze (1784–1864) – the obsessive and more than slightly bizarre neo-classicist who was court architect to Ludwig I of Bavaria. The origins of its style are political, and they lie within the Triple Alliance of the 1880s. In this treaty between Germany, Austria-Hungary and Italy, lasting until the outbreak of the First World War, each great-power member promised to support the others if one was attacked. The general Italian public was unenthusiastic about this. After all, Austria had been the proven enemy of Italian independence: it had shown itself to be a fiercely colonialist power.

Nevertheless the white-column, Greek-revival style of von Klenze spread across Europe. Not only did he do the Glyptothek (sculpture museum) and the Alte Pinakothek in Munich, but he was commissioned by Nicholas I of Russia to design the New Hermitage in St Petersburg and by Ludwig I's son Otto to make designs for the reconstruction of Athens, including the restoration of the Acropolis, so catastrophically damaged in 1687 when a stray Venetian mortar-shell blew up the Parthenon, which was being used as an ordnance dump by the Turks.

Von Klenze provided a convenient, in fact a virtually mandatory template for a neo-classical building that sought to prove Italian links to the classical past. One of his favourite buildings was the second-century BCE Hellenistic altar at the Greek colony of Pergamon (modern Bergama) in Turkey, with its huge stone frieze of the Battle of the Giants, which had been gathered together by German archaeologists in the eighteenth and early nineteenth centuries and shipped, section by damaged section, to Berlin. It consisted of a lower podium, which carried a 113-metre (371-foot) sculptural frieze of the battle between the Gods and Giants described in Hesiod's *Theogony*; on top of this massive base was an open colonnade.* The distant descendant of this weighty and magnificently decorated building was the speaking tribune Albert Speer designed for Adolf Hitler, facing the Zeppelinfeld at Nuremberg (which mercifully lacks Nazi versions of the mighty Pergamene sculptures).

---

* The narrative of gods versus giants probably symbolized the Pergamene conception of its own dynasty defending the Hellenic ethos against 'barbarian' invaders from the North.

One of von Klenze's adaptations of this Pergamon scheme was the U-shaped Ruhmeshalle (Hall of Fame, 1850) in Munich, where he had built other Hellenic-style buildings in a lifelong effort to satisfy the insatiable Graecomania of his monarch. From this, with added memories of the Pergamon altar itself, Sacconi derived his design for the Vittoriano, which was even bigger than the Pergamon altar – some seventy feet longer in plan. Its main difference in layout from both the Pergamene original and von Klenze's Ruhmeshalle is that its crowning colonnade is curved on a concave arc, not straight. It is liberally, indeed fulsomely, endowed with sculpture: not only a ten-metre figure of Emanuele on horseback,* not only two victory-goddesses driving quadrigas, but dozens of white bas-reliefs in *botticino* symbolizing the various districts and cities of Italy now united by the great political event, together with swags, cartouches, eagles and other celebratory props. They remind the visitor how many skilled sculptors were working in Italy at the turn of the century, and how forgotten they all are – a lesson for today. Who now remembers those once noted regional sculptors – Emilio Bisi, who did 'Lombardy', Italo Griselli ('Tuscany') or Silvio Sbricoli ('Abruzzo'), all contributing to what Sacconi called 'the Valhalla of the Gentleman King'? The answer, alas, is nobody, just as nobody will remember most of our own contemporary art when it ceases to be contemporary.

The Vittoriano is also an anti-monument. It celebrates the first king of a united Italy, but, by implication, it marks the end of the temporal power of the Papacy. The last pope to wield this power, in its full measure, was Pius IX, and he was also the longest-reigning pope in the history of the Catholic Church: elected in 1846, he occupied the Fisherman's Throne until his death in 1878. Few popes came anywhere near this record and none equalled it, because they were usually men in their sixties when their reigns began.

* There are photos of the sculptors who worked on the project crammed, rather uncomfortably, around bottles of vermouth inside the cavernous belly of the horse, like tipsy Greeks approaching Troy.

Born Giovanni Maria Mastai-Ferretti, Pius IX began his papal incumbency as a liberal – or so many Catholics thought. Thus he showed sympathy – though not too much of it – for nationalist feeling in Italy, as long as it did not threaten the Papacy or its holdings; he encouraged the drafting of a constitutional framework for Rome, and freed a number of political prisoners who were under indictment from his predecessor, the ultra-conservative Gregory XVI Cappellari.

But such sentiments were not to last. Like many another powerful figure in that mid-century of vehement anticlericalism, he began as a (relative) progressive, to the dismay and suspicion of the neighbouring Austro-Hungarians. Though he did not encourage Protestantism, at least he did not denounce its faithful and even allowed them to worship according to their own rite in the Holy City. He showed a serious interest in social reform within his own fief, Rome, where he began a programme of street lighting and established the first railway, sometimes riding in public view in his own papal carriage – that ancestor of the modern 'Pope-mobile'. He even went to America before his election and was the first pope to have crossed the Atlantic, also visiting some of the South American republics as an assistant to the apostolic nuncio – a gesture that would pay dividends in the later American loyalty to Roman Catholicism. The figures speak: in 1846 there were some seven hundred Catholic priests in North America, by 1878 the country had six thousand.

Nevertheless, it was not long before he began a shift that would take him far to the right. Political feelings in Italy and across Europe in 1848, the 'year of revolutions', were too heated for him to do otherwise. There was nothing opportunistic about this. He genuinely felt the world was slipping away from the stability of the Faith, and felt impelled by conscience to oppose it. In France, there had been an uprising of the workers followed by the abdication of Louis Philippe – who died the next year – and the election of Louis Napoleon as President of the Republic. Revolution in Vienna had forced the resignation of Metternich. In Prague, Czech nationalist revolts were repressed by Austrian troops. Sardinia declared war on Austria. The nationalist Lajos Kossuth rose to power in Hungary.

Most pregnant with direct menace from the pope's viewpoint, however, revolt broke out in Rome. Pius IX's premier, the liberal Pellegrino Rossi, chief minister for the Papal States, was murdered in November on the stairs of the Vatican's exquisite Palazzo della Cancclleria, supposedly by medical students who had practised on a corpse laid out for dissection in order to find exactly the right spot to strike for the jugular vein. The usually reliable Swiss Guards laid down their halberds, leaving the pope essentially unprotected in a Europe of growing nationalism – a barely credible thought, but a fact nonetheless, to which the pope responded by going into exile. Garbed as an ordinary priest he fled south to Gaeta, a fief of the Kingdom of the Two Sicilies, under the aegis of Ferdinand II.

The pope's departure ignited general rejoicing in Rome: a Roman Republic was proclaimed early in 1849, and huge firework displays lit up St Peter's Square on, of all blasphemous dates, Good Friday. Looting and vandalism of papal property followed. Pius responded from the safe distance of Gaeta by excommunicating everyone who had been involved in these outrages and by affirming his devotion to the Madonna, who, he believed, had saved his life. More to the practical point, the new French president Louis Napoleon, who had assured Pius of his unwavering support, sent French troops to Rome and crushed the embryo republic. They would remain there, as a peace-keeping force in support of Pius IX, for twenty years, causing a steady simmer of resentment among Italian nationalists, both in Rome and outside it.

It is sometimes thought that Pio Nono's pursuit of dogma was aimed to combat and reduce the effectiveness of non-Catholic belief. But it was not – not chiefly, anyway. Its main target was 'liberal' opinions held within the Church itself. Nobody who was not a scrupulous Catholic already was likely to care deeply about a detailed, nit-picking document like the Syllabus of Errors, or to regard it as anything but a long list of ecclesiastical complaint and, indeed, desperation. Rather, it was a charter for what came to be called 'ultramontanism'.

Ultramontanism, meaning literally 'adherence to ideas promoted on the other side of the Alps', referred to the geographical location of Rome as against the rest of the Catholic Church, and particularly in contrast to 'Gallicanism', or things happening in France, which denoted non-Roman practices of other Churches and the (in Pius' view) woeful tendency, verging on sinfulness, to give more importance to the traditions and opinions of national governments, national Churches and local hierarchy than to Rome. The ultramontane Catholic was strict, reflexively obedient, and in all things a dogmatist: an unwavering follower of Pio Nono. To him (or her) the views of national governments did not matter a straw compared to the eternal Truth embodied in papal policy. Thus it would not count if some national government – Ireland's, say, or Germany's – wished, under a grant of Catholic emancipation, to veto some episcopal appointment if it thought the candidate politically undesirable; a more flexible Church could put up with that. Not now. Not any more. In particular, the astonishingly ill-timed Syllabus of Errors was aimed at what Pio Nono and the Papal Curia saw as the baleful and enduring effects of the French Revolution, which had happened only a century before.

What were these 'errors'? Some eighty were listed. Some were of the most fundamental kind. It was an 'error' (number 55) to think that 'the Church ought to be separated from the State, and the State from the Church'. It was an 'error' to think that 'the marriage tie is not indissoluble' and that civil authority had the right to grant divorces (number 67). It was an 'error' to suppose that people who came to reside in some Catholic countries had the right to 'enjoy the public exercise of their own peculiar worship', and that was as true for Baptists as for Mahommedans or, for that matter, fire-worshippers. It was an 'error' to hold that the Church lacked the power of 'defining dogmatically' that its religion was the only true religion, or that it needed the 'permission and assent of the civil government' to exercise its authority. And so on, for many clauses and many pages. The capstone was undoubtedly the last, number 80, which in simple purblind majesty pronounced that there was no way in which the Roman pontiff 'can, and ought to, reconcile himself and come to terms with progress, liberalism and modern civilization'.

It is not often that one can say an official document gets everything wrong, but the Syllabus of Errors came as close to that exalted state as anything set forth by the Catholic Church since the death of Luther. To call it antediluvian is to understate its impact. It set Catholic orthodoxy in antagonistic relation not only to the cautiously growing liberalism of the Zeitgeist, but also with the contrary findings of science and recent philosophy from which it would take the Church generations to recover. Indeed some would say, in light of the notorious conservatism of the present pope Benedict XVI, whose habit is to attribute 'virtual infallibility' to all papal utterances, that it has not recovered yet and that the harm done by the Syllabus was permanent.

Inevitably, many Catholic moderates saw it as a blow against the Church's 'ablest and most eloquent defenders', who now, in the words of Odo Russell, the English government's representative in Rome, 'can no longer speak in [the Church's defence] without being accused of heresy ... Silence and blind obedience must henceforth be their only rule of life.' Many believed the pope had placed himself 'at the head of a vast ecclesiastical conspiracy against the principles of modern society', which was indeed true. The French government, whose troops alone stood between the pope and the forces of the Risorgimento, banned the Syllabus. 'If we do not succeed in checking this senseless Romanism,' wrote Archbishop Dupanloup of Orléans, 'the Church will be outlawed in Europe for half a century.'

People embrace religions with special fervour when they yearn for clear ideological security, and the effect of Pio Nono's definiteness was to make the Church more popular, not less, not only in Italy but in the rest of Europe and in both North and South America. Religious bodies, both clerical and lay, expanded; the missionary scope of the Church, in Africa and Asia, increased. Pio

Nono created over two hundred new bishoprics. The life of the Church in France, where it had been devastated by the Revolution, dramatically revived, producing the long outburst of faith and worship that led to a rash of church-building and the growth of such popular Marian miracle cults as that of the healing spring at Lourdes. Given the choice, many people prefer forthright expressions of faith, however irrational and superstitious they may seem, to the qualified utterances of more cautious moral theology, and this received full scope from the papacy of Pius IX, whose Syllabus condemned rationalism, socialism and liberalism of all kinds. A lot of people hated him, but he was still an enormously popular pope. You knew where you stood with him when you were making the sign of the cross.

This helps explain the otherwise puzzling enthusiasm among Catholics for Pio Nono's views and teachings on the subject of the Virgin Mary, Christ's mother, and the prestige her cult enjoyed in Catholic worship during his reign. Little attention was paid to her, or her myth, by the early Church. There is ample evidence for the historical existence of Christ. For that of his supposedly virgin mother, though, there is practically none. Obviously Jesus had a mother of some kind, but we know next to nothing about her and her cult in the Catholic Church – including her much invoked and incessantly lauded virginity, in all its stark unlikeliness – is an accretion for which there is no real biblical sanction. 'Mariolatry', the cult of the Virgin, is basically a variant – though a much inflated one – on ancient cults of the Mythic Mother that long preceded Christianity. She first appears, in art, in third-century CE catacomb pictures of the Annunciation and the Adoration of the Magi. These represent an effort to Christianize an existing pagan deity – Cybele, who had been worshipped originally in Asia Minor, but whose cult as the Mother of the Gods was brought to Rome in the early third century BCE. By imperial times it had grown into a yearly celebration, linked to that of Isis, the Egyptian goddess of fertility, who had her own temple on the Campus Martius. From there it was only a short step to the worship of Mary as the real mother of the god Jesus. This was reinforced by the supposed discovery in the Holy Land of an actual portrait of Mary painted by the Apostle Luke, patron saint of artists. This precious artefact, the so-called Hodegetria, was probably destroyed by the Turks in the 1453 siege of Constantinople, where a special church, the Hodegon, had been built for it. (There were no physical relics of the Virgin Mary, since according to dogma she had been 'assumed' in her entirety into Heaven, so the Hodegetria was the closest thing to a sacred relic of her the Church possessed. Copies were made of it, one of which is in the Pantheon in Rome.)

Five years after the Syllabus of Errors was published, at the end of 1869, Pio Nono convened the assembly of bishops known as the First Vatican Council. Its purpose was to defeat the 'Gallicists' by centralizing power and authority in the hands of the pope and the Papal Curia, and in this it was spectacularly successful. The big question being decided was papal infallibility. Could the pope, speaking *ex cathedra* ('from the throne', meaning with the full official weight of his position, on vital matters of dogma), actually err? Or would God himself intervene to prevent him from doing so? When the votes were counted, God was clearly in favour of 'inerrancy', though not without a lot of heavy politicking from the pope and his Curia.

Pio Nono bullied the bishops relentlessly. Some 350 of the eight hundred or so bishops attending the council meetings were financially dependent on the Vatican, and they were told in no uncertain terms that any dissent from Pius IX's line would bring a complete cut-off of funds. There was no secret balloting. One French delegate, the aforementioned Félix Dupanloup, confided to his journal that 'I'm not going to the Council any more . . . The falsity, vanity and continual lying force me to keep my distance.' The modern Catholic theologian Hans Kung, who was appointed official theologian for the Second Vatican Council in 1962, thought that the First Council 'was so severely compromised' that its infallibility doctrine was null. 'Painful and embarrassing as it may be to admit, this council resembled a well-organized and manipulated party congress rather than a free gathering of Christian people.' Kung would argue that the pope got infallibility translated into dogma for four reasons. 'Pius IX had a sense of divine mission which he carried to extremes; he engaged in double dealing; he was mentally disturbed;* and he misused his office.' Ludicrously but unsurprisingly, the Church in 1979 banned the impeccably scholarly Kung from ever teaching theology in its name.

It says much about Pio Nono's priorities that, having forced through the vote on papal infallibility, he should only have made one other infallible utterance, and that it concerned the Virgin Mary. This was in 1854, when he defined the dogma of the 'immaculate conception' – the belief that Mary, as perfect mother of the Redeemer, had been conceived without the burden of 'original sin'. That inheritance of collective guilt for the fall of Adam and Eve, which the sacrament of baptism was believed to lift from every human soul, had never been laid upon her; she was a completely innocent being, as befitted the Mother of God. Needless to say this was pure fantasy, as statements about those of whom so little is known are apt to be. Nevertheless it became, and remains, Catholic dogma, and a column commemorating it was raised in Piazza di Spagna. Later, Pius XII, another committed Mariolater, would go further and define as dogma the belief that Mary had been saved from earthly corruption by being 'assumed', taken up body and soul, into Heaven. Perhaps she was, but so far the sight of those pristine blue robes in outer space has eluded the world's observatories. (One assumes the robes would be there; the thought of a naked virgin in perpetual orbit is hardly thinkable.)

The life and actions of Pius IX confront the Church historian with an apparent paradox, for despite his innate and growing conservatism Pius IX's papacy marks the beginning of a modern Church: he successfully negotiated the difficult passage of the Church away from temporal power towards purely spiritual dominion, and did so without loss of institutional dignity. For this

---

* 'Mentally disturbed' is perhaps too strong, though the pope did suffer from a well-attested and much-discussed affliction: epilepsy.

he was hated in some quarters – during his burial service a rabble of Italian nationalists tried, but failed, to seize his body and throw it in the Tiber. (This was by no means the first time that such violent disrespect had been thrust on a dead pope. Long before, when papal elections had been more nakedly in the hands of rival factions, the badly decayed corpse of Pope Formosus (reg. 891–6) was disinterred and pulled from his coffin; the fingers with which he had given so many blessings were chopped off; he was dragged through the streets, pelted with ordure and flung in the river; not content with this, the Roman mob threw his successor, Stephen VII, into prison and strangled him there.)

No such violence was inflicted on Pio Nono. He had enemies, of course, but was still much beloved and badly missed by most Italians and by non-Italian Catholics as well. There had been a strong popular move to persuade him to institute constitutional government in the Papal States, but it had come to nothing – Pius held out for the unconditional restoration of papal rule. If there was one principle on which his secular power was set, it was that constitutional government would never be allowed in the *papato*, the 'popedom' or Papal States. Pius' personal following was such that he could do whatever he wanted. He died 'in the odour of sanctity', as the phrase went, leaving behind him an incalculably more popularized Church.

In some ways the man who did most as pope to carry on Pio Nono's legacy was his successor's successor, Pius X, a realist who recognized that further recriminations between the Church and the Italian state were going to produce very little for either side. He stopped publicly calling the state a usurper of the Church's rights (though what he privately thought of the matter is unknown). Giuseppe Melchiorre Sarto (1835–1914) was a man of humble origins, one of ten children fathered by a village postman in the Veneto. By no stretch of the imagination could he have been called an intellectual, but this proved not to matter much and may even have been an advantage: he had a sure instinct for religious populism, and used it to the full. He saw himself as a 'pastoral pope', in direct contact with his flock. He was, in fact, a sincerely charitable man; when a disastrous earthquake hit Messina in 1908 he opened the doors of the Vatican to its homeless victims, putting the secular government of Italy to shame. Perhaps his most famous saying was 'I was born poor, I have lived poor, and I wish to die poor.'

Pius X's special mission, as he saw it, was to expand the living Church by recruiting the devotion of children, through participation in the Sacraments. In a pastoral letter written as Patriarch of Venice, he complained that 'God has been driven out of public life through the separation of Church and State, now that doubt has been raised to a system . . . He has even been driven out of the family, which is no longer considered sacred in its origins.' The remedy for this was divine obedience. 'When we speak of the Vicar of Christ, we must not quibble. We must obey; we must not . . . evaluate his judgements, or criticize his directions, lest we do injury to Jesus Christ himself. Society is sick . . . The one hope, the one remedy, is the Pope.' He wanted Catholic doctrine to impose conformity on the Church, and he would have nothing to do with 'modernism', meaning any kind of synthesis between late-nineteenth-century currents of thought and the supposedly immutable teachings of the traditional Church. The only theology eligible to be taught in Catholic schools and seminaries was that of the medieval philosopher Thomas Aquinas. Hence he would not back the nascent Catholic Action movement, a society of lay Catholics attempting to propagate Catholic influence in society, because even that suggested too much independence by the faithful. Theological debate within the Church was stifled until the reign of Pius XII, when it began to make a shy and tentative reappearance.

In the past, children had been ten to twelve before making their First Communion and lisping out the record of their tiny sins to the priest in the confessional. Pius X decreed the lowering of this age to nine or even seven, thus replicating the traditional boast of the Jesuits, 'Give me a boy before he's nine and he's mine for life.' Boys at their First Communion must wear sashes and rosettes; girls, white dresses and veils. It was a very popular 'reform', increasing the sacramental theatre of childish faith and pleasing all devout parents. It also increased the frequency with which Catholics went to Confession, a necessary prelude to Holy Communion.

Pius X, like his namesake Pio Nono, saw no reason to accommodate simple faith to scientific theories, or to biblical interpretation. He made his views, and the conservative policy of his Church, clear in 1907 in an encyclical letter, *Pascendi Dominici Gregis*, and the decree *Lamentabili*, and the effects of his conservatism would be felt by the Church for some fifty years, right through the papacy of Pius XII. The use of the Index of Forbidden Books now became common, indeed general, throughout the teaching and administration of the Church. All in all, Pius X's papacy spelt hard times for Catholic intellectual life. The threat of excommunication hung menacingly over it. 'Liberal Catholics are wolves in sheep's clothing. Therefore the true priest is bound to unmask them. The Church is by its very nature an unequal society. The hierarchy alone moves and controls ... the duty of the multitude is to carry out in a submissive spirit the orders of those in control.'

Pius X urged his flock to 'be proud' of being called 'papists, retrogrades and intransigents'. He refused to accept France's 1905 Law of Separation between Church and state – which eventually deprived the French Catholic Church of all government funding, and ended with an official diplomatic break between the French government and the Vatican. (His chief intellectual foe within the Church was Father Alfred Loisy, principal theologian at the Institut Catholique in Paris, whose widely circulated book *The Gospel and the Church* argued that the findings of radical biblical criticism dissolved the Protestant threat to faith by dismissing biblical literalism as merely naive, because they implied that there was no getting back behind the tradition of the Church to an 'unmediated' Christ.)

Pius did, however, spell out certain liturgical reforms that the Church needed. Italian Church music had been invaded by opera, stressing bravura passages and ensemble instrumentation.

He would have none of this secular stuff and in 1903 he called for a return to the ancient tradition of plainsong and the classical polyphony of the Counter-Reformation, especially in the Kyriale, Graduale and Antiphonary. Pius favoured a return to Gregorian chant. He also explicitly forbade women to sing in church choirs.

This was all very well, and he backed it up with a programme of restoration of dilapidated churches – always a problem in the Eternal City, which by now was beginning to seem not very eternal – that did little but good.

Initially he even forbade Italian Catholics to vote, on the grounds that the Italian state, being secular, had made the pope a 'prisoner in the Vatican', and that to vote at all for a secular state which had confiscated the enormous papal domains would be to acquiesce in it. But later, when it became obvious that neither Vittorio Emanuele III nor any elected Italian politicians who valued their votes were going to tolerate backsliding on the issue, this was relaxed. From now on the papal domains would remain tiny – although the numerical size of the Catholic Church would be enormous, and ever growing.

This softening on the voting issue did not imply a softening in papal doctrine. In 1907 Pius formally condemned some sixty-five propositions regarding the nature of the Church and the divinity of Christ as wrong and heretical, and soon afterwards compelled all priests to take a sacred oath against modernism in general. 'Modernism' was an extremely wide-ranging term. As understood by Pius and his Curia, it meant any effort to square the ideas of more recent philosophers, such as Immanuel Kant, with the traditional teachings of the Church. Such attempts were viewed with horror by theological traditionalists like Pius X, because they implied that the Church's teachings on faith and morals were neither eternal nor immutable. Gradually the battle-lines between Church orthodoxy and modernism were firming up.

11

FUTURISM AND FASCISM

Poets have seldom had political influence. There have been few exceptions in the twentieth century. In England, none except, just possibly, Rudyard Kipling. In America, none at all. In Russia, one might mention Vladimir Mayakowsky. But the outstanding figure in this regard was Italian: a bizarre, hyperactive and fantastically egotistical writer named Gabriele d'Annunzio (1863–1938), a man hell-bent on turning himself into a living legend, and one who succeeded when most writers who try it fail.

He had been born in Pescara on the Adriatic coast and raised in the Abruzzi, then a brutishly backward part of Italy, with a tiny educated elite and an illiterate, superstitious majority of peasants. This seemed to be the eternal order, and contempt for the masses was to be the mainspring of d'Annunzian politics. His father Francesco Paolo was an intelligent, loathsome bully, whose contempt for the underdog was fully inherited by his son. The world, he wrote, was divided into masters and slaves, with nothing in between: 'To the superior race, which shall have risen by the pure energy of its will, all shall be permitted; to the lower, nothing or very little. The greatest sum of well-being shall go to the privileged, whose personal nobility will make them worthy of all privileges. The plebeians remain slaves, condemned to suffer . . .'

All his life, d'Annunzio would be pursued by the spectre of his own provincial origins and by that of his piggish father's sexual opportunism: sex wasn't real sex unless it was also rape. He married young, but almost as soon as he got to Rome in 1881 to seek his literary fortune he dumped his Abruzzese wife in favour of a string of socialites, whores, *principesse* and actresses, culminating in his prolonged affairs with the two most famous *tra-*

gédiennes of the day, Sarah Bernhardt and her Italian rival, Eleonora Duse. (The wife would presently commit suicide by jumping from a window.) His bed-hopping was ruthless. There was nothing modest about the transfiguration d'Annunzio expected of his sex life: 'The work of the flesh is in me the work of the spirit, and both harmonize to achieve one sole, unique beauty. The most fertile creatrix of beauty in the world is sensuality enlightened by apotheosis.'

D'Annunzio practised most kinds of writing, with increasing public success. He started publishing his juvenilia, verses and short stories, when he was sixteen – and to get publicity for his first book of verses, he sent the newspapers a fake report of his own death in a fall from a horse. He wrote a series of novels, beginning in 1889 with *Il Piacere* ('The Child of Pleasure'), followed in 1891 by *L'Innocente* ('The Innocent One'), *Giovanni Episcopo* ('Bishop John', 1892), *Il Trionfo della Morte* ('The Triumph of Death', 1894), *La Vergine delle Rocce* ('The Virgin of the Rocks', 1896) and *Il Fuoco* ('The Flame of Life', 1900). Most of these were bestsellers in Italy and some in France, where d'Annunzio had also built an avid public. He was constantly in trouble with the Italian clergy, building a hypnotic reputation as a decadent and a sex maniac, which did his sales no harm at all. *Il Fuoco* was a *roman-à-clef* based on d'Annunzio's scandalous and hugely publicized love affair with Sarah Bernhardt. Bernhardt had also prompted him to turn to the theatre, with noisy if variable success. His two great dramatic hits, *La Città Morta* ('The Dead City', 1898) and *Francesca da Rimini* (1901), were written for her as their tragic heroine.

In addition to the plays, the novels and several collections of lushly decadent and hortatory verse published around the turn of the century, d'Annunzio collaborated with the composer Claude Debussy on a musical play, *The Martyrdom of Saint Sebastian*, and even wrote a screenplay for a silent movie based on *Salammbô*, Gustave Flaubert's lurid novel about the fall of Carthage. He also has the distinction of being the only poet in history after whom an airport is named – the Gabriele d'Annunzio Airport, in Brescia.

His poems had their moments, but most were of an old-fashioned sort, echoing English writers like Swinburne, Rossetti and Keats, and tailor-made for the *fin de siècle* fascination with erotic necrophilia:

As from corrupted flesh the over-bold
Young vines in dense luxuriance rankly grow,
And strange weird plants their horrid buds unfold
O'er the foul rotting of a corpse below . . .

You would hardly guess that such sticky period pieces were written by a contemporary of Pound and Eliot. A little of this stuff went a long way, even in the 1890s, and most of it is so overdone in its theatric 'decadence' as to be barely tolerable, even in Italian, a century later. D'Annunzio was addicted to aesthetic posturing; the aesthete-hero of his novels was invariably a projection of himself into the domain of fiction, with all its room for exaggeration. Andrea Sperelli, the protagonist of *Il Piacere*, the novel d'Annunzio published at the age of twenty-six, is the young embodiment of Art for Art's Sake. 'Art! Art!' he sensitively rants to himself; 'This was the faithful Lover, ever young, immortal. This was the Fount of pure joy, forbidden to the multitude, conceded to the elect; this was the precious sustenance that made man like a god. Having set his lips to that cup, how could he have drunk at any other?'

What moved d'Annunzio into the full Italian limelight was not his writing alone, with its relentless emphasis on self-gratification at any cost to others, but his singular aggression and personal bravery. This included a real understanding of mass media and what they could do for a career. D'Annunzio wrote, and was written about, everywhere: he was the only Italian writer, other than the Futurist Filippo Marinetti, who could make headlines in London and New York as well as Rome or Milan.

Whatever one might say about the qualities of his verse – and some of it, allowing for the conventions of the time, was passably good, although the prose strikes a modern eye as unreadably self-regarding – there is no doubting his ardour and toughness as a man. As soon as the First World War broke out, d'Annunzio quit Paris – where he had gone partly in pursuit of Sarah Bernhardt, and partly to escape his growing legion of creditors – and returned to Italy, where he agitated ceaselessly in articles, verses and speeches for Italy's entry on the side of the Allies. He believed that war would rehabilitate his country in foreign eyes: that Italian aggression would cancel his homeland's annoying image as the mother of waiters, tenors and ice-cream vendors. He learned to fly, lost an eye in a landing accident, and reached the climax of his aeronautical career in August 1918 when, with considerable bravery – one should remember that the thing was done in a biplane with an open cockpit and no parachute – he led nine fighters from the 87th Squadron on a seven-hundred-mile round-trip flight from an airfield near Venice to drop propaganda leaflets on the city of Vienna. The Austrian capital had no anti-aircraft guns, but the *volo su Vienna* was still a spectacular achievement that cemented the poet's reputation in Italy as a daredevil, one of the heroes of the early age of Italian aviation.

By the war's end d'Annunzio was seen by his own countrymen (and swooning countrywomen) as a modern *condottiere*, with wings and a Fiat aero-engine instead of a horse. This matched his own opinion of himself: totally without modesty, he was a relentless tuft-hunter, a chaser of awards, citations and medals for bravery, which he sought (and got) not only from Italy but from other Allied countries as well. He briefly heightened this reputation by actually capturing some territory. D'Annunzio's nationalist feelings, like those of many Italians, were offended when at the Paris Peace Conference it was proposed that the ethnically Italian northern city of Fiume be handed over to a newly formed political entity, Yugoslavia. He therefore recruited two thousand hard-core nationalist irregulars, Italian citizens of Fiume, and forced the withdrawal of the British and French occupying forces that were in control of the city.

The Italian government, however, refused to accept Fiume and demanded that d'Annunzio and his men surrender. This the poet refused to do. Instead he declared that Fiume was now an independent state, a sort of Monaco-on-the-Adriatic, ruled and led by himself. He ran it as a military dictatorship, and during this time he invented and put to use a number of devices that were later adopted by Mussolini and the Italian Fascists, ranging from black shirts to forcing dissidents to drink castor oil as a humiliating punishment. Eventually the Italian government, vacillating, weary of d'Annunzio's strutting but uncertain what to do about a national poet-hero, set up a naval blockade. Matters grew tenser by the month. At one point d'Annunzio had Fiume declare war on Italy, one of the more splendid examples of the Mouse that Roared in modern European history. Fiume even issued postage stamps with his head on them and the motto *Hic manebimus* – 'Here we shall stay'. Finally, at the end of 1920, the Italian government had no choice but to accept the declaration and launch a naval bombardment of Fiume, taking care to inflict as little death and damage as possible.

It was all diplomatically resolved in the end. Fiume, no longer a city-state, remained Yugoslavian and then was absorbed into Croatia (it is now known as Rijeka). D'Annunzio went back to his home on Lake Garda and resumed his literary and erotic careers. He never again went into formal politics, though he campaigned vigorously from the sidelines and behind the scenes. But this activity was somewhat curtailed by injuries after he fell, or was pushed, from a window in 1922. The legacy he left was one of political theatre, but it was powerful and became more so when it was taken up by Benito Mussolini. It was d'Annunzio who first made popular the Roman salutes, the black shirts, the speeches from the balcony, the marches and 'oceanic' demonstrations that we associate primarily with Il Duce – a title, not incidentally, that the poet wanted to reserve for himself. He was the first writer, one might say, to grasp the relations between crowds and power. This would make him a valuable role-model for the young Mussolini after the war. D'Annunzio's main theatre was Rome, where he showed an unfailing gift for stirring up street riots and demos against Italy's wartime prime minister, the cautiously neutralist

Giovanni Giolitti, with inflamed and inflaming speeches about how the time for words had gone, the time for action arrived. This, too, would be noted and copied by Mussolini. Did more cautious souls object to these hot harangues? *Me ne frego*, was d'Annunzio's response: I don't give a toss. It became one of the nationally popular catch-phrases of Fascism.

D'Annunzio was himself not a Fascist. He was close to leading anti-Fascists and, in 1922, was better known to many Italians than Mussolini himself. He had the dirt – which never became fully public, but always threatened to – on the 1924 assassination of the socialist deputy Giacomo Matteotti, who had attempted to annul the elections won by Fascism because of their voting irregularities. D'Annunzio was greatly admired by the Fascists for his chore-ography of demos and crowd scenes. Mussolini begged him to help Fascism, but all he got in reply was a letter reproving him for stealing d'Annunzian ideas.

It was hardly a surprise, therefore, that Mussolini, after he came to power, treated this national icon with kid gloves. If you have a rotten tooth, the Duce explained, you either pull it out or fill it with gold; d'Annunzio had to have the second treatment, for otherwise he might become too dangerous. Mussolini got the king to give d'Annunzio the title of 'Principe di Montenevoso', the Prince of Snowy Mountain, which of course the poet lost no opportunity to flaunt. He publicly financed a magnificent edition of d'Annunzio's writings, promoted by the government, on which the poet was paid a 30 per cent royalty, earning a million lire a year from 1924 to 1938 – a time when a lira was still a lira. And he gave d'Annunzio a villa on Lake Garda, Il Vittoriale degli Italiani, which became a memory palace of d'Annunzian achievement, narcissism and, above all, kitsch. It can still be visited and, for its spooky vulgar intensity, it deserves to be. From the ceiling of a music room is suspended the fragile biplane in which d'Annunzio made his celebrated flight over Vienna, dropping leaflets in the midsummer of 1918. Its other exhibits include the *Puglia*, a torpedo-cruiser on which d'Annunzio had once patrolled the Dal-matian coast, which was moved intact to dry land in the cypress gardens overlooking the lake. From time to time her bow guns used to be fired, in salute to the poet's genius. They no longer are, because after nearly a century they (like his verses) have run out of ammunition.

In the gloomy and pretentious spaces of the Vittoriale d'Annunzio conducted the last, rather sordid and perfunctory, affairs of his long amatory career. Women were still falling over one another to reach his bed. It never occurred to d'Annunzio that men should not live off women. Bernard Berenson, who knew d'Annunzio somewhat, liked to tell the story of a silver-haired, highly respectable and immensely rich American woman of advancing years who, seized with the desire to add d'Annunzio to her conquests, let the poet know (through a go-between) that she would pay most generously for a night with him. The poet's response was to ask, 'Is she white all over?'

The d'Annunzian style strongly affected both Futurism and Fascism. Futurism was a culture-bound movement with pretensions to affect everyday life; its leader was Filippo Tommaso Marinetti, 'the caffeine of Europe' as he liked to style himself. He was born in Alexandria, Egypt, in 1876. His father Enrico was a successful corporate lawyer who lived with, but never married, his mother, Amalia Grolli. Unlike most of the poets, musicians and artists in his circle, he was never short of money; for him, private income meant freedom, as it does for most people lucky enough to have one: he never had to swerve from the self-appointed mission of changing the world merely in order to earn a crust, and his attacks on middle-class complacency were made all the bolder by his own class security. As the ringmaster of cultural novelty in Europe, he needed to be everywhere – not only Rome, where he and his family kept a large apartment, but Paris, St Petersburg and Moscow, Zurich, Berlin, London and especially Milan, his chosen home. Such mobility cost money, and Marinetti was one of the few modernists – certainly the only Italian one – who had plenty of it.

He had been schooled by Jesuits, which may well have contributed to his sense of confident exception. This was confirmed when his Jesuit teachers expelled him for cultural rowdiness: he had been passing around copies of Zola's realist novels.

Another factor that seems to have put him at an angle (as one may mildly call it) to middle-class assumptions was his affiliation to Africa, through his Egyptian childhood. Marinetti deeply wanted to be seen as an exotic, and he played it up. Pliny the Elder had written in his *Natural History, Vulgare Graeciae dictum, semper aliquid novi Africam adferre*: 'It is commonly said by Greeks that something new is always coming out of Africa.' This could well have been Marinetti's motto, and it explains the frequent references to the prowess of 'Negroes' (as he called Africans, in the usage of the day) in his writings. Africans were imagined as tough, energetic, fearless, and never at a loss when it came to surprising and disconcerting Europeans. They were, in that sense, natural avant-gardists, which was how Marinetti saw himself. Unlike Picasso, Matisse or Derain, he was never influenced by the 'primitive' art of Africa. He was a writer and performer, not a painter. It is quite possible, though, that there was a link between the languages and chants of the Dark Continent, as imagined by Marinetti and other intellectuals, and the nonsense-onomatopoeia of 'words-in-freedom' that was to become an important part of Marinetti's poetic strategies. Like some other Europeans who wanted to display their difference from the common herd, he liked the bone-in-the-nose, ooga-wooga picture of African savagery.

His father sent him to Paris to study for his *baccalauréat*, which he got in 1893. Then he came back to Italy and enrolled in the Faculty of Law at the University of Genoa, graduating in 1899. But he was never to practise law. Instead he lived the life of a young literary *flâneur*, writing poems, essays, plays and, with increasing regularity and skill, practising journalism in Italian and French. More and more, he gravitated towards literary and artistic circles in Rome, Turin and Milan.

The movement called Futurism was launched with an essay written in French by Marinetti and published, as befitted its international intent, in Paris in 1909. From then on the production of manifestos was going to be Marinetti's chief artform: nobody in

the European cultural world, except for d'Annunzio, had a
stronger instinctive talent for publicity or could excel him at
hectoring.

Certain images recur in his work, and in that of his fellow
Futurists. They are almost all mechanical, and polemically
modern. 'The world's magnificence,' he wrote, 'has been enriched
by a new beauty: the beauty of speed. A racing motor-car, whose
hood is adorned with great pipes like serpents of exploding breath
... a roaring motor-car that seems to run on shrapnel, is more
beautiful than the Victory of Samothrace.' For many people this
is now true. At the very least it is not difficult, more than a century
after this manifesto was written, to find both the sculpture and
the machine beautiful, though not in the same way. But in 1909
such sentiments seemed, to cultivated Europeans who read them,
blasphemous and almost diabolical – they amounted to a contradiction of the 'proper' order of aesthetic experience, because
the car was not beautiful *at all* whereas the sculpture was *nothing
but* beautiful.

The car, object of what one writer called 'autolatry', was the
prime Futurist icon, the emblem, the spectacular object of desire.
The only thing that compared with it was the aeroplane, then (in
1909) in its very early, pioneering stage of development, the Wright
brothers having achieved heavier-than-air flight under power in
1903. The aeroplane of early Futurist dreams was merely a Blériot
monoplane, of the kind that had recently made it across the
English Channel. Trains and fast motorboats also figured, but
they never approached the automobile, whose rapid progress
under personal control (or lack of it) seemed to Marinetti and
other Futurists to confirm the belief of Henri Bergson (1859–1941),
one of their favourite philosophical writers, that reality was in
constant flux: car travel presented the driver and passengers with
one level of experience rapidly overlapping another, so that the
total impression had more to do with *collage* than with a static
view. Consequently Futurist writing and painting, when it turned
to cars, was always highly personal – the 'I' is in the driver's
seat – and invariably centred on exhilarated feelings of directional

energy and rapid change. Needless to say, this arose at a point in history, around the first decade of the century, when the roads were clear of other cars and that emblem of automotive culture, the traffic jam, did not yet exist. What can it have been like to drive a fast car around an Italian city, at night, in those days before the invention of the traffic light? Marinetti's first Futurist manifesto tells us his version, in a stream of Mr Toad-like rantings.

It is 1908. He has been up late into the night with two friends, automaniacs like himself, bloviating about life and culture, when they hear 'the famished roar of automobiles'. '"Let's go!" I said. "Friends, away! Let's be off! ... We're about to witness the Centaur's birth and soon we shall see the first flight of Angels! We must shake the gates of life, test the bolts and hinges!"' This kind of rodomontade would rank high on anyone's list of Invocations That Were Probably Never Invoked (though with Marinetti, it is hard to be sure): in any case, they are soon down at their cars, the 'three snorting beasts, to lay amorous hands on their torrid breasts'. Off they go, vroom-vroom, in a sort of mechano-sexual delirium. 'Like young lions we ran after Death ... There was nothing to make us wish for death more than the longing to be free at last from the weight of our courage!' But alas, some cyclists appear, blocking the road; and Marinetti and his leonine friends have to avoid them. His car plunges upside-down into a ditch, baptizing Marinetti in sacramental filth. 'O maternal ditch ... Fair factory drain! I gulped down your nourishing sludge; and I remembered the blessed black breast of my Sudanese nurse ... when I came up from under the capsized car, I felt the white-hot iron of joy deliciously pass through my heart!'

There is more, much more, in this vein; no one could accuse Marinetti of terseness. One can have a certain sympathy with the annoyed Italian writer who, when asked if he didn't agree that Marinetti was a genius, retorted 'No, he's a phosphorescent cretin', but in fact he was less than the first but a good deal more than the second. Sometimes he could be perfectly idiotic, as in his call to glorify war, 'the world's only hygiene', along with militarism and patriotism; or in his ludicrous exhortations to fill the canals of Venice with the rubble of its demolished palaces. *Let's Kill the Moonlight* was the title of one of his more famous anti-romantic manifestos. And he positively loathed John Ruskin's views on art, nature and (inevitably) Venice. 'When,' he asked his English audience in a speech at the Lyceum Club in London in 1910,

> when will you disembarrass yourselves of the lymphatic ideology of that deplorable Ruskin ... with his morbid dreams of rustic life, with his nostalgia for Homeric cheeses and legendary wool-winders, with his hatred for the machine, steam, and electricity, that maniac of antique simplicity ... [who] still wants to sleep in his cradle and feed himself at the breast of his decrepit old nurse in order to recover his thoughtless infancy?

This must be one of the stupidest diatribes ever launched against Ruskin, but perhaps its defects are ascribable to the limitations of Marinetti's English. Though he was certainly no feminist, he said he stood for 'the semi-equality of man and woman and a lessening of the disproportion in their social rights', which put him ahead (or semi-ahead) of most Italians. He had an acrid realism, sometimes, which contained some hard nuggets of truth: he wanted to see

> disdain for *amore* [sentimentality or lechery] produced by the greater freedom and erotic ease of women and by the universal exaggeration of female luxury ... today's woman loves luxury more than love. A visit to a great dressmaker's establishment, escorted by a paunchy, gouty banker friend who pays the bills, is a perfect substitute for the most amorous rendezvous with an adored young man. The woman finds all the mysteries of love in the selection of an amazing ensemble which her friends still do not have. Men do not love women who lack luxury. The lover has lost his prestige.

Sad, perhaps, but indisputable. Marinetti was an enthusiastic womanizer; if you believe his account of adventures among the beauties of Moscow and St Petersburg on a Russian lecture tour, he was an irresistible sex-god. The preferred attitude of Futurism towards women in general was to see them as primordial forces rather than rational beings. 'Let every woman rediscover her own cruelty and violence that makes them turn on the defeated,' exhorted a Futurist manifesto in 1912. 'Women, become once more as sublimely unjust as every force of nature!' There were, of course, no women artists in the band of brothers who enlisted their talents around Marinetti's peculiar charisma.

As he aged, Marinetti drew closer to the big movement that was developing in Italy: Fascism. Of course, he would not have seen it that way: rather, his view was that the Fascist leaders, including Mussolini himself, drew closer to him, needing the inspiration that only he personally and Futurism in general could provide. In 1918 the political party Marinetti founded, the Partito Politico Futurista, merged with Mussolini's Fasci di Combattimento. Mussolini himself did not have strongly partisan views on visual arts other than architecture, but he was certainly not going to echo the psychotic hatred of modernism as a Jewish plot that animated Hitler and his cultural lieutenants. He never showed any interest in importing Nazism's show of *Entartete Kunst* ('Degenerate Art') to Italy, or encouraging his own people to construct and curate an Italian equivalent. The reason was simple: Mussolini, at first, was not anti-Semitic, and in any case (as he put it in 1923*), with regard to art 'the State has only one duty: not to undermine art, to provide humane conditions for artists' – in short, to get out of the way. Hitler might loathe Futurism, but how could Mussolini do so? Marinetti succeeded in persuading him not to import the *Entartete Kunst* show to Italy. He also

---

* While opening an exhibition of the Novecento [twentieth century] Italian Group, organized by his mistress, the freelance curator and art dealer Margherita Sarfatti.

protested, successfully at first, against the copying of Nazi cultural anti-Semitism by Italian Fascists. As the twenties moved on, Marinetti became more tolerant still: he accepted election to the Italian Academy, tried (but failed) to have Futurism declared the official state art of Italy, took a hand in promoting religious art, and declared that Jesus Christ had been a Futurist – which, given Jesus' more excited and apocalyptic predictions about the transformation of human life in the world to come, may not have been so far off the mark. And no one could say Marinetti himself did not want to practise what he preached: the man who praised war as the world's necessary hygiene volunteered (but was not accepted) for active service in the Second World War, when he was past sixty.

Of the artists associated with the Futurist group and promoted by Marinetti, the most talented were three men: the painters Gino Severini (1883–1966) and Giacomo Balla (1871–1958), and the sculptor/painter Umberto Boccioni (1882–1916).

Along with these one should probably include a fourth, a musician whose work can no longer be assessed because the special instruments for playing it have long disappeared: Luigi Russolo (1885–1947), who was the spiritual ancestor of such eccentric modernists as the English composer Cornelius Cardew. Russolo's belief was that non-musical sounds, as from industry, machines or traffic, could have as much aesthetic value as traditional sounds made by stringed or wind orchestral instruments; his speciality was constructing what he called *intonarumori*, 'noise-makers'. At his first concert, at the Gran Teatro del Verme in Milan in 1914, eighteen of these devices were divided into howlers, cracklers, gurglers, thunderers, hissers, exploders, buzzers and crumplers. Under a hail of vegetables from the indignant audience, they played three of Russolo's compositions, including his *Convention of Automobiles and Aeroplanes*. Other recitals, evoking an equally gratifying anger, were given in London and Paris. Russolo pronounced himself 'satiated' by Beethoven and Wagner; now, he said, 'we find far more enjoyment in mentally combining the noises of trams, backfiring motors, carriages and bawling crowds than in re-hearing, for example, the *Eroica* or the *Pastoral'*. Unfortunately none of Russolo's noise-makers have survived and we have only the sketchiest idea of what sounds they may have produced.

Gino Severini was the creator of one of the major Futurist icons, the congested, jazzy, frenzied panorama of nocturnal pleasure, *Dynamic Hieroglyphic of the Bal Tabarin* (1912). Giacomo Balla, who taught painting to both Severini and Boccioni, was quite widely recognized as an artist by the time he joined the Futurists, and he gave the movement its most popular image, the disarmingly humorous *Dynamism of a Dog on a Leash* (1912). This must rank high among the few core-modernist paintings that are good for a laugh and that almost everyone can recognize – the charming vision of a dachshund, tail a-wag and little legs going frenetically, trotting along the pavement at the feet of its owner. The paintings Balla laid most store by, however, were those of a speeding car. Some were very big – *Abstract Speed* (1913) is fully eight feet wide – and they are suffused with the bellowing romanticism of Marinetti's first manifesto, full of force lines and violent, dynamic curves.

Such work was greatly indebted to photography. The main inspiration was the work of Étienne-Jules Marey (1830–1904), the French scientist who has the strongest claim to be the father of modern cinema. Eadweard Muybridge, wishing to study the movement of humans and animals, had set up a battery of cameras side by side in order to capture isolated phases of movement as single images. Marey, on the other hand, used filmstrips so as to capture on one negative the successive movements of a subject seen from a single point of view by one lens which followed its trajectory. This, not Muybridge's sequences, was the true ancestry of the movie camera.

Boccioni's is an instructive case, because his best-known (and best) surviving work *Unique Forms of Continuity in Space* (1913) is a striding sculpture based upon the very one Marinetti thought inferior to a racing-car – the ancient Greek *Victory of Samothrace*. Its flanges and scooped-out hollows obey Boccioni's conviction that 'Sculpture must make objects live by rendering their extensions in space sensible, systematic and plastic, for no one can imagine that one object ends where another begins ... the pavement can rise up onto our table ... while between your house and the other your lamp spins its web of plaster rays.' But it also illustrates the fact that it is very difficult, and for most talents impossible, to create a work of art that is a hundred per cent new in the way the Futurists prated about novelty. Everything has precedents and their presence does not reduce the intensity of a work of art. Boccioni made at least a dozen sculptures in the same vein which suggest this kind of interpenetration of object and surrounding space. Old photos attest that they are among his most beautiful and complex works, but nearly all of them were destroyed by rain when they were carelessly left outside after his posthumous retrospective of 1916–17. They instinctively accept what contemporary physicists such as Einstein had come to perceive as the truth, however esoteric it might seem at first: that matter is, ultimately, energy. Part of the sculptor's task was to find solid form in which this could be symbolized.

Boccioni despised most contemporary sculpture as derivative, dull and coarse – 'a spectacle of barbarism and lumpishness'. But he made exceptions, chiefly for the Italian sculptor Medardo Rosso (1858–1928), 'who tried,' he argued, 'to enlarge the horizon of sculpture by rendering into plastic form the influences of a given environment and the invisible atmospheric links which attach it to the subject'. Unlike more highly regarded sculptors of the time, with passéist influences – Constantin Meunier (Greek), Antoine Bourdelle (Gothic) and Auguste Rodin (Italian Renaissance and especially Michelangelo) – Rosso was 'revolutionary, very modern, more profound, and of necessity restricted'. Unfortunately his attachment to light Impressionist modelling deprives his art of 'any mark of universality', but his work is much more than a start towards what Boccioni calls 'a sculpture of environment'.

Boccioni was a painter (not 'too') and he struggled to create images of 'universal vibration' which took Impressionist light beyond its normal descriptive aims. He learned much about this from the pointillist paintings of Georges Seurat and Paul Signac. Signac was especially congenial to the Futurists because he was an anarchist, a foe of all established orders, hence an ally of Marinetti's ideas of overthrow and radical change. Some of Boccioni's paintings, conceived in terms of 'Divisionism' (as the dot-painting that derived from Seurat and Signac was called in Italy), appear to be deliberate illustrations of passages from Marinetti's Futurist manifestos. 'We will sing of great crowds excited by work, by pleasure, and by riot; we will sing of the multi-coloured, polyphonic tides of revolution in the modern capitals.' And there was Boccioni's *Riot at the Galleria* (1910), with its jagged confusion of figures struggling under the blinding glare of a café's glass doors. Boccioni's masterpiece in this Divisionist vein was a canvas of industrial work, *The City Rises* (1910–11), originally entitled *Work*, inspired by the sight of heavy industrial construction on the outskirts of Milan. The painting is dominated by an enormous red horse, seemingly half-dissolved into flakes and smears of light. The blue hitching-horn of its harness rises up aggressively to centre the composition. The draught horse strains forward against its hauling cables, as do the human workers that it dwarfs, with the kind of exaggerated effort that will become a commonplace in strip cartoons; its point of departure in 'fine art' is probably Tintoretto's *Raising of Lazarus* in Venice.

Futurist architecture had been imagined, but the only Futurist architect who mattered built nothing. His work survives solely on paper: in the small, beautifully rendered drawings he made for architectural projects that existed in his head but had no commissioning client. Antonio Sant'Elia was born in 1888 and, having bravely volunteered to fight in the war which Marinetti and his friends had exalted as 'the world's only hygiene', was killed in an Austrian attack at Monfalcone in northern Italy in the summer of 1916; he was twenty-eight years old, and his death may be numbered among the culturally unhealable losses of that conflict, along with those of Franz Marc, Umberto Boccioni, August Macke, Henri Gaudier-Brzeska, Guillaume Apollinaire, Wilfred

Owen, and a host of others whose names can never be known because they died too soon for their talent to have a chance to make a mark.

Even the efforts to commemorate him failed. He was buried in a cemetery which he had designed for his unit, the Arezzo Brigade; it no longer exists and his grave is lost. The Futurist painter Enrico Prampolini and the chief architect of Fascist high modernism, Giuseppe Terragni, joined to design a monument to him, and to the dead of the First World War, in the cemetery of Como. (Terragni's canonical building, the Casa del Fascio, is also in Como, though after the Second World War it was shorn of the portrait of Mussolini which adorned its façade.) It is based on Sant'Elia's own designs for larger structures (power stations, apartment blocks and factories), but done on a puny scale and far too small to achieve much impact. For those who have studied Sant'Elia's original drawings, many of which are only a few inches square, it does not matter; since those structures never existed, these drawings are his monument, and a most effective one.

A lot of ingenuity has been expended, mostly by Italian critics, to dissociate Sant'Elia's ideas from those of Marinetti, and one can easily understand why: Marinetti's tolerance for Il Duce, which sometimes approached the level of an intellectual love affair (though a doomed one, in the end), besmirched his postwar reputation and tended to hurt those of his associates. But Sant'Elia was killed before Mussolini's ideas were even born, and long before Marinetti's semi-conversion to them took place in the 1930s. Nothing suggests that Sant'Elia harboured the totalitarian ideas of Fascism, or expressed them in his architecture – though the designs were certainly meant for mass use and occupation. If anything he was a young socialist. (It is still common for some critics, residually enthralled by the promises of radical socialism, to prefer its ideology to that of Fascism – even though the Left, when it achieved power, could be and was as brutal to aspirations of freedom as the Right.)

What he and Marinetti had in common was an ecstatic sense of the possibilities of the modern city – a mighty switchboard of information, manufacture and perception, a social turbine hall, humming away, almost without human interference. To look at the multi-level cities Sant'Elia imagined, with their vast stepped skyscrapers, aerial terraces, bridges and flyovers, is to see the excitement of a supposed future applied to architecture:

> We must invent and rebuild the Futurist city like an immense, tumultuous construction yard, agile, mobile and dynamic in every detail; and the Futurist house must be like a gigantic machine.* The lifts must no longer be hidden away like tapeworms in the niches of stairwells; the stairs themselves, rendered useless, must be abolished, and the lifts must scale the heights of the façades like serpents of iron and glass. Houses of concrete, glass and iron, stripped of paintings and sculpture, rich only in the innate beauty of their lines and relief, extraordinarily *ugly* in their mechanical simplicity ... must rise on the brink of a tumultuous abyss: the street will no longer lie like a doormat at ground level, but plunge down into the earth, with multiple levels ... linked up for necessary interconnections by metal gangways and fast, moving pavements. *The decorative must be abolished* ...

It is unlikely that even Sant'Elia himself could have said what went on in those buildings, space by space, function by function. They are like the cinematic dreams of Fritz Lang – *Metropolis* raised to a high level of aesthetic sophistication. But they pack a romantic wallop, as visionary architectural designs can – and there had been nothing as potent, in Italian architecture, since the (equally unbuilt) fantasies of Piranesi. Perhaps, if they had been built, they might not have lasted well. On the other hand their erosion and decay might not have displeased the Futurists, who liked the idea of temporary architecture anyway because it

---

* Compare Le Corbusier's famous somewhat later characterization of a house as *une machine à habiter*.

accorded with their love of speed and impermanence. They distrusted 'massive, voluminous, durable, antiquated and costly materials'. They hoped to see architecture as a 'rigid, light and mobile art', in Umberto Boccioni's words – although the buildings in Sant'Elia's drawings often look as solid as Egyptian mastabas.

In 1914 Sant'Elia declared in a manifesto* that 'The decorative value of Futurist architecture depends solely on the use and original arrangement of raw or bare or violently coloured materials' – and such materials, as one knows from Le Corbusier and his 'Brutalist' offspring, get very grotty very quickly. But since they existed only on the utopian space of paper, this could not be put to the test. Their extrusion into the world of built architecture was not foreseen by Sant'Elia, who had long been dead when it happened, and it would undoubtedly have repelled him. The ideas – at least his ideas for the single building – were taken over and given a glitzy, theatrical form by two American architects in the 1970s and 1980s – Helmut Jahn with his skyscrapers in Chicago, and John Portman, the architect-developer of huge hotels with see-through glass-pod elevators zipping up and down, making a drama (which quite soon gets tedious, even for the tourists in the lobby) of vertical circulation.

Painting, sculpture, poetry, theatre and architecture were not the only arts that attracted Futurist attention. Because Futurism was meant to be all-embracing, a template for the life to come, it should also – Marinetti insisted – embrace food. Food was not 'subsidiary'. The Futurist, not to coin a phrase, was what he or she ate. To start with, this required a new use of language, one which was fully Italian and not 'corrupted' by linguistic borrowings from elsewhere. What most Italians called a *sandwich*, for example, became in Futurist-speak a *traidue* ('between-the-two'). There would be no more *bars*; they would be replaced by *quisibeves*

---

* Though there is some debate about the exact extent of his authorship and the names of his collaborators, if any, the content of the 1914 *Manifesto of Futurist Architecture* could not have existed without Sant'Elia.

('here-one-drinks'), and staffed not by *barmen*, only *mescitori* ('mixers'); what they mixed were not *cocktails* but *polibibite* ('multiple drinks'). If the Futurist wished to hop in his roaring, rampaging, bellowing, farting, prophetic six-cylinder Fiat and take his girl for a spin in the countryside, they would not eat a *picnic* but a *pranzoalsole* ('meal-in-the-sun').

But Marinetti and (probably to a lesser extent) his brothers in Futurism were not content with mere shifts of vocabulary, which, in any case, never took hold in Italy or anywhere else (much the way not many people are heard ordering 'freedom fries' today). They wanted to change the Italian diet by eliminating *pastasciutta* from it – all forms of macaroni must go and never come back. A more doomed and futile enterprise could scarcely be imagined. Pasta is a sacred food throughout Italy. In Rome there is even a museum of pasta, dedicated to the hundreds of varieties of it, from angel-hair strands to big sheets for *timballi* of the kind so lovingly described by Giuseppe di Lampedusa in *The Leopard*, from pinhead-size semolina to floppy pouches designed to contain ricotta, spinach or purées of chicken in *balsamella*. It is the universal democratic food *par excellence*, as pizza and hamburgers are today.

The very idea of launching an attack on a substance so bound up with Italy's self-image must have seemed like a kind of cultural suicide. But Marinetti hated pasta. He thought it made Italians gross, lazy, complacent, stupid and, worst of all, unfit for combat. The Mayor of Naples could and did go on record as saying that the very angels in Heaven ate *vermicelli al pomodoro*, but that cut no ice with Marinetti. 'Since everything in modern civilization tends towards elimination of weight, and increased speed, the cooking of the future must conform to the ends of evolution. The first step will be the elimination of pasta from the diet of Italians.'

His hatred of pasta came from his army service on the Austrian front. 'The Futurists who fought at Selo, on the Vertoibizza . . . are ready to testify that they always ate the most awful pasta, delayed and transformed into a cold, congealed mass by the artillery barrages of the enemy, which separated the orderlies and the cooks from the warriors. Who could have hoped for hot pasta *al dente*?' Wounded at the Case di Zagora in the May 1917 offensive, he was brought down on a stretcher to Plava, where a soldier cook gave him 'a miraculous chicken broth . . . [although] terrible Austrian shells were crashing down on the battalion kitchen and smashing his stoves. Marinetti had his first doubts then on the suitability of pasta as a food for war.' He had observed that the bombardiers, who were firing their mountain howitzers against the Austrians, never touched the ignoble stuff. Their usual sustenance was 'a lump of chocolate smeared with mud and sometimes a horsemeat steak, cooked in a frying-pan that had been washed out with eau de cologne'. Chocolate, eau de cologne, horsemeat: already the elements of Futurist recipes, which depended so heavily on discord, on the flight from traditional harmonies, were assembling as substances of 'heroism' in Marinetti's mind.

In an interview he gave some time later to an Italian journalist, Marinetti railed against pasta. 'Ugh! What piggish stuff, macaroni!'

To get the message across, paintings, prints, photographs and everything that happens to depict it must vanish from our houses; and publishers must recall their books from the shops to subject them to rigorous censorship, deleting without pity . . . In a few months just hearing its name spoken – macaroni, ugh! – people will throw up. The task is colossal. To destroy something only one hand is needed to light the fuse, but to rebuild it [as a cuisine adapted to our times] thousands and thousands of hands are necessary.

Another journalist, writing in the French magazine *Comoedia* in the early 1930s, echoed Marinetti by blaming *pastasciutta* for the 'languid sentimentalism' with which 'eternal Rome, from Horace to Panzini, has defied the passing of time': 'Today we need to remake the Italian man, for what point is there in having him raise his arm in the Roman salute if he can rest it without effort on his bulging stomach? Modern man must have a flat stomach . . . look at the Negro, look at the Arab. Marinetti's gastronomic paradox aims at education.'

So what would Italians of the future actually eat? 'This Futurist cooking of ours,' trumpeted Marinetti, 'tuned to high speeds like the motor of a hydroplane, will seem to some trembling traditionalists both mad and dangerous; but its ultimate aim is to create a harmony between man's palate and his life . . . Until now men have fed themselves like ants, rats, cats or oxen. Now with the Futurists the first human way of eating is born.'

Thus the 'Aeropainter' Fillia (the pseudonym of the Torinese artist Luigi Colombo) proposed what he termed 'Aerofood'. The diner is served from the right with black olives, fennel hearts and kumquats; and to his left, a waiter places a rectangle made of sandpaper, silk and velvet, which the diner strokes as he eats, enjoying the contrasts of taste and texture. As he or she eats, waiters spray the back of his neck with a *conprofumo* of carnations while, from an unseen source in the kitchen, the violent roar of an aircraft motor (*conrumore*) and some musical accompaniment by Bach (*dismusica*) are heard. Thus all the diner's senses will be mobilized, to ecstasy. Another invention of Fillia's was a dish called 'The Excited Pig': a crazed phallic pun consisting of a whole salami, skinned, standing erect in a dish containing very hot black espresso mixed with 'a good deal of eau de cologne'. A third was titled 'Hunting in Heaven'. Slow-poach a hare in *spumante* mixed with cocoa powder. When the liquid is absorbed, dunk the creature in lemon juice and serve it in a 'copious' *salsa verde* based on spinach and juniper, decorated with silver hundreds and thousands suggestive of huntsmen's shot. The artist Enrico Prampolini, also an 'Aeropainter', came up with an elaborate proposal for a dish he called 'Equator + North Pole'. Poach an 'equatorial sea' of golden egg yolks, from which will rise a cone of stiffly whipped egg white; the peak of the cone to be bombarded with slices of black truffle 'shaped to look like black aeroplanes'. This sounds, at least, conventionally edible, unlike the sexual-metaphor dish proposed by the very minor Futurist art critic P.A. Saladin, 'ManandWomanatmidnight'. Make a large pool of red *zabaglione*.

Arrange on it a 'nice big onion ring', transfixed by a stalk of candied angelica, and two candied chestnuts, presumably symbolizing the midnight lover's *coglioni*.

These dishes, and quite a few others of equal weirdness, appear to have been served at Futurist soirées in Rome and elsewhere organized by Marinetti. It is not known how well they were liked, and one may presume that not a few passéists among the invited guests may have sighed for a nice bowl of *spaghetti alla Bolognese*. Nevertheless the Futurists briefly had their own restaurant, though it was in Torino: the Santopalato or 'Holy Palate', at 2 Via Vanchiglia. It did not last long, but it served such post-industrial delicacies as 'Chickenfiat' – a large fowl, first boiled, then stuffed with steel ball-bearings, sewn up and roasted 'until the flesh has fully absorbed the flavour of the mild steel balls'. It was served garnished with whipped cream, and preferably handed around by 'the woman of the future', who would be bald and wearing spectacles. The Holy Palate was not a commercial success, but Marinetti kept it going for a while to make a point. Its supreme dish – which was also served at Futurist dinners in Rome – was called 'Sculpted Meat', *la carne scolpita*. This was a large cylindrical rissole of minced roast veal, stuffed with eleven kinds of cooked green vegetables. Something must have stuck it together to prevent slumping (perhaps a very stiff béchamel?), but we are not told what. It stood upright on a plate, supported by a ring of sausages which rested, in turn, on three golden spheres of chicken meat. It was crowned with a layer of honey. It claimed to be 'a symbolic representation of the varied landscapes of Italy'.

Just as Futurist efforts to reform the language of food had resulted in substituting lengthy polysyllables for short words, so the food itself had become absurdly elaborate, far beyond the reach of any domestic kitchen, and none too edible in any case. And yet, reading its descriptions, it does seem to have something in common with the crazier fantasies of extreme New Cuisine, as practised by such celebrity cooks as the Catalan Ferrán Adrià. Gustatory fantasists like Fillia represented an absurdist revolt against the vernacular food philosophy of the great normalizers of Italian cuisine like Pellegrino Artusi, whose book *Science in the Kitchen and the Art of Eating Well* had gone through numberless editions by then and was regarded as the Bible of authentic cooking.

One may well ask, what part did the city of Rome play in the development of Italy's one and only important modern art movement? In fact, a very important one. To Futurists, it represented The Enemy – historical consciousness, and all that was summed up in the term 'passéism', worship of the past. The Futurists hated the place for its immense authority, its age and continuity, and of course for its beauty, which they were most reluctant to recognize. To rail against the long achievements of thought, feeling and technique that were summed up in the monuments of Rome was inevitably to look like a beetle whining about a pyramid: it was going to stay in the way, so get used to it. They could indulge their fantasies, of course. One Futurist publication ran a drawing of what Piazza di Spagna might look like without such passéist encumbrances as Bernini's Barcaccia Fountain – in the background, the familiar shapes of S. Trinità dei Monti and the obelisk above the familiar three-stage rise of the Spanish Steps; in the foreground, an ugly blank piazza full of electric tramcars and overhead wires. This was supposed to be Progress.

Of all places on earth, Rome was the one where operatically phrased invective against the past sounded tinniest. The Futurist manifesto on architecture said its authors (mainly Sant'Elia, with input from Marinetti and probably Boccioni) would 'combat and despise' all classical architecture, along with 'the embalming, reconstruction and reproduction of ancient monuments', all perpendicular and horizontal lines, all cubical and pyramidal forms. That more or less took care of everything from the Etruscans to the Vittorio Emanuele monument – 2,500 years, out of the window. No wonder Marinetti and his allies preferred the industrial cities of the north, Milan and Turin.

*

If Cola di Rienzo, in the fourteenth century, was the first pro-
letarian to rise to great political power in Rome, then Benito
Mussolini in the twentieth century was the last.

The parallels between the two men are irresistible: the humble
working-class origins, the force of character and oratorical power,
the belief in oneself as the chosen figure of destiny. Cola was
obsessed with the belief that the ancient glories of the Roman
Empire could be reincarnated in him and revived under his rule.
So was Mussolini, on an even more grandiose scale. Both men
had strong charisma and called forth surging, weeping extremes
of fanatical loyalty from their massed followers.

Both regarded themselves, and were for a time seen by their
fellow Italians, as inspired tribunes of the people, although Mussolini (astutely, for his own political purposes) refused to promote
the kind of class hostility to the rich and titled that marked Cola's
politics, because that idea reeked of Communism and he needed
the support of the rich and powerful.

Each had his intellectual allies and supporters: Cola had the
(episodic) backing of the greatest of Italy's humanist writers after
Dante himself, Petrarch; and whereas no Italian writer of that
stature was at work in the 1920s and '30s, Mussolini had a mentor
and literary figurehead in Gabriele d'Annunzio. Both came to
sticky ends: Cola lynched by a mob under the shadow of the
Ara Coeli in Rome, Mussolini shot by Communist partisans and
strung by the heels from the awning of a petrol station in Milan.
And although there is little doubt that Cola (in his less spiritually
exalted moments) was a nicer guy than the ruthless and stag-
geringly narcissistic Mussolini, the two men incarnated a style
of operatic, self-dramatizing populist leadership that still seems
peculiarly Italian and, truth to tell, still makes many Italians feel
nostalgic.

Benito Amilcare Andrea Mussolini was born under the sign of
Leo on 29 July 1883, in Dovia di Predappio, a small village in Emilia-
Romagna. His father, Alessandro Mussolini, was a blacksmith and
a committed, anticlerical socialist. His mother, Rosa Maltoni, was
a schoolteacher. He was the eldest of three children. His names

bore a heavy load as political emblems: 'Benito' after the Mexican radical Benito Juárez, 'Amilcare' from an Italian socialist, Amilcare Cipriani, and 'Andrea' from another Italian socialist, Andrea Costa. Predappio figures in Italian popular culture only because Mussolini was born there, and various *canzoni* on the later Left stemmed from that:

Se Rosa, illuminata de alma luce,
La notte in cui fu concepito Il Duce,
Avrebbe, in lo fabbro predappiano,
Invece della fica, presentato l'ano,
L'avrebbe preso in culo quella sera
Rosa soltanto, ma non l'Italia intera.

'If Rosa, lit up by divine light / The night The Leader was conceived / There, in the forge at Predappio / Had presented her anus instead of her twat / The one who got it up the ass would be / Just Rosa – not the whole of Italy.'

Young Benito, as a boy, helped his father in the forge; just as there had been nothing false about Adolf Hitler's claims to have served devotedly and bravely at Ypres, so Mussolini's frequent accounts of being a son of the working class were quite true. Just as his father was a passionate socialist, so the son was stubbornly rebellious and a sometimes violent delinquent at his priest-run boarding school. One gesture that made him particularly unpopular with the local citizens was to station himself in plain view outside the village church of Predappio and pelt its worshippers with stones as they filed out after morning Mass. He was bright, his grades were good, but because of his surly and easily inflamed temper he had difficulty finding and keeping work as a schoolteacher when he graduated. In 1902 he moved to Switzerland, with no better luck. His adherence to socialism and his general rowdiness caused him to land briefly in jail and finally to be deported as an unemployed alien.

Back in Italy, he at last fetched up in journalism in 1908, editing the Trento socialist party's newspaper *L'Avvenire del Lavoratore* ('The Worker's Future'). Trento was under the control of Austria-Hungary, which did not take an indulgent view of either Mussolini's anticlericalism or his choleric attacks on Austrian royalty. Eventually he was deported from Trento, back to Italy proper, where he got a writing and editing job with the socialist newspaper *Il Popolo*, followed by another with the more leftist organ *Avanti!* But despite his opposition to the war with Austria, Mussolini was called up by the draft in mid-1915. In all he served about nine months under fire in the trenches until he was severely wounded by an accidental mortar-bomb explosion and, in 1917, invalided out of active service.

It took the Great War to disabuse young Mussolini of his father's dreams of socialism. This catastrophically divisive conflict, this huge international machine for the production of corpses, had put paid to the ideals of voluntary class cooperation across national boundaries that had suffused the socialism of a previous generation. There would be no peaceful *Internazionale* in the bright future. Instead there would be struggle, unremitting and pitiless, whose result would be the abolition of the idea that class war could or should define society's shape. 'Socialism as a doctrine was already dead,' Mussolini later wrote. 'It continued to exist only as a grudge.' What could Italy raise in place of this unrealizable dream? An authoritarian system that would unify the country as ancient Rome had once unified it.

Some of the raw material for such a system already existed in Italy, and in fact had been created by the war. It consisted of the *squadristi* or returned soldiers, the army veterans who could be expected to respect Benito Mussolini as a former comrade-in-arms. They had fought on the winning side, that of the Allies against the Germans, but that could not wipe out the sufferings they had undergone, their dislike of those who had opposed the war (which included most socialists), their contempt for non-combatants – still less the feeling that they had been short-changed in the peace. The solidarity of men-at-arms, in an army drawn from all classes of life, far outweighed the socialist rhetoric of class solidarity.

Mussolini started assembling such an elite. For the workers, he promised a minimum wage, more power for industrial unions – which was quick to disappear once he was firmly in the saddle – and more rights for women. For bosses and bankers, who feared the Communists and socialists more than any other groups, he offered protection from the Red Menace. This was a shrewd and essential move, since it ensured that he could appeal to them for financial support, just as Hitler could in Germany. The emblem of the party was the ancient Roman *fasces*, the bundle of rods bound together around an axe that had been carried as a sign of strength and unanimity by the Roman *lictores*: hence the term *fascismo*. The strong arm of the party was organized by Dino Grandi, an army veteran whose groups of *squadristi*, identifiable by their quasi-military *camicie nere*, black shirts, made them increasingly feared and obeyed throughout the Italian cities and even, by the late 1920s, in country villages. The Fascists refused all alliances with existing parties of the Left, and of the Right as well. Wisely, they always declared their own uniqueness and independence. They were the *terza via*, the 'third way' towards national self-sufficiency. Not surprisingly this group, small at first, swelled into a fully fledged party, the National Fascist Party, within a couple of years and in 1921 its leader, now known to more and more of his adherents simply as *Il Duce*, won official standing by being elected to the Chamber of Deputies. In this and the Fascist rule that followed, Mussolini was greatly helped by the man who would become, in effect, his minister of propaganda and chief image counsellor, Giovanni Starace, appointed in December 1931.

Starace was to the Duce what Goebbels was to Hitler, and just as active in terms of inventing a ruling style. It was he who conceived and organized the 'oceanic' demos of tens of thousands of Romans in Piazza Venezia, beneath the Duce's speaking-balcony with its hidden podium; he who instituted the 'salute to the Duce' at all Fascist meetings, large or small, whether Mussolini was present or not; he who abolished the 'insanitary' handshake in favour of the 'hygienic', snap-to rigidity of the arm-out, Roman-based Fascist salute. He even stood at rigid attention, heels clicked together, when speaking to his leader on the phone.

And he made sure that the orchestrated cheers of the crowd were directed only to Mussolini, since 'One man and one man alone must be allowed to dominate the news every day, and others must take pride in serving him in silence.' Under Starace, uniforms multiplied into a veritable cult; some leading Fascists were required to have ten or even twenty, without a thread of gold braid missing. (This afforded great contrast to British modes of diplomatic dress, which featured the chalk-stripe double-breasted suit and the much ridiculed rolled umbrella *à la* Chamberlain.) In launching the movement which became known, in 1921, as the National Fascist Party, the Duce hinted privately to socialists that he would support them if they were ready to back his brand of populist dictatorship – a lie, but a welcome one to them. Meanwhile Mussolini and his men hugely inflated the numbers involved in the 1922 March (or Train Ride) on Rome to three hundred thousand armed Fascists, of whom, they claimed, three thousand paid for their fervour with their lives. The king was deceptively told that the army was outnumbered by Fascist militiamen and could not possibly defend Rome.

From this point on there was no stopping either the Duce or Fascism. They took over and reaped all the credit. The 1930s seemed to millions of people, and not just to Fascists, miracle years for the image of Italy in general and Rome in particular. Catalysed by the sensations of Futurism, Fascism seemed really to have taken off, in all areas. Faster, higher, further! Italy had the world's fastest seaplane, the supremely elegant Macchi MC 72. Lindbergh had flown the Atlantic, but Italo Balbo, a brute in some respects though indisputably a brave and gifted pilot, leading a squadron of nine twin-engine seaplanes, flew it twice, in 1931 and 1933, between the lagoons of Orbetello north of Rome and Lake Erie in Illinois. In 1931 Italy launched the world's fastest trans-atlantic passenger steamer, the *Rex*. The prestige of Italian cinema seemed likely (at least to the Italians) to be overtaking that of

Hollywood, and in 1932 the first Venice Film Festival was held. In 1934 Italy won the world soccer championship, and the playwright Pirandello, an undoubted Fascist in his idiosyncratic way, was awarded the Nobel Prize. The enormous Italian boxer Primo Carnera, the King Kong of the ring, won the world heavyweight championship by beating the American Jack Sharkey in 1933. (Boxing, one should remember, was then widely rated by Italians even higher than soccer; Mussolini called it an 'exquisitely Fascist means of expression'.) Guglielmo Marconi's inventions in radio and wireless telegraphy were eclipsing those of Thomas Edison. The new models of Italian machinery – both office and domestic – coming off the drawing-boards of Necchi and Olivetti were having their impact on a growing world market.

Perhaps none of these events was quite as epochal as the ever-growing Fascist propaganda machine made them out to be, but together they contributed to a sort of collective exultation, close to national hysteria. Once there had been England. Then there was America. And now, the technological genius of Italy apparently ruled. It was no longer the land of old canvases, mouldy domes and chipped statuary. It was the country of the Future, presided over by a man who was, in Italian eyes, hardly less than a demigod, a modern successor to the ancient Roman god-king Augustus. The most extreme fantasies of Marinetti and the Futurists, thanks to Il Duce, seemed to be coming true in Fascism. It even had a leader who vaunted his athletic prowess. The newspapers and magazines of Italy were enlivened by photographs of Mussolini and his *Bersaglieri* officers actually jogging, a sight which would not be repeated for another half-century, and in America – though a big difference was that Il Duce jogged in full uniform, apparently khaki, wearing riding-boots and an officer's cap, accompanied by brother officers carrying swords and wearing medals gained in the struggle against the Ethiopians. The Fascists understood media and propaganda too. Any country that threatened sanctions against Italy for its bellicose policies against Ethiopia, and later Republican Spain, might be ridiculed with such images as a poster of a small naked boy pissing on the word 'sanctions'. 'Better one day as a lion than a hundred years as a sheep,' ran a much cited slogan, but the lion's day was expected to last for ever. 'If you eat too much, you're robbing your country,' proclaimed a poster that showed a slim, determined cop tapping a greedy diner on his shoulder.

A tough, slender, muscular Italy was part and parcel of the new national image promoted by the Abyssinian (also known as the Second Italo-Ethiopian) war. Behind the uniforms, the slogans and the taste for violence, what did Fascism actually stand for? Was it only another name for social delinquency, as softies and lefties claimed? Mussolini, with some help from his co-author Giovanni Gentile, addressed the question in an entry for the *Italian Encyclopaedia* in 1932. First and foremost, it had to be understood that Fascism was not a pacifist movement, seeking an end to aggression. Quite the opposite. 'Fascism ... believes neither in the possibility nor the utility of perpetual peace. War alone brings up to its highest tension all human energy and puts the stamp of nobility upon the peoples who have courage to meet it. All other trials are substitutes.' That was what Marinetti had been writing a quarter-century before: war as race hygiene.

Fascism conceives of the state as absolute, the individual as relative. And so it can have no traffic with the 'Liberal State', which feebly exalts 'all useless and possibly harmful freedom'. The meaning and utility of freedom can only be decided by the state, never by the individual citizen. Fascism consecrates the idea of empire. Its growth is 'an essential manifestation of vitality, and its opposite a sign of decadence. Peoples which are rising, or rising again after a period of decadence, are always imperialist; and renunciation is a sign of decay and of death.' So it was with Italy, which was rising once more 'after many centuries of abasement and foreign servitude'.

If this rhetoric might seem cloudy, one could always try the ageing Marinetti's descants on 'Fascist poetry', written by way of an introduction to a 1937 anthology assembled by a Sicilian bard, *Il Duce and Fascism in the Dialect Songs of Italy*:

Just as religious poetry, martial poetry, etc. are not resolved in an assiduous exaltation of war or the church, Fascist poetry is not to be explained as poetry in praise of Fascism. On the contrary ... Fascist poetry is that which frames itself in the historical climate created by the Revolution and which means, prefigures or explains the unifying political, moral and economic ideas of the Fascist Corporate State, always constructing (or demolishing to construct), never turning back ... Fascist poetry is thus construction, construction of the Fascist spirit, which is realized in the fervour of fecund work, in human acts of salvation, material or spiritual, always altruistic and, whenever possible, universal. It is a poetry which turns against the orgiastic, the dionysiac, the pessimistic, against everything depressing, mortifying and harmful to the individual as to the collective. It expresses the special state of grace indispensable to the politico-social intuition of the historical moment we are passing through ...

All was now as limpid as the bed of the Tiber, because Fascism stood for the Future, but its way forward was the way backward – to an idealized, purified version of ancient Rome. Equally, because it stood for the Future, it had to have the young, who were the bearers of the Future, on its side. Because it needed to enlist the young, it demanded martyrs and heroes. Fascism was a youth movement, above all else – a fact of which it was not considered proper to remind the young public, in the heady 1960s, with their insane admonitions to trust no one over thirty.

The totalitarian regimes of the last century had young men martyred for their virtuous loyalty to the Cause, like the child-saints of earlier Christianity. The Nazis had Horst Wessel, a young Nazi activist supposedly killed by Communists and the author of a hugely popular song, that of the Sturmabteilung or Brownshirts, which became Germany's national anthem: '*Die Fahne hoch, die Reihen fest geschlossen!*', 'Hold high the Flag! Tightly close the ranks!' A Nazi-fomented legend had it that Wessel wrote both music and words, but in fact the tune came from a German naval song of the First World War. The Stalinists had a repellent teenage ideologue who rose to cult status by denouncing his own father to the secret police for the crimes of disloyalty and deviationism, whereupon the outraged father killed the son: there used to be a bronze statue of this unsavoury young martyr in Moscow, but it was torn down after perestroika.

Italian Fascism, which counted so much on its appeal to youth, had its own historical boy hero too, although not much is known about him. Indeed, there is some doubt about whether he actually existed, at least in the form Fascist propaganda gave him. His name was, or was said to be, Giovan Battista Balilla: the last name meant 'little boy' and was allegedly the nickname of a pre-teen youth named Perasso. He was supposedly a Genoese, and he met his martyrdom during a revolt against the Habsburg forces that occupied Genoa during the Austrian occupation of 1746 – a rising he allegedly started by throwing a rock at some Austrian artillerymen who were struggling to move a cannon stuck in a muddy street.

Many hymns were written by Fascist poetasters to the memory of this semi-legendary child, who came to symbolize Italian victories in the First World War, so precious to Fascist hearts, and the future of Fascism itself, so dear to their hopes. He figured in illustrations, on posters, in murals (though of course nobody knew what he looked like, which hardly mattered since nobody knows what Jesus looked like either). He was the model for masculine Fascist youth. A typical effusion, which won a bronze medal at the song festival of S. Giovanni in Rome, was included in *Li Gioielli d'Italia*, a collection of verse by the Roman dialect poet Pietro Mastini:

Bocce di rose
Fiori Italiani
Future spose
Madri domani
E pe la fede
Che sempre brilla

L'avrai da vede
Quanti Balilla!

'Mouths of roses / Italian flowers / Spouses of the future /
Tomorrow's Mothers / And for the faith / That always
shines / You will see before you / So many Balillas!'

This child-martyr was rewarded with a special distinction: lots
of machinery bore his name. A popular line of low-cost autos –
Italian equivalents to the German Volkswagen, though hardly as
well engineered – was named after him, and so were several sub-
marines. Mussolini appointed a former *ardito*, Renato Ricci, to
create an Opera Nazionale Balilla, intended to train Italian youth
'from a moral and physical point of view', and Ricci went to
England to seek out the founder of the English scouting movement,
Robert Baden-Powell, whose ideas were a more peaceable model
for this militaristic movement of teenagers. Their essential beliefs
were summed up in the 'ten commandments' of the Fascist militia:

1. Remember that those fallen for the Revolution and for
   the Empire go before your columns of march.
2. A comrade is a brother to you: he lives and thinks with
   you, and you will have him at your side in battle.
3. Italy must be served everywhere, always, with all your
   means; with work and with blood.
4. The enemy of Fascism is your enemy: give him no
   quarter.
5. Discipline is the sun of armies; it prepares and
   illuminates the victory.
6. If you go to attack decisively, victory is already in your
   grasp.
7. Total and mutual obedience is the legionary's strength.
8. There are no great or small matters; there is only duty.
9. The Fascist revolution has counted and still counts on
   the bayonets of its legionaries.
10. Mussolini is always right.

This last phrase, *Il Duce ha sempre ragione*, pervaded all Italy and her African colonies. Painted on walls, chiselled in stone, chalked on blackboards, even laid out in pebbles in school playgrounds by Ethiopian peasants, it was the unvarying leitmotif of Fascism, and the vestiges of it were still to be seen in parts of rural Italy up until the late 1960s.

Because a militarized state must have soldiers, Fascism placed great emphasis on the Italian birthrate. In this, if not in everything else, it found common ground with the Catholic Church, which was stonily opposed to any form of contraception. Each year, one of the many ceremonies under the Duce's balcony in Piazza Venezia (which had replaced the Capitol as the emblematic centre of Italian politics, and where huge 'oceanic' demonstrations of loyalty to Mussolini were convened by his minister of propaganda, Starace) was held to honour the country's ninety-five most prolific mothers, assembled with their squalling offspring. Naturally this spectacle gave rise to a good deal of chaffing (though actual satire on fecundity was banned): a cartoon in 1930 showed three flustered but resolute fathers racing towards the finish-line of a track, each pushing a baby-carriage jammed with dozens of infants, egged on by their wives with cries of '*Forza, Napoli!*', '*Spingi, Milano!*' and '*Presto, Roma!*' Mussolini's own view was that Italian families should expand to eight, a dozen or even twenty children: brave cannon fodder for the Empire to come. Each heroically fertile mother was awarded 5,000 lire and a medal.

Other inducements to enlarging the Italian family were devised and tried, as part of the general Fascist application of military techniques of control to civilian life. Thus in 1926, the Duce introduced what amounted to a concealed tax on bachelors, by assessing them at a higher tax level than married men with children. Top posts in education and the civil service were also reserved for such married people. Women, on the other hand, were dismissed from state jobs unless they were war widows. Information on birth control techniques, other than the ever unreliable coitus interruptus, was banned, though condoms remained on sale, since

these reduced the spread of venereal disease. 'There are 400
million Germans,' Mussolini declared in a speech on Ascension
Day (26 May), 1927, '200 million Slavs, and the target for Italians
by 1950 is 60 million, over the present 40 million. If we become
fewer, gentlemen, we shall not build an empire, we shall become
a colony.'

Though he had been born in the provinces, Mussolini when he
came to power wished only to imagine himself as a Roman. That
had not always been so. Though he never made much of a song
and dance about his Predappian origins, unless rhetorical purposes required that he present himself aggressively as a man of
the people, when he was a young socialist Mussolini deplored
Rome as 'a parasitic city of land-ladies, shoeshine boys, prostitutes
and bureaucrats'. But quite soon, as the ideas of what was to be
Fascism took form in his imagination, so did the necessity of
Rome's rebirth. Previous Roman emperors had been born and
raised in distant places like Spain and north Africa, and there
was no possible reason for a young man from Predappio not to
consider himself as fully Roman as any of his ancient forerunners.
Discoursing on architecture to a German journalist named Emil
Ludwig in 1932, the Duce observed that 'Architecture is the greatest of the arts, for it is the epitome of all the others.' 'It is extremely
Roman,' Ludwig agreed. 'I, likewise,' the Duce exclaimed, 'am
Roman above all.' The issue of *romanità*, Romanness, was at the
very core of the ideology and self-definition of the Fascist state.
Fascism viewed Rome as the centre of the world. It had been
before; now, in its new and future-bound incarnation, it must be
again. 'Rome is our point of departure and reference,' Mussolini
declared:

It is our symbol and, if you wish, our myth. We dream of a
Roman Italy: that is to say, wise, strong, disciplined and
imperial. Much of what was once the immortal spirit of
Rome rises again in Fascism: the *fasces* are Roman; our
organization of combat is Roman; our pride and courage
are Roman; *civis Romanus sum* [I am a Roman citizen]. It

is necessary now that tomorrow's history, the history we fervently wish to create, should not be ... a parody of the history of yesterday. The Romans were not only warriors but formidable builders who could challenge their time.

Mussolini thought of himself as a builder too, mainly and always. The poet Ezra Pound paid tribute to this in 1935. 'I don't believe any estimate of Mussolini will be valid unless it *starts* from his passion for construction. Treat him as *artifex* and all the details fall into place. Take him as anything save the artist and you will get muddled with the contradictions.' Il Duce was repelled by the idea of treating Rome just as a museum. It had to show its capacity, not just for commemorating the past, but for continuous life in the present and expansion into the future. Anything less would amount to a silent admission that, in Shakespeare's words in *Julius Caesar*,

> Romans now
> Have thews and limbs like to their ancestors –
> But, woe the while! our fathers' minds are dead,
> And we are governed by our mothers' spirits.

Not the least achievement of Fascism, in the face of the hitherto overwhelming power of the Papacy, was the agreement reached over the Vatican. Benedict XV had already lost an enormous slice of Italy by surrendering the Papal States. Now, after much bargaining with Mussolini, his successor Pius XI found his dependencies reduced to an area one-eighth that of Central Park in New York – a mere 108.7 acres, the size of Vatican City. There were, of course, concessions along with that, such as control over Castelgandolfo and the Lateran, recognition of Canon Law as binding alongside the law of the state, an independent post-office and radio station, Church control of all Catholic marriage, the teaching of Catholic doctrines in state schools, the placing of crucifixes in all classrooms, and financial compensation to the Papacy of 1.75

billion lire. Better still, Mussolini did God's work (as the Church saw it) in suppressing both Freemasons and Communists, sworn enemies of the Church. Pius XI therefore spoke openly (against the advice of his more moderate lieutenant, Cardinal Gasparri) of the Duce as 'a man sent by Providence', and unambiguously told the lower clergy of Italy to encourage their congregations to vote Fascist, which they duly did. This seemed so threatening to the priest-leader of the moderate Catholic Partito Populare, Don Luigi Sturzo, that he fled to London and remained there.

The most far-reaching of Pius XI's utterances, however, was not to do with his relations with Mussolini, though these became thornier as time went by. Nor was it even the 'concordat' or treaty of 1933, which he signed with Adolf Hitler – an ultimately fruitless deal brokered by Eugenio Pacelli, the future Pius XII. It was his encyclical *Casti Connubii* (1930), forbidding artificial contraception between married couples on pain of mortal sin. Naturally this was very much to Mussolini's taste, but its long-term effect was to drive the hitherto faithful away from the Church.

The re-glorification of imperial Rome, and its new linkage to Fascism, required two strategies: excavation and preservation of the ancient past, and the vigorous building of new Fascist structures. Mussolini did not much care about what lay between the ancient and the recent. He was not a friend of medieval, Renaissance or Baroque building, particularly since, despite his diplomatic overtures, he disliked the Catholic Church. Consequently, large amounts of this 'intermediary' city would be demolished if there was a likelihood of laying bare some traces of authentic Roman antiquity below them. This happened with his first large site-clearing, that of the Largo Argentina, originally part of the southern Campus Martius. A sixteenth-century church, that of S. Nicola de Cesarini, stood there – but underneath its foundations archaeologists perceived the ruins of four ancient temples, which dated, they believed, from republican times. Excavation, and the demolition of the church, did indeed disclose these much battered remains, and in the absence of other evidence about them it was supposed that all four were on the line of the start of most Roman

triumphal processions and had been paid for by victorious generals – which ones, it is not known. Nor is it known which gods the
temples might have honoured. But this association with Roman
triumphs, however unclear, naturally would have had great appeal
to Il Duce. 'I would feel myself dishonoured,' he declared, 'if
I allowed a new structure to rise even one metre here.'

What he particularly despised, for symbolic rather than aesthetic reasons, was the Rome of the Risorgimento, the architecture of the half-century between 1870 and his own accession to
power in 1922 – except for the Vittorio Emanuele monument,
which he saw as politically untouchable, since much depended
on amicable relations between Il Duce and the king, Vittorio
Emanuele's son.

Mussolini regarded the nineteenth-century unification of Italy
as incomplete at best, and at worst a sham. How could Italy be
called 'unified' when it was managed by so many local governments, still so hobbled by *campanilismo*, without the central
authority provided by Fascism? He would change all that.
Throughout the 1920s and '30s, Mussolini drew all the main functions of government together in his personal grasp.

In October 1922, Mussolini and his growing force of National
Fascist Party followers staged a *coup d'état*. They assembled at the
Florence railway station, boarded a train and got off in Rome,
heading for the parliament. This train ride was designated the
'March on Rome', though nobody went on foot. To walk all that
way would have been too tiring, sweaty and protracted. The idea
of such a march did not come from Mussolini, either; it was
initiated, but not organized, by d'Annunzio, who wanted to do it
all the way from Trieste with his own men. Supported by the
business class and the military, Mussolini was recognized by King
Vittorio Emanuele III, and the weak but elected prime minister,
Luigi Facta, was ousted.

Italy now had as its prime minister a bellicose man of the people
who nevertheless rejected the idea of class war and had nearly all
Italian businessmen, and the aristocracy as well, strongly behind
him. A minority of socialists and liberals boycotted parliament,

without effect: the king was afraid of political violence from the *squadristi*.

Mussolini's Fasci di Combattimento became part of Italy's armed forces, the Milizia Volontaria per la Sicurezza Nazionale (MVSN). They were now untouchable. In 1923 his Acerbo Law turned Italy into a single national constituency; the result was that, in a 1924 election, the Fascists took some 64 per cent of the vote. It was after this probably rigged election that socialist deputy Giacomo Matteotti tried to have the results thrown out and was murdered by a *squadrista* named Amerigo Dumini, who did several years' jail time but ended being supported for the rest of his life by Mussolini and the Fascist Party. Matteotti's demise caused some weak protest but nothing came of it; this spelt the end of opposition to Mussolini, and the beginning of his absolute control over Italy. Throughout the rest of the 1920s he devoted himself to creating a police state, with himself in charge of foreign affairs, colonies, defence, corporations and internal order.

Naturally, he took personal charge of cultural censorship, vetting up to fifteen hundred plays a year (or so his staff claimed, though it seems hardly credible given the rest of his agenda); among the banned dramas were Machiavelli's *Mandragola*, Rostand's *Cyrano de Bergerac* and Shaw's *Caesar and Cleopatra*. Nobody but the king could remove him. In 1928 further parliamentary elections were abolished and all parties other than the Fascists outlawed.

Meanwhile the Duce began his expansion of Italian power in *mare nostrum*, 'our sea', the Mediterranean. And while brandishing his *gladius Romanus* in Corfu, Albania, the Greek islands and Libya, Mussolini made enormous and unceasing efforts with Fascist propaganda within Italy.

The great propaganda event of the early 1930s was the MRF, or Mostra della Rivoluzione Fascista, which took place in Rome on the tenth anniversary of Mussolini's accession to power, 1932. Its venue was the old 1883 Palazzo delle Esposizioni, which was given a new façade featuring four thirty-metre-high aluminium columns in the form of the fasces, designed by the architects Adalberto Libera and Mario de Renzi. Its theme was how Fascism had united, not divided, the Italian people; how it had prevented class war.

The traditional liberal view is that Fascism was irrevocably opposed to whatever was new or progressive in Italian culture. This became iron doctrine after Italy lost the Second World War, because most Italians by then wanted only to forget about Il Duce and the miseries of his and Italy's defeat. 'Where there was culture it was not fascist,' wrote the Italian intellectual Norberto Bobbio, 'and where there was fascism it was not culture. There never was a fascist culture.' Such a virtuously anti-Fascist view is as perniciously foolish as the cultural doctrines of Fascism itself. Fascism gave hope to millions of people among whom were a number of artists and architects, who fancied (in the words of the architect Terragni) that it was 'the hallmark of the new age ... the harmony which made the Greece of Pericles and the Florence of the Medici great must illuminate the age of Fascism with equal intensity'.

Not only was there a Fascist culture: many of the most gifted Italian painters, sculptors and architects believed wholeheartedly in it and worked devotedly to realize it. Even Giorgio Morandi, the best painter Italy had in the 1930s – and some would say, the best in the whole twentieth century – sincerely thanked Mussolini for the interest he had taken in his work, of which Il Duce had bought several examples. 'It gives me great pleasure to recall His Excellency Benito Mussolini ... The great faith I have had in Fascism from the outset has remained intact even in the darkest and stormiest of days.' From the recluse of Bologna, who was indifferent to public life and knew little about politics, this should hardly be taken as a general endorsement of all the Duce's political actions. True, Morandi never did any official artworks of the kind that Fascism commissioned from the likes of Corrado Cagli, Achille Funi or Mario Sironi – tablescapes of dusty bottles, however beautiful in themselves, were unlikely to raise con- sciousness about Italy's heritage or future. But among the Italian artists who worked, directly or indirectly, for Il Duce were the sculptors Marino Marini and Lucio Fontana, the painters Giorgio de Chirico, Carlo Carrà, Enrico Prampolini and Emilio Vedova, as well as Cagli, Funi and Sironi. The MRF made quite lavish use of some of the best of these. Nobody could say that de Chirico's classical groups of dream-struggle were among his best work – *pittura metafisica* belonged to the teens of the century and was well in the past – but other artists honoured Fascism with convinced and eloquent installations. The architect Terragni, for instance, did the room dedicated to the so-called March on Rome.

But Giorgio de Chirico was the artist most representative of the turmoil of nostalgia kicked up by the modern invocation of imperial Rome, which showed itself most vividly in architecture. He was greatly admired by many Fascists, even did occasional commissions for the Fascist Party, but always indignantly denied that his work had any connection to Fascist ideology. He was also one of the last genuinely influential painters Italy produced in the twentieth century – though his influence, at least in his later years, fell mainly on other Italians. At the outset it was international, since his work had once been a major factor – some would say a determining one – in the development of Surrealism in Paris.

De Chirico was not, by origin, Italian at all, as the French *de* in his name (rather than *di*) indicates. He got quite offended if called 'di' Chirico. He was born in 1888 and raised in the town of Volos in Greece, where his father was a railway planner and engineer. Nevertheless the most crucial encounters of his early development took place in Paris and most of his working life was passed in and identified with Rome, where he had a magnificent studio high on the side of the Spanish Steps with an encompassing view of the piazza with its Berninian ship-fountain, *La Barcaccia*, below. (Of all the urban studios that have been inhabited by modern artists, de Chirico's was perhaps the most enviably sited.) He was truculent about his attachment to Rome. He wanted, he said in his memoirs (1962), 'to remain and work in Italy and even in Rome. Yes; it is here that I want to stay and work, to work harder than ever, to work better than ever, to work for my glory and your damnation.'

The note of anger was unforced. De Chirico loathed the art world, which he believed had deliberately misunderstood and traduced him for its own gain and self-gratification. He had a bad temper and an inexhaustible supply of grudges. That art world, in his eyes, was synonymous with Paris and its artists, 'that group of degenerates, hooligans, childish layabouts, onanists and spineless people who had pompously styled themselves *surrealists* and also talked about the "surrealist revolution"'. The Surrealist painters, of course, were the modernists who derived most from de Chirico, who most admired his early work but, because of their contempt for his later pseudo-classical work, had become his ferociously rejected and disowned children. Chief among de Chirico's villains was the Surrealist leader André Breton, 'the classic type of pretentious ass and impotent arriviste', closely followed in vileness and treachery by the poet Paul Éluard, 'a colourless and commonplace young man with a crooked nose and a face somewhere between that of an onanist and a mystical cretin'. (If de Chirico disliked you, he never forgave or forgot and you would know it soon enough.) This pair and their associates in Surrealism (Yves Tanguy, René Magritte, Max Ernst and Salvador Dalí, the Catalan for whom de Chirico cherished an especial contempt and hatred) had all been inspired by the early 'metaphysical' paintings he made up to 1918 or thereabouts, which turned the image of the city (chiefly Ferrara, where he lived from 1915 to 1918, and Turin, whose towers regularly appear in his paintings) into one of the emblematic sites of the modernist imagination. Its elements click into place as de Chirican property as soon as they are named: the piazza, the hard dark shadows, the statue, the train, the mannequin and of course the arcades.

Many of these are drawn from memories of real places where de Chirico had lived; they are not inventions, and this only adds to their imaginative power. The town of Volos, for instance, was cut through by a railway; hence the recurrent train and its puffs of smoke. But since de Chirico's father was a railway engineer, the train is also a deeply paternal image, and this lends extra meaning to a railway-station painting like *The Melancholy of*

Departure (1914): melancholy, because the father–train is leaving, abandoning the young insecure son to his fears. De Chirico found the epitome of strangeness in classical architecture. It was summed up in the arcade – that receding array of dark arches, that shallow screen. 'There is nothing like the enigma of the Arcade, which the Romans invented,' he wrote. 'A street, an arch – the sun looks different when it bathes a Roman wall in light. And there is something about it more mysteriously plaintive than in French architecture, and less ferocious too. The Roman arcade is a fatality. Its voice speaks in riddles filled with a strangely Roman poetry . . .'

De Chirico cited three words, 'which I would like to be the seal of every work I have produced: namely, *Pictor classicus sum*'. The thought was anathema to the Surrealists, who took unrestrained pleasure in attacking de Chirico for his later work, in which he celebrated the classical world and completely shied away from those elements in his style that were called proto-Surrealist. There were no boundaries to Surrealist hostility, and none to the anger with which de Chirico responded to it. Modern art, he insisted, was now in a state of utter decadence. It had fallen from grace for two reasons. First, it had surrendered to Parisian-style modernism instead of keeping to the real track, which in de Chirico's belief ran from the Old Masters through the artists who had nourished de Chirico himself, the northern painters like Arnold Böcklin. 'If some day someone institutes a Nobel Prize for provincialism, silliness, xenophobia and masochistic lust for *La France Immortelle*,' de Chirico wrote, 'I am convinced that this prize would be awarded to the Italy of today.'

Secondly, painting had forgotten its own basic techniques. Other artists might look back to past painters: Picasso to Ingres, Léger to Poussin, and any number of Italian painters to Masaccio, Piero della Francesca or Lorenzo Lotto. But what de Chirico proposed was not a mere 'looking back', it was a restructuring of art in terms of ancient, now ignored techniques that must somehow be reinvigorated and recovered. And this was not fated to happen, especially not in the terms of gladiator battles and classical façades that came, more and more, to define the subject matter of de Chirico's later painting.

And there was a further complication. De Chirico refused to believe what was an article of faith among the Surrealists and most other foreign admirers of his work: namely, that he had been a better painter in his youth, and that the so-called *pittura metafisica* that he produced up to about 1918 was the real, essential de Chirico, whereas the later work was either cynical self-copying, sold as 'original', or obvious pastiche of older forms of art de Chirico admired – Raphael, Titian and so forth. To make things worse, de Chirico had no inhibitions about selling his later pictures as pre-1918 originals, backdated. Italian art dealers used to say the maestro's bed was six feet off the bedroom floor, to hold all the 'early work' he kept 'discovering' below it. There are, for instance, at least eighteen copies of *The Disquieting Muses* (1917), all painted by de Chirico between 1945 and 1962.

Large marketing efforts have been made to set late de Chirico on an equal footing with the early work, but so far they have been unsuccessful, as indeed they deserve to be. On the other hand, by far the best painter directly associated with Fascism was Mario Sironi, who after the fall of Mussolini would pay dearly for his favoured role in the movement. A leading member of the Novecento group, which had assembled around Mussolini's art-curating mistress Margherita Sarfatti, Sironi had rebelled against liberalism, declaring the fine arts to be 'a perfect instrument of spiritual government' and wholeheartedly placing his work at the service of the Fascist revolution. It ought to be 'intentionally anti-bourgeois'.

Early in his career, just after the First World War, Sironi painted dark, harsh landscapes of industrial Milan, which (consciously or not) reflected Mussolini's early socialist ideas. After Fascism took hold in Italy, Sironi kept stressing that he wanted to be seen as 'a militant artist, that is to say, an artist who serves a moral ideal and subordinates his own individuality to the collective cause'. He wished to leave aside the easel picture and devote himself to large-scale murals and installations. A truly Fascist art, he insisted, was a matter of style in which 'the autonomous qualities of line, form and colour' manipulated reality into 'the medium of political efficacy ... through style, art will succeed in making a new mark on popular consciousness'. Distinctions between high and low culture must go. Sironi hoped that his style, with its archaic monumentalism of rough-hewn forms and its occasional references to ancient Roman bas-reliefs, would play a part in shaping 'the collective will through myth and image', and this equation of formal order with political order became part of the official ideology of Fascism. This idea of 'militant idealism', strongly espoused by Mussolini's first Minister of Education, Giovanni Gentile, became official ideology during Fascism's first decade, the 1920s and early 1930s.

For the Mostra della Rivoluzione Fascista, Sironi designed four powerful galleries around Fascist themes. Perhaps the most moving display was the *sacrario dei caduti*, the 'holy room of the fallen', where, in a dim religious light, the names of the Fascist dead were unrolled while a voice murmured *Presente, presente, presente* and the party's anthem, 'Giovinezza', softly played on hidden, ambient speakers.

For the Fascist faithful this was a guaranteed emotion-jerker. All visitors were taken to it, especially the VIPs: the records of the MRF contain the names of, among others, Franz von Papen, Josef Goebbels and Hermann Goering from Germany, Ramsay MacDonald, Austen Chamberlain, Anthony Eden and Oswald Mosley from England, and the King of Siam. Eden noted in his journal that 'I did not find the place congenial and I did not want to be uncivil to my hosts, so I was glad when the embarrassing ordeal was over.' Nevertheless he felt it was 'less dragooning and pervasive than Nazi rule in Germany'. While it may not have been congenial to foreigners like Eden, it was a smashing popular success with the Italians themselves, particularly since the Fascist authorities organized mass visits to it from all over Italy. These enabled citizens who had never been able to leave outlying home-towns like Grosseto or Acquapendente to get to Rome for the first time. Eventually, some four million visitors came by train and bus to the Mostra della Rivoluzione Fascista, and its run was extended by two full years.

A central idea about art and its purposes was enshrined by the Mostra della Rivoluzione Fascista, and its main promulgator then and afterwards was Mario Sironi. Late in 1933 Sironi joined with three other Italian painters, Massimo Campigli, Achille Funi and Carlo Carrà, to produce a manifesto about the future of art in Italy. 'Fascism is a way of life: it is the very life of Italians.' Art must serve the interests of Fascism: but how? Sironi had nothing but contempt for the vacuous propaganda paintings of German National Socialism. He wanted to see a bony, structural art which would nevertheless have the possibility of wide popular appeal. It would do this by reviving Renaissance ambitions: in the tradition of Italian mural painting of the fifteenth and sixteenth centuries; some revival might take place beyond what was offered by the format of the easel painting. He longed for a collective, community-based art that would unfold on great public walls, under the aegis of the Fascist Party. This would be done in terms of the sober, dark, uningratiating style that Sironi had made so much his own. Its hallmark would be a purposive seriousness, for Sironi had joined with other Fascist-inspired Italian painters such as Carrà and Funi in denouncing all that was less than serious and public. Art must speak directly to the Italian people and 'We are confident that in Mussolini we have the Man who knows how to value correctly the strength of our world-dominating Art.'

It did not dominate the world – there was little chance of that – but it was certainly not as negligible as anti-Fascist feelings made it seem later. Sironi's allegiance to Fascism counted badly against him after Italy lost the war and Mussolini's day ended. Perhaps this was inevitable, but it was certainly not a fair aesthetic judgement. The political beliefs of an artist are no secure basis for judging his, or her, art. What does anyone care, today, about the political convictions of the artists who carved the bulls of Babylon or painted the Madonnas of Siena? It was all very well to deprecate Sironi after the fall of Mussolini for lending his indisputable talents to the promotion of Fascism, but in that case what is one to say of Russian Constructivist artists, like Vladimir Tatlin or El Lissitzky, who wanted to see their work take its role in a national chorus of propaganda-by-monument, whose chief – indeed, only – patron was the new Communist state? There was something very unseemly about the pleasure which the party hacks and Communist sympathizers of the Italian art world took in Sironi's fall, and in the zeal with which they trampled on his postwar reputation. Marxist-Leninism, followed by Stalinism, murdered, imprisoned and exiled millions of Russians, smashed the Russian traditions of free speech and brought illimitable misery to their country and, later, its satellites. If the political allegiances of an artist like Sironi were to be held against him, what could be said against those of one like Tatlin, who laboured to serve the Revolution? The answer, as it emerged after the Second World War, was: nothing. Radical Russian artists who proclaimed their adherence to the deadly fantasies of the Revolution were unanimously forgiven for having been on the 'right' side, the side whose adherents helped destroy Fascism. Indeed, given the dreadful censorship that descended on their work from Stalin, they were exalted by liberal opinion on this side of the Iron Curtain: too much so, given the interests they aspired to serve.

In 1931 Mussolini's government set forth a master-plan for the remaking of Rome. It followed the main lines of a speech Il Duce had made six years before. Its purpose, he had announced, was to reveal Rome as a 'marvellous' city, 'vast, ordered, powerful, as it was in the first Augustan Empire':

> You must continue to liberate the trunk of the great oak from everything that still smothers it. Open up spaces around the Mausoleum of Augustus, the Theatre of Marcellus, the Campidoglio, the Pantheon. Everything which has grown up in the centuries of decadence must be swept away. In five years, from Piazza Colonna, across a great area, should be visible the mass of the Pantheon.

The key to Mussolini's intentions – clarifying the 'true' urban meanings of Rome – was to recover what Mussolini took to be the city's true urban purity: that of the age of Augustus. By exposing and glorifying what was left of the architecture of the glorious Principate, he would present himself as the new Augustus Caesar and show Fascism to be the revival of Empire. To emphasize this message a triumphal avenue, to be called the Via dell'Impero, would link Piazza Venezia – where Mussolini's state offices and apartments were now installed – to Ostia and the sea. This specially levelled avenue, 700 metres long and 30 wide, would be Rome's parade ground. It was somewhat contradictory, since its creation entailed covering up large tracts of recently excavated imperial Roman fora. But, as the Duce put it, 'Rome now has at its centre a street truly designed for its great military parades, which until now have been confined to the periphery or the countryside.'

The 'revival' of the Roman Empire was celebrated in popular song:

Tornan colonne ed archi
I ruderi gloriosi, come un giorno . . .
Dal Campidoglio, fiera, libera l'ale
L'aquila augusta e bronzea
Della Roma imperiale!
Fremon le vecchie mura
Del Colosseo . . .
Un ossana levano di ardore:
Risorgi, o Roma eternal
Torna il littore.

Columns and arches come back / To the glorious ruins, just as before . . . / From the Capitol, the august bronze eagle / Of Imperial Rome, proudly spreads her wings . . . / They shake, the ancient walls / Of the Colosseum . . . / They utter a Hosanna of ardour: / Rise up again, eternal Rome: / The Lictor returns.

In the north would grow a giant development of housing, sports arenas and new roads, to create a gateway to the modern city; it became known as the Foro Mussolini. The southern road to Rome along the Via del Mare would support what was, in essence, a second city, a mass of architectural display, to be known as the EUR or Esposizione Universale di Roma, which the Duce wanted to open in 1942 with what he called an 'Olympics of Civilization'. This immense reshaping of the Eternal City would far exceed, in scale, the efforts of any earlier emperors and popes since Augustus' time. Through it, Rome would 'reclaim its Empire', as a patriotic hymn put it:

Roma revendica l'Impero
L'ora dell'Aquil sono,
Squilli di trombe salutano il vol
Dal Campidoglio al Quirinal,
Terra ti vogliamo dominar!

'Rome reclaims its Empire / The hair of the Eagle has struck / Trumpet blasts salute the flight / From Capitol to Quirinal / Earth, we want to dominate you!'

Many of the new buildings of Fascism were, in essence, quite modernist. They had little to do with the stripped-down Doric, neo-classical manner favoured by Hitler through his court architect Albert Speer. They used curtain walls, floating cantilevers and other attributes of the so-called International style which had gathered momentum in Germany and the USA. Some of them, such as the Casa del Fascio (1932–6) by Giuseppe Terragni in Como, were quite Miesian in spirit.

The most vivid and memorable of the new buildings of Fascism was the so-called Square Colosseum, the severely arcaded multi-storey building which formed the central motif of the EUR. If any building can be called the logo of Fascist architecture, it is this one, in all its polemical purity – the 'Palace of Italian Civilization'. It was much hated in the aftermath of the 1939–45 war, but now there are signs that it is enjoying renewed favour as a landmark and period piece, a situation helped by the fact that it carries no bellicose or excessively nationalist inscriptions – the frieze of letters around the flat roofline praised the peaceful achievements of Italian civilization-makers, explorers, artists, scientists, saints, poets, sailors but emphatically not soldiers. Its main architect was Ernesto La Padula (1902–68), who survived the war but never got a chance to design another official building. His collaborators were Giovanni Guerrini and Mario Romano.

The sculptor Aroldo Bellini was charged, in 1934, with the task of making a gigantic portrait sculpture of Il Duce, a hundred metres tall (as high as the lantern of St Peter's), which would completely dominate the city from the skyline. This monster was never finished, though its head was completed. It was the largest of all Fascist sculptures and it was even expected to house a permanent museum of Fascism.

The grandest Fascist monument, like the grandest monument of ancient Rome, was a road – or rather, two roads. One was the Via del Mare; the other the Via dell'Impero, linking the Colosseum to the Vittorio Emanuele monument, which became the chief parade ground for Mussolini and his *squadristi*. The obvious comparison that all Mussolini's town-replanning projects would have to sustain was with Albert Speer's efforts for Hitler, and nobody would be more conscious of this than the Führer himself, who had met up with the Duce in Venice in 1934 and was scheduled to make a mighty state visit to Rome in the spring of 1938.

It was essential for the Duce to cut a *bella figura* when Hitler arrived, and in February 1938 the dictator made a circuit through Rome to inspect his public works. He started at sites near his political centre, Piazza Venezia: Capitoline Hill, the Palatine, the Circus Maximus. He thought with glee of how impressed Hitler would be. He looked with pride at the great expanses swept clear, 'formerly suffocated by … hovels and alleys'. At his orders, the previously congested site of the Circus Maximus had been cleared of all its shacks and later buildings: nothing was showing except pure ancient Rome. At the far end of the Circus Maximus stood his new Africa building (now the United Nations' FAO offices, whose Fascist architectural origins few remember) and the ancient Obelisk of Axum, brought from Ethiopia after his victories there the year before. As he was driven along the new Via dell'Impero, linking central Rome to the sea, he watched the ancient buildings, now cleaned up, roll by: the Theatre of Marcellus, the Arch of Janus Quadrifrons, the temples of Vesta and Fortuna Virilis. He thought about how the partly finished Via dell'Impero would soon link Rome's centre with the sea, and with the site of the planned EUR complex, whose opening was scheduled for 1942, the twentieth anniversary of the March on Rome. And already, he reflected, his great capital was filling with Fascist buildings: stadia, schools, post-offices and apartments of every kind. It was enough to warm the cockles of any dictator's heart, and in fact many of these structures are still in use, though under other names.

One of the few masterpieces of rationalist Fascist design, in what was then known as the Foro Mussolini, the 1934 Casa delle Armi or Fencing Academy by Luigi Moretti (1907–73), became a carabinieri barracks and had a short afterlife as the site of the heavily secured maxi-trials of the Red Brigades. The new Fascist Via del Mare was reborn, after the war, as the Via del Teatro di Marcello – despite the obvious wish of Italy to erase Mussolini from collective memory, his name remains on the commemorative obelisk of the Foro Mussolini, now the Foro Italico. The Piazzale dell'Impero is filled with skateboarders today – a use Fascism had never contemplated. It is full of mosaics showing Fascist imagery and slogans: 'Many enemies, much honour', 'Duce, we dedicate our youth to you' and, inevitably, 'Better one day as a lion than a hundred years as a sheep'. Mosaics still show the founding of Fascism after 1919, the March on Rome, the Lateran Accords with the Church and the conquest of Ethiopia.

Quite rightly, the postwar authorities of a more democratic Rome have not tried to efface these; instead, others were added after Mussolini's death to celebrate the fall of Fascism in 1943, the national referendum to abolish monarchy in 1946, and the inauguration of the new Italian republic in 1948. Some Fascist monuments had already disappeared; several giant heads of the Duce remain in subterranean storage in Rome, and only the head of a colossal bronze statue of Fascism, 150 feet tall, survived long enough to be melted down for scrap; on the other hand, sport being theoretically apolitical, about sixty giant stone athletes in the Stadio dei Marmi at the EUR are still standing on their original bases. Via Adolfo Hitler, which still ends at Ostiense Station, was tactfully renamed the Via delle Cave Ardeatine, in memory of the massacre of anti-Fascists which took place in revenge for the blowing-up of a squad of marching Nazis. After the war, the Tiber's Ponte Littorio was renamed, in honour of the murdered socialist deputy, the Ponte Matteotti.

There was a certain community of language between Nazi and Fascist works of visual art, but in ideology aspects of Fascism differed crucially from Nazism: it is a common mistake to suppose that they were essentially the same because of later political alliances between the two. The main issue was that of race. Hitler, one need not stress, was completely obsessed by his desire to 'free' the world of Jews. He saw Jewry as the chief evil in German and world society. Even as the battle for a defeated Berlin was entering its last phase and the Russian shells were thundering down on the Chancellery, Hitler's thoughts continued to be of the Final Solution.

Mussolini, on the other hand, was no racialist, and anti-Semitism did not enter his politics either in theory or in practice. 'Race! It is a feeling, not a reality,' he declared in 1933. 'Ninety-five per cent, at least, is a feeling. Nothing will ever make me believe that biologically pure races can be shown to exist today. National pride has no need of the delirium of race.' He pointed out that Jews had lived in Italy since the time Rome was founded, which would have been an inconceivable remark for Hitler to make about Germany.

The National Fascist Party contained Jews – one of them, Ettore Ovazza, ran a Fascist newspaper, *La Nostra Bandiera*, specifically edited to maintain that Italian Jews were patriotic Italians and could continue to be so under Fascism. Certainly, Mussolini had political prisons, some of intolerable severity. But they were never designed, as the German concentration camps were, to annihilate whole social groups, whether Jews, gypsies or homosexuals. His *squadristi* or Blackshirts could be and often were brutal to 'outsiders' and anti-Fascists, but their violence was not designedly anti-Semitic – although it would be naive to imagine that there was no anti-Semitism in Italy, or that it did not come out in blows and shouted insults when some wretched opponent of the regime was being forced to drink castor oil mixed with petrol (a favourite Fascist torture) or to chew up and swallow a living toad.* A lot of this would change later, as Hitler's influence over Mussolini increased in the late 1930s. In *A Manifesto of Race*, issued in 1938, Mussolini copied Hitler's Nuremberg Laws, stripping Italian Jews of their citizenship and their access to the professions. But at the beginning, at least, the new Caesar was no more prejudiced against Jews than the old ones had been. Good Fascists could be compared to Jews, and vice versa, without loss of dignity.

Poets, writing about the March on Rome, frequently and unblushingly compared Mussolini to Moses leading the chosen people into the Promised Land.

Hitler, of course, had other ideas. The comparisons of Mussolini to Moses dropped off sharply after May 1938, when a train containing the Führer and his staff pulled into Ostiense Station in Rome, bringing Hitler on his state visit. Mussolini's *funzionari* had gone to much trouble over Hitler's arrival. They even saw to it that the last few miles of railway track into the station were lined, both sides, with a Potemkin village of stage-sets facing inwards to the train, filled with enthusiastically cheering Romans. This was greeted with a *pasquinato* which ran:

---

* I shall never forget how, forty years ago, I told a young Australian actress of my acquaintance about this Fascist practice. 'Oh, darling,' she exclaimed, 'the poor toad!'

Roma di travertino
Rifatta di cartone
Saluta l'imbianchino
La sua prossima padrone.

'Rome of travertine / Remade in cardboard / Salutes the
house painter / Its next Master.'

The mass media of Italy, which were tightly controlled – one
needed a state-issued licence to practise as a journalist of any
kind, even a fashion reporter, under Mussolini, and he personally
appointed all editors – greeted the arrival of the Führer with an
automatic ecstasy. A good, though minor, example was a cartoon
in whose first panel we see a Nazi officer (no moustache, so he
cannot be Hitler himself) throwing a Nazi salute at the Capitoline
she-wolf and her two foundling babies, Romulus and Remus. In
the second panel the she-wolf, overcome with doggy joy, has come
down from her pedestal and is fawning all over the Nazi, while
the temporarily abandoned but delighted infants are returning
the salute and calling 'Heil Hitler!'

It is impossible to say what effect Hitler's architectural opinions
may have had on Mussolini's changes to Rome. In some respects,
especially at the end of the thirties, the two men thought so much
alike that there is no disentangling their ideas.

However, one project in particular which Mussolini inflicted
on his capital stands out for its Hitlerian character of axial straight-
ness and dumb clarity. This was the approach avenue to the Piazza
S. Pietro, Bernini's overwhelmingly rich symbolic site in front of
the basilica. Before Mussolini, the visitor coming from the Tiber
approached St Peter's along the Spina dei Borghi or 'spine of the
Borgo', a pair of more or less parallel roads that ran into the Piazza
but did not open up the view of the basilica in a suitably spectacular
way. But in 1937, the year before Hitler's first visit to Rome,
Mussolini decided to convert this comparatively gradual revelation into pure, one-point-perspective melodrama. Whether he
planned to impress Hitler with this is hard to say. On balance, it

seems likely: and the result was a giant avenue in the manner of Albert Speer, driving straight for the Vatican obelisk, Maderno's façade and the dome. Surprise, once so vital a part of the approach to the great basilica, was now eliminated. The name of the avenue, the Via della Conciliazione, commemorates the 1929 agreement under the Lateran Treaty, whereby the Vatican – hitherto opposed to Fascism because of Il Duce's anticlerical bias – recognized the Fascist government of Italy while Fascism granted the Vatican complete territorial independence. This would permanently shape relations between Italy's Church and state, whose 'conciliation' the new avenue symbolized.

In the process of the reconciliation of Art and state, every dialect bard from Lake Como to Capo Palinuro, it seemed, was busy telling Italian children to emulate their saviour:

> . . . *anima pura*
> *Va a scola, studia tantu e 'mpara,*
> *E vera fede au nostru Duce giura.*

'Pure soul / Go to school, study hard and learn / And pledge true faith to our Duce.'

The Duce's appearance evoked paeans of awed praise from dialect poets all over Italy. Here is Nando Bennati, writing in Ferrarese dialect, around 1937, addressing his leader simply as *Lu!* – 'You!':

> *La testa, un toc 'd nugara dur massiez,*
> *Taia con al falzzon, cla met i sguiz*
>
> *La front spaziosa larga, ch'fa da ca*
> *A un gran zzarvel, cal pesa purassa;*
>
> *Il zzid come d'arc ruman antig,*
> *Che, si il sa sbassa, a trema i so amig;*

Du' oc' chi fora come du' guciun
E i lez tut i pensier, cattiv o bun;
Al nas come un bec d'aquila, chal s'mov
Par sentr' in tl'aria s'ag fus quell ad nov;

La vos la tocca come 'na frusta
L'ariva in tl'amima come 'na stita –

The head, a hard and massive nut / Hewn with a pruning-hook, which makes one shudder / The high wide forehead, which is the home / Of a large and weighty brain / The eyebrows, like two ancient Roman arches / Which, if lowered, make even his friends tremble / Two eyes which project like two spikes / And read all thoughts, good and bad / The nose like an eagle's beak, which moves / To sniff the air, and see if anything new has come – / The voice that strikes like a whip / And pierces the soul like a dagger-stab.

And so on, for several verses, until the moral is spelt out: *Bisogna obbidirgli e dir ad si!* – 'We must obey him and say yes!'

Not only was Mussolini returning the state to its primal dignity, but he was seen as the man to save Italy from shortages, the one who gave back to Italian food its primordial and sacramental character. Such was the content of *la battaglia del grano*, 'the Battle for Grain', launched by Mussolini in the thirties. The Battle for Grain, which depended on farming the land exposed by the draining of the Pontine marshes – one of Mussolini's most widely hailed projects – was only a partial success and did not live up to its propaganda. Nevertheless, it was constantly saluted by now forgotten Roman Fascist bards like Augusto Jandolo in such poems as *Er Pane*, 'Bread', published in 1936:

Ricordete ch'er pane va magnato
Come si consumassi un sacramento
Co l'occhi bassi e cor pensiero a Dio.

Er Duce ha scritto: 'Er pane
A core de la casa,
Orgoio der lavoro
E premio santo alle fatiche umane.'
Bacelo sempre, fiio, perche in fonno
Baci la terra tua che lo produce,
C'e sempre intorn or ar pane tanta luce
Da illuminacce er monno!

'Remember that bread is to be eaten / As one takes a sacrament / With lowered eyes and a heart thinking of God. / The Duce has written: "Bread / Is the heart of the house / The pride of work / And the sacred rewad of man's labour." / Always kiss it, my son, because in fact / You kiss your land that produces it, / Such light always surrounds bread / As can light the world!'

Even d'Annunzio was moved to write an ode in praise of *parrozzo*, the coarse farmers' bread of the Abruzzi, and dedicate it to his own baker, Luigi d'Amico. However, the bread that resulted from the *battaglia del grano* was often very poor, if one is to believe a famed pasquinade that appeared during the campaign. Some nameless wit hung a rock-like Roman loaf on a string around the neck of a statue of Caesar in the Via dell'Impero, with a message attached:

Cesare!
Tu che ci hai lo stommico di ferro,
Mangete sto pane di l'Impero!

'Caesar! / You who have an iron-gut, / Eat this bread of the Empire!'

Rebuilding this Empire was a dream of Mussolini's, but an impossible one. The main stage for his empirical ambitions was Africa; but too many of the Great Powers already had colonial stakes there. Even Italy had its little bits of Africa – since 1882

Eritrea, and Italian Somalia since 1889. However, they were divided by the independent state of Ethiopia, otherwise known as Abyssinia, with whose ruler Haile Selassie the Duce had signed a non-aggression pact. But with Mussolini, some pacts were made to be broken, and this was one of them.

Italy, it transpired, had been stockpiling ordnance in an obscure oasis named Wal-Wal, which was clearly on Ethiopian territory. A skirmish developed between Ethiopian forces at Wal-Wal and some Somalis attached to the Italian army there; about 150 Ethiopians, it was alleged, were killed by the tanks and aircraft of the Italian–Somali allies. From there the situation worsened, amid Italian claims and counter-claims, until soldiers from Italian Eritrea were on full war footing with the unfortunate Abyssinians. They did not declare war; that formal declaration was left to the Abyssinians, who made it in October 1935. The contest was hopelessly unequal: machine-guns, bombers and mustard gas against half-naked tribesmen armed with bolt-action rifles. Mussolini sent in a hundred thousand Italian troops commanded by General Emilio de Bono. De Bono was soon replaced by a more ruthless commander, Marshal Pietro Badoglio. They overran Abyssinia and even emphasized their complete victory with such propaganda gestures as building, with army labour, a colossal stone-concrete-and-earth portrait of mighty Mussolini as a sphinx, rising from the sand, which today survives only in official newsreels.

In May 1936 the Italian forces entered the capital Addis Ababa; the emperor Haile Selassie, Lion of Judah, fled into exile. The Ethiopians claimed that they lost half a million men in the war; this was probably an exaggeration, but they were dreadfully mauled. Neither side was innocent; both had resorted to torture of prisoners and other war crimes. But there was no doubt which the aggressor was. Italy emerged from this colonial adventure with no credit, and Abyssinia – whose emperor was eventually replaced on his throne by British forces during the Second World War, which broke out shortly after – with very little. To underscore their victory the Italians sent to Abyssinia a cast of the Capitoline wolf, complete with Romulus and Remus. It was installed outside the train station in Addis Ababa, replacing a figure of the Lion of Judah with Solomon's crown on its head, given by a French railway company to the Negus of Abyssinia, which went to Rome as a souvenir of victory. (But after the Allies entered Rome in 1944, the displaced figure of the Lion of Judah, which had been standing in a city park, mysteriously vanished. Someone had shipped it back to Haile Selassie.)

Now Mussolini, realizing that his Ethiopian adventure was not going to earn him credit from England or France, who had their own colonial stakes in Africa, threw his weight behind Franco's Nationalists in the Spanish Civil War. In July 1936 he sent a squadron of Italian planes to Spain to fight for Franco. Naturally this endeared him, to some extent, to Hitler. He accepted Hitler's annexation of Austria in 1938 and his seizure of Czechoslovakia the following year. But this did not mean that Italy became a smoothly working or passive ally of Nazi Germany. It did, however, prepare the way for the Patto d'Acciaio or 'Pact of Steel', an alliance of 'friendship' between Germany and Italy.

There was not much, however, that Mussolini could offer Hitler in the way of practical support – his arms supply was too thin; so when the German invasion of Poland brought a declaration of war from England and France, thus opening the Second World War, Mussolini – at the strong insistence of Italy's king Victor Emmanuel – stayed non-belligerent. This was shortlived. Mussolini soon became convinced that Hitler would win quickly, and sent his Tenth Army under the command of General Rodolfo Graziani to attack the British forces in Egypt. This proved a costly fiasco and ended with the British defeat of Italian forces at El Alamein in 1943. Now the Germans sent the Afrika Korps to north Africa, Germany attacked the Soviet Union and dragged Italy with it, and Italy committed the grave but probably unavoidable error of declaring war on the United States. The descent began in earnest. Allied bombing was pulverizing the cities, factories and food supplies of north Italy. Coal and oil started to run out. Even pasta became a black-market rarity.

On 27 April 1945 Mussolini and his mistress Clara Petacci were captured by Communist Italian partisans as they were fleeing north to Switzerland, hoping to fly from there to Spain. They were taken before they left Italy, at the village of Dongo on Lake Como. They and their fifteen-man entourage were said to have been carrying huge amounts of cash with them. Nobody knows for sure what happened to this money, but the suspicion has always been that it went straight into the Communist Party's coffers; for this reason, the CP headquarters in Rome has, ever since, been known as 'Palazzo Dongo'.

The next day, 28 April, the Duce and his party were driven to the nearby village of Giulino di Mezzegra and shot to death. In a removal van, their corpses were taken south to Milan and dumped in Piazzale Loreto, where they were strung upside-down on meat hooks – in the past, Fascists had done the same in the same place to partisans – to be ritually execrated with stones, vegetables, spittle and curses. After a long game of hide-and-seek with the Duce's corpse, it was at last interred in the cemetery of his birthplace, Predappio, where it continues to be visited by respectful pilgrims to this day.

In the end, what is one to make of Mussolini? He was a narcissistic tyrant; that goes without saying. But he was certainly not a figure of unmitigated evil, like Adolf Hitler. One cannot imagine a new Hitler arising in Germany, but a new Mussolini in Italy is neither a contradiction in terms nor even unimaginable. As Martin Clark put it, 'Mussolini's legacy is a real challenge to contemporary Italian society because his values, though politically incorrect, are so widely shared.' It has to be granted that there was nothing phoney about his beliefs and convictions. His character was, of course, histrionic; but of how many popular leaders can this not be said? Perhaps histrionic talents are essential for political success. Colourless and clerkly figures do not rise to supreme office, though they make the life of spectacular ones easier. To a great extent, what you saw with Mussolini was what you got. The Italians admired his courage, which was not in doubt. He was clearly not in politics for personal gain; he cared

43 Pier Leone Ghezzi
Dr James Hay as Bear Leader, c. 1704–1729
Pen and ink on paper, 36.3 × 24.3 cm; British Museum, London

44 Giovanni Paolo Panini
*Preparations to Celebrate the Birth
of the Dauphin of France*, 1729

Oil on canvas, 1100 × 2520 cm;
Musée du Louvre, Paris

45 Giovanni Paolo
Panini
*Interior of St Peter's,
Rome*, 1731

Oil on canvas,
145.7 × 228.3 cm;
Saint Louis Art Museum,
Saint Louis, Missouri

46 Giovanni Paolo
Panini
*Interior of the
Pantheon*, 1734

Oil on Canvas,
144.1 × 114.3 cm;
Samuel H. Kress
Collection,
National Gallery of Art,
Washington, D.C.

47 Giovanni Battista Piranesi
The Prisons (Carceri), 1745–1761
Etching

48 Anton Raphael Mengs
Johann Joachim Winckelmann, 1755
Oil on canvas, 63.5 × 49.2 cm; Metropolitan
Museum of Art, New York

49 Alessandro Albani
Villa Albani, 1751–1763

50 Henry Fuseli
*The artist moved by the grandeur
of ancient ruins*, 1778–80
Kunsthaus, Zurich

52 Jacques-Louis David
Oath of the Horatii, 1784
Oil on canvas, 326 × 420 cm;
Musée du Louvre, Paris

51 Johann Zoffany
*Charles Townley and his Friends in
the Towneley Gallery, 33 Park Street,
Westminster*, 1781–83
Oil on canvas, 127 × 99.1 cm; Towneley
Hall Art Gallery and Museum, Burnley,
Lancashire

53 Johann Heinrich
Wilhelm Tischbein
*Johann Wolfgang von
Goethe at the window
of his dwelling on the
Corso in Rome*, 1787

Watercolour; Freies
Deutsches Hochstift,
Frankfurt am Main

54 Johann Heinrich
Wilhelm Tischbein
*Goethe in the Roman
Campagna*, 1786–1787

Oil on canvas, 164 × 206 cm;
Staedelsches Kunstinstitut,
Frankfurt am Main

55 Antonio Sant'Elia
The New City, 1913

Ink, pencil and watercolour on paper, 27 × 38 cm;
Private Collection

nothing for money or domestic comfort. They liked his forth-rightness and his willing, indeed eager, acceptance of risk. He had no middle-class background; he was wholeheartedly patriotic and genuinely male – there was nothing forced or mendacious about all those photos of Il Duce striking attitudes on top of tanks or showing his belligerent profile to the lens. The English might mock them; the Italians did not. Hollywood, in the genius of Charlie Chaplin, might set Jack Oakie to play him as 'Benzino Napaloni' in *The Great Dictator* – but it was not a caricature that has ever played well in Italy.

He believed he had a medium's relationship to his country, instinctive and infallible – and much of the time, at least, he was right. 'I did not create Fascism. I drew it from the Italians' unconscious minds. If that had not been so, they would not all have followed me for twenty years – I repeat, *all* of them.' This enabled Mussolini's charismatic mix of presidential omniscience and theatrical posturing to work. To dismiss him as a buffoon, a swollen bullfrog on horseback, as Anglo-American propaganda constantly tried to do, is seriously to underrate him. He under-stood the uses of the media, and grasped them extremely well, at least as well as Winston Churchill; he was particularly well aware of the potential of film as propaganda. In this respect he was ahead of his time, and his career pointed forward to image-managers like John Kennedy and George W. Bush – but most of all to the immensely rich and sexually flamboyant mediacrat who, through his control of national television, was until 2011 the dominant figure in Italian politics, Silvio Berlusconi.

12

ROME RECAPTURED

The capture of Rome, Italy's capital, from Fascist hands was a long time in preparation. It could not be done by direct attack from the north. All previous assaults on Rome, dating back to the time of the Gauls, had come from there. But the German forces made that impossible. It was becoming clear, by 1943, that the burden of keeping the Allies out of Italy was going to fall, more and more, on the German rather than the Italian forces – and on the repulse, which ultimately proved impossible, of a sea and air invasion across the Mediterranean from north Africa.

Mussolini and Hitler, together, had committed Italy to full partnership with Germany in the world war. There is no doubt of the mutual fascination that existed between both men. It had been in place, and strengthening, ever since Mussolini paid his state visit to Germany in 1937 and had been confronted by the full strength of Nazi theatricals – no man as narcissistic as Il Duce was going to be unmoved by the sight of an avenue lined by likenesses of himself and of Roman emperors.

Yet there was no prospect that the partnership of Italy and Germany in a world war could be an equal one. The Italian economy could support only a tenth of Germany's military expenditure (in 1938, $746 million, as against Germany's $7,415 million). Its production of war matériel was small compared to Germany's, despite all the bluster Mussolini and his propagandists made about it. Italian emigration to the US between 1918 and 1938 had been heavy, and the reduction of Italian manpower accordingly large – a problem which obviously could not be solved in the short term by any number of appeals to population growth. And the worst problem of all, from the Axis's point of view, was the difficulty of getting ordinary Italians to hate the Americans and the British. The Allies had fought the Italian army in north Africa in early 1943, and the results were not encouraging for Italy; by May of that year, according to John Keegan, the number of Italians who had been reduced to Allied prisoners in the African wars over Mussolini's 'empire' exceeded 350,000, more than the total garrison assigned to Africa at the beginning. The Allied victory in north Africa was now absolute and irreversible, and this meant that the whole Italian coast was faced, across an intervening sea, by hostile forces, deployed from Casablanca to Alexandria. What Churchill had memorably called 'the soft underbelly of Europe' was now open to attack from sea and air as it had never been in previous history.

Moreover, the royal house of Italy, with most of its ruling aristocracy and officer class, was wavering in its loyalty to Il Duce. Hitler was well aware of this and he felt, correctly, that 'in Italy we can rely only on the Duce. There are strong fears that he may be got rid of or neutralized in some way ... broad sectors of the civil service are hostile or negative towards us ... The broad masses are apathetic and lacking in leadership.'

So they were, and they became more so after the unwelcome news of Operation Husky, the codename for the Allied landings in Sicily – the prelude to Operation Avalanche, a full assault on the Italian mainland. This was a crucial event for Italy's ruling class. It persuaded them to change sides, without telling the Germans so. The Italian troops facing the Allies crumbled, and Badoglio, their commander, had opened negotiations with the Allies, all the while declaring that, as prime minister – for Mussolini had now resigned his office, at the demand of the Fascist Grand Council – he was unshakeably loyal to Hitler. After an uncomfortable meeting with King Victor Emmanuel, who had demanded his resignation, Mussolini was banished to an improvised succession of islands off Italy's west coast, ending at a hotel atop the Grand Sasso peaks in the Apennines. From there, a few weeks later, he was 'rescued' on Hitler's orders by a formidable, duel-scarred SS commando named Otto Skorzeny, who came winging in with a tiny Storch spotter-plane, scooped up Il Duce and flew him off to a reunion with Hitler and refuge, of a sort, in the tiny town of Salò. Here, he was to reign briefly as head of a puppet regime, the Italian Social Republic. Such was the terminus of Il Duce's political career.

The first stage of the Allies' thrust into Italy was a success. The central target of their enormous armada was the ancient port town of Gela – where, according to legend, the Attic playwright Aeschylus had been killed by a falling tortoise, dropped from the beak of an eagle. Much more than tortoises came hurtling down on Gela's Axis defenders from the waves of bombers, the parachutist drops and the naval guns with which the three-pronged assault of Patton's Seventh Army pressed home its attack, out of a limpidly clear July morning. It took the Husky troops just thirty-eight days to win back ten thousand square miles of Sicily from the Axis, fighting with desperation uphill most of the way. By the end of it half a million Germans were dead and when the Allies reached Messina, the north-eastern tip of Calypso's blood-boltered island, the correspondent Alan Moorehead gazed over the narrow strait to the mainland and reflected that 'One was hardly prepared for its nearness ... When one looked across at that other shore, the mainland of Europe, the vineyards and village houses were utterly quiet and all the coast seemed to be gripped in a sense of dread at what inevitably was going to happen.'

What happened, starting in early September 1943, was Avalanche, the Allies' mass landing at Salerno. By now the Italian forces had caved in and all the fighting devolved on the Germans, who held on with the grimmest determination – a determination matched only by that of the invading Allies.

After the hails of fire that had engulfed southern Italy during the Allied crossing from Sicily, after the bitter yard-by-yard struggle up the 'boot' of Italy towards Rome, after the long and murderous transit through Salerno, the 'bitchhead' (as the troops named it) of Anzio and the terrors of the long assault and counter-assault on the venerable fortress and abbey of Monte Cassino, established in the sixth century by St Benedict, the actual fall of Rome in June

1944 came almost as an anticlimax to the Allied army. As the army approached the city, few shots were fired. Rome was almost empty of Germans but full of Romans, all of whom miraculously ceased to be *fascisti* when the first American tanks came rolling over the Tiber bridges; the plug had been pulled and the enemy was draining north, to make its stands above Rome, north of the Tiber.

If Allied bombers had been set loose to attack the city, they could have produced a devastation without limits. With the Allies' air superiority it would not have been difficult to do to Rome what the British had already done to Dresden. But the American high command had to reckon with the reactions of the millions of American Catholics if the American forces were seen to be bombing the pope, even if their target was Mussolini. In late June 1943, General Marshall had allowed that 'It would be a tragedy if St Peter's were destroyed', but Rome still contained a target of high strategic importance: not only was it the capital of Fascism, but through its enormous Littorio marshalling-yards passed most of the rail traffic headed south.

Accordingly, Roman Catholic pilots and bombardiers were given the option of not taking part in the planned raid on the yards. Navigation maps highlighted the Vatican and other historic sites. But there was a limit to what a huge bombing raid could avoid. Five hundred B-26 bombers carrying some thousand tons of high explosive headed for Rome from bases in north Africa. There was a kind of miracle in the fact that they nearly all hit their designated railway targets. Only one church of historical value was hit: S. Lorenzo, a fourth-century structure which was virtually demolished by a single thousand-pound bomb, but has since been rebuilt.

Though thousands of men had been killed on their way to Rome, few Allied soldiers died in Rome itself. The Germans, or nearly all of them, had pulled out in front of the advancing troops. The Allies had suffered 44,000 casualties since the invasion of mainland Italy had begun on 11 May: 18,000 Americans (including 3,000 killed), 12,000 British, 9,600 French and nearly 4,000 Poles. German casualties were higher, estimated at 52,000. Now General

Mark Clark, who had long been obsessed with the capture of Rome, found his conqueror's way through the city to the foot of the Capitoline Hill, up Michelangelo's Cordonata, to the doors of the Campidoglio. Relatively few Romans turned out in the streets to watch Clark's progress through the open city on 4 June – all were afraid, needlessly as it turned out, of being caught in the crossfire of a last-ditch stand by the Nazis as they left. But there was no 'last stand' by the Germans as they quit Rome.

Recovery from the Fascist occupation was slow and incomplete. The end of the Second World War also marked the end of all possibility of Rome's recovery at the head of the static visual arts; culturally, if not dead, Rome was certainly crippled. It is depressing, but hardly unfair, to admit that by the beginning of the 1960s Rome, the city that had produced and fostered so many geniuses in the visual arts across the centuries, had none left – not, certainly, in the domains of painting, sculpture or architecture. None of the painting or sculpture made in Rome since the war even begins to measure up to the grandeur and energy of earlier work done by Roman artists or to commission by Roman patrons. As for another Raphael or Michelangelo rising in Rome, or a Caravaggio, forget it: there are quite simply no candidates.

What had caused this situation? It is impossible to say. Cultures do grow old, and sometimes one of the ominous signs of this can be their frustrated desire to look young. Why this happens may be long debated but remains a mystery. It happened with Roman architecture: one cannot point to a single architectural project built in the Eternal City in the last hundred years or more which could justify comparison with, for instance, the Spanish Steps, let alone Piazza Navona. The sorry truth is that whole cultures, like individual people, do run down; with age, their energies gutter out. They have a collective life, but that life depends entirely on the renewal of individual talent from decade to decade. The mere fact that they once produced extraordinary things guarantees nothing about their futures – otherwise, one could have expected something memorable from (say) Egypt or Mayan America over the last few hundred years.

This is what happened to Rome. The great city gradually ceased to be a place from which one could expect major painting or sculpture to emerge. And in fact no one was watching, because it was simply assumed that the resources of Rome could never be exhausted, and so could be taken for granted. This was not a sudden implosion, but a slow leakage. What Rome had to offer the artist was no longer what the artist necessarily wanted. Who was going to learn about abstract art, the orthodoxy of the postwar years, by looking at Canova and Bernini? The more Rome was visited, the more it was locked into the itinerary of mass tourist spectacle, the less useful it seemed to become to the artist. There had been no doubting the necessity of Rome to the artist in the seventeenth century. Certainly many nineteenth-century French artists could not define themselves or their work without the supreme example of Rome before them, whatever their differences might be among themselves: one need only think of painters who used to be treated as complete opposites, like Ingres on one hand and Delacroix on the other. But the position of Rome became more debatable, and its strength corroded, as Paris took over as the centre of Western art in the nineteenth century. There was, for instance, no Roman equivalent to Manet, and neither Rome nor the prototypes it offered played any significant role in the development of Impressionism or later forms of modernist art, except for Italian Futurism. Then came the twentieth century – and New York, with its even vaster imperial pretensions. In the process, as the Great Tradition of classicism faltered and died, the wonders of Rome slowly became culturally optional.

To a degree not imagined before, Rome had simply run out of major painters, and the artists it did have were running out of energy. Not much of the art made in Rome between the war and the present seems headed for survival.

Giorgio de Chirico may have been the best known and (at least for his early work) the most esteemed Rome-based Italian painter of the twentieth century, but there is little doubt who was the most popular in Italy. He was Renato Guttuso (1911–87), a much younger man than de Chirico and his opposite in every way. De

Chirico's work showed not the least trace of contemporary social interest or awareness. He was entirely focused on nostalgia for a vanished antiquity. Outside the studio he took no part at all in politics. Guttuso, on the other hand, was an ardent Communist from his youth, defiantly joining the Fascist-banned PCI (Italian Communist Party) in 1940 and never deviating from his anti-Fascist beliefs. From 1943 on he was an active anti-Nazi partisan, and the risks he ran from the occupying Germans were real. He saw his work as part of the Italian resistance to Nazism, and to the power of the Mafia. This put him in a good position to be seen as a culture hero, untainted by Fascist sympathy, by younger leftists even before the Allied victory in the war and the fall of Mussolini. After 1945, when an artist's wartime political allegiances were a big factor in his postwar reputation, Guttuso's name became all but unassailable – any demurral from its preeminence was taken, in leftist circles, as a politically motivated assault from the nostalgic right. Guttuso was the only Western artist, other than Picasso himself, who was treated reverentially as an ally and model by official cultural circles behind the Iron Curtain in the 1950s and after, so much so that he was given the Lenin Peace Prize in 1972, the Soviet equivalent of the Nobel (though never accorded such importance in the West). He shared this honour with La Pasionaria of Spanish Civil War fame (Dolores Ibárruri, 1964) and the Italian sculptor Giacomo Manzù (1965), whose speciality, other than lecturing anyone within earshot about the inequalities of the world, was making harmoniously conical effigies of cardinals and designing monumental doors (1964–7) for the Basilica of St Peter.

Guttuso constantly spoke of himself as a Sicilian peasant. 'Sicilian peasants ... hold the primary position in my heart, because I am one of them, whose faces come before my eyes no matter what I do.' This in fact was rather a stretch; he was indeed Sicilian (from the ruinously depressed, Mafia-ridden town of Bagheria, not far from Palermo) but he was from the middle class, was married to a Roman *contessa*, Mimise Bezzi-Scala, and the sales of his paintings made him one of the richer men, and certainly the richest artist, in Italy. Nevertheless, no modern artist could claim to have done more to illustrate the harshly insular, stress-laden and almost furiously vivid conditions of Sicilian peasant life before, during and after the Nazi occupation. Guttuso's best paintings tended to carry a freight of desperation; very much under the influence of Goya, they commemorate revolt against intolerable human conditions. Sometimes they quote and imitate Goya directly, as in *La Fucilazione in Campagna* ('Execution by Firing Squad in the Country', 1938), provoked by the killing of the poet Federico García Lorca by Franco's Falangists, which was based on that archetype of protest pictures, Goya's *Third of May*. Guttuso painted the working class at work: fishermen, textile workers, sulphur-miners. He did so with a fierce and disillusioned sympathy that many Italians, at the outset of his public career, found intolerable at first but later came to expect, more or less as a trademark. When he won the Bergamo Prize in 1942 with his *Crucifixion*, which contains, along with bitter emblems of suffering and torment, indebted equally to *Guernica* and to the Isenheim altarpiece, the figure of a naked woman, there were strident protests from members of the Catholic Church.

His best-known series of paintings inspired by the war, the *Massacres*, was based on a slaughter that took place in a little-frequented suburb of Rome, the Fosse Ardeatine or Ardeatine Caves. These caverns had been used until then as a mine for *pozzolana*, the volcanic dust used in mixing concrete. On 23 March 1944, a squad of German policemen (Eleventh Company, Third Battalion, mostly German-speaking Italians who had served in Russia) was marching along Via Rasella in central Rome when it drew level with a steel refuse-cart which the Italian Resistance, knowing their route, had packed with iron tubes filled with some eighteen kilos of TNT. The resulting explosion, faultlessly timed, killed twenty-eight police and a number of bystanders; others died soon after. (The eventual death toll was forty-two.)

This action, or atrocity as the Germans saw it, threw the Nazis into a frenzy of vengeance. Reprisals were called for: ten Italians for every dead Nazi. (The sixteen Resistance members who had actually planned and helped carry out the action were never caught.) There were difficulties in rounding up enough hostages, and many of those taken into custody not only had had nothing to do with the explosion but knew nothing about it, being already in jail when it happened. But finally, on 25 March, a total of 355 Italians were forced into trucks, driven to the Ardeatine Caves, and shot in groups of five. It took all day and produced indescribable and horrible chaos, particularly since some of the Nazi executioners were themselves so horrified by their task that they had to get drunk on cognac to finish the job, which did not improve their aim. When the last victim was pronounced dead a corps of German engineers sealed the caves with dynamite. They would not be opened for a year, when the Allies entered Rome. But word of the Ardeatine slaughter leaked out very fast, and it was on this that Guttuso based his melodramatically tragic series of massacre paintings, collectively entitled *Gott mit Uns* – 'God with us', the slogan on the buckles of Nazi uniform belts – which could not be publicly exhibited before the liberation of Italy for fear of German reprisals.

Probably his most ambitious painting was done several decades later – his enormous three-metre-square canvas *La Vucciria* (1974), a panorama of the food market in central Palermo. The name of the place derives from the French *boucherie*, 'butcher's shop', and that is essentially how it began: in Italian a *macelleria*, but a gigantic, encyclopaedic one, where everything living or dead, from baby squid to whole hogs, from bunches of laurel to boxes of aubergines, so long as it was edible, was sold for consumption, twenty-four hours a day. Just as the old Les Halles was known as *le ventre de Paris*, 'the belly of Paris', so the Vucciria is and was the belly of Palermo, growling, grumbling, restlessly teeming and always alive. *E balati ra Vucciria 'un s'asciucanu mai*, runs a common Sicilian saying, 'The paving-stones of the Vucciria are never dry', meaning that the place is always in use, always being swilled and hosed down. Or, if you want to make a promise of delivery that neither you nor your hearer will believe, you can say 'When the stones of the Vucciria dry out.' Into this painting Guttuso packed his feelings and observations about Palermo; the city was, as he painted it, what the city ate, an enormous and phantasmal, chaotic slaughter-house: dead lambs, tuna split open to disclose their ruby flesh, harsh contrasts of purple aubergine, tomatoes so red-ripe as to seem on the verge of explosion, sardines awaiting their transformation into *pasta con le sarde*, pyramids of shining lemons – a massive compost of life and death.

If Guttuso's form of social realism, victims, big backsides, spaghetti-haired women and all, proved popular with orthodox Communists and rich Italians in and out of Rome, it failed to excite much imitation – and none of any quality – among Italian painters in the postwar years, and was looking decidedly tired by the 1960s.

The new rage, it seemed, was for abstract painting, and in particular for the work of Alberto Burri (1915–95) and Lucio Fontana (1899–1968). But Burri's work now seems to have been overtaken by the more subtle paintings of the Spaniard Antoni Tapiès, and Fontana's has come to look monotonous. (There are those who, remembering Fontana's early enthusiasm for Mussolini and Fascism, to which he was a convinced adherent, would regard this as a just punishment.) How much mileage can an artist extract, and for how long, from ripped, paint-drenched, charred burlap? The work of these 'informalist' painters only reminds us, decades later, that when paintings have little or no anchorage in the world as seen, they will end up looking pretty much the same; the 'freedom' of so much abstract art actually leads to monotony. Nine times out of ten, the thing that underwrites variety is a certain degree of faithfulness to things as they appear, to a world whose enormous and constantly invigorating and challenging differences cannot be surpassed by the more limited experience of a painter.

Fontana was the kind of artist whose work passed through a phase of seeming radical almost to the point of aggression and alarm, and then slumped into a semi-decorative sameness. From early Cubism onwards, artists had achieved certain effects by adding material to the canvas – collaged newsprint, glued-on objects. Fontana's rhetorical device was to take material away from the canvas, leaving holes in it – either poked or slashed in its paint-burdened surface. These were christened, rather pretentiously, Concetti Spaziali ('Spatial Concepts'), because they showed emptiness behind the stretched canvas. Fontana's admirers saw in this an invigorating sign of pent-up energy, though today this seems more a figure of art-speech than a physical reality. Looking back on it, how pointless it seems! The real surface of Italy was full of holes, craters, gashes, all inflicted on it by the bombs of the raiders and the shells of the panzers. It was one huge landscape of damage. Little could have been more gratuitous than to take canvases and punch holes in them, as though this could add some meaning to what the real world had undergone, whose traces were so much more eloquent than anything an 'advanced' artist could do to surfaces in his studio. Fontana's work could not escape the fate of novelty art which outlives its novelty.

In general, Italian painting in the 1960s seemed caught in an insoluble bind: anxious to escape the heavy, elegant burden of inherited culture, plagued by memories of its own glorious past, it could not invent a convincing way of looking brutal. In Rome it entered a phase of complacent, pseudo-radical Mannerism which made the frigid exercises of such painters as the Cavaliere d'Arpino, three centuries before, seem positively exuberant. The Italian art world, seemingly disoriented by the war and by the rise of American art to prominence (and then to imperial glory in the fifties), tended to treat as 'major figures' artists whose talent and achievements were quite nugatory. One example among many was Mario Schifano (1934–98), an 'Italian Pop' artist who briefly enjoyed the reputation of being Italy's answer to Andy Warhol – as if an answer were needed! – before wrecking his slender talent and eventually killing himself with massive intakes of cocaine. Schifano was the next-door neighbour of the great Italian aesthete and English scholar Mario Praz, author of The Romantic Agony, The House of Life (a long meditative essay that circled around his enormous collection) and other works. Praz loathed Schifano, who was the noisiest of neighbours and, as a friend of the Rolling Stones and a devotee of rock 'n' roll, represented everything Praz found most noxious and threatening in sixties culture. Schifano, on the other hand, worshipped Praz, and bombarded him with invitations to meet. He wanted, in particular, an inscribed copy of *The House of Life*. Eventually one was left outside Schifano's door, and it was indeed inscribed by the great scholar. *A Mario Schifano*, the dedication ran. *Così vicino, ma così lontano*. 'To Mario Schifano, so near but so far away'.

The 1960s–70s were a hospitable time for conceptual art in Rome, particularly given the Italian talent for obfuscatory theory. The most 'radical' of these gestures – one whose sharpness is most unlikely ever to be surpassed, and which out-Duchamps Duchamp in a small way – was Piero Manzoni's *Merda d'Artista*, which is (or possibly is not) what it says it is: the artist's shit, a small lump of turd weighing about thirty grams, sealed in a small tin can and for ever invisible.

Manzoni was born near Cremona in 1933 but lived in Rome; he had no art training, and did not need it, since his work existed entirely of ideas about art rather than the making of aesthetic objects. One part of this field was his *achromes* ('no-colours'), white canvases covered with white gesso that was scratched or scored with parallel lines. (They did not have to be canvases; other *achromes* of Manzoni were made of white cotton wool and even bread rolls – white bread, naturally, rather than the grainier brown Italian *pane integrale*.) The chief influence hovering behind these was that of the French artist Yves Klein, whose show of mono-chrome canvases, all painted the same IKB or 'International Klein Blue', Manzoni had seen in Paris in 1957. Another was that of Robert Rauschenberg, who had done a group of all-white canvases as far back as 1951; and one should not forget the Russian Male-vich's *White on White* (1918).

Manzoni did single lines, drawn on a roll of paper of a precise length, such as a kilometre; these scrolls were rolled up and kept in polished metal drums. He designated friends (one of whom was the writer Umberto Eco) as living works of art, issuing them with certificates of authenticity. He exhibited red and white balloons which he had blown up himself and then tethered to wooden bases, under the title *Artist's Breath*; these were intended as relics or souvenirs of 'creativity', though of course they did not last long; the rubber perished. In 1961, he installed an iron block in a Danish park; its title, *Base of the World*, was inscribed on it upside down, so that the viewer could imagine the whole world reposing on the block, rather than vice versa. Thus before his early death from a heart attack in 1963, Manzoni had created a small, wry, sharp body of work; how things might have developed from there is of course unknowable. Probably, one suspects, not so very far.

But the little can of excrement was the signature of his career, as nobler things had been of Gianlorenzo Bernini's. Rumour insists that he got the idea from Salvador Dalí, but in any case it was a neat conceptual *jeu d'esprit*. Opening the can would, of course, destroy the value of the artwork. You cannot know that the shit is really inside, or that it is really shit. The obvious target of this object, or gesture, is the overvaluation of art as a fragment of the artist's being – the idea that, in buying a work of art, one also comes to own not just a made object but a part of a creative personality. It is the kind of thought that tends to dissipate when explained, as good jokes do. It is also a point which can only be made once, which redoubles the 'uniqueness' that Manzoni's idea proposes. The edition size is ninety cans, and so far none has been opened; it seems unlikely that any will be, since the last can of Manzoni's *Merda d'Artista* to go on the market fetched the imposing sum of $80,000 – no shit, one is tempted to add.

Other artists gathered under the umbrella of *arte povera* produced objects of some modest interest. Probably the best of them was Giuseppe Penone (b. 1947), who hit on the memorable idea of taking a wooden construction-beam with knots showing and then, starting from the exposed knot-ends, whittling back into the substance of the wood to disclose what had originally been the younger form of the tree, hidden inside – an intriguingly poetic reversal of time and growth.

There was, however, a limit to how much conceptual art the

Italian market and its public could continue to absorb with interest. No matter how many art followers might admire such products of *arte povera* as Mario Merz's igloo constructions of metal, glass, neon and other mixed materials (praised at the time for their allusions to 'nomadic' and 'primitive' cultures), or Jannis Kounellis's *Twelve Horses* (just that: twelve live horses, straw, bridles, horseshit and all, displayed in Rome's Galleria l'Attico in 1969), which one postmodernist art historian called 'the model of pre-linguistic experience, as well as ... non-discursive structures, and non-technological, nonscientific, non-phenomenological artistic conventions' – enough dry jargon to choke any pony – people still seemed to want something to hang on their walls, which one could not easily do to a horse or an igloo. Enter, at this point, a brief temporary salvation in the form of the Transavanguardia.

This clunky neologism was coined by the Roman art historian Achille Bonito Oliva, who acted as ringmaster for a group of young painters, of whom the most prominent were Sandro Chia (b. 1946), Francesco Clemente (b. 1952) and Enzo Cucchi (b. 1949). It meant absolutely nothing definable but pointed to a mood of eclectic revivalism, of eager neophytes shoring fragments – of archaeology, of religion, of what you will – against their ruins. But at least it meant painting, for which a surfeit of conceptual art seldom fails to excite nostalgia, especially if the painting is of human figures. These, the Transavanguardisti supplied in some quantity. Their quality was a different matter. It produced interest in America – indeed, it was the only new Italian art to stimulate excitement on the American market. Nevertheless this was quite short-lived.

The most dramatic painter of the three was Cucchi, who did large doom-laden panels of frantic chickens caught in what appeared to be mud-slides in a cemetery, with shovelfuls of brown and black paint two inches thick.

Chia, on the other hand, had a curiously revivalist flair. In the early 1980s he appeared to be influenced by an almost forgotten figure, the Fascist painter Ottone Rosai (1895–1957), whose roly-poly figures – buttocks like blimps, ladylike coal-heaver arms –

had been part of a conservative reaction against Futurism. Chia was running what appeared to be more light-hearted variations on Rosai's fatness. In the same way he alluded to de Chirico – not the early master of strange cityscapes, but the de Chirico of the 1930s, kitschy antiquities and all. If these padded boys and dropsical nymphs were to meet the demands of real classical art, it would seem a breach of etiquette. But in the stylistic context of Chia's work, such demands could hardly be made. Everything looked so ebullient, juicy and harmless that non-Italians thought it 'typically Italian', like a painted cart or a singing gondolier.

But at least it was less pretentious than the work of the third Transavanguardista, Francesco Clemente. Clemente spent part of each year in Madras, in southern India, and his work is a stew of European and Indian quotations, full of quasi-mystical teases. He acquired a reputation as a draughtsman, quite undeserved: Clemente's figures are boneless and his conventions for the human face – he is fond of portraiture – are close to a joke, with their poached-egg eyes and strained, one-expression mouths. These effete masks suggest no ability to peruse a face and its particularities. They are nothing more than figuration cut adrift and stripped of its reason for being.

One can hardly blame Clemente for this – he clearly can't do any better. And at least he isn't quite the pseudo-classical pasticheur that other Italian postmodernist contemporaries are, with their slimy parodies of neo-classical profiles and flaccid musculature. But the blame, if any, should go to the mechanisms of late modern taste, the flaccidity induced by the market acting in concert with the supposition that the new can only be the good. It is probably true that the person with a serious curiosity about contemporary art can bypass Rome on his or her travels. Anything of that kind there is seen, as it were, under licence; it has come from other galleries in other countries of Europe, or from New York. An air of distinct second-handedness and second-rateness prevails. Rome today originates nothing. If a pilgrimating artist in the seventeenth century, when Rome was incontestably the school of the world and all works of art were certified by their relation to the great city, had been told that this would happen within less than three hundred years, he would have recoiled in disbelief. Time was when the opportunity to exhibit or do a commission in Rome would have been regarded, and rightly, as the climax of an artist's career; today it hardly matters, because the Mandate of Heaven (in that expressive old Chinese phrase) has moved elsewhere, and did so many years ago.

No Italian painter or sculptor after (say) 1960 had anything like the same effect on other artists in his medium that Italian film-makers did in theirs. Film was where the creative vitality of Italy, driven underground by the Second World War, re-emerged in force. First, it was visible in the neo-realist movement. And by the end of the 1950s it was crystallized in one splendidly imaginative figure.

That person, of course, was Federico Fellini, who may well have been the last completely articulate genius Italy produced in the domain of the visual arts. Fellini was not the only Italian movie-maker of exceptional talent working in Rome immediately after the war. There were other, perhaps slightly less gifted figures: Roberto Rossellini and Vittorio de Sica come to mind. Others may yet appear, and one should never assume that the long history of Roman painting is permanently closed, deep as its hiatus now looks – the 'death of painting' is constantly announced, though it never quite happens. But certainly they have not appeared yet, and even the most sanguine tour of the horizon does not reveal another talent of Fellini's order in the art of film. Not yet. Perhaps not ever.

The most enduring gift Mussolini made to Italian culture had been the creation of Cinecittà, the studio complex erected in 1937 just outside Rome. As the Duce so correctly pointed out, 'Cinema is the most powerful weapon' for propaganda purposes, including a people's understanding of its own history. Within six years of the official opening of Cinecittà, a ninety-nine-acre spread which had large facilities for training, production and post-production – it was in effect Europe's only full-service production centre –

almost three hundred films had been made there, partly government-financed. That number is now closer to three thousand; and of course these vary extremely in quality.

Because of the disruption of war, there was little security for Cinecittà. When Italy surrendered in 1943, the whole complex was intermittently bombed by the Allies, though not heavily enough to destroy its production capability altogether. The Germans, retreating, looted Cinecittà's equipment and facilities. Immediately after the war, when it became clear that bombing the sets and sound-stages was of little strategic use, the Allies converted Cinecittà into a camp for refugees and other displaced persons. It was, in effect, closed down; and Italian film-makers, deprived of its facilities, took to the streets, using contemporary Rome as their setting and amateur actors as their players. The result was 'neo-realist' cinema, which amounted to a complete rebirth of the medium in Italy. One 'classic' of this type was the film that made Roberto Rossellini's reputation, *Roma Città Aperta* ('Rome, Open City'), starring Anna Magnani and co-scripted by the as yet little-known Federico Fellini, and released in 1945; it was partly shot as documentary during the actual liberation of Rome, and created a sensation when it took the Grand Prize at the 1946 Cannes Film Festival. Another neo-realist landmark was Vittorio de Sica's *Ladri di Bicicletta* ('Bicycle Thieves'). The masterpiece of the neo-realist genre was, however, Rossellini's film. As not infrequently happens in times of shortage, its moody newsreel style was partly an accident due to a lack of film stock, so that its unexplained variations in image consistency are now agreed to have been produced by poor processing and insufficient fixing. Had it not been for the war this belt-tightening would not have taken place, and Cinecittà would probably have kept turning out the inferior, anodyne *telefono bianco* romances and comedies that had provided much of its staple fodder in the late 1930s and early 40s. But as things stood after the triumph of *Roma Città Aperta*, a new form of hybrid cinema had been created, partly by design and partly by accident; and quite suddenly, Italy – whose influence on movies had been slight, at best, before – was creating world standards for film from its local industry. The influence of *Roma Città Aperta* would be felt for more than twenty years, in such works as Ermanno Olmi's *Tree of Wooden Clogs* (1978) and Michael Cimino's much underrated *Heaven's Gate* (1980).

It would be quite wrong to suppose that most of the productions at Cinecittà followed suit. After a grittily realist start, the movies found their natural home in a ready-made ancient Rome touched up with plaster, among what one of their titles (1984) called *Le Calde notti di Caligola*, 'The Hot Nights of Caligula'. Certain historical figures kept cropping up: one of the earliest Rome-set features, long antedating Cinecittà, was *Spartacus* (1914). It was followed by *Spartaco* (1953) and Stanley Kubrick's excellent *Spartacus*, starring Kirk Douglas (1960), then *Son of Spartacus* (1962; played by that doughty American weight-lifter Steve Reeves, effortlessly tossing huge chunks of foam plastic around the Forum); and, as further spin-offs from the gladiator mode, *The Revenge of Spartacus* (1965), *Spartacus and the Ten Gladiators* (1964) and *Triumph of the Ten Gladiators* (1964) and, perhaps inevitably, *Gladiatress* (2004). Some sixteen features, between 1908 and 2003, bore the title of *Julius Caesar*, and Gérard Depardieu even played him in French (*Astérix et Obélix: Mission Cléopâtre*, 2002). The most famous and ruinously expensive of all the Rome reconstructions was Joseph Mankiewicz's 1963 *Cleopatra*, the cheapest and sluttiest was the Warholish *Cleopatra* (1970), starring Viva and Gerard Malanga, and the silliest was the British *Carry On Cleo* (1964). The first of the Antony and Cleopatra movies was released in 1908 and it was followed by more than twenty bearing the lady's name.

In the 1950s, thanks to the cheapness of Rome production and the attractions of the city itself – what American star wasn't going to prefer living in a grand Roman hotel to working in Hollywood? – giant international co-productions were filmed there, such as *Ben-Hur* (1959), the 1951 *Quo Vadis*, and *Spartacus* (the fourth version, 1960). But the film director whose name is most strongly, indeed indissolubly, linked to the Via Vittorio Veneto was, again, Federico Fellini, and the movie that provided the link was his best-known one, *La Dolce Vita*.

No film has ever fascinated me more. This really was Europe on celluloid. It seems odd that Rome would have been rendered more attractive to a writer in his hot-potato twenties by seeing a film as intensely pessimistic as *La Dolce Vita*, but it was, and for a double reason. First, I was a callow and inexperienced romantic, yearning for foreign parts; second, Fellini's film was a real (if flawed) masterpiece about places and situations that seemed overwhelmingly exotic to me. There was no gainsaying either.

Shooting on *La Dolce Vita* had begun in March 1959 and the film was released in a storm of publicity and controversy early in 1960. It broke all box-office records; *L'Osservatore Romano*, the Vatican's official paper, called for its censorship; crowds queued for hours to see it and Fellini was physically attacked at a screening in Milan. For those who have not watched it, it is about the sexual and emotional experiences of a peripheral journalist, Marcello Rubini, played by the iconically handsome Marcello Mastroianni, who makes his living purveying trivial gossip about celebrities to the Italian press. (Originally the producer, Dino de Laurentiis, had wanted Paul Newman to play Marcello to guarantee his investment; Fellini adamantly insisted against it.) In order to gather the gossip he peddles, which is never of the least political or cultural significance, he hangs out around the bars and cafés of the Via Veneto. (At the time Fellini was making this movie in the late 50s, the Via Veneto was not yet the caricature of urban glamour *La Dolce Vita* turned it into. But it was getting there, and the success of the movie cemented the process in the 1960s. Indeed, a stone plaque on one of the buildings acknowledges Fellini's role in 'creating' the Via Veneto as everyone came to know it.)

Marcello is a weakling, one of the class of people who create nothing substantial or even authentic but to whom things merely happen and create a brief, tinny resonance – the essence of voyeurism, which is how Fellini portrays journalism in general. His companion, the Sancho Panza to this ineffectual and passive Quixote – for all gossip papers need photos – is an irrepressibly cheery, fast-footed and pea-brained photographer named Paparazzo (Walter Santesso) – whose name, such being the film's

enormous afterlife, was to become generic for gossip pho-
tographers from then to now. (The name came from Paparazzo,
a character in a long-disregarded novel set in Italy by the semi-
bohemian English novelist George Gissing, *By the Ionian Sea*, but
that title seems to have no bearing on the film. Gissing's Paparazzo
does not even have a camera.)

The atmosphere of fraudulence leaking from on high is set in
the very first shots – a clatter of rotor blades that announce the
coming of Christ, not the real redeemer, of course, but a hideous
and vulgar ten-foot-high effigy with its loving arms extended in
blessing, being hauled across the skyline of Rome by a rented
helicopter, ready to be lowered on to the top of some column or
dome. The pervasiveness of phoney religion is as much a theme
of *La Dolce Vita* as that of manipulated emotion, and as a newly
hatched ex-Catholic I loved every minute of it: it looked and felt
like revenge, which indeed it was – Fellini's own.

La Dolce Vita loosely unfolds through eight episodes, which are
taken to typify the folly and emptiness of Roman life at the dawn
of the 1960s. It shows the impulse to religious faith, of which
Rome was the traditional centre, becoming dried-out and descending into the merest superstition. It shows family relationships – those between son and father – dying, more or less,
on the branch. It shows Rome as a place given up to sterile and
passing pleasure. It shows the death of fame – its descent into
mere raucous celebrity. All in all, it sketches a city which can no
longer nourish its human contents and yet exercises a magnetic
fascination over them, so that they can no longer break from the
orbits in which they hold one another.

Despite all its human oddity and theatrical décor, the weirdest
moment of *La Dolce Vita* was, for me at least, the fish in the net at
the end of the film. I have seen it three or four times and, although
I am pretty good at identifying fish, I have no idea what this sea
beast was: some kind of large ray, I suppose. One does not glimpse
its whole body; only a glaucous eye, staring damply in close-up at
the lens. Its gaze seems both judgemental and indifferent, as no
doubt Fellini meant it to be. The party-goers cluster around it.

What is this oddity? Where does it come from? 'From Australia,' someone off-camera suggests. On hearing this I felt mildly buoyed with semi-patriotic pride. My homeland's tiny, whispered impact on Rome! It seemed like an omen of some kind. I identified with that fish in its strangeness, even though it looked so unappetizing, like a lump of mucus entangled in twine. Like me, it had come all the way from Australia to Italy, in quest of . . . something or other. Who could know or guess what (if anything) it had been expecting, as it blundered slowly and slimily about on the bed of the Tyrrhenian? Certainly it had been haunting Fellini's imagination ever since, in 1934, he saw a huge, ugly fish stranded on a beach near Rimini.

Fellini went on to make several more movies which became classics of the Italian imagination; the most beautiful and complex of these were 8½ (1963), his extraordinary meditation on the creative process itself – he wanted 'to tell the story of a director who no longer knows what film he wants to make' – and *Amarcord* (1973), a convoluted essay on childhood memory. ('*Amarcord*' was Riminese dialect for *Io mi ricordo*, 'I remember'.) But though these were loaded with honours from festivals and the industry, *La Dolce Vita* has a special place in film history which no Italian paintings of the period can conceivably rival, and no Italian movie made in the foreseeable future is likely to equal its wide cultural impact.

The vision Fellini released of Rome as a kind of tragic playground, filled with the promise of sensuous delight but shadowed by the impossibility of true gratification, proved to be very haunting. It also played beautifully, and to a large extent truthfully, against the Rome the visitor came to know fifty years ago. The Eternal City was a far more agreeable place to be in the early 1960s than it is today.

Of course, this may have been (in some degree) an illusion, fostered then by my own ignorance of the Italian language and by my excessively optimistic belief in the continuity of Italian culture. At the time, those decades ago, it seemed entirely promising and real. The past fifty years have yielded little of interest, culturally, politically, and especially artistically. But the fact that

Rome, at the start of the twenty-first century, has been gutted by the huge and ruthless takeover of its imagination by mass tourism and mass media, does not mean that continuity didn't exist – once upon a time, when the city was slightly younger.

People, Italians included, never run out of complaints about the decay of Roman culture, both high and popular. It is gross. It is pandering. You only need to turn on the TV in your Roman hotel room to see that. Do so and you will at once be immersed in what you might call the Id of the owner, Silvio Berlusconi – a nightmare territory to you perhaps, but to most Italians a sort of paradise, filled with fictions of 'knowing' – the ceaseless diet of gossip and chatter and scandal and unembarrassed glitz that passes for news, the relentless barrage of sports and commentary on sports, the parade of cushion-lipped, big-breasted blonde babes who serve as announcers, the wrestling matches, and all the rest of it. After all, it is only in Italy that a stripper named Cicciolina (briefly famous in the outside world as the spectacularly ill-treated wife of the artist Jeff Koons, and mother of their little son Ludwig) could acquire a seat in parliament. It is easy, after passing an idle evening with this stuff (one evening will suffice; it is pretty much all the same, whichever evening you pick), to assume that Italian popular culture has sunk below some IQ level it once occupied in the past. This is an illusion. Italian television – one is tempted to say Italian popular culture in general – is crap, always has been, and will never be anything else. It may not be the absolute worst in the world, but it is certainly way down there.

But then, has Italian 'popular' art ever been much better? We are inclined to sentimentalize about it, but should we? Reflecting on this, I sometimes find myself strolling in the galleries formerly occupied by mosaics from the Baths of Caracalla. In their heyday these enormous *thermae*, whose stage was big enough to allow a four-horse chariot to be driven on it (this is still done in some productions there of *Aida*), were elaborately decorated with mosaics of the third century CE. Many of these have now been transferred to the pagan museum of the Lateran Palace and reapplied to its walls. Some are not without their archaeological and narrative interest, but what a vision of lumpish coarseness they present! They are gross muscle-men, naked gladiators brandishing weapons that look like, and presumably were, heavy bronze knuckle-dusters with protruding flanges, the better to put out an opponent's eye or smash in his teeth. Watching a pair of these brutes belting away at one another might have slaked most of the thirst for pleasure in violence that was satisfied by more lethal encounters with sword and trident. But as studies in heroic nakedness these stumpy mosaic figures have nothing going for them. They are pure demonstrations of the human body as a weapon of meat. They have little in common with more gracefully formalized Greek pugilists or wrestlers. And this was what the Romans liked: violence without frills, just glaring and bashing. And rubbish, too. The floor of the dining-chamber depicted is covered with rubbish. Not ordinary droppings such as might be left after a banquet of extremely messy guests, but unswept kitchen filth: fruit-skins, the bones of a fish and suchlike. Walking on it (which you cannot do, since this is a museum) you half expect things to go squidge and crackle underfoot. Except that they cannot and will not do so, being a couple of thousand years or so old.

When we talk about classical Roman art, the word 'classical' does not really mean what it might mean in Greece. It tends to signify something heavier, more grossly human, and definitely less ideal.

We cannot make the mistake with Romans of supposing that they were refined, like the Greeks they envied and imitated. They tended to be brutes, arrivistes, nouveaux-riches. Naturally, that is why they continue to fascinate us – we imagine being like them, as we cannot imagine being like the ancient Greeks. And we know what they liked best to do was astonish people – with spectacle, expense, violence or a fusion of all three. As Belli put it, writing about the exultant firework display that rose each year above the cupola of St Peter's at the pope's behest,

Chi ppopolo po' esse, ec chi sovrano,
Che cciàbbi a ccasa sua 'na cuppoletta,
Com'er nostro San Pietr' in Vaticano?
In qual antra scitta, in quàl antro stato,
C'è st'illuminazzione bbenedetta,
Che t'intontissce e tte fa pperde er fiato?

What people could there be, and what ruler,
That could have in its house a cupola
Like our own Saint Peter in the Vatican?
In what other city, in what other state,
Could there be this blessed light
That astonishes you and makes you lose your breath?

The answer is still essentially what it was back then, in 1834:
Rome, and only Rome. So too, 'classical', in the Roman sense,
suggests something solider, more enduring, than the Greek. For
all its glories and for all the legacy it left in art, thought and politics,
Greek civilization did perish. That of Rome is still somewhat with
us. One would need to be strangely indifferent not to appreciate
what Ammianus Marcellinus (*c.*330–95 CE), writing after the effective collapse of the great Empire, had to say about Constantine's
arrival there in the early fourth century CE, for there is a little
Constantine left in all our reactions, in our undying sense of
astonishment at this city of prodigious and overweening ambition
(italics my own):

> Then, as he surveyed the sections of the city and the suburbs
> . . . he thought that whatever first met his gaze towered above
> all the rest; the sanctuaries of Tarpeian Jove so far surpassing
> as things divine excel those of earth; the baths built up in the
> manner of provinces; the huge bulk of the Amphitheatre,
> strengthened by its framework of travertine, to whose top
> human eyesight barely ascends; the Pantheon like a round
> city-district, vaulted over in lofty beauty; and the exalted
> columns which rise like platforms to which one may mount,

and bear the likeness of former emperors; the Temple of the City; the Forum of Peace; the Theatre of Pompey, the Odeum, the Stadium, and in their midst the other adornments of the Eternal City. But when he came to the Forum of Trajan, a construction unique under heaven, as we believe, and admirable even in the unanimous opinion of the gods, he stood fast in amazement, turning his attention to the gigantic complex about him, beggaring description and *never again to be imitated by mortal men.*

EPILOGUE

That summer evening of 1959, standing before the great statue of Marcus Aurelius during my first trip to Rome, I was struck with the sense that the Rome I was standing in was the Rome it had always been, and would continue to be; a pervasive naiveté, I see now, born of crude imaginings. It has been interrupted, that sense of continuity broken by the foul, corrosive breath of our own century. For their own protection from terrorism, the horse and rider have now been removed to the Capitoline Museum and they have been replaced on Buonarroti's pedestal with a replica. It won't matter that many passers-by won't see that it is a replica. Just knowing it is will spoil the pleasure of its viewing.

What makes it worse is that whoever installed the great sculpture inside the Capitoline deprived it of its base and placed it slantwise, cantilevered out on an inclined ramp. This is vandalism. It is absolutely intrinsic to the meaning of the *Marcus Aurelius* that the horse and rider should be level and horizontal; otherwise their firm authority is lost. In its new installation, slanting meaninglessly upwards in a way Michelangelo would never have countenanced for an instant, the sculpture becomes a parody of the huge bronze of Peter the Great by the French sculptor Étienne-Maurice Falconet (1716–91), the 'bronze horseman' of Pushkin's poem, riding up his rock in St Petersburg. It would be very hard to imagine a more stupid treatment of a great sculpture than this: 'design' run amok, vulgarizing the work it was meant to clarify, ignoring all ancient meanings for the sake of an illusion of 'relevance' (to what?) and 'originality' (if you don't know the Falconet). But sadly, that's Rome now – a city which, to a startling extent, seems to be losing touch with its own nature, and in some respects has surrendered to its own iconic popularity among visitors.

The 'tourist season' of Rome used to be confined, more or less, to the months of July and August, when the city was filled with visitors, when restaurants were overcrowded, hotels jammed and reservations for anything hard to get. The principal 'sights', such as the Vatican museums and the Sistine, were best skirted during those eight weeks or even avoided by the clued-in traveller. That is no longer feasible. Today this season has lengthened to embrace the whole year. And if you think the Sistine Chapel is a tad over-crowded now, just wait another five or ten years, when post-Communist prosperity has taken hold in China and expresses itself as mass tourism. A good preparation in the present would be to visit the Louvre (if you haven't done so already) and make for the gallery in which the *Mona Lisa* is displayed to the crowd: a fortress wall of blinking, clicking cameras, all taking bad, vaguely recognizable photos of the picture, whose function is not to pre-serve and transmit information about Leonardo's painting but to commemorate the fact that the camera's owner was once in some kind of proximity to the insanely desired icon. All the high points of Rome will be like that, I gloomily think, before so very long. Some will survive it – at least partially; others cannot and will not, because it is not in the nature of works of art to do so. The closed spaces – museum galleries, churches and the like – will suffer most; it will not make much difference to one's experience of the Forum, not at first. But who can tell what the big outdoor spaces of Rome will begin to feel like once they have twice as many people in them, and their perimeters are jammed even more thickly with buses?

The degree to which the Sistine Chapel is overcrowded represents the kind of living death for high culture that lurks at the end of mass culture – an end which Michelangelo, of course, could not possibly have imagined, and which the Vatican is com-pletely powerless to prevent (and would not even if it could, since the Sistine is such an important source of revenue for the Vatican). You cannot filter the stream. Either a museum is public, or it is not. To imagine some kind of cultural means-test and try to impose it on people who want to visit the Sistine Chapel is, of course, unthinkable. But since the Sistine is one of the two things (the other being St Peter's Basilica itself) that every tourist in Rome has heard of and wants to see, the crush there is numbing; it defeats the possibility of concentration. At least the basilica is huge enough to accommodate crowds of people. The Sistine, and the way into it, are not.

It was not always like that. One reads in Goethe's *Travels in Italy* his account of walking more or less casually into the Sistine to escape the baking heat of the Roman summer, two hundred years ago. A cool, approachable place where one could be alone, or nearly so, with the products of genius. The very idea seems absurd, today: a fantasy. Mass tourism has turned what was a contemplative pleasure for Goethe's contemporaries into an ordeal more like a degrading rugby scrum. The crowd of ceiling-seekers is streamed shoulder to shoulder along a lengthy, narrow, windowless and claustrophobic corridor in which there is no turning back. At last it debouches into an equally crowded space, the Chapel itself, which scarcely offers the room to turn round. These are the most trying conditions under which I have ever looked at art – and over the past fifty years I have looked at a lot of art. Some of the arts benefit from being shared with a large audience. All kinds of music, whether rock 'n' roll or piano recitals, seem to. Dance sometimes does, and so might theatre and poetry readings. But the visual arts, especially painting and sculpture, do not. Throngs of other people just get in the way, blocking your view and exasperating your desire for silence with their overheard comments, which are always a distraction, even if they are intelligent – which they seldom are. Fellow humans are fellow humans, endowed with certain inalienable rights which we need not go into here, but you no more want to hear their reactions in front of a Titian or below a Michelangelo fresco than you would like to have your neighbour in a concert hall beating time on the arm of his seat or humming the notes of '*Vesti la giubba*' along with (or just a wee fraction ahead of) the singer, to prove his familiarity with the piece. (When this happens it is an invitation to murder.)

Painting and sculpture are silent arts, and deserve silence (not phoney reverence, just quiet) from those who look at them. Let it be inscribed on the portals of the world's museums: What you will see in here is not meant to be a social experience. Shut up and use your eyes. Groups with guides etc., admitted Wednesdays only, 11 a.m.–4 p.m. Otherwise, just shut the fuck up, please pretty please, if you can, if you don't mind, if you won't burst. We have come a long way to look at these objects too. We have not done so to listen to your golden words. *Capisce?*

The only way to circumvent this Sistine crowding is to pay what is in effect a hefty ransom to the Vatican. After closing hours it now runs small tour groups through the Vatican museums, guaranteeing the visitor about two hours (start to finish) with Michelangelo and Raphael and, of course, a guide, whose silence is not guaranteed; 'normal' viewing time in the Chapel itself is about thirty minutes, which is a good deal more than the usual visitor, harried and chivvied, is going to get. The tour groups, at present about one a week, are made up of about ten people, though there may be as many as twenty. (The very first time I went to the Sistine there were, by my rough count, about thirty people in the whole Chapel, but that, I repeat, was some fifty years ago. It felt a little crowded then, but not intolerable.) Each visitor, under the new tour system, pays up to $500 – some 300 euros per person – for the privilege, and the deal is done through outside contractors, not directly with the Vatican itself. How the fee is split is not known. Of course this is highway robbery. If you don't like it, you can always write to the pope; or else buy some postcards and study those in the calm and quiet of your hotel.

What happens inside churches also happens outside, on a vaster scale. No European city that I know has been as damaged, its civic experience as brutally compromised, by automobile and driver as Rome.

The traffic of Rome used to be bad, but now it is indiscriminately lethal. Parking in Rome used to be a challenge that required special skills, but now it is almost comically impossible. Of course, it is rendered all the more difficult – in contrast, let's say, to parking in Barcelona – by the near-impossibility of discovering an underground public garage: such amenities do exist, but they are rare, since the city government cannot dig below ground level without invariably encountering some ancient, illegible and archaeologically superfluous buried ruin from the time of Pompey or Tarquin the Arrogant, an unwelcome discovery which will freeze all future work on the site for all ages to come, *in omnia saecula saeculorum* as the Church used to say before it abandoned the Latin for the vernacular Mass.

The most astonishing thing about the city used to be, until recently, the Romans' cavalier disregard for the chief thing that brought so many people there – namely, its deposit of art. People are apt to suppose that a nation which has been left enormous cultural legacies by its ancestors can be presumed to be highly cultivated in the here and now.

Italy is one big proof that this is not true. Most Italians are artistic illiterates. Most people anywhere are; why should Italians be any different? Though once they pretended not to be, today most of them can't even bother to pretend. Many of them see the past as a profitable encumbrance. They like to invoke the splendours of their *patrimonio culturale*, but when it comes to doing anything about them, like turning their considerable energies towards preserving that inheritance in an intelligible way, or even to forming a solid and organized constituency of museum-goers, little or nothing is done and nothing or little happens.

What the Italian public really cares about is *calcio*, soccer. If an Italian government were crazy enough to try to ban soccer matches, those astounding orgies of hysteria in which hundreds of thousands of fans explode into orgasms of loyalty for this team or that team, the nation would cease to be a nation; it would become ungovernable. Not only does high culture not function as a social glue in this country, it probably has less local pride invested in it than anywhere else in Western Europe. What really count are sport and TV, and their pre-eminence is assured by the fact that the former Italian prime minister, Silvio Berlusconi, is a multi-multimillionaire from ownership of both and seems to have no cultural interests, let alone commitments of any kind, apart from top-editing the harem of blondies for his quiz shows. That is why most Italians can contemplate, with relative equanimity, the very real prospect that their Ministry of Culture's already beleaguered and inadequate budget will be slashed, as is now being suggested, by the year 2012, while its director has been replaced by a former chief of McDonald's.

You might say that it has always been this way, but actually it has not. It has got worse since the sixties with the colossal, steamrollering, mind-obliterating power of TV – whose Italian forms are among the worst in the world. The cultural IQ of the Italian nation, if one can speak of such a thing, has dropped considerably and the culprit seems to be television, as it is in other countries. What is the point of fostering elites that few care about? It bestows no political advantage. In a wholly upfront culture of football, 'reality' shows and celebrity games, a culture of pure distraction, it is no longer embarrassing to admit that Donatello, like the temperature of the polar ice-cap or the insect population of the Amazon, is one of those things about which you, as a good *molto tipico* Italian and nice enough guy, do not personally give a rat's ass.

Perhaps (one hopefully adds) it takes only two or three artists to reanimate a culture. One cannot simply write a culture off because it has gone into recession, because recessions – as history amply proves – can turn out to be merely temporary. Nevertheless, at this moment, it doesn't look terribly likely. Do I feel this only because I am older, somewhat callused, less sensitive to indications of renewal? Perhaps. Or do I feel it because the cultural conditions of the city itself have changed so radically – because, in a word, the Rome of today is no longer (and cannot possibly become again) the Rome of Fellini? That, too, is possible, and indeed more likely. In the meantime, there are at least compensations. The energies of what was once the present may no longer be there. They may have been something of an illusion, as promises and first impacts are fated to be. But the glories of the remoter past remain, somewhat diminished but obstinately indelible, under the dreck and distractions of overloaded tourism and coarsened spectacle. Like it or lump it, Rome is there; one cannot ignore it.

There is always a level of delight on which Rome can be enjoyed – unashamedly, sensuously, openly. Is there a solution to the present difficulties and enigmas of Rome? If there is, I freely confess that I have no idea what it might be. So many centuries of history are wound inextricably into the city and confront the visitor, let alone the resident, with apparently insoluble problems of access and understanding. It wasn't built in a day and can't be understood in one, or a week, or a month or a year – in however much time you may allot to it, a decade or a guided bus ride. It makes you feel small, and it is meant to. It also makes you feel big, because the nobler parts of it were raised by members of your own species. It shows you what you cannot imagine doing, which is one of the beginnings of wisdom. You have no choice but to go there in all humility, dodging the Vespas, admitting that only a few fragments of the city will disclose themselves to you at a time, and some never will. It is an irksome, frustrating, contradictory place, both spectacular and secretive. (What did you expect? Something easy and self-explanatory, like Disney World?) The Rome we have today is an enormous concretion of human glory and human error. It shows you that things were done once whose doings would be unimaginable today. Will there ever be another Piazza Navona? Don't hold your breath. There is and can be only one Piazza Navona, and happily it is right in front of you, transected by the streams of glittering water – a gift to you and to the rest of the world from people who are dead and yet can never die. One such place, together with all the rest that are here, is surely enough.

BIBLIOGRAPHY

Adcock, F.E. (1960; reprint, 1940) *The Roman Art of War under the Republic*. New York: Barnes and Noble

Ademollo, A. (1883) *Il Carnevale di Roma nei secoli XVII e XVIII*. Rome: A. Sommaruga

Ades, Dawn et al. (eds). (1996) *Art and Power: Europe under the Dictators 1930–45. The Age of Neo-Classicism*. Catalogue to Council of Europe exhibition, London, 1972

Alberti, Battista. (1965) *On the Art of Building in Ten Books*. Trans. J. Rykwert et al. Cambridge, Mass., and London: Alec Tiranti

Amadei, E. (1969) *Le Torri di Roma*. Rome: Palombi

Amy, R. and Gros, P. (1979) 'La Maison Carrée de Nîmes' in *Gallia-Supplément*, xxviii. Paris: Éditions du Centre national de la recherche scientifique

Anderson, James C. (1997) *Roman Architecture and Society*. Maryland: Johns Hopkins University Press

Angeli, D. (1935) *Roma Romantica*. Milan: Treves

—— (1939) *Le Cronache del Caffè Greco*. Milan: Treves

Appian. *Civil Wars*. *c.*135

Argan, Giulio Carlo et al. (1992) *Canova: A European Adventure*. Catalogue to exhibition at Correr Museum. Venice: Marsilio Publishers

Atkinson, Rick. (2007) *The Day of Battle: the War in Sicily and Italy, 1943–1944*. New York: Henry Holt

Augustus. *Res Gestae*. *c.*14 CE

Aurelius, Marcus. *Meditations*, vol. 2. *c.*170. Trans. Maxwell Staniforth (2005). New York: Penguin Books

Bailey, C. (ed.). (1947) *The Legacy of Rome*, 7th edn. New York: General Books LLC

Ballo, Guido (1958) *Modern Italian Painting, from Futurism to the Present Day*. Trans. Barbara Wall. New York: Praeger

Baracconi, G. (1906) *I Rioni di Roma*. Princeton: Princeton University Press

Barilli, Renato (ed.). (1982) *Gli Annitrenta: Arte e cultura in Italia*. Milan: Mazzotta

Barnes, T.D. (1982) *The New Empire of Diocletian and Constantine*. Massachusetts: Harvard University Press

Barrett, Anthony. (1998) *Caligula: The Corruption of Power*. Connecticut: Yale University Press

Baynes, N.H. (1972) *Constantine the Great and the Christian Church*. London: British Academy Publications

Beard, Mary and Henderson, John. (2001) *Classical Art from Greece to Rome*. New York: Oxford University Press

Belli, G.G. (1952) *I Sonetti Romaneschi*. 3 vols.

Bergmann, B. and Kondoleon, C. (eds). (2000) *The Art of Ancient Spectacle*. NGW-Stud Hist Art

Besso, M. (1903) *Roma e il Papa nei Proverbi e nei modi di dire*. Florence: Leo S. Olschki

Black, J. (ed.). (2003) *Italy and the Grand Tour*. Connecticut: Yale University Press

Blunt, A. (1940) *Artistic Theory in Italy*. Oxford: Oxford University Press
—— (1979) *Borromini*. Massachusetts: Harvard University Press

Boardman, J. et al. (1988) *Oxford History of the Classical World*. Oxford: Oxford University Press

Boatwright, M.T. (1987) *Hadrian and the City of Rome*. Princeton: Princeton University Press

Boccioni, U. (1912) *La Scultura Futurista*. Milan: Corso Venezia
—— *Technical Manifesto of Futurist Sculpture*. Milan: Corso Venezia

Boethius, A. (1960) *The Golden House of Nero*. Ann Arbor: University of Michigan Press
—— (1978) *Etruscan and Early Roman Architecture*. Harmondsworth: Penguin Books

Boni, Ada. (1983) *La Cucina Romana*. Rome: Newton Compton

Bonner, Stanley. (1977) *Education in Ancient Rome*. Berkeley: University of California Press

Borgatti, M. (1980) *Castel S. Angelo, Storia e descrizione*. Rome: Florence

Borghese, D. (1955) *Vecchia Roma*. London: Prince Olsoufieff

Bosticcio, Sergio et al. (1970) *Piazza Navona, Isola dei Pamphili*. Rome: Fratelli Palombi

Bowder, D. (ed.). (1980) *Who Was Who in the Roman World, 753 BC–AD 476*. Ithaca: Cornell University Press

Bowersock, G.W. (1981) *Augustus and the Greek World*. Oxford: Oxford University Press
—— (1997) *Julian the Apostate*. Massachusetts: Harvard University Press
—— (1999) *Late Antiquity: a Guide to the Postclassical World*. Massachusetts: Belknap Press

Bowron, E.P. and Rishel, J. (eds). (2003) *Art in Rome in the Eighteenth Century*. London: Merrell Publishers

Boyle, Nicholas. (1992) *The Poetry of Desire*. New York: Oxford University Press

Bradley, K.R. (1987) *Slaves and Masters in the Roman Empire: A Study in Social Control*. New York: Oxford University Press

Brady, F. and Pottle, F. (eds). (1955) *Boswell on the Grand Tour, 1765–66*. London: Heinemann

Brentano, Robert. (1974) *Rome before Avignon*. Berkeley, Los Angeles, London: University of California Press

Brigante Colonna, G. (1925) *Roma Papale*, Florence: Le Monnier

—— (1936) *La Nipote di Sisto V.* Milan: Mondadori

Broude, Norma. (1987) *The Macchiaioli, Italian Painters of the Nineteenth Century*. Massachusetts: Yale University Press

Brown, F.E. (1961) *Roman Architecture*. New York: George Braziller

Brummer, Hans. (1980) *The Statue Court in the Vatican Belvedere*. Stockholm: Haskell, Francis, and Nicholas Penny

Brunt, P.A. (1988) *The Fall of the Roman Republic*. New York: Oxford University Press

Bruschi, Arnaldo. *Bramante*. (1977) London: Thames and Hudson

Campbell, Colen. (1717) *Vitruvius Britannicus, or the British Architect*. Mineola: Dover Publications

Campbell, Duncan. (2003) *Greek and Roman Siege Machinery, 399 BC–AD 363*. Oxford: Osprey Publishing

Canons and Decrees of the Council of Trent, 5th Session, 3/4 December 1563, *On Sacred Images*

Carcopino, J. (1939) *La Vie Quotidienne à Rome*. Paris: Hachette

Carducho, Vicente. (1865) *Diálogos de la Pintura*. Madrid

Cary, M. (1949) *The Geographic Background of Greek and Roman History*. Oxford: Clarendon Press

Cattabiani, A. (1990) *Simboli, miti e misteri di Roma*. Rome: Newton Compton

Caven, B. (1980) *The Punic Wars*. New York: Palgrave Macmillan

Ceroni, G. (1955) *I misteri di Roma*. Rome

Cerquiglini, O. (1939) *Curiosità e Meraviglie di Roma*. Rome

Chisholm, Kitty and Ferguson, John. (1992) *Rome, the Augustan Age: a Source Book*. New York: Oxford University Press

Christiansen, Keith. (2007) 'The Critical Fortunes of Poussin's Landscapes', in 'Poussin and Nature', *Journal of Art History*, vol. 4

Cicero. *De Oratore* II. 55 BCE

—— *On the Consular Provinces. c.*52 BCE

—— Letters to Friends, 55 BCE

Cipriani, Giovanni. (1993) *Gli obelischi egizi: politica e cultura nella Roma barocca*. Florence: Leo S. Olschki

Clark, Martin. (1998) *The Italian Risorgimento*. New York: Longman Publishing

—— (2005) *Mussolini*. London: Pearson

Clarke, Georgia. *Roman House – Renaissance Palaces: Inventing Antiquity in Fifteenth-century Italy*. Cambridge: Cambridge University Press

Clementi, F. (1939) *Il Carnevale di Roma*. 2 vols

Clements, Robert J. (1963) *Michelangelo's Theory of Art*. New York: New York University Press

Cochrane, E. (1981) *Historians and Historiography in the Italian Renaissance*. Chicago and London: University of Chicago Press

Condivi, Ascanio. (1969) *Life of Michelangelo*. Trans. Alice Wohl. Pennsylvania: University of Pennsylvania State Press

Connolly, Peter. (1981) *Greece and Rome at War*. New Jersey: Prentice-Hall

Connors, Joseph. (1982) 'Borromini, Francesco', in *Macmillan Encyclopedia of Architects*, vol. 1. New York, London

Cowling, Elizabeth and Mundy, Jennifer. (1990) *On Classic Ground: Picasso, Léger, de Chirico and the New Classicism, 1910–1930*. Oklahoma: Tate Publishing

Croon, J.H. (ed.). (1965) *The Encyclopedia of the Ancient World*. New Jersey: Prentice-Hall

Cunliffe, Barry. (1978) *Rome and Her Empire*. Ohio: McGraw-Hill

Daly, Gregory. (2002) *Cannae: The Experience of Battle in the Second Punic War*. London: Routledge

D'Annunzio, G. (1992) *Le Cronache della Tribuna*. Bologna

D'Arrigo, G. (1962) *Roma: Miti, Riti, Siti, Tipi*. Rome: New Sword Publishing

—— (1964) *Uomini, cose, fatti e leggende di Roma*. Rome

Davey, Peter. 'Outrage – the Vittorio Emanuele II Monument in Rome', *Architectural Review*, Oct. 1996

De Chirico, Giorgio. (1971) *The Memoirs of Giorgio de Chirico*. Trans. Margaret Crosland. Miami: University of Miami Press

—— (1985) *Il Meccanismo del Pensiero*. Turin: Giulio Einaudi

Della Pergola P. (1962) *Villa Borghese*. Rome: Istituto Poligrafico dello Stato

De Santis, L. (1997) *Le Catacombe di Roma*. Rome: Newton Compton

De Tuddo, I. (1969) *I Diavoli nel Pantheon*.

Di Castro, E. (1962) *Trastevere*

Dio Cassius. *History of Rome*. c.200 CE

D'Onofrio, Cesare. (1962) *Le Fontane di Roma*. Rome: Staderini Editore Roma

—— (1967) *Roma Vista da Roma*. Rome: Liber

—— (1967) *Gli Obelischi di Roma*. Rome: Bulzoni

—— (1968) *Visitiamo Roma mille anni fa: la città dei Mirabilia*. Rome: Roman Society Publishers

—— (1970) *Il Tevere e Roma*. Rome: Ugo Bozzi

—— (1973) *Renovatio Romae: storia e urbanistica dal Campidoglio all'EUR*. Rome: Edizioni Mediterranee

—— (1974) *Scalinate di Roma*. Rome: Stadineri

—— (1978) *Castel S. Angelo e Borgo tra Roma e Papato*. Rome: Ugo Bozzi

—— (1980) *Il Tevere: l'Isola Tiberina, le inondazione . . .* Rome: Cremonese

—— (1989) *Visitiamo Roma del Quattrocento: La città degli Umanisti*. Rome: Roman Society Publishers

Duff, J.W. (1960) *A Literary History of Rome from the Origins to the Close of the Golden Age*. South Carolina: BiblioBazaar, LLC

Duffy, Eamon. (1997) *Saints and Sinners: A History of the Popes*. New Haven: Yale University Press

Dumézil, G. (1970) *Archaic Roman Religion, with an Appendix on the Religion of the Etruscans*. Chicago and London: University of Chicago Press

Earl, D.C. (1980) *The Age of Augustus*. Exeter Books

Ellis, P.B. (1980) *Caesar's Invasion of Britain*. New York: New York University Press

Ellis, Simon P. (2000) *Roman Housing*. London: Duckworth

Ettlinger, L.D. (1965) *The Sistine Chapel before Michelangelo*. London: Oxford University Press

Eutropius. *Breviarium ab Urbe Condita. To AD 364.* 10 vols

Everitt, Anthony. (2003) *Cicero: The Life and Times of Rome's Greatest Politician*. New York: Random House

—— (2006) *Augustus: The Life of Rome's First Emperor*. New York: Random House

Fagiolo dell'Arco, Maurizio, and Carandini, Silvia. (1977–8) *L'Effimero Barocco*, 2 vols. Rome: Bulzoni

Favoretto, Irene. (1992) 'Reflections on Canova and the Art of Antiquity', in *Antonio Canova*

Ficacci, Luigi. (2000) *Piranesi: the Complete Etchings*. Cologne: Taschen

Fichera, Filippo. (1937) *Il Duce e il fascismo nei canti dialettali d'Italia*. Milan: Edizione del Convivio

Finley, M.I. (ed.). (1968) *Slavery in Classical Antiquity*. New York: Penguin Books

—— (1987) *Classical Slavery*. UK: Frank Cass

Fontana, D. (1590) *Della Trasportazione dell'Obelisco Vaticano*

Fossier, Robert (ed.). (1986, reprint) *The Cambridge Illustrated History of the Middle Ages, 1250–1520*. Cambridge: Cambridge University Press

Fowler, W.W. (1911) *The Religious Experience of the Roman People*. London: Macmillan

Frontinus. *The Water Supply of Ancient Rome*. 97 CE

Fronto, Marcus Cornelius. *Elements of History*. c.150 CE

Futurist Manifesto, *The Futurist Sensibility* (1913)

Gabucci, Ada (2002) *Ancient Rome: Art, Architecture and History*. Trans. T.M. Hartmann. Los Angeles: Getty Trade Publications

Galassi Paluzzi, C. (1975) *La Basilica di San Pietro*. Bologna: Cappelli

Gianeri, Enrico. (1945) *Il Cesare di cartapesta: Mussolini nella Caricatura*. Turin

Gillespie, Stuart. (1988) *The Poets on the Classics: an Anthology of English Poets' Writings on the Classical Poets and Dramatists*. London: Routledge

Giusto, Gerolamo. (1933) *La Marcia su Roma*, Milan

Gnoli, U. (1935) *Alberghi e osterie Romane della Rinascenza*. Rome: Spoleto

—— (1940) *Cortigiane della Rinascenza*

Goethe, Johann Wolfgang von (1982) *Italian Journey, 1786–1788*. Trans. W.H. Auden and Elizabeth Mayer. New York: Penguin Classics

—— *Conversations with Eckermann, April 14, 1829*. New York: North Point Press

Gooch, John. (1986) *The Unification of Italy*. London: Methuen

Goodman, Martin. (1997) *The Roman World, 44 BC–AD 180*. London: Routledge

Grafton, Anthony (ed.). (1993) *Rome Reborn: The Vatican Library and Renaissance Culture*. New Haven: Yale University Press

Grant, F.C. (1957) *Ancient Roman Religion*. London, New York: Macmillan General Reference

Grant, Michael. (1970) *The Climax of Rome*. New York: Plume Publishing

—— (1974) *The Army of the Caesars*. Macmillan

—— (1978) *The History of Rome*. New Jersey: Prentice-Hall

—— (1985) *The Roman Emperors: a Biographical Guide to the Rulers of Imperial Rome*. New York: Charles Scribner's Sons

Greenhalgh, Michael. (1989) *The Survival of Roman Antiquities in the Middle Ages*. London: Duckworth

Gregorovius, F. (1972) *Storia della città di Roma nel Medioevo*. 6 vols. Rome: Newton Compton

Gregory, Timothy. (2005) *A History of Byzantium*. Hoboken, New Jersey: Wiley-Blackwell

Gulisano, Paolo. (2000) *O Roma o morte! Pio IX e il Risorgimento*. Rimini: Il Cerchio

Gutman, Daniel. (2006) *El amor judio de Mussolini: Margherita Sarfatti. Del Fascismo al exilio*. Buenos Aires: Lumiere Publishing

Hager, June. (1999) *Pilgrimage: a Chronicle of Christianity through the Churches of Rome*. London: Weidenfeld and Nicolson

Hammond, N.G.L. and Scullard, H. H. (1970) *The Oxford Classical Dictionary*. New York: Oxford University Press

Haskell, F. and Penny, N. (1981) *Taste and the Antique*. New Haven: Yale University Press

Hayter, Alethea. (1968) *Opium and the Romantic Imagination*. Berkeley: University of California Press

Hibbard, Howard. 'Bernini, Gian Lorenzo', in *Macmillan Encyclopedia of Architects*, vol. 1. New York, London

—— *Michelangelo*. (1974)

Hibbert, C. (1987) *The Grand Tour*. London: Putnam

Hobhouse, Penelope. (2002) *The Story of Gardening*. London: Dorling Kindersley

Hodge, A. Trevor. (1992) *Roman Aqueducts and Water Supply*. London: Duckworth

Holt, Elizabeth. (1982) *A Documentary History of Art*, vol. 2. Princeton: Princeton University Press

Horace. *Odes* I. III, *c*.23 BCE Trans. J. Michie (1965). London: Penguin

Howatson, M.C. (ed.). (1989) *The Oxford Companion to Classical Literature*. New York: Oxford University Press

Hulten, Pontus (ed.). (1986) *Futurismo & Futurismi*. New York: Abbeville Press

Jannattoni, L. (1990) *Roma intima e sconosciuta*. Rome: Newton Compton

Jenkyns, Richard (ed.). (1992) *The Legacy of Rome, a New Appraisal*. New York: Oxford University Press

Johns, Christopher. (2000) 'The Entrepot of Europe: Rome in the Eighteenth Century'. Catalogue to *Art in Rome in the Eighteenth Century*. Pennsylvania: Philadelphia Museum of Art

Jones, F.L. (ed.). (1964) *The Letters of Percy Bysshe Shelley*. London: Oxford University Press

Julian. Letter XL, Loeb Classical Library. *c*.332–63 CE

Justinian. *Digest*. *c*.529–34 CE

Juvenal. Book III. *c*. early second century

Kagan, D. et al. (1962) *Decline and Fall of the Roman Empire: Why Did It Collapse?* Boston: Heath

Keegan, John. (1994) *History of Warfare*. New York: Vintage

Kinney, Dale. 'Roman Architectural Spolia', in *Proceedings of the American Philosophical Society*, vol. 145, no. 2, June 2001

Krautheimer, R. (1980) *Rome, Profile of a City*. Princeton: Princeton University Press

Lactantius. *On the Deaths of the Persecutors*.

Lanciani, R. (1901) *The Destruction of Ancient Rome*. London: Macmillan

La Stella, M. (1982) *Antichi Mestiere di Roma*. Rome: Newton Compton

Lebreton, J. and Zeiller, J. (1949) *The History of the Primitive Church*. 2 vols. New York: Macmillan

Lechtman, H. and Hobbs, L. (1986) 'Roman Concrete and the Roman Architectural Revolution', in *Ceramics and Civilization*, vol. 3, *High Technology Ceramics: Past, Present and Future*, ed. W.D. Kingery

Leeds, Christopher. (1974) *The Unification of Italy*. New York: Putnam

Legge, F. (1915) *Forerunners and Rivals of Christianity*. 2 vols. Cambridge: Cambridge University Press

Leppmann, Wolfgang. (1970) *Winckelmann*. New York: Knopf

Levi, Peter. (1998) *Virgil, His Life and Times*. New York: St Martin's Press

Lewis, D.B. Wyndham and Lee, Charles. (1960) *The Stuffed Owl: an Anthology of Bad Verse*. London: J.M. Dent

Lewis, Naphtali and Reinhold, Meyer. (1990) *Roman Civilization, Selected Readings: The Republic and the Augustan Age*. 2 vols. New York: Columbia University Press

Livy. *The History of Early Rome*. Trans. Aubrey de Sélincourt (1972). Las Vegas: Heritage Press

Longhitano, Rino. (1938) *La Politica Religiosa di Mussolini*. Rome: Cremonese

Lugli, G. (1946) *Roma antica, il centro monumentale*. Rome: G. Bardi

McDonald, A.H. (1940) *The Rise of Roman Imperialism*. Sydney: Australasian Medical Publishing Company

MacDonald, W.L. (1976) *The Pantheon: Design, Meaning and Progeny*. London; Cambridge, Mass.: Harvard University Press

—— (1982) *The Architecture of the Roman Empire*, I. *An Introductory Study*. New Haven: Yale University Press

MacDougall, Elizabeth B. (ed.). (1981) *Ancient Roman Gardens*. Washington, DC: Dumbarton Oaks Research Library and Collection

—— (1987) *Ancient Roman Villa Gardens*. Washington, DC: Dumbarton Oaks Colloquium

Mack Smith, Denis. (1969) *Garibaldi*. New Jersey: Prentice-Hall

—— (1981) *Mussolini*. New York: Knopf

—— (1985) *Cavour*. New York: Knopf

—— (1988) *The Making of Italy, 1796–1870*. New York: Palgrave Macmillan

McKay, A.G. (1975) *Houses, Villas and Palaces in the Roman World*. London: Thames and Hudson

McManners, John (ed.). (1990) *The Oxford Illustrated History of Christianity*. New York: Oxford University Press

MacMullen, R. (1981) *Paganism in the Roman Empire*. Cambridge: Yale University Press

—— (1984) *Christianizing the Roman Empire*. Cambridge: Yale University Press

Madonna, Maria Luisa (ed.). (1993) *Roma di Sisto V.* Rome: Edizioni de Luca

Magnuson, Torgil. (1986) *Rome in the Age of Bernini*. New Jersey: Humanities Press International

Malizia, G. (1990) *Le Statue di Roma*. Rome: Newton Compton

—— (1994) *Gli archi di Roma*. Rome: Newton Compton

Mandowsky, E. and Mitchell, C. (1963) *Pirro Ligorio's Roman Antiquities*. London: Warburg Institute, University of London

Marcellinus, Ammianus. *History*. c.353–8 CE. Loeb Classical Library

Marchetti Longhi, G. (1960) *L'Area Sacra di largo Argentina*. Istituto Poligrafico dell Stato; Rome: Libreria dello Stato

Marinetti, F.T. (1991) *The Futurist Cookbook*. San Francisco: Chronicle Books

—— (1992) *Selected Writings*. Ed. and trans. R.W. Flint. Los Angeles: Sun and Moon Press

Mariotti Bianchi, U. (1977) *I Molini del Tevere*. Rome: Newton Compton

—— (1978–83) *Perche a Roma si Dice . . .* 3 vols.

Martial. *Epigrams*. c.103 CE Book II (Loeb Classical Library) LXVIII

Masson, Georgina. (1972) *The Companion Guide to Rome*. West Link Park, Doughcloyne: Collins Press

Mastrigli, F. (1929) *Acque, acquedotti e fontane di Roma*. 2 vols. London

Mazzini, Giuseppe. (1845) *Italy, Austria and the Papacy*. London

Meissner, W.W. (1994) *Ignatius of Loyola: The Psychology of a Saint*. New Haven: Yale University Press

Melani, Vasco. (1979, rev. edn) *Itinerari Etruschi*. Pistoia: Tellini

Menen, Aubrey. (1960) *Rome for Ourselves*. New York: McGraw-Hill

Mollat, G. (1949) *The Popes at Avignon 1305–1378*. Trans. J. Love. London: Nelson

Momigliano, A. et al. (1963) *The Conflict between Paganism and Christianity in the Fourth Century*. Oxford: Clarendon Press

Moore, John. (1792) *A View of Society and Manners in Italy, with Anecdotes relating to some Eminent Characters*. A. Strahan and T. Cadell, London

Morgan, Philip. (2007) *The Fall of Mussolini: Italy, the Italians and the Second World War*. Oxford: Oxford University Press

Morrogh, Michael. (1991) *The Unification of Italy*. New York: Palgrave Macmillan

Murray, Peter. (1963) *Donato Bramante*. New York: Praeger

Mussolini. (1951–62) *Opera Omnia*. Florence: La Fenice

New Testament: Paul, Thessalonians II; Matthew 24:7; John 20:41

Nicholas, B. (1962) *An Introduction to Roman Law*. Oxford: Clarendon Press

Nichols Fr. (1986) *Mirabilia Urbis Romae*. New York: Italica Press

Nicoloso, Paolo. (2008) *Mussolini Architetto: Propaganda e paesaggio urbano nell'Italia fascista*. Italy: Giulio Einaudi

Ogilvie, R.M. (1976) *Early Rome and the Etruscans*. New Jersey: Humanities Press International

Oldenbourg, Zoé. (1998) *Massacre at Montségur*. New Haven: Phoenix Press

Onians, J. (1988) *Bearers of Meaning: the Classical Orders in Antiquity, the Middle Ages and the Renaissance*. Princeton: Princeton University Press

Osborne, John (trans.). (1987) *Master Gregorovius: The Marvels of Rome*. Toronto

Ovid. *Metamorphoses*. Trans. Rolfe Humphries (1954). Bloomington: Indiana University Press

—— *The Loves*. Trans. Rolfe Humphries (1957). Bloomington: Indiana University Press

—— *Tristia*. Trans. J. Ferguson (1980)

Oxford Classical Dictionary. (1970) 2nd edn

Painter, Borden W. (2005) *Mussolini's Rome: Rebuilding the Eternal City*. New York: Palgrave Macmillan

Palladio, Andrea. (1997) *The Four Books of Architecture*. Cambridge: MIT Press

Parks, George B. (1954) *The English Traveller to Italy*. 2 vols. Palo Alto: Stanford University Press

Pepper, D. Stephen et al. (1988) *Guido Reni, 1525–1642*. Navora: Istituto Geografico de Agostini

Perowne, S. (1966) *The End of the Roman World*. London: Hodder & Stoughton

Petrie, A. (1961) *An Introduction to Roman History, Literature and Antiquities*. London

Pietrangeli, Carlo et al. (1992) *The Sistine Chapel, a Glorious Restoration*. New York: Abrams

Pliny. *Natural History*. *c*.77 CE

Plutarch, *Life of Aemilius Paullus*. 75 CE

—— *Life of Cato the Elder*. 75 CE

—— *Life of Crassus*. 75 CE

Pollio, Vitruvius. *De architectura*. *c*.25–23 BCE

Polybius. *Histories* I, III.xx; VI.li – lii, xix – xlii

Pomeroy, Sara. (1975) *Goddesses, Whores, Wives and Slaves: Women in Classical Antiquity*. New York: Schocken

Pontiggia, Elena (ed.). (1997) *Da Boccioni a Sironi: Il Mondo di Margherita Sarfatti*. Milan: Skira

Pound, Ezra. (1935) *Fascism as I Have Seen It*. New York: Stanley Nott

Propertius, *Elegiae*. *c*.15 CE

Rawson, E. (ed.). (1985) *Intellectual Life in the Late Roman Republic*. Maryland: Johns Hopkins University Press

Rendina, Claudio. (1984) *I Papi, Storia e Segreti*. Rome: Grandi Tascabili Economici Newton

—— (1987) *Il Vaticano, Storia e Segreti*. Rome: Grandi Tascabili Economici Newton

—— (1991) *Pasquino, Statua Parlante*. Rome: Grandi Tascabili Economici Newton

—— (2006) *Guida Insolita ai misteri . . . di Roma*. Rome: Grandi Tascabili Economici Newton

Riall, Lucy. (1994) *The Italian Risorgimento: State, Society and National Unification*. London: Routledge

—— (2007) *Garibaldi: Invention of a Hero*. New Haven: Yale University Press

Richardson, E. (1976) *The Etruscans, Their Art and Civilization*. Chicago: University of Chicago Press

Richardson Jr, L. (1992) *A New Topographical Dictionary of Ancient Rome*. Maryland: Johns Hopkins University Press

Rizzo, Maria Antonietta (ed.). (1989) *Pittura Etrusca al Museo di Villa Giulia*. Rome: De Luca Edizioni d'Arte

Robinson, J.H. (1904) *Readings in European History*. Essex: Ginn & Co.

Rose, H.J. (1948) *Ancient Roman Religion*. London: Hutchinson University Library

Rosenberg, P. and Christiansen, K. (2008) *Poussin and Nature: Arcadian Visions*. New Haven: Yale University Press

Rostovtzeff, M. (1960) *Rome*. New York: Oxford University Press

Schiavo, Alberto. (1981) *Futurismo e fascismo*. Rome: Giovanni Volpe

Seltzer, Robert M. (ed.). (1987) *Religions of Antiquity*. New York: Macmillan

Seneca. *Moral Epistles*. *c*.3 BCE–65 CE

Sozomen. *Ecclesiastical History*. *c*.440–3 CE

Stack, Frank. (1985) *Pope and Horace: Studies in Imitation*. Cambridge: Cambridge University Press

Starr Jr, C.G. (1982) *The Roman Empire 27 BC–AD 476*. New York: Oxford University Press

Statius. *Silvae*. *c*.40–95 CE

Stockton, D. (1979) *The Gracchi*. New York: Oxford University Press

Suetonius. *The Life of Caligula*. Trans. J.C. Rolfe (1902). 110 CE. Cambridge, Mass.: Harvard University Press

—— *Claudius*. Trans. J.C. Rolfe (1914). 121 CE. New York: Macmillan Co.

—— *Augustus*. Trans. R. Graves (2003). 121 CE. New York: Penguin Classics

Tacitus. *Annals*. 109 CE

Thompson, David (ed.). (1971) *The Idea of Rome from Antiquity to the Renaissance*. Albuquerque: University of New Mexico Press

Tinniswood, Adrian. (1998) *Visions of Power: Ambition and Architecture from Ancient Rome to Modern Paris*. UK: Mitchell Beazley

Tinterow, Gary and Conisbee, Philip (eds). (1999) *Portraits by Ingres: Image of an Epoch*. New York: Metropolitan Museum of Art

Torselli, Giorgio (ed.). (1981) *Trastevere*. Rome: Multigrafica

Toynbee, A. (1965) *Hannibal's Legacy: the Hannibalic War's Effect on Roman Life*. London: Oxford University Press

Ullmann, Walter. (1955) *The Growth of Papal Government in the Middle Ages*. London: Methuen

Valerio, Anthony. (2001) *Anita Garibaldi: a Biography*. Westport: Praeger

Valla, Lorenzo (1518) in *De falso credita et ementita Constantini donatione declamatio*, Mainz

Varro. *De Lingua Latina*. V.143

Vasari, Giorgio. (1550) *Le Vite*. Rome: Florence

Virgil. *Aeneid*. Trans. C. Day Lewis (1952). 29 BCE. London: Oxford University Press

—— *Georgics* II. 29 BCE

——*Fourth Eclogue*. Trans. C. Day Lewis (1962). London: Oxford University Press

Vitruvius. (1970) *De Architectura libri decem*. Ed. F. Granger. 2 vols. London

Walpole, Horace. (1786) *Anecdotes of Painting in England*. IX. London

Wardman, A. (1976) *Rome's Debt to Greece*. London: Paul Elek

Weiss, R. (1969) *The Renaissance Rediscovery of Classical Antiquity*. Oxford: Basil Blackwell

Westermann, W.L. (1955) *The Slave Systems of Greek and Roman Antiquity*. Philadelphia: American Philosophical Society

Westfall, Carroll W. (1974) *In This Most Perfect Paradise: Alberti, Nicholas V and the Invention of Conscious Urban Planning in Rome 1447–55*. University Park: Pennsylvania State University Press

Wheeler, R.E. (1965) *Roman Art and Architecture*. New York: Praeger

Wilken, R.I. (1984) *The Christians as the Romans Saw Them*. New Haven: Yale University Press

Wilkinson, L.P. (1968) *Horace and His Lyric Poetry*. Cambridge: Cambridge University Press

Wilton-Ely, John. (1978) *The Mind and Art of Giovanni Battista Piranesi*. London: Thames and Hudson

Wittkower, R. (1988) *Architectural Principles in the Age of Humanism*. London, New York: St Martin's Press

Zanker, P. (1988) *The Power of Images in the Age of Augustus*. Ann Arbor: University of Michigan Press

Zei, Giuseppina. (1979) *Canti dell'Italia Fascista*

Zonaras, *Epitome*, VII. *c*.twelfth century

ILLUSTRATION SOURCES

INDEX